MW00626960

Beyond The Lines

Beyond The Lines

An Autobiography

Kuldip Nayar

Lotus
Roli

Lotus Collection

© Kuldip Nayar, 2012

All rights reserved. No part of this publication
may be reproduced or transmitted, in any form or by any
means, without the prior permission of the author.
First published in India in 2012

First published in June 2012
Second impression, July 2012
The Lotus Collection
An imprint of
Roli Books Pvt. Ltd
M-75, Greater Kailash II Market, New Delhi 110 048
Phone: ++91 (011) 40682000
Fax: ++91 (011) 2921 7185
E-mail: info@rolibooks.com
Website: www.rolibooks.com
Cover photograph: Kavita Chopra Dikshit

Also at Bangalore, Chennai, & Mumbai

ISBN: 978-81-7436-910-9

Typeset in Perpetua by Roli Books Pvt. Ltd
and printed at Sanat Printers, Haryana

Dedicated to

Bharti, my wife, my two sons, Sudhir and Rajiv, their wives, both Kavita, three grandchildren Kanika, Mandira, and her husband Ratish; and Kartik and his wife Kanika.

Contents

Preface

This book, an account of my life, has taken far longer than I had anticipated. I began writing in 1990 when, as India's high commissioner, I had some leisure. That tenure did not however, for political reasons, last long and I was back in the mill to resume work on my syndicated column.

I wish I could have said more about myself and less about the events that were engulfing me. There were some constraints. For one, I was conscious that I was willy-nilly, writing a contemporary history of India, Pakistan, and Bangladesh — countries I had seen and experienced from the time they came into existence. Two, I wished, as far as possible, to minimize the personal pronoun in order to avoid accusations of projecting myself and propagating punditry.

I have seen the great, the despotic, and nonentities among politicians, bureaucrats, and industrialists, media magnates, and journalists. The performance of a majority has disappointed me, and my experience has been that most who occupied high positions were unworthy of them; they were authoritative but lacked substance.

I do not claim to know of all that has happened in India, Pakistan, and subsequently Bangladesh, prior to Partition or after, but I have written honestly and frankly about all that I do know. My problem was to reduce all that I had seen, sensed, or known in a book of reasonable length, and this has meant leaving out a great deal.

In the course of my life I have endeavoured to have as wide an experience as possible, and have tasted failure in many of my efforts. Had I had greater energy I might have achieved many more of my dreams.

The book opens on the day the Pakistan Resolution was passed in 1940 when I was a school student of 17 years, present in Lahore where it happened. This book encapsulates much inside information which would not otherwise have been known, from Partition to the government of Manmohan Singh.

It has taken me almost two decades to write this book because I would select an episode, write about it, and leave it at that. As I was not working to a deadline I could afford to do so until I realized a few years ago that I was not immortal. As I write in long hand it takes me time to complete a manuscript.

It was difficult to decide when the book should begin. Should it be from the day I reached Delhi on 14 September 1947, as a refugee from my home town, Sialkot in Pakistan? However, many people I consulted, both in India and Pakistan, insisted that I should write about Partition because they wanted to know why and how India came to be divided. I have told all because I have lived through that period and have helplessly witnessed the events as they unfolded.

I have depended largely on my memory to write my memoirs, but the notes I maintained were useful as were my articles which I have had bound, beginning in 1968 when I left the United News of India (UNI), a news agency, and joined the *Statesman* as its Delhi editor.

If I were to identify a watershed moment in my life, I would say it was my detention during the Emergency when my innocence was assaulted. I began my life in India with Rs 120 which my mother gave me when I left home. Although Partition compelled me begin life afresh, I was then young and took whatever happened in my stride. The Emergency woke me up from the cocooned life I had led and obliged me to face the realities of politics, prejudice, and punishment.

That was also the time when I began to feel for the violation of personal liberty and human rights. The young boys interned in jail for no fault of theirs who were made to wait upon politicians in detention shook my conscience to the core. It lessened my faith in the system. I have seen how our political masters are violating it, not just the mafia who, in any event, cannot be expected to have any respect for human life or individuals' rights.

Readers will find much discussion on India–Pakistan relations. Improving them has been my passion as well as my prayer. Mine is a commitment, not just nostalgia. I hope one day I am able to see a region of friendly states working together for their mutual benefit.

I have seen Bangladesh developing from the days when it was liberated. My contact with many people in Pakistan and Bangladesh are personal and I am proud to own the relationship. I believe that some day all the countries in South Asia will form a common union like the European Union (EU), without abandoning their individual identities, and this will help fight against the problems of poverty and to span the ever-yawning gulf between the rich and the desperately poor of all our countries. I am convinced that South Asians will one day live in peace and harmony and cooperate with one another on matters of mutual concern such as development, trade, and social progress.

This is the hope I have clung to amidst the sea of hatred and hostility that has for far too long engulfed the subcontinent.

I have won many awards, including one named after Lord Astor awarded to the best journalist in the Commonwealth. What I value most is my membership of the Medill Hall of Achievement, the American school from where I earned an M.Sc in journalism, and the doctorate in journalism I received from Nagarjuna University, Andhra Pradesh. I was conferred PhD in philosophy by Guru Nanak Dev University, Amritsar.

I can honestly say that failures have not deterred me from pursuing the path I have considered correct and worth fighting for. I have suffered in consequence and I carry many raw wounds. What has sustained me is faith: *Hum honge kamyab ek din* [We shall succeed one day].

I have no idea of what the art of living is. I have lived just following my usual daily routine. Circumstances have buffeted me from one situation to another, and I have tried to adjust myself to them, often wondering whether I control my life or whether life controls me. Time has passed by like an unfettered stream, just flowing.

Occasionally, I am shaken when I pass through a slum or when a poor helpless child spreads his hand before me for alms. 'How do they live? Why do they live?' I ask myself. I often imagine myself engaged in a slew of activities to transform their destiny; a genie fighting against evil. Wishful thinking perhaps, but the tedium and tension involved in the very process pushes aside such cogitations and I return to a self-centred life of good meals and an air-conditioned room.

I believe that perhaps some day everything will miraculously right itself. Some magic wand will help wipe tears from every cheek and awaken the people to something deeper and nobler. How? When? These questions gnaw at my conscience. I try to push them away but they keep reappearing, each time with greater force, like a refrain from a piece of forgotten music, leaving me feeling sad, shaken, and helpless. I wish I could find a peg to hang my worries and doubts on. If only I had faith. Those who believe the present life is a continuation of a past one and that we are now reaping what we had sown have some explanation to cling to. Others have prayers as their anchor. At least they are not a rudderless ship like me. What is the purpose of life?

My mind goes back to the time when I had just begun life. Would I be an entirely different person were I to begin all over again? Then what about my critics and supporters? In some way, how similar they are.

I do not think my time is up. I am buoyed up by the feeling that I still have time to do something worthwhile, and this elates me. If I only knew what would be worthwhile; and how I should go about it!

It is beyond my capacity to describe what has goaded me to go on and on for over eight decades: destiny or determination? Could it be both? After all, the show must go on, and I concur with the great Urdu poet, Ghalib who wrote: '*Shama har rang mein jalti hai sehar hone tak* [The flame flickers in every colour until the morning].'

I had titled the book, A Lifetime is not Enough. But the publisher preferred *Beyond the Lines*, taking a cue from my column, 'Between the Lines'. I am indebted to Shyam Bhatia, Seema Sirohi, R. Ramachandran, and Manjur Ali for the valuable suggestions they have made and to Gopal who has repeatedly and tirelessly typed and retyped the manuscript. Even so, the book would not have taken the form it has but for the meticulous editing by Adil Tyabji sahab and the advice given by Nandini, my first pupil in journalism, and Mandira Nayar, my granddaughter, who alone in the family has taken up journalism.

1

CHILDHOOD AND PARTITION

Every new beginning in life is unique and my example is worth recalling because it was unplanned; I stumbled into journalism by accident. My chosen profession was law, in which I had a degree from Lahore, but history intervened and before I could enroll myself as a lawyer in my hometown, Sialkot, India was divided. Making my way to Delhi, I found a job in an Urdu daily, *Anjam* (meaning end). That is why I always say that I entered the profession of journalism from the end, not the beginning: *Mere sahafat ka agaz Anjam se hua.*

Were the Almighty to take me back to 15 August 1947, the day of India's Partition, and ask me what I would like to be, a journalist or a lawyer, I would choose the former. That is not because I have done well in this profession but because it has given me an opportunity to write what I have considered to be correct, notwithstanding multiple pressures. Ironically, I failed to pass a journalism diploma course in Lahore, and also the optional paper in Urdu for the bachelor of arts degree.

After Partition, we were among the very few Hindu families who did not want to migrate to India. We mistakenly thought that as large numbers of Muslims would continue to live in India, the same would be true of Hindus in Pakistan. Our resolve was strengthened when a few days prior to Partition, Mohammed Ali Jinnah, founder of Pakistan, categorically pronounced that people were free to go to their mosques or temples and practise their faith because the state would never mix religion with politics. He reinterpreted his thesis of two nations, Muslims and Hindus, to mean Pakistanis and Indians.

Jinnah's encouraging statement apart, there was his gesture to select a Hindu poet, Jagan Nath Azad, to compose the national anthem of Pakistan. The anthem was changed after Jinnah's death for communal considerations: a Hindu writing the national anthem of a Muslim state appeared unthinkable.

Moreover, our family's lifestyle was also so comfortable that we did not wish to uproot ourselves. We had substantial property and my father was a leading medical practitioner in Sialkot. How could he, then past sixty, begin his practice afresh in a new city? He had already spent most of his savings a few months prior to Independence building a new house, a new dispensary, and an array of shops.

I have fond memories of my home, at Trunk Bazaar, a two-storey house with a garden at the back where there was an old grave which my mother said was the *kabar* of some *pir* (saint). The grave was like a family shrine where we prayed in our own way and sought refuge from the outside world. It was here that we lit a lamp every Thursday and made an offering of sweets which we, the children, subsequently distributed amongst ourselves. A few years before Partition, some Muslims demanded a passage to the grave on the plea that they should have free access to their religious site. We had to yield to the demand but the passage, which cut through our property, was rarely used.

Ours was a joint family, with my grandmother as the effective head. My grandfather was alive but he took a back seat. Grandmother was a great one for astrology. She had horoscopes of every child prepared by a leading pandit, forecasting the future. I recall one occasion when the pandit dropped in at the house. A visit from him was always eagerly awaited because he would also read our palms. He said that I would read the *malechh vidya* (a language of foreigners), thereby meaning English. He also predicted that I would travel a lot by *udhan khatola* (plane). When my youngest brother Sindhu showed his hand, he was dismissed in a second with the remark that the lines on his hand had not properly developed. This was perhaps his way of saying that Sindhu would not live long.

When my grandmother died, I rode a horse alongside the cortege of family and friends who carried the coffin to the cremation ground. Women, some of them hired, rhythmically beat their breasts. Brahmins were fed one day and the poor of the locality on another. My grandmother apparently evoked a great measure of respect because scores of people were gathered at the cremation ground. I remember I went to Haridwar with the family to immerse her ashes in the Ganga. I do not recall crying because the whole ceremony of her death wore an aura of festivity. This was the custom among Hindus when a woman died at a ripe old age.

My immediate family comprised my father, mother, and four brothers – Rajinder, Hardip, Surinder, and a sister, Raj, who lived in Jamshedpur at the time of Partition. Sindhu had died of cholera a few months earlier. I can never forget his last moments: he passed away with his head resting on my lap. He called me *bhapa* (elder brother), and when his moment came, he asked me to hold him tight so as to prevent anyone from taking him away. I held him tight, but I could feel his body going limp. His last words were, '*Bhapa* leave me, I can see the light. I am going there,' and then he was gone. His loss left me distraught for a long time.

His parting words often make me wonder whether there is indeed a higher power controlling the universe. The light, to which Sindhu referred, represents a power which eventually leads us in our journey from life to death. Why, how, and when, I cannot say, but notwithstanding my leftist leanings I have come to believe that there is power beyond: be it god or any other name you may choose to give it. I have oscillated between faith and doubt for many years but have come to accept that there is a force which I feel within but which I cannot explain. I am neither an atheist nor an agnostic; I am a believer, but notwithstanding this I have failed to curb my doubts and misgivings, and prayer has not helped either.

I envy those who have an implicit faith in god. They do not have to seek explanations because they don't need any. I am convinced that there is something called destiny which makes you choose a particular path from the many before you. In my own life, I have preferred one option over another without really knowing why, and that has made all the difference. I studied law but settled on journalism. I tried to join the Indian Administrative Service (IAS) but failed to make it. Had I been successful I would have retired 25 years ago, but this is destiny. Perhaps my faith springs from something I read many years ago inscribed on a tablet on a restaurant wall near Jama Masjid in Delhi: *Waqt se pehley nahin, Mukaddar se ziada nahin* [Not before your time, nor more than your destiny].

My wife, Bharti, is quite the opposite. She has implicit faith in god and is a practising Hindu who goes to the temple every day and fasts on the days enjoined by her religion. She organizes *havans* for her children and grandchildren on their birthdays and has dragged me along to many pilgrimages, from Amarnath in the north to Rameshwaram in the south.

I have, however, always believed in the *pir* buried in the back garden of our house in Sialkot. I respect him as a family elder or patron, protecting us all from any unpleasant events. Even when I left Murray College at Sialkot to join Forman Christian College in Lahore (Government College refused me admission), I carried with me the blessings of the *pir*, my unseen guardian. I feel he represents something spiritual; something akin to bhakti or sufism. Did this dependence make me a coward? Anyone could bully me. I accepted beatings in the brawls in which I was unwillingly involved. A physically strong person always impressed me. Aptly, my mother had nicknamed me Bhola (innocent).

Over the years, I developed a taste for classical music, both Indian and Western. My wife helped me appreciate the nuances of Indian classical music, particularly the ragas. I have, however, been unable to assimilate or appreciate even the rudiments of the other fields of art. I have no skill whatsoever in assessing a drawing or a painting.

I once had a humbling experience when I tried to buy some paintings. Many years ago, near Charminar in Hyderabad there were some shops offering a variety of small paintings. Pretending to be an expert, I went to a shop and selected twelve from which I thought I would shortlist three. The shopkeeper, a venerable old man, watched me intently and after some time he stopped my selection. He curtly told me that I did not understand the paintings and those I had selected had little merit.

Hurt but dumbfounded I looked at him. He took back all the paintings I had put aside and reached for a small one on the shelf I had scanned. 'Take this,' he said, handing over the painting. 'This is a present from me on the promise that you will never buy a painting on your own.' I have kept that promise and the painting I was gifted has been praised by many, and adorns one of the walls of my sitting room.

Much later in life once M.F. Hussain came to my house in New Delhi. He was transporting canvases on a bicycle while walking alongside it. He requested me to buy at least one painting and the price he sought, if I recall correctly, was Rs 100 or so. I refused because I could not afford it then, and in any event I remembered the advice of the Hyderabad shopkeeper that I should not buy any painting on my own.

✿

My mother, Puran Devi, was very particular about customs. She really believed that antiquity gave them credibility. She burnt her spinning wheel when my first son Sudhir, her grandson, was born. The custom had it that a grandmother would be so occupied by her grandson that she would not have time to sit at the spinning wheel.

A practising Sikh, my mother regularly attended the gurdwara regularly. Marriages between Hindus and Sikhs were common in those days. She would read us the Guru Granth Sahib every Sankrant (the first month of the Indian calendar) and give us halwa prepared at home. My father had 'Singh' affixed after Gurbaksh, his first name. However, unlike the Sikhs, neither he nor my grandfather had long hair. It would be fair to say that we blended the traditions of Sikhism and Hinduism.

The first name of my brothers, like mine, was chosen by a *granthi* (preacher) from the Granth Sahib, the holy book of Sikhs. There was no such custom for girls. My sister got her name from my grandmother. My name at birth was Kuldip Singh but I dropped the 'Singh' after Partition, not wishing people to think I was a Sikh when I wasn't one. I also saw no validity in claiming to be a Sehajdhari (a term used for people who have cut hair or shaven beard but believe in the Sikh Gurus and Guru Granth Sahib).

In keeping with the intermingling of the two faiths in our daily lives, we celebrated both Hindu and Sikh festivals. Diwali was the biggest celebration in our house, and then my parents would insist that we wore new clothes. There was always a Lakshmi puja which my mother performed and subsequently the tradition was followed by my wife. Once, a Muslim couple, family friends of ours, dropped in while we were performing the ritual Lakshmi puja. My mother abruptly stopped the puja, and requested them to join in. They did, in the sense that they sat quietly on the floor and watched the proceedings.

The idol of Lakshmi (goddess of wealth) was placed on a pedestal and everyone bowed before it. My mother asked them to do the same. They just smiled and kept a distance. She did not realize even later that for a Muslim to bow before Lakshmi was tantamount to idol worship, which is prohibited in Islam. Our Muslim friends were, however, well aware that my mother didn't mean to hurt their feelings. She was just ignorant of their religious practices. This was true of most Hindu and Sikh families who lived in the midst of a Muslim majority in Sialkot. All that they knew was that Muslims ate halal meat, unlike Sikhs who relished *jhatka*, but we respected communal sensitivities.

My mother was a liberal and bore no prejudice against Muslims. She would say that they were just like us. She however practiced discrimination without even realizing that she was doing so when it came to the untouchables. She would not allow the girl who swept the floor at home to enter her kitchen. Once when she did by mistake, I heard my mother shouting at her endlessly while washing the kitchen floor with buckets of water, which ironically were brought by the same girl from a nearby well.

I would watch the girl intently. Wearing a thin white dhoti, she showed her shapely legs and a swash of thick hair between. I was twelve or thirteen then, and felt an indescribable surge of desire whenever I saw her nakedness. I did not go near her, not because she was a dalit, the preferred term today, but because of fear of what the family might think. I was just scared.

The untouchable girl, however, made me conscious of the caste system in Hinduism. Even in my school, some boys sat on the bare floor while we had the benefit of jute mats. Once I startled my teacher when I asked him why everyone couldn't have a jute mat. He gave me the stock reply that they did not pay the full fee. However, when he saw that I was not convinced, he said it was because they were untouchables. I found it revolting but did not raise my voice. Upper castes remained upper and lower castes lower. This had been accepted for centuries and even those who felt repulsed did not challenge the practice. I did however wonder how long this order would survive.

My mother gave me an explanation of sorts: The untouchables were those who had committed 'sins' in their previous life and were paying for them in this birth. I did not accept the rationale then and I continue to be confused about the philosophy of inflicting punishment now for deeds committed in another life. The philosophy of karma, as preached by the Gita, is what the Hindu philosophy is about. It made me somewhat smug but not accepting of injustice or inequity.

Despite the somewhat tense atmosphere in Sialkot, we led a normal life until the announcement of Partition on 12 August 1947 which changed everything. I was twenty-four year old. It was like a spark thrown at the haystack of distrust. The subcontinent burst into communal flames. The north was the worst affected and to some extent Bengal. Pent-up feelings among both Hindus and Muslims, stirred by the communal propaganda disseminated over several years, gave vent to widespread anger. This was aggravated by the fact that the administrators were divided along religious lines.

Trouble began almost simultaneously on both sides of the new border on 13 August. Lahore and Amritsar got engulfed after the killing of Sikhs at Rawalpindi and of Muslims in the Sikh-ruled states in East Punjab. Soon it became a bloodbath, with furious mobs roaming the bazars with weapons. People went on a rampage of killing, looting, and kidnapping, especially of women and children, and setting homes ablaze. Even the sky of the relatively quiet Sialkot was radiant. We helplessly watched the fires in the distance. My mother tiptoed to me and whispered in my ear: these are only lights; today is your birthday (14 August).

Initially, we had taken shelter with the jailor, Arjun Das, who later supervised the hanging of Mahatma Gandhi's assassin, Nathu Ram Godse, at Ambala Cantonment.

I did not witness India becoming an independent state on the night of 14–15 August because I was with my family in Sialkot. Radio Pakistan played nationalist songs which were Islamic in tone. I switched over to All India Radio and heard the replayed version of Nehru's speech. His words still resound in my ears: 'Long years ago, we made a tryst with destiny, and now the time comes when we shall redeem our pledge, not wholly or in full measure, but very substantially....'

Our family decided to visit India for some time till the communal frenzy subsided. Even for one-bag travel I had to return to the house to bring my clothes. My brothers and parents too needed some things. My mother and I hired a tonga at Sialkot cantonment, a comparatively safe place where we had taken shelter, after moving from Arjun Das's residence, at a bungalow owned by Ghulam Qadir, a multi-store owner and a friend of my father.

My mother and I did not know the tongawalla, who was a Muslim. It was a distance of some 10 km from the cantonment but not even once did it occur to anyone that someone could attack us on the way at a time when people were baying for each other's blood.

When we had hurriedly left home on 14 August, my mother had carried with her a precious shahtoosh shawl. She carefully folded it and put it back in her trunk, taking with her an ordinary Kulu shawl. She said she did not want to spoil her good shawl by taking it to India. I had taken with me the hardback edition of *Jean Christopher* by Romaine Rolland. I put it back on the shelf and picked up a paperback which I thought I could afford to throw away in India before returning home. My mother packed three suitcases, one for me, the other for my two brothers, and the third for my father and herself.

My mother and I sat for some time at the dining table. We were sad, probably struggling to avoid the thought that we might never return, not to mention the feeling that we would have to start our lives afresh in India. Neither of us realized that it would be our last visit to our home.

I wish I had words to describe the poignancy of those moments. How can I express the thought of leaving everything behind? It was akin to being crushed in the embers of memory. I feared that everything had been reduced to ashes. My mother did say when, locking the outer door, that she had a strange premonition of never returning again.

On 12 September, when we were discussing our travel plans, a Hindu army major who had decided to go to India came to bid my father goodbye. He was indebted to him for the medical attention given to his children. The major inquired if he could do anything for him. 'Take my three sons with you,' was my father's request. The major was obviously embarrassed. He said he wished he could but there was no space in his jeep. At best, he could accommodate only one person with a handbag.

The entire family insisted that I should be the one to accompany the major but when they found I was unwilling, my father suggested we draw lots. Whether it was managed or accidental, I was the reluctant winner. I tried my utmost to wriggle out but everyone said that it was destined. I could not sleep that night, and after a long time I put my head in my mother's lap, asking her to caress my hair as she used to when I was a child. I was afraid to face the future.

I wanted to return to the days when I had no worry, no fear. Now I wanted to cling to each member of my family, apprehending that I might never see them again. Even before embarking on the journey, we had heard innumerable stories of migrants being killed on their way to Pakistan or India. On many trains in Pakistan, all non-Muslim passengers were killed, while Muslims were butchered on trains in India. I imagined the worst as I fell asleep. We had decided not to travel together, only one at a time.

The major's jeep arrived with his wife and two children on the morning of 13 September. It was crammed with luggage and there was also an orderly sitting at the back. My mother had packed two trousers and two shirts for me in a handbag. She also gave me Rs 120. With tears rolling down her face, she reminded me to stay at Daryaganj, Delhi, with her sister, Kunto *masi*, who was married to a head clerk at the central secretariat.

It was an avalanche of migration. Humanity in its entirety appeared to be on the move on both sides. No one expected it; no one wanted it, but none could prevent it. The two countries blamed each other as they tried to grapple with the unexpected tragedy and the other concomitant and chaotic problems of Partition after experiencing a few heady days that Independence had brought.

Jinnah picked on the Sikhs whom he had tried to wean away from India on the promise of an autonomous state (Azad Punjab) on the border of Pakistan and India. His secretary, K.H. Khurshid, many years later told me in Lahore that Jinnah had never visualized such large-scale massacre and migration occurring after Partition. His idea of Pakistan, Khurshid said, was that of a parliamentary democracy where there would be no difference between Muslims and non-Muslims on the basis of religion.

In India, Vallabhbhai Patel was anxious that all Hindus and Sikhs should leave West Pakistan; he cared little for the Muslims who he thought had better leave India as they had achieved what they wanted: Pakistan. For Jawaharlal Nehru, secularism was a matter of faith and he was known to personally chase away Hindus looting shops owned by Muslims in New Delhi.

The refugees carried with them not only bitterness and vengeful thoughts but also stories of atrocities in the cities and villages where they had lived peacefully with other communities for centuries. If Partition was on the basis of religion, the killings only served to carve deep furrows.

Whoever was to blame, or rather, more to blame, these few weeks of madness on both sides of the border embittered relations between the two countries for decades into the future. Three generations have already suffered and one does not know how long this dark alley is. The two countries have differed on every subject, at every step. Fear and mistrust of each other has made even trivial matters major issues.

So wide was the hiatus soon after Partition that Jinnah thought at one time of breaking off diplomatic relations with India. He confided to his chief of staff, Lord Ismay, in September 1947, that 'there is no alternative but to fight it out'. Jinnah genuinely believed that India wanted to dismember his country, a fear that haunts Pakistan to this day.

As I got into the jeep, I looked towards my mother who was trying to hold back her tears. My father was stunned and distraught. However, they were relieved that at least one member of the family would be making it to safety. My brothers were laughing but how unreal their laughter sounded! Wistfully, I looked towards them and waved my hand in farewell.

The journey to Sambrial, about 20 miles from Sialkot, was uneventful, but as soon as the jeep reached the main road it stopped. A wall of men blocked the road. It was a stream of Hindus and Sikhs from distant towns trekking to India. It was a harrowing sight. They looked haggard: gaping wounds, torn clothes, and meagre belongings all told the story of their suffering. They were victims but not of 'riots', a word that fell far short of describing what had happened. A sadistic desire to kill each other had overtaken the two communities.

I still remember an old Sikh with a flowing beard flecked with grey, nudging me and trying to hand over his grandson. 'He is all we have in the family,' he implored, 'take him to India. At least someone from the family should live.' A young woman thrust her child into the jeep. 'I shall search for you and collect my son,' she said. How could I take their children into the jeep when I did not know about my own future? I just kept silent. How could I explain? How? How?

Leaving these helpless people behind was heart-wrenching but there was nothing I could do. It seemed as if we had lost the past but were not sanguine about the future. I was worried about my parents. I wished I could tell them that there was no going back to our home. They must come out quickly and forever. We had to start from scratch.

※

The catholicity of Hinduism and the compassion of Islam: if such sentiments survived, they made no difference. Villages after villages had been annihilated, the Muslim habitations destroying and burning the Hindu–Sikh ones and Hindus and Sikhs, in turn retaliating or taking the initiative in wiping out the Muslims. I had a glimpse of all these as I travelled in the jeep.

Riots, in fact, had erupted in Punjab in March 1947 itself. Rawalpindi and Jhelum were the most affected, where many Hindu and Sikh women jumped into wells to save themselves from rape and kidnapping. Lahore became a battleground between Hindus and Sikhs, on the one side, joining hands, and Muslims on the other. This was the city where Master Tara Singh, a Sikh leader, had unsheathed a sword in front of the state assembly building and had raised the slogan of Khalistan.

The killing of Sikhs in Rawalpindi as well as the rape of women who did not jump into wells to save their chastity was the turning point for the community. Till then Master Tara Singh, their leader, was equivocal in his thinking, wondering whether to stay on in Pakistan where Guru Nanak Dev, the founder of Sikhism, was born, or migrate to India where the Master was confident of security because of Hindu–Sikh religious kinship. Both shared the same beliefs and held sacred more or less the same gods and goddesses. The Sikhs had not forgiven or forgotten the Mughal atrocities at the hands of Aurangzeb and some other Muslim emperors. Similarly, the Muslims recalled the killings perpetrated by Hari Singh Nalwa, Maharaja Ranjit Singh's chief of the Sikh army. I have often wondered why the Punjabi Muslims never cultivated the Sikhs. Both were *ahle kitab* (people of the book or scripture), the Sikhs have the Guru Granth Sahib and the Muslims the Quran-i-Sharif. Neither suffer from the caste system or prejudice.

I saw corpses lying on both sides of the road and empty suitcases and bags which bore testimony to the looting that had taken place either before or after the killing. The storm of fury seemed to have blown over. There was nervousness as we neared Wagah.

The men in khaki – the army, the police, and other services – were meant to bring the riots under control but they too were infected by the communal virus. To expect them to be impartial and punish the guilty from their own community was to hope for the impossible. They had lost all sense of right and wrong. These custodians of the people knew they would go scot-free in their 'own country' after the transfer. I think it was a blunder to give the choice to civil servants, the police, and the armed forces to opt for India if they were non-Muslims and Pakistan if they were Muslims. A mixed administration would have behaved differently and infused the minorities with confidence.

Jinnah would not believe the reports that thousands of people were migrating from both sides of the border. Both the Congress and the Muslim League had rejected the proposal for an exchange of population and had insisted on Muslims and non-Muslims staying back in their homes. Jinnah remained sullen for a few days and then accused India of seeking to undermine Pakistan. Even so, he was deeply concerned not only about the migration of people but also recurrent news that several lakhs of people had been butchered on either side of the border.

One day when Jinnah was in Lahore, Iftikhar-ud-din, Pakistan's rehabilitation minister and Mazhar Ali Khan, editor of *Pakistan Times*, flew him in a Dakota over divided Punjab. When he saw streams of people pouring into Pakistan or fleeing it, he struck his hand on the forehead and said despairingly: 'What have I done?' Both Iftikhar and Mazhar vowed not to repeat the remark. Mazhar took his wife Tahira into confidence and told her what Jinnah had said, and she communicated Jinnah's comment to me long after her husband's death.

☙

It was late in the afternoon when our jeep reached the outskirts of Lahore. It halted, but nobody knew why. Word was that a convoy of Muslims had been attacked in Amritsar and that Muslims in Lahore were waiting to take revenge. We waited in silence. There was some stray shooting in the distance and from nearby fields came the stench of decomposed flesh. We heard cries of '*Allah ho Akbar, Ya Ali, Pakistan Zindabad*' but there was no attack. Our fears were proved unfounded.

It was then that we heard '*Bharat Mata Ki Jai*'. That was it; the end of the line. We drove past the hurriedly erected, whitewashed, overturned drums and the Indian national flag aloft a bamboo pole marking the border. There was rejoicing and people hugged one another. It was great to be alive. The major's wife in the jeep distributed sweets from a packet which she had apparently been hiding under her seat. It was still daylight.

As I looked around, I saw people huddled in trucks and many on foot passing us going in the opposite direction. They were Muslims. Our jeep stopped to make way for them. I got down to see around, just to see. No one spoke, neither they nor I, but we understood each other; it was a spontaneous kinship. Both had seen murder and worse; both had been broken on the rack of history; both were refugees. I hoped the new India would know no killings in the name of religion. How wrong I was proved!

I was taken for a Muslim in the second-class compartment in which I travelled from Amritsar. Non-Sikh Punjabis on both sides looked alike. They spoke the same language and dressed in the same way; ate the same food and even behaved in the same manner. Everyone was condemning their leaders for letting them down, but I was abusive and that too at the top of my voice. I undoubtedly attracted attention, but also some hostile glances.

My bare right arm flashed the crescent and star which I had got tattooed at Sialkot at the insistence of my friend Shafquat. I heard whispers of suspicion about my identity. Was he a Muslim abusing loudly to cover up his religion? The tattoo heightened the suspicion and convinced more and more people that I was a Muslim.

I was pulled out of the compartment at Ludhiana, coincidentally the city where most people from Sialkot had migrated. Burly Sikhs with spears and swords joined a hostile crowd around me at the platform, asking me to prove that I was a Hindu. I could see blood in their eyes. Before I could pull my pants down, a halwai from Sialkot, from our very locality, came to my rescue. He shouted that I was Doctor Sahib's son. Another joined him to confirm this and the unbelieving crowd dispersed. This ended my agony as well as the excitement of the spectators. I was let off, but those few minutes still haunt me. There was no mercy in those days.

Meanwhile, my parents and two brothers came separately through another route, across Narowal rail bridge which had to be negotiated on foot to reach the Indian soil. My father, who was carrying all the jewellery and cash the family had in a small suitcase, was pushed at the bridge. A young man snatched the suitcase and melted away into the crowd. My parents, by then in their sixties, had to start their life all over again in Jalandhar where they decided to settle. They borrowed money and bought earthenware pots and pans to enable my mother to cook.

My father, however, narrated to me how some Muslim youth at Sialkot had saved them. One day, not knowing the fate of their children, both he and my mother boarded a train for Narowal. Some Muslim youths recognized my father and asked him not to travel by that train. When my parents resisted, they told them that the train would be attacked 10 km ahead, and that was what actually happened. All the passengers on that train were butchered. The youths took my parents back to the house and brought them back the following day, ensuring them a safe journey.

There were many such instances of Hindus saving Muslims and Muslims saving Hindus. A report by Ashis Nandy, a leading Indian academic, has analyzed many incidents and says that the number of Muslims saved by Hindus in India and Hindus by Muslims in Pakistan averaged 50 per cent, an equal number on both sides.

Estimates of the scale of the killing and migration vary, but one figure generally accepted is: one million killed and 20 million uprooted. Lord Louis Mountbatten, who was the last governor general of free India, put it between two and three million. The enormity of what occurred is beyond conjecture. In the two Punjabs there was a wholesale transfer of populations, which amounted to ethnic cleansing. The city of Lahore, former capital of Ranjit Singh's kingdom and a great centre of Sikh culture, became an exclusively Muslim city within a matter of days, while Delhi, the capital of successive Muslim empires, saw most Muslim families leaving for Pakistan. It was an irony of the times that the grounds around the great Red Fort, built by Shah Jahan as a symbol of Mughal power, became a refugee camp for Delhi's Muslim community. Even so, many Muslims argued that the British had seized rule from Muslims and should have returned the country to them.

The unbounded ferocity witnessed on both sides of Punjab was exceptional. Bengal did not experience that, nor did Muslim-minority provinces, the United Provinces (now Uttar Pradesh), Bihar, or the Central Provinces (now Madhya Pradesh). However, bulk of the Muslim middle class from these states migrated in huge numbers to the urban centre of Sindh where they came to be known as Mohajirs, a description that still lingers.

Nonetheless, all across India, Muslims were under considerable pressure to go to Pakistan. Still, with the exception of East Punjab, Muslims, by and large, stayed back, and the migration of people was limited and mostly voluntary. The Muslims who remained in India constituted about 12 per cent of the population in comparison to 2 or 3 per cent Hindus and Sikhs who stayed back in Pakistan.

The fact was that from the very day the two countries came into being, recriminations began piling up. Pakistan, in particular, blamed India for not letting it establish itself. When the riots disrupted train services, delaying the dispatch of government records from Delhi to Karachi, Pakistan saw it as an Indian plot to destabilize the administration of the new country. The delay, however, helped Karachi because it was able to avoid excessive red tape.

The Joint Defence Council was disbanded on 30 November 1947, four months earlier than scheduled. This caused the Pakistani government to infer that it was a ploy to deprive it of military stores. I was greatly disturbed by the growing hostility because I wanted the two countries to settle down to normalcy and talk about cooperation rather than engage in confrontation. New Delhi still had not sent all the equipment and stores pledged to Pakistan when the assets were divided.

Even Field Marshal Sir Claude Auchinleck, commander-in-chief of India before Independence, accused India of having designs to 'prevent Pakistan receiving her just share or indeed anything of arsenals and depots in India'. It was Sardar Vallabbhai Patel who was the stumbling block. He would say that India could not send Pakistan weapons in the midst of a war in Kashmir. When Mahatma

Gandhi's advice to Patel to release Pakistan's assets had no effect, Gandhi went on a fast, forcing New Delhi to honour its pledge. Even then India returned only Rs 20 crore as part of Pakistan's assets out of the fixed Rs 75 crore.

⚛

Delhi was in the throes of rioting when I reached the city on 15 September 1947. Our train was rerouted and detained at Meerut for 24 hours because of the riots. Muslims were fleeing the city as Hindus and Sikhs had been doing from West Punjab. It was a replay of the same bloody drama, only the victims had changed. I had not witnessed killings in Pakistan because I had left home only a month after Partition but I saw it in India's capital, New Delhi.

As Muslims were not safe on the streets of Delhi, most of them were moved to Purana Qila for security. Rioters went to the residence of diplomats in search of Muslim cooks and bearers, and this was rationalized as retaliation. The majority of the troops in Delhi were Hindus and Sikhs. The government suspected they were partial and were not wrong. The communal virus had infected many. By contrast I saw soldiers from southern India restoring law and order, without any favour.

Strangely, both Patel and the president of the constituent assembly, Dr Rajendra Prasad, reacted strongly to Jawaharlal Nehru's proposal to reserve certain residential areas in Delhi for Muslims. Nehru wanted to employ Muslims to protect the Muslim refugees. A few years later, when I, as the home ministry information officer, was part of the team escorting Rajendra Prasad after his retirement to Patna, his home town, he confirmed that he had written a letter to Nehru to warn him that 'his proposal would lead to undesirable and unexpected results'.

I could not understand the objection as the arrangement to house Muslim refugees was a temporary measure in order to make them feel secure. It reflected the general anti-Muslim bias, which I never imagined would exist at the level of Rajendra Prasad. He told me that he did not like Nehru's exhortations to his countrymen to behave in a civilized manner after hearing the news of killings from across the border. Prasad said that Nehru's speeches had only defamed India. I failed to understand the logic of remaining silent when dastardly acts were tearing asunder the fabric of pluralism in India.

Nehru found himself isolated in governance. Firstly, he had never thought that Pakistan would come into being. Secondly, he was confident that there would be no communal trouble after the British left. 'Was I not wrong?' he admitted later to a foreign dignitary. Nehru, however, pulled himself together and began depending upon Abul Kalam Azad and Rajkumari Amrit Kaur, the two minority members in the cabinet. Patel and Shyama Prasad Mukherjee invariably opposed him.

Gandhi supported Nehru's efforts to protect the minorities but he could not help him in the administration. Nehru constituted an emergency committee of the cabinet and got Mountbatten to preside over it, feeling it was beyond his capacity to handle 'so many problems at the same time'.

Mountbatten's version was that Nehru and Patel jointly appealed to him to handle the situation for them, and that he agreed provided his active role was kept secret for the time being and, while he would go through the motions of consulting his ministers, what he decided would be final. These conditions were accepted.

Patel also joined issue with Nehru on the powers of cabinet ministers. According to Patel, the prime minister could not interfere with the functioning of a ministry. He was only a leader among equals. If the prime minister wanted to overrule a minister, he (the prime minister) must bring the matter before the cabinet for its collective verdict.

❀

I could not live in the past. Whatever my agony, I had to start my life afresh. After leaving my bag at *mausi*'s place in Daryaganj, I went to Birla House where Mahatma Gandhi lived. I wanted to see him, not only because he had won us freedom from the British but also because he had given us dignity. I remembered how in my early teens in Sialkot, a white soldier in a sola topi had caned me because I was part of a procession shouting slogans for *azadi*. I did not approach the Mahatma but looked at him from afar. He was walking up and down in a veranda with his arms on the shoulders of two young women. I thought that one day I would tell my children and grandchildren that I had seen Gandhiji with my own eyes.

He would address a daily prayer meeting, when in Delhi, in the garden of Birla House. After a couple of bhajans, there were recitations from the Bible, the Quran, and the Gita, in that order. The venue was largely thronged by Punjabis who had come from Pakistan. The day I attended the meeting, one person objected to the recitation of the Quran. Many of us requested him to sit down but he kept standing. Gandhiji said that there would be no prayers because of the objection raised.

The following afternoon, the person withdrew his objection. Addressing the gathering, Gandhiji said he knew that many in the gathering had lost everything, even family members, but the country 'we are trying to build will be pluralistic and democratic' in character as envisioned during the freedom struggle. Taking off his spectacles, he said: 'Remember, Hindus and Muslims are my two eyes.' I live with those words to this days.

Jama Masjid, near Daryaganj was an area which I most frequented during those days. The non-vegetarian food there was cheap and delicious. Conspicuous was a red flag atop a building opposite the masjid. This was the headquarters of the Communist Party in Delhi. I went up the rickety staircase to inquire about my radical friends who had worked with me in the Students' Federation at Lahore and received no worthwhile information because the bespectacled Mohammed

Farooqi, then secretary of the party's Delhi unit, lectured me instead on the British designs to stay back in India using the maharaja of Kashmir and the nizam of Hyderabad as their proxies. Subsequently, I learnt that the Communists had been advised by Moscow to wage a war against the Indian bourgeoisie who had taken over the country. The Communists went underground and then resurfaced to participate in the first general election in April 1952.

Farooqi asked me to go and sell the Communist weekly, then called *People's Age*. I stood at a corner of nearby Sadar Bazar with a bundle of newspapers. A middle-aged woman approached me and began crying. She gave me a ten-rupee note, remarking that she did not know that the Doctor Sahib's family had reached the stage of selling newspapers. Apparently, she knew my parents. I tried to explain that it was not what she had imagined but she went on wiping her tears. I returned to the office and told Farooqi that I wanted a job. He asked me whether I knew Urdu. I was a graduate in Persian.

Farooqi was the person who, unwittingly, initiated me into journalism. Any job was good enough at that time and it did not necessarily have to be in the legal field. An affluent Muslim, Mohammed Yasin, who had stayed back in India, was the owner of an Urdu daily, *Anjam*. He had requested Farooqi to look for a Hindu who knew both English and Urdu. His was a pro-Muslim League and pro-Pakistan daily, which had poured venom against the Hindus but the paper felt rudderless after Partition.

Alongside the job at *Anjam* I also had to teach English and Mathematics to Yasin's two sons. He was more interested in my religious credentials than in my educational qualifications, viewing me as a liaison man who could help him secure his brother's property which had been sealed after the latter's departure to Pakistan.

When my visiting cards were delivered, I was surprised to see the designation of joint editor. In the proprietor's estimate, a joint editor would open more doors in the government than a low-level reporter. The office was located in Ballimaran, a Muslim locality, which looked forlorn; the atmosphere seemed congealed with submerged personal tragedies; the suffering of a community without any tangible sense of hope.

The Muslims felt cheated, not having realized that they would have to pay the price of Partition: a pronounced bias against them and the Hindus' demand that they go to Pakistan. Even today the same thing echoes in the ears of some of them. Muslims were afraid and confused, yearning to turn a new leaf but the Hindus were too bitter and too hostile to allow them any quarter.

The attitude of my Muslim colleagues at *Anjam* towards me indicated what was going on in the mind of the community. They treated me as if I was a first-class citizen and they were second class. Their dependence on the generosity of the majority community was pathetic. They behaved like people with a hat in hand, little realizing then that Pakistan was the cross they would have to carry for generations.

It was futile to argue who was responsible for the partition of the subcontinent. With the sequence of events stretching back decades, such an exercise could only be an academic distraction. It is, however, clear that the differences between Hindus and Muslims had become so acute by the mid–1940s that something akin to Partition had become inevitable.

🙏

Nothing has had a greater impact on me than Partition because it severed me from my roots and forced me to live in a new environment, embark on a new life. It is an irony of history that Muhammad Ali Jinnah, the founder of Pakistan, himself had not wanted it this way. He had fought for the creation of Pakistan but did not favour an exchange of population. Over the years what I have learnt is that Partition could have been averted. In any event, Jinnah was not happy with the way India was divided. From what I have heard, he regretted the events because in the final analysis he was uncertain about the way Pakistan would shape in the future.

K.H. Khurshid, Jinnah's private secretary, a Kashmiri who spoke fluent Punjabi, narrated to me years later an incident that occurred a few days after Partition. Jinnah was at the helm of affairs as Pakistan's first governor general. Sitting for lunch in the palatial residence in Karachi were Jinnah, his sister Fatima, Khurshid, and a young naval officer attached to the governor general. The officer was very perturbed because he had heard that his parents had been killed in India as they were trying to get to Pakistan.

He asked Jinnah bluntly: 'Sir, was creating Pakistan the right thing to do?' There was an eerie silence in the room. Jinnah paused a while before replying: 'I do not know young man. Only posterity will judge.'

Jinnah, it seems, had in mind some arrangement for free travel between the two countries. His reply to the Indian high commissioner in Karachi, Dr Sitaram, indicated as much. Jinnah had a sprawling house at Malabar Hill in Bombay (now Mumbai). Before declaring it to be evacuee property, Nehru wrote to Sitaram to find out from Jinnah what he wanted to do with the house. Jinnah's reply at that point was that he would like to retain it because he proposed spending a few weeks a year in Bombay.

The house remained in his name for a long time until it was taken over by the government of India. Subsequently, Pakistan tried its best to convert it into a consulate but New Delhi hedged all pressure. At one time the government of India had decided to hand over the house to Islamabad and even conveyed its decision but in the end changed its mind. Jinnah's daughter, Dina Wadia has raised her claim to it and the case is pending before the Bombay High Court.

The late Louis Heren, South Asia correspondent of the *Times,* London, who was stationed at Delhi in 1947–48 told me that Jinnah was not willing to accept the onus of Partition. I met Heren at his office in London in 1971 when I was collecting material for my book, *Distant Neighbours* (1972), a story of

India–Pakistan relations. I asked him if he had ever met Jinnah after Partition. He said, 'Yes'. Soon Heren was reminiscing about the past. He described an evening he had spent with Governor General Jinnah at Kohat, a cantonment in the North West Frontier Province (NWFP). Heren complained to him how unhappy he was over the division of the armed forces. To this Jinnah responded: 'Do not blame me; blame Nehru.'

In a letter to me dated 3 October 1971, Heren wrote: 'We [Jinnah and I] had a drink together one evening when, while acknowledging the creation of Pakistan and the political necessity for it, I regretted the partition of the Indian subcontinent. I can recall referring to the tragedy – for anybody who knew it in the past – of the division of the old Indian Army and the ICS. Strangely, he acknowledged all this and then went on to blame Nehru for Partition, as I said when we met in London.'

Heren recalled Jinnah's words: 'Had he [Nehru] agreed to the Muslim League joining the UP Congress government in 1937, there would have been no Pakistan.' He went on to add: 'Maulana Abul Kalam Azad, a venerable old leader of the Congress, regretted that Nehru's rejection gave the Muslim League a new lease of life.' Jinnah's allegation, according to Heren, suggested 'that Nehru's judgement was impaired by Purushottam Das Tandon, a Hindu nationalist who was a senior Congress leader in UP'. Azad said more or less the same thing in his book, *India Wins Freedom* (1988). He regretted that even Mahatma Gandhi did not intervene 'as he should have done'.

I personally do not know whether the refusal of two seats to the Muslim League in the UP Congress government hurt the Muslim community so acutely that it went on to demand a country of its own. Nehru's point of view came to be known many years later, in 1959. He maintained that Azad was wrong in his assessment. He was hurt by the Maulana's description of him as 'a vain person', the words which were mentioned in the 30 pages withheld for 30 years in consonance with Azad's wishes. The pages were released for publication in 1988, 24 years after Nehru's death.

Humayun Kabir, Azad's secretary, who gave the manuscript to the archives seven months after Azad's sudden death, told me that Azad did not want to publicize his views at that time because he felt it might weaken Nehru. However, the pages, when finally released, did not even create a ripple. Azad's judgement about Patel being pro-Hindu was well known. In the unreleased pages he said that the role Patel played was not always consistent with the ideals of the Congress. In fact, Azad's comments on Krishna Menon, who later became defence minister, were more telling. Azad considered Menon 'not trustworthy' and wanted his actions as high commissioner of India to the UK be investigated before appointing him a minister. Azad felt so strongly about this that he sent in his resignation when Nehru first spoke of including Menon in the cabinet in 1954.

Khaliq-ul-Zaman, a leading Muslim leader, would have been a member of the UP cabinet had the League been given the two seats. He supported Azad.

However, when I met him many years later in Karachi when he was suffering from protracted illness, I found him lamenting India's division and nurturing a sense of guilt as if he had betrayed the Muslims he had left behind in his home state of UP. He was far from being the only top Muslim League leader who regretted the formation of Pakistan. The party's treasurer, M.A.A. Nawab of Mehmoodabad, too shared the feeling that the division was a mistake. He wrote from London, where he had settled after Independence, to a well-known physician A. Faridi, a friend of his who lived in Lucknow, that 'the experiment we made was wrong'.

Regardless of these afterthoughts (there were thousands of Indian Muslims who regretted Partition) 90 per cent of them had supported the demand. I was in Lahore where a resolution was passed on 23 March 1940, supporting the formation of a country for Muslims on the basis of religion. (Ironically, Israel is the only other country to have been founded on the basis of religion.) The name 'Pakistan' was not mentioned in the resolution, but it subsequently came to be known as the 'Pakistan Resolution'. I was 16 years old then. The chief reporter of *Tribune*, A.N. Bali, a family friend, had taken me along to cover what proved to be a historic occasion.

I vividly recall that the *pandal* where the All India Muslim League session was being held, was metaphorically on fire with the radical idea of creating a new and independent Islamic country dividing the subcontinent. Thousands of people thronged the venue, traditionally used as an arena for wrestlers. What struck me was the mood. Those participating were defiant but disciplined, noisy but resolute, emotional but determined. This was no ordinary crowd but a multitude of people who had their eyes set on the stars. The Muslim League was not popular in Punjab in those days, although the party was taken more seriously than the other two formations: the authoritarian 'Khaksar' and the somewhat liberal 'Ahrar'.

Volunteers in green shirts, the hallmark of the Khaksars, carried *belchas* (shovels) and unsheathed swords as they conducted the League's president, Mohammed Ali Jinnah, thin and straight as a spindle, dressed in a tight-fitting black sherwani, to the dais amidst deafening slogans of 'Pakistan Zindabad'. The other person who was accorded a similar unsheathed sword reception was the bulky Bengal premier Fazl-ul-Haq.

Lahore, a national centre of learning, was the capital of Punjab. Even so, its premier, Sir Sikander Hayat Khan, a known Jinnah supporter, was conspicuous by his absence at the inauguration. Hayat, head of the unionist party of zamindars, represented a viewpoint which favoured the integration of Muslim-majority provinces into a separate state with 'some form' of central government for the whole of India, and with at least a common defence policy. The army had a strange fascination for the British. Hayat, who was close to them, reflected their way of thinking. He visualized a series of autonomous states in India within the British Commonwealth. This was, indeed, the plan devised by Professor Reginald Coupland, a renowned constitutional expert, and adviser to the Cabinet Mission which came to India six years later. Hayat had declared earlier that he would have nothing to do with Pakistan if it meant Muslim rule in some states and Hindu raj in the rest of the country.

I must admit that I did not take the demand for Pakistan seriously at the time. How could a mere resolution tear apart the Hindus and Muslims who had lived together for over a thousand years? They had shared a life which had over the years evolved into a unique subcontinental culture, with the communities retaining their identity and yet meshing into an ethos of coexistence. How could a mere piece of paper make them strangers, and how could my bosom friend Shafquat be alien to me? Both of us had studied together in the same school, the same Murray College, and lived in the same city, Sialkot, since childhood, like two members of a family. Still, the frenzy that I witnessed frightened me. Religious slogans like 'Yah Ali' were repeated time and time again, giving the entire atmosphere a religious tinge, suggesting that Pakistan would be a theocratic state.

In his address, Jinnah reiterated:

> Hindus and Muslims belong to two different religions, philosophies, social customs, and literature. They neither intermarry nor inter-dine, and, indeed, they belong to two different civilizations that are based mainly on conflicting ideas and conceptions. To yoke together two such nations under a single state, one as a numerical minority and the other as a majority, must lead to growing discontent and final destruction of any fabric that may be so built for the government of such a state.

A.K. Fazl-ul-Haq, the then chief minister of Bengal moved the Pakistan Resolution (also known as the Lahore Resolution), little realizing that the Muslim independent state he was endorsing would 31 years later split into two countries (Pakistan and Bangladesh). The resolution, passed by a show of hands, stated that no constitutional plan would be workable in the country or acceptable to the Muslims unless it was designed to follow certain basic principles. These were that geographically-contiguous units should be demarcated into regions with such territorial readjustments into areas where the Muslims were in a majority, as in the north-west and east, making up 'independent states in which the constituent units would be autonomous and sovereign'.

My reading is that Jinnah intentionally selected Fazl-ul-Haq as the mover of the Pakistan Resolution, fearing that East Pakistan might one day try to secede from Pakistan and hoping that he, coming from Bengal, would block any such move. Similarly, the selection of Punjab as the launching pad for the demand for Pakistan was intentional. This province had only a paper-thin Muslim majority. Jinnah could, however, foresee that if and when Pakistan came into being, Punjab would be its mainstay.

The use of word 'states', implying more than one Muslim country, was not noticed until the following day when Jinnah clarified that the word was a typographical error and should have been 'state'. Khaliq-ul-Zaman commented that the president on his own could not change the wording of the resolution. Years later, after the liberation of Bangladesh in 1971, Zulfikar Ali Bhutto, the then president of Pakistan, quipped during an interview to me at Rawalpindi: 'Quite a costly typing mistake. I must be careful about my stenographer.'

The use of the word 'states' might have been deliberate on the part of the top Muslim League leaders (not Jinnah) who drafted the resolution with the idea of constituting Muslim states on either side of the majority Hindu India. Many years later I found in the archives at London a document spelling out the same concept of two Muslim states: one in the north-west (Sind, Baluchistan, NWFP, and Punjab, together with Delhi after amalgamation with Punjab); the other in the Northeast (Assam and Bengal, excluding the districts of Bankura and Midnapur together with the district of Purnea from Bihar). The document was prepared by a Muslim League committee appointed soon after the adoption of the Pakistan Resolution. Surprisingly, the committee did not say a word about Kashmir, the state which subsequently drew India and Pakistan into three wars. This committee probably had in mind a federal structure in the subcontinent because its document suggested a central machinery concerned with external relations, defence, communications, customs, and safeguards for minorities.

It was in fact the unity of Muslims that the speakers underlined at the League's session in Lahore. They shared Jinnah's belief in the two-nation theory. Virtually all the speakers criticized Maulana Abul Kalam Azad, then the Congress party president, who they said, was opposed to a Muslim homeland although himself a Muslim. He was dubbed a 'show boy of Hindus'. The remark surprised me because it reflected almost unbridgeable differences between the two communities.

In his presidential address at the Congress session held earlier, Azad had vehemently criticized the two-nation theory as it suggested religious separatism. He had exhorted Muslims to preserve a united India as both Hindus and Muslims were Indians who shared deep bonds of brotherhood and nationhood. He had said:

> Islam has now as great a claim on the Indian soil as Hinduism. If Hinduism has been the religion of the people here for several thousands of years, Islam also has been their religion for a thousand years. Just as a Hindu can say with pride that he is an Indian and follows Hinduism, so also can we say with equal pride that we are Indians and follow Islam.

The idea of Pakistan was nothing new. I had heard of it earlier. The bulky and overbearing Mohammed Iqbal, an eminent Urdu poet from Sialkot, had proposed the amalgamation of Punjab, the NWFP, and Baluchistan into a single, free Muslim state. On the other hand, he wrote to the Punjab governor that he was not the author of the Pakistan idea, which came from Rahamat Ali, living in London. I wondered how the same person who had written '*Sare Jahan Se Achha, Hindustan Hamara*' could also articulate a proposal for India's division and subsequently write: '*Muslim hain hum watan hai sara jahan hamara.*' Did Iqbal ride two horses at the same time or did he undergo a metamorphosis? Significantly, when meeting Jawaharlal Nehru in Lahore, Iqbal remarked: 'What is common between you and Jinnah? You are a patriot and he is a politician.' Iqbal embraced Nehru, hailing him in Punjabi: '*Mera sher puttar* [my lion son], *mera dilare puttar* [my courageous son].' Iqbal's point of pride was that Nehru's ancestors, like his, came from Kashmir.

My friend Shafquat, who lived near Iqbal's house, took me there once to meet the poet. Iqbal was sitting on a charpai which was touching the floor under the strain of his weight. He was hurling such vulgar abuses in chaste Punjabi that we literally fled from there.

The Pakistan Resolution became widely popular among Muslims, exceeding even Jinnah's expectations. It was like an avalanche that swept away all other ideas and threw up the Muslim League as the most influential body among Muslims. Only the Pathans in the NWFP were unaffected. They had been grounded in pluralism by an austere, secular Muslim leader, Khan Abdul Ghaffar Khan, popularly known as 'the Frontier Gandhi'. Baluchistan too remained distant, opposing the League. Punjab was interested in a general way, but there was no evident enthusiasm.

The Muslims who were truly dazzled by the demand for Pakistan were from the Urdu-speaking UP, Bihar, and Delhi, the areas which it was apparent would never form a part of Pakistan if ever it came into being. Their psyche was not difficult to understand. They considered themselves the ones who had ruled India for thousands of years, and could not reconcile themselves to the idea of a post-British dispensation where they would not enjoy superiority, either in numbers, power, or status. The dream of being rulers blinded them to the reality that in a democratic polity the majority would be at the helm of affairs.

Jinnah relentlessly kept elucidating his two-nation theory. Muslims and Hindus should have their own separate countries after the departure of the British. He would argue that Muslims didn't want to live in a country where Hindus would be in a majority and hold the reins of government. Nehru, however, pointed out several times that when even a small village had Hindus and Muslims living together, how was it possible to separate them? The Pakistan idea, I found, was more captivating in cities, not in the countryside.

When Jinnah's opponents questioned the economic viability of the proposed state, he would say: 'Then leave us to our fate.' When some spoke nostalgically about the composite culture of Hindus and Muslims, he would answer: 'Our sense of values and objectives in life and politics differ greatly.' When Hindus referred to the Pakistan demand as 'vivisection of their motherland', he said that for the Muslims it was 'a struggle for survival'. The parting of ways had begun, I regretfully noted. Nastiness in discussions had also entered the political discourse.

Pakistan became 'the promised land' and Jinnah its Moses. As time passed, Muslims from different walks of life and from different age groups rallied behind him. They saw in Pakistan a realization of their dreams. Educationally and economically, Hindus were far ahead of the Muslims who were primarily tillers of the land or artisans; Hindus controlled industry and business. I recall that the Mall, Lahore's posh shopping centre, had only one shop owned by a Muslim.

Economic backwardness apart, I saw Muslims coming around to believing that Islam itself would be in danger in India with a vast Hindu majority. Bengal, on the one hand, and UP, Bihar, and Delhi, on the other, would express such views openly. Little thought, I could see, was given to the fate of those Muslims who would remain in 'Hindu Hindustan' after Pakistan was created. Azad would warn in vain that the Muslims would 'awake and discover overnight that they have become aliens and foreigners. Backward industrially, educationally, and economically, they will be left to the mercies of what would then become an unadulterated Hindu Raj.' His warning touched many hearts.

Many years later, a central government minister, M.C. Chagla, Jinnah's lawyer-friend from Bombay, told me that when he asked Jinnah what would happen to the Muslims left behind in India, his reply was that they would have nothing to be afraid of as 'Hindus would be living in Pakistan just as Muslims in India'. This hostage theory advanced in the early 1940s frightened me. I thought Nehru had a point when he said that the division of India would not solve the problem of 'two nations' because both communities were spread throughout the country. Even so, I could sense the atmosphere getting polarized by the day.

Some British experts warned that once broken into separate and independent entities, India would lapse into a welter of contending powers in which free institutions would be suppressed and in which no one element would be able to defend itself against an external attack. They thought a federation was a better solution.

I found that the Congress leaders did not oppose the idea of a federation. Their only condition was that the British should stay out. Even the Indian States' Peoples' Conference, a Congress-led body, agitating for people's rule, did not outrightly reject the federation proposal. However, Jinnah told Lord Linlithgow, the then viceroy, that the League could not support any federal scheme which would 'produce a Hindu majority'. I feel that India and Pakistan becoming a federation or a confederation did not fit in with the Muslims' demand at that time. Pakistan had first to be created for these ideas to take shape. Such proposals came to be mooted in Pakistan many years later.

I don't think that the opposition of the League or the Congress was material because the central player in this scheme of things was the comity of princely states. When they rejected the idea of a federation, the British put the proposal in cold storage.

Lord Mountbatten told me later when I met him in the UK that if the princes had not been so 'foolish' as to reject the federal idea, India would not have been partitioned. I met him after his retirement in his sprawling mansion, Broadlands near London. This assertion was strange because the princes had no entity of their own. They were marionettes in British hands. My experience told me that whenever the Congress intensified the Independence movement in the princely states, the British responded as if the Raj was under attack and bolstered their support to the rulers. I think London changed its mind about the idea of a federation because of Jinnah's pressure.

In the 1940s, a change, more psychological than real, began manifesting itself in relations between Hindus and Muslims. The two began to feel more at home with members of their own community. Social contacts began wilting. Many Hindus still sent sweets to their Muslim friends on Diwali, as my mother did, and Muslims, in turn, sent us meat after a Muslim festival like Bakr-Id but many wondered whether the practice had outlived its utility.

However, the Muslims in the north had a different perspective from those in the south. The latter had got integrated with the Hindus and had developed a composite regional culture. Muslims in the north had a complex of superiority having once been rulers. Islam unified the Muslims in the north and south. Jinnah had sensed this and used religion to forge unity within the community and create a sense of a separate identity.

Surprisingly, public discussion on Pakistan was rare. The dialogue was between the leaders of the Congress and the Muslim League. College students like us avoided the subject. Nonetheless, loyalty to the idea of Pakistan was expected from Muslims, just as opposition was assumed from Hindus. Some Muslims would themselves scoff at the whole idea, particularly the word 'Pak' which meant 'pure'. My Persian professor at Forman Christian College, Lahore, opposed the concept on that ground alone. Azad told me after Independence that the very term of Pakistan went against its grain. It suggested some portions of the world were pure while others were impure.

Yet, fear impregnated the minds of Hindus; fear of the unknown. My family, peaceful in every way, thought of protecting itself. My father travelled by train to Multan to obtain a double-barreled gun through Nakul Sen, the deputy commissioner transferred from Sialkot. It was a hush-hush job and I never saw the gun. It remained hidden till my younger brother, Hardip, fired it in a room out of curiosity. It made such a loud bang that people gathered outside our home to find out what had happened. However, aware of my father's Gandhian traits, no one suspected us of having a gun. The speculations, however, reached our ears and it became a problem to decide what to do with the weapon. Finally, we dumped it in a well in our premises.

Some Muslims questioned what Pakistan was supposed to achieve when more Muslims would be left behind in India. Jinnah did not spell out the concept of Pakistan because he wanted both London and the Congress to concede equality between the two communities.

I watched the demand for separation slowly becoming a rallying point for Muslims who saw in Pakistan a panacea for their economic, social, and political backwardness or what had been 'denied' to them. To blame only Jinnah for the differences that divided the Hindus and Muslims would be unfair. He merely gave shape to the latent estrangement between the two communities.

The hiatus between them had been visible, at least in the urban areas, for a long time. They lived in separate localities, had separate eating places, and separate places for social gatherings. Railway stations had separate water pitchers, with 'Hindu' or 'Muslim' written in bold letters. A similar segregation was visible in government offices. There were no protests against the practice; no indignation. In hostels, the kitchens were separate. Whenever I wanted a better-tasting mutton curry, I would get food from the Muslim kitchen and Muslims would order vegetables from the Hindu kitchen.

The demand for Pakistan also evoked among Muslims a longing to find their roots. They would trace them to earlier Afghan and the Mughal regimes in India. Otherwise too, Muslims looked back to the days when they had ruled India for 600 years. They became conscious of how 'different' they were from 'the polyglot, caste-ridden Hindus'. Urdu, a language born around Delhi, gave them a sense of superiority. The British, who exploited these differences, were shocked in 1857 when Muslims and Hindus united to fight a liberation struggle. The British crushed it brutally but were shaken by the solidarity between the two communities.

In 1909, when the British introduced separate electorates, with Hindus voting for Hindu candidates and Muslims for Muslim, along with reservations in the services on the basis of religion, the division between the two communities became institutionalized. From then on, they rapidly began drifting apart. Azad wished the Indian Muslims had led the national struggle for freedom. He said that Arab and Turk revolutionaries, with whom he was in touch in the 1920s, could not understand why Indian Muslims were mere camp followers of the British. The demand for Pakistan, some believed, covered up the stigma.

Being the idealist I was, I imagined that the differences between Hindus and Muslims would disappear once the British left. However, my five years in Lahore, two in Forman Christian College and three in Law College, convinced me that the mistrust between them was so deep that either they would sit across the table one day to thrash out their differences once and for all or they would continue to live in hostility.

Jinnah recognized the scenario much earlier than the Congress, which was totally absorbed in the struggle against the British. To begin with, Jinnah appealed to Hindus to accept the Muslims' demand for separate electorates to win the confidence and trust of the community. Until then, the Congress had not formally accepted the proposal, whether for legislatures or the central assembly. Jinnah rationalized: Separate electorates were not a matter of policy but a necessity for Muslims who needed to be raised from the torpor into which they had sunk. The Congress slowly came around to accepting the proposal. This only gave a new edge to the two-nation theory and widened the chasm between Hindus and Muslims. Whenever we, the Hindus, discussed the separate electorates, we felt it would alienate Muslims from us.

There was a narrowing of the gap when Mahatma Gandhi brought about Hindu–Muslim unity in 1920 over the Khilafat movement, which supported a sectarian demand for a caliph among Muslims. The demand ended when Kamal Pasha of Turkey jettisoned the entire idea. Yet, the brief togetherness between the two communities was a welcome development.

Muslims stayed away from the Congress for numerous reasons. They feared that their historical and religious culture would be submerged in a Hindu-majority party.

A chasm was already growing between the Hindus, who had taken advantage of English-language education and Western thought to widen their horizons and improve their economic conditions, and the general run of Muslims who had not. Then there was the well-crafted policy of the British government to keep the Muslims down after the 1857 uprising where they had been in the forefront. Gandhi's emphasis on the worship of cow, which the Muslims ate as part of their daily diet, did not help matters. A vast majority of Muslims considered Islam as much an ideology as a religion. Islam provided them with a system that was complete in itself.

Culture and religion were so fused in Hinduism that there was hardly any distinction between the two. Thus Indian nationalism had come to acquire a somewhat Hinduized character, and Muslims could not stomach this. Many years later, in 1938, when the Muslim League appointed Raja Sayed Mohammed Mehdi of Pirpur to examine the Congress governments' performance, it was 'proved' that Muslims had been 'maltreated'. This was an exaggeration but there was some truth in the allegation that the Congress rule in the states had given Hindus a sense of superiority. It was reflected in the governance. A few chief ministers of the Congress-run states had, indeed, behaved in a partisan manner.

Muslims saw in Pakistan an alternative to Congress rule. They were belatedly supported by the British who helped Muslim landlords and wealthy members of the community to form the All India Muslim League on 30 December 1906 as they had done in the case of the Indian National Congress on 28 December 1885 with A.O. Hume, a Britisher, as its leader. He was asked by the British rulers to create a forum to ventilate grievances. They believed such a step would take the wind out of sails of the aspiring nationalists who were still stuck on the glimmer of freedom that had flickered in the 1857 uprising.

The Muslim League had little impact or respect until Jinnah took over in 1916. He had left for London in disgust because he did not feel at home with most of his colleagues in the Congress party, who mixed religion with politics. His greatest grievance was against Gandhi who spoke of Ram Rajya and political emancipation in the same breath.

On his return from London Jinnah said his experience in the Congress party had taught him that Muslims had to fend for themselves. His terminology came from Islam as did his politics. He soon emerged as the Muslim's Quaid-e-Azam (Great Leader), a title bequeathed by Gandhiji. I heard Nehru explaining at a meeting that Jinnah 'had left the Congress, not because of any difference of opinion on the Hindu–Muslim question, but because of his failure to adapt 'to the new and more advanced ideology, and even more so because he disliked the crowds of ill-dressed people, speaking in Hindustani, who filled the Congress'. Once hailed by Congress leader Sarojini Naidu as the best ambassador of Hindu–Muslim unity, Jinnah was now considered an inveterate separatist. He, however, had the satisfaction of knowing that he was uniting the Muslims of India into one nation and giving them a platform and a voice.

Jinnah used the Pirpur report to highlight the differences between Hindus and Muslims, and made it appear as if the Congress governments had been wreaking vengeance on 'the helpless Muslim minority'. On the other hand, he joined issue with Gandhi and Nehru, making it clear to them that he would plough a parochial furrow. When Gandhi wrote to Jinnah to inquire: 'Are you still the same Mr Jinnah, the staunchest of nationalists and the hope of both Hindus and Muslims?' he shot back, 'Nationalism is not the monopoly of any single individual and in these days it is very difficult to define it'.

I think the personal rivalry between Jinnah and Nehru was not limited to issues, and this made the scene murkier. They were two very different personalities. Both were brilliant in their own way and had a magnetic appeal for the masses but ideologically they were poles apart. I feel one of the reasons Jinnah left the Congress was that there was not enough space for both him and Nehru. Gandhi was inclined towards Nehru and Jinnah realized that Nehru would inherit the Congress mantle.

Two letters exchanged between them, underlined the differences between Nehru and Jinnah. In reply to Nehru's letter of 16 April 1938, contending that 'the Muslim League is an important communal organization but the other organizations, even though they might be younger and smaller, cannot be ignored', Jinnah said: 'Your tone and language again display the same arrogance and militant spirit, as if the Congress is the sovereign power'. Unless the Congress recognized the Muslim League on an equal footing and was prepared to negotiate a Hindu–Muslim settlement, Jinnah said he would depend upon 'our inherent strength'.

Jinnah also objected to the Congress using 'Vande Mataram' as the national anthem. This was odd because people were used to singing it at every meeting held to call for India's Independence. Nehru argued that his party could not compel large numbers of people to abandon what they had come to associate with the freedom movement. The song was adapted from a Bengali novel, *Anandamath*, which personified the motherland as Goddess Durga. This was repugnant to Muslims who opposed idol worship. The first two stanzas of the song, which the Congress used, should not have caused any offence because there was no reference to the goddess, but that did not mollify Jinnah. I found it ominous that whatever he said would become normal vocabulary for the Muslims.

After Independence India adopted the song as an alternative national anthem. Humayun Kabir, subsequently appointed education minister in Nehru's cabinet, once told me: 'It was very unfair for a secular India to have adopted "Vande Mataram" because of its religious overtones.' I was unable to understand why Muslims objected to the compromise of using only the first two stanzas which appealed to nationalist sentiments alone.

While Gandhi travelled from one civil disobedience meeting to another, Jinnah propagated his two-nation theory from one Muslim League platform to another. The latter repeatedly plugged the same line: Gandhi was fighting for the supremacy of Hindus and the submergence of Muslims within the Congress party. Gandhi posed a question: Did he become a different nation overnight if he embraced Islam; Jinnah did not respond.

However, the British were overjoyed with all these developments. It gave them a credible excuse for remaining on in India. They cited the growing distrust between the two communities as an argument to convince people abroad that British Raj had to stay. Hindus and Muslims were at daggers drawn and needed the overlord to maintain peace.

The Muslims who supported the Congress were known as nationalist Muslims but they became increasingly equivocal in their attitude towards the party because of Jinnah's pre-eminence in the community. The distance between the Congress and nationalist Muslims would become more visible during the election. The latter constituted a unity board, thinking that this would have greater appeal for the Muslim electorate but the strategy annoyed Hindus, embarrassed the Congress, and evoked little support among Muslims. I felt helpless when the Indian press, largely owned by Hindus, was hard on nationalist Muslims whenever they tried to distance themselves from the Congress. Even their opposition to the demand for Pakistan was considered dubious. They suffered silently for their commitment to the Congress ideology and opposition to the creation of Pakistan.

Strangely, Jinnah did not shake hands with Azad while doing so with Nehru and Patel after a meeting. Azad was different. Many years later, when his plane was stuck at Karachi on its way to India, he went to Jinnah's mausoleum to say prayers (Fateha).

My disappointment knew no bounds when I found the All India Students' Federation, a left-of-centre group, supporting the demand for Pakistan. Even some leading Muslim communists joined the League. Subsequently, I learnt that this was at the instance of the Soviet Union, which by then had sided with the Allies in their war against Germany. Supporting the British in India was Moscow's policy, and so was that of the communists. Only a few days before the Federation had labelled the demand for Pakistan 'an imperialist ploy' but it was now hailing it as 'a genuine expression of Muslim identity'. Those who protested against the volte-face were denounced as votaries of vested interests. However, those who supported the demand for Pakistan, nawabs or zamindars, were hailed as progressive. It was a dialectical materialism of sorts.

Khan Abdul Ghaffar Khan was labelled an agent of the capitalists because he opposed the demand for Pakistan. How could the comrades consider feudal lords in the Muslim League, such as the Nawab of Mamdot and Sir Feroze Khan Noon from Punjab, as progressive? I asked. The reply was that after the Soviet Union joined, the scenario had changed the Allies. True, it did not mean that the rich had become the proletarians but the League, unlike the Congress, did not oppose the British rulers for having pushed India into the war without consulting it.

꽃

I would proudly mention in public the names of Jayaprakash Narayan, Aruna Asaf Ali, and Achyut Patwardhan, the three left-of-centre leaders, who had kept alight the flame of defiance against the British through an underground movement following the wholesale arrest after Gandhi's slogan of Quit India. I was, however, crestfallen when Patwardhan told me several years later that the Quit India Movement was 'a waste of time and energy'. India, he said, would have achieved independence in any case after the war as the British were in no position to sustain the empire, and neither had the money or manpower required to suppress a turbulent India. Patwardhan's words were: 'We had many people killed and imprisoned unnecessarily.'

I admired the manner in which Aruna Asaf Ali infused life into the Quit India Movement while remaining underground. Her dodging the best security arrangements and flying the Congress flag at Gowalia Tank Maidan of Bombay on 9 August 1942, the Quit India Day, was a daring act. Millions admired her for it, especially at a time when they felt leaderless as Gandhi and other top Congressmen had been detained a day earlier.

Aruna was a picture of rebellion even when I met her many years later as the owner of *Patriot,* a daily newspaper, and *Link,* a weekly magazine. She was among the very few who disseminated the Left perspective in India which had adopted a mixed economy model under Nehru's prime-ministership. She said she was proud of being associated with the Quit India Movement and recalled how she, along with her husband, Asaf Ali, had met Bhagat Singh in jail a few days before he was hanged. For her, he was a role model. She called me once when some of her staff were trying to take over her publications. I was of little help but she was able to retain ownership.

Britain tried to limit the increasing unrest among the people following the Quit India movement by sending a senior cabinet minister, Sir Stafford Cripps, to meet the Congress and the Muslim League leaders. His mission in 1942 was to offer India 'power' after the end of the war. At the heart of his proposal was the creation of a de jure cabinet at the Centre, to be called an Executive Council under the viceroy who would be the the de facto boss. The proposal had the seeds for germinating Pakistan because it said that any province which did not want to accede to the union, could remain outside it as a separate entity.

Gandhi, who guided the Congress, rejected the proposal outright and characterized it as a post-dated cheque drawn on a failing bank. There was, however, more to it than that. The reality was that Gandhi did not want to be part of the war, not only because of his faith in non-violence but also because he honestly believed that the Allies would be defeated. From his perspective, accepting Cripps' proposals meant participating in a war, which he thought the US and Britain had almost lost. Nehru, for his part, was in favour of Cripps' proposals because he wanted to join the global democratic alliance against fascism. He was keen to re-establish his credentials as a liberal democrat which some in the West had begun to doubt when the Congress imposed conditions for joining the Allies.

Jinnah, known to be a personal friend of the then British prime minister, Winston Churchill, was equivocal on Cripps' proposals. He wanted to know what the Congress had in mind because he often played his cards after the Congress had announced its decision. He knew that without Congress backing, Cripps' proposals were as good as dead. Accordingly, he too rejected them when the Congress said 'No'. The real reason for the rejection, as Azad, the then Congress president, recounted, was the last-minute change in the proposal by Britain: from an undertaking to grant Independence at the end of war to a mere favourable consideration of India's demand for freedom.

My own view, as I recall those critical days, was that if the Congress had accepted Cripps' proposals, it would have saved India from partition. True, the proposals held the seeds of division but the federal structure that the proposals provided would have forced the Congress and the Muslim League to work together for a single country. It would have meant depending on British goodwill, but that would have been temporary. Any one could see that London would be in no position to maintain its hold over India after the Second World War.

Following the failure of the Cripps' Mission, a group of Hindu extremists suddenly emerged on the scene and warned that the millions of Muslims who continued to live in India after the formation of Pakistan would pay the price of 'Bharat Mata's vivisection'. In other words, the Muslims left behind in India would have to face the 'consequences'. Azad angrily scotched the thesis of hostages. Yet, in a way, he was proved wrong because the Muslims in India after Partition were victims of reprisals in the form of prejudice, neglect, and mistrust. They continue to face the same fate.

The atmosphere in the subcontinent became increasingly murky. Both Hindus and Muslims, primarily those living north of the Vindhyas, began to feel that the parting of ways was inevitable. It was not as if the country was sharply divided into Hindus and Muslims. There was a vast grey area, but it was shrinking rapidly. The desire for separation had overtaken most of the Muslims. They increasingly flocked to the League, which was emerging as the only representative body in the community.

Nearly a year before the creation of Pakistan, Azad described what would happen to the Muslims in an interview to an Urdu magazine, *Chetan,* in Lahore:

Today the Muslims are not walking, they are flowing. The problem is that Muslims have not learnt to walk steady; they either run or flow with the tide. When the group of people loses their confidence and self respect, they are surrounded by imaginary doubts and dangers and fail to make a distinction between right and wrong. The true meaning of life is realized not through numerical strength but through firm faith and righteous action.

He cautioned Muslims that the formation of Pakistan would stop the spread of Islam in India.

Despite acute differences between the Congress and the League, a flicker of hope appeared when they joined hands to defend members of the Indian National Army (INA) put on trial in Delhi in 1945. The INA was a roughly 20,000-strong force drawn from Indian soldiers captured by the Japanese after the fall of Malaya and Burma. Led by the fiery former Congress President Subhash Chandra Bose, a passionate advocate of Indian Independence, the INA was in a way an anti-colonial movement. Bose was not bothered about the niceties of method, an article of faith with Gandhi, but with the ends alone. Bose said he would achieve Independence without violence, if possible, but would use arms if necessary. This approach distanced him from Gandhi. He stealthily left his home in Calcutta where he had been detained by the British. I have seen the place in Kabul where he stayed before slipping into Europe. It was a solitary room on top of a dilapidated building when I visited it some 40 years ago. His escape, first to Germany and then to Japan was applauded by India.

Nonetheless, I had reservations about the INA which, however nationalist, was dependent upon Japan, a fascist country fighting against the democratic world. I was happy that the INA had demanded India's freedom but wondered whether the Japanese would have freed us had they won. My fears were somewhat allayed when Gandhi praised Bose, recalling not only his bravery and patriotism but also his contribution to the freedom struggle. He did not criticize the creation of the INA. Subhash Chandra Bose never returned to India, dying in 'an air crash'. The authenticity of the accident is still doubted even after three probes at the behest of the Indian government.

The trial of three INA officers (between November 1945 and May 1946) – Shah Nawaz, a Muslim; Prem Sehgal, a Hindu; and Gurbax Singh Dhillon, a Sikh – forged a unity of sorts. There was a joint countrywide demand for their release. This had its impact because the British government bowed to the pressure and released all three. It was one of the rare occasions when Nehru, who had a law degree from London, donned his lawyer's robe to appear in court. The way in which Hindus, Muslims, and Sikhs came together at the time was proof that the Congress and the League could overcome their internecine quarrels on an issue that transcended their differences.

However, not a single member from the INA was taken back into the army. The British top brass refused on grounds of 'morale and discipline'. Nehru could have insisted on absorption of the INA men into the Indian army and the nation would have backed him, but he faltered and went along with the British who made it an issue. The nationalists, and 20,000 soldiers of independence lost the opportunity to be integrated in the armed forces.

A similar angry outburst, national in scope and secular in character, was visible in the wake of the Royal Indian Navy uprising in February 1946 against the general conditions in the naval force. Once again, both Muslims and Hindus stood together to defy the British. Nearly 3,000 ratings from the two communities marched on the streets of Bombay. There was an exchange of fire between the British soldiers and the 'mutineers'. Sardar Patel, the Iron Man of the Congress, was against the uprising. Nehru joined him to condemn the 'mutiny of ratings'. It was called off but the bourgeois character of Congress leaders became ever more visible. This made me wonder if a post-Independence Congress government would respect popular agitations and ideological challenges.

The INA trial and the Ratings uprising made us feel good. A pleasant mood of expectancy over, the country looked towards London for some important announcement on India's future. The Labour party's victory in the 1945 British elections strengthened the impression that Britain's policies would change. This proved to be true. London announced fresh elections in India. The British also held out the promise of an 'early realization of full government'. Both the Congress and the League expressed their disappointment over the wording of the announcement; the former missing any reference to Independence and the latter to Pakistan.

Yet, whatever their reservations, the two parties participated in the polls to prove their support among the electorate. The League likened the polls to a referendum on Pakistan; the Congress characterized them as a path to

Swaraj (self-rule or Independence). The Communist Party of India, which otherwise opposed communalism, clung to the old formula of supporting whatever the Soviets wanted. In this case it was the creation of Pakistan. The Hindu Mahasabha fought on the platform of Akhand Bharat (United India). I recall that Nehru, accompanied by Sheikh Abdullah, then popularly called the Kashmiri Gandhi, came to address an election meeting in Sialkot. Both, clad in khaddar achkans, urged the gathering, which had waited for five hours to listen to them, to vote for the Congress. The two travelled together in many parts of India.

The results of the poll held in 1946, a year before Partition, demonstrated that 90 per cent Hindus were with the Congress while 90 per cent Muslims supported the League. Of the 102 elected seats in the Central Assembly, the Congress won 57 and the League 30. Every Muslim seat in the Central Assembly went to the League. It also won 442 out of the 509 Muslim seats in the provincial assemblies. Once again, the League lost the NWFP assembly where nationalist Muslims won a majority. Baluchistan too rejected the League and in Punjab, the pro-agriculturist Unionist Party took seven Muslim seats away from the League. It was obvious that a line had been drawn between Hindus and Muslims. Meanwhile, London announced the visit of the Cabinet Mission to India.

2

THE NEHRU YEARS
The Road to Partition

In this chapter I have dealt in detail with the Cabinet Mission's plan because I believe it was the last scheme, and the last opportunity, to save India from division. The Mission's three ministers – Frederick Pethick-Lawrence, then secretary of state for India; Sir Stafford Cripps; and A.V. Alexander – arrived in India on 24 March 1946. Cripps was an old hand and friendly to India. Pethick-Lawrence was more sold on India's independence than Cripps. Alexander was, however, a Churchillian who could not brook the thought of the British losing India, the jewel in the crown. The Mission's thinking was clear from its observation at the first press conference: the British wanted Indians to set up an 'acceptable' machinery to realize full independent status and to put interim arrangements in place. That Jinnah stood for India's partition was no secret for the Mission. It did not, however, know how far the Congress was willing to accommodate him. It therefore initiated its talks with the Congress to get a sense of where the party stood.

To the Mission's surprise, Nehru spoke about a plebiscite in the border districts as if his party had already accepted the idea of division. Jinnah also mentioned partition, and told a Punjab Hindu delegation that in his scheme of things Ambala would not form part of Pakistan. Azad, still the Congress president, was on a different wavelength. He ruled out both Partition and a unitary structure. His thesis, which Gandhi had approved, was that a federal constitution would give full autonomy to the provinces and transfer all subjects to them except defence, foreign affairs, and communications. If they so desired, the provinces could delegate more subjects to the Centre. This was, to use Pethick-Lawrence's words, 'a new solution of the communal problem'. He liked Azad's proposal: provinces getting full autonomy and, at the same time, retaining links with the Centre to keep the country a single entity.

Azad's effort was to allay the fears of the Muslim majority provinces. He wanted to ensure a secure position for the community in a free India. However, at the same time he wanted the community to play a pivotal role in creating a pluralistic society. 'The basis of Pakistan,' he argued, 'was the fear of interference by the Centre in Muslim majority areas since the Hindus would be in a majority at the Centre.' He tried to counter these fears by proposing full autonomy to the provincial units and also vesting in them the residuary power. Two lists of central subjects were contemplated, one compulsory and the other optional. The provinces would administer all affairs, excluding the three subjects given to the Centre: foreign affairs, defence, and communications.

I liked Azad's scheme because it kept India united and at the same time gave autonomy to the provinces. I imagined that there was something called the Indian civilization, 5000-years old, to which the Muslims had also contributed. If and when the chips were down that pull of civilizational links would prevail and India would stay one. I was however proved wrong. Hindus and Muslims had drifted too far apart. One person who could make the difference was Jinnah, and he did not want a centralized government, however federal in character.

Azad's formula was a midway solution. It gave space to both the provinces and to the Indian union. Azad wanted to avoid the shortcomings of the Pakistan scheme which would leave roughly 12 per cent Muslims in India with 80 per cent Hindus.

Azad called a meeting of senior Congress leaders to stress that after attaining freedom India would forget the days of communal suspicion and conflict, and face the problems of modern life from a modern point of view. Opposition among political parties would continue, but it would be based on economic and political issues, not religious. Class and not community would be the basis of future alignments, and policies would be shaped accordingly. I hoped such thinking would become a reality. Both Azad and Khan Abdul Ghaffar Khan were too optimistic and failed to realize that the poison of communalism had penetrated too deeply into India's body politic.

Cripps asked Azad whether the Muslim-majority provinces could align themselves to administer subjects other than those delegated to the Centre. Azad's reply was that this was 'worth considering'. He was not opposed to the idea but did not give a categorical reply at that time because Patel had made it clear before Azad's meeting with the Mission members that every comma and full stop of the scheme had to be discussed and approved by Congress leaders before anyone could say anything on behalf of the party. Patel's obvious reference was to Azad.

I believe Patel's suspicion was that Azad and Nehru were in league and would bypass him. Even during the Cripps Mission in 1942, he was tormented by similar thoughts. C.P. Ramaswami Iyer, a distinguished scholar from south India, with whom I briefly worked on a committee on Hindu temples to ensure their proper administration, told me that Patel 'interpreted the Cripps

Mission as an organized stunt by Nehru to get himself into the forefront so that he could become the prime minister of India'.

Azad's meeting with the Cabinet Mission was discussed threadbare by the Congress Working Committee (CWC) when it met on 12 April 1946. Members voiced their doubts over the federal structure. Gandhi came to Azad's rescue and silenced the critics by saying that a federal solution alone could work in a country of India's size and diversities. When Patel said that subjects like currency and finance should be in the hands of the Centre, Gandhi intervened to say that it would be in the interest of the provinces to have a unified policy in such matters but it was not necessary to include such subjects in a compulsory central list.

The Mission was clear on its purpose. It wanted a united India, with a status somewhere between a federal structure and autonomous provinces. When the Mission invited Jinnah for talks it placed two options before him. One was the constitution of a separate state of Pakistan embracing Sind, the NWFP, Baluchistan, Punjab, Assam, and the Muslim-majority districts of Bengal minus Calcutta, linked to India in a mutual defence alliance.

The other option was to group together more or less the same areas with a strong Centre. There was a provision for a central government with an equal number of Hindu and Muslim ministers to administer defence, foreign affairs, and communications. After 15 years, either group could secede from the union. The princely states could either join India or Pakistan or remain separate.

Alexander in his diary, which I read in the archives many years later, had jotted down on 2 April 1946 that Jinnah did not define what he meant by Pakistan. Neither did M.A. Ispahani and the Raja of Mahmudabad, the two Muslim League stalwarts who met the Mission. Jinnah first showed interest in the second option, a central government with a parity of ministers but later refused to commit himself. As always, he wanted to see the cards the Congress held before playing his hand.

The representatives of the Sikhs, according to the Mission's own records, 'don't know what they want but are worried and alarmed'. One leader, Giani Kartar Singh, felt that the Sikhs would be unsafe whether they were in Pakistan or in a united India. Master Tara Singh favoured a Sikh state, or an autonomous province which Sardar Baldev Singh, later defence minister of India, elucidated should include Ambala, Jalandhar, and Ludhiana divisions of Punjab.

The Mission wanted an all-India commission, drawing members from the Centre and the provincial assemblies, first to work on the constitutional guarantees for the minorities and then to consider whether India should be one or two countries. Jinnah and Nehru were consulted. Both rejected the scheme, which was then not made public at all.

The Mission members also picked up the thread with Gandhi who wanted an undivided India, and with Azad who saw in their efforts the last hope of keeping India united. Azad sincerely believed that Partition would divide and harm Muslims more than Hindus. C. Rajagopalachari, a top Congress leader from the south, wanted the issue of Pakistan to be referred to an international arbitration committee with the Soviet Union as a member.

Thus far, the Mission's proposal had been a matter of conjecture. It was only known that the British had decided to leave, but the formula of their departure was made public only on 16 May. The Mission respected the wishes of both Gandhi and Azad to keep India united but tried to please Jinnah too by giving him 'the Muslim zones'.

It was a three-tier structure. At the top was the 'union of India' embracing the entire country, including the princely states, to deal with three subjects: foreign affairs, defence, and communications. The middle tier was that of provinces grouped as (i) Madras (now Tamil Nadu), Bombay (split into Maharashtra and Gujarat), Bihar, the Central provinces (now Madhya Pradesh), and Orissa; this was the Hindu-majority group; (ii) Punjab, the North-West Frontier Province, and Sind; this was the western Muslim-majority group; and (iii) Bengal, Assam; the eastern Muslim-majority group. Each of these groups was to be autonomous and frame its own constitution for all subjects apart from defence, foreign affairs, and communications. After elections under the new constitution, any province, if its legislature so decided, could leave any group in which it had been placed. The bottom tier was that of princely states. They were treated as provinces which could join either India or Pakistan or stay independent. The Parsis declared in a statement that despite their differences, they would stay with the Congress on the question of India's freedom.

The Mission rejected the suggestion of 'partitioning' Punjab and Bengal on the ground that it would be 'contrary to the wishes of a very large proportion of the inhabitants of these provinces', and that it 'would of necessity divide the Sikhs'. Strangely, a few months later, Lord Mountbatten, repudiated this thesis while partitioning the two provinces, although Nehru was equivocal on this point at some stage.

The Muslim League accepted the Mission's proposal on 6 June as 'the compulsory grouping of the six Muslim provinces' was considered 'the basis and the foundation of Pakistan'. Khurshid, Jinnah's secretary, told me that Jinnah accepted the Cabinet Mission plan 'honestly' and admonished his critics in the League who wanted nothing but Pakistan. However contradictory, Jinnah wanted a Muslim state within undivided India.

The Congress endorsed the plan on 26 June 1946 but interpreted the grouping of provinces to mean that they 'shall make their choice whether or not to belong to the group in which they are placed'.

The reservation on the part of the Congress sounded the death knell for the proposal. After its ratification by the All-India Congress Committee on 6 July 1946, Nehru, who had by then taken over the party's presidency from Azad, said his party would be free to suggest in the constituent assembly modifications to the proposal. He hinted at changing both the grouping of provinces and the powers given to the Centre. He was echoing the fears of Gopinath Bardaloi, then Assam's chief minister, who did not want Assam to stay in Group Three in which Muslims were in a majority.

Azad differed with Nehru's interpretation. He regretted having resigned from the Congress presidency, which he described, in Gandhi's words, as a Himalayan blunder. Azad realized that he should have given his charge to Sardar Patel who would have implemented the Cabinet Mission plan. Azad stressed that it was incorrect to assume that the Congress was free to modify the proposal as it pleased. According to him, the Congress could not unilaterally change the grouping of provinces and the Central subjects without the consent of the other parties to the agreement.

When the matter was referred to the Mission's members, Pethick-Lawrence said that the parties could not go outside the terms in the constituent assembly. Cripps explained that a province could opt out of its particular group after elections had been held under the new constitution. The British government suggested that the matter could be referred to the Federal Court of India to advise on the Congress interpretation that a province need not join a group from the very outset. The Congress rejected London's proposal.

Jinnah reacted sharply and blamed Nehru for repudiating the grouping of provinces and the limited Centre, the 'basic form' on which the scheme rested. He made the All-India Council of the Muslim League change its earlier resolution by rejecting the proposal. He accused the Mission of 'bad faith' and the Congress of a 'pettifogging and haggling attitude'. When I met Azad many years later, he held Nehru responsible for Jinnah's reversal. In chaste Urdu, Azad said: '*Woh tala jo kabhi khul nahin sakta tha Nehru ne uski chabi Jinnah ke hath main de di* [Nehru gave to Jinnah the key of the lock which could not be opened].'

In any event, Jinnah was chafing over the results of the elections to the constituent assembly which had given the League 76 seats as against 292 to the Congress. There was, however, nothing he could do as the scheme was based on electing one member for every million of the population. This gave Hindus a head start given their greater numbers. Jinnah had yet another grievance: The Mission shelved the formation of an interim government at the Centre. Here, he was himself to blame because he had insisted that Muslim members should be from the Muslim League alone.

The pluralistic Congress claiming to represent the nation as a whole could not agree to this demand. However, it accepted that the cabinet should have an equal number of Hindu and Muslim ministers. I wish the Cabinet Mission plan had borne fruit, this being the only way of keeping India united. Defence, foreign affairs, and communications with the Centre would have ensured a federal structure with the states enjoying autonomy. I apprehended that after Partition the two countries would treat each other as enemies, given the estranged relations between Hindus and Muslims. These fears were not unfounded.

The Congress assured the League that any major legislation would require the support of a majority of Muslims in the Central legislature. This was yet another undertaking to assure the Muslims that their voice in a united India would be crucial. The proposal did not, however, appeal to Jinnah who was looking for an opportunity to withdraw his support to a scheme suggesting togetherness. Observations made by the Congress, particularly Nehru, that the constituent assembly could amend the Mission's recommendations gave Jinnah an opening to forcefully renew his demand for Pakistan. He realized that the constituent assembly would have a preponderant Hindu majority.

Jinnah gave a call for Direct Action, not against the British but as a show of strength on the part of Muslims as the Congress had treated their demand with 'defiance and contempt'. He argued the Congress was not willing to accept even the proposal conceding only a 'limited Pakistan'. This was false propaganda because the Congress had come round to accepting the Cabinet Mission plan, but after raising doubts that made Jinnah wary. That might have been why, when Mountbatten offered a partition proposal a year later and asked Jinnah whether he would accept some links with India, he said: 'I do not trust them now.'

When asked whether Direct Action would be violent or non-violent, Jinnah said: 'I am not going to discuss ethics.' Direct Action was undertaken only in Calcutta and that too merely for a day (16 August 1946). The Muslim League government in Bengal declared a public holiday on that day, despite warnings and protests by the Opposition. The League organized a 'grand rally' over which Chief Minister Shaheed Suhrawardy himself presided. Bands of Muslim League National Guards forced their way into Hindu areas and asked for subscriptions, sometimes as much as Rs 1,000. Returning from the rally, the League's National Guards began looting Hindu shops for not paying subscriptions or not responding to the League's call for a hartal on that day. Hindus and Sikhs were attacked and the entire event appeared to have been pre-planned.

Soon Calcutta was engulfed in a communal riot, with Hindus and Sikhs retaliating against Muslims. Parts of the city were reduced to rubble. Over 5,000 people lost their lives in less than three days in what came to be known as the 'great Calcutta killing', a phrase coined by the Statesman, the influential British-owned newspaper. Jinnah laid the blame on the Cabinet Mission, the Congress, and Gandhi. Surprisingly, Jinnah found no fault with his National Guards who had pledged themselves before the carnage 'to strive for the achievement of Pakistan and glory of the Muslim nation'. The Statesman laid the blame on the British governor and Chief Minister Suhrawardy. 'Arson, looting, murder, abduction of women, forced conversions and forced marriages are everywhere and by every investigator spoken of as the characteristics of lawlessness.'

Such large-scale killing and looting should have been a warning to Jinnah that the tension between the two communities had reached dangerous levels.

A haystack of hatred was just waiting to be lit. When Jinnah came to Law College in 1945 in Lahore where I was in my second year and was part of the audience he addressed, I told him we would jump at each other's throats after the departure of the British. This was before the Direct Action Day. He disagreed with me and said some nations had killed millions of each other's nationals and yet an enemy of today was a friend of tomorrow. 'That is history.' He told me how France and Germany had fought for hundreds of years, 'But today they are best friends. We shall be friends,' he assured me.

I knew he was wrong and could envisage what would happen once the British left. Surprisingly, Jinnah did not see things that way. I asked him another question. If a third country attacked India, what would be Pakistan's response? He said the Pakistani soldiers would fight side by side with Indian soldiers to defeat the assailants. 'Young man, remember blood is thicker than water,' he said, another statement that proved to be false.

Before the great Calcutta killing, the viceroy had revived the proposal to constitute an interim government at the Centre as the Cabinet Mission had suggested. The Congress had accepted it and had joined the Viceroy's Council. The League, which had rejected it, now indicated its willingness to join. The Council was reorganized on 15 October to include the League's nominees.

Stories in the press told us that the presence of both the Congress and the League ministers in the central government had not in any way improved relations between Hindus and Muslims. I could see the killings in Calcutta had set in motion riots in Bihar, UP, Punjab, and elsewhere. With the communal virus contaminating the lower echelons of the administration, including the police, controlling the riots had become still more difficult. Over the years, the number of British officials considered 'neutral' had decreased because there had been no British recruitment to the civil services in India since 1939 when the Second World War broke out. Even those who were in India were losing interest as they could see the end of the Raj.

Thousands died in the riots. The British government was so perturbed over the disastrous events that it asked the viceroy to prepare a secret plan for withdrawal. The plan, appropriately called, 'Mad House', was for the evacuation of British troops and British civilians by March 1948, beginning the process from southern India.

London was concerned over Jinnah's call to the League members not to take their seats in the constituent assembly which was to meet in Delhi from 9 December. A final effort was made to get both the Congress and the League to participate in its proceedings. Nehru, Jinnah, Liaquat Ali, and Baldev Singh, the Sikh minister at the Centre, were invited to London on 3 December. The meeting ended in a fiasco. After three days in London, Nehru returned home disappointed. It was clearer to him than ever before that His Majesty's Government would not withdraw from India unless the Muslim League joined in framing the new constitution, and the former made no secret of this.

That meant that even if the constituent assembly were to declare India a sovereign republic, the British would not be bound by the decision if the Muslim League did not concur. This took the wind out of the Congress sails as the party had announced that the constituent assembly was a sovereign body. How then could it give the veto power to London or the League?

The Congress went ahead and elected the constituent assembly. At a public meeting on 15 December in Banaras, Nehru said: 'We have not entered the constituent assembly in order to place our decisions on a silver plate and dance in attendance on the British Government for their acceptance.' The Objective Resolution he moved in the constituent assembly stated: 'The Constituent Assembly declares its firm and solemn resolve to proclaim India an independent sovereign republic and to draw up for her future governance a Constitution.' The Muslim League boycotted the constituent assembly but continued to remain in the interim government, its only way of forming a part of the administration. Nehru complained to Archibald Wavell, the penultimate viceroy of India, that the League could not be part of a government which it was committed to oppose. Patel publicly declared that if the League members were to remain in the interim government, the Congress members would resign.

Even otherwise, the experiment of the interim government was not working in spirit to bridge the distance between the Congress and the League. Nehru was exasperated because only a united government could give support to an independent foreign policy, build a strong defence apparatus, and formulate a plan for economic development. What persuaded Nehru and Patel to accept Partition was not Jinnah's arguments, but the unworkability of the joint interim government. The two Congress leaders were convinced that India would not be able to move forward if the 'intransigent' League was yoked with the Congress at the wheel. On 13 February, Nehru formally wrote to the viceroy demanding an immediate dismissal of the Muslim League members. There was no response.

Wavell could see the division of India coming. He prepared a scheme for Partition and sent it to London. This came in handy when India was actually divided. Anxious, Attlee announced the replacement of Wavell with a new viceroy, Lord Mountbatten.

Attlee did something else. On 20 February 1947 he announced that the British would quit after transferring power to Indian hands 'by a date not later than 6 June 1948, whether as a whole to some form of central government for British India or in some areas to the existing provincial government, or in such other way as may seem most reasonable and in the best interests of the Indian people'. The future the of princely states would be decided after the date of the final transfer was finalized.

Cripps's elaboration in the British parliament was: 'We could not accept the forcing of unwilling provinces into a united India,' implying that the creation of Pakistan in some form was on the cards. This was not acceptable to the

Congress, but it could also see that the Pakistan of Jinnah's dream would not be possible because the party would insist on dividing Punjab and Bengal. After Attlee's announcement, Nehru told Krishna Menon, who was heading the freedom movement in London, that a truncated Pakistan would hardly be worthwhile for Jinnah who might join the Indian Union on 'special terms'.

Nehru personally approached Liaquat Ali Khan, Jinnah's second-in-command, pleading that they should not speak to each other 'from a distance' because the British were fading out. Liaquat did not respond. In the meantime, Mountbatten replaced Wavell who went unsung. Azad was one of the few who appreciated Wavell's efforts and wrote him a letter of appreciation, which was disapproved by other Congress leaders.

Mountbatten, while still in London, felt that there was 'no escape from Pakistan' after meeting the Mission leaders and Attlee. He told me this when I interviewed him in 1971 for my book *The Distant Neighbours*. He said he had not even heard of Pakistan until the offer of viceroyship was made to him. By the time Mountbatten arrived in New Delhi on 23 March 1947, the Congress and League ministers in the interim government were thoroughly sick of each other, the League thwarting the Congress at every turn. It was in the government yet against it.

Unwittingly, the Congress was itself responsible for the situation. At the time of the interim government's reconstitution, following the League's decision to join, Wavell had indicated that either home or finance, preferably the former, should go to Jinnah's men, but Patel, who was then home minister, did not want the intelligence department and the police to go to the League. Patel said he would rather quit the government than give up the ministry. Azad, however, favoured handing it over to the League.

Rafi Ahmed Kidwai, a senior nationalist Muslim leader, who later became India's most successful food minister, said that finance was such a technical subject that the League itself would say 'No' when it was offered. Little did the Congress leaders realize that Chaudhary Mohammed Ali, a brilliant Muslim officer in the finance ministry at that time, had secretly contacted the League and assured its leaders that he would make the Congress rue the day when it parted with finance.

This proved to be true. Every proposal of every government department had to go to the finance ministry for funds. So much so, that the Congress ministers could not appoint even a petty clerk without the sanction of the ministry. Patel, who himself had preferred home to finance, felt so exasperated that he began saying openly that it was far better to divide India than to face a situation where the Congress was paralysed. The League pressed its advantage hard by presenting a central budget on 28 February 1947 which, while appearing to reflect some of Nehru's progressive thinking, hit the Hindus hard because they were comparatively rich. When the Congress protested against a particular section of people being 'purposely' targeted, the League retorted that the Congress was upset because industrial houses like the Birlas and the Tatas, which had contributed money to its coffers, were affected.

For Mountbatten, this was an ugly situation at the start of his innings. He, however, felt gratified that the Congress party was so exasperated that it was willing to accept 'anything' to be independent of the League. Patel was the most disgusted. Mountbatten saw the prospects. He appointed V.P. Menon, then the reforms commissioner and a close confidant of Patel, to his staff. Menon's job was to remain in touch with Patel and report on how his mind was working.

'Wavell committed the mistake of bypassing Patel, but we depended on him, and that explains why we succeeded,' Campbell-Johnson, Mountbatten's press secretary, told me years later in London. 'Patel conveyed to Mountbatten through Menon that whatever they wanted to sell to Nehru they should do it through him [Patel].' Indeed, it was Patel who helped Mountbatten (through Menon) evolve the Partition plan. The viceroy could never imagine that Partition, like a ripe apple, was ready to be plucked. He wanted to test the waters.

Mountbatten began with Gandhi who, after hearing the word 'partition', did not want to know anything further. Before leaving the room he told Mountbatten that the British should hand over power to Jinnah and leave. What he proposed was that Jinnah be appointed as India's first prime minister. Nehru and Patel opposed the idea and found it 'impractical'. Both were now together to win power, even if it came to dividing India.

Mountbatten told me that 'Whenever he [Gandhi] entered my room I felt an aura of holiness around him'. Azad's grievance was that Gandhi did not speak out against Partition when he should have. He blamed Patel for ensuring the consolidation of Hindus in one country.

In his own mind, Mountbatten was quite clear: a united India, if possible, or Partition, if necessary. He preferred, as he told me, to have a central authority responsible for the subjects of defence, external affairs, communications, and possibly food. Before long, however, Mountbatten realized that the Congress party did not favour a solution with even a hint of separation. On the other hand, Jinnah did not want to accept any ties, however loose, with even a hint of a Centre. It was a complex scenario.

Mountbatten concentrated on Nehru, by now declared by Gandhi as his successor and accepted as such by Patel. Mountbatten promised both of them the partition of Punjab and West Bengal. They made the CWC resolve on 6 March 1947 that if India were to be divided then Punjab and Bengal would be partitioned, the Muslim-majority area going to Pakistan and the Hindu- and Sikh-majority areas to India. In fact, Patel said in a letter to a friend at the time that if 'the League insists on Pakistan', India's only alternative is to insist on 'the division of Punjab and Bengal'. Still, the Congress rejected the two-nation theory despite agreeing to the Muslim areas going to West Punjab and East Bengal and the Hindu areas coming to East Punjab and West Bengal.

This from the Congress that had fought the Independence movement on the thesis that Hindus and Muslims were one nation; one people fighting against the British.

For Nehru, the Congress resolution was a stratagem rather than an acceptance of the fact of Partition. I wonder why Nehru thought that sooner or later India would have to function as a unified country, even when he accepted Partition. The best explanation I can think of is that he felt that India had to go through some form of partition to forge unity in the long run.

This was clear in a letter Nehru wrote to brigadier, later General K.M. Cariappa, that he was convinced that eventually there would be a strong and united India: 'We often go through the valley of the shadow before we reach the sunlit mountain tops.' Nehru was a dreamer and thought of a united India when in reality the country was close to division.

That may be why the property left behind by the Muslims in India was called 'evacuee property'. It came to be known as 'enemy property' only in 1965 after Nehru's death. India and Pakistan had fought a war that year.

In the partition of Bengal and Punjab, Nehru thought Jinnah would see the logical consequences of his demand for Pakistan. However, for Gandhi, who intentionally did not attend the CWC meeting where the resolution accepting the division was passed, Mountbatten's suggestion to divide Punjab and Bengal was based on 'communal grounds and the two-nation theory'.

Therefore, when the demand for an independent, undivided Bengal was raised, Gandhi extended his full support. He saw in it a step towards restoring a part of India's unity, already crumbling before his eyes. What was cited as 'Greater Bengal' or a 'Sovereign United Bengal' was the suggestion of Suhrawardy, whose reputation had been soiled by the great Calcutta killing. He said: 'The two-nation theory should be suitably modified so as to be adaptable to local conditions as the situation demanded.'

Some Hindu leaders, led by Sarat Chandra Bose, also saw Bengal's ruin in the partition of the state. Jinnah welcomed the proposal of a United Bengal. His comment was: 'They [the Bengalis] would be much better off by remaining united and independent.' He even suggested a referendum for the independence of Bengal. He believed that the dalits, till then called the untouchables, would vote for the Muslims. When Mountbatten was sounded, he said he would let the people in the state decide. The then British governor of Bengal also suggested to the viceroy that the state be given the option to become independent.

At this juncture Suhrawardy sought Gandhi's intervention. The latter's reply was that the future of Bengal could only be decided by the joint will of the Hindus and Muslims in the state. Shyama Prasad Mukherjee, a Hindu Mahasabha leader from Bengal, who joined the central cabinet after Independence, met Gandhi to oppose the whole idea of a sovereign Bengal state. Even then the Congress and the League in Bengal came to a tentative agreement that if and when a Greater Bengal came into being, 'every act of its Government must carry with it the support of at least two-thirds of the Hindu minority in the executive and the legislature'. This was intended to allay the fears of Hindus who would be in a minority in a United Bengal.

A leader of Bengali Muslims, Abdul Hashim, later said: 'Whether Hindu or Muslim, a Bengali is a Bengali. Both hated to be ruled by the Pakistanis from over a thousand miles away.' The statement met with an apt reply: If the concept of a United Bengal made sense, why didn't the idea that all Indians live together, however different in faiths, made any?

The move of one Bengal, undoubtedly failed at the time but in 1971 a small group, headed by Tajuddin Ahmad, a liberation struggle leader, founded an émigré Bangladesh government where a manifesto was adopted to ensure that the policies of Bangladesh and West Bengal would be enmeshed and based on a progressive economic and social programme. This was a promise for one Bengal of sorts.

Punjab, which was also partitioned, saw no similar move to unite the state. One reason was that the state had neither a Rabindranath Tagore nor a Nazrul Islam to bind the people through poetry, culture, or language. There was nothing like Punjabi nationalism to string together Hindus, Muslims, and Sikhs. In comparison, Punjab's great poet, Iqbal, was himself the author of the idea of Partition. The Punjabi language, even though spoken by the people as a whole, was written differently by the three communities: in Arabic (Urdu) script by the Muslims, in Devnagri (Hindi) by the Hindus, and in Gurmukhi (Punjabi) by the Sikhs. The only culture attributed to Punjab was 'agriculture', a disparaging remark that still is thrown at Punjabis.

For Mountbatten, there was no question of either a united Bengal or a united Punjab. He was quite clear that if the country was to be divided, splitting the two states was inevitable. He was, however, still hopeful that he might be able to persuade Jinnah to agree to a minimal Centre because partition of Punjab and Bengal would mean 'a moth-eaten Pakistan'. He was, however, unable to persuade Jinnah to dilute the concept of Pakistan.

The prospect of partitioning both Punjab and Bengal shocked Jinnah and he opposed the suggestion. He argued that they were Punjabis or Bengalis first and anything else afterwards, but the idea of a united India was even more repugnant to him. What he was aiming at was a separate identity and a territory for the Muslims. That being the purpose, even a truncated Bengal and Punjab mattered little. To Nehru and Patel, splitting Bengal and Punjab seemed logical. Jinnah paid Mountbatten back when he refused to accept him as a common governor general.

Two Sikh leaders, Master Tara Singh and Giani Kartar Singh, whom Mountbatten described in his papers as 'two unkempt junglee-looking old men', pressed the viceroy to agree to the transfer of population if the state were to be divided. Finally, they persuaded him to agree that in the eventuality of Partition, the Sikhs be given the option of joining either India or Pakistan to enable them to negotiate better terms. The Muslim League offered the Sikhs a Sikkim-like status (unlike other princely states, Sikkim became a tributary of India, in which India controlled its external defence, diplomacy, and communication).

When Jinnah refused to accept any link with India, Mountbatten got Liaquat Ali to agree to 'an overall Defence Headquarters', above the separate headquarters of the military in the two countries. They were to finance the 'overall Defence Headquarters' in proportion to their respective populations. Mountbatten wrote in his notes on 19 April: 'I have the impression that Liaquat Ali Khan intends to help me find a more reasonable solution than this mad Pakistan.'

However, this scheme did not mature. How could it when Jinnah insisted on a communal division of the armed forces, despite Lord Ismay (Jinnah's personal friend) pleading him to accept a division on numerical lines, keeping regiments intact. A similar exercise had been conducted before the arrival of the Cabinet Mission. That was resurrected when the time for division came. Jinnah did not agree and Liaquat Ali had no standing of his own in the party and therefore the scheme proved to be a non-starter. At one time, Jinnah himself had hinted at the possibility of a defence alliance between Pakistan and India according to the minutes of the viceroy's meeting on 23 April 1947.

When it was clear that there was no alternative to Pakistan, Mountbatten presented his partition plan to the leaders of political parties. The boundaries of the two countries were to be demarcated by a commission. The princely states were free to join either country. Power would be transferred on the basis of dominion status and either government could withdraw from the Commonwealth if it so desired. The date for the end of British rule was fixed as 15 August, nearly ten months ahead of the time limit set by Attlee in his first statement on the transfer of power.

Mountbatten's proposal, aptly named 'Plan Balkan', was to transfer power to the provincial governments, leaving them to come together to form a central government if and when they chose to do so. The states, released from British authority, would also be free to make such arrangements as they wished. Nehru was furious when Mountbatten showed him the plan because he saw in it many Pakistans. Nehru's consent was essential if any settlement was to take place.

Mountbatten felt defeated and was summoned to London. What would he tell Attlee? V.P. Menon sought Mountbatten's permission to try out his plan which he claimed had Patel's blessings. Mountbatten had seen it and told him to go ahead but Menon found it difficult to meet Nehru before Mountbatten's departure. However, Edwina Mountbatten managed to arrange an appointment for Menon. Azad had proposed this to Menon. Nehru was not opposed to the Partition plan provided it meant transfer of power to the two countries, not to provincial governments. After the failure of the Cabinet Mission plan, Menon, who had limited educational qualifications, had sketched an alternative and had obtained Patel's approval. He had sent a copy to the India Office in London. The plan called for the acceptance of Partition, including the division of Punjab, Bengal, and Assam first and the formation of two central governments of India and Pakistan later, each having its own constituent assembly. The transfer of power was to be effected to two central governments.

The London office had with it Menon's alternate sketch, but it learnt the details only when Mountbatten arrived after obtaining the consent of the Congress and the Sikhs in writing and that of Jinnah orally. Had the British cabinet rejected Menon's plan, Mountbatten would have resigned, as he told some friends before leaving for London.

Describing his meeting with the British cabinet, Mountbatten told me that he gave them no explanation for the plan. He said he knew that they depended upon him and they 'had to do' what he said. They were all exasperated; had no alternative to Partition. Attlee wanted to quit India as soon as possible and therefore agreed to divide the country without any emotion or remorse. Nehru admitted that Partition was 'evil' but then he changed his mind. There was no document or letter to explain why he did so. According to Azad, in his book, *India Wins Freedom*, there was 'the influence of Lady Mountbatten' on Nehru. This could well be true, but there was something in the argument that Nehru and Patel, like other top Congress leaders, were by now very tired. They lacked the stamina and will for another round of agitation and imprisonment. They were therefore keen to implement what the Congress had been fighting for decades: building a prosperous India. Nehru wanted at least some of his dreams to be realized during his lifetime. He was already 58 years old.

Whether Lady Mountbatten had any influence over Nehru or not, the general impression was that she had. I recall a post-Independence meeting of chief ministers at the house of Govind Ballabh Pant who was then the home minister, I was his information officer. The topics for discussion included a letter which Lady Mountbatten had written to Nehru to explain why she was late for the Red Cross meeting in Bombay over which he had presided. Her husband had retired by then but Red Cross work had brought her back to India. The reason for the delay was that she had to wait at a crossing while Nehru's cavalcade passed by. Nehru had sent her complaint to Pant.

As soon as Pant mentioned the name of Lady Mountbatten there was loud laughter in the room, followed by sarcastic comments. There was no doubt in their minds that Nehru was having an affair with her. Nehru had suggested to the home minister that roads should not be closed for the prime minister; instead the traffic should be regulated. B.C. Roy, then the West Bengal chief minister and a prominent Congress leader, said that they did not have to listen to Nehru. They were responsible for the prime minister's security and would be justified in taking whatever steps they considered necessary. I learnt for the first time that there was a Blue Book setting out the steps for the security of the president and the prime minister. The chief ministers wanted the guidelines in the Blue Book to be stricter.

⚜

My interest in finding out about Lady Mountbatten's influence on Nehru did not slacken with time. I picked up the thread when I was India's high commissioner in London in 1990. I learnt that Air India flights would carry Nehru's daily letter, which the high commission dutifully delivered to Lady Mountbatten and daily collected her reply and forwarded it to Nehru. Nehru took officials to task whenever her letter was delayed.

I wished I could see the letters. Was it mere journalistic curiosity? No, it was more than that. Edwina Mountbatten, who, as Azad said, had influenced Nehru to accept the Partition formula must have been an extraordinary woman and a wonderful correspondent; an intelligent human being, honest in her advice.

During my stint in the UK, I met her grandson, Lord Romsey, who headed the Nehru Trust, which Mountbatten had constituted in London to arrange an annual lecture in Nehru's memory. As high commissioner, I was an ex-officio member of the trust. Lord Romsey and I met many times in that connection. After meeting him a few times, I thought I had developed a sufficient equation to talk to him about his grandmother. He did not seem to mind.

I once broached the subject of Nehru's letters with him. I said: 'Nehru wrote beautifully.' His reply was that his grandmother too wrote beautifully. I told him I would love to see at least one of her letters. I had seen Nehru's writings but not hers. He said that Rajiv Gandhi and he had exchanged copies of his grandmother's and Nehru's letters. There were two sets, one with him and the other with the Gandhi family. I realized then that it would be difficult to obtain access to them.

Nonetheless, I bluntly asked him one day whether his grandmother and Nehru had been in love. First he laughed and then wondered how he could describe their relationship. He paused for a while and said: Theirs was 'spiritual love'. Then he changed the subject. I let the matter rest there. Lord Romsey subsequently said: 'They fell in love; a kind of chivalrous love which was understood in the olden days. Nowadays when you talk of love, you think of sex. Theirs was more a soul-to-soul kind of relation. Nehru was an honourable man and he would never have seduced a friend's wife.'

Back in Delhi I tried to get access to the letters. I went to the Nehru Memorial Library and asked for the correspondence between Jawaharlal Nehru and Lady Mountbatten. The librarian looked surprised. 'You have to get permission from Mrs Sonia Gandhi,' he said and closed the topic. I wrote a letter to Sonia Gandhi stating that I was working on a book on the

Mountbattens and would like to see Nehru's papers. She did not reply but Natwar Singh, then the state minister for external affairs, said that I could go to the library and consult the letters. I could hardly believe it. When the librarian placed before me a bundle of papers in a secluded room I thought my efforts had borne fruit. I spent many hours sifting through the pile, but they proved to be Nehru's letters and notes to Krishna Menon, who got him to change many policies on foreign affairs. My mission was however different. I approached the librarian who said that my permission was for the 'C' grade papers. For this I would have to obtain Sonia Gandhi's specific instructions.

I wrote to her again. Once more Natwar Singh was the channel of communication. He told me the papers could not be made available to me. There was no explanation. All he said was that they were her property and she alone could decide. I think Nehru's letters are the nation's property and should be made available to the public because they throw light on matters meaningful to our history. But this does not seem to be the general policy. The government of India has not yet made public the papers relating to the transfer of power by the British to India while the UK has.

Recounting events of the last days before Partition, Azad told me that he was convinced the division of India could have been prevented had Gandhi come out openly against it in the CWC. He repeated the charge that the argument of Hindus consolidating in one country had silenced the committed secularists. Azad said that Gandhi had veered around to accepting 'Partition'. Azad's claim was, however, challenged by Abdul Ghaffar Khan. The latter said that 'Gandhi was the only person who never agreed to partition'. Gandhi just remained silent, Khan said, when he saw that both Nehru and Patel were on same side and keen to immediately occupy the seat of power.

Azad's contention that Gandhi had become a convert to the idea of Partition was refuted by Mountbatten too, who told me that Gandhi never agreed to it. Historian H. V. Hudson and Mountbatten's press secretary Alan Campbell-Johnson, whom I met in London, also confirmed that Gandhi did not accept Partition, yet both said that he went along with pain etched on his face because Nehru and Patel, his two lieutenants, had already agreed to it. Even so, the fact remained that the same Gandhi who had declared that Partition would take place over his dead body did not threaten any fast when the British agreed to partition the subcontinent. He did not express his opposition to the formula in public and seemed reconciled to the idea.

Gandhi's secretary, Pyarelal, has defended him and recorded on 1 June 1947 in his diary: 'Let it not be said that Gandhi was a party to India's vivisection. The Congress has practically decided to accept Partition and as Gandhi said they have been handed a wooden loaf in this new plan. If they eat it, they die of colic. If they leave it, they starve.' In his book, *India Wins Freedom,* Azad states he was against Partition and claims to have warned Nehru that 'history would never forgive us if we agreed to Partition. The verdict would be that India was not divided by the Muslim League but by the Congress.'

However, Acharya Kripalani, a top Congress leader, challenged this contention: 'I do not know what private conference he [Azad] had with Gandhi. All I know is that Azad never opposed the partition resolution at the Congress Working Committee or the All-India Congress Committee.' Kripalani made no secret of this observation and repeated it to me even during Azad's lifetime. Kripalani in fact went beyond this and claimed that had Azad and other nationalist Muslims opposed Partition, it might not have taken place. 'But they were always obsessed with the right of self-determination for the Muslims,' Kripalani alleged.

At the CWC meeting, Khan Abdul Ghaffar Khan said with tears in his eyes: *'Ham to tabah ho gaye* [we are ruined]. Before long we shall become aliens in Hindustan. Our long fight will end with the creation of Pakistan.' Ghaffar Khan at this stage sought a third option: an independent state of Pakhtoonistan, but this was not in Mountbatten's scheme of things. He gave only two choices to the NWFP: to remain in India or join Pakistan. A plebiscite on these options was bound to favour Islamic Pakistan. Gandhi did try to intervene on his behalf but nothing came of it.

Subsequently, when the plebiscite was held in the NWFP, Ghaffar Khan and his brother Khan Sahib called upon their followers to boycott it because the propaganda at that time was that the Muslims could either support the Quran or the *Gita*. It was Islam versus Hinduism. The one-sided plebiscite culminated in a vote that favoured Pakistan.

Baluchistan, another unit of the proposed state of Pakistan, was never in consonance with Jinnah's philosophy. For centuries the Baluchis had not considered themselves a part of the Indian subcontinent and insisted on a special status in their relationship with British India. Mir Ahmad Yar Khan, the then Khan of Kalat, argued that they were not in any way akin to the people of India. During the visit of the Cabinet Mission he submitted a memorandum: 'Kalat is an independent and sovereign state. Kalat is not an Indian state. Regions under British control should be handed over to the Kalat state and on the lapse of British sovereignty; the rights hitherto vested in the British Crown should automatically be transferred to the Kalat government.'

On 11 August, three days before the inaugural session of Pakistan's constituent assembly, a meeting was held under the chairmanship of representative of the Crown, Lord Azuma, with Jinnah, Liaquat Ali, the Khan of Kalat, and Sir Sultan Ahmad, the legal advisor. The government of Pakistan recognized Kalat as an independent and sovereign state. It was also announced that talks on defence, foreign affairs, and communication would soon be held at Karachi.

The Kalat government made a formal declaration of its independence and on 12 August 1947 hoisted its national flag. Jinnah proposed a merger of Kalat state with Pakistan but the Khan refused. Jinnah issued an order on 15 April 1948 ending the Khan's authority. Prince Abdul Kareem Khan, the brother of the Khan of Kalat, revolted against the merger of Kalat. A compromise was reached with the creation of 'Baluchistan States Union', which meant the creation of a union of the former states of Baluchistan, separate from the one unit of West Pakistan. With the approval of the Government of Pakistan, the Baluchistan States Union was announced on 9 April 1952. However, the struggle for autonomy by Baluchis continues to this day. 'If we had common border with you we would have joined India long ago,' a top Baluchi leader told me in 2009.

The AICC met on 14 June 1947 and accepted the partition plan, but only after a heated discussion. Both Patel and Pant, respectively, who moved and seconded the resolution, were on the defensive. All they said was that partition was the only possible solution under the existing circumstances. Gandhi spoke about political realism, not on the merits of the proposal. He said: 'The Congress has signed on your behalf. You can disown them, but you should do so only if you can start a big movement. I do not think you can.' Pant told me, when I was his information officer, that they should not have accepted Partition because this aggravated the 'Hindu–Muslim problem'.

What disturbed me was the hostage theory which was influencing more and more people. Even secular-minded Congressmen repeated it many times at the AICC meeting: 'The Hindus in Pakistan need not have any fear as there would be 45 million Muslims in India and if there was any oppression of Hindus in Pakistan, the Muslims in India would bear the consequences.' The argument had communal overtones. India was fighting for Independence, a secular dispensation, and the Congress advocated a pluralistic society. It never even hinted at a Hindu state so why did some Congressmen talk in terms of the hostage theory? The only explanation is that a majority of Congressmen at the meeting lacked a firm commitment to secularism, regarding it only as a policy not a faith. This lack of commitment continues to trouble post-Independence India.

The resolution on Partition was adopted on 15 June 1947. Of the 218 members present, 157 voted in favour and 29 against. The loudest dissenter was Aruna Asaf Ali, who said that the proposal was a 'victory for Jinnah and Churchill'. The All-India Council of the Muslim League had already accepted the plan in principle at its meeting on 9 June and had authorized Jinnah to 'work on all the details' as the partition of Punjab and Bengal was not to their liking.

The League's representatives from UP, Bihar, and other provinces, the states which were to stay in India, were concerned about the fallout: the inevitable hostility of a Hindu majority which was vehemently opposed to the Muslims' demand for a separate homeland. The fact that Pakistan would have two wings with no land connection worried them. Jinnah had once suggested a 800-mile long corridor to link West and East Pakistan, but neither the British government nor the Congress took the proposal seriously, nor did he himself pursue it.

One person who met Mountbatten before the announcement of an agreement by the Congress and the Muslim League to Partition was Azad. He implored Mountbatten to defer the implementation of his formula by a year to 15 August 1948, instead of 15 August 1947. Mountbatten refused. Perhaps things might have taken a very different turn had Partition been so postponed. The two figures dominating the political scene at the time died within a year of Partition: Gandhi was assassinated by a Hindu fanatic on 30 January 1948 and Jinnah died of cancer on 11 September 1948, although his ailment was common knowledge six months earlier. (It is said that Britain knew about it before Partition but did not want to reveal it because the Churchillian elements wanted to leave Partition as their parting gift.)

Humayun Kabir, who edited Azad's biography, told me that Azad thought the Congress leaders (Nehru was then 58 years old and Patel 72) accepted Partition because they had grown too tired and old to resort to yet another agitation to free India. In fact, almost all the Congress and League leaders were in a hurry to come to power. Even a truncated India was acceptable to Nehru and Patel just as a truncated Pakistan was to Jinnah.

The process of division was clumsy and hurried, particularly when Mountbatten advanced the date from 3 June 1948 to 15 August 1947. Why did he do this? He understood the enormity of the task and the appalling difficulties involved but still decided to go ahead. His papers, too, failed to throw any light on this. I asked several historians and politicians in India and the UK about why he preponed the date.

Campbell-Johnson told me that Mountbatten selected 15 August because it was the day when the Japanese surrendered to the Allies, ending the Second World War. Mountbatten remembered hearing the news of the Japanese surrender for the first time in Churchill's room and hoped to associate Britain's 'surrender' to India with himself playing a leading role.

Some British Foreign Office hands disagreed with this reasoning. Their argument was that Mountbatten was lobbying for a more senior position in the Royal Navy and did not want his appointment in India to block his aspiration. He eventually got the appointment he sought as naval commander of Southeast Asia in 1955.

When I checked with Mountbatten himself, he said he had to change the date because he could not hold the country together. 'Things were slipping from my hands,' he said repeatedly. 'The Sikhs were up in arms in the Punjab, the Great Calcutta Killing had taken place, and communal tension was prevailing all over. On top of it, there had been the announcement that the British were leaving. Therefore, I myself decided to quit sooner.... This was not to the liking of Lord Attlee,' Mountbatten added, 'but he had given me full powers.'

'But your act of advancing the date by ten months resulted in the killing of over a million on both sides of the border,' I charged. It was as if I had touched a raw nerve because he suddenly became pensive and lapsed into silence. After a while he said that in the 1947 Partition riots nearly 2.5 million people had died but he had saved three to four million people from starvation during the 1943 Bengal famine by giving 10 per cent of the space on his ships for the transport of foodgrains to Calcutta despite Churchill's opposition. 'Well, before Providence I can say that the balance is in my favour,' said Mountbatten, adding: 'Wherever colonial rule has ended, there has been bloodshed. This is the price you pay.' (Some books subsequently revealed that Churchill had intentionally denied food grains to India.)

Mountbatten told me about the message Rajagopalachari sent him as early as 1948: 'If you had not transferred power when you did, there would have been no power to transfer.' To my mind, Mountbatten's explanation was flimsy and an indirect admission of guilt. His haste created panic and an atmosphere of unease and distrust began growing. It was a dangerous time, but he took no precautions to relieve the pain of migrants, much less protect them. He took things far too lackadaisically.

Initially, two constituent assemblies, one for India and the other for Pakistan, were established to draft the constitution of either country. Both the Congress and the Muslim League nominated persons for the assemblies. It was clear that the minorities in both the countries would stay where they were and enjoy equal rights. Khaliq-ul-Zaman was nominated to India's constituent assembly and Bhim Sen Sachar to Pakistan's. In actual fact, the constituent assembly in India was already in session.

This was too orderly in a disorderly scene. Leaders on both sides were totally unaware whether this was a reality. Living in an atmosphere of communal tension for seven years after the Pakistan resolution was passed in 1940, an undefined wall of suspicion and separation had enshrouded all. People were not sure whether they could live peacefully in their homes at a time when propaganda was focusing on their different religions; their different ethos. They were bound to search out people of their community to experience a sense of safety, especially when even civil servants, the police, and the armed forces of their religion left for the other side.

Prime Minister Margaret Thatcher showed me during my tenure at London an oblong teak table at 10, Downing Street, where the transfer of power was discussed and the Independence Act finalized. This is where your country's future was decided, she said, or something to that effect. I looked at the table longingly, recalling in my mind India's history of struggles and triumphs. Did the table bear the testimony to those events? I wish there was a plaque to signify the transfer of power.

When the Independence Bill was debated in the British parliament, Winston Churchill had angrily remarked, 'Power will go into the hands of rascals, rogues, and freebooters. Not a bottle of water or a loaf of bread shall escape taxation; only the air will be free and the blood of these hungry millions will be on head of Attlee.'

Looking back, I cannot but blame Mountbatten for doing virtually nothing to ensure the protection of the minorities notwithstanding his assurances to Azad: 'I shall not merely use the armed police, I will order the army and the air force to act and will use tanks and airplanes to suppress all those who want to create trouble.' He did not deliver on his promise.

When rivers of blood flowed in Punjab and elsewhere in the subcontinent, and fires of destruction engulfed homes and hearths, ruthless action was required to stop the carnage but there was only paralysis. On 23 June Jinnah begged Mountbatten to 'shoot Muslims', if necessary. On the other side, Nehru suggested handing over cities to the military, but Mountbatten's response was wanting. He did not wish to annoy either India or Pakistan because his dream was to become the common governor general of the two countries. Jinnah rejected the proposal of a common governor general and Pakistan suffered the consequences of his refusal. It lost a fair division of assets, the delivery of which a common governor general would have ensured. Jinnah's predicament was that any joint supervision might suggest a link with India and he wanted a clean partition with no room for confusion.

It was not as if the Boundary Force, formed on 1 August, to quell the riots, was short of manpower; its strength was 25,000 including competent officers like Brigadier Mohammed Ayub Khan, who later became Pakistan's president. Even so, the force had a high proportion of British officers who had no interest in what happened to either India or Pakistan, and were keen to return to Britain and didn't want to be caught in an operation which might tie them to the subcontinent for an indefinite period. The British commander of the force, General Thomas W. Rees, had given specific instructions 'not to get involved and to protect only European lives'. This callous attitude and lack of interest proved to be the undoing of the force.

The report submitted by the Boundary Force after Independence was brutally frank: 'Throughout, the killing was pre-medieval in its ferocity. Neither age nor sex was spared: mothers with babies in the arms were cut down, speared, or shot. Both sides were equally merciless.' There was, however, no explanation of why the Boundary Force had so criminally neglected its responsibilities and duties. The problem of delineating the boundaries of a divided Punjab and divided Bengal stared the Congress and the League sternly in the face. After failing to get the UN to nominate the Boundary Commission's members, Jinnah, who had heard Cyril Radcliffe, an outstanding lawyer, arguing complex legal cases in London courts, suggested his name to Mountbatten. Nehru approved his name after consulting 'that sneaky fellow Krishna Menon', as Radcliffe put it when I met him in London on 5 October 1971.

Hindus were expecting Lahore to be included in India and Muslims had the same expectation about Calcutta going to Pakistan. Both were disappointed. Radcliffe told me that he never had the slightest doubt from the very outset that Calcutta (Jinnah had said it was no use having East Bengal without Calcutta) should go to India. I was astonished when Radcliffe said: 'I first gave Lahore to India but then realized I had to give Muslims some big city in West Punjab because they had no capital so I changed my proposal.' When I told him that the Muslims in Pakistan were unhappy over the line he had drawn, he said that they should be 'grateful' that he gave them Lahore, although his initial decision was different.

When I complained to him that this was a strange way of dividing the subcontinent, Radcliffe explained that he was so rushed that he had no time to go into the details. Even district maps were not available and the ones there were, were incorrect. What could he have done in one and a half months? he asked.

I could understand Radcliffe's predicament. Still, I was horrified at the way the subcontinent was divided and the future of its people decided. When I asked Radcliffe if he had any regrets, he said he had none, adding that he had done injustice to non-Muslims in Punjab and Muslims in Bengal. Both should have been given more territory than they got.

The land of the five rivers, with its magnificent irrigation systems, which was ruled for so long by the Punjab Unionist party, representing all three communities, had become a land of divided communities and divided waterways. It was one thing to draw a line; quite another to deal with the severing of age-old relationships and long-established patterns of trade and communication. Still, Radcliffe hoped for joint control over river headworks.

I told Radcliffe about the controversy over Kashmir. He had read about it in the press after his return to London, he said. He had never imagined that Kashmir or, for that matter, Gurdaspur or Ferozepur, would create any problem. He denied having had any talks on this matter with Mountbatten who was supposed to have 'influenced' him to 'alter' the dividing line in northern Punjab to give India access to Kashmir.

Nevertheless, there is an intriguing letter dated 8 August 1947 from George Abell, private secretary to Mountbatten, to Stuart Abbott, private secretary to the Punjab governor, Evan Jenkins. The latter had asked for advance information on possible boundary lines to enable him to make necessary arrangements to check bloodshed. The letter said: 'I enclose a map showing roughly the boundary which Sir Cyril Radcliffe proposes to demarcate in his award, and a note describing it. There will not be any great change from this boundary, but it will have to be accurately defined with reference to village and *zilla* [district] boundaries in the Lahore district.' (*The Radcliffe Report* was said to have been finalized on that very day, 8 August, although it was published five days later.)

Abell's letter added: 'The award itself is expected within the next 48 hours, and I will let you know later about the probable time of announcement. Perhaps you would ring me up if H.E. the Governor has any views on this point.' In the map, the *tehsils* (sub-districts) of Ferozepur and Zira in India were shown as part of Pakistan. On 11 August, Jenkins received a cipher telegram from Mountbatten's office reading: 'Eliminate salient,' which meant that these two areas had been transferred to India. This gave credibility to Pakistan's allegation that Mountbatten had made Radcliffe change the award in favour of India.

Some years later, a Pakistani diplomat at a party reminded Radcliffe of Abell's letter and insinuated that he had acted in a partisan manner. Narrating the incident to me, Radcliffe said: 'I told the Pakistani diplomat that Pakistan got more than what it should have had.' Radcliffe went on to tell me that it was a 'tragedy' that Punjab had to be divided. He also said: 'Patel was very unhappy about the Chittagong hill tracts going to Pakistan, but why, I do not know.' He added that most of the population in Chittagong hill tracts was not Hindu, and the entire economy of the area depended upon East Bengal.

Indeed, Patel was so concerned about the hill tracts that on 13 August he wrote to Mountbatten that any award in that area, 'without any referendum to ascertain the will of the people concerned, must be construed as a collusive or partisan award and will therefore have to be repudiated by us.'

Radcliffe was criticized by both sides, but this, as he said, was the best he could do in the time available to him. The real fault lay with Mountbatten who appointed the Boundary Commission very late. In fact, both the Hindu and Muslim members of the commission were frank enough to tell Radcliffe that they would not have agreed to any boundary even if they had felt that the award was fair. They admitted that their concurrence would annoy the new rulers they would be serving in the two countries after Partition.

Radcliffe had a word of praise for Meherchand Mahajan, who served as a member on behalf of the Congress and for M.C. Setalvad, who presented India's case before the Boundary Commission. He, however, had nothing to say about the League's members. He related an anecdote to me: One Muslim member had met him separately and asked for 'the inclusion of Darjeeling in East Pakistan'. When Radcliffe insisted on knowing the reason, this member said: 'My family and myself have come to be rather fond of Darjeeling over the past years where we have been holidaying' (Darjeeling ultimately went to India).

Both the Congress and the Muslim League had agreed that there would be no migration of populations but the people on either side had no alternative but to move because violence had erupted. No one envisaged that the situation would deteriorate to such a degree that virtually the entire population of non-Muslims in Pakistan would be forced to seek shelter in India and lakhs of Muslims in Pakistan.

Delhi and Karachi celebrated Independence in their own way. The refugees had no sense of triumph over the British. They faced a future of uncertainty in the new country. In a way, Gandhi shared their grief. He was in Calcutta on 15 August and fasted while the country was cut asunder.

He had earlier gone to Noakhali in East Bengal (7 November 1946) to mitigate the sufferings and fears of Hindu families who had lost their bread-winners because Muslims had killed them. The attackers were fanatics but he could foresee the pattern of killings initiated by extremists of one community with the other retaliating. Noakhali was where Gandhi had tried his 'experiment with brahmcharya'. When his grand-niece Manu came to Noakhali, Gandhi resolved on a brahmcharya test with her as his partner. Gandhi's grandson said: 'it was not an experiment but a yagna; a sacrificial offering of his sexuality to god'.

If neither Gandhi nor Manu felt the sexual urge despite sharing the same bed, the *yagna*, Gandhi claimed, would purify him. When the news of his 'experiment' was made public, both the Hindu and Muslim communities were aghast with embarrassment. Nehru was dumbfounded. One of Gandhi's biographers wrote: 'The people in India were less interested in the problems of brahmcharya and ahimsa than in the knowledge of whether they would live or die'. Was Gandhi trying to escape facing the situation when he had failed to prevent the division of India and control Hindu–Muslim riots? Pyarelal reported that Gandhi muttered to himself: 'There must be a serious flaw deep down in me.'

Comparatively fewer people left the two sides of Bengal. There were killings in Bengal but nowhere near on the scale of the carnage seen in Punjab. The one-man boundary force, Gandhi, succeeded in Calcutta and the city quickly returned to normalcy. An incident there spoke volumes about Gandhi's philosophy. In response to his appeal to surrender all arms, the killers queued up to lay down their weapons. One Punjabi, the last one, threw a big knife at Gandhi's feet, complaining that Muslims had killed his 12-year-old son, his only child. Gandhi told him to adopt a Muslim orphan of the same age and bring him up as a Muslim to put the community to shame.

Partition was the greatest tragedy humanity had ever witnessed. The entire cultural fabric that Hindus, Muslims, and Sikhs had shared for centuries was in tatters. Was this the dawn of freedom, as Faiz Ahmad Faiz, a famous Urdu poet, wrote: '*Yeh dagh-dagh ujala, yeh shab-e-gujida sehar—woh intzar tha jiska yeh woh sehar to nahin* [this stained light, this night-bitten dawn; this is not the dawn for which we yearned this is not the dawn for which we set out so eagerly]'. True, it was stained with the blood of the innocent.

Jinnah's vision of Pakistan was of a tolerant, progressive, and modern state. It is another matter that it has become a purely Islamic one. He believed that the creation of Pakistan was the best way of protecting the interests of Muslims. With Nehru, secularism was a matter of faith and he believed that pluralism was a sine qua non for democracy. Patel had no such commitment, although he believed in democracy. Both openly differed on how to check migration from East Pakistan. West Bengal Chief Minister B.C. Roy and Patel joined hands to request Nehru to tell Pakistan that India would turn out Muslims in proportion to the Hindus coming from East Bengal. Nehru stood firm and refused to compromise with the principle of secularism.

The differences between Nehru and Patel were ideological. The former was a social democrat, seeking to move the country forward by giving the commanding heights of the economy to the public sector. Patel was a staunch rightist not only in terms of economic development but even in political matters, representing Hindu nationalism. The Congress party was under Patel's control but no occasion ever arose when the two had to measure their respective strengths. I think Nehru's popularity was so great that he would have supervened had he ever been challenged.

Gandhi knew his country well. He said that if Indians were to take up guns to kill the British, given India's great religious and ethic divisions, they would continue using the same guns to kill each other long after the British had left. He said he did not want India's freedom if it meant Indians would be free to slaughter each other.

When it came to the division of assets between India and Pakistan, both sides wanted the last penny to be accounted for. The worst fallout was on the armed forces. Even a pacifist like Dr Rajendra Prasad insisted on splitting the military to the last soldier. Almost all Hindu defence officers opted for India and Muslims for Pakistan.

Bereft of officers of their own community, Muslims in India and Hindus and Sikhs in Pakistan experienced the worst type of partisan administration. New Delhi realized the error and Nehru asked the states to recruit Muslims, particularly in the police. It was, however, too little too late and India is reaping the bitter harvest to this day. Muslims in India were disillusioned, but Azad had warned them.

In 1945, I had once heard Azad in Lahore. I had never seen him before but had admired him for his sagacity and courage. He stood firm when the tides of communalism were sweeping leaders off their feet. He said:

> I am prepared to overlook all other aspects of the problem and judge it from the point of view of the Muslim interest alone. It seems that the scheme of Pakistan is a symbol of defeatism and has been built on the analogy of the Jewish demand for a national home. It is a confession that Indian Muslims cannot hold their own in a united India and would be forced to withdraw to a corner specially reserved for them.

Azad's words came true. Muslims of the subcontinent were the greatest losers. He had predicted the secession of East Pakistan from West Pakistan.

Muslims are now spread over three countries: India, Pakistan, and Bangladesh. Imagine the influence their numbers and their votes would have commanded in an undivided subcontinent! They would have constituted over one-third of the total population. No democratic country could have ignored them.

Sometime after Partition, my father was keen to return to Sialkot despite the killings. Fida Hussain, chief secretary of Pakistan's Punjab, was visiting Delhi to discuss problems between the two countries. He was once deputy commissioner at Sialkot and knew my father, who had been his family physician at the time. I took my father to meet him. He was very frank and told him that Pakistan's policy was not to have any non-Muslims back. That ended the matter. My father's dream was shattered and he realized that there was no going back. However, neither he nor my mother were the same after having lost their home in Sialkot. They felt that their life had really ended when they left their home.

3

EARLY PANGS OF GOVERNANCE
Kashmir, Gandhiji's Assassination,
and the Integration of the Indian States

As the division of the country had been on the basis of religion the fallout was inevitable. Muslims in India did not escape the privations which they as Muslims had to suffer. I have often told Pakistanis that Indian Muslims paid the price for constituting the new country. Pakistanis do not deny the charge but rationalize that Indian Muslims knew they had to suffer for a Muslim country to be hewn from India.

Helpless and abandoned, Muslims in India recalled Maulana Azad's warnings that after Partition their importance would be reduced to nothing. They rallied around him but it was too late. Hindus maintained a streak of respect for him, no matter how angry they were with Muslims in general. This was clear when he died on 22 February 1958. A ceaseless queue of non-Muslims flowed into his house through the night to pay respects. I was one of them. Nehru himself selected the site for Azad's burial near Jama Masjid. Azad had left behind piles and piles of books and papers which I tried to access in vain. I finally located the papers over forty years ago in a trunk in the custody of the family of Ajmal Khan, Azad's private secretary. I wish someone would retrieve them because the papers belong to a significant period of our national struggle.

There was no money in Azad's bank, nor was there any at home. Significantly, another Muslim cabinet minister, Rafi Ahmad Kidwai, too died penniless. The fact that these Muslim ministers had no assets spoke a great deal about the integrity of nationalist Muslims.

I recalled how, prior to Partition, Muslim students from the Aligarh Muslim University had once spat on Azad's face when the train stopped at Aligarh station. Was this a precursor of the hatred that Azad had predicted in Pakistan? He told Shorish Kashmiri, a leader from Lahore, in an interview a few weeks before Partition:

An entity conceived in hatred will last only as long as that hatred lasts. This hatred will overwhelm the relations between India and Pakistan. In this situation it will not be possible for India and Pakistan to become friends and live amicably unless some catastrophic event takes place. It will not be possible for Pakistan to accommodate all the Muslims of India. It will not be possible for the Hindus to stay especially in West Pakistan.

People were still migrating from one country to the other when I heard of tribesmen infiltrating into Kashmir within months of Independence. I recalled our family's annual visit to Pahalgam, pitching a tent on an expansive, undulating terrain and watching a lazy stream flowing a few yards away. The sojourn at Pahalgam during the summer was common among Punjabi Hindu and Sikh families. It was taken for granted that Kashmir would be a part of India.

When Maharaja Hari Singh of Jammu & Kashmir declared independence, New Delhi wanted him to come to terms with Sheikh Abdullah, Kashmir's popular leader, who was heading the Quit Kashmir Movement for a democratic dispensation to replace the monarchy.

My impression is that had Pakistan been patient it would have got Kashmir automatically. India could not have conquered it, nor could a Hindu maharaja have ignored the composition of the population, which was predominantly Muslim. Instead, an impatient Pakistan sent tribesmen along with regular troops to Kashmir within days of Independence.

While its true that Nehru was keen on Kashmir's accession to India, Patel was opposed to it. Sheikh Abdullah told me in an interview later (21 February 1971) that Patel argued with him that as Kashmir was a Muslim-majority area it should go to Pakistan. Even when New Delhi received the maharaja's request to accede to India, Patel said: 'We should not get mixed up with Kashmir. We already have too much on our plate.'

Nehru's anxiety was clear from his letter to Patel (27 September 1947), three days before Kashmir's accession to India: 'things must be done in a way so as to bring about the accession of Kashmir to the Indian union as rapidly as possible with the cooperation of Sheikh Abdullah'. Nehru wanted Indian forces to fight against the Pakistan tribesmen and others advancing in the Valley. It was Mountbatten who asked Nehru to get the instrument of accession signed first before sending troops.

From the very outset the maharaja's preference was for independence. Failing that, he wanted a merger with India. His fear in relation to the second alternative was that with Nehru at the helm of affairs, he would be reduced to a mere figurehead, and Sheikh Abdullah would be the one with real power. When Patel, otherwise close to the maharaja, suggested that he should 'make a substantial gesture to win Sheikh Abdullah's support', the maharaja knew his fate was sealed.

On the other hand, Pakistan was anathema to the maharaja. First, as a Hindu, he was opposed to joining an Islamic country, and secondly, he was afraid that once he did that, his loyal supporters, the Hindus and Sikhs, would leave the state. Pakistan did offer him a Sikkim-like status, with defence and foreign affairs remaining with Karachi. The maharaja did not even consider the offer because he had no trust in the Pakistani leaders.

As far as I am aware, there is nothing on record to prove that the maharaja had a secret agreement with India as is alleged by Pakistan. If there was one, Nehru, on hearing reports about Pakistan's proposed invasion of Kashmir, would not have written to Patel before the maharaja signed the Instrument of Accession, that 'once the State accedes to India it will become very difficult for Pakistan to invade it officially or unofficially without coming into conflict with the Indian Union'.

Pakistan's allegation of a secret agreement with India was on the basis of papers carried by one of Hari Singh's cousins, Thakore Harnam Singh, whose plane had to land in Lahore because of engine trouble. The papers reportedly contained a promise that the Indian Union, in return for Kashmir's accession, would build communications from Pathankot to Jammu and station troops at Gilgit in the north of Kashmir. This may well have been a temptation for the maharaja but does not constitute proof of a secret agreement. The accession would have automatically meant not only the building of lines of communications but also of stationing troops.

Mountbatten later told me that Patel had agreed to let Kashmir go to Pakistan if the state so wished. 'By sending its irregular troops into the state, Pakistan spoiled the whole thing,' added Mountbatten. He was, however, worried that Nehru's Kashmiri ancestry would lead him to unwise decisions. (Nehru is reported to have confessed to a British officer: 'In the same way as Calais was written on Mary's heart, Kashmir is written on mine.')

However, Pakistan could not wait. Kashmir had always been a part of the concept of Pakistan and the letter 'K' in its name stood for Kashmir. As the Pakistan minister for Kashmir affairs said in 1951, and this has been repeated by many ministers to this day, 'Kashmir is an article of faith with Pakistan and not merely a piece of land or a source of rivers'. Jinnah, too had tried to win over Sheikh Abdullah when the two met in Lahore. Recalling his meeting with Jinnah, Sheikh Abdullah said: 'I told him that I was opposed to the idea of Pakistan and it would not help the situation. Muslims were scattered all over India and they would face greater difficulties if certain portions were taken away from the country and declared independent. If they (Muslims) were not safe in the entirety of India how would they be safe in a small enclave?'

This was more or less what Azad had said when airing his opposition to the creation of Pakistan. One other remark attributed to the Sheikh for not going to Pakistan was that 'There are too many Muslims there'.

When Pakistan made no progress either through talks or pressure which it applied on the maharaja by slowing down the supply of necessities, it implemented a scheme in September 1947 which was prepared while Douglas David Gracey, Pakistan army's second commander-in-chief, was away in London on leave. In brief, the plan was to send tribesmen followed by Pakistan's regular forces into Kashmir.

Shiv Saran Lal, who was at that time deputy commissioner, Dera Ismail Khan, NWFP, reported to New Delhi that Pakistan had sent 'armed tribal people (half a million) to the Pakistan–Kashmir border and the Pakistan government provided transport in civilian and military lorries'.

After the accession, the maharaja provided New Delhi with more evidence (plans bearing proper seals and names) to prove that 'a conspiracy for the establishment of a new Muslim State by the Muslim League in Jammu and Kashmir' was hatched as early as 1945.

Tribals and regular troops from Pakistan invaded Kashmir while both Delhi and Srinagar were in the midst of negotiations relating to the accession. Jinnah gave his consent to the invasion. Allen Campbell told me that when Mountbatten met Jinnah at the latter's invitation in Lahore, Pakistan tried to persuade him to agree to India withdrawing its forces fighting against tribals from Pakistan and regular Pakistan forces. In fact, Jinnah's invitation was to Nehru who had purposely stayed back and had feigned illness. When Mountbatten asked for a guarantee that the tribal invaders would agree to withdraw, Jinnah said he would 'call the whole thing off if Indian forces withdrew'. This was an admission of sorts. Mountbatten wrote to Patel quoting Rees as his source, that tribesmen were advancing towards Uri in the Baramulla district. Mountbatten informed him later that ex-INA officers were involved in the incursion.

It was on the evening of 24 October that India received definite confirmation about the infiltration of Pakistani tribesmen into Kashmir. Nehru was hosting a dinner at that time in New Delhi in honour of Thailand's foreign minister. Thus far, India had not taken any military action. Mehr Chand Mahajan had written to Patel on 23 October that the raiders had penetrated deep into the state. He said: 'The help that you kindly promised has not arrived and we are surrounded on all sides.' New Delhi was still caught on the horns of a legalistic dilemma although Mahajan had urged in the same letter: 'you will agree with me it is hardly the time to think of any constitutional issues'.

Records of the Defence Committee's meeting on 25 October show that Mountbatten, who was in the chair, favoured Kashmir's temporary accession to India on the understanding that the people's wishes would be ascertained after the restoration of law and order. Nehru and Patel found nothing to prevent India from sending assistance even in the absence of accession. They argued that India was duty-bound to provide assistance to Kashmir because it was the successor state to the British in the same way as the British were successors to the Mughals. Therefore, India exercised suzerainty over the entire subcontinent excluding those parts which had acceded to Pakistan.

By this time, Sheikh Abdullah was out of jail and organized people's resistance against the invaders (he was released in September 1947). The maharaja sought India's help which was denied until he signed an instrument of accession. Once Srinagar had legally accepted New Delhi's requirement, Indian troops, in the face of Mountbatten's reluctance, flew to Srinagar which at that time was within shooting range of the invaders. The two countries were at war now and India began pushing Pakistanis out of Kashmir.

The first Indian contingent arrived in Srinagar airport when 'the raiders' were at its outskirts. An army major was killed on the tarmac. Had the tribesman not wasted time in looting and raping women in Baramulla, they would have been successful in capturing the airport, without which it would not have been possible to land Indian troops. A daring army officer, Major-General K.S. Thimayya, who later became chief of the army staff, drove a detachment of tanks to Zojila Pass at a height of 11,575 feet during winter, hastening the end of the war.

Gandhi blessed the operation on the ground that if cowardice came in the way of saving a community, it was better to fight to do so. This was his reply to those who wondered how he could support an armed conflict.

'Why did you stop and not take over the whole of Kashmir?', was a question I posed to Lt Gen. Kulwant Singh, who headed the Kashmir operation, many years after the ceasefire. He said the prime minister had instructed him to go up to the area where the population spoke Kashmiri. Nehru did not want the army to go into the Punjabi-speaking territory (now Azad Kashmir). In a sense, Nehru wanted only the Kashmir Valley: His thinking was clear from what he offered Liaquat Ali Khan at the Commonwealth Prime Ministers' Conference in London in October 1947. It was the division of the state with certain areas in western Poonch and the north-western part of the state of Jammu & Kashmir going to Pakistan.

Hostilities in Kashmir escalated into a fully-fledged war between India and Pakistan. The fighting was still going on when Liaquat came to Delhi for a meeting of the Joint Defence Council on 26 November. He and Nehru agreed that Pakistan should persuade the tribesmen to cease fighting and leave Kashmir as soon as possible and that India should withdraw the bulk of its forces, requesting the UN to send a commission to hold a plebiscite.

It was New Delhi which referred the case of Pakistan's attack to the UN, as Mountbatten had advised Nehru. It proved to be a mistake. There were many Indian leaders who did not wish the case to be referred to the UN, afraid that the British would play their old pro-Pakistani games. In this they were not proved wrong.

India suffered a major setback when the case came before the UN Security Council. This was primarily due to the brilliant advocacy by Pakistan foreign minister, Zafarullah Khan, an Ahmedi (his entire community was subsequently declared non-Muslim). Pakistan was able to refute all the charges levelled against it and contended, quite effectively, that India was hostile to Pakistan. He however admitted that Pakistani troops were fighting in Kashmir. The entire complexion changed and the UN passed a resolution (13 August 1948) calling for, (1) a ceasefire; (2) Pakistan to withdraw the tribals and place its troops under the command of local civilian authorities; (3) India to withdraw the bulk of its troops; (4) UN observers to supervise the ceasefire; and (5) holding of the plebiscite.

The resolution was not entitled Kashmir, as was India's endeavour, but related generally to peace and security. India was unhappy. Nehru believed that this couldn't have been possible without the help of Philip Noel-Baker, an 'Old Labour' minister in the Attlee government at the UN. It was apparent that the UK had decided to adopt a pro-Pakistan stance not because of any merit in the case but in the belief that the country was essential to its Middle-East policy. Baker was also personally prejudiced against India. He never forgave Nehru for not consulting him or even seeking his advice on disarmament, the subject on which he won a Nobel Prize in 1959.

When the British argued that Kashmir was a 'territory in dispute', the US first disagreed and stated that they 'found it difficult to deny the legal validity of Kashmir's accession to India'. The US opposed Noel-Baker's resolution at the UN to allow Pakistan to deploy its troops in Kashmir. However, under pressure from the UK, the US eventually agreed to a draft resolution which would permit the entry of Pakistani troops into Kashmir 'only if India concurred'.

Subsequently, the UK and the US joined hands. They did not want Pakistan to take any action to stop the invaders until a formula was found for a solution of the Kashmir problem acceptable to her. They also favoured removing the Sheikh Abdullah government and bringing Kashmir under the UN's control and the subsequent organization of a plebiscite.

Nehru was furious at the British machinations. He wrote to Vijayalakshmi Pandit on 16 February 1948:

> I cannot imagine that the security council could probably behave in the trivial and partisan manner in which it had and it is not surprising that the world is going to pieces ... and the US and Britain have played a dirty game, Britain being the chief actor behind the scenes.

Nehru originally thought the Western bias was due to the US pursuit of concessions in Pakistan, but after a briefing by Indian officials at the UN, he realized that Noel-Baker was the 'villain of the piece'. Nehru complained angrily to Attlee that Noel-Baker had in a conversation with Sheikh Abdullah dismissed as untrue the charge that Pakistan had assisted the raiders in entering Kashmir. Six decades later, Prime Minister Gordon Brown publicly admitted that London was misled by its UN envoy, Noel-Baker.

Nehru was, however, so incensed with the UK that India's membership to the Commonwealth became a question mark. However, his friends, the

Mountbattens, were keen on having India on board. How could a republic accept the Queen as its head? The question tormented Nehru. The acceptance of Commonwealth membership in 1947 was independent India's first major foreign policy decision. It constituted a watershed in the evolution of the Commonwealth, establishing a precedent for non-white republican membership. The Mountbattens, as I learnt, were gratified.

The intelligentsia was against India joining the Commonwealth which was a reminder of our slavery. The British had committed so many atrocities that our association would give the impression of cowardice. They had not even asked for forgiveness or offered apologies. Many Congressmen too didn't favour the idea of being hitched to British rulers in one way or another. Nehru's defence was that it augured well for the future and that the old conflict between India and the UK had been resolved in a friendly and honourable way.

Nehru felt belittled by the attitude of both London and Washington towards the ceasefire proposal he had submitted to the UN. Subsequently, in December 1950, India rejected the UN offer to mediate in Kashmir. Nehru said at a press conference, at which I was present, that

> the people who run the government of India have a record in the past of standing for what they consider to be right regardless of the consequences for the last thirty years and they propose to do that in regard to Kashmir and any other matter.

Nehru was opposed to a plebiscite but on different grounds. He told Mountbatten that 'with the troops of the Indian Dominion in military occupation of Kashmir and with the National Conference under Sheikh Abdullah in power, such propaganda and pressure would be brought to bear that the average Muslim would never have the courage to vote for Pakistan.'

Without clearance from the government of India, Mountbatten suggested to Jinnah a plebiscite under the UN, with an advance complement of observers and organizers preparing the 'necessary atmosphere'. Jinnah instead suggested that he and Mountbatten were 'the only two who could organize the plebiscite'. To this, Mountbatten's comment was that he had no authority to do so; Lord Ismay, who was Mountbatten's chief of staff in India, added that Attlee would not give his consent.

Chester Bowles, then the US ambassador, told me that India would have won the plebiscite if it had held it before 1953. Then New Delhi had popular backing in Kashmir, but things changed subsequently, he said. He was probably referring to the arrest of Sheikh Abdullah.

The record of the talks, given by Mountbatten to Nehru in the form of a report, which I have seen, said that at the end of the meeting Jinnah was quite pessimistic and said 'India was out to throttle and choke the Dominion of

Pakistan at birth'. At that time, Claude Auchinleck, in a cable, sent a similar assessment to London: 'I have no hesitation in affirming that the present Indian cabinet are implacably determined to do all in their power to prevent the establishment of the Dominion of Pakistan on a firm basis.'

The conflict in Kashmir was still raging when Hyderabad became a point of concern. Landlocked as it was, the state could not accede to any other country other than India although the Nizam's preference was for Pakistan. The British had rewarded him with the title of 'His Exalted Highness' for his services. The Nizam's grandiose idea was to declare himself a rightful descendant of the great Mughal dynasty. He also imagined India was too embroiled in Kashmir to pay any attention to Hyderabad.

The Kashmir war prompted New Delhi to stop the transfer of Karachi's share of the cash balances of an undivided India. The Arbitration Tribunal had given Pakistan Rs 75 crore but New Delhi had paid only Rs 20 crore. Patel explained that India could not reasonably be asked to make a payment when an armed conflict was in progress. Pakistan's reply was that at no stage of the negotiations was the Kashmir question mentioned or considered. Therefore, linking the two was an 'unfriendly act'.

A large section of the Indian government wanted to adjust Pakistan's share against the property which the Hindus and Sikhs had left behind. A rough estimate was that the evacuee property in Pakistan totalled Rs 500 crore ($375 million) as against Rs 100 crore ($75 million) in India, a ratio of five to one.

Mahatma Gandhi was appalled over the non-payment of dues to Karachi. Patel never forgave Gandhi for forcing the issue, nor did the extremist Hindus. They found him in the way of their design to set up a Hindu state. They conspired, and one of them shot him dead on 30 January 1948.

Patel submitted his resignation from the cabinet because he felt personally responsible for Gandhi's assassination. His resignation was also intended to mollify the general opinion that pointed fingers at him. Everyone was aware that he was unhappy with the Mahatma who had gone on a fast to pressurize New Delhi to transfer the assets due to Pakistan. Failing to provide any security to Gandhi even after the bomb thrown by a person named Madan Lal a few days earlier (on 20 January 1948) was unforgivable. I was present at that prayer meeting. Gandhi acted as if nothing had happened. Everyone, including I, thought it was a cracker but learnt the next day from newspaper reports that it was a bomb.

Patel was known to be soft towards the RSS (Rashtriya Swayamsevak Sangh), which was suspected of involvement in Gandhi's assassination. Patel banned the RSS but withdrew the ban soon after. It was as if he was going through the motions. Patel's papers say that the Hindu Mahasabha, not RSS, was to blame. I do not think there is any difference between the two.

Nehru implored Patel not to resign and said that 'in the crisis we face after Bapu's death, I think it is my duty, and if I may venture to say, yours also, to face it together as friends and colleagues'. Patel was touched by this expression of affection and even abandoned his stand that every ministry was autonomous.

I was then working with *Anjam,* and 30 January 1948 was like any other normal winter day, sunny and cool. The PTI teleprinter was belching out words relentlessly in a corner of the office. The desk-in-charge, Sabri sahib, gave me a long copy datelined London, for translation. The peon had placed before me a cup of tea, hot and sugary. I was sipping it slowly when the teleprinter's bell rang. I rushed to the teleprinter and read the flash: *Gandhi Shot.*

A colleague of mine with a motorbike immediately drove me to Birla House. It wore a sombre, forlorn look. I could hear from afar the chant 'Gandhi *Amar Rahe'.* There was no one at the entrance to check the people entering. Swathed in white khadi, a group of men and women stood around Gandhiji's body. They were his immediate followers who stayed with him. Many who had come early for the afternoon *prarthana* (prayer) had stayed back.

There was not much of a crowd. I could see Nehru, Patel, and Defence Minister Baldev Singh overcome by grief and their loss was palpable. I saw Azad sitting beneath a tree all on his own, lost deep in thought. Unfortunately he, an important voice before Partition, had ceased to count after Independence. Nehru continued to consult him and respect his advice but Patel would often relate how the Maulana's influence had been reduced to nothing. By contrast, Gandhi invariably sought his advice.

I saw Governor General Lord Mountbatten arriving and saluting the body of the Mahatma, placed on a dais at the centre of the compound. 'Thank God, he was not a Punjabi,' Baldev Singh told Mountbatten. 'He was not a Muslim either and we are broadcasting this fact.' This would, I thought, stop the rumour that the assassin was a Muslim. Besides the dark cloud of gloom, anger and vendetta could easily have engulfed the country. Gandhi represented unity and pluralism.

By now the police presence was building into a large force. Gandhi had never liked the fuss of security. Leaders should not shun the public, he would say. Although the men in khaki had taken over the place, no one pushed me or any other person out of the circle of mourners around the body. Birla House still looked forlorn even though a sea of humanity surrounded it. A few devotees were singing Gandhi's favourite bhajan: 'Ishwar, Allah tere naam.'

I saw Nehru climbing a boundary wall and wiping his tears. In a broken voice, he said: 'The light has gone out of our lives. Bapu is no more. A glory has departed and the sun that warmed and brightened our lives has set and we are left to shiver in the cold and dark.' Nehru broke down, as did the crowd. There was hardly a face with dry eyes. The man who had guided India's destiny for decades was gone. Who would the nation turn to now? Who would span the distance between Nehru and Patel who were drifting apart?

I did not see Nathuram Godse, who had shot the Mahatma thrice from close range. He had probably been locked up in a room in Birla House or been taken away by the police. I was too overwhelmed with grief to concern myself with where the killer of the apostle of non-violence was. I saw a trickle of blood and some flowers crushed on the path which Gandhi always took from the building to the place of prayer. Even with scores of people around, the path looked desolate. One man's absence had made all the difference.

I tried to comprehend the meaning of the loss while struggling with a surge of emotion. I could see history exploding before my eyes. Perhaps I was too soft, too sentimental, too raw and too new to journalism and had not been hardened even by the carnage that I had witnessed during Partition. I wept unashamedly.

It was a catharsis of the anger which had swelled within me after seeing the killings during the days of Partition. I felt blank. I remembered the time when I saw the Mahatma on my arrival in Delhi from Pakistan. He epitomized for me all of India's sufferings and dreams. Only a week earlier Gandhi had told B.C. Roy, the tall Congress leader: 'What's the good of my living? Neither the people nor those in power have any use for me. "Do or Die" becomes me more in the circumstances. I wish to die in harness, taking the name of God with my last breath.' It is believed that when he collapsed under Godse's bullets, he uttered the words '*Hey Ram*'.

I walked up to the place of prayer and stood there for a long time. It exuded an air of asceticism and spiritualism. It touched me within as if I was a part of the audience, the Indian people, whom Gandhi was counselling to renounce violence. Would the nation follow his voice, which a fanatic Hindu had silenced? Would his mission for secularism be completed after his sacrifice? At least, for the time being, the loss had fused the different religious communities – Hindus, Muslims, Sikhs, and Christians – into one multitude of sorrow; as one nation in mourning. The miracle of Gandhi would remain, I was confident.

Pakistan did not join India in mourning Gandhi's assassination. Even Jinnah's reaction was lukewarm: 'He was one of the greatest men produced by the Hindu community.' I have not found any recognition of Gandhi's greatness in Pakistan, as if doing so would belittle Jinnah.

※

Sardar Patel withdrew his resignation on Nehru's insistence. Post Gandhi's death the differences between Patel and Nehru had become more apparent. On Nehru's part, he compromised with Patel on the creation of an Indian Administrative Service (IAS). The two had a different outlook on civil servants. Nehru did not want the Indian Civil Service (ICS) to continue as it was a relic of the past, of British imperialism. He had been hurt by the behaviour of the ICS during the freedom struggle. He felt they lacked patriotism. Patel changed the nomenclature, ICS, into Indian Administrative Service (IAS), but did not agree to disband it. He considered the service a steel frame, essential for governance. Many years later when I was the home ministry's information officer, Bhola Nath Jha, home secretary, told me that the service should have been disbanded. His view was that the chief ministers in the states would be so powerful one day that they would use the IAS for their purpose, belittling the service. They would prefer obedient provincial cadres to the embarrassment and helplessness of a centrally administered All India Service like the IAS.

Nehru was, however, impressed by a few members of ICS working under him in the Ministry of Foreign Affairs. To K.P.S. Menon, a senior ICS officer, he wrote, 'their efficiency appeals to me'. He surprised everyone when he appointed Girja Shankar Bajpai, an ICS officer, secretary-general in the Ministry of External Affairs (MEA) and came to depend upon him because he was highly impressed by his opinion and advice.

However, the gulf between Nehru and Patel was never bridged. Before China began encroaching on Indian soil, Patel warned Nehru that one day China would stab India in the back.

❁

The constituent assembly was not my beat but I followed its proceedings with great diligence. It met for the first time on 9 December 1946. It was an open secret that Nehru and Patel between them decided on the principal issues and got them approved at the Congress meeting held virtually every evening. Although they had studied many constitutions and the law advisor, B.N. Rao, travelled around the world to garner all the information he could for the benefit of the constituent assembly, the eventual choice was the British parliamentary system with various modifications. Even our national movement had felt at home with the British parliament. The difference was that, as in the case of the US, ours was a written constitution unlike its British counterpart based on precedents and tradition. Our precedence and traditions dated only to the days when the British ruled us. The result was a strange mis-match that did not adequately translate the aspirations of people for a secure livelihood: Gandhi had promised everyone food, clothing, and shelter.

True, Dr B.R. Ambedkar, the dalit leader representing the poor, piloted the Constitution Bill but he differed very little from Nehru and Patel. Ambedkar's strongest objection was to reservation for scheduled castes and scheduled tribes considering them to be 'crutches'. It was with greatest difficulty that he was persuaded to agree to reservations for a period of ten years.

However, a committee, headed by Patel, offered reservations to Muslims in the constitution. But Muslim leaders rejected the offer and reportedly remarked that they did not want anything that would convey a sense of something separate or special being granted to them. They said they had suffered sufficiently for following a separatist agenda.

Nehru proposed Hindustani as India's official language at a meeting of the Congress party held on the eve of constitutional assembly vote on Hindi.

His apprehension was that Hindi might give rise to communal feelings because it had come to be associated with Hindus adding that Mahatma Gandhi favoured Hindustani.

Though Nehru's proposal was defeated by just one vote, that of Gurmukh Singh Musafir from Punjab, Pant gave me a different version. He said that the division was on whether the numerals should be in Roman or Devnagri. Musafir voted for the Roman script and that was incorporated in the constitution. There was an overwhelming majority in favour of Hindi, said Pant. In the constituent assembly, the resolution to have Hindi as the national language was adopted without much opposition because Congressmen, in a majority in the constituent assembly, went by what their party had decided earlier.

Nehru was very particular about spelling out fundamental rights for the people and a provision that any citizen could approach the highest court for protection. This was an undertaking given by his father, Moti Lal Nehru, as far back as December 1927 when he was asked by the Congress session at Madras 'to draft a constitution for India on the basis of the Declaration of Rights'.

I was present at one of the last sittings of the constituent assembly. Dr Rajendra Prasad, who was in the chair, said that theirs was the best constitution in the world and the finest minds would interpret it, by which he meant the judges. He went on to say that the best of men, meaning advocates, would argue on the different provisions but it was a pity that those who would frame the laws (members of parliament and state legislatures) were not required to have any educational qualifications.

Prime Minister Nehru said in reply that he agreed with Rajan Babu on the distinctiveness of the constitution which the best of minds would analyze and interpret. His problem, he said, was that when India was fighting for Independence, the best minds were the toadies of the British. The illiterate, the poor, and the backward were on our side, sacrificing all for the country. Should he prefer the toadies to them after India's Independence?

Humayun Kabir and I would blame Jinnah for dividing the country on the basis of religion. The discussion sometime meandered to Nehru. Kabir would say that the fact that Nehru and Jinnah did not like each other personally was largely responsible for the Partition. He would criticize Nehru for not being 'practical' and for grafting his Western ideas on to the entirely different conditions in India. This mismatch, he said, was costing the nation heavily.

Kabir believed that Azad had come to realize after seeing Nehru's functioning that Patel should have been India's prime minister and Nehru the president of India. Coming as it did from an inveterate opponent of Patel, it was a revelation. Apparently, Azad, a great admirer of Nehru, had learnt after serving in his government that Patel, though conservative in his outlook, was pragmatic and down to earth. Nehru was too much of an idealist. A year earlier, Rajagopalachari had said the same thing: Nehru should be appointed governor general and Patel prime minister.

Patel was not the same after Gandhi's death. His health was deteriorating rapidly. However, when Nehru created a ministry of states to deal with princely rulers, Patel asked for the charge as if he wanted to do something that would go down in history. Indeed, the country will always remember him for merging the princely states in India. When the British left, there were 564 princely states spread across India administering their own affairs under the supervision of British agents.

Rajas, maharajas, and nawabs, as they were addressed, ruled the states. The British had nurtured them to milk from them as much wealth they could. Later, when the British were about to quit India, they offered the Indian states three alternatives: one, to accede to India; two, to Pakistan; or to remain independent. London underlined the composition of the population and geographical proximity as being important when making their choice. The alternative given of remaining independent was the parting kick of the British who sought India's balkanization after their departure.

Rulers vainly tried to group themselves into unions. Gandhi did not favour the idea, although Nehru was equivocal. Even before the British withdrawal, the Nawab of Bhopal, representing the chamber of princes, had made it clear (2 April 1946) that the Indian states wished to continue their existence with the maximum sovereignty possible. Many wanted to govern themselves. It was a combination of impudence and confusion.

Patel and V.P. Menon, once in Mountbatten entourage, began 'disciplining' them. Through pressure, persuasion, and allure, the two were able to get nearly all the princely rulers to join India. In reality, it was a show of strength. Menon, so to speak, had a pistol in one hand and the instrument of accession in the other. Rulers were permitted to have control over all subjects, except defence, foreign affairs, and communications. Even this leeway was, however, only on paper as they were to subsequently discover. They were given a privy purse on integration with India and the title of Rajpramukh. How could such a title remain permanent in a democratic republic? I could see some resentment over the purse and the title, even though there was a widespread sense of relief that a coherent India had emerged. Both, the privy purse and the titles were abolished after some years. Justice M.C. Chagla, who served as a union minister, characterized the abolition as a 'betrayal of contractual obligation'.

Indeed, the integration of states was a stupendous task, which Patel, with the active participation of Menon, largely brought about through finesse but partly through threat of force. Menon described the process thus: There was 'aviary which possessed a rare collection of birds'. They were 'captured' one by one, apparently 'on the principle of ahimsa'. Whatever Menon's observation, the approach could best be described as accession at the point of a gun.

Menon had a long story to tell about Junagarh. Nawab Mohab Khan Rasul Khan Ji and Diwan Abdul Kadir Mohammad Hashim declared the state's accession to Pakistan on 15 August 1947 itself. India was greatly perturbed because Junagarh was in the heart of Kathiawar, a preponderantly Hindu belt. Junagarh itself was a Hindu majority state. According to Menon, he had letters to prove that Jinnah had advised the Junagarh ruler in early 1947 to stay 'firm' and not to accede to India. However, when Patel sought military action, Nehru stopped him. Mountbatten wanted the matter to be referred to the UN. To stay 'firm', the nawab had appointed in early 1947, Shah Nawaz Bhutto, father of Zulfikar Ali Bhutto, as the dewan. Under pressure from the Kathiawar rulers and New Delhi, the nawab flew to Pakistan, emptying the entire treasury but was soon disillusioned and wanted to return to Junagarh. He approached India's high commissioner to Pakistan, Sri Prakash, to convey that he acceded to Patel's wishes but New Delhi never responded. On 20 February 1948, a referendum was held in the state in the presence of foreign journalists. Only 91 votes were cast in favour of Pakistan against over two lakhs in favour of India.

❖

Soon after the announcement on the transfer of power, the Nizam sent a message to Jinnah to find out if he would side with Hyderabad against India. Jinnah's reply was that he would not endanger Pakistan for 'a handful of effète nobility'. A few weeks later, Jinnah said the same thing to Mountbatten: 'The Hyderabad question is for the Nizam and his own government to decide.' However, the regal manner in which Pakistan treated Ittehad-ul-Muslimeen, representatives of an organization of diehards from Hyderabad, evoked doubts about the Muslim League's intentions. In fact, after one meeting with Jinnah at Karachi, the delegates remarked that they were going back to Hyderabad 'fully satisfied'.

Patel reportedly offered Kashmir to Pakistan in exchange for Hyderabad's accession to New Delhi. Liaquat Ali was inclined to accept, not knowing when the elusive Kashmir would be Pakistan's. Patel and Liaquat Ali were on the same wavelength. The former was not interested in Kashmir and the latter disinterested in Hyderabad.

Jinnah declined Patel's suggestion because he believed Kashmir would eventually come to Pakistan but the defiant Hyderabad would remain a thorn in India's flesh. Lest his prime minister, Liaquat Ali Khan or anyone else should compromise over Kashmir, Jinnah wrote in his notebook on 30 November 1947, as published in a book (*Jinnah-Liaquat Correspondence*, Ed. Muhammed Reza Kazimi): 'Kashmir no commitment ... should be made ... without my approval of settlement. Mr Liaquat has agreed and promised to abide by the understanding.'

Sensing New Delhi's determination to merge Hyderabad with India, the Nizam played with the idea of an autonomous state, relinquishing external affairs (minus foreign trade), defence, and communications to New Delhi. However, he could not go beyond the negotiating table because he was unable to stand up to threats by Qasim Razvi, chief of the Razakars (an irregular body of men in the Nizam's police force). Razvi was leading the extremists who claimed to maintain 'the supremacy of the Muslim power in the Deccan'.

The impression was growing that Hyderabad was being converted into a 'Mini Pakistan'. People felt helpless and they looked to Patel because he was considered pragmatic in comparison to Nehru, who tended to get lost in diplomatic niceties.

So strained was the atmosphere that even Nehru had to say at a Congress party meeting (24 April 1948): 'There are two courses now open to Hyderabad – war or accession.' He later contradicted the report because the situation in the state had begun attracting world attention. Mountbatten assured New Delhi that he would have the Nizam issue a firman to hold a plebiscite.

I have studied the Partition documents published by the US State Department. They reveal that Hyderabad attempted 'to establish direct relations with the British Crown, presumably to maintain a status completely separate from that of the rest of India'. There may be some truth in this, because a few London firms did enter into industrial agreements with businessmen from Hyderabad.

The activities of the Razakars irritated New Delhi. When they attacked Hindus travelling by train at Gangapur station in Hyderabad (22 May), they incensed people throughout India who were already criticizing the government for being 'soft' towards the Nizam. New Delhi asked the Nizam to allow entry of Indian troops at Secunderabad, Hyderabad's twin city, to restore law and order but he, instead, appealed to the UN Security Council for intervention.

Reports circulating at the time said that even then Nehru was not in favour of marching troops into Hyderabad lest the matter be taken up by the UN. One story was that Nehru heard about the 'police action' only after troops had entered Hyderabad. When he tried to contact Patel, he was not 'available' and was told this was not possible because he was ill. Maniben, Patel's devoted daughter, writes in her diary that Nehru tried his best to delay the operation.

It is true that Patel chafed at the 'do-nothing attitude of the Indian government' but it is inconceivable that a decision to send in troops could have been kept back from the prime minister. Nehru had an eye on international opinion to whose notice he wished to bring the Nizam's intransigence.

Rumours were many. One was that India decided on its 'police action' on 13 September 1948, a day after Jinnah's death, so as to obviate the possibility of Pakistan's intervention (a *Daily Telegraph* correspondent told India's high commissioner at Karachi at that time that but for Jinnah's untimely death Pakistan would have intervened). K.M. Munshi, then New Delhi's representative at Hyderabad, says in his book that the date was 'set on 9 September, because the army authorities wanted three days' notice in order to move troop's right to their final position'.

The entire action, called 'Operation Polo', lasted five days. In his 'Report of the Governor-General' Mountbatten said that the operation plans were worked out during his visit to Burma from 8 to 16 March 1948. General Francis Robert Bucher, then India's commander-in-chief, was opposed to the operation and asked Patel to postpone the action as there was a possibility of Pakistani air attacks on Ahmedabad and Bombay.

The quick end of the operation defused any possibility of the Security Council or, for that matter, any foreign power discussing the problem. As Nehru wrote to Patel in a letter (27 October) from Paris: 'It was very fortunate that we could dispose of it rapidly. Otherwise reactions would have been very much adverse to us as it is very difficult to explain everything and the simple fact of a large country attacking a small one impressed people.'

Pakistan tried to initiate a debate on Hyderabad in the Security Council thrice on 6 October, 21 November, and 6 December 1948, but members showed little interest, particularly when the Nizam had himself withdrawn the complaint.

Many months later, when Laik Ali, once the Nizam's prime minister, who had fled to Pakistan by then, was present at a party, Ghulam Mohammad, then Pakistan's governor general, introduced him to India's high commissioner saying: 'He was your prisoner,' to which the high commissioner retorted: 'He is your prisoner now.'

Goa remained under the Portuguese for thirteen years after Independence. I think all pimples of colonialism should have been wiped clean soon after winning freedom. The French behaved better, first giving New Delhi de facto charge of Pondicherry and its other territories, and then transferring their *de jure* control. A plebiscite was held only in Chandannagar and the people chose India. (In May 1950, the French allowed the Indian government to assume *de facto* control over Chandannagar.)

I visited Pondicherry (now Puducherry) many years after its merger. The famous Ashram was the centre of attention and the Mother headed it still. I stood in a queue to receive a flower from her; one that was of a different colour than is usually the case. This meant the Mother was 'pleased' with me. How? I had never met her before. There was a serene tranquillity about her, although her neck was shaking because of Parkinson's disease. Pondicherry still retained something of a French ambience. Apart from the buildings, the Ashram had an air of spiritualism. I felt at peace there. This has happened to me rarely – when something within had tugged me to sit in a lonely place and pray.

The French had left behind goodwill. This was in contrast to Lisbon's behaviour. Portugal, under Antonio Salazar, a dictator, refused to vacate Goa. Nehru expected Lisbon to withdraw before long. When that did not happen, many in India felt Nehru was afraid of annoying the West, which they suspected was ganging up against India on Goa.

In one way this was correct. I felt the US was exerting pressure on Nehru. He was himself against a forcible takeover lest it should mar his image as a conciliator in settlement of international disputes. To allay angry public opinion in India, he would say that solving a problem by hitting an adversary with a club was not the right way. When his opponents raised a crescendo of criticism against him, he said he did not wish to resort to arms.

The US suggested India buy Goa from Portugal as the US had done with France in the case of Louisiana. Nehru was considering the proposal favourably when Portugal made it clear that it was unwilling to part with Goa at any price. The deadlock continued. Nehru's attitude agitated members of parliament and exasperated the country. Even so, he refused to use force, following Gandhian principles.

However, as I discovered, Nehru's policy was in deference to the US wishes. Its ambassador, John Kenneth Galbraith, who had direct access to Nehru, pleaded with him not to blot his record. India's moral voice, he argued, would cease to count if it moved the army into Goa. President J.F. Kennedy followed Galbraith's advice with a message regarding his general concern over the use of force, particularly in Goa. Washington even suggested that India approach the UN and request it to settle the 'dispute'. Nehru regretted his decision to go to the UN over Kashmir and could not afford to make a similar mistake. Still, he was willing to postpone the action. Strangely however, it was Defence Minister Krishna Menon who informed Nehru that the advance party of the Indian army had already moved in (17 December 1961) and that the governor general of Goa had surrendered without a fight. Menon had eyes fixed on his election from Maharashtra and did what Patel had done in the case of Hyderabad, informing Nehru after initiating the military operation.

When told about the army's entry into Goa, Kennedy was so upset that he remarked that 'a priest [meaning Nehru] had been found in a prostitute's house'. Kennedy was loud and persistent in his criticism because he feared other countries, particularly those in Africa, would follow India to roll out colonialism.

Kennedy was talking like an imperialist. I think it would have been a welcome action if the African countries had followed India's example. I could not understand the logic of the West. It did not want to give up imperialism peacefully on its own but expected the colonies not to revolt because the use of violence was 'out of date'. What really hurt Nehru was the criticism within India. The opposition leaders said that Goa had been annexed because of the impending Lok Sabha election.

Nath Pai, a socialist MP who lived opposite my house at Tughlak Road in New Delhi, told me that India would not have acted had scores of Indian volunteers not crossed into Goa despite the hails of bullets from the other side. Madhu Limaye, a top socialist leader who had crawled into Goa through barbed wires, had to be dragged back because the Portuguese soldiers were on the point of shooting him. Had it not been for the socialists, I still believe Menon would not have taken action because Nehru's Congress party favoured a wait and watch policy.

Goa was able to retain Portugal's culture even after many years of its merger with India. Today, it is only a tourist resort. A few structures still remind you of Portugal but the builders from Delhi and Bombay have squeezed out whatever existed of bygone days. Indeed, Goa has lost its soul but is happy that it has not become part of Maharashtra, a demand occasionally heard in political circles of Mumbai.

4

MY TRAINING AND APPRENTICESHIP
IN ENGLISH JOURNALISM

The proprietor of *Anjam,* Yasin, dismissed me because I had failed to
recover for him the property that his brother had left when he migrated
to Pakistan. Sabari, a colleague in *Anjam,* got me a similar job at *Wahadat,*
another Urdu daily, also published from Ballimaran, not far from the house
where Mirza Ghalib, India's greatest Urdu poet, had lived.

At the *Wahadat* office, I met Maulana Hasrat Mohani, a leading Urdu poet
and a freedom fighter, who took a liking to me. He was an austere person with
leftist leanings, who had been in the Congress for years and had gone to jail
many times at Gandhi's call. A little before Partition he had however joined the
Muslim League. 'Why did you do that and support the demand for Pakistan?' I
asked him at our second meeting. He admitted it was a blunder. He explained
that the concept of Pakistan he had supported had proved to be very different in
reality. He had expected it to be a liberal pluralistic state, similar to India.

After he got to know me for a few weeks, he advised me one day to abandon
Urdu journalism because it had no future in India. He gave me another piece
of advice: to stop attempting to write Urdu poetry. I had shown him some of
my verses. He described them as '*tuk bazi*' or mere rhymes. I still remember
one of the couplets I wrote:

Uneh dekh kar hum ibadat ko bhule
Jo dekha uneh to ibadat bhi karli
Khudai ab to bula lo Qurab mein
Gunaho se hamne to toba bhi karli

(I forgot my prayers after seeing her. Yet I said my prayers when I saw her. God
call me at least now near you [because] I have vowed not to commit any sin).

I took Mohani's advice on both counts. I gave up writing Urdu poetry and also resigned from *Wahadat* to join the United States Information Service (USIS). The new job enabled me to go to the US where I earned a master's degree in journalism from the Medill School of Journalism, Northwestern University.

I had sought the assistance of Norman Cousins, editor of the *Saturday Review of Literature,* New York, who had hired me as an interpreter in Delhi when he came to India soon after Partition to write about the sufferings of refugees. When he was speaking to some of the refugees at Kingsway Camp one person intervened to exhort the crowd not to meet Americans who had helped the British to divide India.

What has, however, remained etched in my memory is C.D. McDuggal, a tall, austere looking man, who taught us interpretative reporting. The US was in the midst of anti-communist hysteria initiated by Senator Joseph McCarthy. He was a liberal and withstood all the accusations and abuses showered on him by those who saw red in every expression of dissent.

I felt the journalism course in the US was pedestrian. It was too remote from Indian requirements and I learnt nothing useful. All that I recall – which explains today's America – is one press conference, which I covered as a student of journalism in Chicago. I asked an industrialist who was addressing the press conference what the effect would be on the US economy if there was no demand for military weapons? He said: 'We will always seek wars to keep our industry going.' He was quite right.

I was unable to get money from home because my wife and I had a bank balance of Rs 1200 only and my parents were struggling to make both ends meet in Jalandhar. I must admit that working my way through university was tough. On some days I had to be content with only a loaf of bread and water. It was, however, great fun because I came to be known as the fastest dishwasher on the campus! In three terms I earned an M.Sc in journalism.

On my way back to Delhi I stopped in London to appear before the Union Public Service Commission for the job of information officer in the Ministry of External Affairs but was rejected. Ironically, 35 years later, I returned to London as India's high commissioner.

Newspapers in India had a prejudice against a degree in journalism in those days. An M.Sc was of little help and I drew a blank at most offices. The *Times of India*, Bombay, was then in the midst of setting up its own news service. D. Thomas, a god-fearing Christian, who later became a good friend, interviewed me. All that he asked me was whether I could rewrite copy, still a rare quality in the Indian media. I do not recall what I said but he must have been satisfied because I received a letter of appointment. As in every profession, however, and this is particularly true in journalism, the tale-carriers became active and the appointment letter was withdrawn before I could join the newspaper. J.C. Jain, general manager of the paper, was told that I did not know how to write, a stigma that has hounded me throughout my journalistic career.

My efforts to obtain a position in the *Hindu* of Madras also came to naught. The closest I could get to the editor was his secretary who gave me every hope until he found that I was a Nayar from Punjab, not from Kerala. At that time the *Hindu* was a closed, insular place. The USIS, for which I had worked before going to the US, had no opening but it helped me find an assignment at its Technical Cooperation Mission in Delhi.

I did not, however, survive there. The US Embassy traced my connections in Lahore to the Students' Federation, which was considered a communist organization. I was dismissed and remained unemployed for nearly a year. I was not willing to start at the bottom rung of a newspaper and I lacked sufficient experience to claim a higher position. The few articles which I sent to newspapers came back with a printed regret slip.

I did not want to return to Urdu journalism and found no opening in English newspapers. I approached Humayun Kabir for help. He asked me to write for his feature agency which published my first article: 'To Every Thinking Refugee.' Three newspapers used it. This was my debut in English journalism. Almost 35 years later I began syndicating my weekly column, 'Between the Lines', to almost 80 newspapers in 14 languages in India and abroad.

In those days an ad hoc recruitment by the publicity unit for the Five-Year-Plan gave me a job in the Press Information Bureau (PIB), a central government organization. My work as a features writer took me to different parts of the country.

This was the first time that I truly experienced India: the lovely texture of fields, the sturdy strands of faiths, the diversity of local cultures, and the modest huts of hardy farmers. I saw dams, factories, and laboratories rising in the wilderness which Nehru described as the new temples of modern India. Probably, they were. Many years later, I discovered the futility of big dams. When I joined Medha Patkar's movement, I realized that small dams could harness the same benefits without creating the havoc of uprooting huge numbers of people.

The widespread poverty, illiteracy, and disease which I witnessed during my travels in India left an indelible impression upon me. It appeared to be an impossible task to defeat hunger on the scale that it was prevalent in the country. Even so, I had an unshaken faith that we would one day overcome our problems of poverty and of parochialism based on class, community, and caste. I have always believed that optimism is a moral duty.

I felt more settled in the government when I was sent as regional officer of the PIB to Jalandhar, which was the centre of the then Punjab, embracing Haryana and Himachal Pradesh. It was a sort of homecoming because it was in Jalandhar that my parents had settled after migrating from Sialkot. My father was once again a leading physician in the city, which was also the state's Fleet Street. As many as 23 daily newspapers in Urdu, Hindi, and Punjabi were published from there, rather like Lahore before Partition.

The Urdu press dominated Punjab in the 1950s. Although the language was no longer taught in schools, a fallout of Partition politics, Urdu was still the language of communication in the courts and government offices. Both Hindus and Sikhs aired their differences in Urdu. Hindus, who constituted a majority in the state at that time, declared Hindi to be their mother tongue. Their reasoning was that Punjabi was only a dialect of Hindi. Sikhs resented this. The Hindus were also afraid that if ever Punjab was divided on the basis of language, they might have to leave the Punjabi-speaking area with a Sikh majority, a fear ingrained after Partition.

Still suffering from the ravages of Partition, the Hindus disowned Punjabi to ensure that the Sikhs who embraced it as their language would not benefit. This however proved to be unproductive for them. Many years later, when Punjab was divided on the basis of language, the Hindus in the Punjabi-speaking area, now Punjab, were reduced to a minority. They realized then that had they affirmed Punjabi, which they spoke at home, as their mother tongue in the census, they would have been part of a larger bilingual state because it would have been difficult to determine the line of separation as Punjabi was spoken right up to Sonipat, the outskirts of Delhi.

The repudiation of Punjabi by the Hindus became a grievance of the Sikhs who convincingly argued that if the Hindus could go to the extent of disowning their mother tongue from prejudice or fear that the Sikhs would gain, there was little left for the two communities to share. Even so, both constituted the warp and weft of the same Punjabi culture and could not be separated, as subsequent events have shown. I have, however, maintained that the two communities with no future in India are Punjabi Hindus and Kashmiri Pandits.

The majority of Sikhs were upset because their demand for a linguistic state on the basis of the Punjabi language had been rejected in 1955, by the States Reorganization Commission which argued that 'to take a decision regarding the future of this area on the assumption that the Hindus and Sikhs are destined to drift apart will be short-sighted and unwarranted in these circumstances'.

The commission's point was that 'the whole of Punjab from the Sutlej to the Indus was obviously intended by nature to be a single natural area'. Strangely, these ideas were expressed eight years after Punjab was partitioned following the birth of Pakistan in August 1947.

The demand for a Punjabi *suba* generated bad blood between Hindus and Sikhs. Hindus felt that it would lead to the foundation of Khalistan. The Sikhs were not mollified by mere talks. Nehru had promised them a place where they would feel the glow of Independence. They wanted autonomy and some leaders confided in me that if Hindus could get Hindustan and Muslims Pakistan, why not Sikhs their Khalistan?

Together with my friend Sadhu Singh Hamdard, editor of *Ajit,* I tried to stop the division of East Punjab. At his initiative I met Congress President

K. Kamaraj, Haryana leader Bhagwat Dayal, and the Akali leader Sant Fateh Singh. Hamdard's and my proposition was to take Hissar out of Punjab and constitute the rest of Punjab as a single state with Punjabi in Gurumukhi script as the official language. Kamaraj, who was for a united Punjab, supported our proposal on the assumption that the Akalis would agree to it. Bhagwat Dayal said that he would make noises on forgoing the formation of Haryana but would eventually remain silent.

The key was Fateh Singh, the president of the Akali Dal. When I placed the proposal before him he rejected it and stuck to the idea of a Punjabi *suba*. He said he wanted it to be a small state and only for those who believed in the philosophy underlying a Punjabi *suba*. 'You mean the Sikhs?' I asked. He denied the charge. I warned him that he would not be able to ensure that Punjab would be a Sikh-majority state because the constitution gave the right to people from other parts of the country to move freely to any place in India for jobs, business, labour, or residence. Not only the Sikhs but even the Punjabi-speaking population would be reduced to a minority one day, I argued. I was, however, unable to convince Fateh Singh. He was convinced that he could convert a Punjabi-speaking state into an autonomous unit and keep out non-Sikhs. Many years later Jarnail Singh Bhindranwale picked up the thread from where Fateh Singh had left it.

Before I could see the end of the debate on the Punjabi *suba* issue, I was transferred to Delhi to serve Govind Ballabh Pant as his information officer.

I was already married when I became information officer to Pant. Bharti, my wife, was the daughter of a top Congress leader, Bhim Sen Sachar and sister of Rajinder Sachar, my best friend since our college days in Lahore. Rajinder married my sister, Raj, several years later. He wrote at the instance of the government a report, known as the Sachar report published in 2006. It revealed the extent of Muslim deprivation in India. He found that the plight of Muslims were worse than that of dalits. It was a pitiable condition in which the Muslims in India lived. He was most critical of the communist-run West Bengal where he said that the employment of Muslims by the state was only 2.1 per cent as against 5.4 per cent in Gujarat. He did not recommend reservations for dalits among Muslims and Christians but observed that their plight was no better than the plight of Hindu dalits. Muslims did get reservations on the basis of backwardness but not on the basis of religion which is banned in the constitution.

5

GOVIND BALLABH PANT
AS HOME MINISTER
Linguistic Reorganization, Administrative Reforms, the
Sino-Indian Border Question, and the Indus Waters Treaty

When I stood before Home Minister Govind Ballabh Pant as the new information officer, I was nervous, daunted by his stature in public life. My spirits had sunk after a wait of five hours in the durbar-like surroundings where job-seekers, hapless bureaucrats, and petty politicians queued up to solicit crumbs of favour.

Pant, sensitive to public opinion, attached great importance to the information officer. He was concerned when a newspaper criticized him. There was a practice to send him press clippings of what the PIB felt would interest him. He read each of these and often acted on the information provided.

Once in a while he liked to tease. On a clipping from *Current*, a tabloid, he wrote: 'Please speak.' It was a news story that declared in bold letters: 'Sardarji duped.' What Pant was trying to get at were the words 'semi-clad' used to describe the Minister of State Tarkeshwari Sinha who had 'allowed' her name to be used by a friend to 'cheat' a Sikh seeking a favour. Pant asked me, with a twinkle in his eyes, what the phrase 'semi-clad' meant. I was nonplussed because he had never before indulged in loose talk. Noticing my embarrassment, he wondered how a woman could appear 'semi-clad' in public? Alternatively, did the paper mean that she always wore clothes that made her look 'semi-clad'? Then he burst into paroxysms of laughter.

Nonetheless, he took the press seriously. Once when the *Evening News*, a tabloid from Delhi, published a picture of local sweepers on strike, he sent me to the editor who was understandably rude. When I quoted Pant's words that such photos fomented discontent, the editor said, 'Mind your own business'. Pant did not realize that my visit might be misconstrued in a society that took pride in a free press. I returned embarrassed but the editor did not survive long in his position.

Pant was, however, particular about not coming between a proprietor and a journalist, accepting the delicacy of the relationship. Frank Moraes, when ousted from the editorship of the *Times of India*, met him to seek his intervention but Pant did not oblige; indeed, he admonished me for having invited Frank to a dinner party, the only one Pant hosted during his tenure. He thought Frank's presence at the party conveyed the message that the government was taking sides.

His reaction at the dismissal of Durga Das from the editorship of the *Hindustan Times* was somewhat similar. Both had known each other from the days when Pant was the UP chief minister and Durga Das a special correspondent at Lucknow. Birla appointed S. Mulgaonkar as editor. Pant did not intervene despite Durga Das's pleas. I suspected that Mulgaonkar's friendship with Krishan Chand, Pant's only son, endearingly called Raja, could have been a factor because no journalist was closer to Pant than Durga Das. However, when I asked Pant he simply said that Mulgaonkar was a better editor.

As regards his own publicity, Pant naively believed that it depended upon the resourcefulness of his information officer. Once when I congratulated him for his speech at Amritsar, he merely said: 'I have done my duty, you do yours.' I used to badger the Press Trust of India (PTI), a news agency, to disseminate as complete a version of his speech as possible. Pant was always overwhelmed by the coverage he received in the south. This was because reporters there were conversant with shorthand and would reproduce virtually all that he said.

One of Pant's drawbacks was that he was seldom on time, although he kept his watch half an hour ahead. Once when he wanted to leave for a cabinet meeting, his driver was nowhere to be found. He asked me to drop him at Parliament House where the cabinet meetings were held. My small car could not muster the speed he sought, so he remarked: 'Does your car have no engine and why are you so nervous?' Indeed I was nervous and he should have known why.

I believe that Dr Rajendra Prasad, India's first president, showed his displeasure at Pant's late arrival by asking him to come again the following day at the same time. Some allowance should, however, be made given Pant's disability: he had been beaten mercilessly by the police during the demonstration against the visit of the Simon Commission to India and as a result could not walk properly and his hands would shake all the time; so much so that he had parliament's permission to remain seated when addressing it.

Soon I realized that Pant wanted me to be at his house after my work at the PIB. This would mean working till late into the night. I must admit that I had no family life those days and hardly spent any time with my two sons. One of them said on a Sunday when I was at home: Why don't you marry Pant?

Pant was still the chief minister at Lucknow when he told Nehru that he had his doubts about Sheikh Abdullah. Indeed, the relation between Nehru and Abdullah had begun falling apart after the signature of the 'Delhi Agreement' in July 1952. The Delhi Agreement had several clauses. One was that hereditary rule would be abolished; two, the constitutional head of state would be called Sadar-i-Riyasat and elected by the state assembly from among the state's citizens; three, citizenship rights would not be conferred on non-state subjects; and fourth a separate flag for the state would fly alongside the national flag.

The assurance to the centre was what the Jammu & Kashmir Constituent Assembly elected in 1951 had stated: 'The State of Jammu and Kashmir is and shall be an integral part of the Union of India. This section cannot be legally amended as per provisions of the constitution.'

Sheikh Abdullah's warning that the Centre's role should not extend beyond the three subjects agreed upon, i.e. defence, foreign affairs, and communications, led to his clash with Delhi. Nehru sent Union Minister for Food and Agriculture Rafi Ahmed Kidwai to Srinagar to find out what Abdullah was up to. Kidwai returned unhappy, not only because Abdullah had treated him shabbily but also because he found him defiant. Sheikh Abdullah told him that India could arrest him but not silence him.

After some days Nehru sent Maulana Azad to talk to Sheikh Abdullah. He insulted him too, well aware that Nehru held Azad in high esteem. At a meeting with Azad, Sheikh Abdullah said that he regretted his decision to support Kashmir's accession to India.

Nehru was perturbed but did not know what to do because of his friendship with Sheikh Abdullah. Nehru entrusted the matter to the cabinet where Sheikh Abdullah had no supporter. The cabinet was all for removing him from Kashmir which it apprehended could rise in revolt if Abdullah was allowed to get his way. The home ministry alleged that Sheikh Abdullah was in touch with Pakistan.

This charge was not correct as Sheikh Abdullah later discussed the developments of those days with me. He said that New Delhi was trying to exceed the terms of accession and wanted a say in the domestic affairs of the state. He did not blame Nehru but 'others' who carried 'tales' to him. Sheikh Abdullah argued that he told both the union ministers who met him that he did not want his state to be 'slave of India'. Nehru came round to accept Azad's advice that it would be better to remove Sheikh Abdullah from the Valley than to face the resultant complications.

Sheikh Abdullah was arrested on 9 August 1953. This was the day when Gandhi had launched the Quit India Movement against the British in 1942. Sheikh Abdullah was flown to Coimbatore from where he was taken to cooler Kodaikanal in the south.

⚜

After dealing with Sheikh Abdullah, Delhi took up the task of redrawing the map of the Indian states on a linguistic basis. Nehru had brought Pant especially to Delhi to pilot in parliament a bill on the recommendations, of the States Reorganization Commission. Long before Independence the Congress had given an assurance to the country that it would undertake this. Left to themselves Nehru and Pant would have wriggled out of this commitment, realizing the error of opening up a Pandora's Box of claims and counter-claims for separate states at a time when the country was facing innumerable problems. The Congress could not, however, retract from the repeated assurances it had given. At the last minute Nehru, Pant, and Pattabhi Sitaramayya, the then Congress president, decided to defer the question for ten years to allow the atmosphere to cool down, but it was too late.

In fact it was Nehru who stoked the fires of linguistic claims by making a number of statements in favour of redrawing India's map. I recall that what rushed the decision was the fast unto death by a political worker, Potti Sriramulu, who wanted the grouping of Telugu-speaking areas, hitherto part of Madras state, to be formed into a separate state. New Delhi dilly-dallied but his death created panic. The government announced a State Reorganization Commission (SRC) with Fazl Ali as the chairman and K.M. Panikkar and H.N. Kunzru as members, even though Andhra Pradesh had been constituted a short time earlier.

The commission's constitution silenced agitators from different parts of the country making varied demands. However, the report (1955) reignited agitations and revived claims for separate states. Those who did not get what they sought raised the standard of revolt. The impression that gained ground was that the greater the pressure, the greater the likelihood of it being accepted. The situation got aggravated when Nehru said that the recommendations were not 'sacrosanct'. Pant was unhappy about the remark, not because he wanted the commission's recommendations to be implemented in full but because it compounded the confusion.

Pant wanted to go down in history like Patel, who had integrated some 560 princely states into India. A daily meeting of home ministry officials would take place at Pant's residence to discuss the report. No other report received as much attention as did the SRC. The cabinet discussed it fourteen times, apart from long discussions in the parliamentary select committee and the two Houses of parliament.

Even so, the SRC report was like an unwanted child which troubled the government. Pant was really unhappy over Panikkar's dissenting note, advocating trifurcation of UP, Pant's home state. There was indeed no love lost between the two. Pant distrusted Panikkar for his communist leanings and was never reconciled to his appointment as India's ambassador to China. The home minister believed that Panikkar had purposely kept Nehru in the dark about the Chinese building a road through Indian territory to link Sinkiang with Tibet.

Panikkar's dissenting note was thrown out without discussion, with Pant calling it 'mischievous'. Hari Sharma, the SRC secretary, recalled how both Fazl Ali and Kunzru had tried to prevail upon Panikkar not to press his proposal. Panikkar's argument was however that the federal concept of the Indian constitution would be imperilled if UP remained as large as it was. Once he remarked: 'I do not want UP to rule the country all the time.'

Over 25 years later the then home minister, Choudhary Charan Singh, also from UP, supported Panikkar's proposal to trifurcate UP. He was, however, at loggerheads with most of his colleagues in the cabinet, including Prime Minister Morarji Desai. Another 25 years later, the then Home Minister L.K. Advani succeeded in bifurcating the state, grouping together the hilly parts into Uttarakhand as a separate unit. In 2011 Chief Minister Mayawati proposed to split UP into four states. It was an election stunt but it went down well with the people of UP keen to have an administration in greater proximity.

Pant was very upset over the Akalis' threat to begin an agitation to revive their demand for a Punjabi *suba*, which the commission had rejected on grounds that such a state would lead to greater communal disharmony.

Indeed, the report plunged the nation into linguistic warfare. Pant blamed Nehru who admitted that the death of Potti Sriramulu had exerted such a weight on his mind that he had appointed the commission. Even so, the Congress never expected the issue to boil over to such a degree as to appear as if the country was falling apart at the seams. India had not faced a crisis on this scale since Partition. However, India continued to have supporters such as Yehudi Menuhin, famous American violinist, who wrote to Nehru:

> [W]hen I myself think of India, I think of a quality specially Indian which in my imagination holds something of the innocence of the fable and symbolic Garden of Eden. To me India means the villages, the noble bearing of their people, the aesthetic harmony of their life: I think of Gandhi, of Buddha, of the temples, of gentleness combined with power of patience matched by persistence, of innocence allied to wisdom, of the luxuriance of life from the oxen and the monkeys to the flame trees and the mangoes; I think of innate dignity and tolerance of the Hindu and his tradition. The capacity of experiencing the full depth and breadth of life's pleasures and pains without losing a nobler resignation, of knowing intimately the exalted satisfaction of creation while remaining deeply humble, are characteristics peculiar to these villages.

Nehru and Pant met to discuss how to stall demands for separation and agreed upon a strategy to initiate anti-linguistic movements. Pant telephoned the two Congress stalwarts, West Bengal Chief Minister B.C. Roy and Bihar Chief Minister A.N. Sinha (Anugraha Babu), to propose the merger of West Bengal with Bihar, integrating the Bengali-speaking area with a Hindi-speaking state to become a larger unit called Purva Pradesh. A formal letter Sinha wrote to Roy, who agreed to the proposal, was released to the press. I was told to propagate the idea that people in the two states were agog with excitement over a bilingual rather than a unilingual state.

Nehru, as expected, hailed the proposal as 'the great lead'. 'We have had enough folly in this country during recent weeks and it was time that we turned our face away from it.' The idea of a 'joint family' of Bengalis and Biharis caught the imagination of many people. They backed Roy's argument that language was not as important as food or clothing, but when the entire opposition in West Bengal walked out from an assembly session, the proposal was dropped.

But the juggernaut of state reorganization had picked up too great a momentum to be halted. The horse had bolted from the stable by the time the leadership thought of shutting the gates. In linguistic states, people saw separate entities for themselves. Pant was opposed to the formation of small states, an idea which the Gandhian leader Jayaprakash Narayan had floated to implement the idea of direct democracy. Still, Pant accepted Fazl Ali's note suggesting that the union territory of Himachal Pradesh be converted into a fully-fledged state. Its merger with Punjab, Pant thought, would be 'locally unpopular'.

One recommendation which received the most attention and ignited prolonged agitations concerned Maharashtra. Pant did not favour the creation of Vidarbha but agreed with the commission that the Marathi-speaking region and the Gujarati-speaking areas in Bombay state be kept together, joining together a maritime community with a mercantile class; the vibrant with the wily.

Nehru toyed with the idea of separating the Marathi-speaking areas from the Gujarati-speaking areas and constituting Bombay city, India's largest financial centre, as a separate entity directly under the Centre, as was the case with Delhi. He was chided for being influenced by money bags, and retaliated by saying: 'We are children of revolution not of money bags.'

I wish Bombay had become a union territory. This would have stalled the parochial agitation by Bal Thackeray, and his *parivar*, the Shiv Sena, to oust non-Marathis from Maharashtra. The harm that the Shiv Sena has inflicted on our secular ethos is immeasurable. It is responsible for initiating violence in the name of preserving a language and culture in a pluralistic society.

After speaking to Nehru, Pant put before the cabinet a proposal to divide Maharashtra into three states, namely Maharashtra, Gujarat, and Bombay City. C.D. Deshmukh, the then finance minister hailing from Maharashtra, agreed to the proposal at the cabinet meeting but when Nehru announced that Bombay city would be under central administration, Deshmukh resigned from the government.

While explaining the reason for his resignation in parliament, Deshmukh also attacked Nehru for having such ministers whose sons were linked to the corporate sector. When challenged, he named one. In a letter to Nehru, Deshmukh mentioned K.C. Pant, Govind Ballabh Pant's son. When I learnt this, I went straight to Pant's house where he was closeted with the ministry's top officials. When he saw me at the door he asked them to leave. After hearing that Deshmukh had named Raja, his son, Pant said he wished he were dead. 'In the evening of my life,' he said, 'I did not want to see this day.'

The press did not publish Deshmukh's allegation. I wondered why. Was it because Raja occupied a room at the home minister's residence from where, after returning from Germany he ran a consultancy? Nehru requested Chief Justice S.R. Das, the Supreme Court judge, father-in-law of Ashok Sen, law minister, to hold an inquiry. K.C. Pant was exonerated to his father's relief but I was shocked when Ashok's wife said that she had to remonstrate with her father to get Raja absolved. I had gone to call on them at their house in London when I was Indian high commissioner in 1990.

The decision to place Bombay city under the Centre reignited the struggle for a greater Maharashtra under the leadership of the Samyukta Maharashtra Samiti, a new version of the Samyukta Maharashtra Parishad (SMP). It announced that it would fight for a state of Maharashtra comprising all contiguous Marathi speaking areas.

However, the bulk of the population in western Maharashtra got disgusted with the vacillations of local Congress leaders and turned to S.M. Joshi and S.A. Dange, the two non-Congress leaders, who organized Satyagraha. The Samyukta Maharashtra Samiti achieved its goal on 1 May 1960 when the bilingual state of Bombay was divided into the Marathi-speaking state of Maharashtra and the Gujarati-speaking state of Gujarat.

The SRC found the argument advanced for the creation of Telangana weightier than that in favour of Vishal Andhra. That the latter would cut deep into the pockets of Telangana was convincing. Equally so was the commission's feeling that it would be better administratively to set up Telangana. 'Hyderabad State' was the name suggested when the new state of Andhra was enmeshed with the problem of integration of services.

The commission's recommendation was that it would be better 'for the present' to constitute Hyderabad state with a provision for its unification with Andhra after the general elections scheduled for 1961. The condition for unification was that a two-third majority of the legislature of the residuary Hyderabad state should express itself in favour of it.

Politically, Telangana did not find favour with either Nehru or Pant. Deliberations over the formation of Telangana in the ministry were animated. The majority was in favour of a separate state of Telangana, as the SRC had recommended. Even so, Pant had the self-immolation of Potti Sriramulu at the back of his mind and Nehru too concurred with Pant's suggestion that the question should not be reopened lest the other parts of Andhra Pradesh should go up in arms again.

A Major fallout of the states' reorganization was the disappointment of territories comprising Assam. Six of them wanted to go it alone with the status of union territory. Were one to go by history, one would infer that Assam and the North-east hill districts were intended by nature to be the meeting place of many tribes and races, with migration to the state from sundry areas. Till 1931, the linguistic tabulation showed that Assamese was not the language spoken by the majority in the state.

Indeed, a former Assam governor during the Raj compared the Brahmaputra valley with a broad central corridor or hall, from which small rooms corresponding to the hill districts opened out on both sides with no connecting door between them. Even today, Guwahati provides access between India and six hill states. The ambitions of several hill state leaders were probably a clear warning. Still, Raj Bhawan in Shillong has embossed these words on the entrance: 'Your uncle is not greater than my country.'

Pant's predicament was how to keep the state of Assam united while giving the hill districts a sense of being their own masters. He camped at Raj Bhawan in Shillong for nearly a week. Nehru had told him not to entertain the claim for a hill state because its creation would lead to a separation between Assam and its tribal people. The key to the problem was Rev. Michael Nicholas, a widely respected man. Chief Minister Bimala Prasad Chaliha had annoyed him but Nicholas was respectful to Pant. My job was to issue a daily press release recording Pant's meetings.

No doubt, there was a deadlock between Chaliha and the hill leaders. One of Pant's strong qualities was his ability not to throw up his hands in despair. He had a great deal of patience and I often thought that he won because he would tire others out. He evolved the idea of autonomy within Assam: the Scottish pattern of government, as he called it. Hill districts were offered a council, an assembly of sorts, enjoying control over subjects such as health and roads.

The arrangement did not work for long because the spirit of sharing of power was lacking. Pant's assurance to the hill districts remained only on paper. Particularly annoying to them was the imposition of Assamese, which in one form or another was spoken in the entire region but by now had come to be equated with Assamese chauvinism.

The writing on the wall was that if the Assam government did not mend its ways, the state would split. Chaliha rode the crest of populism generated by his stand that the Assamese language could not be bartered for territory. The state subsequently paid the price when it was split and when illegal migration from the then East Pakistan reduced the Assamese-speaking population in Assam to a minority.

It was not Chaliha who had initiated the issue of illegal migration but his senior in the Congress, Fakhruddin Ali Ahmad, who rose to be India's president. In fact, the entire party was guilty. Its simplistic solution was to win elections in Assam by allowing would-be settlers from across the border into the state thus creating a vote bank.

Pant knew that large numbers of people were coming from across the border. After all, his party had connived at the migration since Independence, but he wished to ascertain its exact extent. He sent Asok Mitra, then the census commissioner, to ascertain numbers. Mitra conducted a mini-census in some of the border districts of Assam and West Bengal and found the infiltrators numbering 2,50,000 in Assam and 1,16,000 in West Bengal.

Pant decided to expel them as quietly as they had come. Some were expelled but protests from Pakistan that Muslims were being ejected from Assam and West Bengal brought the issue out into the open. Several Muslim leaders from Assam were perturbed. The fact that some Indian Muslims had been thrown out also contributed to a stoppage of the process of reconciliation between India and Pakistan. Nehru too remarked: 'To take rash action is no help and may even make the situation worse.'

Those were the days when the Naga hill district was still a part of Assam, although more or less at the behest of underground Nagas. Jayaprakash Narayan and the Rev. Michael Scott, a British missionary, tried to help Chaliha find a solution. The demand for independence by the Nagas, however, stalled a settlement.

Indeed, the government was sensitive about the Nagas, and Nehru had outlined a policy to integrate them with India. The idea of the British, the Coupland plan, to join the Naga hills with the upper part of Burma and make it into a crown colony had made no headway. There was no doubt that the British did not administer the area and that it was not integrated with the rest of India during their rule. New Delhi's policy was, however, to convert the area into a state within the country, but at the same time Nehru wanted the Nagas to follow their own culture and introduced a permit for permission to enter their territory.

Till the mid-1950s the Naga hills were administered by the Ministry of External Affairs under Nehru but were transferred to the home ministry when Pant came to head it. He would say that the problem in Nagaland was one created by missionaries and instructed the home ministry not to extend the tenure of visas to foreign ones. Many of them were expelled notwithstanding a spate of protests from foreign churches.

Pant did not, however, alter Nehru's policy of keeping the Nagas separate, keen that they preserve their culture and their way of life and thereby retain their identity. He was, however, opposed to their being isolated from Indian culture.

The demand of the Nagas for independence was repeatedly rejected by New Delhi. A.Z. Phizo, their leader, took to arms and the Indian forces met the challenge they posed until a ceasefire was declared. A white flag near Kohima flew for many years. I found during my visits there that the flag gave the Nagas a sense of equality as though New Delhi had accepted their demand for independence. This impression came in the way when New Delhi held serious talks with the Nagas to reach a settlement.

New Delhi did not forgive the Nagas for having walked out of the meeting which the prime minister of Burma, U Nu, and Nehru jointly addressed in 1953. Pant took advantage of Nehru's umbrage and changed the policy of treating the Nagas as 'an anthropological specimen', an idea propagated by Verrier Elwin, a British missionary and anthropologist, who was Nehru's adviser on tribal matters. Pant kept Elwin out of the picture while he strengthened his ministry's grip over the Naga territory.

The Nagas and the Kashmiris are similar in one respect, as people seeking to secede from India. There is, however, one difference between the two. The Kashmiris raised the demand for independence after the ruler merged his state with the Union of India. The Nagas have maintained all along that they were never a part of India.

The Kashmiris have realized the futility of violence and have adopted non-violence as their means to achieve their goal. The Nagas have not, but have continued the ceasefire under the delusion that both India and they are equal and speak to New Delhi on joint defence and the type of links that exist between two sovereign countries. The reality is however different. Nagaland is as much under New Delhi as any other state in India. New Delhi, having constituted Nagaland state, sits pretty because whatever the level of protest, the Nagas willingly participate in state and parliamentary elections with a polling percentage of around 70 per cent each time.

Whenever in Kohima I have found the intellectuals busy adumbrating the thesis that the Nagas are not Indians. This may perhaps be true, but New Delhi has treated them just like the people in the rest of India and has been continually strengthening its military presence there. Undoubtedly, many atrocities have been committed by the security forces but there is little protest in India except by a few groups of human rights activists. Public opinion does not get as agitated as it does in the case of other states barring Kashmir because the feeling is that the Nagas are trying to break up the country.

Phizo escaped to London to continue his struggle for independence and was aided by some missionaries but no country in the world, and at least not the UK, joined issue with New Delhi on Nagaland, in particular when Nehru was the prime minister.

I wondered whether New Delhi's policy on the Nagaland issue had been realistic. Nehru kept the area separate and isolated in order to preserve the culture of the people living there. The result was that it was cut off from the mainstream, telling upon their emotional integration with India. The economic development of the area also suffered in consequence, and the youth in particular have felt alienated and many among them have taken to the gun in desperation.

Phizo died in 1990 in London when I was India's high commissioner to the UK. The high commission sent his body to Kohima and defrayed travel expenses to enable members of his family to travel to Nagaland. A few weeks after Phizo's death, Khoday-Yanthan, Phizo's old comrade-in-arms who had been living in the UK since the days of insurgency in Nagaland, met me. He said he wanted to advise his old friends to abandon violence and seek a solution within the framework of the Indian constitution. According to him Phizo had changed his approach and had wanted to settle the Nagaland question within India.

Khoday-Yanthan complained that his visa application had been rejected by the embassy. I called the officer in charge to find out what our position was in relation to this. He had written 'Naga' in the nationality column. I told the officer that Nagas were Indians and asked him to issue a visa to Khoday. I was confident that he would be a moderating influence on the extremists. I informed New Delhi about his visit which unfortunately took place when the V.P. Singh government was facing a no-confidence motion in parliament.

I wished I had met Phizo, I was told that he had died long before this had been publicly disclosed. My journalist friend Harish Chandola (married to Phizo's niece) who was then in London, tried in vain to obtain his death certificate to ascertain when exactly Phizo died. I also asked high commission officials to obtain this information but was unable to do so.

It was eight years after the ceasefire in Nagaland that I met T. Muivah, a top Naga leader in New Delhi. His colleague, Issac Chesi Swu, had left him a few months earlier. The two and New Delhi's emissary had held several rounds of talks when I met Muivah. What amazed me was the cursory manner in which the central government or, for that matter the successive governments in New Delhi, had gone about the whole thing, year after year, without tackling the fundamental problem of independence, which was germane to the discussion.

The first and foremost demand by the Nagas, said Muivah, was the integration of 'their people' who lived outside Nagaland. What this meant was that parts of Assam, Manipur, and Arunachal Pradesh inhabited by the Nagas would be cut off from those states and merged with Nagaland. 'We do not want our people to live under the Assamese, Manipuris, or others,' said Muivah. 'Our places were forcibly occupied. We want them back to protect and pursue our own culture, our own way of living, and our own traditions. How can the Nagas be ruled by foreigners?' There may have been something in what he said, but on the other hand how could the states be asked to surrender the areas inhabited by the Nagas which were integral limbs of states like Manipur and Assam.

I must confess my inability to convince Muivah that the Indian constitution did not allow for alteration of the boundaries of any state without its consent. The constitution would need to be amended entailing a two-thirds majority in either House of parliament. No political party or leader would have the courage to even raise the issue, much less convince a state to part with its territory. Muivah told me that on advice from New Delhi, they had approached Assam, Manipur, and Arunachal but found them hostile to the very idea. That was not in the least surprising. Some boundary disputes, from the days of the states' reorganization in 1955 were still pending because no state wanted to give up territory that the States Reorganization Act had allotted to them.

The Nagas' proposal for integration, however, brings to the fore a larger question: How insecure do ethnic groups feel in places where they are in a minority? People of different climes are spread throughout India but still we have seen Tamils having suffered in Karnataka over the water dispute. Kannadigas in Tamil Nadu, and the Bengalis in Assam have faced occasional outbursts of anger from the local people due to rising parochial feelings in India despite the fact that the constitution recognizes only common citizenship for the entire Indian population, with equal rights and opportunities to all Indians throughout the union.

I gave Muivah the example of my own state, Punjab. It was divided and redivided. Some parts of Punjab constituted Himachal Pradesh and some Haryana. The Punjabis living in the two states, I argued, could not say that they must be grouped together with Punjab. People belonged to wherever place they lived in.

Muivah also raised the old point that the Nagas were not Indians and had never been part of British or post-British India. This might be true, but the Hydari agreement (27 June 1947), which the Nagas had accepted, stated that they would be free to rule and choose the pattern of administration of their choice within the framework of the Constitution of India. They went back on the undertaking when the constituent assembly incorporated the conditions of the agreement in the Sixth Schedule to safeguard Naga demands. The Nagas could of course say that they did not accept the Sixth Schedule.

Muivah did not contradict me when I told him that Phizo favoured a solution within the framework of the Indian constitution. He however said that the Nagas would be willing to accept India's currency, a role in defence, and dual citizenship. This may be a good beginning but it is important for the Nagas to realize that it is not possible for New Delhi to expand Nagaland at the expense of Assam, Manipur, and Arunachal Pradesh.

꙳

Pant was relieved that the stirs relating to the reorganization of states more or less subsided except in Punjab. The Sikhs were particularly agitated. Nehru was so perturbed that he wrote a letter to the chief ministers of states with a copy to Pant, that if people went ahead and did not accept a decision unless it was in consonance with their predilections, then that would be tantamount to a negation of democracy.

Pant would at times feel depressed about the fallout of the formation of linguistic states. The SRC had sought to assuage the fears of linguistic minorities by providing safeguards, such as the right to instruction in their mother tongue and the use of the minority language for official purposes in the area where they constituted 30 per cent of the population. That the state governors could be entrusted with the task of protecting the minority interests was fine as an idea but difficult to implement and time evidenced that it was mere wishful thinking. Pant's frequent warning to the ministry that the reorganization of states might create more problems than it would solve proved to be true.

A Linguistic Minorities Commission was constituted to safeguard minority interests but it remained on paper because those who wielded power in the states ran the administration in a way that consolidated their own interests and their own vote bank. While the linguistic commission reported directly to parliament, in its annual reports it regularly expressed its helplessness against the 'tyranny' of linguistic majorities. Even minor officials snubbed the commission by refusing to meet the chairman. Many chairmen have complained to me that their recommendations received no attention from the government and were just filed by the home ministry.

Anyone could read the writing on the wall that linguistic states would in due course become islands of chauvinism and eventually the sons-of-the soil theory would supervene and linguistic minorities would feel insecure.

Anticipating that 'outsiders' would feel handicapped in not being conversant with the local languages, the home ministry ruled that the state language could be learnt after getting a government job. This was not adhered to because the states insisted on proficiency in the regional language as one of the qualifications for employment.

The SRC had feared that the provisions of common citizenship of the entire Indian people with equal rights and opportunities throughout the union would get diluted after the territorial redistribution. This proved to be only too true. The solution, which the SRC suggested, such as the creation of an Indian Service of Engineers, an Indian Forest Service, and an Indian Medical and Health Service was sought to be implemented. Only the Indian Forest Service came into being.

Pant also drew a blank on his proposal to have a 'central pool' of officers who would occupy important positions in Delhi and not return to the states in order to maintain continuity in the central administration. The states did not favour the scheme because they saw in it an attempt to retain the best talent or those who could pull strings in New Delhi. Even before its creation, the 'central pool' came to be known as the 'cesspool' and dropped.

Top officers working at the Centre were disappointed because most of them had managed to find themselves a place in the pool. Pant clung to the idea for a long time but Nehru's lukewarm response ensured its demise.

Pant depended upon the bureaucracy a great deal but Nehru had a poor opinion of it. Both had different viewpoints on administration. Nehru, as he said, had no patience 'for the jungle of rules and regulations' and openly criticized the red tape. Pant believed that rules and regulations were the contours that obliged a government to take well-conceived action and inculcated a salutary discipline which, if harsh, needed to be followed.

Pant in fact wrote a long note on administrative reforms, justifying the checks and balances. This was in response to a letter he received from Nehru, who had been influenced by Paul H. Appleby, an eminent expert on public administration. Assessing India's bureaucracy at Nehru's behest, Appleby had pointed out in a report that there were 'too many forms of class, rank, and prerogative consciousness'. He had found the government procedures 'cumbersome, wasteful, and dilatory'. After examining the Appleby report Nehru wrote to Pant: 'We have worked too much in the rut and carried on old traditions which have little significance today. If we are to work for a welfare state, the whole of our administrative service has to function somewhat differently and, indeed, has to think differently...'

Nehru's letter was curt in tone and irritated Pant. Nehru had written that he would like the reorganization of the administrative structure 'soon'. Pant passed on the note to Home Secretary K.K. Jha, who just filed it despite the word 'soon'. His remark was that the starry-eyed Panditji had utopian ideas.

Jha had a poor opinion of politicians who, he said, learnt elements of administration from bureaucrats and then behaved as if they knew everything. He gave me the example of his trainee, Lal Bahadur Shastri.

Sensing that corruption had come to taint the bureaucracy, Pant one day called a closed-door meeting of all secretaries to the government. Top officials turned up in their buttoned-up jackets. He praised them for their good work but regretted that their integrity had come into question. 'We cannot sit idle and see this happening,' he said.

His strong words sent a shock wave throughout the room and there was dead silence. One senior ICS officer, H.K. Patel, who later became a union minister, stood up and told Pant that no official would resort to anything illegal unless there was pressure from above. Some officers might be lacking in integrity, he said, but what about ministers? The rot began at the top. I could see Pant seething with anger but he remained silent. When three more officers got up and spoke in the same vein, Pant wound up the meeting with soothing words such as cooperation between ministers and bureaucrats. He said the two were like two wheels of a carriage; both had to carry the load equally. With these words the meeting ended. No one subsequently spoke about the meeting or corruption and the press had no inkling of the discussion.

Jha was unhappy about the class of officers working in government. His criticism dwelt on one particular issue: there was too much élitism in the civil service. I realized how true his remarks were when I once visited the IAS training school at Metcalfe House in Delhi. Joint secretary of the home ministry, Senapati Bapat, who headed the school, told me that they purposely wanted the service to be élitist. The probationers were the best in the country and they should not mix with the ordinary lest they be in any way influenced by the latter, he argued.

I had a bitter experience of both the training academies at Mussorie and Hyderabad, the former for the IAS and the latter for the IPS. The Mussorie academy invited me for a talk. My friend, Rajeshwar Prasad, Shastri's former secretary, was the director. During my speech, I mentioned how Muslims had been treated as second-class citizens after the Partition. Some members of the audience objected to my remark, which was natural, but I was never invited to the academy again. At Hyderabad, it was even worse. When I told the senior police officers I was addressing that none of them had stood up to object to the excesses during the Emergency, not even against illegal arrests, they were sullen. None of them spoke to me even during the tea break. The academy has never invited me since.

I had an almost similar experience at the Staff College in Delhi. There was a discussion on India–Pakistan relations. While the entire panel was vehemently critical of Pakistan, I pointed out certain examples of India having rubbed Pakistan the wrong way. That college too never invited me again.

Over the years I have felt that both the IAS and IPS have developed a kind of feudal class consciousness that does not go well with the service to the people that India needs. Their initial idealism begins to diminish within a few years of service and they gradually become part of the furniture.

Once I asked a young IAS officer attached to me at Raipur, on tour of some projects, why the high principles infused in them when they entered the service wore thin within a few years. He said that the day the commissioner rang you up to tell you to collect money to be sent 'above' was the day when the disillusionment set in. He said his first place of call to collect money was the fair price ration shop. That officer became the resident commissioner in Delhi. He had superseded some officers to get the appointment, and from this I inferred he had mastered the art of rising rapidly up the ladder.

Pant had another ticklish question to settle: the Language Commission's official report. Whether he came out well from the ordeal of the States Reorganization Commission was a moot point although Nehru congratulated him for 'the miracle' he had achieved. However, producing a unanimous report on the vexed language question was a miracle indeed.

As set out in the constitution, a language commission was appointed in 1955, five years after the republic came into being, to assess whether Hindi had developed sufficiently and spread to the degree necessary to replace English as the union language. The switch over date was 26 January 1965 – 15 years after the adoption of the constitution. The commission reiterated the constitutional obligation to switch over to Hindi from English on 26 January 1965 but it left the decision to the government in terms of the preparations it had made. The commission recommended that every student should be taught Hindi till the age of fourteen and that the teaching of Hindi should be made 'necessary' up to the middle level throughout the country.

The commission did not approve a suggestion that knowledge of any other south Indian language should be made compulsory for students from Hindi-speaking areas. It sought to make it mandatory that court judgements should be delivered 'in the language of the country' but that a translation in the regional language should be attached to all proceedings and records, decisions, and orders of the Supreme Court and the high courts.

There were two important dissenting notes by Dr P. Subbarayan from Madras and Dr Suniti Kumar Chatterji. They observed in their respective notes, occasionally the words used were identical, that Hindi had been adopted by the constituent assembly and not by a parliament consisting of directly elected representatives of the people.

To scrutinize the commission's recommendations, a constitutional obligation, a parliamentary committee was appointed. It met for the first time in 1957 and Pant was elected as the chairman.

The very first meeting of the committee seemed to indicate that it would be the last. Both the Hindi chauvinists and representatives from the non-Hindi speaking areas jumped at each other's throats and threw cold water on the prospect of a compromise. As the home minister's information officer, I was deputed to brief the press, but no one was interested in my briefing because the members held their own press conferences and gave out their own versions of the meeting.

Pant was horrified by the press reports on the meeting, fearing that the entire language question would be reopened, particularly the constitutional provision that Hindi would replace English.

The first governor general of India, C. Rajagopalachari, who was from the south, began a crusade against Hindi even though he had once supported it. Pant gave me a copy of Rajaji's foreword in a Hindi primer, which pleaded that the southern states should learn Hindi. The foreword was written many years earlier when Gandhi had begun a movement in the south to popularize Hindi.

At my instance the foreword was reproduced by the *Hindustan Times*, ironically the daily edited by Rajaji's son-in-law and Mahatma Gandhi's son Devdas Gandhi. Rajaji reacted adversely to the reproduction and criticized the government for adopting unfair methods. The foreword did not, however, have any impact on the committee members. Pant was particularly concerned about the press carrying the committee's acrimonious discussions. My request to editors, on his behalf, not to publish any report on the committee's deliberations met with no success. No one was willing to black out a crucial discussion concerning the language question and members of the committee refused to end their press briefings despite Pant's request.

I came up with an idea which worked. I told the correspondents that the committee's discussions were privileged and not one of them had checked whether that was indeed the case. It was a committee of members of parliament discussing a report and not a house committee entitled to the privilege of secrecy, but the pressmen in their indolence failed to check the actual position. They stopped reporting on the committee meetings, even though members told them that I was bluffing about the violation of privilege. My warning therefore paid off and nothing appeared until the report was out.

While distributing copies of the final report to the correspondents, I offered my apologies and explained to them the difference between a parliamentary committee and a committee constituted by the House. The correspondents cursed me but by then it was all over. Was my act unethical? Probably, it was. But I saved the nation from an acrimonious debate which might have reopened the settled issue of a switch over to Hindi.

The first few meetings of the committee were uneventful, confined to formalities. Very soon, however, there was a cleavage between those who wanted to do away with English straightaway and those wishing to retain it indefinitely along with Hindi. Some members even questioned the propriety of having Hindi as the Indian union's language. Pant intervened to say categorically that they were not writing on a blank slate and that the constitution had already provided for Hindi as India's union language.

Purushottam Das Tandon, once the UP Speaker, led the Hindi protagonists. They wanted the transition from English to Hindi on 26

January 1955 itself and were not willing to wait until 1965 as provided for in the constitution.

The opposing point of view, shared by virtually all the members of the non-Hindi speaking states, was voiced by Lakshmanaswamy Mudaliar from Madras. He accepted the constitutional obligation to use Hindi as the official language but wanted the date of transition to be postponed indefinitely. He argued that a prolonged period of bilingualism would eradicate fears from the minds of non-Hindi speaking people. They thought that Hindi was being thrust on them before they had time to learn it. Frank Anthony, an Anglo-Indian member and Pramatha Nath Banerjee, a communist member from West Bengal, were the only two in the 26-member committee to completely oppose the switch over from English.

Realizing that the switch over was the most crucial issue, Pant left it to be taken up at the end of the deliberations on the report. It was like starting from the wrong end but it at least saved him from facing the ceaseless debate on the transition. His approach was that the switch over from English to Hindi should be endorsed by the committee and did not mind as many steps as possible to facilitate transition. Pant frequently said that the date mentioned in the constitution was not mandatory. Mudaliar, to Pant's relief, was not opposed to Hindi, seeking only an indefinite period for preparations. This irked the pro-Hindi members who wanted a firm date.

The battle royal began when the committee discussed the recommendation that government servants should be required to learn Hindi and qualify in an examination within a reasonable period of time. Mudaliar expressed the fear that the non-Hindi speaking population would be handicapped in finding jobs. The proponents of Hindi were so eager for an immediate switch over that they were even willing to agree to a quota in the services for the Hindi and non-Hindi speaking populations. Pant was horrified at the suggestion. He said that such a step might one day lead to the pernicious pre-Partition arrangement of separate electorates.

A quiet, lacklustre P.T. Thanu Pillai from Kerala saved the situation. He spoke passionately against the quota system, warning that the principle, once accepted would be applied in all fields, not the services alone. This would be a great disservice to the unity of the country and that future generations would never forgive them. There was applause after his speech, a rare gesture on the part of the committee. Even the Hindi-speaking members found it difficult to press the suggestion. Tandon realized his error and withdrew the proposal.

Pant's forte was patience. He never lost his temper. Even when Tandon told him to his face that 'you are a traitor' to the cause of Hindi at the concluding meeting, Pant did not retaliate. He merely said: 'I place India's unity above Hindi and I am sorry if I have not come up to the standard of Tandonji.'

Pant, who had accomplished the miracle of having achieved unanimity on Hindi, did not want to spoil things by rushing through the last phase. He allowed members take their time to express themselves, and said he did not want to pressurize anyone. The strategy worked and it was left to Pant to write the report.

The recommendation of the committee, with the exception of Frank Anthony, was unanimous. It said that Hindi should be the principal language from 26 January 1965, and English a subsidiary one, with no target date for the switch over. It was truly a feather in Pant's cap.

Before the report was finalized, Pant sent the draft to Nehru for his comments. The use of the word 'subsidiary' for English infuriated Nehru, who argued that the word, subsidiary, meant English was the language of 'vassals'. Pant backed up his preference for the word by sending Nehru various equivalents of 'subsidiary' in English. That day I ransacked every library in Delhi to collect as many dictionaries as possible. Some of them said that the word 'subsidiary' also meant 'additional'.

Pant tried to argue with Nehru that the two words meant more or less the same thing. He also pointed out that the Madras government's report had itself used the word 'subsidiary' for English. It was possible by 1965 to promote Hindi to the status of the principal official language of the union if a provision was made for the continuance of English as a subsidiary official language thereafter. Nehru disagreed with Pant and worse, he was quite indignant and reportedly made some harsh comments. Finally, the word subsidiary was substituted by additional. Pant told me, 'Mark my words, Hindi will not come to the country'. He was dejected. That very evening, Pant had his first heart attack.

Once the report was out of the way, Pant decided not to have any further commissions or committees on the official language. Article 344 (1) of the constitution stated that 'the President shall at the expiration of five years from the commencement of the Constitution, and thereafter at the expiration of ten years from such commencement, by order constitute a Commission'. Both the home and law ministries concluded that the word 'shall' could be interpreted as 'may'. Therefore, the president was not bound to appoint a commission after ten years. Another commission, which should have been constituted in 1960, was not appointed, and none has been since.

Meanwhile, in the Lok Sabha, on 6 August 1959, Nehru gave an assurance that there would be no time limit and that the non-Hindi-speaking areas would themselves decide the date when the switch over from English to Hindi should take place. For the non-Hindi-speaking people, the assurance was like a safety belt in the swirling waters of language chauvinism. There was genuine fear amongst the non-Hindi-speaking population that they would be excluded from government jobs.

The states began to switch over to regional languages because they felt more at home with their own language than either English or Hindi. The link between the different linguistic regions was weakened, but even so English remained the only language linking together the north and south, east and west.

There was, however, a growing feeling that a democratic government could not function indefinitely in a language which was understood only by a small fraction of the population. The Hindi-speaking states made it clear that they would not indefinitely continue to communicate with the Centre in a foreign medium.

Regional languages began taking the place that rightly belonged to Hindi. No one realized that if and when Hindi became the only official language of the union it would not be able to push out regional languages from the position they had occupied, which rightly was the prerogative of the union language. The protagonists of Hindi viewed the growing use of regional languages as an indirect support to their cause, rather than as a threat.

Soon after Hindi was declared as the principal language of the union in 1965, a candidate in the UPSC (Union Public Service Commission) examination for the All India and Central Services answered his question papers in Hindi and prefaced his answers with the slogan: *'Hindi mata ki jai'*. The UPSC was not moved by this emotional outburst and awarded him zero.

Although the law ministry justified the UPSC marking, arguing that it was like a club framing its own rules of entrance, the home ministry was afraid that the aggrieved student might go to the Supreme Court. Realizing the danger, the cabinet decided to permit all the languages, as many as fifteen mentioned in the Eighth Schedule of the Constitution, to be used as a medium of expression in examinations. English, which was not listed in the Eighth Schedule, was also to continue as an alternative medium.

Pant had hardly met the demand of the student for the use of Hindi when another complained to him that he had failed in the UPSC competitive examination because he had not passed the personality test even though he had secured nearly 90 per cent marks in the written examination. Pant felt it was unfair to fail a person solely on the basis of the personality test and ordered that the viva-voce would be considered another subject but not an essential one. Marks of the personality test would be added to the total but would not disqualify the candidate if he or she had failed in it.

Nehru watered down the police clearance which every candidate was required to have. The purpose of this was to ascertain whether the candidate had a communist background. The cases of three probationers were sent to Nehru because their antecedents showed their Left inclinations. He overruled the police report and allowed the probationers to complete their training. They were subsequently absorbed in the Indian Administrative Service. This notwithstanding, the verification of the antecedents of candidates by the intelligence bureau to ascertain a leftist background continues.

Giving awards – the Padma Sri, Padma Bhushan, Padma Vibhushan, and the Bharat Ratna – was Nehru's idea, but was implemented by the home ministry in 1954. Although the constitution barred any titles being conferred on individuals, the distinction made was that these were awards and not titles like Rai Bahadur or Khan Sahib, which the British doled out to toadies. I saw the exercise from close quarters when I was the information officer in the home ministry for six years till 1964. The ministry would receive names from individuals or organizations who were close to the Congress party. Central and state ministers also sent the names of their favourites.

A deputy secretary in the home ministry and I would prepare the list of names alphabetically and summarize their biodata. It was a clerical job and the entire exercise was arbitrary. There were no rules to guide the exercise or any norms to follow. Both of us would drop names that sounded odd to us. The list was sent to the home secretary who whetted it and then forwarded it to the home minister.

It was left to me to prepare the citation. I used to place before me a dictionary and *Roget's Thesaurus* to avoid repeating the same adjectives. It was a piquant situation when Pant was awarded the Bharat Ratna. I prepared the citation which went to the home minister but he did not like it. Then the home secretary tried his hand but even his version was not to Pant's liking. Then the entire staff of the home ministry sat down to prepare a new one but Pant rejected that too. We were all downhearted till I convinced Pant that the Bharat Ratna was beyond description. All the words used to praise him fell short of his achievements and therefore there should be no citation for the Bharat Ratna. That year the brochure's page for the citation for the Bharat Ratna awardee, Pant, was blank.

The prime minister and the home minister jointly decided on the final list. The president, who authorized the gazette notification, rarely amended the list.

However, Dr Rajendra Prasad, the then president made an exception on one occasion. He added 'Miss Lazarus from the south' in his own hand to the list. We, in the ministry worked hard to find out who she was. There was an educationist by that name in Chennai and we informed her about the award of the Padma Shri. However, when the list went back to Dr Prasad, he wrote that she was a nurse and returned the list. His ADC informed us that she had treated him when he fell ill travelling by road from Vijaywada to Hyderabad. We were eventually able to locate her, and that year two ladies with the name Lazarus received the award.

The screening committee for these awards is a relatively recent phenomenon. There was a public interest litigation to challenge the awards on the ground that they were banned. The Supreme Court, however, did not regard civil awards as titles. It did, nonetheless, suggest the constitution of a screening committee, and here the ruling party has really muddied the waters. The committee is presided over by the prime minister's secretary and its members are government nominees. That is why some awardees are unknown people without any distinction whatsoever because at some stage someone slipped in their name.

The Janata party government abolished these titles on the ground that they were a relic of British rule. So long as the Janata party remained in power no awards were given. After the Janata party rule, awards have resurfaced with a vengeance and so have the fawning flatterers and sycophants. Once again the award has begun to appear on the letterheads and visiting cards of the recipients despite instructions to the contrary.

There have however been many persons who have refused to accept awards. Maulana Abul Kalam Azad was sounded out for the Bharat Ratna. He declined the award, reportedly telling Nehru that it was altogether improper for those deciding on the awards to pin the medal on themselves.

Despite Azad's objection, the government went ahead and gave awards to other Congressmen. Many years later the Bharat Ratna was awarded to Azad posthumously. This had not been provided in the original Act.

The selection of awardees by different governments, when analyzed, shows a clear tilt towards the people who suited them. Critics or opponents never figured anywhere. For instance, Ram Manohar Lohia, the socialist leader, or the Marxist E.M.S. Namboodripad were not even considered for any award. The BJP-led government saffronized the list of recipients and gave awards even to RSS *pracharak*s. Some have refused to accept awards like the late Nikhil Chakraborty, a journalist; Rajinder Sachar, a retired chief justice; and the Gandhian Siddharaj Dhadda.

After so many decades I still cannot figure out how Rabindranath Tagore accepted the title of 'Sir' during the British period. True, he returned it after the Jallianwala Bagh massacre, but why did he accept it in the first place? Freedom fighters were dismayed by it and to that extent, Tagore's stature fell several notches.

It was in the home ministry that I first heard about the Chinese incursion into our territory. I was sitting with Fateh Singh, deputy secretary in charge of foreigners, when his aide came with a sheaf of papers relating to China and wanted to know what he should do with them. They related to the illegal construction of a road in Ladakh. Without even looking at him, Fateh Singh said: 'Put them in the "border file"'.

It was an odd description for reports. Fateh Singh explained that telegrams, messages, and reports dealing with China's incursions were stacked in files, without any action being taken. Prime Minister Nehru saw them and marked them to the home minister after initialling them. They eventually landed up in the section dealing with foreigners. In fact, there was a joke in the home ministry that if some official did not wish to take any action on a particular complaint he would say 'Put it in the border file'. I heard this euphemistic description of inactivity very frequently even at the joint secretary level.

Fateh Singh told me how China was nibbling away our territory in Ladakh and the guilt he felt that the nation had not been informed. China had built a road in the Indian territory of Aksai Chin. Police official Lakshman Singh was the first person in 1954 to inform New Delhi about the road. As our trade representative, he used to visit Tibet every year. His contacts were wide and he had learnt about the road from some labourers who had built it. (An Indian air force plane accidentally flying over the area at that time confirmed the road on the basis of a photograph.)

New Delhi doubted Lakshman Singh's version. There was a division of opinion between Pant and Nehru. Pant wanted air reconnaissance to be undertaken to verify the report. Nehru claimed that this would serve no purpose. He did not want to even lodge a protest about the alignment of the road without being certain about its existence. After many discussions, Nehru agreed to send Indian maps to China which depicted Aksai Chin as part of the Indian territory, and even this he asked the foreign secretary to do informally. He was reluctant to annoy China.

However, when there was no response from the other side, Pant persuaded Nehru to send a patrol which found that the road had indeed been constructed in Aksai Chin and was being patrolled by Chinese soldiers. Sighting the Indian patrol, they captured it and tied its members to the tails of horses and dragged them along the road. New Delhi lodged a protest which was rejected with contempt.

It was apparent that Nehru did not wish to irritate China, particularly when he had himself introduced Prime Minister Chou En-lai at the conference of non-aligned nations at Bandung in Indonesia in 1955. What, however, riled Nehru was that Chou En-lai now treated him with far less respect than he had done at their earlier meetings. The latter had not even responded regarding Nehru's proposed visit to Tibet. The Dalai Lama had invited Nehru and wanted to take Chou En-lai along with him on the visit. Nehru had also noted the abusive language that China used in criticizing Yugoslavia. If Beijing could go to that extent in the case of a communist country, Nehru was not surprised that China had treated India's protest with disdain.

Nehru nonetheless rationalized that China's posture was like that of a young communist country which had cast off the past and was impatient to pursue the future. He assured the angry Indian parliament, which learnt from the press about the road built by China in Aksai Chin, that it was Indian territory and there was no dispute about it. To mollify critics, he told them that China would never wage a war against India, and if it ever did, there would be a world war. How wrong Nehru proved to be, his wishful thinking costing the nation dearly.

Never before had I heard such vehement criticism of Nehru in parliament which for years I regularly covered. While replying on the China question, Nehru would sound like a person who had been betrayed, but this did not return Aksai Chin to India. The nation was indebted to him for his leadership since Independence. Institutions like parliament, the judiciary, and the executive he had built made the people proud of their country and their leader. They never forgave him for his soft attitude towards China. He was the hero who had failed them.

I dug out from Nehru's letters one that Patel had written to him before his death. I was then planning to write my first book, *Between the Lines* and reproduced the letter as an annexure to it. Patel had warned Nehru to look ahead because 'the Chinese government had sought to delude us by professions of peaceful intentions'. Patel had a dig on the Indian communists he loathed, categorizing them as a security risk and alleging that they 'can safely depend on communist arsenals in China'.

China's aggressive posture became clear when it denounced the old border maps and refused to accept the traditional alignments depicted on them. To India's dismay our maps showed some of our territory as part of China. The home ministry wrote to the states asking them to burn the maps or at least smudge the border with China on the Assam side because they did not accurately delineate the Indian border.

The Chinese exploited our confusion and used our maps to question our claim. Nehru was still in favour of accommodating China on the question of the Aksai Chin road. Pant proposed a long-term lease, but China responded by occupying Khurnak Fort in Ladakh. *China Pictorial,* Beijing's official publication, once again published a small-scale map showing a large part of north-eastern Ladakh within the borders of China. Nehru wrote to Chou En-lai to express his surprise at the Chinese attitude 'which was contrary to what he had been led to believe since 1949'.

It was a bitter personal blow to Nehru. Despite the warnings from Congress leaders that China was deceitful, he relied on his judgement that China would not betray his confidence and would agree to the traditional border with a few minor adjustments. He had recommended a Security Council seat for China even when the West wanted India to occupy it. A communist country, he imagined, would never be hostile to a third world one, and particularly one wedded to socialist ideals.

China too was keen that the two countries should not come to the point of war. Chou En-lai flew to New Delhi in 1960 for talks to improve relations. Nehru told him that public opinion was very hostile and his own colleagues in the cabinet felt that his policies had led China 'to occupy territory that belonged to India'.

In the meanwhile, Nehru ordered that police check-posts be established to register India's presence in the Ladakh area. As many as 64 posts were built, but they were not tenable. Home Secretary Jha told me that it was the 'bright idea' of B.N. Malik, the director of intelligence, to set up police posts 'wherever we could', even behind the Chinese lines, in order to 'sustain our claim' on the territory. This was Nehru's 'Forward policy', but then, Jha said, 'Malik does not realize that these isolated posts with no support from the rear would fall like ninepins if there was a push from the Chinese side. We have unnecessarily exposed the policemen to death.' He went on to say: 'Frankly, this is the job of the army, but as it has refused to man the posts until full logistical support is provided, New Delhi has pushed the police.'

Indeed, all the posts did fall like ninepins when China attacked India on 21 October 1962. Finding not a semblance of common ground with China, Nehru ordered the army to eject the Chinese forces from India.

I recall that before hostilities broke out, a 'solution' of the border issue was suggested by Krishna Menon, but he was overruled by Pant. Menon had met Chen Yi, China's foreign minister at Geneva, and told him that India might accept Peking's suzerainty over the area in Aksai Chin as well as a buffer of 10 miles to the road. In exchange, China must officially accept the McMahon Line in the East and India's rights to the rest of Ladakh.

China had reportedly accepted the idea but Pant stood in the way. He got the government to formally withdraw the offer through a resolution in the cabinet. Even leasing out the Aksai Chin area was not acceptable. The fact was that Pant, like Vijayalakshmi Pandit, Nehru's sister, did not trust Menon and considered him an inveterate communist.

Pant's meeting with Prime Minister Chou En-lai was the best presentation of India's case on China. I recall how, before the meeting, Pant donned his long coat and had the sitting room rearranged for the meeting. I heard Krishna Menon saying after the meeting that Pant was rude to Chou En-lai, but this was not true. Pant rejected Chou En-lai's plea outlining how important the Aksai Chin road was for China to link Sinkiang with Tibet. Pant said that India would allow the passage of civil traffic but not part with its territory. Chou En-lai remained silent but did hint at consequences fraught with danger. It was clear that the two sides stood far apart on the issue.

Starting from the Ladakh side, Pant tried to establish the watershed theory that the point from which water flowed to either side was the dividing line. This line could not be straight, he argued, and would naturally swerve from one side to the other depending upon the flow of water. Chou En-lai said very little, with the help of an interpreter. Until then my impression was that the dispute was over the Aksai Chin road but Chou En-lai twice or thrice even questioned the validity of the McMahon Line. Pant began with the presumption that the McMahon Line was a settled fact, but Chou En-lai did not accept this, making it very clear that it was open to interpretation. China's subsequent claim to Arunachal Pradesh confirmed that.

At that very meeting, it was agreed that some scrutiny of the different claims would be necessary. Eventually, an official team was appointed with S. Gopal and Jagat Mehta as members from the Indian side. Gopal travelled to London to obtain material to support India's case. He was happy to have found relevant documents but there was additional material the British government would not part with but made photostat copies available. The Chinese tried their best to sabotage this project but the Mountbattens were a great help. The story that the Chinese attempted to snatch some material from Gopal on his return flight was incorrect, and he contradicted this when I subsequently asked him for confirmation.

Gopal and Mehta carried a load of material to Peking. A set of copies of the entire data was prepared and left in Delhi lest 'theft' or some other untoward occurrence' might destroy the valuable evidence. They had prepared a convincing report but the Chinese rejected it.

I got a hint of how little was expected from the meeting from the Polish ambassador, whom I had met at diplomatic parties, even before the official team left India. I was only the home ministry's information officer and had no official locus standi, but it was obvious that the Polish ambassador was on a mission. He invited me for a chat at his chancery and expected me to convey what he had said to Pant. At the beginning of the conversation he said that the proposal he would make had the support of all Communist countries, and specifically mentioning the Soviet Union.

His proposal was that India should accept a package political deal, getting recognition for the McMahon Line in exchange for handing over control of some areas in Ladakh to China. He said that the areas demanded had never been charted, and nobody could say to whom they belonged. What was being claimed to be India's was what had been forcibly occupied by the UK. No power could honour 'the imperialist line', nor should India insist upon it. Whatever the odds, China would never part with control of the road it had built. That was the lifeline between Sinkiang and other parts of China, he argued. I conveyed the proposal to Pant who gave me no reaction, his or that of the government.

❀

As the Sino–Indian relationship began unravelling, India was inclined to seek friendship elsewhere. General Mohammad Ayub Khan, who had taken over Pakistan, also feared the 'inexorable push of the north'. Soon after assuming power he proposed a defence pact between India and Pakistan to defend the subcontinent.

To this Nehru asked, 'Defence against whom?' This no doubt angered Ayub Khan but Nehru was reminding Pakistan of its membership of the CENTO and NATO defence arrangements which were directed against the Soviet Union, India's friend. Also, how could India, with its policy of non-alignment, join any defensive arrangement?

Ayub Khan later explained to me in Islamabad that what he meant by joint defence was that the two armies should not be in a position to stab each other in the back; instead of looking inwards, they should be looking outwards. 'I never suggested any formal defence arrangements. How could I have when big problems like Kashmir and the canal waters remained unresolved?'

Even so, my feeling was that Ayub Khan was doing all this because he needed time to reorganize and re-equip his army. Therefore, at the suggestion of his foreign minister, Manzur Qadir, former chief justice of West Pakistan who was a great admirer of Nehru and who had many Indian friends, Ayub Khan agreed to meet Nehru. New Delhi's high commissioner to Pakistan at that time was Rajeshwar Dayal who too, bred in the composite culture of UP, was a dove on Indo–Pakistan matters. He also considered Ayub a friend: they had served together in a UP town long before Partition. Dayal and Qadir arranged a stopover for Ayub at Delhi airport on his way to Dhaka. Nehru readily agreed to meet him there. By this time Nehru had realized that Ayub was firmly in the saddle and that it would be worthwhile to know his mind.

They met on 1 September 1960. This meeting, Qadir told me later in an interview at Lahore, proved to be a 'disaster' though newspaper reports had described it as a success. According to Qadir, both sides had agreed to strike 'a favourable note' in public and, therefore, the truth was never revealed at the time. Nehru, according to Qadir, listed four outstanding problems: (i) evacuee property; (ii) border disputes; (iii) distribution of river waters; and (iv) Kashmir. To Ayub's disappointment, Kashmir came last.

Nehru's elucidation of the first three points, Qadir said, was 'fair and comprehensive', but Kashmir was only mentioned, not elaborated upon. Ayub raised the question and said that a 'satisfactory' solution of the Kashmir problem was vital. When he did not get any response, Ayub was visibly annoyed and 'huffed and puffed like military chaps,' as Qadir put it. Ayub's version, as I got it from him, was that Nehru did not 'disagree with his ideas' on Kashmir and favoured only the creation of goodwill and understanding to eliminate border incidents.

Even though the meeting was not much of a success, Ayub accepted Nehru's proposal to make the boundaries firm. India and Pakistan constituted a ministerial committee to demarcate the border and take other steps that would put an end to border disputes and therefore localized incidents.

Ayub appointed K.M. Sheikh and Nehru, Swaran Singh, to discuss the differences between the two countries. Nehru had wanted Pant to be India's representative but the latter expressed his inability. Pant's reluctance was due to his conviction that the ministerial committee would fail. Little did he know that Ayub had instructed Sheikh Abdullah to go more than halfway to seek an agreement. By the time Dayal informed Pant about it, Nehru had already announced that Swaran Singh would be India's representative.

The Swaran Singh–Sheikh meetings, held in the wake of the Nehru–Ayub talks, were a success. Even if they had not been, the very fact that a dialogue was held was an achievement. India and Pakistan agreed that 'all border disputes between the two countries, if not settled by negotiation, would be referred to an impartial tribunal for settlement and implementation'.

This was indeed one of the good phases in Indo–Pak relations. So relaxed was the atmosphere that when Ayub spoke about Kashmir to Nehru during the Commonwealth Prime Minister's Conference in London, he thought he could afford to be personal. Ayub told Nehru that there was a general belief that the latter's attitude towards Kashmir was 'governed by certain emotional considerations'. Nehru laughed and said that if that were so 'the valley could have been turned into a kind of Switzerland for him to visit as often as he chose'.

This informal spirit spread to other areas too. Radio Pakistan and All India Radio changed their vituperative tone; the two governments instructed them to avoid such broadcasts as would adversely affect Indo–Pakistan relations. Political leaders became circumspect and spoke less of differences and more of amity, and newspaper editors from both sides met to agree to forsake 'hate' campaigns.

This atmosphere of goodwill was more pronounced after Nehru and Ayub signed the Indus Waters Treaty at Karachi on 19 September 1960. The treaty divided the six Indus rivers – the Sutlej, Beas, Ravi, Chenab, Jhelum, and Sindh – between India and Pakistan. The waters of the first three rivers were to go to India and of the other three to Pakistan. It was stipulated that Pakistan would continue to receive water even from the rivers allotted to India for ten years or so by when Karachi was expected to construct alternative channels. The treaty also created an Indus Basin Development Fund of $900 million to finance Pakistan's replacement programme. The Western powers, including the US and UK, were to contribute roughly $725 million and India $175 million in ten equal installments.

The water dispute was as old as Partition itself. When the Radcliffe Boundary Commission award split the composite irrigation network of Punjab between India and Pakistan, the irrigation canals went to Pakistan, and the rivers feeding them to India, while the controlling headworks were evenly divided. The Boundary Commission Chairman, Radcliffe, had hinted at 'some joint control' which Nehru had rejected at that time as 'a political recommendation'.

As there was no 'joint control', the two countries had argued endlessly over their respective rights. Pakistan had said that the rivers were common to the subcontinent and hence India could not do anything unilaterally. New Delhi had maintained that it was the sole owner of the waters and the headworks in its territory. Karachi had suggested that the matter be referred to the International Court of Justice, but Nehru had rejected the proposal on the ground that it would be 'a confession of our continued dependence on others'.

This was an amicable settlement of the dispute. In 1951, when Pakistan was on the point of bringing the dispute before the Security Council, an article by David E. Lilienthal, former chairman of the US Tennessee Valley Authority, was published in an American magazine, suggesting a comprehensive engineering plan under which India and Pakistan could jointly develop the entire Indus basin, 'perhaps with the World Bank's assistance'. Eugene R. Black, then heading the World Bank, had been consulted before Lilienthal wrote the article, and the US gave the proposal its blessings. As the proposal suggested a way out and was also laced with money, both India and Pakistan accepted it.

In response to the formal proposal by the head of the World Bank (November 1951), a 'working team' of engineers was appointed to discuss the problem outside the political arena. India gave a guarantee not to disrupt supplies until the end of the negotiations, and it kept its word though Pakistan continued to make allegations to the contrary. For nine years the negotiations between India and Pakistan covered a long, tortuous route, and even in the last stages, both Nehru and Ayub had to intervene to put the talks back on track when the prejudice and cussedness of officials appeared to be derailing them.

Nehru had to face criticism within India on agreeing to continue deliveries till Pakistan had built its alternative channels. Indian engineers had prepared a formidable case to prove that both Punjab and Rajasthan would be virtually ruined if India were to give water to Pakistan for a ten-year transitional period. Opposition from political quarters was organized by Morarji Desai, then a member of Nehru's cabinet. Even Pant, who was very loyal to Nehru, expressed his unhappiness over India's 'heavy contribution' to the Indus Basin Development Fund. He wanted to get it adjusted against the value of the property that Hindu refugees had left in Pakistan.

Nehru brushed aside all objections. He was anxious to build good relations with Karachi, and settlement of the water disputes could serve as a foundation upon which would be built a durable structure for Indo–Pak amity.

Ayub's problem was not politicians, because they were discredited at that time, but the bureaucrats upon whom he lent heavily. Some thirty or forty engineers and administrators, who were fomenting trouble, accosted him at Lahore. He explained to them that in the absence of a settlement, India could decide to divert the waters and starve Pakistan, 'If we can get a solution which we can live with, we will be very foolish not to accept it'. He said: 'Since the Indian army was three times the size of our army, the dice was loaded against us. It was not a good bargain but I had no choice in the circumstances and I accepted it.'

Before the treaty was signed there was a hitch. Ayub was not happy over India's insistence on using in Kashmir 'some water' from the Chenab, a river allotted to Pakistan. 'It appeared as though the entire arrangement would break down,' later Dayal told me. New Delhi deputed him to talk to Ayub, and after a great deal of persuasion, he was able to get him to agree to the proposal. Nehru had no time to sit back and feel gratified by the Indus treaty because China's aggression was gaining momentum.

6

LAL BAHADUR SHASTRI AS HOME MINISTER
Foreign Policy, the Sino-India War, Kashmir, and the World of Journalism

After Govind Ballabh Pant's death on 7 March 1961, Lal Bahadur Shastri was appointed home minister. He changed virtually the entire personal staff, the two survivors being the driver, who drove very fast, and I whom Shastri described as that '*lamba* presswala who publicized Pant ji so much'. In time I became so close to him that he confided to me many political secrets, and I read all his mail. His secretary, Rajeshwar Prasad, became a friend and would share with me all the information he received. During Pant's time too I would see letters and notes but usually secretly and not openly as was the case with Shastri.

I also felt more comfortable with Shastri and wasn't in awe of him as was the case with Pant. Shastri's simplicity and modesty were in their own way as impressive as Pant's sagacity and maturity. Both represented the best of the Indian independence movement and its traditional values. They wanted to do all they could to take the country forward, personal interest never so much as crossing their minds. How diminutive in comparison were the leaders of political parties whom I saw from close quarters forty-five years later as a member of the Rajya Sabha.

After India gained Independence, Nehru, as the first prime minister, began building the edifice of foreign policy, brick by brick. He was clear in his mind that the Cold War necessitated India distance itself from the two political blocks, the Western led by the US and the Eastern headed by the Soviet Union. He developed the concept of non-alignment with the idea of bringing together the small and economically backward countries. Leading the Non-Aligned Movement (NAM) were India, Egypt, Indonesia, and Yugoslavia.

Nehru had organized the First Asia Conference in 1946 when he was prime minister of the interim government and had declared that Asia as an entity would assert itself against the colonial powers. He hoped that the Asian countries would develop close relations with one another and eschew mutual hostilities.

He developed India's policy towards Pakistan only after he realized that its troops were complicit in the attack on Kashmir. Till then his attitude was friendly despite Karachi's pinpricks. He knew that anti-India feeling was what united Pakistan's Punjabis, Sindhis, Pathans, and Baluchis. He also began to see Pakistan as a pawn of the great powers when both the UK and US supported it on Kashmir. Nehru held his ground and found the great powers 'bereft of principles and decency' in their utterances and activities.

Stalin in the Soviet Union and John Foster Dulles in the US, although mutually opposite in character, spoke the same language of power and allies. Nehru found very little space for small or weak countries in the Cold War between the two blocks. His advocacy of non-alignment, he felt, was the Gandhian approach suited to his country.

Towards China, Nehru adopted a 'cautious friendly' policy in order to woo it from the Soviet sphere of influence At the same time, he did not want any quarter for Beijing's enemies because he was confident of his ability to win over Beijing to his side and was satisfied by the 'Hindi–Chini Bhai-Bhai' thesis.

When Nehru visited the US in November 1961, he did not openly discuss with President John F. Kennedy India's soured relation with China. Kennedy wanted Nehru to discuss this because the US was aware of China's aggressive stance towards India and he himself was disturbed by China's indirect aid to Vietnam. He entreated Nehru, his icon, to advise him on what the US should do in Vietnam. In response, Nehru looked at the ceiling, as he was wont to do when he was disinclined to discuss something. He, however, told M.J. Desai, then foreign secretary, accompanying him, to convey to the US president that they would get stuck in Vietnam if they did not withdraw soon. Kennedy organized a breakfast meeting between Nehru and top US economists and foreign policy experts. First he was late and then monosyllabic in his responses. The breakfast ended in 20 minutes. Some of them reported this to Kennedy who remarked in the presence of his aides that Nehru had 'lived too long'. President Lincoln was fortunate that someone killed him, said Kennedy.

Nehru depended a great deal on Shastri who literally worshipped him. He was circumspect when dealing with the dynasty: Nehru's two sisters, Vijayalakshmi Pandit and Krishna Hatheesingh, and daughter, Indira Gandhi. As commerce minister, Shastri had allowed a car presented to Krishna Hatheesingh in West Germany to be brought to India without her paying the customs duty.

As home minister he was startled when he received a copy of a letter Vijayalakshmi Pandit had written to Nehru that the Raj Bhawans (she was then governor of Maharashtra) were being used as dak bungalows by central ministers. Shastri received the complaint after he had stayed at Raj Bhawan,

Bombay. From then onward, Shastri and his staff would stay at the airport even at night, with all the attendant discomforts, but never at any Raj Bhawan.

Shastri, who like Nehru belonged to Allahabad, was conscious that he was way down in the social ladder in comparison to the Nehru family. After all, Motilal Nehru, Jawaharlal Nehru's father, was an iconic figure and a dashing social figure while Shastri was a struggling lower middle-class individual. I recall Indira Gandhi's remark about 'middle-class living' when she visited Shastri's residence to consider whether she could move there after his death.

Shastri was impressed with English-speaking intellectuals who he thought came from highly educated families. Once he wrote a note on the Punjab situation and asked me to read it. I thought he wanted me to see whether his analysis tallied with mine as I came from Punjab, but to my surprise he wanted to know whether the note was well written. As I began reading it, Shastri said that even L.P. Singh, his favourite joint secretary, had praised his writing style.

Shastri's note to Nehru on Punjab did not create any stir, but his letter on Vladimir Nabakov's racy novel *Lolita*, did. One Congress leader had written to Shastri that *Lolita*, which had reached bookshops in India, was so lewd that it should be banned. Shastri accordingly wrote to Nehru (the draft was provided by L.P. Singh) that the book should be banned. Prompt came Nehru's reply the following morning (he replied to all correspondence within 24 hours) arguing at length why he thought *Lolita* should not be banned and why D.H. Lawrence's *Lady Chatterley's Lover* should continue to be. *Lolita* was not banned.

Shastri was not a moralist but he was a traditionalist. When he watched *Swan Lake* performed by the Bolshoi Ballet group in Leningrad he was uncomfortable. At intermission I asked if he was enjoying the show. He said he had felt embarrassed throughout because the legs of the dancers were naked and *amma*, the word with which he addressed his wife (Lalita Shastri), was sitting by his side. He was equally embarrassed at the reception hosted by Kamal Amrohi in Bombay at the sets of his film, *Pakeeza*. Meena Kumari, then at the peak of her career, garlanded him and read out a small speech in his praise. Before responding he took me aside and asked who the lady was. I was flabbergasted and told him that she was Meena Kumari, the leading film star in the country. He began his speech in Hindi: Meena Kumari ji *mujhe maaf karen* [should forgive him] for admitting that he had heard her name for the first time in his life.

My intimacy with Nepal began when Shastri took me to Kathmandu as part of Nehru's bid to improve relations which were far from happy. Harishwar Dayal was our envoy. Like his predecessors, he treated Nepal as if it was a backyard of India. Shastri ignored him and asked his secretary Rajeshwar Prasad and me to prepare a draft of a joint statement. Dayal sheepishly sat with us. Through the statement Shastri was able to eradicate Kathmandu's impression that New Delhi was dictating it on foreign policy.

I also recall the day B.P. Koirala, founder of the Nepali Congress, called me to the All India Institute of Medical Sciences, where he had been convalescing for a few weeks. Surprisingly, he was not bitter against the king who he referred as Maharaj. I found him keen to find a place in his country's politics. He was eventually to become Nepal's prime minister.

I heard that Nepal wanted to merge with India when King Tribhuwan Bir Bikram Sah took shelter in New Delhi. I checked this with Koirala, who said that Nehru was clear in his mind that Nepal should remain a sovereign democratic state with a freely elected parliament. Nehru did emphasize that the two countries should have soft borders and act closely militarily and economically. That more or less reflects the policy today.

These days, whenever I visit Nepal, I find people voicing many grievances in the form of anti-India sentiments. New Delhi's Ministry of External Affairs is largely to blame for this because most Indian ambassadors posted to Kathmandu have acted like viceroys of the British raj, dabbling in Nepal's internal politics. This attitude has boomeranged and Nepal has fallen under the influence of pro-China Maoists. Beijing has moved close to Nepal, extending large loans and building railway lines and roads to Kathmandu to bridge the distance between them.

However, the real irritant for the Nepalese is the 1953 treaty which New Delhi signed with Kathmandu. The treaty is loaded in favour of India and has defined security relations as if Nepal is a vassal of India. Although both countries are inclined to alter the treaty of 1953, it still hangs like an albatross round their necks. The monarchy has gone and Nepal has become a secular republic in which Hinduism is no longer the state religion. It is difficult to say how Nepal's proximity with China will affect the people there but there is little doubt that relations between Nepal and India will continue to be close through their shared culture, heritage, and even religion. Provided India plays its cards right, there should be no room for misunderstanding between the two.

These few distractions did not lessen Shastri's attention on China. He agreed with Sardar Patel's warning to Nehru that the Chinese government was trying to delude us by a declaration of peaceful intentions. Shastri told me that China would one day betray India and it was a pity that Panditji, as he referred to Nehru, did not see the writing on the wall.

Nehru was a hero to me and I imagined there must be a good reason why he did not want to join issues with China. He was perhaps reluctant to divert his attention from development, because manning the 2,400-mile Sino–Indian border meant huge expenditure on the purchase of arms. He could perhaps envisage the consequences of an armed conflict with China, akin to a clash between 'two giants' as Nehru put it. He wanted to avert the confrontation, the tremors of which, he would say, would be felt throughout the world.

Whatever the reason, Nehru opted for quiet negotiation through diplomatic channels. Indian officials wrote to their Chinese counterparts, politely pointing out that Peking was ignoring India's traditional boundaries. What concerned New Delhi most was that Peking had depicted part of Bhutan as its territory within Tibet.

The Chinese in their reply reiterated that the alignment in their maps was based on old ones, which would be corrected after fresh consultations and surveys. This, however, proved to be a ruse to gain more time to prepare to attack India. When there was no communication from China in answer to the questions New Delhi had raised, Nehru grew suspicious.

By mid-1961, Chinese border forces had advanced 70 miles west of the Sinkiang–Tibet road from the position they had held in 1958. This meant the occupation of 12,000 squares miles of Indian territory. Krishna Menon told me many years later that nobody in India appreciated the fact that India 'encroached on 4,000 sq. m. of territory belonging to China'.

The war was, however, preceded by a string of events. I am reconstructing the story after having spoken to General P.N. Thapar, the then chief of army staff and Defence Minister Krishna Menon. Somewhat peeved by the criticism, Nehru ordered Thapar to evict the Chinese from the posts they had built within Indian territory. The army chief was reluctant to do so because he thought it would be like 'disturbing a hornet's nest'.

A meeting was held under the chairmanship of Krishna Menon, who was all for action. Thapar argued that the Indian army did not have the necessary strength, the ratio being six Chinese to one Indian. Menon responded confidently that he had met Chen Yi, the Chinese deputy premier, at Geneva and had been assured that China would never fight India over the border issue. When I asked Menon specifically whether this information given to me by General Thapar was true, his reply was: 'That toothless old woman; he did not know how to fight a war.'

Thapar had submitted a note to the government when he took over as chief in 1960. In it, he had pointed out that the equipment with the army was in such poor condition and in such short supply that China or Pakistan could easily defeat India. This was in sharp contrast to Nehru's statement, which I heard from the press gallery: 'I can tell the House that at no time since Independence has our defence been in better condition and finer fettle.'

It appeared as if the government was determined to fight the Chinese without reorganizing or re-equipping the army. At Menon's meeting, Thapar was supported by only one person, V. Vishwanathan, then the additional secretary in the home ministry. He said that if Gen. Thapar felt that India was unprepared there was no point in being foolhardy, but Menon was obdurate about attacking China.

Faced with no option other than an immediate military operation, Thapar sought an interview with the prime minister to seek his intervention. A few minutes before his departure for Nehru's house, S.S. Khera, then cabinet secretary, met him and said: 'General, if I were you, I would not express my fears before Panditji for he might think that you are afraid to fight.' Thapar's curt reply was that he must tell the prime minister the truth; the rest was for him to decide.

Before Thapar got into his car, Khera once again said that he must realize that if India did not fight, the government would fall. Thapar did not argue further but was more convinced than ever that the decision to resist China was motivated by political considerations.

Thapar repeated to Nehru how the Indian army was unprepared, untrained, and ill-equipped for the operation it was being asked to undertake. (Menon told me before he became defence minister that there was no army worth the name and no equipment worth the mention.)

Nehru said Menon had informed him that India was itself producing a substantial part of the army equipment it required. Thapar emphasized that India was nowhere near the stage of even assembling the weapons required for war. He then mentioned the note he had submitted, complaining about the poor shape of the army and its equipment. Nehru said he had never seen it.

To reassure Thapar, Nehru told him that he had received reliable information that the Chinese would not offer resistance if there was a show of force to make them vacate the check-posts. Thapar knew from where the information had come. Obviously, the government had not taken any note of the Chinese warnings that 'the Indian aggressor must bear full responsibility for the consequences of their crimes'.

The general was still not prepared to take the risk. He asked Nehru to speak to some of the army commanders. Lt Gen. Prodip Sen, commanding-in-chief Eastern Army Command, who was in Thapar's room in the defence ministry at that time, was summoned. He supported Thapar and said that the army was far from prepared. Nehru repeated that his information was that the Chinese would not retaliate.

Thapar took heart from this. If that was true then even his unprepared forces might wear the crown of glory. No general can resist the temptation of marching at the head of a winning army, and Thapar was no exception. He began preparing for action. Thapar told me on 29 July 1970: 'Looking back, I think I should have submitted my resignation at that time. I might have saved my country from the humiliation of defeat.'

Shastri took me along when he flew to the Northeast to make an assessment on the ground, as he had been asked to do by Nehru. When we reached Tezpur in Assam, Lt Gen. Harbaksh Singh was in command. B.N. Kaul, the controversial commander, had gone to Delhi on leave. Hostilities were yet to begin. Harbaksh Singh explained to us how the Indian forces would do better despite many handicaps. He assured Shastri that it would not be a walkover for the Chinese. Shastri was happy and told me on our return flight that he would request Panditji to let Harbaksh Singh stay on in place of Kaul. However, in the evening we heard on the radio at Calcutta that Kaul was back from leave and had resumed charge.

Menon's specific instructions were not to move a single soldier from the border with Pakistan. India's assessment since Independence had been that it would have to fight Pakistan one day. Detailed plans of 'projected action', if ever it became necessary, had been prepared in the defence ministry and kept ready. The border between China had however been left unprotected because no attack was expected from there.

Even as late as August 1962, a few weeks before the Chinese attack, Menon was talking of Pakistan's preparations against India. In those days, Rajeshwar Dayal, India's high commissioner to Pakistan, was in Delhi. One morning Dayal, as he told me, received a call from the defence ministry for a meeting. When he reached the ministry, he was ushered into a room where Menon was sitting with the army commanders, including Thapar.

Dayal had barely taken his seat when Menon asked him to tell the commanders about the preparations that Pakistan was making along the Indian border. Before Dayal could reply, Thapar told him in Punjabi, which Menon could not understand, that Dayal should not allow himself to be tricked because the projected danger from Pakistan was part of a larger plan.

Dayal said that he knew nothing about the preparations and that he had found no such sign at the border on his way to Delhi. Menon was annoyed and asked Dayal to send him a report to confirm that there was no evidence of preparations by Pakistan to invade India.

Against this backdrop, Thapar had been reluctant to ask for the withdrawal of any troops from the Pakistan front, but now conditions were different. He wanted a division to be withdrawn from that sector. Nehru immediately conceded to his request.

'Normally, the time given to the defence forces to attack is a fortnight and an attack is timed at the break of daylight,' said Thapar. The Chinese attack came on 20 October, at 5 a.m. in the eastern sector where the sun rose early, and at 7 a.m. in the Ladakh area where daylight was late to arrive.

As the war began, the Shah of Iran sent Nehru a copy of letter he had written to Ayub Khan, suggesting that he send his soldiers to fight alongside Indian forces against the 'red menace'. (I have seen the copy.)

I recalled what Jinnah had said at Law College in Lahore when I had asked him what Pakistan's reaction would be if a third power were to attack India. He had said that his soldiers would fight alongside Indian soldiers. Ayub told foreign powers who wanted him to help India that the fact that Pakistan did not take advantage of India's vulnerability was a form of assistance and a sufficient gesture.

At the end of hostilities, Shastri recalled the Shah's letter and said that had the Pakistani soldiers fought alongside us and 'shed their blood with Indian soldiers', it would have been difficult to say 'No' to Pakistan even if it had asked for Kashmir (*Agar wo Kashmir bhi mangte to na karna mushkil hota*). Probably he was right because emotions played a substantial part in our decisions.

Nehru had appointed a Citizen's Council to generate public opinion against China's attack and Shastri was a member of the council. I attended the meetings as the press officer. Indira Gandhi headed this council, an example of Nehru's way of building up his daughter, and I met her there for the first time. As days passed we got to know each other so well that she started calling me by my first name.

As desired by the council, Shastri addressed many public meetings, not only to criticize China but also to defend Nehru who was being pilloried for having trusted China. At one public meeting in Delhi, Shastri asked for donations of ornaments to meet defence expenses. I was so moved by his speech that I immediately handed him my wedding ring, and he for his part announced my gesture at that very meeting. When I told my wife about the wedding ring she just remained silent. I thought she supported my decision but many years later she told me that I could have given money instead of the ring. A wedding ring was after all a wedding ring, she said quietly.

By the time Thapar went to meet Menon towards the end of October 1962, the Indian post at Dhola (3 kilometres north of the McMahon Line) had fallen and the Chinese forces were rushing downhill further into North East Frontier Agency (NEFA). Menon had already known about it because one copy of every signal to the chief of the army staff was going directly to the defence minister.

Thapar did not indulge in 'I-told-you-so'. He simply reported what had happened and said, 'Now we must plan what to do next'. Menon, brooding over a cup of black tea, only remarked: 'How could I have known that they would come like an avalanche?'

Thapar told the defence minister that Indian forces should now fall back and hold out at Se-la Pass, about 40 miles from Dhola. Menon sarcastically remarked: 'General, why not Bangalore?' They talked very little after that and awaited the defence committee meeting over which Nehru was to preside.

Before the meeting, B.N. Mullick, the intelligence chief, came to Thapar to apologize for being so wrong in his intelligence reports in which he had said that the Chinese were too tied up with the Khampas in Tibet to spare men for the border. The general's reply was that it was the future which was more important.

Never before had India sought armed assistance from abroad, but after China's attack it did. Nehru sent a frantic message to President Kennedy through B.K. Nehru, India's ambassador in Washington. The latter told me that Kennedy met him without any delay, despite his preoccupation with the Cuban missile crisis, and found him, to his surprise, engrossed in studying a blow-up of a map of India. Kennedy had top civil and military officials with him.

The then Secretary of State Dean Rusk suggested the use of tanks to stall China's advance. B.K. Nehru explained that the tanks would have to take a long, circuitous route to reach the place. Rusk asked why they could not go there straight. B.K. Nehru said that it would not be possible because East Pakistan lay in between. The secretary of state said: 'You are defending your country, not having a picnic. March your tanks through.'

Kennedy further asked whether Krishna Menon was still the defence minister. When B.K. Nehru replied in the affirmative, Kennedy remarked that this would make things difficult at home. He also asked B.K. Nehru to approach Khrushchev and tell him either to 'put up or shut up'. (The latter had blamed the West 'who wish to line their pockets by engineering a military clash between India and China'.) However, the comment of a top US official, after seeing the long list of armaments India sought, was that 'Churchill with virtually no weapon worth the name had won the war but you want all the weapons while retreating'. He was pointing out India's lack of combative spirit to confront China.

When Bomdi-la fell (19 November 1962), General Thapar was at Tezpur. He flew to Delhi and went straight to Nehru to say that in the best traditions of the Indian army he, as a defeated general, would like to submit his resignation. For the first time in many days Thapar saw a smile on Nehru's face. Holding his hand tightly, he said: 'Thank you, but this is not your fault.'

However, when Thapar met him the following morning Nehru said: 'General, you remember what you said to me last night. I would like to get it in writing.' Thapar came home and got the letter of resignation typed by his daughter and sent it within two hours. I saw Nehru in the Lok Sabha waving the letter of resignation. This did lessen the anger of members who were targeting Nehru. He thought that Thapar's exit would assuage parliament's anger against Krishna Menon. It did to a degree when Nehru changed Menon's portfolio from defence to defence production.

Thapar wished to issue a statement in his defence, but Nehru dissuaded him from doing so and assured him that he would one day get an opportunity to tell his side of the story.

Later in September 1970, Thapar approached Indira Gandhi, then the prime minister, to allow him to see the report of the Australian-born Indian official Lt Gen. Henderson-Brooks who, along with Brig. Prem Bhagat, was appointed to inquire into the reasons for India's defeat against China. She did not however concede to his request. (When I was a Rajya Sabha member from 1996, I wanted the report to be made public. The government refused do so 'in public interest'. My hunch was that the report had so severely criticized Nehru that the government, even though headed by the BJP, did not want to face the public anger that would have been generated.)

Lt-Gen. M. Chaudhuri was appointed to officiate as chief of the army staff and Thapar was given 'sick' leave before being compulsorily retired. Nehru repeatedly inquired from Thapar whether Chaudhuri was a good choice. Thapar said he was a competent soldier but there were rumours about 'his conduct' when he was the military governor of Hyderabad following India's police action against the state in 1950.

Nobody knew where and when the Chinese forces would stop as they were facing very little resistance. Only the *Statesman* editor N.J. Nanporia was repeatedly reporting that the Chinese would offer a ceasefire unilaterally. (After the war, Nehru asked him the reason for his assessment. Nanporia said that his reading was they wanted to punish India, not occupy it.) The Indian army was preparing to retreat to Assam. Nehru said at that time: 'my heart goes to the people of Assam'. The Assamese took these words as a sort of goodbye and abandonment by India. They have never forgiven Nehru.

On 20 November 1962 Shastri was preparing to leave for Tezpur at the instance of Nehru to see things from close quarters. I was the first to reach Palam airport and found the newspaper stall unusually crowded. With great difficulty I was able to buy a copy of the *Statesman*. It carried the dramatic offer of a unilateral ceasefire by the Chinese.

Peking's statement said: 'Beginning from November 21, 1962 (midnight) Chinese frontier guards will withdraw to positions 20 km [12.5 miles] behind the lines of actual control which existed between China and India on November 7, 1959.' The 'unilateral withdrawal' announcement was preceded about an hour earlier by flashes from news agencies that an 'important announcement' was expected from Peking. The announcements came early enough to catch the morning editions of Indian newspapers, but sufficiently late to prevent them from carrying any reactions from New Delhi.

In any event, the bureaucracy in New Delhi seemed blissfully unaware of press timings. A colleague in the *Statesman* recalled that he received a call from an external affairs ministry official at around 4 a.m., saying that they wanted to issue a statement countering Chinese claims on their advance. The official was surprised when told that the Chinese had already announced a unilateral ceasefire.

L.P. Singh and M.M. Hooja, joint director of intelligence, reached the airport just before we left for Tezpur. I showed them the announcement. Surprisingly, the bosses of the home ministry and the intelligence bureau were unaware of the ceasefire offer. Hooja rang up the IB to confirm the news. The home minister, who reached soon after, also did not know about the ceasefire. After reading the news, Shastri said: 'This does make a difference. I may have to cancel my visit, but let me find out from Panditji.'

A cavalcade of cars moved to the prime minister's residence. Nehru had just woken up and was totally unaware of the Chinese offer. This was typical of our intelligence agencies and of the functioning of the government. Though the statement on the ceasefire had reached newspaper offices just before midnight, the government was unaware of it. Even the official spokesman whom the pressmen awoke for a reaction expressed ignorance. What a way to fight a war, I thought.

Nehru's first remark in Hindi after hearing the news was: 'Has it happened? I was expecting it.' He, however, wanted to see the newspaper. Shastri asked him if he should cancel the trip to Assam. Nehru's reply was: 'No, we cannot give up our plans. But you should come back soon.'

Shastri was not in favour of accepting the Chinese proposal. He told me that we would emerge as a tough nation if we did not seek a soft option. He was in favour of continuing the war despite the reverses.

When we reached Guwahati, Assam Chief Minister Bimala Prasad Chaliha was at the airport. According to Bhagwan Sahay, the state governor, Chaliha smiled for the first time in many days. Indira Gandhi, who was also in town, found the last paragraph of the ceasefire statement objectionable because, according to her, Chinese control would enable them to indoctrinate the people against India.

From Guwahati we flew to Tezpur. The airport had been saved in the nick of time. One day's delay would have been too late because a decision had been taken to blow up the airport. The deputy commissioner of the area had fled, burning the files. Burnt currency notes were lying on the floor of the treasury. Private cars had been requisitioned to evacuate government officials and army vehicles were found to be carrying even the poultry of the bara sahib, but had no space for ordinary people. Prisoners had been released, including mental patients. There was little food, even for children.

We were received by a contingent of army officers. I met Lt-Gen. Kaul for the first time. How meek he looked, in contrast to the controversial figure he had become. I had expected him to be stouter and younger. His face was pudgy and his manner appeared reserved. My encounter with him was brief and formal, but he squeezed my arm to express friendship. Kaul told Shastri that India must have peace at any cost. Shastri, who never favoured his appointment on the Chinese front, paid him scant attention.

Kaul told our pilot that he was travelling in a helicopter carrying food, clothes, and medicines to contact his men who were cut off when Bomdi La unexpectedly fell. I knew this information was meant for me to be passed on to Shastri.

The passenger lounge was still displaying a board 'Beer Sold Here' and had been converted into a map room. We were told how the debacle took place and where the Chinese soldiers now stood. The position was worse than we had expected.

I met young army officers sitting in another corner of the lounge. They were bitter and openly spoke of how every requirement of senior officers – soldiers had to carry commodes – were met at the last picket post even while the firing was going on. A captain admitted: 'We are no longer fighters. We think of clubs or restaurants even in the trenches. We have gone too soft; we're no good.'

One major who spoke in favour of fighting to the last drop of blood was from my home town, Sialkot. I had known him. He asked me to carry a trunk to Delhi so that he could fight without bothering about the luggage. When his wife collected the trunk and opened it before me, I was aghast to see it filled with smuggled imported goods. I had unknowingly carried the smuggled goods in the home minister's plane.

The advice of General Thimayya, now the retired chief of the army staff, was: 'One year is necessary to recoup.' Even those who were keen on avenging the defeat were in favour of the ceasefire. The government had no choice. It activated a few non-aligned nations, led by Sri Lanka, to intervene and formalize the ceasefire on the line India and China held at that time. India withdrew its troops by 20 kilometres as required by the ceasefire proposal but the Chinese did not do so.

Krishna Menon resigned from the government. I got to know him well when he was in the wilderness. I once asked why he didn't tell his side of the story. He said: 'My story must die with me because I would have to lay the blame on Nehru, and I do not want to do so because of my loyalty to him.'

❀

Nehru was still awaiting the US response to a request for an air-umbrella. The inevitable fallout of seeking assistance from Washington and London was to accept their insistence on talks between India and Pakistan on Kashmir. I had seen this happening after every occasion when Washington and London had done New Delhi some favour. Whatever the reason, the West, particularly the US, tended to support Pakistan, even when ruled by military dictators who had staged coups against democratically elected governments.

Kennedy's personal envoy, Averell Harriman and Duncan Sandys, secretary of state for Commonwealth relations and the son-in-law of Winston Churchill, who were in New Delhi assessing India's military requirements, urged Indian leaders to talk to Pakistan on Kashmir. They tried to play Shastri against Nehru by giving the former the impression that he was more forthcoming and that they counted more on him than Nehru. Sandys, however, assured India that there was no question of handing over the Valley of Kashmir to Pakistan. What he had in mind were only marginal changes.

The then high commissioner to Pakistan wrote from Karachi (Shastri received a copy) that all the officials he had met had told him that India and Pakistan could be friends if the Kashmir problem was solved. He warned that India might have to part with some part of the Kashmir Valley.

Nehru and Ayub Khan jointly issued a statement (29 November 1962) to announce that their ministers would meet to make a renewed effort to resolve 'outstanding differences'. This provoked Khrushchev to send a personal note to Nehru regretting that India was raking up the subject of Kashmir every now and again to its detriment.

The Indo–Pak talks could hardly have been held at a worse time. New Delhi, after its defeat by China, was not prepared for further concessions, and Pakistan's morale was high because of its friendship with Peking. The demand in Pakistan was that a political settlement 'must be one which, when implemented, will see its flag hoisted on every housetop in Kashmir'.

After the failure of the talks, the number of ceasefire violations in Kashmir increased. Pressure began mounting within Pakistan. Bhutto was in the front line to fan the fires of protest and frenzy. 'Kashmir must be liberated if Pakistan is to have its full meaning,' was the clarion call he sounded. Ayub warned India that Pakistan might enter into a military pact with China. True to its words, Rawalpindi signed on an agreement with Peking (August 1963) but it was limited to flights by the Pakistan International Airlines to Canton and Shanghai.

Shastri was keen on representing India, and Pakistan too wanted him. However, Nehru nominated Swaran Singh, who he knew was adept in the art of talking for the sake of talking. The ministerial talks began in Karachi on 20 December 1962. Bhutto, then foreign minister, represented Pakistan. On 20 December itself, there was an announcement that Pakistan and China had reached an 'agreement in principle' on the alignment of the border between Sinkiang and Azad Kashmir. (Pakistan gave away 2,200 sq. m. of Gilgit–Balistan in Kashmir.) Some officials accompanying Swaran Singh suggested that he should break off talks on the grounds of Pakistan's gift of land to China and return home. On the other hand, the UK and US envoys, ever present at the venue of the talks, argued with Swaran Singh that the talks should continue. He decided to stay on. After all, his brief was to keep the talks going without giving in on fundamentals.

Ayub explained to me that it was only a coincidence that the announcement on the border settlement with China came on the day the Indo–Pakistan talks began. He said that the timing had been decided upon by China, and Pakistan had nothing to do with it. However, the impression I got from Bhutto's associates was that the announcement was timed to convey to New Delhi that if the talks did not succeed both Pakistan and China might force a solution on India.

Ayub said,

> You know, Nehru asked me for the copy of the Chinese border map on which we had based our claim and I sent him one, even though my officials were opposed to it on the ground that the enemy should not be given information on the terrain for defence reasons.

Even before the first round of talks began, Ayub sent letters to both London and Washington that Nehru had agreed to talks under pressure and that nothing would come of them. Harold Macmillan then prime minister of the UK, in turn wrote to Nehru that a breakdown of the talks would dampen the enthusiasm of the people in the UK and US to support India. He also advised New Delhi not to prolong the talks lest the public get impatient.

Nehru's reply to Macmillan was on the same lines as that to Kennedy. He wrote: 'Even if Kashmir were to be handed over to Pakistan on a platter, Pakistan would think of some other way to keep its quarrel with India alive because Kashmir was only a symptom of a disease and that disease was hatred for India.'

John Kenneth Galbraith, then US envoy to India warned Kennedy that in his view 'Kashmir is not solvable in territorial terms but it can be by holding up the example of the way in which France and Germany have moved to soften their antagonism by the common market and common instruments of administration'.

Galbraith had undertaken what he called a Harvard Exercise (named after the university at which he had taught before taking up his assignment in New Delhi). He suggested the reopening of the road between Rawalpindi and Srinagar through Baramulla, Uri, and Murree, and the resumption of trade and tourist traffic, while India's military rights in the Kashmir Valley were to remain intact. Strange, the suggestion that the road be opened and trade resume came largely true some forty years later.

Sheikh Abdullah's proposal was bolder. He told me in 1969 that the border should be 'soft' so that Pakistanis had easy access to the Valley. Bhutto more or less dittoed the idea of making the ceasefire line into a line of peace. He elucidated his proposal during an interview I had with him in March 1972 after the Bangladesh war.

Nothing came of the six rounds of talks spread over six months (till 16 May 1963). The specific points which the two sides covered were: (a) Swaran Singh's proposal that Poonch town and a few other places (about 3,000 sq. m.) be handed over to Pakistan; and (b) Bhutto's suggestion of a boundary which would give India Jammu, plus a small tract of land in Kashmir.

Would the presence of Sheikh Abdullah at the talks have made any difference? While it would have expanded the scope of the talks, the participation of Kashmiris might have helped reach a settlement. Abdullah was however in detention at that time.

In the meanwhile, Pakistan renewed the demand for a plebiscite under the aegis of the UN. India warned that even a partial plebiscite would stoke the fires of Hindu–Muslim differences. It was argued that if the vote were to go in favour of Pakistan, Hindus would be annoyed with Muslims in India and this might even damage the concept of secularism. Nehru had drawn the attention of the world to the same danger after the Security Council's last debate on Kashmir in 1957. India proposed a political settlement and suggested a readjustment of the ceasefire line. It was however made clear that the proposal should be regarded only as the beginning and that it did not represent India's final position.

A week before the breakdown of the talks, Bhutto said in Dhaka (9 May 1963) that Pakistan was firmly opposed to the partition of the Kashmir Valley or its joint control by India and Pakistan. Shastri too, when he was prime minister, was against dividing the Valley or having joint control over it.

The proposal to divide Kashmir, as I discovered, was suggested by the US. The division of the Valley was to be carried out in such a way as to leave Srinagar in India to give it access to Ladakh. Earlier, the USIS in Delhi had issued a statement (20 December 1962) that:

> India's only supply route to Ladakh, where so much is at stake, runs out of the vale of Kashmir. The old fortress city of Srinagar is a major supply base. For India, the fertile vale is the lifeline to Communist-threatened Ladakh… Any settlement of the Kashmir issue as a whole involves an agreement on access to the valley.

Why the USIS, an information outfit, would issue such a statement was noted by New Delhi with suspicion.

America's other scheme was for a condominium over Kashmir, and this was mentioned (April 1953) by Walt Rostov, then US presidential adviser, to Nehru, who rejected it. Pakistan tried its best to sell India the UK suggestion for internationalization of the Valley, but India refused to entertain the idea. It repeated its basic objection that it could not allow any third-party intervention. (This is its current stand because Pakistan had agreed to the bilateral approach at Shimla in 1972).

The issue on which the talks really failed at the fourth round in Calcutta (12 March 1963) related not to Kashmir but to the question of Pakistan's boundary agreement with China. As Nehru put it, India could not agree to the boundary agreement between China and Pakistan over 'the areas illegally occupied in Kashmir'.

New Delhi's quiet reply was to integrate Kashmir further with India. Article 370 of the constitution, which gave special status to Kashmir, underwent further erosion. The pattern of Kashmir's representation in parliament, hitherto through nomination by the Jammu & Kashmir state assembly, was given up in favour of direct election by the people.

❀

Domestically, Nehru was smarting under the criticism by key cabinet ministers on his China policy when Congress President K. Kamaraj suggested he let his top cabinet members work in the organization to strengthen the party. My information was that Kamaraj was only mouthing Nehru's sentiments. Morarji Desai and Jagjivan Ram, the two principal critics, and Shastri, were dropped from the cabinet to work for the party organization.

I asked Shastri why he should have been 'Kamrajed' when he had been loyal to Nehru. Shastri said that Panditji had been obliged to do so because he did not want to be accused of using the Kamaraj Plan to get rid of his critics. According to Shastri, Punjab Chief Minister Pratap Singh Kairon was one of the state chief ministers who was to resign, but, apparently to Shastri's disappointment, Nehru retained him at the last minute.

On the day Shastri was asked to leave the government, I went to his bungalow in the evening as usual. We had developed a personal relationship and I wanted to remain in touch with him. It was dark at Shastri's house, with only the drawing room lit. I thought he was not at home because the one-man guard was also not on duty.

I found Shastri sitting in the drawing room all by himself, reading a newspaper. I asked him why there was no light outside. He said that from now onwards he would have to pay the electricity bill for his house himself, and could not afford extravagant lighting.

From the absence of visitors at Shastri's house, it was clear that he was no longer in office. My experience is that once a person is not in the *kursi*, people generally shun him as he is no longer in a position to be of any benefit to them. The trait is colonial in character and also reflects the days when we were ruled by emperors. Our instinct is to bow our heads before those in power, partly out of fear and partly out of greed. There is little respect for a person without authority, even though he may have served the country well. A worse fate meets academicians, economists, and scientists who retire. Politics has tarnished everything; every value.

I was still with the home ministry when the new home minister, Gulzarilal Nanda, signed a document to assume charge at 11.55 a.m., as his astrologers had told him it was the most auspicious time. It was a comical scene because everyone, from the home secretary downwards, sat waiting with their eyes fixed on the clock in the room. Nanda signed a document before him at the fixed time although he put up an act to indicate he was in the midst of an animated discussion with ministry officials.

After Shastri's departure from the cabinet, I left the home ministry and had a brief stint in the Planning Commission as its information officer. The Planning Commission was a jungle of offices and statistics. Its members were supposed to be path finders in the economic wilderness in which India was. They were, however, quarreling among themselves all the time. There was a recurring battle between Tarlok Singh and V.K.R.V. Rao, the two senior members of the commission. Their differences would be over trivialities but they consumed many sittings of the commission.

I thought that the cabinet secretary's trip to Colombo to develop close relations with Sri Lanka was newsy. I rang Tarlok Singh to ascertain details and he felt insulted that a junior officer had rung him. He complained to the planning secretary who, in turn, admonished me for directly ringing up the cabinet secretary. What probably annoyed the secretary was that I did not address him as 'Sir'. Although I had become a government servant, I had not imbibed the hierarchical culture of the bureaucracy because addressing a senior officer as 'Sir' is a British relic to which we have faithfully adhered.

The journalist within me did not permit me to sit idle. I got hold of the report by Wolf Ladejinsky, a Ford Foundation hand. He had been deputed to assess the extent to which India had instituted land reforms. His report vehemently criticized the government for having reforms on paper but doing very little on the ground. Nehru had taken some steps to stop the zamindars from evicting the landless but Ladejinsky had found them 'too inadequate'. Surprisingly, it was Nehru who had stopped the report from being made public. I made it public at a briefing to journalists attached to the Planning Commission. The leakage shocked the commission members. I was summoned by Deputy Chairman Chandu Lal Trivedi, who had been told that I had leaked the report. I did not deny the charge but argued that the report, front-paged by the press, would exert pressure on the government to take legal steps to institute early land reforms. In any event, I joined the United News of India (UNI), a news agency, the following day.

Nehru abandoned the proposal to initiate drastic land reforms when he found that the states were opposed to the measure. This sent a wrong message to the country and proved yet again that he hated to join issue when vested interests were involved.

I do not think that Nehru was a true socialist although he claimed to be one. His policies were at best Fabian. He was, however, keen that the Socialist Party, headed by Jayaprakash Narayan, already dubbed as Nehru's second eleven much to their dismay, should merge with the Congress. Jayaprakash Narayan suggested to Nehru that he nationalize bank insurance and mines before the socialists could consider an alliance with the Congress. Nehru advised a pragmatic approach which they rejected. Little did they anticipate that his daughter, Indira Gandhi, would nationalize banks and insurance companies, albeit for political reasons.

Nehru's approach was 'step by step'. He was not certain of the human material in the country to implement a Left-oriented programme. It was clear to the socialists that he wanted them in the party to destroy them and their agenda. They began levelling personal attacks on Jayaprakash Narayan. Nehru preferred to part company with him. Nehru realized that he had better consolidate the Congress because he found that many state chief ministers of his party were opposed to socialism. That may be why the Congress used the phrase of 'Socialistic pattern of society'. It was clear to the party that in a country where the preponderant majority were poor, a posture of being Left went down well with the bulk of them.

When relations between Nehru and the socialists were deteriorating Congress felt no compunction in winning over Tanguturi Prakasam and appointing him chief minister of a Telugu-speaking state separated from Madras. I met him when the state's capital was Kurnool. He was a simple man, austerely dressed. He was sitting on a charpai. He said he was a socialist and did not see any contradiction in heading the Congress legislature party. His defence was that the Congress was at heart a socialist and praised Nehru for building socialism in the country.

The Socialist Party reacted with hostility. Prakasam's switch over to the Congress was the proverbial last straw for the socialists. They described the Congress and Prime Minister Nehru as the greatest enemies of the poor. Nehru too began attacking the Socialist Party, without naming Jayaprakash Narayan (JP). Some twenty years later, JP picked up the thread where he had left it to join issue with Indira Gandhi.

The curious thing is that both Nehru and JP were disillusioned by socialism towards the end of their lives. Nehru said that socialism was a means to an end and the not end which could provide welfare to man. A month before JP died, he rang me from Patna to ask me to bring together some economists and thinkers to devise an Indian way of development because he had concluded that ideologies like socialism and communism had lost their purpose because they had failed to uplift the people.

Recollection of certain events is meaningful. One such was the second meeting of the National Development Council, sometime in the early 1950s. All the state chief ministers were present. Nehru was pushing the agenda which would combine his form of socialism with the private sector. No one at the meeting understood what he was getting at. The chief ministers and members of the Planning Commission requested Nehru to write the introduction to the Second Five Year plan, spelling out his vision for the future.

In his piece, Nehru envisaged the commanding heights of the economy being in the hands of public sector undertakings and said that a poor country like India had no option but to turn towards the Left. After two years of the Second Five Year Plan he assured the nation: 'I will not rest content unless every man, woman, and child in this country have a fair deal and attains a minimum standard of living.' What struck me was his remark: 'Wait for another ten years and you will see that our plans will change the picture of the country.' Nehru lived nine years after that speech but the condition of the common man did not improve.

I once asked JP whether Nehru was a socialist. He recalled how Nehru, while wanting the socialists back in the Congress fold had argued that 'an attempt at premature leftism may well lead to reaction and disruption'. JP was critical of Nehru who, he said, wanted to build socialism with the aid of capitalism.

The national income over the First and Second Five Year Plans (1951–61) rose by 42 per cent, but whom had it benefited? Nehru appointed a committee to find out why the common man had not benefitted. P.C. Mahalanobis (founder of the Indian Statistical Institute) headed the committee. The committee found that the 'concentration of economic power in the private sector was greater than what could be justified as necessary on functional grounds'. It questioned 'how far this is an inevitable part of the process of economic development, how far it can be justified in terms of economy of scale and full utilization of scarce managerial and entrepreneurial resources ... and how far the growth which has taken place is unhealthy and anti-social in its consequences'. A report on the current pattern of economic development, if prepared, would arrive at the same conclusions.

Even though the radicals found the Mahalanobis report to be grist to their propaganda mill, they could not make a convincing case against the private sector because the report itself was not categorical on its role. Therefore, the phrase, socialistic pattern continued to be used by the Congress.

Yet, what Nehru had in view was the building of heavy industry for the production of capital goods as a base for a modern, strong country, and on the wide expansion of village industries for the manufacture of consumer goods and provision of large-scale employment. Many years later, Manmohan Singh, leading the government, adopted something similar with less emphasis on village industries.

Vote-bank politics had already begun in Nehru's time. Maulana Azad enquired which constituency he should contest from and was told by Nehru to choose a place with a substantial Muslim population. Azad opted for Gurgaon constituency, including Mewat where there was a substantial Meo (Muslim Rajput) population. When Zakir Hussain heard about this he said that Azad should have contested from a Hindu-majority seat so that if they were to defeat even a person like him, they would have proved that their avowed faith in secularism was a sham.

Nehru found little time for the party organization and still less for the Gandhians who were annoyed that they were not being consulted on any policies or programmes being formulated by the government. After waiting for years, Acharya Vinobha Bhave, Mahatma Gandhi's closest disciple, invited Nehru and Pant to his Paunar ashram, near Wardha in 1959, to exchange views. Vinobha told them that they had strayed away from the 'Gandhian path'.

Nehru had liked Vinobha's Bhoodan movement, that had motivated landlords to donate a part of their land for distribution among the landless. When Sheikh Abdullah had distributed land to the tillers in Kashmir without compensation to the landowners, Nehru had congratulated him. Nehru had himself effected the first amendment to the Indian constitution when the Supreme Court had held that the requisition of land for public purposes should be on the basis of 'just compensation'. The amendment required the government to lay down the principles of compensation.

Nehru was not against compensation but argued that the land owned by the zamindars was given to them by Britain for their loyal services to the Raj. He couldn't accept feudalism in a country which they were determined to convert into a welfare state. Subsequently, the land acquisition act was passed in 1984 when the quantum of compensation was considered to be the market price. Both governments at the Centre and in the states have played havoc with the right to acquire the land for public purposes.

The discussion at the ashram degenerated into heated arguments, and Nehru found the questions taking the form of an inquisition. Vinobha said in general terms how difficult it was for any government or individual to match up to Gandhi's standards, but the real attack was launched by an elderly lady at the ashram. She said that the government had betrayed Mahatma Gandhi's principles. I could see Nehru's face first showing discomfort and then annoyance. He could not contain his anger and told her that he too knew about lapses and irregularities in the working of the ashram and the Bhoodan movement. He had purposely kept silent but 'if you want to discuss economic development, you should give me the chance to point out the humbug that went in the name of Gandhiji'. Pant controlled the situation by taking the lady to task for levelling vague charges, and the discussion ended on a sour note.

This was where I first heard that Congress President V.N. Dhebar was resigning and Indira Gandhi was taking over. Pant had supported Nehru at Vinobha's ashram but not at the CWC when Indira Gandhi was nominated as the party president. He was careful not to oppose Nehru's daughter directly but argued that her frail health would come in the way of the extensive travels the Congress president was required to undertake. Raising his voice, Nehru told Pant that 'she was healthier than both of us' and could put in longer hours of work. The subsequent discussions, as I noted, were to fix the date on which she would assume charge. This was the first time that dynastic politics came to the fore, and the Congress since then has been following the practice of invariably having a member of Nehru family at the helm of affairs. It assumed a ridiculous form when Robert Vadra, husband of Priyanka, daughter of Sonia Gandhi recently during the UP legislative assembly election in early 2012 said that he was willing to join politics 'if people wanted'.

Left to Nehru, he would have liked Indira to succeed him as prime minister, but too many Congress leaders, with a long stint of sacrifice and struggle for the country's freedom, were still on the scene at the time. Nehru did not possess the dictatorial traits necessary for him to ignore them.

How simple, in comparison, was Shastri can be deduced from a single incident. He was the home minister when we were returning from the Qutub after a function. One single security man sat in the front seat of the Ambassador car, the vehicle which all ministers, including Prime Minister Nehru would drive in.

When we reached what is now the All India Institute of Medical Sciences, the railway crossing was closed. Shastri saw a sugar-cane crusher selling juice. 'Why not have some juice until the gate opens,' Shastri said. Before I could say anything, he got down and went to the sugar-cane stall. Both of us had a glass each, Shastri paying for it. Strangely, no one recognized us, not even the sugar-cane juice vendor. Even had he entertained any suspicion about the identity of his customer, he must have cast it aside because he could not have imagined that the home minister would come to his stall for juice.

Shastri found it difficult to make both ends meet as the salary of an MP was small. I persuaded him to write for newspapers. His first article was on Nehru, understandably all laudatory. I organized his syndicate service on the lines on which I had set up mine some thirty-five years later. The article was placed with the *Hindu* in the south, with *Amrita Bazar Patrika* in the east, the *Hindustan Times* in the north, and the *Times of India* in the west. Each paper paid Rs 500 per article. An additional income of Rs 2000 made a big difference. Shastri's second article was on his hero Lala Lajpat Rai. Before he could write the third, Nehru had a stroke in Bhubaneshwar at the AICC meeting in 1962. Shastri was recalled to the cabinet and I returned as his information officer.

Shastri in his quiet way began dealing with the files marked to Nehru. Indira Gandhi did not like her father's choice and would see important files herself before returning them. Shastri learnt of this but did not protest. Nehru had treated him with affection and he did not wish to create a situation in which Nehru would have to choose between him and Indira Gandhi.

Nehru's recovery was slow and a rumour meanwhile spread that he was seriously ill. I also acted as Nehru's information officer when the person attached to him went on a week's leave. I had Nehru photographed in a side profile in which he looked healthy and released the pictures to the press. The rumour died, but I knew that the stroke he had suffered had left a permanent mark and he would not live for long.

My first face-to-face meeting with Nehru was in 1963, when I reported to him what Chester Bowles, US ambassador to India, had said at a press conference. I was nervous and spoke rapidly in English. He asked me to repeat it slowly and in Hindustani. The gist of Bowles' remarks was that America wanted India to take the initiative to foster good relations with Pakistan. Nehru did not react.

A few days later, when the prime minister visited Jaipur, I accompanied him in his car from his residence to the airport. The newspapers had reported his advice to IAS probationers. Vijayalakshmi Pandit, accompanying him up to the airport, asked him about the speech. Nehru pointed towards me from the back seat and said: 'This was his doing.' I had briefed the press on the advice he had given the probationers that they should pay special attention to the common man.

One night in winter the Bharat Sevak Samaj, a voluntary organization, requested Nehru to accompany them when they distributed blankets among the homeless. Nehru agreed to distribute the blankets, sometimes wrapping them around those sleeping in the open. His remark while doing so was: 'Why don't they revolt?'

This incident might prick the conscience of today's leaders. Bhim Sen Sachar, then chief minister of Punjab, approached Nehru with an embarrassing request. Vijayalakshmi Pandit had stayed at the Shimla Circuit House, then part of Punjab, and had not paid the bill of Rs 2500. Sachar was told by his governor, C. Trivedi, to put the expense under some miscellaneous state government account. However, Sachar was a stickler for propriety. Nehru said that he could not clear the bill at one go but would pay the Punjab government in installments. Nehru sent the amount in five installments, each time drawing a cheque on his personal account.

When I was still Nehru's information officer (1963) I saw Shastri, then out of the government, waiting for his turn to meet the prime minister. I complained to N.K. Sheshan, Nehru's private secretary, that Shastri had been waiting for an hour for the meeting. Sheshan took me aside and said that he had twice sent the message upstairs to Nehru's bedroom. 'What can I do when she [Indira Gandhi] is not calling him,' said Sheshan, and advised me to keep away from 'their politics'.

Morarji Desai expressed his indifference to Shastri's entry into the cabinet; Jagjivan Ram made it publicly known that he opposed Shastri being taken back. Recalling the Kamaraj Plan, he said quite indignantly that on the carrom board of politics Nehru had used Shastri as the 'striker' to drive out the men he did not like.

When Nehru tried to make Shastri, leader of the House, there was opposition within the party, particularly from Morarji Desai, and the proposal had to be dropped. Nehru did not want a contest lest the party should split during his lifetime. He devalued the post and a relatively unknown person was appointed leader of the House.

Shastri was dejected, but from that day he realized that he would have to brave Desai's firm opposition if he was to become prime minister. Shastri had a knack of keeping his own counsel and therefore never showed any disrespect to Desai, nor did he project himself as a candidate. He, however, tilted still more on the side of the old guard (the syndicate) in the Congress while, at the same time, giving an impression of being a non-factional, non-controversial individual.

If Shastri nurtured the belief that his ministership was a stepping stone to prime-ministership, he was mistaken. As soon as Nehru recovered slightly, all important files and papers went direct to him and Shastri would learn about their disposal many days later through the courtesy of some indulgent deputy secretary or joint secretary. 'I am only a glorified clerk,' he often said.

One day he received a request from Kenya to nominate a delegate to an international labour conference. He suggested the name of Abid Ali, a

Congress leader known for his standing in Labour circles. Rajeshwar Dayal, then foreign secretary, did not accept the recommendation and went directly to Nehru to have the name changed. Shastri learnt about the rejection of his recommendation only through routine papers and felt humiliated.

As the days went by, such instances piled up. In fact, he had to wait even to get an appointment with Nehru and at one point thought of resigning from the ministry. Once he told me that he would return to Allahabad. 'There is nothing for me here now,' he said. He then added woefully: 'If I continue to stay in Delhi I am bound to come into a clash with Panditji. I would rather retire from politics than join issue with him.' Two considerations however made him stay. One, the syndicate did not want him to give up the position of vantage he occupied as cabinet minister, even though No. 4 in rank. Two, by quitting, Shastri did not want to erase the impression that he was the successor because that was how he was viewed when he was brought back to the government.

Many people told him that Nehru's behaviour was influenced by Indira Gandhi's 'hostility' towards him. Initially Shastri would never encourage such doubts but later he would go out of the way to find out if that was true. In due course, he became convinced that he was not uppermost in Nehru's mind as his successor. Indira Gandhi was more open about ignoring him and would herself take important files to Nehru.

I ventured to ask Shastri one day: 'Who do you think Nehru has in mind as his successor?' '*Unke dil main to unki saputri hai* [In his heart is his daughter],' said Shastri, 'but it won't be easy,' he added. 'People think you are such a staunch devotee of Nehru that you yourself will propose Indira Gandhi's name after his death,' I said. 'I am not that much of a sadhu as you imagine me to be. Who would not like to be India's prime minister,' was Shastri's reply. Krishna Menon did not think that Nehru was grooming Indira Gandhi for a bigger role. He told me that 'the impression got around when she became the Congress president. Nehru really wanted democratic procedures to take their own course'.

Nehru was steadily declining in health. The Congress party spoke in whispers about his possible successor. Top Congress leaders, K. Kamaraj from Madras state, N. Nijalingappa, from Karnataka, N. Sanjiva Reddy from Andhra Pradesh, and Atulya Ghosh from West Bengal, all opponents of the intractable Morarji Desai, vowed at the temple town of Tirupati to have Shastri as Nehru's successor. He was the key that fitted all locks.

Even so, there was an atmosphere of uncertainty. Only a week before his death, Nehru had jokingly said at a press conference in New Delhi that his life was not ending 'so very soon'. Why didn't he appoint a successor? To this question of his successor, Nehru usually said: 'If I nominated somebody that would be the surest way of his not becoming my successor. Winston Churchill nominated Anthony Eden and Eden did not last long.'

Nehru was, however, impressed by Shastri's gentle yet effective approach in tackling volatile situations. He had sent him to calm the tense situation that had developed in Kashmir after the disappearance (December 1963) of the holy relic *(Moe-e-Muqadas)*, a lock of Prophet Mohammad's hair, from the Hazratbal shrine near Srinagar. As a result there were demonstrations in Kashmir and Calcutta witnessed a Hindu–Muslim riot. B.N. Malik, then India's intelligence chief, was sent to Srinagar to assess the situation. He submitted an alarming report, and saw the hand of the interned Sheikh Abdullah behind the theft. However, Bakshi Ghulam Mohammed, the outgoing prime minister of Kashmir, alleged that it was the doing of his political opponents, G.M. Sadiq and D.P. Dhar.

On receipt of Malik's report, New Delhi seriously considered the imposition of rule by the Sadar-e-Riyasat in the state but held its hand when it realized that with Bakshi Ghulam Mohammed in the opposition the Kashmir government might not garner sufficient votes in the Assembly for ratification of such an order, which had to be put into effect within six months of the suspension of popular rule.

Fortunately, the holy relic was traced when it was being smuggled to Pakistan. However, Maulvi Mohammed Farooq, a Kashmiri leader who had constituted an 'action committee' to trace the relic, alleged that the 'recovered relic' was not genuine. Once again tension began building up. Shastri's predicament was how to arrange a *deedar* (display) to establish the identity of the relic.

It was indeed a tense atmosphere when we reached Srinagar in January 1964. Shastri, in heavy winter clothes (the overcoat was Nehru's) paced up and down the ground at Hazratbal where patches of snow defiantly remained despite the sun. The identifiers were a little late. Anxious, Shastri, who was not given to revealing his emotions, smiled in relief when they eventually arrived. As soon as the relic was declared *haq* (genuine), Shastri informed Nehru. This averted the worst because New Delhi was even prepared, if need be, to declare martial law in the state.

After the relic's recovery, Pakistan found that it was whipping a dead horse. The situation improved so greatly that Nehru sent orders for the release of Sheikh Abdullah (8 April 1964) whose detention always bothered him because they had been close friends. The only contact between the two in eleven years took the form of a couple of messages from Nehru which Abdullah insultingly ignored. However, when the Chinese attacked India in October 1962, Abdullah wrote a letter to Nehru to remind him that his warning of Chinese 'untrustworthiness' had been proved correct.

The long detention had made Abdullah bitter. I invited him and Mirza Afzal Beg, Abdullah's close associate, to lunch one day after their arrival in New Delhi. He said that the ratification of the state's accession by the constituent assembly was not valid because he was not present there. He compared Kashmir to a beautiful woman whom both India and Pakistan 'wanted to ravish'.

Nehru asked Shastri to hold talks with Abdullah on Kashmir but nothing came of these meetings. How could it have when Abdullah's mind was filled with the idea of an independent Kashmir? When Shastri could not pin him down to any specific demand, he asked him: 'Sheikh Sahib, what you have in mind is independence?' Abdullah said: 'Yes.' Shastri was so perturbed by this reply that he said in public later that India would not allow Abdullah to propagate independence for Kashmir.

Abdullah now worked hard on Nehru. Once a respected guest at the prime minister's house, he was back there. Abdullah told me that he found Nehru 'genuinely sorry about what he had done to me'. The result of the reunion between the two was that India initiated another effort to contact Pakistan to resolve the Kashmir problem. When Abdullah suggested that he should visit Pakistan and meet Ayub Khan to find a solution, Nehru concurred. By that time Abdullah told me he (Nehru) had realized that 'he should not leave the Kashmir problem unresolved'.

Ayub Khan and Abdullah met in Rawalpindi on 24 May 1964. According to what Ayub told me, Abdullah brought no specific proposals but wanted 'me and Nehru to meet'. Ayub's version was:

> I asked Abdullah what made him think that a meeting would bring about a solution of the Kashmir problem. His reply was that Nehru was a changed man. I knew that Abdullah was wrong but I did not want to disappoint him. My impression is that Nehru wanted to tire me out.

However, in his book, *Friends Not Masters* (1967) Ayub Khan wrote: 'Abdullah brought the absurd proposal of a confederation between India and Pakistan and Kashmir.' Refuting Ayub's claim, Sheikh Abdullah later told me that no specific proposal was placed before Pakistan. Checking government records and Nehru's papers on his talks with Abdullah, I found no mention of the confederation proposal.

The version of K.H. Khurshid, president of Azad Kashmir and formerly Jinnah's private secretary, whom I met in Lahore, was that he met Abdullah for nearly four hours during his visit to Pakistan and did not find any evidence that Abdullah was proposing a confederation. 'What he was seeking was a soft border between the two parts of Kashmir so that people on both sides could travel, meet, and trade freely,' Khurshid said. 'This might have led to other things.' I thought Khurshid was right.

Whatever the proposal might have been, it proved to be a non-starter because Nehru died when Abdullah was still in Pakistan.

Those were days when the Government of India was experimenting with inducting experts from the private sector to head ministries. Mantosh Sondhi was hired as secretary of the ministry of steel. I too suggested to my ministry that if the government could bring persons from outside to man ministries why could it not loan its employees to the private sector. This was in the context of my wishing to have a stint in the private sector. The then Information Minister Satya Narain Sinha agreed to my suggestion and gave me two years leave with a lien on the PIB job. That made it easy for my family to let me join UNI, but I never returned to the government.

UNI's principal handicap was that it did not have a good address. It had started its operations from a flat in Khan Market (then a sleepy little market and now one of the most expensive commercial areas in the world to rent). As the sponsors were keen to start a news agency without any delay, any premises would do. The key sponsors of UNI were: the *Hindu*, *Hindustan Times*, *Amrita Bazar Patrika*, *Hindusthan Standard* cum *Anand Bazar Patrika* and the *Nation* from Patna. Later, *Deccan Herald* too joined them. I was able to persuade Shastri to allot UNI a government bungalow near the office of the Indian Eastern Newspaper Society (IENS), an association of newspaper proprietors.

Though started on a very positive note, UNI was soon making such a loss that the sponsors wanted to close it down. S. Mulgaonkar, editor of the *Hindustan Times*, then chairman of the UNI board, was in favour of running it a little longer in order to see whether the agency could emerge as a competitor to the Press Trust of India (PTI), a premier news agency.

He had once offered me the editorship of *Searchlight*, a paper which the Birlas, owners of the *Hindustan Times*, had started from Patna. He asked me whether I would like to try my hand at running UNI and was confident that he could persuade the sponsors to continue with the agency for another six months and extend the period if it showed improvement in its operations. I accepted his offer despite my wife's opposition to my leaving the PIB.

UNI had limited staff which was conscious of the sword of damocles, i.e. closure, hanging over its head. The agency's outside stations were generally manned by a single individual who functioned as a journalist-cum-teleprinter operator. My first job was to boost their morale and inspire them with the expectation that UNI could survive.

I wanted to make a mark and this occupied my thoughts. It could be effected by breaking news first and giving short tight copy to lessen the burden of editing in newspaper offices. As I had maintained contacts with the home ministry I could do exclusive stories. My friend, Rajeshwar Prasad, Shastri's secretary, helped me, both wittingly and unwittingly. For politicians, I was a familiar figure because they had seen me first with Pant and then with Shastri. This enabled me to get to know and report on what was happening in the government and the Congress party.

Our best bet, I told the staff, was the economic field which was beginning to yield news and catch attention. The Planning Commission was the principal source of this. One UNI reporter covering the beat, after obtaining permission from me, regularly paid an operator who gave us a copy of every document he cyclostyled. We broke stories on economic subjects almost everyday. Tarlok

Singh, a senior member of the Planning Commission, knew me well. He called me once because UNI had carried a top secret note from the ministry of commerce which it had sent to the commission for its comments. He asked me how I got the information. He was too much of a gentleman to threaten me but he used every other method at his command. My reply was that journalists never disclose their sources.

What was frustrating for the editor and general manager, the title I used, was to wait outside the rooms of editors and proprietors to sell the UNI service at a pittance. Ram Nath Goenka (RNG), proprietor of the Express group, was a difficult nut to crack. Along with Shanti Prasad Jain, owner of the *Times of India*, he had started a news agency which had failed within a few weeks. Goenka was wreaking his vengeance, although the *Times of India* had become one of the agency's sponsors. Many months of patient waiting resulted in Goenka eventually buying the UNI service.

The Express group of newspapers was forced to buy UNI because it felt that it was missing stories, as Goenka told me. Doing political stories with inside information and taking the path which news agencies did not follow made newspapers and politicians take notice of what UNI transmitted.

We would freely report on cabinet meetings. Once Indira Gandhi held a two-day meeting of the cabinet without officials to ensure there was no leakage. She did not suspect her ministers when we reported discussions in cabinet meeting in detail. She remarked that it seemed as if Kuldip was sitting in at the cabinet meeting.

The best compliment came from the PTI within six months of my joining UNI. The then general manager, Ram Chandran, approached me to come to an arrangement whereby the two agencies did not compete but divided their spheres of activity. His proposal was that UNI should cover world events and have exclusive contracts with foreign news agencies. PTI, he said, would confine itself to domestic affairs; the Indian scene. I declined his offer because a news agency which did not cover its own country had no role.

News agencies were in a way indebted to the establishment because a substantial amount of money in our form of subscriptions came from the government. All India Radio was the top buyer. There was no TV those days.

The government was, however, annoyed with UNI because of our story on the negotiations that the government was holding with the Nagas in Delhi. For days, newspapers reported only the daily press note that the talks were being held in a cordial atmosphere. Nothing more was mentioned. I met members of the Nagas National Council conducting the dialogue, and found that there was a deadlock. The Nagas had stuck to their original demand for independence and the government had once again rejected it. It was a situation which I thought the public should know about. I told the PIB that UNI would be running what the Nagas had said, but would like to include the government's version in the story. The PIB told me not to run the story because it was not in the 'country's interest'.

We ran the story that the Nagas had not abandoned their demand for an independent sovereign state. The Government of India, the story said, had rejected the demand outright. When Prime Minister Indira Gandhi saw the story, she was livid. Yashpal Kapoor, then Indira Gandhi's aide, asked me over the phone to withdraw the story. We knew each other well. I had advised him to get into the Foreign Service which was being constituted some years earlier. He had replied that he saw no reason to accept a clerical post when Indira Gandhi would be the prime minister one day. He proved to be correct. His long service with her had enabled Kapoor to acquire considerable political weight, which he used at her bidding.

I told Kapoor that we were willing to run the government version, an offer we had made earlier. The government never came back to us but the cabinet presided over by Indira Gandhi rejected the UNI application for an increase in subscription. Raj Bahadur, then minister for information and broadcasting, telephoned to inform me that Indira Gandhi was angry about the Naga story. The note he had put up before the cabinet had proposed Rs 2 lakh as the subscription, and Indira Gandhi had slashed this to half. He said the story had cost UNI a lakh of rupees a month.

⚜

When in the home ministry, I found that it maintained tabs on the various political parties. Information about them, received from the intelligence bureau, was maintained and updated. Every political party, except the Congress, was profiled and an assessment made of how close it was either to the communist views or communalists' views.

The emphasis on the communist relations was greater in relation to China than the Soviet Union. A section of a note, captioned 'Anti-national Propaganda by Communists in Border Areas', prior to China's attack on India, is reproduced below:

> The Communist Party has launched a systematic propaganda in the frontier districts with a view to subverting the local population. The modes of propaganda are, holding of meetings, enacting of dramas and circulation of publication. The extension of the party's influence is carried out by formation of Kisan Sabhas, Student Fronts and Unions of low-paid workers. To ensure their support, local issues are invariably exploited.

State inspector generals of police still discuss the Left movement at their annual meeting in Delhi. Of course, the focus is now on Maoists from the law and order point of view.

7

LAL BAHADUR SHASTRI AS PRIME MINISTER

Nehru Passes Away, Succession, the Indo-Pak War and the Tashkent Declaration

Pandit Jawaharlal Nehru died on 27 May 1964. His physician, Dr K.L. Wig, had given specific instructions that he should not be left alone and yet there was no one with him when Nehru went to the bathroom, where he fell and died. Wig told me that Panditji must have been lying on the floor for over an hour before he was found in that condition. It was pure negligence, he said. Though his poor health was no secret, nobody expected him to die so soon.

The news of Nehru's demise spread throughout India like wildfire. The nation was numbed; a sense of insecurity and uncertainty prevailed. After the cremation, I rewrote the introduction of the UNI story: 'The man who was Jawaharlal Nehru was now a handful of ashes.' For me, he represented all that India was after Independence. In sixteen years he had built institutions, public-sector undertakings, and a polity that was open, democratic, and secular. Above all, he had been instrumental in giving the nation a constitution that would ensure the fundamental rights of individuals, which his daughter, Indira Gandhi, suspended eleven years later.

For the cremation, priests were flown in from the temple town of Varanasi to chant Sanskrit mantras. Water was brought from the holy Ganga to be sprinkled over the body. Fragrant sandalwood was stacked over the pyre. As is customary among Hindus, the closest younger male relative present, Sanjay Gandhi, then 18 years old, lit the pyre.

All this was in stark contrast to what Nehru had stood for. He had declared in his will, written a decade earlier, on 21 June 1954:

> I wish to declare with all earnestness that I do not want any religious ceremonies performed for me after my death. I do not believe in any death ceremonies and to submit to them, even as a matter of form would be hypocrisy and an attempt to deceive ourselves and others.

That Nehru was opposed to religious mumbo-jumbo was narrated to me by his private secretary M.O. Mathai, who was one of the two signatories to Nehru's will, and had served him for almost fifteen years until 1960. He blamed Indira Gandhi for disregarding his wishes. 'This was all Indira Gandhi's and officiating Prime Minister Gulzarilal Nanda's doing; it was they who had earlier arranged at Teen Murti House (then the prime minister's residence) the *jaap* for Nehru's long life,' Mathai said. A Delhi-based astrologer, who performed the *jaap*, claimed that Indira Gandhi ensured Nehru's presence during these ceremonies.

According to Mathai, Vijayalakshmi Pandit was also opposed to such religious ceremonies but 'she was helpless'. When I inquired about this from Nanda, he said that the recitation of 'the death-conquering mantra' was done 4,25,000 times with Nehru's 'understanding', and he would often attend the ceremony.

Nanda claimed that the *jaap* did help lengthen Nehru's life by four to five years. 'Nehru would have lived longer,' he said, 'had he not taken a particular individual into his cabinet after his illness at Bhubneshwar.' On the astrologer's advice, Nanda said, 'Nehru had tried to withdraw the name but by then the list had reached the president.' Nanda was of course referring to Lal Bahadur Shastri. I did not believe Nanda because the prime minister could always have altered the list before the swearing-in ceremony.

Tiruvallur Thattai Krishnamachari (TTK), who was a close associate and a minister in Nehru's cabinet for almost a decade, once told me that Nehru had 'become religious' in his last days. 'In 1954 he refused to go into a south Indian temple when asked to take off his shirt but at the time of his death copies of the *Gita* and the Upanishads were at his bedside,' TKK said.

Whether the *Gita* and the Upanishads are scriptures or philosophical treatises is a matter of opinion. For Nehru, as he once wrote, 'there was a compelling reality about them', and he considered them to have been written not by any supernatural power but by human beings, 'very wise and far-sighted but nevertheless ordinary mortals'. He always carried with him a copy of the *Gita* and an abridged version of the UN charter.

Was his religion godless like the Buddha's because he found himself incapable of thinking of a deity or of any unknown supreme power in anthropomorphic terms? Mathai told me that if he adhered to any faith at all it was Buddhism. Otherwise, Nehru's religion was like the Deist Movement in England, barely distinguishing God from Nature. Alternatively, was his religion merely humanism? A painting of beautiful Kullu hills adorned his study. André Malraux, a French intellectual and author told me in New Delhi that Nehru had once said: 'It may be that Truth is my supreme value. I don't know, but I can't do without it.'

Someone once asked him: 'What do you think of God and man's relation to God?' Nehru reflected for a moment and then answered ponderously,

It is a difficult question to answer precisely. Man's conception of God itself is not fixed and constant throughout the ages. For example, God is conceived in the Old Testament as a disdainful, fearful father, as a wrathful creature, a punishing agent for every sin and sacrilege committed by Man. But in the New Testament, the conception of God changed. Here God is conceived as a loving, benign father; he is ready and willing to forgive you even if you commit wrong. This change in concept was a development that shaped man's ideas about God throughout the course of human civilization.

Agnostic or believer, people loved him. I was present at Nehru's funeral, a dot in an ocean of mourners who had been swelling on the bank of the Jamuna in the rapidly-gathering gloom of 27 May 1964. A vast stretch of the riverside, including Raj Ghat, 300 metres from where Mahatma Gandhi, Nehru's political guru, was cremated sixteen years earlier, was inundated with people. As smoke rose from the pyre, I heard the sobbing of thousands and watched their faces wracked with agony. Grief had fused us all – Hindus, Muslims, Christians, and Sikhs – into a community of sorrow.

I believed Nehru always chose soft options, making compromises when he should not have and was painfully slow in changing India's economic contours which made poverty indelible. He was, however, my hero and I would rationalize the deficiency on the ground that he had to carry with him all interests, regions, and religions to keep the country united. Even so, I felt that after Patel's death and before the rupture with China, Nehru had twelve years when he could have taken India on the path of development and laid deeper foundations for a welfare state.

There was too much of Gandhi in him to convince him that only through harmonizing different interests, characterized by him as a mixed economy, he could lead the country to rapid growth which, to use the phrase of my friend Raj Krishna, had remained anchored to the Hindu rate of growth of 3.5 per cent.

A man of the world, a man of the masses, a master of the written and spoken word; innumerable images flashed through my mind at this death. I was stirred by his thoughts which combined the modern with tradition. I went back to his *Discovery of India* to read: 'Life is a continuous struggle of man against man, of man against his surroundings; a struggle on the physical, intellectual, and moral plane out of which new things take shape and fresh ideas are born.'

How Nehru would cope with poverty was the nation's dilemma. I thought, and wished, he would follow Gandhi's concept of self-sufficiency, with villages as the base. At the same time I wanted India to be a modern developed country like the US and UK with a large middle class with pronounced socialist policies. Was the Gandhian way of ushering in preeminence of villages possible, employing democratic, non-violent methods?

Even as Nehru's body lay at his residence, talk of who would succeed him began. The syndicate, as elderly Congressmen were described, was united behind Lal Bahadur Shastri, a minister without portfolio. Home Secretary V. Vishwanathan read too much into the succession battle, and sent a message to all state governments that there was great tension in Delhi. This was quickly followed by his directive that the security forces should take all precautions against subversive activities. Military officials and men were recalled from leave. This notwithstanding, there was never even a whiff of a coup d'etât.

In fact, the Chief of the Army Staff General J.N. Chaudhuri suffered a heart attack on the day of Nehru's funeral. It was true that he had summoned 6000 troops from the Western Command to Delhi, but they were called solely for ceremonial purposes, to line the route and control the mammoth crowd at Raj Ghat. Moreover, General Chaudhuri had informed the president, Dr Radhkrishnan, about the movement of these 6000 men. Vishwanathan claimed that he had ordered the army's march past to scotch any rumours.

Nehru might not have designated his successor but he left behind a durable political structure which could smoothly elect a leader, and this happened quite seamlessly. The real hotbed of activity on Nehru's cremation day was Morarji Desai's residence at Thyagaraja Marg. The lawn and the veranda were thronged with people, and at least two of his supporters, Tarakeshwari Sinha, minister of state for finance, and Kanti Desai, Morarji's only son, were armed with a list of Congress MPs, with a tick or a question mark against their names to indicate whether they supported Desai or Shastri as the next prime minister.

As a newsman, I went to Desai's house to confirm his candidature for prime-ministership. Though I could not meet him his supporters were very clear: 'Come what may, Morarji will contest and win hands down.' One person even took pains to explain how strong men like Pratap Singh Kairon from Punjab, Biju Patnaik from Orissa, Balwant Rai Mehta from Gujarat, C.B. Gupta from UP, and P.C. Sen from West Bengal, all state chief ministers, had already pledged their loyalty and support to him. 'Tell your Shastri not to contest,' said Kanti, who knew I had served as his information officer.

I reached Shastri's house late in the evening. He said: 'I would prefer a unanimous election,' and after a pause, added: 'Were a contest to become inevitable, I would like to stand against Morarji*bhai* because I can defeat him, not Indiraji.' Then, as if he was speaking of an ideal arrangement, he said: 'We need a person like Jayaprakash Narayan to head the government at this juncture.' Shastri then asked me to carry a message to Morarji suggesting an agreed choice. Shastri proposed two names: Jayaprakash Narayan and Indira Gandhi, in that order.

I went to Morarji's house and conveyed Shastri's proposal to him. About Jayaprakash Narayan, Morarji's remark was: 'A confused person' and about Indira Gandhi: 'That chit of a girl.' He made it plain that the only way to avoid a contest was to accept him as the leader. It was Congress President K. Kamaraj who intervened and persuaded the party to choose a consensus candidate and was entrusted with the task of finding one.

After assessing the atmosphere in the two camps, I put the following story on the UNI ticker:

> Mr Morarji Desai, former finance minister, is the first one to throw his hat in the ring. He is believed to have told his associates that he is a candidate. Mr Desai is understood to have said that there must be an election and he for one will not withdraw.
>
> The minister without portfolio, Mr Lal Bahadur Shastri, is considered another candidate, though he himself is reticent. According to circles close to him, he would like to avoid a contest as far as possible.

I did not realize that this news item would do as much damage to Morarji as it did. Coming from the government's Press Information Bureau (PIB), I could not visualize the impact of the printed word. His supporters said that it cost them at least 100 votes. Word went round that Morarji was so ambitious that he had not waited even for Nehru's ashes to get cold before making a bid for leadership.

I realized subsequently how much the story had helped Shastri. Kamaraj whispered in my ears, while walking down the steps of Parliament House, 'Thank you'. Shastri called me to his house to say: 'No more story; the contest for leadership is over.' He meant that the story had swung the pendulum in his favour and that he was as good as elected.

I tried to explain to him that the story was never meant to help or harm anyone. He concluded the meeting by placing a finger on his lips. Later, when he was elected leader of the party, he embraced me on the steps of Parliament House in the presence of everyone as an expression of gratitude.

Shastri asked me to rejoin the PIB and become his press information officer. I told him I was prepared to return provided he gave me the status that the press secretary of the US president enjoyed. Shastri said he could do so but then 'Morarji Bhai will say that I have repaid your debt'. I did not join his staff.

Even so, Morarji remained convinced for the rest of his life that I wrote the story to favour Shastri. Whenever I broached the topic with him, he would say: 'Shastri had his own way of using people, even without their realizing it.' In fact, Morarji should have blamed his own supporters, who were confiding in everyone on the day of Nehru's cremation that the prime-ministership was in their pocket. That kind of talk horrified other members of parliament.

Kamaraj declared that the consensus was behind Shastri, and he was formally elected as the party leader and appointed the new prime minister. Morarji never accepted the verdict and alleged that Kamaraj had manipulated the consensus.

Unlike Nehru, who submitted a handwritten list of his ministers, Shastri had it typed and did not show it even to Kamaraj before sending it to the president. Indira Gandhi was reluctant to join the cabinet and Shastri too was not keen to give her an important portfolio, always conscious of the challenge she posed.

Without doubt, the meek had inherited the earth. A man who during the 1942 Quit India movement lost his typhoid-stricken daughter because he had no money to buy her medicines was now India's prime minister. When Shastri was out of government under the Kamaraj Plan, he reduced his meals to one dish and gave up eating relatively expensive potatoes, the vegetable he liked most. Poverty had, however, taught him humility, and people found that an endearing trait. It stood him in good stead in the political field which was full of men of arrogance, conceit, and false pride. He had learnt from experience that cooperation was far better than conflict. He quoted to me Gandhi's observation on the assumption of office: 'Sit light, not tight.'

Within days of becoming India's prime minister, Shastri had a mild heart attack, his second. Unofficially, I was still looking after his publicity. I gave out that because of excessive strain the prime minister had been advised by his doctors to rest. I was among the few visitors who met Shastri within a few days of his illness. He looked a touch pale but he was otherwise fine.

I told Shastri that there was a book by an American journalist Welles Hangen, entitled *After Nehru Who?* (1963). The Almighty would give him a long life but the question was 'After Shastri Who?' He became a bit pensive and said: 'If I was to die within one or two years, your prime minister would be Indira Gandhi, but if I live three or four years, Y.B. Chavan will be the prime minister.' (Several years later, when I told Chavan about Shastri's prophecy, he said 'Kuldip, you must write about it in one of your columns'.)

Shastri asked me who in my view would be the best foreign minister as doctors had advised him to give up the portfolio which he, like Nehru, had retained. I suggested the name of Indira Gandhi. Shastri said: 'Nayar Sahib, you do not understand politics. She wants to be the prime minister. The portfolio of foreign affairs would make her more important.' I then proposed the name of M.C. Chagla, education minister in his cabinet. Shastri said that he wanted to have good relations with Pakistan. Chagla, being a Muslim, would bend backwards to be anti-Pakistan to demonstrate his impartiality.

The portfolio was subsequently entrusted to the experienced Swaran Singh. Though Indira Gandhi joined the cabinet she wanted a light portfolio. She got information and broadcasting. (She was upset when she saw her ministry issuing a calendar showing Nehru with his hand placed on Shastri's shoulders looking much like the leader and his protégé.) In a country where Nehru was regarded as a god, this step to add to Shastri's stature and standing was not to her taste.

Shastri was reticent about speaking about himself. With great effort I was able to find out why he resigned as rail minister in 1956 because of a stray accident. He said that as the portfolio was under him he felt personally responsible for what went wrong. Ministers must take moral responsibility when departments under them seriously falter.

When I told him that there were complaints of a trade connection relating to his elder son, Hari, Shastri said that Hari would have to leave the house. Shastri's wife was livid and had it communicated to me that I had no business in interfering in their family affairs. I knew that Hari was asked to leave the house although he returned within a few weeks. He was able to convince Shastri that the complaints were unfounded.

President of Pakistan, Gen. Ayub Khan welcomed Shastri's succession as a 'Good augury for Indo-Pakistan relations'. He told me that Shastri was 'really keen to have friendly relations with Pakistan but did not live long enough. 'Nehru was not serious about burying the hatchet with us.' He, however, added poignantly, 'It is a strange irony that when Nehru realized that he should probably make up with Pakistan, he died, and when the climate was favourable after the Tashkent Agreement, Shastri died.'

Shastri had repeatedly told me after the 1962 debacle that India would be able to normalize relations with Pakistan but not China. He saw an opportunity to hold talks with Pakistan when returning from Cairo after attending the meeting of non-aligned nations in October 1964. On his own initiative, Shastri met Ayub Khan at Karachi. It was a goodwill gesture but Pakistani officials tried to use the occasion to reiterate their position on Kashmir.

Rajeshwar Dayal, once India's envoy to Pakistan, was asked to draft a joint communiqué on the talks in conjunction with Zulfikar Ali Bhutto, then foreign minister, and Aziz Ahmed, then Pakistan's foreign secretary. Dayal had to seek Shastri's intervention as the two Pakistani representatives argued that a joint communiqué had no meaning unless Kashmir was specifically mentioned. Ayub Khan, at Shastri's request, told his team not to insist on Kashmir's inclusion in the communiqué and therefore it was not eventually mentioned at all.

Even though Ayub Khan agreed to Shastri's suggestion, he reportedly made a contemptuous remark about Shastri: 'How can I have any talks with a person who does not have even physical stature?' After Nehru's death, Ayub Khan thought he had inherited his mantle in Asia; Pakistan was also becoming something of a success story at that time. Viable economically and militarily, the country had begun to be noticed. Pakistan was content with Shastri's assurance that he would like more time to initiate steps to end the tension between the two countries. Ayub Khan reportedly said that he was willing to wait but in the meantime nothing should be done to 'further integrate the state [Kashmir] with India.' According to Dayal, with whom I checked, no such assurance was ever given or sought.

Shastri was very concerned about corruption, which was then beginning to rear its head. He set up a committee under K. Santhanam, a senior Congress leader, to suggest ways to stop corruption. For government employees he converted the Special Police Establishment (SPE), a department in home ministry, into the Central Bureau of Investigation (CBI). The SPE was intended to process complaints against central government employees and investigate their conduct. The scope of the SPE was expanded to look into corruption of contracts in the award by the central government. The SPE had a small office in the penthouse of North Block above the home ministry office. Shastri seriously considered the appointment of a Lokpal (ombudsmen) as Santhanam had proposed.

The CBI assumed importance only during Indira Gandhi's time. For her it was a machinery to chastise her critics and harass her opponents. The CBI then became an instrument of tyranny, used for all purposes it was not intended for. This has remained the practice and no government after Shastri's has kept it above politics. The BJP-led government was no exception even though the party tried to occupy a high moral ground.

Several CBI directors have told me, and many have written books, to cite cases in which the prime minister had directly intervened to save the guilty because they wielded political power. Chandra Shekhar, even during his brief stint as prime minister, ordered the then CBI director not to pursue cases against Chandraswami (the 'godman'), who was later arrested on charges of repeated financial irregularities.

The CBI has no jurisdiction over the states. It operates only if a particular state gives it permission to undertake an investigation or seeks its services. Its powers are still governed by the charter that the SPE held. The Centre has tried to extend the scope of CBI investigations to other parts of the country but very few states have agreed to this.

Following the policy of giving no quarter to the corrupt, however high, Shastri took action against Punjab Chief Minister Pratap Singh Kairon on the basis of the S.R. Das Commission Report within a few days of its submission. The commission had held him guilty. Shastri sent his cabinet secretary to Chandigarh to seek Kairon's resignation. However, Kairon claimed that Shastri had punished him because of his friendship with Morarji Desai (Rajinder Puri, the famous cartoonist, drew a cartoon to comment on Kairon's exit: 'It was not Das Commission's report but a UNI report').

My disclosure of Justice H.R. Khanna's inquiry report on allegations against Biju Patnaik, former chief minister of Orissa, was equally upsetting and drew wide attention.

The probe covered the period when he occupied office. Shastri appointed a Committee of three cabinet ministers, TTK, M.C. Chagla and Ashok Sen, to examine the inquiry report and recommend action, if any, to the government. Though the press reported on the committee's meetings almost everyday, it did not disclose anything about the report.

One evening I went to meet Ashok Sen, whom I knew well, and asked if I could borrow the report for an hour to go through it. To my surprise, he agreed on the condition that I would return it the following morning. This was a big task because the report was voluminous.

Returning to the UNI office, I called all the teleprinter operators and reporters known for their typing speed and distributed the pages from the report among them. We worked through the night and made five copies of the report. As promised, the following morning, I returned the report to Sen. (Photocopying machines had not yet come to India; I am talking of a time as far back as forty years.)

Before releasing our story, I met Patnaik at his residence on Aurengzeb Road in New Delhi. I told him that I wanted his version so that I could run both, the report and his defence. First, he threatened to sue me and UNI for rupees one crore each. Then he offered to buy shares of UNI and also purchase the service for his daily paper, *Kalinga*, provided I did not release the story. It was a tempting offer because UNI was then a struggling news agency, not even earning enough to cover the salary bill. I told him that I would await his response for 24 hours. If I did not hear from him, I would run the story.

When I did not hear from him I ran the story. Many papers used it on the front page.

True to his word, Biju sued me and UNI. What could we do? Legal experts advised us to establish the authenticity of the report. This, they said, could be done if it was made public. One way of doing this was to place it on the table of any of the two Houses in parliament. I entrusted this work to the bulky, the senior-most correspondent in UNI.

Our effort to place the report in the Rajya Sabha was foiled by the then chairman S. Radhakrishnan. He expressed his unhappiness over the attempt. Finally, Joshi was able to persuade the stormy petrel H.V. Kamath to place the report on the Lok Sabha table.

Kapur Singh, the Speaker was not too happy with the ruling Congress and gave permission to Kamath to place the report on the table of the House. Suddenly it was all over.

Our rival news agency, PTI, had to run the report because it was a big disclosure. When the then home minister Gulzarilal Nanda was asked in parliament whether the report placed on the table was genuine, he said he could neither deny nor confirm it. This was quite an embarrassing moment for the government. Parliament was up in arms. Prime Minister Lal Bahadur Shastri ordered a CBI inquiry into the matter.

Aware that he was unfamiliar with modern finance, Shastri picked L.K. Jha, an economic expert, as his principal secretary. He was the founder of the PMO, which during Nehru's time was confined to one officer, Tarlok Singh.

Jha's first job was to reconstitute the Planning Commission which he had wanted to join but had failed to do. He restricted a member's tenure to five years. Tarlok Singh, by then the seniormost member, had to leave.

Shastri was not in favour of a planned economy but wanted to convey in deference to Nehru that there would be no break with past policy. He did not reverse any economic programme but declared a one year 'holiday' for the Plan. What this meant was that rather than taking up new projects or programmes, the old ones would be strengthened to consolidate gains.

🕉

I could sense Shastri's approach when I discussed with him the questions he might face at his first press conference as prime minister. He held only one in Delhi throughout his tenure, unlike Nehru who had fixed the first Wednesday of every month for a press conference. Spelling out his approach, Shastri told me that his government's priority would be to bring down food prices. This would allay the hardships of the common man. The second step, he said, was to have projects broken up in terms of jobs. He would ask all ministries to translate the outlay into the number of people they would employ. He did not speak about socialism but would often speak about the Gandhian concept of self-sufficiency in rural India.

Shastri's first encounter in foreign affairs was his participation in the non-aligned conference at Cairo in 1964. I found him cautious and a little overawed. He felt he did not enjoy Nehru's stature. Still, he was determined to leave his own imprint, however hazy. He did quite a commendable job but was always compared to Nehru.

Shastri's simplicity was his forte. I thought I would help him to highlight that image through my dispatches for UNI on whose behalf I had gone to Cairo. As I had direct access to him, I found that his frugal meal was prepared in his hotel room. I sent a story that Shastri was cooking his own food at the Hilton in Cairo. The story boomeranged and the Hilton management issued a statement that it would sue the Indian prime minister for blackening the walls of the hotel room with soot.

Gamal Abdel Nasser, president of Egypt, came to the airport to bid goodbye to Shastri. Chou En-lai, the first premier of the People's Republic of China was also at the airport at the same time, returning from an international conference. Nasser asked Shastri whether he would like to meet Chou En-lai, but Shastri declined the offer. He told me that he was tempted to meet him but feared the repercussions at home.

Shastri was keen on projecting himself on the world stage. Before going to Cairo he received Chester Bowles, the US ambassador who extended President Lyndon B. Johnson's invitation to Shastri to visit the US. Bowles added that the First Lady wanted to meet Lalita Shastri too. However, before Shastri could collect his thoughts on the US visit, Johnson withdrew the invitation.

Pakistan had reportedly exerted pressure on the US not to enter the picture at a time when Ayub Khan was trying to build a new equation with India after Nehru's demise. Shastri never forgave Johnson for the insult and rejected his subsequent invitation to stop in Washington when flying to Canada. Bowles told me that Johnson was sorry to have withdrawn the invitation to a person he described as 'god's man'.

Shastri, instead, went to the Soviet Union. Soviet leaders were at home with 'socialist Nehru' but wanted to know more about Shastri because they prized their relationship with New Delhi. It was also apparent that Russia did not want all its eggs in India's basket in the post-Nehru period and wished to normalize their relations with Pakistan.

Shastri was specifically told that Soviet support to India on Kashmir would continue. A few years later, Moscow changed its stand when it stopped saying or publishing anything that might hurt Pakistan's susceptibilities and damage their relations.

Nonetheless, when overzealous Gulzarilal Nanda, then home minister, proposed to extend Articles 356–7 of the Indian constitution to Kashmir, there were loud protests in Pakistan that Shastri had 'betrayed' the promise to Ayub Khan. The two Articles were intended to enable the president of India to extend the Centre's rule to Kashmir in the event of a breakdown in the constitutional machinery of the state and to empower parliament to make laws during that period. The Indian Ministry of External Affairs was, however, opposed to the changes because it feared that they would again attract the attention of the international community which had more or less accepted the status quo in Kashmir. Nanda, however, had his way and got Shastri to sign the papers which he had kept pending for many weeks.

Pakistan called it an 'annexation' of Kashmir. Foreign Minister Zulfikar Ali Bhutto, who was trying to build his image as a tough anti-Indian leader, prepared a working paper, which came to be known as the Bhutto Plan, to argue that if India was to be tackled at all, now was the time. He was able to impress the army with his plan for a war with India.

The extension of the two Articles irritated the Kashmiris because it meant greater proximity to Delhi, which was anathema to them. Nibbling away at Kashmir's autonomy, I think, was against the spirit of the accession. When Kashmir joined the Indian union, Srinagar gave New Delhi control over only three subjects: defence, foreign affairs, and communications. It was for Kashmir to expand these, not for the Union to unilaterally appropriate more. India's one-sided steps created a lot of trouble for it many years later.

Kashmir was not a priority for Shastri. He was more concerned about the language controversy. An enthusiastic official in the home ministry, with Nanda's (who was minister of home affairs) approval had issued a circular stating that Hindi would become the principal official language of the Union and English an additional language from 26 January 1965, a formula which the Parliamentary Committee on Language had devised but Nehru had rejected it outright. The *Gazette of India* appearing on that day for the first time had the Hindi masthead: *Bharat Ka Raj Patra.*

A directive on greater use of Hindi in the central government departments indicated that notes on certain files would begin to be written in Hindi, although an English translation would be appended for the benefit of those who were not proficient in the language. A letter received in Hindi would be answered in Hindi. Official circulars and communiqués would be issued in both Hindi and English. It was an effort to establish the pre-eminence of Hindi as the national language.

I considered the *Gazette* notification contrary to Nehru's assurances to non-Hindi speaking states and feared trouble. I was not wrong. The southern states regarded the home ministry's circular as a violation of Nehru's undertaking that the switch over to Hindi would take place only when non-Hindi speaking states were ready for it. To appease the Hindi-speaking population, Nehru had said 'English cannot be in India anything but a secondary language in future; in the nature of things, mass education will be in our language.'

Ironically, the circular on language was issued on Republic Day when a 21-gun salute welcomed President Sarvepalli Radhakrishnan to a colourful parade in New Delhi. However, in his home state, Tamil Nadu, there were riots: in Madras, a youth burnt himself to death, a grim form of protest that most people had till then associated only with South Vietnam.

The circular was not only withdrawn but also disowned. Shastri was personally in favour of Hindi because that was the language in which he felt most at home (unlike Nehru who, according to his colleague Maulana Abul Kalam Azad, muttered in English even in his sleep). In the face of the agitation in the south, which had primarily supported Shastri's prime-ministership, he had no choice other than to give an 'official assurance' that the introduction of Hindi for 'the official purposes of the Union' would be regulated in a way that would not cause any hardship to people who did not know the language. C. Subramaniam, the union minister for food, resigned from the central cabinet in protest. He told me that it was Shastri, not Nanda, who had clandestinely tried to impose Hindi.

When O. V. Alagesan, another cabinet minister from Madras state, submitted his resignation, Shastri said in a broadcast that Nehru's assurance 'will be honoured in letter and in spirit without any qualification or reservation'. Shastri told me that he had wanted to accept the resignation but 'the two presidents [Radhakrishnan and Kamaraj] did not allow him to do so'.

Waiting for an opportunity to strike at Shastri, Morarji said that giving legal sanction for the implementation of Nehru's assurance extended at the time of the agitation in the south would be a 'surrender to violence'. Forever seeking a consensus, Shastri then convened a meeting of chief ministers of all states. Those from the Hindi-speaking states clashed with those from the non-Hindi ones. As a concession, Shastri offered to fix a quota in the All India Central Services for each state so that knowledge of Hindi would not be an advantage for the Hindi-speaking states. The home ministry was asked to process the proposal which the union cabinet found 'retrograde' and 'harmful' to the country's integrity. The riots subsided after Shastri's assurance but the agitation of 1965 led to major political changes in Tamil Nadu – the Congress lost the 1967 assembly elections to the DMK and has not been able to regain power since.

❁

The language stir had barely subsided when Shastri and the country had a more vital problem to face: Pakistan's incursions in the Rann of Kutch in Gujarat. The border in this area, which was a swamp for seven months a year, had remained un-demarcated.

Pakistan's action united the nation as the attack by China had done in 1962. New Delhi had known about the incursions since 25 January 1965 when a Gujarat police patrol had noticed a freshly laid 32 kilometre heavy-vehicle track 2.4 kilometre inside the Indian territory. It must have taken Pakistan some time to lay the track. This had a familiar ring, because the Aksai Chin road built by the Chinese, north of Ladakh, was also discovered only when it was nearing completion after months of construction. There was, however, one difference. In the case of the Aksai Chin road, the government took five years to take the country into confidence, but in the case of the road in the Rann of Kutch, Shastri, who was all for good relations with Pakistan, did not keep the nation in the dark, as Nehru had done in order to foster friendship with China.

Logistics favoured Pakistan because it had an airport near the border. Rawalpindi deployed a complete infantry division, one regiment each of medium and light tanks including some US Patton tanks, and some other paramilitary units. Pakistan also brought two squadrons of US F-86 fighter bombers to the nearby airport.

When Islamabad brought in US fighters, New Delhi protested to Washington because the planes were obtained by Pakistan through the US military aid programme. In 1954 the US had supplied arms to Pakistan in a bid 'to contain Communism'. President Dwight D. Eisenhower had written in a personal note to Nehru:

> What we are proposing to do and what Pakistan is agreeing to is not directed in any way against India and I am confirming publicly that if our aid to any country, including Pakistan, is misused and directed for aggression I will undertake immediate act in accordance with my constitutional authority, and take appropriate action both within and without the UN to thwart such aggression.

Philip Talbot, then US assistant secretary of state, had assured B.K. Nehru, India's envoy to Washington, that Pakistan was only authorized to use the arms against Communist aggression.

India produced a photograph of Patton tanks on the Kutch border. Washington asked Rawalpindi to allow a US observer to visit the site of conflict. To this, Gen. Ayub Khan's reply was that Pakistan was entitled to use all its arms to defend its territory. However, at a garden party in Karachi a few days later, Ayub Khan told Walter McConaught, then US ambassador to Pakistan: 'You can send a military observer any time. We have nothing to hide.'

At Shastri's insistence, Washington did send a team and found the Pakistani brigade in the Rann equipped partly with the weapons that the US had sent. Had the US been firm at that time and told Pakistan not to use the arms they had supplied against India, the subsequent war between India and Pakistan might have been averted. Moscow's post-Khrushchev policy to befriend Rawalpindi also encouraged Pakistan to flex its muscles. Russia had not yet supplied arms but the fact that the leader of the Soviet Union had welcomed Pakistani leaders to Moscow caused Rawalpindi to believe that if it ever came to a conflict between Pakistan and India, the USSR would remain neutral. New Delhi suspected that this might well happen, and I could see that Shastri was disturbed about the prospect.

India claimed that Kanjarkot, Chhadbed, and Birabet in Kutch had always been part of its territory but Pakistan said that the Rann of Kutch was a disputed area and even according to international practice the boundary must run through the centre of a waterbody (the Rann).

New Delhi wanted to go all out to recover the area but the army chief, Gen. J.N. Chaudhuri was against it. The army was not yet ready for a war against Pakistan, an eventuality that Chaudhuri embarrassingly faced. Dr Ram Subhag Singh, an articulate MP, one day chided Gen. Chaudhuri in his room: 'You Bengalis are probably afraid to fight. We Biharis are not.' Chaudhuri handed him a machine gun lying in his room, which Dr Singh found even difficult to lift!

I knew that Shastri was not in favour of India–Pakistan hostilities. He had frequently told me so. At a cabinet meeting, while discussing the Rann of Kutch, he said he could not reconcile himself to a war between India and Pakistan. Harold Wilson, the British prime minister, used all his tact and pressure to persuade Shastri, who was then in London to attend the Commonwealth Prime Ministers' Conference, to agree to arbitration. For India to agree to the Rann of Kutch being labelled disputed territory and to accept a third party award was a great concession on it's part. The award, announced on 18 February 1968 did not uphold India's claim to the entire Rann of Kutch. Of a total of 3,500 sq miles, 350 sq. miles were given to Pakistan.

Shastri felt that war would spell disaster for the subcontinent, and in fact repeated the offer of a no-war pact to Pakistan, as Nehru had done at one time. Pakistan, however, rejected the offer. All this seemed to have exhausted Shastri's entire fund of goodwill for Pakistan during those days. He explained to me later:

> Pakistan mistook my desire not to fight as a sign of weakness. It thought that I would never go to war and Pakistan tried to take undue advantage in Kashmir. When it did so, I was convinced that Pakistan was not serious about good relations and peace with India. I decided to act.

The award, criticized by the public and the press alike, also affected Shastri's thinking. Hardly had the ink on the Kutch ceasefire agreement dried when incidents on the Kashmir border increased (to almost 300 a month). There were vague intelligence reports that Pakistan was training infiltrators to be sent into Kashmir. Each report was different from the other and therefore the government found it difficult to gauge the nature of Pakistan's preparations. It was, however, inferred that something serious was brewing across the border.

A top-level meeting of military officials, at which the army chief was himself present, was held in Srinagar on 2 August 1965 to study the situation. Surprisingly, they concluded that Pakistan posed no immediate threat. Two days later, the army received clear evidence of infiltration from Pakistan.

Mohammad Din, a young farmer had reported to the police that while tending to his cattle near Gulmarg, 40 miles north of Srinagar, he had met two armed strangers wearing green *salwar* and *kameez*. They offered him Rs 400 for information on the location of Indian army posts. In Mendhar sector, Jammu, a few suspicious looking armed men had contacted another person, Wazir Mohammed. Both men, pretending to cooperate with the Pakistanis, had reported the matter to the Indian authorities.

The army immediately sent patrols which encountered a few raiders who, after some resistance, fled back to the other side of the ceasefire line. Three days later, on 8 August, two Pakistani officers, both captains, Ghulam Hussain and Mohammed Sajjad, were captured. During interrogation, they admitted that a large scale infiltration was planned and that they were the lead team of the Pakistani forces planning to seize Jammu & Kashmir by force. This was corroborated by documents found in their possession.

The documents revealed that the plan for massive infiltration was hatched as early as January 1965. At that time, through a presidential ordinance, a *mujahid* force was formally constituted, and its training began in May 1965 under the overall direction of Maj. Gen. Akhtar Malik, then general officer commanding Pakistan army's 12th Infantry Battalion. The raiders were to enter the state in small groups between 1st and 5th August, gather at central points, and then attack the Valley from various directions. The raiders expected to mingle unnoticed with the thousands of people congregating to celebrate the festival of Pir Dastagir Sahib on 8 August.

On the following day, which coincided with the anniversary of Sheikh Abdullah's arrest by Nehru, the raiders were first to join a demonstration scheduled in Srinagar, and then to capture the radio station, airfield, and other vital centres. A few other columns of infiltrators were to cut the roads connecting Srinagar with other parts of the state in order to isolate the capital. Eventually the raiders were to form a 'revolutionary council', proclaim themselves the lawful government, and broadcast an appeal for recognition and assistance from all countries, especially Pakistan. A copy of the proclamation was to be broadcast over Radio Kashmir on 9 August. The 'broadcast' was to be the signal for Pakistan to move in for the kill.

The early detection of infiltrators accentuated the pace of events. There was a spate of serious incursions throughout the Jammu & Kashmir border, all aimed at capturing the Valley. It appeared that the infiltrators had been given specific tasks such as destruction of bridges, disruption of lines of communication, attacks on military formations, and the distribution of arms and ammunition to local civilian sympathizers. The invaders set about their task, with missionary zeal and were confident of a spontaneous response from the people who they had come to 'liberate' but the local population kept themselves aloof.

On 8 August the infiltrators managed to enter the suburbs of Srinagar. The state government panicked and suggested the Centre to impose martial law in Jammu & Kashmir. Accordingly, the central government asked the army to take control of the entire state. The army commanders, however, dissuaded the government from such an action and assured it that the situation was not as bad as had been painted by the state government.

On the night of 8–9 August 1965, for the first time, the entire ceasefire line exploded with intensive and continuous firing from across the border. In the Poonch area, Pakistan shelled selected targets with 25 lb guns. The infiltrators, roughly 3,000 in the state, made a daring raid on the brigade headquarters but there were no casualties. Pakistan, through the press and radio, was at great pains to explain that the events in Jammu & Kashmir were 'a spontaneous local insurrection' in which it had no hand.

During the night of 9–10 August there was a comparative lull in the Valley. That very night some infiltrators were fired upon when attempting to slip back into Pakistan. This was the first indication of the infiltration of traffic in the reverse direction. Once the infiltrators met with resistance, they withdrew. The operation had failed.

Lt Gen. Harbaksh Singh, heading the Western Command, said in his report to the government:

The Pakistanis borrowed a leaf from the teaching of Mao Tse-tung in their plan to instigate an insurrection in J&K under the guise of a spontaneous 'Liberation Movement'. But it was in the implementation of the Chinese doctrine on the subject that the Pakistani leadership faulted and fell. To succeed in this form of subversive warfare, requires meticulous organization, detailed planning, a high standard of training, aggressive leadership, and universal local support. Without these basic essentials, a liberation movement is bound to fizzle out – as it did in J&K.

Meanwhile, New Delhi intensified its diplomatic initiative to garner foreign opinion against the infiltration from Pakistan. B.K. Nehru met US Secretary of State Dean Rusk, and explained, as did other Indian envoys in the countries to which they were accredited, that Pakistani army officers were leading 'massive infiltration' in gross violation of the ceasefire line. Rawalpindi claimed that no Pakistani soldier was involved. Kewal Singh, Indian high commissioner to Pakistan, met Zulfikar Ali Bhutto who said it was only an 'uprising' in J&K.

The UN secretary general, to whom India complained, described the situation as a 'dangerous threat to peace' but did nothing beyond summoning Lt-Gen. R.H. Nimmo, head of the UN military observers' group in Kashmir, for consultation. His interpretation was that the ceasefire agreement applied only to the armed forces on either side, not to civilians, armed or unarmed. However, in a subsequent report, he did confirm that armed Pakistani infiltrators had crossed the ceasefire line in an attempt to destroy strategic communication targets.

Shastri was surprised to receive a letter from Soviet Prime Minister Alexei Kosygin, who did not side with India. Kosygin wrote (4 September) that 'the rights and wrongs of the present situation were hardly of any importance at the moment ... The main efforts should be concentrated on the immediate termination of military operations and stop tanks and silence the guns.' His letter equated New Delhi with Rawalpindi and blamed both the countries for playing into the hands of 'American imperialism'. Indeed, Moscow's tilt towards India had ended.

General J.N. Chaudhuri, then chief of the army staff, told me:

> After 5 May 1965, I was working out the appropriate moves to attack Pakistan if and when it attacked Kashmir. The day Pakistan moved its regular troops, infantry and armour into the Jammu sector, I was in Kashmir. As I was coming back, in the plane to Delhi, the Director of Military Operations who was in the aircraft with me started writing out the required signals to go to the formations concerned. On landing he sent them out and I immediately went to see the Defence Minister who formally confirmed my action. I then informed the Prime Minister.

Disappointed, Shastri was now on the side of the hawks who maintained that Pakistan must be taught a lesson. Rawalpindi had launched a massive attack on 1 September in the Akhnur–Jammu sector by crossing the ceasefire line. Two days later, on 3 September, Shastri ordered the Indian army to cross the international border and march into Pakistan. The actual attack came on 6 September, and would have come a day earlier had not the Indian air force wanted to pound the 'enemy' bases first. It hardly did so. The Pakistan air force attacked Pathankot airport on the afternoon of 6 September and destroyed thirteen Indian planes.

After the war, I asked Shastri who gave the specific order to cross the international boundary. 'I did,' he said. According to Shastri, Chaudhuri and others were taken aback when he asked them to march into Pakistan. Harbaksh Singh told me that the army could never forget 'this tallest decision by the shortest man'.

In 1966, a few days before Nehru's birth anniversary (14 November), when I met Indira Gandhi, I asked her who took the decision to march into Pakistan? She said: 'We, the Cabinet Committee on Defence did when the army commanders told us that it was necessary to engage Pakistan forces elsewhere to relieve pressure on Jammu & Kashmir. Shastri accepted the advice of the army commanders.' I asked what her father would have done. 'He would have also gone by the advice of the army commander,' said Indira Gandhi. I am sure that Nehru, a stickler for the rights and wrongs in the world affairs, would not have crossed the international border.

Some critics think that Shastri, who was 'diminutive physically and otherwise', wanted to do something extraordinary to add to his stature and, therefore, went to war against Pakistan. His explanation was however that the war was forced on him. It is true that the action against Pakistan made him a hero. Before the war, I would hear titters from the audience at cinema halls when his picture appeared on the screen. His image soared after the war.

The fact was that Shastri had very little choice. He had to open a second front in Pakistan to relieve pressure on Indian troops greatly outnumbered and out-positioned in the Chhamb sector and the Poonch–Rajouri and the Jammu–Srinagar roads. The only link with the Valley was threatened. If the road had been cut, all Indian forces in Jammu & Kashmir would have been isolated: Indian units were operating in difficult terrain in that area and could only use light tanks while Pakistan was in a position to move in its heavy ones.

'I want to reach Lahore before they enter Kashmir,' Shastri told Gen. Chaudhuri. Plans to attack Pakistan already existed because at the time of the Kutch confrontation the two countries had almost reached the point of war. In fact, a few days earlier, Gen. Chaudhuri had told Lt. Gen. Harbaksh Singh, as he confirmed to me, that India should be ready to attack Pakistan across the international border within 48 hours because of the pressure on it to take Chhamb. This was exactly what happened.

Lt. Gen. Harbaksh Singh was clear that India must move towards Pakistan if the latter ever 'marched' on Kashmir. Therefore, when Chhamb was attacked, and in the process Pakistan crossed nearly a quarter of a mile of international border, he repeated Nehru's warning that any attack on Kashmir was an attack on India. Harbaksh Singh's argument was weighty, particularly when it was difficult to hold Kashmir because of the way Pakistani forces were advancing in the Chhamb sector.

'Operation Riddle', a three-pronged attack on Pakistan was mounted from Amritsar, Ferozepur, and Gurdaspur, and two days later, on 8 September, the Sialkot front was opened. Sialkot was the base from where Pakistan had planned its attack on the Chhamb sector. They, however, did not have an armoured division. General Tikka Khan, Pakistan's army commander, told me that they were able to hoodwink the Indian army through field phone conversations that Indians intercepted, indicating that the armoured division was positioned at Sialkot. 'But this was not true. You could just have walked in,' he said.

Harbaksh Singh told me that Gen. Chaudhuri wanted him to withdraw the forces behind the Beas for better defence but he refused. When I checked with Chaudhuri, he said that he was not the kind of general who would brook disobedience. The explanation probably was that Chaudhuri 'wanted' Harbaksh to withdraw but never ordered him to do so.

It was really a border war because the theatre of hostilities did not go beyond 15 miles on each side; India occupied 470 sq. miles of Pakistan's territory and 270 sq. miles of Pakistani-occupied Kashmir (PoK). Pakistan's gain of Indian territory was to the extent of 210 sq. miles The Indian forces did not disturb East Pakistan because what they had sought to achieve in the western region was already beyond their capacity.

I must confess that most of my insight into the 1965 war was based on Harbaksh Singh's report which he sent to the Statesman to be published when I was its resident editor. I used some of it in my book, The Distant Neighbours, a book on India–Pakistan relations. He approached eminent lawyer Nani Palkhivala to sue me. Palkhivala told him that he did not wish to take up the brief because 'both of you are my friends' and advised him to make up with me. Thereafter, Harbaksh Singh did not speak to me for five years.

When the two sides stopped fighting, both had exhausted most of their ammunition. For Pakistanis it was a jehad against Kafir Hindus. One example was that of a wounded young Pakistani officer, captured in the Ferozepur sector, who refused to accept blood transfusion, saying: 'I would rather die than accept the blood of a Kafir.' That officer died, but there were instances of jawans on both sides being looked after by soldiers from the villages to which they had belonged prior to Partition.

Once at a seminar I asked Gen. Chaudhuri why India's advance was so slow. His said that India wanted to destroy Pakistan's armour; not to occupy territory. Subsequently, Air Marshal Arjan Singh reiterated that India essentially fought a war of attrition; what really mattered was the extent of damage inflicted on Pakistan's armed forces. Harbaksh Singh also told me that the decision taken before attacking Pakistan was not to take Lahore. 'That was not our military aim.'

Gen. Chaudhuri confirmed that the Indian army never wanted to occupy Lahore. He was aware that Lahore was well defended and that a great many Indian troops would be tied up in the occupation of the city which by itself would have achieved little. Later, he said during a discussion with journalists, that the occupation of Lahore would have meant feeding a civilian population of almost one million.

The real reason for not going into Lahore was the fear of street fighting for which the Pakistan government had prepared the population: 'Fight with doors, windows, sticks, knives, or whatever you can find,' was the call to the streets of Lahore and the people responded to it. The fact that India was unable to capture Lahore led other countries to believe that the war was a draw.

During the war Shastri used RSS volunteers to regulate traffic in Delhi. The organization approached him and he saw no harm in posting its men at different points. This, however, conveyed a wrong message to Muslims who were already feeling insecure. In fact, Muslims became suspect in the eyes of many Hindus as soon as the tension with Pakistan rose over the Rann of Kutch. It got aggravated after the 1965 war.

The limited war was over on 23 September. Four days later, Shastri said to the disgruntled soldiers in the Ferozepur sector that he had to agree to the ceasefire because of foreign pressure, particularly from the US upon whom India depended for food and economic aid. Surprisingly, he did not mention the Soviet Union which also wanted us to end the war.

Those were the days when Washington began reconsidering its policy on Kashmir and had second thoughts about whether a plebiscite would be the correct solution to the problem. The US now believed that India and Pakistan must reach a solution between themselves and that outside interference would not help. More recently in November 2010, President Barack Obama declared the same stand in public.

India's war with Pakistan made one thing clear to all: India did not consider Kashmir a disputed territory but an integral part of the country. Nehru's 1952 New Year message had come true: 'If Pakistan by mistake invades Kashmir, we will not only meet them in Kashmir but it will be a full-scale war between India and Pakistan.' This made people like Jayaprakash Narayan change their stand on Kashmir completely. He used to say that the future of Kashmir was to be determined by discussions among New Delhi, Srinagar, and Islamabad. Now he issued a statement to announce that Pakistan had lost its locus standi in Kashmir and that the parties to the dispute were Delhi and the people of Kashmir.

The two foreign powers which sullied their reputations in India's eyes during the 21-day war with Pakistan were the UK and China, particularly the former. Shastri had gone to the extent of hailing the Commonwealth as 'an association which can help to further peace and friendship amongst nations'. This was in line with what Nehru told the state chief ministers when India accepted membership of the Commonwealth: 'It was desirable to maintain some form of association with the UK and the Commonwealth because this seemed to me advantageous, both from the national point of view and that of world peace at large.'

Here, however, was Harold Wilson of Britian, the hub of the Commonwealth, accepting Islamabad's version and saying in a prepared statement on 6 September 1965 that 'he felt deeply concerned, especially at the news that Indian forces have today attacked Pakistani territory across the international frontiers in the Punjab'. While Shastri criticized London privately, Indira Gandhi attacked it publicly: 'One of the strange quirks of the contemporary scene is that countries who are pledged to democracy and freedom so often lend their support to dictatorships and to censure freedom.'

As regards China, it first sent a note that Indian troops had violated the Tibet–Sikkim border. Subsequently, on 18 September, it issued an ultimatum that New Delhi should either dismantle its 56 military installations in Sikkim within the next three days or face 'grave consequences'. The ultimatum rattled New Delhi and Shastri did fear an attack from China. However, after shelling some posts in Sikkim and Ladakh, the Chinese gave up their game of bluff with the claim that India had itself demolished the military structures in question.

Peking's behaviour was strange because Shastri had heard only a few months earlier from Edgar Fauré, a former prime minister of France, after a visit to China, that he thought conditions existed for 'fruitful talks' between India and China.

Shastri was worried but felt reassured after India's chargé d'affaires, Jagat Mehta, a distinguished foreign service officer, sent a three-page telegram from Peking to argue why China would not attack India. Shastri congratulated him after the ceasefire for his correct reading.

The US gave an assurance to Shastri that it would not allow India to go under. Between themselves, Washington and London reportedly discussed plans to provide India with air cover in the event of China attacking so that the IAF would be free to strike Chinese targets: Nehru too had requested air cover towards the end of the Sino–India war in 1962. Shastri told me that Nehru had written letters to President John F. Kennedy seeking air cover.

One of Nehru's letters: 'begged for US help not just in "our fight for survival" but for "the survival of freedom and independence in this subcontinent and the rest of Asia".'

The Soviet Union had always favoured bilateral talks, and Kosygin successfully brought the two sides together across the table in Tashkent after the UN Security Council failed to get them to withdraw their forces from each other's territory. The US had tried to host such a meeting but Shastri was not enthusiastic about their involvement. To Ayub Khan, Kosygin wrote that Tashkent was famous for its pullao; to Shastri, a vegetarian, Kosygin's invitation spoke of the historic background of the town.

India's initial reaction was unfavourable and a cable was sent to T.N. Kaul, then India's ambassador to the USSR, to communicate a refusal to Moscow. He did not forward the reply and instead sent a long cable to Delhi requesting the prime minister to reconsider the decision against the background of the Soviet support on Kashmir and the fact that Moscow was staking its prestige in proposing such a conference. The Indian cabinet thereafter reconsidered its earlier decision and asked the ambassador to accept the proposal.

Pakistan's inside information was that India would refuse, but when it sent its acceptance, Rawalpindi had no choice but to agree. Shastri justified his acceptance to newspaper editors by arguing that he would try to retain Hajipir and Tithwal, the vantage positions in Kashmir which India had captured during the war. The best thing, he said, would be to have a conference in order to persuade Pakistan to commit itself to 'certain things' in exchange for withdrawal from the territory India had occupied. I felt he was preparing the country for a withdrawal from Hajipir and Tithwal, the posts which India was extremely keen on retaining as they were important for the control of Kashmir.

Before leaving for Tashkent, Shastri asked his finance minister, T.T. Krishnamachari to resign, suspecting that he had made fun of him behind his back. Of greater concern for Shastri was that TTK and Indira Gandhi had formed a united front.

This was not the first time that TTK was obliged to leave the cabinet. Seven years earlier he had resigned following certain questionable transactions undertaken by the Life Insurance Corporation, a public sector undertaking that had allegedly taken orders from him. At that time Nehru had told his colleagues that TTK had to leave because 'the minister must shoulder the responsibility for any decision or action of his secretary'. Nehru had then written to the state chief ministers to praise TTK's 'great ability and perseverance', adding that 'his leaving us had been a great blow to me and to our Government'.

TTK's exit from the Shastri government was also said to be because of pressure from the US. The story that went around was that President Lyndon B. Johnson got rid of two ministers in the subcontinent: TTK from India and Bhutto from Pakistan, both anti-American. When I asked Bhutto if he was crowded out by Ayub Khan at Johnson's insistence, his reply was:

> I am one of the few politicians who have staged a comeback after having been eliminated by both great powers [US, USSR]. Poor Krishna Menon alienated one of them and he never could effect a recovery.

After TTK's resignation, Indira Gandhi observed that it was only matter of time before she too would be crowded out under pressure. According to a senior Congress leader, Dinesh Singh, then very close to her, she even spoke in terms of settling down in the UK and inquired about the cost of living there and the royalty that the books written by Nehru earned. Indira Gandhi realized that Shastri had gained new strength and was receiving a hero's welcome wherever he went. He even introduced a new salutation, *Jai Jawan, Jai Kisan* (victory to the soldier; victory to the farmer) which went down very well with the masses.

When Shastri went to Tashkent he took along with him two plane-loads of journalists and told me that those from the English language press were bound to oppose him but those from the vernacular press would right the balance. He expected me to help him strike this balance.

Shastri was well aware that he would have to vacate Hajipir and Tithwal. The Security Council's unanimous resolution (20 September 1965) called upon India and Pakistan to withdraw 'all armed personnel back to the positions held by them before 5 August 1965', and both the US and Russia were insistent it be implemented. How long would he be able to withstand the pressure from them given India's dependence on both of them?

From the very outset of the Tashkent Conference (beginning 4 January 1966) it was clear that Pakistan's aim was to revive the question of Kashmir and India's to avoid it. In his inaugural speech at Tashkent, where I was present, Ayub Khan said that he would sign a no-war pact with India once the 'basic problem', meaning Kashmir, was resolved. Shastri did not oppose a no-war pact, which he said would help 'improve the totality of relations between India and Pakistan'.

Bhutto, the foreign minister, was in sour mood from the very outset. While the Pakistani delegates greeted Shastri's inaugural speech with loud cheers, Bhutto sat impassively with his arms crossed. After the speeches, Ayub Khan, at Shastri's instance, walked to a private room reserved for discussions, Bhutto wanted to join them. Ayub Khan, however, gestured in the negative, making Bhutto visibly angry.

The meeting was brief, and Ayub Khan suggested a formal agenda for the talks. Shastri did not think this was essential because he could foresee what this would imply a discussion on Kashmir which he wished to avoid. However, Kosygin was able to persuade him to discuss Kashmir by arguing that Ayub Khan too had to cater to and mollify public opinion in Pakistan.

Shastri conceded and, as quid pro quo, Ayub Khan agreed to a discussion on a no-war pact. Obviously, Kosygin had done some arm-twisting in arranging this. Shastri was annoyed with me for having reported all this through UNI for which I worked, although I unofficially also looked after Shastri's publicity.

News agencies have a continuing deadline, either breaking news or updating it and need to be the first off the blocks. This was at the back of my mind when I bought time, thrice a day, on Tashkent Radio to be able to read out my stories to my staff. They received my dispatches at the Post and Telegraph reception centre at Delhi and disseminated it quickly. As India and Pakistan had severed diplomatic relations after the 1965 war, all messages had to pass through London. This took a lot of time which a news agency could ill afford. My rival, PTI, was filing stories through Reuters, London. I had an advantage over them because my channel was instant, enabling us to reach our subscribers way ahead of PTI. However, the disadvantage was that my last broadcast was at 4 p.m. and I was unable to send any material after that.

The talks broke down on the very first day when Shastri and Ayub Khan met alone. Indian journalists surrounded Shastri who refused to say anything. I went up to him and inquired whether the talks had failed. I could read his face having worked with him for so many years. He asked me to wait. T.N. Kaul, the Indian ambassador in Moscow, rushed towards us and said that the talks had been successful and the two countries had never before been so close. Shastri looked towards me helplessly, not saying anything.

On Kaul's information, I filed the story that the talks had been successful, but I was wrong. I expressed unhappiness at the briefing that Foreign Secretary C.S. Jha held. I complained that the government should not lie to us when it was unable to speak the truth. I named Kaul, who was present, for misleading me. The reality was that the Pakistani journalists had been told to prepare to return as the talks had failed.

Shastri's reactions to my dispatches were always on my mind but I covered the Tashkent meeting with no thought of the All India Radio subscription or the government's reaction. I was conscious that I had a lien on my government job, having taken two years' leave, that ended in 1966, but that was just a technical issue because I had decided not to return to the PIB.

Shastri was upset with me, because he did not like the UNI coverage. He thought that I, being close to him, would be well-disposed to his government. My predicament was that I had to report what happened, not what Foreign Secretary Jha or Ambassador Kaul told us. My sources included the Pakistani journalists who were taken into confidence by their government. I must admit that the briefing by Altaf Gauhar, the Pakistan information secretary, was more accurate and comprehensive than ours. Indian officials told us what suited the government and therefore lacked authenticity.

Shastri told Ayub Khan that India would withdraw from Hajipir and Tithwal said provided Pakistan vacated Chhamb. Ayub Khan's said that his forces would leave Chhamb if Indian forces withdrew from the entire Pakistani territory. Shastri pointed out that Chhamb was in Jammu & Kashmir and so were Hajipir and Tithwal and should therefore be taken up together and the rest separately.

Ayub Khan stuck to his point: both sides should withdraw from all territories they had occupied during the conflict. The talks between the two leaders were in Hindustani, a mix of Urdu and Hindi, although the Pakistan government claimed that the two spoke in Urdu.

The talks had reached a deadlock. Shastri told Ayub Khan, and later Kosygin, that India would be willing to withdraw from all the territories occupied by it if Pakistan were to agree to sign a no-war pact. Ayub Khan was ready to consider the suggestion.

Meanwhile, the talks on the preparation of an agenda at the ministerial level between Foreign Minister Swaran Singh, who had accompanied Shastri, and Bhutto, got embroiled in a discussion on Kashmir. Bhutto insisted on this discussion on the plea that no peace between India and Pakistan was possible until the Kashmir issue was settled. Swaran Singh said that the sovereignty of India over the state was not a matter for mediation, arbitration, or negotiation.

Swaran Singh expressed his willingness to discuss other matters which Bhutto believed 'were peripheral'. India's approach was that by resolving other problems first, there would be so much goodwill generated that it would be easier to tackle even Kashmir.

Under 'other matters', Bhutto mentioned the 'eviction of Muslims from Assam and West Bengal'. In the 1950s India discovered that Muslims from East Pakistan were surreptitiously entering Assam and West Bengal for economic reasons. Many Indians were also inadvertently expelled in an attempt to control this influx and eventually the government had to set up special courts to examine appeals against expulsion orders. Swaran Singh readily agreed to a discussion on such subjects, but proposed that it be taken up in a discussion between the home ministers of India and Pakistan.

The deadlock between the foreign ministers, on the one hand, and between Ayub Khan and Shastri, on the other, caused Kosygin to once again shuttle between the Indian and Pakistani camps. Ayub Khan was willing to meet Shastri on the basis of a draft agreement which Pakistan had prepared and Shastri was willing to consider it. Therefore the two met again.

Ayub Khan brought with him a two-page typed draft that principally discussed the modalities for the withdrawal of Pakistani and Indian forces and the post-withdrawal steps. There was no mention of a no-war pact but there was reference to a renunciation of force. Shastri consulted Swaran Singh, and Defence Minister Y.B. Chavan sent his formal acceptance of the declaration within two hours of the conclusion of the meeting. Ayub Khan, however, went back on his word and communicated that the draft agreement was not acceptable.

In the Pakistani camp, Ghulam Farooq, the commerce minister, was agreeable; Shahabuddin, the then information minister, was half inclined, but Bhutto was dead set against the proposal and threatened to return to Pakistan alone and take 'the nation into confidence'.

When Ayub Khan's rejection reached Shastri's camp, Andrei Gromyko, Soviet Union's minister of foreign affairs, was with the Indian delegation. He admonished Bhutto who had called him over the telephone to communicate Ayub Khan's reply. Bhutto said that when Ayub Khan agreed to renounce the use of force, India had had promised to show some concession on Kashmir.

Gromyko said, 'It is a lie'.

The conference was virtually over so the effort now was to examine whether an innocuous joint statement was possible. The Indian spokesman was still waiting and said that the talks had reached 'a delicate stage'. The Pakistani delegates were, however, quite outspoken and said that they were packing their bags to go home.

Kosygin once again tried to retrieve the situation. He told Shastri that the UN charter enjoined upon all members to use peaceful methods and that he should not specifically ask for the renunciation of force. 'Then you will have to talk to some other Indian prime minister,' said Shastri, whereupon Kosygin hastily withdrew his observation remarking: 'This is what Ayub said.'

Kosygin asked Shastri to make some 'concession' on Kashmir. Shastri did not agree, not even to a statement that he and Ayub Khan would meet later to discuss Kashmir. Finding Shastri quite firm, Kosygin exerted pressure on Pakistan. Eventually, Ayub Khan relented and he and Shastri met for a 'final' session. Ayub's typed draft stated that 'all disputes between the two countries should be settled through peaceful means in accordance with the principles of the United Nations charter'. Shastri persuaded him to write in his hand 'without resort to arms' (copy on facing page). This document is in the archive of our foreign office. Probably, Ayub Khan's handwritten assurance was what Bhutto referred to in his speeches as a secret clause of the Tashkent Declaration. At the back of Ayub Khan's mind was the fear that the breakdown of talks would mean that Pakistan would have to rehabilitate thousands of refugees who had fled the areas under India's occupation and from elsewhere.

Shastri wanted a separate and specific reference to the no-war proposal but agreed to a compromise when Kosygin made it clear to him that the Soviet Union would support any step that the Security Council took to implement its resolution on the unconditional withdrawal of forces by the two sides. (Later, Shastri confided to the Indian journalists that in the face of Kosygin's stand, the Security Council would have gone to the extent of imposing sanctions against India if it had not agreed to withdraw its forces. 'I didn't have much choice,' he said.)

Thus Kosygin, on 10 January 1966, got the two sides to sign the Tashkent Declaration (Pakistan refused to call it an agreement). Shastri and Ayub reaffirmed their obligation 'not to have recourse to force and to settle their disputes through peaceful means'. The declaration also stated:

> The Prime Minister of India and the President of Pakistan have agreed that all personnel of the two countries shall be withdrawn not later than 25 February 1966 to the positions they held prior to 5 August 1965, and both sides shall observe the ceasefire terms on the ceasefire line.

The Indian Foreign Secretary C.S. Jha told me that the agreement largely tallied with the draft they had taken with them from Delhi. The words, 'all

The President of Pakistan and the Prime Minister of

India agreed that conditions should be created for the

establishment of good neighbourly relations between India

and Pakistan and to that end all disputes between the two

countries should be settled through peaceful means (in

accordance with the principles of the United Nations Charter.

Photostat of a part of the Tashkent Declaration draft with Ayub's addition, in his own hand, of the words "without resort to arms." The change was made to satisfy Shastri (see p. 122).

personnel' were taken by the Indian side to include the armed infiltrators. The Pakistan spokesman at Tashkent, however, denied this interpretation, adding that the armed infiltrators 'were not sent by Pakistan' and that Rawalpindi did not accept the responsibility for evicting them.

Bhutto was more forthcoming, and briefed Pakistani journalists not to write in favour of the declaration. He said it was intended only to get Pakistan's territories vacated. He began sabotaging the Tashkent Declaration from the day it was signed. It was alleged that Ayub encouraged him to do so. However, when Kewal Singh, Indian high commissioner to Pakistan, returned to his post in Rawalpindi, Ayub told him that the Tashkent Declaration must be honoured. It was, however, clear that Ayub was under pressure, particularly in view of the fact that the people were asking what they had gained after 'losing thousands of people in the war'.

Pakistan was in a predicament. This was clear when the ministers of the two sides met at Islamabad on 9–10 February for a follow-up exercise. There was no agreement on normalization of relations, not even the resumption of direct flights between the two countries. Pakistan insisted on a 'meaningful' dialogue on Kashmir, thereby suggesting some 'concrete' concessions. The Pakistani ministers and officers privately told the Indian delegation that they would not be able to face public opinion if they were to normalize relations without getting 'something' on Kashmir.

I covered the conference at Islamabad. While waiting at the airport, I wanted to verify whether the airport had been damaged as claimed during the war. I found no evidence of even the slightest damage. Aware that I looked no different from other passengers, I asked a person standing nearby what damage had been inflicted on the airport. He was embarrassed and said that he was from the CID, assigned to keep an eye on me.

The Indian ministers met Ayub Khan before their departure for New Delhi. Swaran Singh, at his suave best, explained that they could make no progress because the Pakistani delegation was insisting on 'concessions' on Kashmir. Ayub Khan was rude to say the least 'What do we do? You do not want to settle Kashmir. That is the basic issue.' Swaran Singh quipped on the return flight: 'How can they expect to get at the negotiating table what they were unable to win on the battlefield?'

However, all that Ayub sought was New Delhi's permission for Pakistani planes to overfly India to enable Pakistan to maintain contact between the eastern and western wings. Once he obtained that, though Kewal Singh had to go to Indira Gandhi to obtain it after the refusal of the external affairs ministry, Ayub did not appear interested in implementing the Tashkent Declaration. By that time, Indian forces had vacated Hajipir, Tithwal, and the other territories they had captured during the war. Pakistan had now nothing more to gain from the Tashkent Declaration.

Once it appeared that even the Kashmir question could be settled at Tashkent itself. Kosygin requested Shastri to resolve the Kashmir issue there and then, and he agreed and spoke to Lt Gen. Kumaramangalam, then India's chief of the army staff designate. Shastri told Kosygin that India would be willing to make some adjustment in the ceasefire line and give some territory of the state to Pakistan. (Before Shastri left for Tashkent, G.M. Sadiq, the chief minister of Kashmir, had also requested him to settle the Kashmir issue if possible.)

Kosygin conveyed to Ayub, Shastri's offer of adjustment on the ceasefire line. The Pakistan president said he would consider it and reply later which he never did. Whatever be the difference over Kashmir, Shastri was so conscious of maintaining the spirit of the declaration that he told me at his farewell reception in Tashkent that even meeting Khan Abdul Ghaffar Khan, as he planned to do at Kabul on his way back to India, might well be an 'anti-Tashkent act' as Pakistan considered Ghaffar Khan a 'traitor'.

I met Shastri for the last time on 10 January 1966 at the reception given by the Indian embassy in the prime minister's honour. He said that the return journey would be early because Ayub had invited him to have tea with him at Islamabad.

❦

Shastri asked me to ascertain the reaction of the Indian press to the Tashkent Declaration. I noticed some anxiety on his face. Some of it was understandable because two or three Indian journalists at the press conference held earlier in the day had been 'rude' in their questioning. They asked why he had agreed to hand Hajipir and Tithwal back to Pakistan. He argued that he could not retain the 'fruits of aggression', as Soviet Union, India's best friend, had expressed it. One journalist went so far as to call Shastri anti-national. I had to intervene to remind journalists that they were addressing the prime minister of India. Shastri said he was in their hands. The dispatches they sent would formulate public opinion. What took place at the press conference weighed heavily on him.

When I returned to my hotel I found that the party hosted by the Soviets to celebrate the signing of the declaration had already begun. It meant a lot to them. They could not have afforded to fail because the eyes of the world were focused on Tashkent. Whisky was flowing like water at the party and there were pretty girls posing as interpreters. I did not stay there long because I wanted to retire to bed early as Shastri's plane was scheduled to leave at 7.00 a.m.

That night I had a premonition that Shastri was dying. I dreamt about him dying. I got up abruptly to a knock on my door. A lady in the corridor told me: 'Your prime minister is dying.' I hurriedly dressed and drove with an Indian official to Shastri's dacha which was some distance away.

I saw Kosygin standing in the verandah. He raised his hands to indicate that Shastri was no more. Behind the verandah was the dining room where a team of doctors were sitting at an oblong table, cross-examining Dr R.N. Chugh who had accompanied Shastri.

Next to it was Shastri's room. It was extraordinarily large. On the huge bed, his body looked like a dot on a drawing board. His slippers were neatly placed on the carpeted floor. He had not used them. In a corner of the room, however, on a dressing table, there was an overturned thermos flask. It appeared that Shastri had struggled to open it. There was no buzzer in his room, the point on which the government lied when attacked in parliament on its failure to save Shastri's life.

Our official photographer and I spread the national flag, which had been neatly folded up near the dressing table, over the body, and placed some flowers to pay homage to him. I then went to meet Shastri's assistants. It was a few yards away and one had to walk through an open verandah to reach it. Shastri's personal secretary, Jagan Nath Sahai, told me that Shastri had knocked on their door at around midnight and wanted water. Two stenographers and Jagan Nath helped him walk back to his room. This was fatal, Dr Chugh said.

I heard Gen. Kumaramangalam in the adjoining room, giving instructions over the phone (a hotline between Tashkent and New Delhi) about the arrangements for the reception of Shastri's body. After he had finished his call I took the receiver from him and gave the operator the UNI telephone number.

Sunder Dhingra, on late night duty, received the call. I told him to send a flash: 'Shastri Dead'. This was after midnight when the newspapers had been put to bed. Dhingra began laughing over the phone and told me that I must be joking because he had just cleared Shastri's speech at the evening function. I told him not to waste time and send the flash immediately. He still did not believe me and I was obliged to resort to some harsh words in Punjabi to get him to act. He then showed agility and rang up the newspaper offices in Delhi to inform them about Shastri's death. Many papers stopped the press to include the news. It was a UNI scoop; PTI got the news much later.

Sitting in another room were the two leaders, Y.B. Chavan and Swaran Singh, and senior officials discussing who would succeed Shastri? When Swaran Singh asked me to join them, his first question was who the next prime minister would be. I told them what Shastri had himself said that if he lived for another three or four years, the next prime minister would be Chavan but if he were to die in a year or two, Indira Gandhi would be the prime minister.

After sending the flash on Shastri's death, I went back to his assistants' room to learn the details about his death. Bits and pieces of information gathered together indicated that Shastri, after attending the farewell reception, reached his dacha around 10 p.m. Jagan Nath, with Shastri's servant Ram Nath and some other assistants, trooped into his room. They had heard about Ayub's invitation to tea in Islamabad. Loyal and devoted as they were, they said that he should not overfly Pakistan because Pakistanis might engage in mischief.

Jagan Nath recalled how Gujarat Chief Minister Balwant Rai Mehta was killed during the India-Pakistan conflict when 'a Pakistani plane had downed his Dakota'. (Forty-six years later Qais Hussain, a distinguished Pakistani pilot, wrote to the daughter of the IAF pilot who was flying Mehta, admitting that he mistook the plane for a Beechcraft.)

Shastri dismissed Jagan Nath's apprehension: 'Now we have an agreement. Moreover, Ayub is a good person.' Shastri told Ram Nath to bring him his food which came from Ambassador Kaul's house, prepared by his cook, Jan Mohammed. He ate very little: a dish of spinach and potatoes and a curry. While he was eating a call came from Delhi, which Jagan Nath took. It was from Venkataraman, another of Shastri's personal assistants. He said that the reaction in Delhi to the Tashkent Declaration was favourable but Babuji's (as he was called by the family and the staff) own household was not happy. Surendra Nath Dwivedi, the Praja Socialist Party leader and Atal Bihari Vajpayee, the Jana Sangh leader, had also criticized the withdrawal of Indian forces from Hajipir and Tithwal. Shastri said that the Opposition was bound to criticize the declaration.

Jagan Nath asked Shastri if he should connect him to his residence as he had not spoken to his family for two days. Shastri first said 'No', but then changed his mind. This was around 11 p.m. (Tashkent time, half an hour ahead of New Delhi). First, his son-in-law, V.N. Singh, spoke, but he did not say much. Then Kusum, Shastri's eldest and favourite daughter, took the phone from her brother-in-law. Shastri asked her: *'Tum ko kaisa laga?* [How did you react to it?]' She replied: 'Babuji, hamein achha nahin laga. [I did not like it]'. He asked about Amma, the word by which Lalita Shastri was referred to in the house. 'She too did not like it', was Kusum's reply. Shastri observed: 'Agar gharwalon ko achha nahin laga, to bahar wale kya kahengae? [If people in the family did not like it, what will outsiders say?]'.

Shastri asked his daughter to hand the telephone to Amma. Despite Shastri's many requests, Lalita Shastri did not come on the phone. He then asked for the morning newspapers to be sent to Kabul, where an Indian air force plane was reaching the next day to collect him.

The telephone call, according to Jagan Nath, appeared to have upset Shastri. The Indian press too had been rough on him. He began pacing up and down in his room. This was not unusual as Shastri would often do that when talking to people who came to meet him at his residence in Delhi. For one who had suffered two heart attacks earlier, the telephone conversation, the journalists' attitude, and the walk must have been a strain.

Ram Nath gave Shastri milk which he used to drink before retiring at night. The prime minister once again began pacing up and down and later asked for water, which Ram Nath gave from the thermos flask on the dressing table. (He told me that he had closed the flask.) It was a little before midnight when Shastri told Ram Nath to retire to his room and get some sleep because he had to get up early to leave for Kabul. Ram Nath offered to sleep on the floor in Shastri's room but Shastri told him to go to his own room upstairs.

The assistants were packing the luggage at 1.20 a.m. (Tashkent time), Jagan Nath recalled, when they suddenly saw Shastri at the door. With great difficulty Shastri asked: 'Where is doctor sahib?' It was in the sitting room that a racking cough convulsed Shastri, and his personal assistants helped him to bed. Jagan Nath gave him water and remarked: 'Babuji, now you will be all right.' Shastri only touched his chest and then became unconscious. (When Lalita Shastri was told by Jagan Nath in Delhi that he had given him water she said: 'You are a very lucky person because you gave him his last cup of water.')

Dr Chugh, his physician, who had arrived by then, felt Shastri's pulse and tearfully said: 'Babuji, you did not give me time.' He then gave him an injection in the arm and later put the syringe straight into the heart. Finding no response, he attempted reanimation through artificial mouth-to-mouth respiration. Dr Chugh asked Jagan Nath to call for additional medical help. The Soviet government had posted a security guard who, after hearing the word 'doctor', ran to call them. A lady doctor arrived ten minutes later, followed by more physicians. They found Shastri dead. The official time of death was declared as 1.32 a.m. (Tashkent time); in India it was just after 2 a.m. on 11 January 1966.

Gen. Ayub was genuinely grieved by Shastri's death. He came to Shastri's dacha at 4 a.m. and said, looking towards me: 'Here is a man of peace who gave his life for amity between India and Pakistan.' Later, Ayub told the Pakistani journalists that Shastri was one person with whom he had hit it off well;

Pakistan and India might have solved their differences had he lived,' he said.

Aziz Ahmad, Pakistan's foreign secretary rang up Bhutto to inform him about Shastri's death. Bhutto was half asleep and heard only the word, 'died', and apparently asked, 'Which of the two bastards?'

When I returned from Tashkent, Lalita Shastri asked me why Shastri's body had turned blue. I replied: 'I am told that when bodies are embalmed, they turn blue.' She then inquired about 'certain cuts' on Shastri's body. I did not know about those because I had not seen the body. Even so, her remark that no postmortem had been conducted either at Tashkent or Delhi startled me. It was indeed unusual.

Apparently, she and others in the family suspected foul play. A few days later I heard that Lalita Shastri was angry with the two personal assistants, who had accompanied Shastri, because they had refused to sign a statement which alleged that Shastri did not die a natural death.

Kamaraj rang me up not to discuss Shastri's death but to find out whether the family had the resources to sustain itself. I told him that as far as I knew they had nothing to fall back upon. He had a legislation passed to provide free accommodation and an allowance to the wife of the deceased prime minister.

As days passed, the Shastri family became increasingly convinced that he had been poisoned. In 1970, on 2 October (Shastri's birthday), Lalita Shastri asked for a probe into her husband's death. The family seemed to be upset that Jan Mohammed, T.N. Kaul's cook at the time, had cooked the food, not Ram Nath his personal servant. This was strange as the same Jan Mohammed had prepared food for Shastri when he visited Moscow in 1965.

Following newspaper reports, the old guard Congress party supported the demand for a probe into Shastri's death. I asked Morarji Desai towards the end of October 1970 whether he really believed that Shastri did not die a natural death. Desai said: 'That is all politics. I am sure there was no foul play. He died of a heart attack. I have checked with the doctor and his secretary, C.P. Srivastava, who accompanied him to Tashkent.'

The news of Shastri's death had spread throughout Tashkent. It was one of those gloomy sunless days such as that which Balzac describes as 'a beautiful blind woman'. People had lined both sides of the road leading to the airport. Only a few days earlier they had cheered as they welcomed him and today they wept for him. The overwhelming silence that enveloped the route was broken only by muffled drums as the funeral procession, with Ayub Khan as one of the pall-bearers, inched through the streets of Tashkent. Friendly hands stretched towards us journalists as we wended our way along the road to catch a special plane. I could imagine thousands of my countrymen waiting in Delhi to receive the body and have a darshan of the man who in 19 months had left a mark which was not only deep but earthy.

To some he might appear as a small man figuratively as he was physically, without a guiding philosophy or vision, to the leftists he might be a man 'without conviction', and to many others his tenure might have been only a 'parenthesis in Indian history', as TTK put it. Even so, as Shastri would himself say: 'Nobody can succeed Nehru. We can only try to carry on his work in a humble way.' It was during his tenure that the Indian army, which had been humiliated at the hands of China in 1962, regained its self-confidence and rekindled national pride. Pragmatism took precedence over ideology, corruption charges against persons in high places were pursued to their logical conclusion. The Punjab chief minister, Pratap Singh Kairon, had to resign after a Supreme Court judge held him guilty, Orissa Chief Minister Biren Mitra and former Chief Minister Biju Patnaik had to face prosecution on the basis of a report by another Supreme Court judge, H.R. Khanna. Finance Minister TTK had to resign because he did not want the chief justice of India to examine the chargesheet against him.

⚜

TTK was still in the cabinet when Shastri assigned to me the task of finding out from Shanti Prasad Jain whether he would be willing to sell Bennett Coleman, which published the *Times of India*, *Nav Bharat,* and other publications. They were being run by a board that the government had appointed when TTK told Nehru that the owners had been found indulging in malpractices.

Shanti Prasad and his talented wife, Rama Jain, were known to me as we played bridge together. Shanti Prasad had told me to start a Hindi UNI service which he promised to subsidize. I was embarrassed to have to carry Shastri's message to him. He was upset. He told me that even if he had to sell all his businesses, including the house in which he was living, he would never sell the *Times of India*. Shastri returned Bennett Coleman to him.

For sixteen of the nineteen months of his tenure Shastri remained vulnerable to the pressures and pulls within and outside the Congress party. It was a pity that he died just when he had acquired the stature to withstand the pressure. The ordinary man was beginning to feel that India's prime minister could be a common man, one of them.

I never suspected any foul play at Tashkent till many years later, when during Indira Gandhi's rule, an independent MP, Dharamyash Dev, alleged in the Lok Sabha that Shastri had been poisoned. The charge shook the nation and the government was in the dock. T.N. Kaul was then the foreign secretary. He was attacked for having been 'party' to the conspiracy. It was a ridiculous charge that he wanted the pro-Soviet Indira Gandhi to come to power and had poisoned Shastri's food, which had come from his house.

As there had been no postmortem of Shastri's body, the allegation of poisoning gained currency. Without any authentic rebuttal, Kaul called me at the *Statesman* to request me to issue a statement that Shastri's death was due to a heart failure. He pressed me when I told him that I did not want to get mixed up with the debate in parliament.

From that day, particularly because of Kaul's repeated requests, I have wondered whether Shastri really did die of heart failure. I tried to pursue the matter when I was India's high commissioner in the UK. The collapse of the Soviet Union had resulted in many things, one of them the opening of its archives. A busybody from Moscow known to the high commission met me to ask for his annual air ticket to Delhi and back. I took the opportunity to request him to find out whether the papers relating to Tashkent had been released. He said he had already gone through the papers relating the Tashkent meeting and had not found anything on Shastri's death. Were the relevant papers destroyed or withheld? He did not know. The mystery deepened because the Ministry of External Affairs refused access to papers relating to Shastri's death. The ministry also rejected in 2009 the information sought through the Right to Information Act 'in public interest'.

8

INDIRA GANDHI
AS PRIME MINISTER

Succession, Foreign Affairs, Clash with and Victory over the
Syndicate, *Garibi Hatao* and Constitutional Amendments

Lal Bahadur Shastri's death caught us all unaware. The nation was initially in a
state of shock and then of stupor, unable to realize the full implications of yet
another succession at the centre. I recalled Shastri's prophecy that if he were to
die within one or two years, Indira Gandhi would become the prime minister.

Once again the responsibility for selecting the prime minister fell on the
shoulders of Congress President K. Kamaraj, who flew to Delhi for the
purpose in a chartered plane. R. Venkatraman, his interpreter since the days
he was chief minister of Madras state, accompanied him. He told me that
Kamaraj went to sleep as soon as the plane took off, but awoke fifteen minutes
before landing and said that Indira Gandhi would become prime minister, as
if he had already pondered over the question in his sleep.

When I asked Kamaraj several months later how he had arrived at the
decision, he said, 'The choice was really between Indira Gandhi and Gulzarilal
Nanda. My colleagues, particularly N. Nijalingappa, then Mysore's chief
minister, and S.K. Patil from Bombay were in favour of Nanda. I, however,
thought he was a confused person and would ruin the country so I selected Mrs
Gandhi.' Kamaraj added: 'All warned me against the choice. Krishna Menon
also told me not to trust her, but I thought she was better than Nanda.'

Kamaraj presumed there would be collective leadership. 'To me she
appeared to be the right choice,' he said, admitting later that he was proved
wrong. She wanted all power for herself; and collective leadership was
something she totally opposed. She made it a point to establish the prime
minister's pre-eminence, and for that reason was immediately in conflict with
the old guard.

There was strong opposition to her, particularly among senior party bosses.
Some even called her 'incompetent'. Her record as minister for information

and broadcasting was considered to have been at best 'mediocre'. There were many who had been slighted by her during Nehru's days in power. N. Sanjiva Reddy, a minister in Shastri's cabinet, recalled how she had treated him 'like a doormat' when he was Congress president.

The old guard, the syndicate, thought it would be better if one of them were in office. Why not Kamaraj? He was aware of his limitations. He told me in broken English: 'An Indian prime minister should know both Hindi and English. I know neither.' However, M. Bhaktavatsalam, his successor as chief minister, offered me another explanation: 'What deterred Kamaraj was the possibility of a contest in which he knew he could not defeat Morarji, a north Indian, while Mrs Gandhi from Uttar Pradesh could.'

For the first time in the history of the Congress parliamentary party, there was a contest for leadership. Indira Gandhi secured 355 votes and Morarji Desai 165, less than half. There was no doubt about Indira Gandhi's popular support. For most people, it marked the continuation of the Nehru legend, briefly interrupted by Shastri. They missed Nehru but consoled themselves with the thought that their hero's daughter, Nehru's *bitiya* (daughter) was at the helm of affairs.

The reaction of political parties was on predictable lines. The rightists suspected her of harbouring communist leanings. Both the Jana Sangh and the Swatantra Party which C. Rajagopalachari had founded to espouse a rightist ideology, openly said that she was pro-Soviet. To the leftists, she was more acceptable than Morarji, although they had scores to settle with her. As the Congress president she had forced Nehru to dismiss the communist government in Kerala even though it had a majority in the legislature. E.M.S. Namboodiripad, the then chief minister, who went all the way to Shimla to seek Nehru's intervention, told me on his return that he found him 'unhappy and helpless'.

Like Shastri, her first policy statement was vaguely worded, with a pledge of secularism, democracy, and socialism. She rejected the demand of persons like Krishna Menon that 'Either we become a socialist society or we become a capitalist society; there is no other way.' She said she would follow the path shown by Mahatma Gandhi, her father, and Shastri.' It was a measure of Shastri's popularity after the 1965 war that forced her to mention his name. She had been critical of him throughout his years in office.

Indira Gandhi's first decision as prime minister in 1966 was how to deal with Lalita Shastri's insistence on having the words *Jai Jawan Jai Kisan* engraved on Shastri's samadhi. This was the popular slogan that he had coined during the 1965 war. Left to Indira Gandhi, Shastri would have been cremated at Allahabad, his home town. She suggested this to Kamaraj who did not agree. Indira Gandhi's opposition to his cremation in Delhi caused Lalita Shastri to threaten a fast unto death. Indira Gandhi relented, and Shastri's samadhi was built in the Rajghat area with the slogan engraved on it.

Despite her assurance that she would usher in a socialist pattern of society, she chose the US, a capitalist country, for her maiden foreign trip as prime minister. To placate critics, she included at the last minute a short stay in Paris to meet General Charles de Gaulle before reaching Washington, and stopped at London and Moscow on her return journey. (Whitehall noted that it was for the first time an Indian prime minister making a maiden trip abroad without first stopping at London.)

Once she agreed to devalue the rupee, she found all doors in Washington open. President Lydon Johnson said he was her guardian. He made an unusual gesture by staying back for dinner at the Indian embassy in Washington after his talks with Indira Gandhi.

Whatever the Soviet Union might have thought of her visit, it was not popular with the Indian communists. Though they had not opposed her till then, they now jibed at her and said that Johnson had 'ordered her' to come. The Congress party, not yet under her thumb, also resented 'American dictation'. Kamaraj told me that had India stood firm and not yielded on the devaluation of the rupee, 'We would have developed much needed self-reliance'.

Indira Gandhi had to give the Congress an assurance of sorts, and it was strangely worded: 'We can and shall do without it [US assistance] and in any case we will not debase ourselves to get it.'

Indira Gandhi defended devaluation on the ground that Shastri had agreed to it in principle and had accepted a package of aid and a loan from the World Bank. Asoka Mehta, a socialist who joined her cabinet, told me that it was Shastri who had conveyed his willingness to devalue the rupee. I did not find any evidence to support this contention of Indira Gandhi or Mehta. I think they were looking for a scapegoat when devaluation did not work.

After devaluation, I found a deluge of statements, mere statements, by the US businessmen that they would invest in India in a big way and set up many ventures. Raw materials and spares that the Indian industry required were also released. Manubhai Shah, then commerce minister, told me: 'It was we who flinched. Otherwise Washington was willing to give us $4,500 million it had promised for devaluation. Our problem was that we could not absorb all that money in industry which was at a nascent stage.' Donor countries were also surprised to find that New Delhi was repaying the loans that they were willing to reschedule or write off.

The general impression was that India would have to abandon her socialist policies if it were to tie itself to the US. Hurt by such comments, Indira Gandhi explained that socialism did not become any less acceptable if it was achieved through foreign aid. The common man would suffer if foreign aid was rejected, she argued.

Because of devaluation, Kamaraj had Morarji Desai inducted in the cabinet. Kamaraj told me on the day the rupee was devalued, 'I decided that there must be some person in the cabinet to balance her.' Having successfully met the attacks on devaluation, Indira Gandhi thought of building a new house for the prime minister in the President's Estate at Rashtrapati Bhawan but subsequently abandoned the idea in favour of moving into Teen Murti House. By then her proposal for a new official residence for the prime minister was before the cabinet. She absented herself from the cabinet meeting. Morarji Desai, by then deputy prime minister, told me that 'at her instance' he scotched the proposal. Nehru too had a proposal at one time. This was to build flats for ministers on either side of the road, now called the Rajpath, New Delhi's lungs, from which he was dissuaded by his cabinet.

Because of its newfound pro-US bias, New Delhi found no objection to the proposal of American industrialists that in the fertilizer plants in which they would collaborate they would hold 51 per cent shares, as in the case of the Cochin Oil Refinery. One could see the new shift reflected elsewhere. At one time, the government had changed the title of a US film *From Russia with Love* to *From 007 with Love* so as not to offend Soviet sensibilities. Now Moscow's protest that *Dr Zhivago*, a film relating to the days of the Russian Revolution, was 'unfriendly and incorrect' did not evoke any response beyond a couple of inconsequential cuts.

Asoka Mehta continued to follow Indira Gandhi but not Ashok Mitra, an angry liberal, who was her secretary when she headed the ministry of information and broadcasting. He leaked to me the news about *Voice of America* installing a transmitter in India, which appeared to be at Washington's dictation, in return for aid. The reaction of Indira Gandhi's own friends was unfavourable. Kamaraj rang me to confirm whether the news was correct. He was annoyed. It was given out that the deal with the *Voice of America* had Nehru's approval, but this could not have been true because he had opted for a high-power medium wave transmitter from Russia on rupee payment.

Flushed with confidence after receiving US assistance, Indira Gandhi stopped at London and Moscow on her way back from Washington. At both places, she was told that devaluation was against India's interest. What upset the Soviet leaders was the fear that Indira Gandhi might align India with the US. They showed their annoyance by telling her to implement the Tashkent Declaration which included talks with Pakistan on Kashmir. This came as a surprise to Indira Gandhi. She said that she was not opposed to a discussion on Kashmir so long as it was understood that the territory was an integral part of India. The Soviets had come a long way from their earlier stand that Kashmir was part of India and that India had only to 'whisper' and 'we would be there'.

Indira Gandhi took the opportunity of talks with the Soviet leaders to check on reports that Russia was thinking of supplying arms to Pakistan and was assured that this was not true. However, the Russians had not stated the correct position because by then the equipment had already been earmarked for Islamabad. Nevertheless, Moscow repeated the line that it had tried to sell to Shastri: it would be in India's own interest if Russia were to 'retrieve' Pakistan from China's influence.

New Delhi followed up on Alexei Kosygin's suggestion that they hold talks with Sheikh Abdullah. Ayub Khan had reportedly told the Soviet prime minister that if New Delhi could effect a settlement with the Sheikh, Pakistan might accept it. The Sheikh met Indira Gandhi but both chose to be cautious. If Morarji's speech at Jammu at that time was any indication, the government was not willing to dilute Kashmir's integration with the Indian Union.

New Delhi, however, realized that it was helpless to do anything in the state against those who in the name of 'plebiscite' worked against the country's integrity and never sought separation which would fall within the ambit of law. The home ministry had another look at the Unlawful Activities Act. Woefully, it realized that it should have stuck to the original bill which empowered the government to ban a party or organization working against the integrity of the country. The Centre had at that time added the qualifying word 'territorial' before 'integrity' to placate the Opposition which feared that any demand for regional autonomy might be interpreted as a challenge to India's integrity.

However, the fact that the legislation had specifically mentioned 'territorial integrity' did not discourage hostile Nagas and Mizos, against whom it was primarily directed, from continuing to fly the standard of revolt. Nehru would say that the Nagas were not 'tactfully' handled, which was true to an extent. What they had in mind was the 'Coupeland Plan' (1946) under which the hill tribes of the Indo–Burmese frontier were to be grouped into a separate British colony. The entire scenario changed when the British left without any specific announcement for the Nagas.

I was still heading UNI when K. Rangachari, resident editor of the *Statesman*, met me to ascertain whether I would be available for a job in his newspaper. I imagined he was offering me the post of political correspondent but to my surprise the position offered was that of resident editor who was to be second-in-command to Pran Chopra, selected to be the newspaper's editor based in Calcutta, the *Statesman*'s headquarters.

The salary offered was more than double of what I was drawing at UNI. It was not so much the money as the opportunity to be the editor of a leading newspaper that excited me.

What made me delay my decision to quit UNI, which I had built from scratch with the help of ill-paid employees, was the close relationship I shared with the staff. The agency was financially weak; so precarious was the situation that if All India Radio, the lead buyer, did not send the subscription payment of a lakh of rupees, on the first of the month, salaries to staff were delayed. I always received mine two months late.

During the switch over in 1967, I met Dr Ram Manohar Lohia, the socialist leader. He had heard that I was joining the *Statesman* and chided me in Hindi about how I had not yet overcome my 'love for the British even after their departure'. 'UNI was something Indian and turning back on it was like leaving something of your own India,' he said. I told him that the sponsors were not willing to put in more money which would have enabled me to increase the pittance that the employees were paid.

I met Lohia many months later when he was lying on his deathbed in a government hospital. He did not refer to UNI or the *Statesman,* only saying, 'Kuldip I am dying because of doctors'. This proved to be true, in that his illness was incorrectly diagnosed.

I was able to persuade, not convince, UNI employees to let me go. They feared that the agency would not last after I left, but I knew their misgivings were mistaken. I went to say goodbye to Prime Minister Indira Gandhi. She had already heard that I was joining the *Statesman.* She said: 'Kuldip, *maa kabhi bache ko bhi chorti hai* [Does a mother ever leave her child?]' I was overwhelmed by her remark and told her that UNI had made a niche for itself.

In contrast, the *Statesman* was a well-oiled machine, with the employees earning substantial salaries. On the very first day I realized it was a classy organization. I wanted some water which the peon refused to bring, instead going all the way to the kitchen to ask someone to serve me water. The peon explained to me later that such chores were assigned to the people of a particular caste. Those walls crumbled but it took me some time to accomplish that.

What made me happy was the start of my weekly column, called 'Between the Lines', which I have continued for the past forty-five years with a break of a year when I went to London as India's envoy. My first book was also entitled, *Between the Lines,* a title which the distinguished editor Chalapathi Rao (editor of the *National Herald* for over 30 years) had suggested.

In the *Statesman* I did not have to run after ministers to seek information. It was quite the other way round. Ministers were keen to see a speech or photograph of theirs in print. The newspaper enjoyed far greater prestige than its circulation warranted. A typical example was that of a union minister requesting me to publish his wife's photograph when distributing prizes at a sports function. When I pointed out to him that I had seen the photograph used in a Hindi newspaper that had over three times the circulation of ours, he said that the intelligentsia read the *Statesman.*

When in the *Statesman* I founded the All-India Urdu Editors' Conference and said in my presidential address that any language that was not linked to people's livelihood was bound to suffer. I wanted it be declared the second language in UP, Bihar, Andhra Pradesh, Punjab, Haryana, and Delhi.

Urdu was my first love. I do not think one ever gets over his first love. I had begun my career in journalism in Urdu and I was keen that the language received recognition in India which was jettisoning it on the ground that it was the language of Pakistan. True, Urdu was Pakistan's official language but it was born on the outskirts of Delhi. It represented the Ganga–Jamuna culture, our secular ethos.

The central government appointed several committees to find out how Urdu could be helped to flourish. Many Urdu academies were opened but they, as my friend Ahmad Faraz, one of the leading Urdu poets of the subcontinent, after visiting the academies, described as mere 'translation bureaus'. This is true even today because very little original work comes out of these academies. Pakistan spends less than India on the development of Urdu and the language alas continues to languish there. Maulana Azad once said that Urdu lost its case after Partition. This happened because the language was associated with a particular religious community. There is a deep-seated prejudice against Urdu and the Hindutva elements consider anything done for its promotion to be tantamount to appeasement of Muslims.

Within a month of my joining the *Statesman*, Pran Chopra, the deputy editor, was appointed the newspaper's first Indian editor. The proprietors, a group of industrialists, including the Tatas, created a trust, above the board of directors, to ensure the freedom of the newspaper, and particularly of the editor who was responsible for its contents. Motilal C. Setalvad, former attorney general of India, was appointed the trust's chairman.

The board also appointed a managing director, C.R. Irani, who chaired the board. He was a nephew of Nani Palkhivala, lawyer to the Tatas. The trust was authorized 'to safeguard the policy' which was laid down by the board of directors 'to uphold the principle of democratic government as set out in the Constitution of India and specially the fundamental rights provided by it'. The trust was also intended to protect the 'reasonable customary and necessary editorial freedom given to the editor by the board'.

The board was not happy with Pran's editorial policy, and particularly unhappy about the news disseminated in relation to the United Left Front (ULF), which came to power in West Bengal in 1967. J.R.D. Tata and Palkhivala met Setalvad and argued that Pran's handling of news and editorials 'showed a communist bias'. They wanted Chopra to go. The trust discussed the comments and the news with Pran Chopra and came to the conclusion that he had 'in no manner' deviated from the newspaper's policy.

Then all of sudden, the trust was abolished. Palkhivala, as a lawyer, knew that the board he chaired could do so. Though Setalwad regretted the trust's dismissal, he could not legally do anything to save it.

The disbandment of the trust and the way it was effected gave the *Statesman* a bad name. During that period I ran into S. Sabawala, a journalist who had become Tatasons director. He too was worried about the criticism of the *Statesman* for having wound up the trust without giving any reason. He had heard of this in the drawing rooms of New Delhi. I told him that the *Statesman*'s prestige would be retrieved if Pran Chopra were to stay on as its editor. He had to be persuaded to take back his resignation which he had submitted in protest against the disbandment of the trust. His argument was that by doing so the board had unilaterally changed his conditions of service. The following day I received a call from Bombay that J.R.D. Tata would like to meet me. It was obvious that Sabawala had spoken to him. I rang Pran to inform him that JRD had summoned me to Bombay.

JRD was sitting with Palkhivala when I was ushered into his office. I could make out that both had been discussing the *Statesman* when they were told about my arrival. No pleasantries were exchanged, and JRD came straight to the point and asked me why Pran was leaving the newspaper. I said that Managing Director Irani and Pran had not been getting along well. Pran's fears were that in the absence of the trust, Irani would dictate terms and interfere in the editorial freedom of the editor. His experience of Irani had not been pleasant and he would rather leave now than be forced to do so later.

JRD looked at Palkhivala and said: 'I told him [Palkhivala] that I did not like the look of that man [Irani].' Palkhivala first remained silent, but when JRD repeated his criticism of Irani, Palkhivala said 'Why should Irani interfere. I will see to it that he doesn't.' JRD was not satisfied. He asked me if I knew the terms on which Pran would agree to continue to remain as editor. I told him I did not.

JRD said that he had a proposal which I should convey to Pran Chopra: JRD would deposit in his (Pran's) personal account the salary and other emoluments for the unfinished period of his contract (probably two and a half years). Pran Chopra would then be entitled to decide how and when his editorial freedom had been curtailed. Whenever he felt that, the money deposited in his account would be his. He could walk out without explaining how he felt that his editorial freedom had been violated.

I thought it was a fair proposition: Pran would himself be the judge. After returning to Delhi, I telephoned him to convey JRD's proposal. He was not interested in the offer. I pleaded with him to accept it because I thought it was fair and left it to him to decide whether he had been restricted as editor. I also told him that the paper needed him at that time to provide it with the stability that it required. I did not know the reason for his rejection. True, Irani was an opinionated individual with strong right-wing views while Pran was liberal and tended to tilt towards the Left, a point of view that went down well in West Bengal.

The case went to court. Pran would have fought on but withdrew it when the judge told him that the case would drag on for years before a decision was forthcoming. Pran was paying lawyers from his own limited resources while Irani was fighting on behalf of the *Statesman*.

JRD was disappointed with Pran's rejection of his offer and took no further interest in the newspaper. Pran was dismissed and he launched the *Citizen* in Delhi. I attended the launch party and signed the register of invitees. Whether Irani liked it or not bothered me little. However, the *Citizen* flopped.

A few years later when Irani pushed me out of the *Statesman*, I wondered whether my presence at the launching of the *Citizen* had remained with him, but there was yet another reason: I had refused to be party to Irani's scheme to oust N.J. Nanporia whom he had brought in as editor from the *Singapore Times*. Nanporia was a professional and had no commitment to any view, but Irani's ambition was to control both the editorial and the managerial side. That was why he removed first Nanporia, then Amalendu Das Gupta, and finally Nihal Singh.

Irani succeeded, but in the process he ruined the newspaper, probably the best in India. He saw to it that the paper was run by mediocrities who were 'his men'. He eventually came to own the newspaper because the proprietors were so scared of being associated with the *Statesman* during the Emergency that they sold their shares to him at their face value. I met him to buy some shares when he said he had no money to pay all the owners. He bluntly refused, although he gave me a pair of cuff links for my 'role' during the Emergency.

JRD rang me up twice when I was still the Delhi editor. Once he requested me not to publish anything against the Shah of Iran. The latter had telephoned him to protest over a story that portrayed him in poor light. I recall JRD telling me that he had never faced as much trouble in running any of his ventures as he had in associating himself with the *Statesman*, and wondered why the news had spread that he owned the newspaper when in reality he had less than 10 per cent of the shares.

The second time when JRD called me was regarding our printing in the Delhi edition, of Rajinder Puri's cartoon on Indira Gandhi watching a puppy, the press, barking at her. (Nanporia had stopped using him in Calcutta.) JRD phoned me and said that he had received a call from Indira Gandhi objecting to the cartoon. Puri, who had been given the rank of assistant editor, was a regular employee of the newspaper. I did not say anything to him. A few days later, Puri drew a cartoon showing Indira Gandhi in a haughty mood, again with a dog barking in the background. I did not use the cartoon. He was so angry that he accused me in his book of suppressing the freedom of the press by withholding the cartoon. I never told him about JRD's telephone call.

The *Statesman*'s circulation of the Delhi edition was only 30,000. We commissioned a study to examine why the circulation was so low. We found to our embarrassment that the general complaint was that its English was too difficult, requiring readers to consult a dictionary. The general impression was that the newspaper was edited by the British. The truth however was that there was no British hand involved with the Delhi edition. There was an Englishman in Calcutta but he too had been there for over thirty years and had become an Indian citizen.

One thing I introduced to increase the newspaper's circulation was to encourage reader participation by the inclusion of a local page entitled 'We have a grievance sir'. This was just twice a week but the response was poor. I thought that the follow up on the readers' complaints would interest them.

'Redress' was added on the basis of complaints that readers had against organizations such as the municipal corporation or life insurance companies, and this gave the column momentum.

Another effort which did not work was on instances of individual enterprise in relation to voluntary work. We devoted quarter of a column every week and captioned it: 'Brick by Brick'. Even after I announced a prize of Rs 25 for the story accepted, there was little response. We were able to sustain the column for only three months because readers did not send anything. This was positive journalism of sorts.

The *Statesman* had, however, other political developments to cover. Punjab was very much in the news because of agitation for a Punjabi suba. Indira Gandhi saw no alternative to this and Punjab was divided into Punjabi-speaking Punjab and Hindi-speaking Haryana. This was a long-standing demand of the Sikhs who had launched an agitation.

Nehru had stood firmly against Punjab's division, arguing that the people in the region were the 'warp and weft' of the society as it existed. The Sikhs, who then constituted 65 per cent of the population, were happy over the majority which, however, went on falling as a consequence of the influx of labour from outside, particularly from Bihar and Kerala.

Indira Gandhi's decisiveness was a strong point but the streak of authoritarianism in her make-up became palpable when she revived the Preventive Detention Act, apparently to silence her critics. There were critics too to contend with. To her delight, she found virtually all state chief ministers telling her individually and collectively that they found it difficult to administer their states without a detention law. She had earlier allowed legislation of that nature to lapse in deference to the communists.

She revived the measure by issuing an ordinance. Five weeks later, when parliament met, she had the Maintenance of Internal Security Bill passed in the face of vociferous and heated protests from the opposition who dubbed it a '*Kala Kanoon*' (Black Bill), and so it proved to be because she used it indiscriminately. How different she was from Nehru who had doubts on passing such a law, saying that any suppression was painful.

The communists were however happy when Indira Gandhi began the promised amendments to the constitution. Nehru too had Article 39 altered when the Zamindari Abolition Act was thrown out by the Supreme Court. To him, the constitution was not sacrosanct, and in this context he wrote to the chief ministers:

A Constitution must be held in respect, but if it ceases to represent or comes in the way of the spirit of the age or the powerful urges of the people, then difficulties and conflicts arise. It is wise therefore to have not only stability and fixity of purpose, but also a certain flexibility and pliability in a Constitution.

With Bharti (sitting in the centre) and her parents Bhim Sen and Lalita Sachar and other family members after our wedding in Shimla, 1949.

My wife Bharti's family at Raj Bhavan, Hyderabad where my father-in-law Shri Bhim Sen Sachar (sitting third from left) was the state governor from 1957 to 1962. Bharti is sitting extreme right.

With my with elder son Sudhir.

Bhim Sen Sachar, my father-in-law
was member of the India National
Congress and played an active role
in the freedom movement.

In Jalandhar, 1958 Where I was sent by
the Press Information Bureau (PIB).

With Bharti and our elder son Sudhir.

Participating in a journalism orientation course at Medill School of Journalism, Northwestern University, in the US, 1949.

With Lal Bahadur Shastri (standing in centre) and M.L. Bharadwaj (principal information officer standing extreme left) during Lok Sabha election in 1957.

With India's first Prime Minister Jawaharlal Nehru in the election room during Lok Sabha election in 1957.

With my father Dr Gurbaksh Singh and mother Puran Devi.

With Bharti at Raj Bhawan, Hyderabad.

Picnic with friends at Srinagar in 1949.

With Lal Bahadur Shastri (standing first from left) and B.V. Keskar (second from left), India's first minister of information and broadcasting.

With Chief Minister of West Punjab Feroz Khan Noon (second from left) and Bhim Sen and Lalita Sachar at Noon's residence in Lahore, 1955.

With president of Pakistan Gen. Zia-ul Haq during one of the interviews. Gen. Zia was the president of Pakistan from July 1977 to his death in August 1988.

Shaking hands with Haile Selassie I, emperor of Ethiopia from 1930 to 1974, at Rashtrapati Bhawan, during his visit to India in 1956.

Prime Minister Indira Gandhi at a press conference.

With V.K. Krishna Menon, defence minister from 1957 to 1962.

With friends Romesh Thapar (centre) and Nikhil Chakravarty (right).

With George
Fernandes, popular
trade unionist leader.
Fernandes was a
member of Janata Dal
and later founded the
Samata Party.

With Y.B. Chavan, a prominent leader of the Indian National Congress.

Visit to China with Bharti in 1972.

Interacting with students in China, 1972.

Farewell by I.K. Gujral, minister of external affairs on the eve of departure for London as India's high commissioner in 1990.

Inauguration
of Nehru
Gallery at
London
by Queen
Elizabeth in
1990.

As the new Indian high commissioner on way to present credentials to the Queen at Buckingham Palace, London.

With President R. Venkatraman at London, during his state visit to the United
Kingdom in April 1990.

With a group of retired ICS officers at London.

With President R. Venkatraman on a state
visit to the United Kingdom in April
1990.

With Bharti meeting British Prime
Minister Margaret Thatcher.

Official residence of the Indian high
commissioner in Kensington Palace
Gardens, London.

With Amjad Ali Khan and his family during their visit to London.

Bharti with Pandit Shivkumar Sharma (left) and Bhim Sen Joshi (right) at the high commissioner's residence, India House.

Farewell function at London. Also seen in this picture is deputy high commissioner Mr Salman Haider.

Bharti with our two daughters-in-law at the wedding of our younger son Rajiv.

With Justice V.M. Tarkunde (first from left), a prominent lawyer and civil rights activist.

At the first Indo-Pak meeting of editors at Islamabad in 1979. Also seen in this picture is Khushwant Singh.

With Vice President Bhairon Singh Shekhawat.

Lighting of candles at Wagha Border in 1992. This was the first time candles were lighted on the night of 14/15 August.

With members of the Indian cricket team at London in 1990. Also seen in the picture are Bishen Singh Bedi and Dilip Vengsarkar (from L to R).

At the Wagha border.

Being felicitated by the Shiromani Gurdwara Prabandhak Committee in 1998.

With former prime minister Chander Shekhar (extreme left) and Rabi Ray (second from right), former Speaker of Lok Sabha (December 1989 to July 1991).

With senior leader of the Bhartiya Janata Party, L.K. Advani.

Receiving an award from **President** Giani Zail Singh at Tirupati.

With my brother-in-law Rajinder Sachar. A distinguished lawyer and former Chief justice of the Delhi High Court, he has been a strong advocate of human rights and civil liberties.

With Bharti on a holiday near river Beas.

My two sons Sudhir and Rajiv (sitting from L to R) with their wives, both Kavita.

At Lahore with other human-rights activist.

Getting honoured by Sankaracharya of the Kanchi muth.

Honorary PhD conferred by chief minister of Punjab Prakash Singh Badal at Guru Nanak Dev University, Amritsar.

At my office in Delhi

With President A.P.J. Abdul Kalam at the Rashtrapati Bhawan.

A recent family outing to Agra: With Bharti and our children and grandchildren.

This is in sharp contrast to today's argument that a demand must be within constitutional provisions.

Indira Gandhi's outlook was there for all to see when the first amendment of the constitution she effected was in Article 24 to make it explicit that parliament had the power to amend all parts of the constitution, including those relating to fundamental rights. Surprisingly, this did not raise any objections. The 25th amendment however evoked loud protests. It introduced a new clause 31 (c), under which, after parliament had certified that a bill was intended to ensure equitable distribution of wealth or prevent the concentration of economic power (39 (b) and 39 (c) of the Directive Principles) it could not be challenged either under Article 14 (equality before the law), Article 19 (right to property, freedom of association, speech, etc.), or Article 31 (no deprivation of law except under the authority of law).

Subsequently, the Supreme Court held in a majority judgement in the Keshavananda Bharati case that the basic structure of the constitution could not be changed, even by parliament, and this continues to hold good to this day.

What I found galling about Indira Gandhi's government was its insistence on 'commitment' from people in high places in the judiciary, the bureaucracy, parliament, and the state legislatures which basically implied personal loyalty to her. Like some others, I would argue that there should be total commitment to the nation and the constitution but not to an individual, however high. Ministers in her cabinet, particularly Mohan Kumarmanglam, minister for steel, known for his pronounced communist views, was her alter ego. He explained to me that commitment represented an outlook. Bureaucrats, he said, should bear in mind the preference of the ruling party's philosophy and ideology in their decision-making. Through Law Minister H.R. Gokhale, and on the advice of former West Bengal chief minister, Siddharth Shankar Ray, whom she inducted into her cabinet for his 'progressive views', she selected the Supreme Court to show what she meant by commitment.

The three seniormost judges, Justice I.M. Shelat, Justice K.S. Hegde, and Justice A.N. Grover were superseded for 'their outlook'. They heard the news of their removal over the radio at 5 p.m., half an hour or so after they returned from the court in the same car. Justice Ajit Nath Ray, their junior, was appointed chief justice. All the three had been on the bench which had ruled that the basic structure of the constitution could not be altered even by parliament.

All the three, in separate interviews to me, said that 'the supersession was her doing'. It created a furore in the country, many characterizing it as a 'rape of democracy'. Kumaramanglam defended the government's action on the ground that it had to take into account 'not merely the legal knowledge and skill which we do but also the philosophy and outlook of the judge'. Never had the judiciary been subjected before to such ideological considerations.

Indira Gandhi attributed the propaganda against her to the congress old guard. She decided to join battle with them but awaited an appropriate opportunity to humble them. Congress President N. Nijalingappa, the ebullient former chief minister of Mysore, who often invited me to breakfast, told me that she had to be disciplined. He and some others among the old guard felt she was 'too dictatorial'. Nijalingappa showed me what he wrote in his diary on 12 March 1969: 'I am not sure if she deserves to continue as PM. Possibly there may be a showdown.' The opportunity arose when there was a vacancy for the position of the president of India following the death of Dr Zakir Hussain on 3 May 1969.

Indira Gandhi did not wish to go by the advice of elderly Congress leaders or even make a pretence of consulting them. Kamaraj, who had brought his senior colleagues around to vote her in as prime minister felt small. He would rationalize that he had no alternative. What Kamaraj did not admit was that he preferred her because she was the daughter of Nehru, his icon. Nijalingappa said he was pretty sure that Nehru had his daughter in mind as his successor. In his diary, he wrote on 15 July 1969 that Nehru 'was always grooming her for the prime-ministership obviously and patently'. This was more or less the same thing that Shastri had told me six years earlier.

S.K. Patil, from Bombay, was more categorical and told me that 'Nehru would have seen to it that she became prime minister after his death but he realized that she needed experience and expected her to take over some day.'

Indira Gandhi's defence, as she spelt it out to me, was, 'Had I been in my father's mind, surely he would have wanted me to be elected to parliament. In fact, whenever I made the suggestion he would say that I should not go into parliament.'

The problem before the elderly leaders, the syndicate, was how to stop her from splitting the Congress party when they had blocked her nominee, Jagjivan Ram, from being appointed president of India. Their own candidate, N. Sanjiva Reddy, whom they had sponsored as the official Congress candidate, had been defeated and there was no doubt that Indira Gandhi had been responsible for that. She had got an independent candidate, V.V. Giri, to file his nomination papers when her nominee, Jagjivan Ram, was not adopted by the Congress, and got Giri elected.

The old guard wanted to take disciplinary action against her for defeating the party's official candidate. Her argument was that the question at issue was the prime-ministership. She said in a statement: 'It is presumptuous on the part of these handful of men to take disciplinary action against the democratically elected leader of the people. Are we to submit to them [the party bosses] or clean the organization of these undemocratic and fascist persons.'

It was an entertaining time for us in the press. Both sides would issue a statement close to the night deadline of newspapers, each expecting that its press release would be the last story that the morning paper could accommodate. Thank God, there were no television channels then, otherwise they would have been breaking news all the time.

Nothing seemed to be able to avert the split in the Congress party because the old guard was not willing to compromise on the point of discipline. Indira Gandhi, on the other hand, was determined to have a showdown. Both sides began assessing their relative strength in the Lok Sabha. The House had a total of 523 sitting members. The press was told by Indira Gandhi's side that it had with it 330 members. This was meant to demoralize the opponents and to win over those who were sitting on the fence.

We, in the *Statesman*, headlined the story, 'Presence of 330 at meeting claimed'. I was informed that Indira Gandhi did not like the headline, and later, at a public meeting, without mentioning our newspaper by name, she said that headlines in newspapers were suggested by their proprietors. Today this might be true but it was not the practice at that time.

Indira Gandhi's actual strength proved to be 220 which did not give her an absolute majority in the Lok Sabha. She was nonetheless confident of the support of 46 Communist members who were egging her on to fight against 'the vested interests'. According to them, the process of polarization between the Left and Right had begun and they had no hesitation in backing her.

A regional party from Tamil Nadu, the Dravida Munnetra Kazhagam (DMK), saw in the split an opportunity to play a part at the Centre. Subsequent events proved that the party's calculations in supporting Indira Gandhi were not wrong for she gave Rs 17 crore (nearly $16.5 million) from Central funds to Tamil Nadu to meet the DMK's exaggerated claims of damage to the crop from drought.

Other political parties also saw their opportunity in the split and took sides. The Jana Sangh confined largely to north India, lent tacit support to the Congress party bosses but not because it liked them. The split evoked a vague hope for an alternative government in which the Jana Sangh saw an opportunity for participation. A similar expectation welled up in the heart of the Swatantra Party.

In the camp of the old guard too there were some members who preferred the 'dynamism and courage' of Indira Gandhi. The threat of disciplinary action subdued them because they were told that she might not be in the Congress party for long.

The Praja Socialist Party (PSP) was in a predicament. It did not want to miss the bus of socialism, which Indira Gandhi claimed to represent, but was uncertain whether the time to ride it had come. Even so, it was inclined to go along with Indira Gandhi. However, given that the Communists were on her side, caused the PSP, known for its anti-Communist stance, to distance itself from her.

The overall picture was too jagged, too confused for a call, but it was apparent that by and large the Left-inclined parties had lined up behind Indira

Gandhi and the rightist ones behind the syndicate. This gave an impression of polarization which was not altogether correct. There was, however, a palpable fear that the split Congress, the party which had won Independence for India, would unleash such forces that might destroy individual freedom, if not freedom itself.

Indira Gandhi set the ball rolling by asking Morarji Desai to give up his finance portfolio. As she explained to him in a letter, he had come to be 'identified with certain basic approaches and attitudes'. D.P. Mishra, Indira Gandhi's principal political strategist, told me that the person who deceived her was Y.B. Chavan because he had sided with the syndicate at the parliamentary board to defeat Jagjivan Ram. 'But Chavan's image was that of a radical,' and as they had made the split appear to be a separation of the progressives from the rightists, Morarji was the correct target.

Ideology hardly played any role in the split, although Indira Gandhi was able to exploit the bogey. She would point out that the party bosses had among them Morarji who, as Indira Gandhi told me in an interview, 'has a public image of a rightist which is not erased by his denials'.

Morarji, however, countered it by telling me: 'I am more socialist than she is.' He recalled how, in reply to a remark by Alexei Kosygin during his visit to Delhi in January 1968, that the general impression about him (Desai) was that of an anti-public sector person, he had replied: 'This is the propaganda by the Communists in India; otherwise give me one instance where I have opposed the public sector.' Many years later, when he was on a visit to the Soviet Union as prime minister, he asked Kosygin why they financed the Communists in India. I was sitting behind them in the plane. Kosygin denied the charge, but when Morarji said that he had evidence of this, Kosygin remained silent.

Indira Gandhi wore the halo as Nehru's daughter and she was acceptable to most. Hers was an India-wide image and her reputation was that of a person who was personally honest despite Ram Manohar Lohia's allegation that she had once accepted from Russia a mink coat as a gift.

Indira Gandhi refurbished her 'progressive' image by nationalizing the banks and insurance companies and banning the entry of foreign capital to fields in which local technical know-how was available.

That she did not like members of the syndicate, particularly Kamaraj who placed her in the *gaddi*, was apparent when they wanted details about the government's functioning. She thought that they were trying to run the government from the back seat, and in an interview to me, she once observed that it eventually depended upon the people to decide whom they liked, them or her. Kamaraj specially rang me to find out whether she had made the comment in those words. I played the recorded interview.

She individually explained to editors that Morarji's outdated views did not fit in with the finance portfolio. I was left out because I was critical of her. Inder Gujral, information minister and a member of her kitchen cabinet, prevailed upon her to call me. She told me that Morarji could not come to terms with progressive measures. I tried to defend him by arguing that he was honest and had brought values to politics. She inquired how long I had known him. Before I could reply, she uttered a single word to describe him: 'Humbug'.

Morarji did not accept the change in his portfolio and decided to resign. The syndicate was caught on the wrong foot, having been angered by the unceremonious way in which Desai had been ousted but was helpless (Desai told Nijalingappa that he must be reinstated and given back his portfolio). Any protest would give them a bad name.

After all, nationalization of banks had been an integral part of the Congress party's manifesto for the past two decades. How could they now suggest, even by implication that they were not in favour of the measure? In a country where money was hard to come by, the nationalization of banks was considered a step towards making money. Every individual, from a business executive to a cab driver, saw in it an opportunity to draw money from banks, invest it in his or her business or just spend it. Was this the dawn they had been long awaiting? Her defeat at the hands of the party bosses in Bangalore was forgotten and overnight she appeared taller than anyone else in public perception. She was a champion of the people. The government-controlled All India Radio helped her to blow her trumpet.

Although late, the syndicate decided to act. They could hardly acquiesce to the dubious precedent of 'free voting for members on "a vital political issue" involving the party's very existence'. What had happened was that Indira Gandhi, Jagjivan Ram, and Fakhruddin Ali Ahmed had voted against Sanjiva Reddy, the official candidate of the Congress and were asked to explain why they had worked against the official candidate.

S.K. Patil said in public that Indira Gandhi and her supporters had used 'the propaganda technique of the Communists and Hitler' and that Giri was 'basically a Communist candidate and perhaps for that reason the favourite candidate of the prime minister'. When I interviewed Giri, he said he was not 'a rubber stamp', although he praised Indira Gandhi for her support and never differed with her throughout his tenure.

Indira Gandhi began explaining to her party MPs in groups, often breaking into tears when in the process of speaking, that she had fought back 'not because I was involved but because the dignity of prime minister of India was involved'. She said she knew what anguish her father, Nehru, had suffered during his last years because he could not stop the Congress party from straying from the socialist path. Thus it was not she who was leading the people to socialism but it was the factional behaviour of leadership that was resulting in it.

The syndicate now openly said that Indira Gandhi was a communist and pointed out the way in which the communists had rallied behind her. This angered her more and she hit back by saying that the party bosses had given the communists a foothold in India. I thought she was not wrong in saying this. The states of Kerala and West Bengal had slipped from the hands of the Congress because the party bosses had quarreled among themselves and had put up wrong candidates in elections.

That unity was necessary to save the party was the line adopted by her supporters in the Congress. Y.B. Chavan, who had voted with the syndicate and had annoyed Indira Gandhi, wanted a position at the Centre. His belief was that he would be acceptable for prime-ministership if and when the Congress split. Nijalingappa was ready to rescind the show-cause notice provided she withdrew her charge against him for aligning with the Jana Sangh and the Swatantra party. She refused to take back her allegation because this was her trump card. After much wrangling she agreed to have the words 'while it is painful and unfortunate that a large segment of the Congress voters failed to support Reddy's candidature' incorporated in the resolution.

A week after the unity resolution, D.P. Mishra told her that even though she had won by defeating Sanjiva Reddy, she must control the organization if she wanted to remain in power. He suggested that a meeting of the All India Congress Committee (AICC) be requisitioned to consider a no-confidence motion against Nijalingappa.

Indira Gandhi was initially indifferent to the suggestion. When Mishra left Delhi, the signature campaign for the requisition stopped, but later even she realized that she needed to capture the organization for her own survival. People saw in her 'the leader of the new generation' and 'a friend of the poor', and even her critics conceded that she was a 'man among women in the party'. She also plugged the line that the top Congress leaders were against her because she refused to compromise on 'matters vital to the interest of the people'.

Shankar Dayal Sharma, who was later rewarded with the office of the country's president, kept Indira Gandhi informed about the discussions within the syndicate. He was the party's general secretary who pretended to be on the side of the old guard. She asked four junior ministers, Parimal Ghosh, M.S. Gurupadaswamy, Jagannath Pahadia, and J.B. Muthyal Rao, considered to be supporters of the syndicate, to quit.

The atmosphere was now building up to a climax. The waning lustre of bank nationalization bothered Indira Gandhi but she was still the only leader who had an all-India image. Morarji was confined to Gujarat, Nijalingappa to Karnataka, and Kamaraj to Tamil Nadu.

The party bosses did not mistake Indira Gandhi's intentions this time. They tried to win back Chavan but he preferred to stay with her. He had changed his loyalty once, had earned a bad name, and did not want to repeat that. He told me that leaving Indira Gandhi was his biggest mistake. Moreover, he could not run away from the fact that Indira Gandhi's opponents were those with a rightist image while he stood left of centre.

The syndicate expelled Indira Gandhi from the Congress party and she in turn blessed the meeting of the members who were on her side. They (441 of the 705 elected party members) met in Delhi on 22 November 1969 and passed a vote of no-confidence against Nijalingappa. It was followed up with a larger session in Bombay for confirmation of this. Others met near Ahmedabad and also put up an impressive show.

Now there were two Congress parties and both claimed to be the 'real Congress'. In newspaper offices it was a problem differentiating one from the other. We in the *Statesman* thought that we should call the syndicate's Congress 'old' and Indira Gandhi's 'new'. We however abandoned this idea because the word 'old' had a connotation of something outdated, and this would not be fair to the party bosses. Still, we settled for (O), meaning thereby the Congress organization. Once, when I referred to the syndicate's side as the Congress (organization) during an interview with Indira Gandhi, she objected to it: 'What do you mean by organization? We are the organization.' For Indira Gandhi's side we used the word Congress (R) which really meant the party of requisitionists, but (R) came to be known as the ruling party.

Her claim was that she stood for 'progressive and pro-people policies while the syndicate represented feudalism and capitalism; that she had parted company with the party bosses for the sake of India's development.

Who was correct? Probably both. She wanted her leadership to be supreme and the party bosses did look like leaders steeped in outdated policies. In the process, however, the two sides murdered a party which provided a centre. Now the field was open for the extreme Right, particularly the Jana Sangh, and the extreme Left, particularly the Marxists. Subsequent events testified to this polarization in the country although Hindutva gained more ground than Marxism.

To bolster her image, Indira Gandhi effected an amendment to Article 26 of the constitution to provide for the abolition of the privy purses and other princely privileges. M.C. Chagla told me that this amounted to the government going back on its solemn pledge at the time of the states' integration. Indira Gandhi's real purpose was to play to the gallery and she exploited the populist measures to the hilt.

However, before Indira Gandhi could make use of such amendments to lessen disparities, her government became embroiled in what came to be known as the Bangladesh problem. Already, New Delhi's relations with Islamabad had suffered a setback when an Indian plane was hijacked from Jammu to Lahore where it was allowed by Pakistan authorities to be set on fire. New Delhi still did not make it an issue. On the contrary, its informal suggestion was that the two countries should support each other whenever there was an election for any UN agency. Pakistan considered this a peripheral issue as all it wanted was to discuss Kashmir.

India continued its goodwill gesture by allowing the surplus waters of the Beas and Ravi to flow to Pakistan even after the expiry of the date, 31 March 1970, mentioned in the Indus Waters Treaty (the water still flows to Pakistan). This was in consonance with Nehru's views. He had said in a note on the Indus waters even before the treaty was signed: 'In this matter we have proceeded with extreme patience and far greater caution than I myself am perhaps capable of. It had never been our desire to injure Pakistan, much less to make the large number of people there suffer.'

Yahya Khan, who by this time had seized power from Ayub Khan after he resigned following serious rioting in Peshawar, was reluctant to open a dialogue with New Delhi. Elections were due in Pakistan and he did not want politicians to make capital out of the talks and accuse him of trying to build an image for himself at the expense of 'Pakistan's honour'.

9

THE BANGLADESH WAR

India's problem was that there was an exodus of refugees to West Bengal from East Pakistan. As many as one million of them, largely Hindus and some Muslims, had arrived for relief and rehabilitation, entailing relief measures on a massive scale. There was also an incipient movement for freedom in East Pakistan.

Indira Gandhi sent Jayaprakash Narayan, the prominent socialist leader, around the world to acquaint other countries with the burden India was shouldering on account of the massive influx of refugees. He also explained how difficult it was for a Bangladeshi to live in East Pakistan because of the persecution at the hands of West Pakistan.

In the National Assembly poll (17 December 1970), the Awami League, which was leading the movement for autonomy, won 167 of the 169 seats in East Pakistan, giving the party an absolute majority in the House of 313. Zulfikar Ali Bhutto's Pakistan People's Party (PPP) won 88 out of the 144 seats in West Pakistan. The Awami League won no seat in West Pakistan and the PPP any in East Pakistan. The people voted either as East Bengalis or as West Pakistanis. According to Bhutto, the entire Hindu vote went to the Awami League.

The Awami League chief Sheikh Mujibur Rahman, who had swept the polls, now demanded provincial autonomy and the prime-ministership on the basis of his majority in the National Assembly. There was no prospect of a compromise between the two, or for that matter between the two wings of Pakistan.

Yahya Khan and Bhutto joined hands to fight what they considered a secessionist movement to divide Pakistan. Mujib was arrested and his party, the Awami League, was declared unlawful, and a reign of terror let loose in East

Pakistan which by then (26 March 1971) had declared itself an independent country, Bangladesh.

The military crackdown by Islamabad resulted in murder, rape, and plunder. The trickle of refugees flowing into India became a torrent. New Delhi thought of sealing the border (Swaran Singh repeatedly pressed for this) but the proposal was rejected on the ground that it would go against the grain of India's policies, and it would be inhuman to close its doors on people who were of the same stock. Even Nehru had taken a stand on this: 'if a demand comes to us for protection, more specially from women and children, who are in danger of death or worse, it is difficult and ultimately impossible to remain unaffected by not to do something for them'.

India took a policy decision at that time. New Delhi's first high commissioner to Bangladesh, Subimal Dutt, told me so when I met him at Dhaka after the liberation war. The decision was to support the uprising against West Pakistan and help the movement for the creation of Bangladesh. This would ensure that no power would attack India from that side. As for 10 million Hindus living in that country, Dutt said, it was agreed to leave them to their fate. New Delhi's estimate was that many would migrate to India, some would embrace Islam, and some would reconcile to the living conditions in Bangladesh. It was cold-blooded logic but there it was.

That the two wings shared very little became more and more apparent as the days passed. The language, customs, and way of life of East Pakistan were totally different from West Pakistan's. The only connect was Islam. The moment the religious fervour for the creation of Pakistan cooled down the contradictions began erupting and acquired assertiveness. To cap it was Mohammed Ali Jinnah's observation at Dhaka that East Pakistanis would have to learn Urdu, Pakistan's national language. The language issue became a rallying point for East Pakistan to express its resentment against West Pakistan.

New Delhi began giving assistance to Bangladesh guerrillas in terms of training and arms, much as Pakistan had done when some Nagas and Mizos rose in revolt against the Government of India. The Border Security Force (BSF), led by military officers, gave them a helping hand.

For every ill they suffered, East Bengalis blamed West Pakistan which, in turn, developed a feeling that whatever good West Pakistan did for East Bengalis, remained unacknowledged. 'Left to me,' Ayub Khan said when I interviewed him in 1972, I:

> would have told East Bengal in 1962, when a new constitution was introduced, that if they wanted to go they could do so. It was no use keeping them if they did not want to remain with us. In fact, once I had a plan to ask them straightway whether they wanted to secede. Were they to say "Yes", that would have ended the problem there and then but certain things came in the way and I could not go ahead with my scheme.

Although East Bengali Muslims could be roused against Hindus, especially when communal riots occurred in India, there was no hiding their ire against West Pakistanis. Over the years it became clearer that the Bengali Muslim disliked West Pakistanis more than Bengali Hindus. Similarly, the West Punjab Muslims found Hindus more akin to them than Bengali Muslims.

East Pakistan's alienation was visible to Jinnah. His naval ADC, Colonel Mazhar Ahmed, several years later wrote about the conditions in those days:

West Pakistan's order (1952) to make Urdu, nearer to Arabic and hence to Islam as Pakistan's first language, was greatly resented in East Pakistan which even taunted that Bengali was akin to Sanskrit and hence to Hinduism. East Bengal Muslims and Hindus stood side by side against the West. (East Bengal ultimately won and equal status for Bengalis).

Secularism was strengthened by the emergence of a fatherly figure, Sheikh Mujib-ur-Rehman, on the scene. Although an associate of H.S. Suhrawardy, who was Bengal's chief minister at the time of Great Calcutta killings of 1946, Mujib was openly on the side of secular and progressive forces. He had spent half his adult life in jail for agitating for a better deal for his people. West Pakistan thought it would strengthen its hands if it brought a federal type of constitution (1954) to appease the Eastern wing, but the scheme was shelved. The idea that the Bengalis would have a majority in the constituent assembly was dismissed. Punjab, NWFP, Sind, and Baluchistan were grouped into 'one unit' so that, the integrated province would be at par with East Pakistan.

The Pakistan government's attempt to foil Mujib's secular appeal by arousing Islamic fervour for the 'liberation' of 'Hindu-subjugated' Kashmir evoked very little response, and even that soon died. Kashmir was too distant to stir up the Bengalis. In fact, they increasingly felt that the problem of Kashmir had been perpetuated to maintain the military machine monopolized by the West Pakistanis.

Mujib formulated a charter of demands which provided the bricks on which the structure of Bangladesh was built. West Pakistan saw the 'hidden hand of India' behind the demand and told this to the people in East Pakistan. They however cared little about the propaganda because they had faced exploitation and discrimination at the hands of their Muslim brethren from West Pakistan, not India.

The Agartala conspiracy case was trumped up against Mujib, who was already in jail under the Preventive Detention Act (20 January 1968). He was held responsible for a secessionist plot, obtaining weapons from India via Agartala, the capital of Tripura. To give it credibility, Pakistan declared (January 1968) P.N. Ojha, first secretary in the Indian High Commission, persona non grata, accusing him of having attended a meeting of the 'conspirators'. It was true that Mujib had crossed into India in 1965 when he found the going difficult in East Pakistan, but he did this on his own. When the Indian government learnt of it, he was sent back.

The Pakistan government could not substantiate the charge and had to release Mujib unconditionally. After his release, Mujib said that if ever there was a conspiracy it was 'a conspiracy against me', and that the case was designed 'to sabotage the just demands of East Pakistan'. The Agartala trial added to Mujib's stature, and he now epitomized the Bengali resentment against West Pakistan. From then onwards, Mujib's slogan was: 'We want to be the brothers of West Pakistan, not its slaves.'

Tajuddin Ahmed, who was Mujib's right-hand man, told me that the autonomy movement really began with the Agartala conspiracy case against them. 'We realized then that we could not live with West Pakistan,' he said, 'and when we found that the allegation of conspiracy with India did not bring us down in the public esteem, we were emboldened.'

To appease East Bengalis, Yahya Khan announced (28 November 1969) the break-up of a 'one unit' West Pakistan and restoration of the old provinces and abolition of parity between East and West Pakistan. Subsequently, he fixed a time limit of 120 days for framing the constitution, and said that he would be the final authority to endorse or reject it.

The solution sought was too vague and too late. Two things shook the confidence of East Bengalis further. One was a report by the Pakistan experts that in 1959–60 the per capita income in West Pakistan was 32 per cent higher than that in the East and in 1969–70 the gap had widened by another 30 per cent.

The other reason was West Pakistan's nonchalant attitude when a devastating cyclone hit East Bengal (12 November 1970), killing a million people and making East Pakistan's weak economy still more feeble. Very little was done by Islamabad to help the victims. India offered helicopters to send them medicines and food but Islamabad rejected the offer. It was, however, alleged later by West Pakistan that the East Bengalis had been 'won over' by India with 'money it had smuggled in' during the relief operation.

Up to this point, East Bengal was only seeking autonomy within Pakistan. Even the election manifesto that Mujib's Awami League adopted took a pro-Pakistan stand on Kashmir. The manifesto stated: 'We accord the highest importance to the settlement of the Kashmir dispute on the basis of the UN resolutions adopted on this subject. We should continue to support the rightful struggle of the people of Jammu & Kashmir for the realization of their international rights of self-determination.'

However, when I met Mujib in April 1972, after East Pakistan had won Independence, he said that Kashmir was India's in entirety and that the controversy was only about that portion of the state which was still with Pakistan. He did not want to say this publicly then because he said he could perhaps serve as a bridge between the Indian government and Sheikh Abdullah.

Bhutto threw the first stone when he announced that his party would not attend the National Assembly's session fixed for 3 March 1971. He explained to me that it was neither a boycott nor a threat; was only intended to win time to reach 'a broad settlement' with Mujib before going to the Assembly.

Indicating that Bhutto and Yahya were in league, the latter postponed the Assembly session. (Yahya told the Hamood ur-Rehman Commission, appointed to inquire into the causes of Pakistan's military debacle, that he was forced by Bhutto to postpone the session.) The postponement triggered off an uncontrollable chain of events. There were riots in East Bengal, particularly in Dhaka. Mujib again said at a public meeting (7 March 1971) that 'we can live like brothers if we solve our problems peacefully and amicably'. However, before attending the assembly session, now fixed for 26 March, he wanted a withdrawal of all military personnel to their barracks as well as lifting of martial law and an immediate transfer of power to the elected representatives of the people.

Mujib also said that the East Bengalis felt the geographical distance during the 1965 Indo–Pakistan war, when the east was completely cut off from the west, devoid even of an air link. Partly to exploit this feeling and partly to keep the theatre of war restricted, India had not attacked East Pakistan at that time. (Bhutto, however, claimed that East Pakistan was saved only by Peking's ultimatum to New Delhi.)

The US was keen on a settlement between East and West Pakistan. Secretary of State Henry Kissinger took a hush-hush trip to Delhi in July 1971 and met Indira Gandhi. Her plea to him was to stop the influx of refugees. She had asked Gen. Sam Manikshaw to come in his uniform and wait in her office. He was called in and Indira Gandhi introduced him to Kissinger who got the message that India was even proposed to go to war.

New Delhi announced its recognition of Bangladesh on 6 December 1971 and set up a joint command of the Mukti Bahini and Indian forces. It was clear in October itself that we were involved in some way or the other. A meeting of the secretaries of defence, external affairs, and home invited some editors and took them into confidence to say that the die had been cast. They thanked us for not having disclosed the location of Mujib Nagar, which we were aware was on the outskirts of Calcutta but we carried reports of incursions as if Mujib Nagar was in East Pakistan.

One editor pointed out to the secretaries that it would have been better had India sought to have a commonwealth of Pakistan with Bangladesh as an autonomous unit in it. He feared that Bangladesh was a 'bottomless pit' and it would not be possible for India to provide adequate assistance. One secretary said in reply that he agreed with him but the decision had already been taken.

There would always be a black mark against the Indian press for the coverage of the initial events in Bangladesh. During the first few days, whatever came in the hands of the press was published, even hearsay. It was true that the freedom fighters had put up 'great resistance'; far in excess of what anyone had expected, and it was probably difficult for Indians to put themselves in place of Bangladeshis who fought the liberation war staking everything and sacrificing all that they had. The response in India was emotional, not even recognizing what the Bangladeshis were going through at that time.

The two principal Indian news agencies (PTI, UNI), had a field day and vied with each other in purveying exaggerated accounts of war, mentioning very little about the 'enemy' the Bangladeshis were pitted against. Not many correspondents were familiar with military terms and there were ludicrous mistakes in the reporting. By the time the press realized that its credibility had been severely dented it was all over.

The *New York Times'* correspondent met me around that time to inquire whether there was informal censorship of the stories relating to Bangladesh. I told him there was 'none'. This was true. Nobody from the government had told us what to report on Bangladesh and what not to. I admitted to him that the press during such situations acted on its own in a jingoistic way and became the custodian of 'national interest'. 'Perhaps we are too near slavery,' I said. Many years later the Western press, including the *New York Times,* behaved even more abominably during the Iraq war. For the first time, the journalists reported the war on the basis of what the commanders of the US and the UK forces told them.

To India's relief Pakistan attacked India on 3 December 1971 and bombarded Pathankot airport destroying all the planes. The Pakistan military was a divided house. Rumours were that Gen. Yahya Khan, the military chief, wanted to end the fighting but was virtually a prisoner of his aides. The Indian military too was not a cohesive force till then. However, before the operations, the three chiefs, General S.H.F.J. Manekshaw, Air Chief Marshal P.C. Lal, and Admiral S.M. Nanda, met and decided to have Manekshaw as the overall commander. At that meeting, Nanda reportedly said that whatever differences of opinion there were should remain within the four walls of the meeting room.

'Thank god Pakistan has attacked,' was Mrs Gandhi's reaction the moment she was informed about Pathankot. India was already prepared.

Chittagong harbour and Dhaka airport were bombed and the Pakistan air force in the East was put out of action. A sea blockade was also put into place, cutting off all assistance to the Pakistani forces and blocking all escape routes.

As for the navy, it bearded Pakistan not only in its home waters but also within its naval base at Karachi. Such was the confusion caused that the Pakistanis sank one of their own vessels mistaking it to be an Indian one. In reply to my question, I was told officially by Pakistan that the section which picked up the SOS from the Pakistan navy was headed by a Bengali official who 'out of loyalty to Bangladesh' did not forward the message. The oil installations at Karachi were bombarded, and when I visited the port three months later I saw the evidence of extensive damage.

From the outset, India's plan was to outflank Pakistan's prepared positions along the border, to cross the Meghna and the Padma rivers, and reach Dhaka, as Maj. Gen. J.F.R. Jacob, chief of staff of the Indian Eastern Command, told me after the operation. However, retired Lt Gen. Harbaksh Singh maintained that the conduct of the operation in the early days did not suggest that Dhaka was the principal target and his charge was that too much time was wasted in capturing areas in the north which were of no military consequence.

Pakistan first thought that India's aim was to win a border strip to rehabilitate the refugees, and this indeed was New Delhi's initial plan. When Swaran Singh went abroad, he had hinted at the creation of a 50-mile belt along the border to settle the refugees temporarily, under UN auspices, until a permanent solution was found. The US and UK did not however agree to this.

Apparently, Pakistan was led to believe that India planned only a limited action. Lt Gen. A.A.K. Niazi, commander of Pakistan's forces in the East, said later, during interrogation, that he did not expect a major Indian attack and felt that Indian efforts would only be to capture a chunk of territory for the establishment of a Bangladesh government. That was the reason, he explained, for his initial deployment of troops and decision to wage battle close to the border. However, when the Indian forces bypassed fortified Jessore city and raced towards Dhaka, Pakistan realized that if ever there was a plan merely to 'free' some territory it had been discarded. By then it was too late for Pakistan to change its strategy. Indian troops drove rapidly towards Dhaka and contact soon established with the liberation forces inside East Bengal.

The government of India was giving daily briefings on the war. I would take down notes and run to Lt Gen. Harbaksh Singh who explained the moves and their significance. I began in the *Statesman* a daily front-page column under the byline 'A military expert'. Ashoka Mehta rang me to find out the name of the military expert and was somewhat disappointed when I said that it was I who wrote the column.

New Delhi learnt via Moscow that Washington would attempt to evacuate Pakistani troops from a point near Barisal and Narayanganj, where they had begun to gather after their long retreat. Gen. Manekshaw, in a broadcast, warned the Pakistani forces that they would not be able to escape as all outlets had been sealed. It was better for them to surrender, he said, and he gave his word as a soldier that they would be well treated. A message intercepted at that time said that Gen. Niazi had escaped, handing over charge to Rao Farman Ali, deputy martial law administrator. There was, however, no truth in it; the message was planted to facilitate Niazi's escape but did not work.

Although India began tightening the noose around Dhaka, it appeared that it was taking a long time. Not many Pakistani troops were surrendering and it appeared that they were making a planned withdrawal for a last-ditch stand around Dhaka. Moscow was concerned over the Indian forces' slow progress in completing the operation. It did not want Bangladesh to become a Vietnam for India. Vasily Kuznetsov, first Soviet deputy foreign minister, rushed to Delhi post-haste, but he was soon convinced that the morale of the Pakistani forces, completely alienated from the Bangladesh population, had been broken and that the surrender was only a question of three or four days.

Pakistan frantically got in touch with the US for supply of arms and ammunition. Washington seriously considered the request and thought of ways of delivering arms despite India's blockade of Pakistan's ports. Asked by correspondents whether the US would respond, President Richard Nixon's press secretary simply said: 'There is no news.' This equivocal reply was in contrast to his earlier statement that the US would remain neutral in any armed conflict between India and Pakistan.

Washington thought of invoking the 1964 Mutual Security Pact between the US and Pakistan to provide assistance. Indira Gandhi took the first opportunity to warn the US at a public meeting:

> I hear that some countries are trying to threaten us and saying that they also have some treaties and agreements with Pakistan. I did not know this earlier because whatever the agreement was, as far as I know, it had been forged to form a pact against Communism. It was not a pact to fight against democracy. It was not against the voice of justice. It was not meant to crush the poor. But if that was so, then they had told a big lie to the world.

Nixon first sent a 'warning' to India and then ordered the Seventh Fleet, led by the nuclear-powered aircraft carrier *Enterprise,* to go to the Bay of Bengal. Information of this first came from Moscow, which had monitored a message to the Seventh Fleet in the Tonkin Gulf, off the coast of North Vietnam. Soon the Indian embassy in Washington too confirmed it; a senior US marine officer had unwittingly revealed it in conversation with an Indian embassy official. I ran into an Arab diplomat in New Delhi at the time and he openly spoke about the fleet moving to the Indian Ocean, supporting America's 'punitive action', as he put it.

Swaran Singh at the UN telephoned New Delhi to complete the operation expeditiously. The Soviet Union had told him that it would not be able to stall the ceasefire resolution for long. Even so, Moscow urged the UN for 'a political solution'. Had Pakistan accepted it there would automatically have been a ceasefire. New Delhi hurriedly recognized the provisional government of Bangladesh (8 December 1971) and Jacob, who was spearheading the operation, received a telephone call from a US diplomat a day before the surrender that both Niazi and Farman Ali had submitted the ceasefire proposal to the US. Henry Kissinger kept the document with him, hoping that Pakistan would retake some of the territory occupied by India in West Pakistan.

In comparison to India's contribution, the role of the people of Bangladesh and the Mukti Bahini was greater. I have no doubt that they would have won their independence on their own. Mujib had declared that East Pakistan was a free country which had severed all its ties with Pakistan. This was in the wake of brutal attack on Bengalis, particularly Hindus. The Bangladeshis would have found it difficult without India's support and it would have taken them somewhat longer but their determination and capacity to suffer should never be underestimated.

Some three million people were killed and ten million uprooted from their hearths and homes. Pakistanis have little knowledge about the atrocities committed by the Pakistan army. Thousands of doctors, lawyers, academicians, and journalists were murdered in cold blood prior to the surrender. This was confirmed by the Hamood-ur-Rehman Commission report.

I cannot understand why Pakistan has not apologized for the atrocities committed by its army at that time. It could not be because of lack of knowledge. If the US has apologized to Japan for dropping an atom bomb on Hiroshima and Nagasaki, why not Pakistan.

In its finding, the Hamood-ur-Rehman Commission stated that the principal reason for the Pakistan army's debacle was 'lust for wine and women and greed for land and houses resulting in senior officials losing their professional competence and the will to fight'. The commission, while questioning Lt Gen. Niazi, asked him:

"General Niazi, when you had 26,400 troops in Dacca alone and the Indians only fought on for at least two more weeks, the UN was in session and had you fought on even for one more day, the Indians would have had to go back, why did you accept a shameful, unconditional public surrender and provide a guard of honour commanded by your ADC?"

Niazi replied: "I was compelled to do so by General Jacob who blackmailed me into surrendering."

Niazi repeated this in his book, *Betrayal of East Pakistan* (1998). The reason why Niazi blamed Jacob was because the latter was able to bulldoze him into surrendering with his 93,000 men to the Indian army and not the UN. Jacob told me that on the morning of 16 December, General Manekshaw asked him to obtain a letter of 'surrender'. The UN Security Council was in session. 'I had sent a draft Instrument of Surrender to Manekshaw some days earlier, which the latter declined to confirm. I took this draft that I had earlier sent to Delhi with me to Dhaka', said Jacob.

At Dhaka, Jacob was met by representatives of the UN, Marc Henry and Kelly, who asked him to accompany them to take over the government. Fighting was still on in Dhaka between the Mukti Bahini forces and the Pakistani army. Jacob thanked them but refused their offer and went ahead in a Pakistan army staff car accompanied by a Pakistani brigadier. A few hundred yards down the road the Mukti Bahini fired at the car. Jacob was unhurt but they wanted to kill the Pakistani brigadier, till Jacob persuaded them to let them proceed.

Jacob negotiated the surrender with Niazi at his headquarters. The draft Instrument of Surrender that he had earlier sent to Delhi had remained unconfirmed. Jacob converted the Instrument of Surrender into an unconditional laying down of arms by 93,000 troops in public.

The surrender was announced on 15 December 1971, although Islamabad vainly tried to lay down arms in the presence of the UN. Pakistan wished to avoid the word 'surrender', but Jacob was able to mastermind a public surrender in the full view of the people of Dhaka. Lt Gen. J.S. Aurora flew from Calcutta to preside over the ceremony. Why was the public surrender to Lt Gen. J.S. Aurora of the Eastern Command done later when Jacob had effected it earlier? When I asked Jacob about it, he did not mince words: 'New Delhi wanted to humiliate Islamabad by showing that Muslim country had laid down arms before a Jew.' (Jacob is a Jew.)

Unfortunately, some Indian soldiers and officers looted the best of houses in Dhaka. Indira Gandhi was furious but a greater cause of concern to her was a rumour that Manekshaw was planning a coup in the wake of his acclaim and popularity for having won the Bangladesh war.

This is what Manekshaw told me: 'She [Indira Gandhi] rang me to check the rumours. I went to her and told her that there was nothing like that. She should do her business and let me do mine.'

India took 93,000 Pakistani soldiers as prisoners of war and occupied 479.96 sq. mtr. in Azad Kashmir, 373.93 sq. mtr. in Punjab, and 4,76.17 sq. mtr. in Kutch and Sind.

Bhutto, after being sworn in as Pakistan's president (20 December 1971), got in touch with Mujib, who had been earlier saved by him when Yahya Khan ordered Mujib's killing. I spoke to both Sheikh Mujibur Rahman and Zulfikar Ali Bhutto to find out what had transpired between the two. Of course both gave different versions. I met Bhutto first, and this was the conversation which I recorded on tape. Bhutto said:

On December 23 when we [he and Sheikh Mujib-ur-Rahman] met for the first time, Mujib took out the Quran and said: "I am a good Muslim. I still want Defence, Foreign Affairs and Currency to be central subjects between the two regions." On 27 December, when we met for the second time, he was very vague. He said: "I cannot say the number of subjects to be given to the Centre and what kind of subjects, but I want to retain links." I [Bhutto] was sceptical. I told Mujib: "As you know, you are saying this here and I take you at your word, but when you go there, see the atmosphere and see all the young men with rifles around you and having come back from the grave, you won't be able to do it. But even if you maintain some fictional links, I would be satisfied." He [the Sheikh] was positive. "No, No." He said, "I am the leader – *main leader hoon, main theek kar doonga*" [I am a leader; I shall set things right]. You know, I like him. The point is that there are so many problems and I don't think he bargained for half of those.

The Sheikh, whom I recorded after Bhutto, had an entirely different version:

I had come to know from my jailor, a God-fearing man, that Bangladesh had been liberated. Therefore, when I was removed from my jail, I suspected that it must be for the purpose of holding talks. I thought I would not indicate any prior knowledge of the liberation of Bangladesh. Within a couple of days of my arrival at the dak bungalow, Bhutto appeared there one afternoon. I asked him: "Bhutto, how are you here?" He said: "I am the President of Pakistan." I began laughing and said: "You, Bhutto, Pakistan's President! That place belongs to me; you know. I won the majority of seats in the Pakistan National Assembly." As if he wanted to frighten me, he said that he was also the Chief Martial Law Administrator. Bhutto said: "I have come to talk to you." To this my reply was that I would not talk unless he [Bhutto] were to say that I was free. He said: "Yes." Then we talked. He blamed Yahya for all that had happened, although I knew that he [Bhutto] had been at the back of everything. He really wanted the eastern wing to go its own way so that he could become the president of what was left of Pakistan. Bhutto came straight to the point. He wanted me to agree that the three subjects, Foreign Affairs, Defence and Communications, would be managed jointly by Pakistan and Bangladesh. I told him it was not possible, but when he went on pressing, I said that it was difficult for me to decide anything without consulting my people. There was yet another meeting, the last one between us. That time also he pressed for the same thing and asked me to try my best. I replied: "Let me see."

When I told Mujib what Bhutto had said, particularly his assertion that Mujib had sworn by the Quran to allow joint control of some subjects, Mujib said: 'Bhutto is a liar. I am grateful to him for saving my life, but that gives him no right to spread lies.'

The versions were as different as the personalities of the two. Bhutto was flamboyant, dapper, and not straight. Mujib was retiring, simple, and forthright. The former blew hot and cold in the same breath; the latter showed trust and steadfastness.

At least one thing emerged from the talks between the two. Mujib was released unconditionally on 8 January 1972. He was requested to go to any Arab country and then fly to Dhaka or Delhi or wherever he pleased. He however preferred to go to London before returning to Dhaka via New Delhi.

After the meeting between Mujib and Bhutto, the follow-up dialogue was reported to have been continued between Bhutto and Kamal Hussain, foreign minister of Bangladesh. He was also released from a West Pakistani jail after Mujib was set free. Kamal was supposed to have carried a message for Mujib on links between Pakistan and Bangladesh. Islamabad spread this report, but Mujib denied its truth when I met him at Dhaka.

'You know they are not real Muslims; they are only converts,' was the remark I often heard in Pakistan after the constitution of Bangladesh. 'You, a Punjabi, are nearer to a Pakistani than is a Bengali because, even though a Hindu, you speak the same language, eat the same food, and have the same habits,' I was told in Lahore and Islamabad.

Bhutto told me that Pakistan lost because it was not prepared. In his broadcast before hostilities, he said:

> "We don't want war, and I am sure the Indians don't want war also." And I kept pressing that line. So when I met him [Yahya Khan] next he said: "Why are you saying this. You are queering my pitch. You are trying to give the impression that I am telling a lie." I told him: "I am saying this because you are going to lose." He asked, "Why should we lose?" I said: "For nine months the army has been engaged there in the East in one form or another; they are tired. You cannot maintain the lines of communication, and secondly, more important than that, for the last three years you have been active in politics. Ayub withdrew the army from politics; there was some involvement, but not much. He brought the army fully into politics. He thought that by doing that he was consolidating his own position. For three years, therefore, the army was engaged actively in politics.

Bhutto's purpose in releasing Mujib-ur-Rehman ('a nightingale which I allowed to go scot-free unnecessarily', as Bhutto put it to me) was to retrieve in the eyes of international community at least something of Pakistan's image which had been shattered by the events in Bangladesh. Bhutto spoke Yahya Khan's language and in his first broadcast as president (20 December 1971), he said: 'We will continue to fight for the honour and integrity of Pakistan … East Pakistan is an inseparable part of Pakistan.'

Also keeping up the fiction was Radio Pakistan, which continued to begin its daily transmission with the announcement of the time, not only in West Pakistan but also in 'East Pakistan'. West Pakistani newspapers which used to have editions published from Dhaka continued to claim on their mastheads simultaneous publication in 'East Pakistan'. Whenever Rawalpindi spoke of convening the Pakistan National Assembly, it took pains to mention 'the representatives of East Pakistan' among the members attending it. Pakistan changed its stance only after the Shimla Conference between Prime Minister Indira Gandhi and Bhutto.

Yahya Khan's explanation before the Hamood-ur-Rehman Inquiry Commission, appointed by Pakistan to find out the reasons for its debacle in East Pakistan, was that there was nothing wrong in his strategy. He knew that whatever forces might be deployed in East Pakistan, the area could not be defended unless the big powers intervened on Pakistan's behalf. In West Pakistan, he said, the Indians were not able to make as big an advance as military observers all over the world had thought they were capable of. He also pointed out that actually in 1965 India had made larger advances in Azad Kashmir and West Punjab than during the Bangladesh war.

I went to Dhaka for the first time towards the end of April 1972, never before having felt the necessity to visit the city. I saw at the airport a frustratingly long queue inching past the immigration authorities and confusing piles of baggage. It was also hot. Notwithstanding this, I heard passengers shouting, 'Jai Bangla (Long Live Bengal)'. They looked like people returning to the Promised Land. In the city, I found signs of strain and poverty, but pride was writ large on every face; each seeming to say: 'I have done it.' There was a sense that Bangabandhu, the title bestowed upon Mujib, would solve all their problems.

Narrating the sequence of events of those days, Mujib told me how he was pushed to a point where he had no alternative other than to give a call for a free country; a free Bangladesh. Tajuddin Ahmed, who had set up the émigré government of Bangladesh on 17 April 1971, and Kamal Hussain, the then foreign minister of Bangladesh, the two persons who had held negotiations with Lt-Gen. S.G.M.M. Peerzada, Yahya's principal staff officer, for a settlement, admitted to me that West Pakistan was not sincere about parting with power. Tajuddin said:

> There was no disagreement on any point with Yahya's negotiating team. On 24 December, two days before the Pakistan army struck, we came to an understanding about the new constitution; only one or two minor points remained. When we pressed for their finalization, Yahya's men dilly-dallied and said that they would call us for the final meeting the next day.

Indeed, Yahya had no plans to transfer power to East Bengal. Mujib added that Yahya was willing to go to the extent of having a commonwealth of Pakistan, with the eastern and western wings as its two units. (This was the US suggestion which it imagined would be acceptable to India.)

Bhutto's version was:

> The draft plan on which Yahya's men and Mujib's representatives worked envisaged a withdrawal of martial law and transfer of power to the provinces

without affecting a similar transfer to the central government. The National Assembly was to be divided ab initio into two committees, one for West Pakistan and the other for Bangladesh. The committees were to prepare separate reports within a stipulated period and submit them to the National Assembly.

The 'two-committee proposal' contained the 'seeds of two Pakistans'. The PPP rejected the proposal and thus ended the prospect of any settlement.

Nine months of operation by the Pakistani army, when it utilized all the organs of government to crush defiance, had almost wrecked the administrative machinery. What could his government have done when Pakistan, as Mujib told me, had tried to 'kill every Bengali and destroy Bangladesh'?

Destruction and disruption on a colossal scale made restoration of normal life impossible. However rational the explanation for the delays, it made little impression on the people. They wanted transformation in their lives and expected another miracle like that of the birth of Bangladesh: the eradication of poverty. To add to the disenchantment of those who had fought the liberation war, there were pronounced differences between those in Dhaka and those who had demonstrated defiance from Mujib Nagar. The more radical among them had little hope for the desired improvement and doubted the credentials of some elements in the leadership. They wondered whether they would once again have to take the gun.

Indeed, guns were available aplenty. It was not the radicals alone who found them handy; innumerable plain brigands would not part with their arms. Mujib's personal appeals worked only up to a point: 100,000 to 200,000 arms were not surrendered, creating a major law and order problem. Violence lay latent in the land.

The most disconcerting development for the Bangladesh leaders was an incipient anti-India feeling. 'I wish I could die now because relations between India and Bangladesh are so good today that I do not want to see them deteriorating,' Tajuddin told me.

Mujib was not concerned when I met him. He said:

I know that some elements assisted by international interests are indulging in a whispering campaign against India. They cannot however sabotage the relationship between your great country and Bangladesh. A Bengali does not forget even those who give him only a glass of water. Here your soldiers laid down their lives for my people. How can they ever forget your sacrifice?

In 2011, Bangladesh posthumously presented to Congress President Sonia Gandhi the highest state award 'Bangladesh Swadhinata Sanmanona' in the name of Indira Gandhi, who had helped them in their war of liberation.

The administration in the country was weak. Bhutto had warned me that Mujib was a good leader but a poor administrator. Things were slow to improve.

Internal political dissensions took most of Mujib's time which should have been concentrated on the country's economic development. In due course he abolished all political parties and introduced a one-party system in the country. Similarly, he closed all newspapers with the exception of four papers like the Soviet Union's *Pravda* and *Izvestia*, much to the embarrassment of his colleagues and the criticism of his opponents. As he explained, the country needed strong governance, not the distraction of challenges all the time. His popularity graph began plummeting.

One group in the army misread the situation and made much of Mujib's unpopularity. In any event, this group, belonging to pro-Pakistan elements in the army, had not reconciled itself to the snapping of all ties with Karachi.

On 15 August 1977 (thirty years earlier, both India and Pakistan came into being on the same date) this group staged a coup and murdered Mujib and his entire family at their residence in Dhan Mandi at Dhaka, using the six tanks which Egypt had gifted to Bangladesh. (D.P. Dhar had emphasized that when the Indian forces left they would not leave a single tank behind because he feared that it could be a temptation for the army to take over the country.) The coup had the blessings of the then military chief, General Zia-ur-Rahman. He had told the conspirators that he would not lead the coup but if they succeeded he would back them. True to his word, he assumed power and protected the perpetrators of the crime.

I was in jail when I heard about Mujib's assassination because India was still under Emergency rule. I subsequently heard that New Delhi had warned Mujib that its intelligence had reported that there could be a murderous attack on him. He had reacted by saying: 'Who in Bangladesh will kill me?'

New Delhi's problems with Bangladesh began when Zia-ur-Rahman took over. His sympathy was with 'the collaborators' who had sided with Pakistan during Bangladesh war. India had planned to develop a close relationship with Dhaka so that the development of Bangladesh would be integrated with India's economic progress. New Delhi was hasty in scratching all those blueprints because after the liberation, Dhaka most needed India. Walls of hostility grew between the two countries and anti-India elements from among the Nagas and Manipuris would shelter in Bangladesh after operations in India.

Zia's regime would be remembered for one proposal he made: a regional cooperation arrangement between the countries of South East Asia under the nomenclature SAARC (South Asian Association for Regional Cooperation). It comprised Bangladesh, India, Sri Lanka, Pakistan, the Maldives, Bhutan, and Nepal. Subsequently, Afghanistan and Myanmar too become members. The SAARC, however, never took off because of the hostility between India and Pakistan.

Zia met the same fate as Mujib did, and in a similar way. On 30 May 1981 the ambitious Maj. Gen. Abul Monjur staged a coup and killed Zia who was then the president. All this was carried out with the reported blessing of the then Army Chief H.M. Ershad who took over the reins of government. For a dictator, I found in him human qualities. When he once took me in his plane to distribute relief among flood victims, I was impressed by his concern and the humane way in which he treated the victims.

I first met Sheikh Hasina when her Awami League sought to capture power. I recognized in her some traits of her father, Mujibur Rahman: courage, consistency, and callousness. She had understandably trained her guns against the Bangladesh National Party (BNP) headed by Khalida Zia, wife of Zia-ur-Rahman. We met frequently and I told her during one of our meetings that she should join hands with Hasina to first get rid of Gen. Ershad and his military rule in Bangladesh and restore democracy.

The first time I met Khalida Zia was in her house at the cantonment. She was surrounded by her advisors and their sole target was Hasina. They were careful not to say anything against India, although their pro-Pakistan slant marked them out. I would meet both Hasina and Khalida whenever I visited Dhaka.

The two begums were forever at war. As I had told Hasina, I advised Zia that her greatest enemy was Gen. Ershad, the then army chief. I was happy when I found, after a few months, that both, Khalida and Hasina had buried the hatchet and had jointly raised the standard of defiance against the general.

So concerted and massive was the agitation against Ershad that he had to resign and order elections. Once elections were declared both Hasina and Khalida were again at loggerheads. My feeling is that Bangladesh lost, with time, the exuberance and idealism of Independence because of the constant and bitter contestation between the two begums.

I have met both of them in office and have found Hasina pro-India and Khalida anti-India. The latter also brings religion into all her agitations and is very close to the Jamat-e-Islami. The Jamat has polluted the secular ethos of Bangladesh and makes no secret of its criticism of Mujib for having founded Bangladesh after defeating Pakistan. Both Hasina and Khalida have alternated in heading the government in the country.

After the return of Hasina to power on 6 November 2008 (she secured three-fourths of the seats in parliament) she took several bold decisions, among them, extending transit facilities to India. Khalida's public protests related to the cancellation of all the deals Hasina had signed with India. I do not see a consensus developing in Bangladesh because Khalida believes that an anti-India line sells in her country and that fundamentalism gives her a position of strength.

The Tripura government has raised a memorial to commemorate the sacrifices of Bangladeshis who gave their lives for the liberation of their country. This is a gesture which should have been made long ago. In the same way, the invitation by Hasina to Lt Gen. J.S. Aurora, before his death, to honour the Indian soldiers killed in the Bangladesh war was belated. I have no doubt that New Delhi and Dhaka will one day in the not too distant future become close and friendly neighbours.

As for Bangladesh, I do not see the army taking over the country. I feel it has had an unhappy experience when the military extended the rule of the caretaker government. The army sought to clean up the administration and took action against the corrupt leaders of both the Awami League and BNP and their followers.

Where the army went wrong was in trying to drive both the begums, Hasina and Khalida, under detention, out of the country and ultimately out of politics. The two have roots too deep to be severed and their support amongst the public is substantial.

I met the chief advisor Fakhruddin Ahmed, heading the caretaker government, at Dhaka in those days. He refused to be drawn into any discussion on the Awami League or the BNP but believed that the task of cleansing the administration which had been undertaken by initiating corruption cases against virtually all the leading politicians would be wasted once the 'democratic structure' was restored. He has been proved right.

During the rule of the caretaker government, Muhammad Yunus, the founder of the Grameen Bank (a micro-finance organization and community development bank), and Nobel laureate, thought of floating a third party. The army was all for it because it feared that its relinquishment of the administration would result in a revival of the same old corrupt and chaotic politics.

Mohammed Yunus eventually decided that he was not up to the type of politics in Bangladesh. He had however never reckoned with Hasina's rage over his mere consideration of the prospect of joining politics. She never forgave him and thought of punishing him when she came to power, and did so by retiring him from the project he had spent a lifetime setting up and nurturing, and one for which he had won worldwide acclaim. The effect of this was so far-reaching that Secretary of State Hillary Clinton was even willing to fly to Dhaka to personally request Hasina not to humiliate Yunus. However, Hasina did not agree. New Delhi also tried to effect an honourable exit for Yunus but she was determined to humiliate him.

Another person Hasina never forgave was Kamal Hussain, a colleague of her father and the first foreign minister of Bangladesh. He committed the cardinal sin of criticizing her for a departure from ethos of the country. He measured every step she took in the scale of secularism and democracy and also deplored her treatment of the old freedom fighters. He was loyal to her but more loyal to the principles for which they had fought during the liberation of Bangladesh.

Hasina was furious with him and pushed him into a position where he could no longer remain a close associate and not even an important member of the Awami League. He bore this humiliation with courage. I asked her why she had treated him in this way. She said: 'He was supposed to be my uncle but he stabbed me in the back,' without giving me any further explanation. Kamal Hussain did not take things lying down for long and set up a party with the help of some other liberals. He was however roundly defeated. Bangladesh was yet not ready for an alternative to Hasina or Khalida.

What may rock Bangladesh in future is Hasina's constitution of the war crimes tribunal. The BNP is dead against it, but most people want the collaborators to be tried.

After the massive win in 2008, Hasina's first statement was on the 'bogus cases' against her. All the Awami League leaders who had been indicted for corruption plugged the same line. The BNP was more vehement because Khalida's son Tariq, another Sanjay Gandhi, was hauled up for corruption. The two parties did not agree on anything else except that the cases of corruption were 'a vendetta' against the politicians. Hasina has been elected and has dropped cases against members of her party but most BNP men continue to face prosecution in the old cases.

Relations between New Delhi and Dhaka have had their ups and downs. They are generally up when Hasina is in power and down when Khalida returns. Hasina depends upon India and expects it to help her country overcome the handicap of limited resources and territory, and a burgeoning population.

The bureaucracy in both the countries is not imbued with the lofty ideal of bringing the two countries closer to each other. Volatile public opinion, fuelled by BNP's anti-India propaganda and the Jamat's fundamentalism may turn against Hasina for her tilt towards India.

When I visited Bangladesh after Hasina's electoral win (2008) I found that whatever good the caretaker government had done had been more or less undone. My disappointment was that authoritarianism had become part of Hasina's personality, a streak, unfortunately, reflected in her father's, the Bangabandhu's actions. People however accepted it from him as their liberator but they might not react as charitably in her case.

I am afraid this attitude may come in the way of Bangladesh's progress which requires consensus and trust. Khalida and her party are forever on the look out for an opportunity to pounce on her, but Hasina, whatever her limitations, presents Bangladesh with its best visible prospects. Her move to put anti-liberation leaders on trial, however morally correct has confused the nation. The BNP is, of course, vehemently opposed to such a trial and in addition there so are many others who feel that the process might divide the nation.

It was during Khalida's regime that several groups from India's Northeast found refuge and a base in Bangladesh aided by Pakistan's ISI and Bangladesh's intelligence agencies. The anti-India campaign and violence against the minorities assumed new dimensions. Scores of Hindus were killed and thousands crossed the border for safety. They have not returned.

My feeling is that the sustenance of the atmosphere of goodwill between India and Bangladesh is more dependent on India than Bangladesh. If ever relations between the two deteriorate that would also be due to the mindset of the bureaucracies on either side.

What would cement relations between the two countries is Dhaka's return to its secular ethos. Hasina got an opportunity to delete the amendment to the constitution effected by Gen. Ershad declaring Bangladesh to be an Islamic state. However, she retained the amendment even when she made other changes in the constitution when Bangladesh was founded. Mujib did not declare it an Islamic state although there was a great deal of pressure on him to do so from within the country and from Muslim world.

China's interest is a new factor in Bangladesh. This may some day affect Indo–Bangladesh relations. China's plan is to tie a ring around India, and Bangladesh is an important territory in this effort. Much will however depend upon Dhaka and how it protects India's sensitivity. In turn, New Delhi will need to ensure that Bangladesh receives every assistance it can provide to enable the country to develop. It already has a growth rate of 6.5 per cent and should never be made to feel that India is exploiting it in the name of assistance.

Prime Minister Manmohan Singh's visit to Dhaka in September 2011 was a limited success. True, the two countries signed many agreements for cooperation, particularly the transfer of a few enclaves of Assam to Bangladesh, its rightful owner (the BJP has already made it an issue). The absence of agreement on the Teesta Waters undercut much of enthusiasm in Bangladesh which almost ignored other generous agreements that Dr Manmohan Singh signed. The last minute cancellation by West Bengal chief minister Mamata Banerjee of her visit to Dhaka along with the prime minister proved a wet blanket. Although she had indicated to the Centre the share of Teesta Waters she was willing to offer Dhaka, Mamata did not want to go through with the commitment because of the threatened agitation by her rival, the CPM. CPM leader Jyoti Basu had come around to sharing the water at the Farakka Barrage even at the expense of the accumulation of silt in the Hooghly making it impossible for large ships berthing at Kolkata. Mamata may one day come around to sharing the Teesta waters with Bangladesh. Till that happens this issue will be a major irritant between Dhaka and New Delhi.

10

THE SHIMLA CONFERENCE

As soon as the Bangladesh war ended I sent a request for an interview through the Swiss embassy to the then Pakistan President Zulfikar Ali Bhutto. We had no diplomatic relations at the time. When I arrived at Lahore airport I was put back in a flight to Kabul as the immigration authorities had no information about my visit. At that time, I met Salman Haider, India's ambassador at Kabul, who was subsequently my deputy in London.

I took the opportunity to visit the Frontier Gandhi, Khan Abdul Ghaffar Khan, in the one-room tenement in which he lived. He was squatting on a charpai when I bowed to say salaam. The room was bare, a kurta and salwaar hung on a string drawn from one wall to the other. A few earthen vessels with a *chulah* lay in a corner. I told to myself that here was an individual who could have occupied any position in India but had preferred to stay in Afghanistan because his struggle for Pakhtoonistan was not over. (Nearly thirty years later, his grandson, Asfandyar Wali Khan, elder son of Wali Khan who led the Awami National Party, had the NWFP renamed Khyber Pakhtoonkhwa.)

Ghaffar Khan was bitter about Jawaharlal Nehru who, he said, had promised to fight for Pakhtoonistan. 'Are you people banias who calculate all the time about the gain and loss in what you do?' he asked rhetorically. I remained silent. After a pause, he asked me whether it was true that many Muslims had been killed in Gujarat (in the communal riots of 1970). I told him it was. He sorrowfully remarked that their assessment was that once Independence was won and the British left, communal violence would be a thing of the past. 'But Gujarat is the land of Gandhi,' he added, looking disillusioned and helpless. A few days later I crossed into Pakistan through Peshawar.

After Pakistan's central government had moved from Karachi to Islamabad, a city founded by Gen. Ayub Khan, who had the area aerially sprayed with seedlings to provide a green cover, and indeed the city was deliciously green. I spent the morning at Rawalpindi Club with local journalists. They were all critical of India for its role in the creation of Bangladesh but did not sound unhappy at having lost it. One journalist said in Punjabi – most of them were Punjabis – that they had had a taste of living with the Bengalis and that India was welcome to do so.

Aware that the loss of Bangladesh represented a humiliation for Pakistan, I teased them with the question: Were we, the two Punjabs, to get together, what would happen? Pat was the reply: Were that to happen we would conquer the entire subcontinent.

Before meeting Bhutto, I had fixed an appointment with Gen. Ayub Khan. A well-built Ayub was clad in a bush shirt and trousers and looked the picture of health. He was however a broken man because he had been forced to resign his position as president of Pakistan by what he described as 'Bhutto's tricks'. He told me that the students' agitation outside Peshawar, given out as the principal reason for his resignation, was inspired by Bhutto and 'openly supported by officials and the police'. Morarji Desai had faced greater problems but did not have to quit, Ayub Khan said.

Ayub Khan was reluctant to talk about the 1965 war, which he characterized as 'Bhutto's war'. He told me: 'You should ask him about it when you meet him.' He however remarked that he knew the Kashmiris (*Hatus*, as he called them) would never rise. He proved to be correct at that time because the infiltrators in 1964 were unable to motivate the Kashmiri rebels.

'What choice did I have?' Ayub Khan asked me when I wanted to know why he handed over power to Gen. Yahya Khan, Pakistan's army chief. He was on the defensive and sounded unhappy about his successor's actions. Ayub Khan carried within himself a strong element of statesmanship notwithstanding his military background. I wonder whether the army would have indulged in the cold-blooded murder of thousands in Bangladesh had Ayub Khan been in power. Sometimes Yahya Khan appeared to be so enamoured of his rule that he seemed to be making a fetish of it.

Even now a Bengali is 'That Bengali' in Pakistan. Ayub Khan said:

> West Pakistan did its best to help Bengalis to develop and find avenues of employment but whatever industries were started in East Pakistan, would be in the red because there was no managerial talent, no skills, and no hard-working people available. The real talent lay with Bengali Hindus.

Ayub Khan went on to say: 'Whenever I visited Dhaka I would tell the Hindus that I could have utilized them if they had been Muslims.' Was he suggesting conversion?

The Pakistan government was conscious of this. A deliberate policy of discrimination against Hindus in East Pakistan was launched soon after

Partition. S.A. Karim, once a top Pakistani civil servant and subsequently Bangladesh's foreign secretary, admitted to me in April 1972 at Dhaka that there were specific government instructions to push out Hindus. In consequence it became impossible for Hindus to find work, set up a business, or find a vocation; they could not obtain export and import licences unless they took Muslims as partners. The Indian deputy high commissioner reported to New Delhi (30 April 1948) a systematic 'Government requisition of Hindu houses, even though they were occupied by the owners themselves'.

Many Hindus began to migrate to India. Some changed their lifestyle, took to Muslim attire, and outwardly adopted Muslim forms of behaviour and speech to avoid persecution. Many of those who stayed back looked to New Delhi for succour.

Ayub Khan was bitter not only at having lost his *gaddi* but also because of Pakistan's surrender at Dhaka in 1971. That might be why he said that he had no doubt that 'One day you will come to this side [West Pakistan] to conquer it. But we will always be a thorn in your flesh. You would recall how we did not allow the interim government before Independence to function.' I assured him that India has no such intention. He, however, insisted that there was such a plan at India's military headquarter.

When I met Bhutto, I asked him whether the 1965 war was his doing, as Ayub Khan had alleged. Bhutto did not deny it and assumed responsibility for the war. I knew he had prepared a working paper to argue that if India was to be tackled at all, now was the time before Indian ordinance factories went into full stream. He reiterated this thesis and gave me an extended explanation which I recorded on tape (I told Benazir Bhutto later that I would one day present the tape to the Pakistan archives). I reproduce relevant section below:

> There was a time when militarily, in terms of the big push, in terms of armour, we were superior to India because of the military assistance we were getting. That was the position up to 1965. Now, the Kashmir dispute was not being resolved, and its resolution was also essential for the settlement of our disputes and as it was not being resolved peacefully and as we had this military advantage, we were getting blamed for it. So it would, as a patriotic prudence, be better to say, all right, let us finish this problem and come to terms, and come to a settlement. It has been an unfortunate thing so that is why up to 1965. I thought that with this edge that we had we could have morally justified it. Also, because India was committed to self-determination and it was not being resolved, and we had this situation. But now this position does not exist. I know it does not exist. I know better than anyone else that it does not exist and that it will not exist in the future also.

Bhutto was also taken in by certain occurrences in India before embarking on the 1965 war. He interpreted the Madras DMK demand for autonomy, the

Akali Sikh movement for a Punjabi *suba,* and the Maharashtra–Mysore border dispute as evidence of India falling apart. His case therefore, was: the sooner Pakistan decided to 'settle its scores' with India the better.

On the Tashkent Declaration, Bhutto said:

> Let me tell you, I told both Ayub and Kosygin [at Tashkent], that if you put a thousand years of history in a capsule and think you can swallow it and digest it, you are sadly mistaken. You cannot clear the decks of history in one sweep. There can be no clean sweep in the subcontinent. We know the subcontinent, you know the subcontinent. Why did Ayub not know it?

He also defended Gen. Tikka Khan who had allegedly committed atrocities in East Pakistan. 'He is a good soldier,' said Bhutto, 'but India thinks he is some Halaku Khan.'

Bhutto did not allow normalization of relations with India beyond the restoration of high commissioners. He saw to it that Pakistan did not associate itself with India in getting the Tashkent Declaration registered at the UN and also had the Indo–Pakistan ministerial meeting in Rawalpindi (9–10 February 1966) sabotaged. Pakistan insisted on a 'meaningful' dialogue on Kashmir, suggesting thereby some 'concrete concessions' while India wanted to address other issues first. The tables were turned five years later when India insisted on settling Kashmir first and other issues later.

Bhutto was encouraged in his anti-Indian stance by the response he received from the nation. The more intractable the position he took, the more popular he became. Persistent propaganda by a series of regimes against 'Hindu India' (Pakistan still refers to India as 'Bharat') had conditioned the minds of Pakistanis to such a degree that for them India was an embodiment of evil. The controlled information media had shut out the truth about India and fed Pakistanis with falsehoods and exaggerations.

School history books played up the wars between Hindus and Muslims, with the latter always emerging victorious. Mohammed Bin Qasim and Mahmud Ghaznavi, the first two Muslim invaders of India, were glorified for destroying kafirs. In fact, Pakistan's history began with the arrival of Islam in India, ignoring Taxila and Mahenjodaro which were not only located in Pakistan but were also relics of the thousand years' old culture of the Aryans and Hindus.

The Hindu period was dismissed in a single sentence: 'The Hindus were not much interested in history and we have a very few historical records of this period,' was the reason advanced. Babur was described as changing the architecture of the Hindus because he 'did not like it', finding 'the rooms so small that they were dark even in the daytime'. The Muslim buildings 'were much larger and airy'. In one of the books it was mentioned that India was once part of Pakistan.

After having spoken to Bhutto I met his press attaché, Khalid Hussain. He made every evening of mine meaningful because he invited Faiz Ahmed Faiz who regaled a few of us with poetry recitations and anecdotes. This was after the liberation of Bangladesh. He blamed nobody but regretted that one portion of Pakistan was no more part of it. He was then a member of Bhutto's delegation. He was hurt by the stories of atrocities that he had heard from Dhaka. He recited to me the first couplet of the poem that he wrote after his visit to Bangladesh:

And will there be a spring when the green is all unblighted
And how many rains must fall before the spots are washed clean

Once he spoke in Lahore about radical Islam. As he was a leftist but not an atheist, he argued how Islam and the ideology of the Left, were on the same page. 'Lal Islam' is the phrase he used.

What surprised me was Faiz's contention that Pakistan would eventually become a 'Red Islamic polity'. I asked him how he thought that Islam was ideologically anywhere close to Marxism. His reply was that 'the Muslims of Pakistan would prove it'.

On my way to Delhi, I stopped at Lahore. When I contacted the information department they inquired if they could be of any assistance to me. I asked them whether it would be possible to meet actress and singer Noorjahan. I loved her songs and had not seen her since I had watched her as Baby Noorjahan in one of her films. They located her at Model Town, Pakistan's Bollywood.

I was ushered into a room where two fat ladies were sitting who looked alike. My guide nudged me and pointed out Noorjahan to me. I sat next to her and felt awkward beginning the conversation. I opened with a general enquiry about the number of songs she had so far recorded. She became pensive and replied: *'Na to recardo ka shamar hai aur na hi gunahon ka - ye aap log maaf kar dainge our woh Allah mian* [There is no count of records or sins. You would forgive the first and Allah the other]'. She sang for me a Punjabi song which she had prepared to urge Pakistanis to join in the war against India. She meant no offence but communicated the mood of her nation.

On my return to Delhi, Indira Gandhi called me to ask about my visit to Pakistan. She was aware through diplomatic channels that Bhutto was keen to meet her. She had even decided to send D.P. Dhar to Islamabad to prepare the ground for talks. What she was keen to learn from me was whether India should first return the territory it had captured and the 93,000 prisoners of war it had taken.

'Both,' was my short reply. I explained that just as the Chinese, after defeating us in 1962, had returned our men and territory (China retained what it claimed belonged to it), they created such a situation for the men in khaki that they had to remain indoors for many days because they were jeered at by people who thought they had been cowardly and had given India a bad name. If the prisoners were returned now, I told her, they would be hooted in the streets of Pakistan. The longer the Pakistan prisoners were detained, I argued, the greater would be the halo surrounding them. (Bhutto had chided me that they would remain Muslim for whatever period we held them in jail.)

We neither returned the territory nor the prisoners at the time but both were returned in due course. I felt that the generous step of returning both after the ceasefire would have gone down well with the people of Pakistan who had been fed on India's squeamishness and 'baniya-like' mentality.

My session with D.P. Dhar, who was looking after Bangladesh and Pakistan, lasted for three hours. His bright and conscientious officer, Ashok Chib, then heading the Pakistan division in the Ministry of External Affairs, was sitting with him. They wanted every minute detail of my visit to Pakistan. I told them that what struck me was Bhutto's suggestion that the ceasefire line be converted into a 'line of peace'. They pursued the idea with Bhutto at Shimla but found that he did not attach great importance to his suggestion. He said: 'It was one of many.'

The talks between Indira Gandhi and Zulfikar Ali Bhutto began in Shimla on 28 June and ended on 2 July 1972. Indira Gandhi wondered why Pakistan had brought in the UN Declaration or Principles of International Law during the talks. She said that all matters between India and Pakistan should be bilaterally resolved without any direct or indirect third-party intervention. She argued that the subcontinent should refuse to be a pawn in the game of the great powers. Bhutto said that he too was not 'going to rush around the chanceries of the world, because even after twenty-five years of doing so the world had not helped'. He assured her that the reference to the UN was never meant either to involve the international organization or any third party.

Bhutto had in his team many intellectuals, including my friend Mazhar Ali Khan, the editor of *Viewpoint,* a weekly he published from Lahore. One person who attracted unusual attention at Shimla was the young and attractive Benazir Bhutto, then just around 17 years old. Bhutto had brought her along perhaps in a first attempt to groom her for politics. Subsequent years of Pakistan wrangling testified that he had exposed her to politics at the right time.

Bhutto told Indira Gandhi that he had to get the POWs released and assured her that he would demobilize them. On Bangladesh, he gave an undertaking that Pakistan's recognition would be formalized, when he met Mujib 'by the end of this month' (July). She told him that India had no hesitation in releasing the prisoners but the concurrence of this by Bangladesh was necessary as they had surrendered to a joint command of the Mukti-Bahini and the Indian army.

Bhutto had told me earlier in an interview:

We can make the ceasefire line a line of peace and let people come and go between the two Kashmirs. After all, why should they suffer? Let there be some free movement between them. Then one thing can lead to another. After all, simultaneously we hope that there will be exchanges of visits, of officials and non-officials.

Indira Gandhi felt that Dhar, who was helping her during the talks, was not direct in his approach, often introducing other subjects. She therefore replaced him with P.N. Haksar, her principal secretary tracing his ancestry to pandits in Kashmir. It was given out that Dhar was not 'feeling well'. It was probably Haksar's straight talking that made Bhutto feel that the change from Dhar to Haksar was intended to convey a harder line.

Bhutto's officials would tell their Indian counterparts that if he returned empty-handed his position in Pakistan would be greatly weakened. A few non-officials accompanying Bhutto went further and warned India that the failure of the Shimla Summit would mean the beginning of Bhutto's downfall and the return of the army. This disappointed the Indians, but both sides were so entrenched in their positions that it was thought that the best way out was a joint communiqué to break the news of failure as gently as possible. The communiqué read, inter alia:

Both Mrs Gandhi and Bhutto discussed all major issues affecting the relations between the two countries. They also specifically talked about Jammu and Kashmir. They expressed the hope that a mutually agreed settlement of all outstanding issues would be possible and that the process of reconciliation initiated in the first meeting of the Heads of the Governments would continue.

At the last minute Haksar spoke to Indira Gandhi and told her 'to trust' Bhutto who was down and out. India decided to accommodate Pakistan on the question of the territory occupied during the war. Besides being a gesture, it would convince Bhutto of India's sincerity in seeking a durable peace, a status which Dhar had discussed with his Pakistani counterpart, Aziz Ahmed, in Murree.

The reason for returning the territory was because New Delhi did not have to seek Dhaka's concurrence to do so. The Indian army was also finding it difficult to remain in the desert territory which it knew it would eventually have to vacate. New Delhi's stand in international forums was that after a conflict the victor should never be allowed to retain the fruits of aggression.

When Pakistan was informally sounded out, it was found that its priority was in fact territory. As Aziz Ahmed explained, most of Pakistan's army was drawn from its five Punjab districts, and that Tikka Khan had personally found, after talking to the people in those areas, that they were more concerned about the loss of territory than the POWs. It was known that they were being well treated and in any event they visited their homes only once a year during their army career.

In exchange for territory, India wanted to see whether Pakistan would agree to, (a) joint inspection teams to ensure that the war machinery in both countries was kept within reasonable proportions; and (b) adjustments in the international border after mutual consultations.

Pakistan was keen to institute a self-executing machinery (mutual discussion followed by mediation and adjudication) to settle disputes if there was no mutually agreed settlement. India firmly rejected this. Aziz Ahmed again cautioned the Indians against the failure of talks. The Indian delegation said that they could only go on striving to save the talks. Bhutto was vehemently opposed to the two proposals of having joint inspection teams and agreeing to convert the ceasefire line into the international border. When he met Indira Gandhi for a farewell call on 3 July he said that he would be willing to sign an agreement provided these two proposals were dropped.

India had included these proposals only as a bargaining counter and did not mind deleting them, but was determined to convert the new ceasefire line into a stable international border to which Pakistan was not willing to concede.

New Delhi had for some time been wanting the UN observers on the ceasefire line to leave because their presence was tantamount to interference by a third party in the affairs of the subcontinent. A new ceasefire line, agreed to by India and Pakistan, would make their role redundant, and that was exactly what New Delhi declared after concluding the agreement with Rawalpindi.

Bhutto agreed to respect 'the line of control resulting from the ceasefire of 17 December 1971', but added after this sentence in his own hand in the draft agreement, 'without prejudice to the recognized position of either side'. India did not object.

The agreement was signed at 12.40 a.m. on 3 July 1972 after almost everyone had assumed that the summit had failed. So late and unexpected was the development that no typewriter was at hand to prepare a corrected copy of the agreement, nor was the Pakistan government's seal available, having been packed in a box and sent by road to Chandigarh with the other heavy baggage which could not have been transported by helicopter from Shimla. As the Pakistan seal could not be affixed on the document, India too did not affix its own.

Haksar told me that there was an oral agreement according to which Bhutto accepted the ceasefire line as an international border, meaning thereby that Pakistan would retain the territory it held in Kashmir, called Azad Kashmir, and India the rest of the Valley, Jammu, and Ladakh. Haksar said that Bhutto did not want to be part of the agreement because he wanted to break the news in his own way. After having lost East Pakistan, Bhutto reportedly argued with Indira Gandhi that if he were to announce the acceptance of the status quo in Kashmir he would face a military coup.

The oral agreement has been denied by Pakistan's leaders, foreign office, and others. Every time I have asked even people at the top they have categorically denied its existence. New Delhi swears that Bhutto gave his word and Haksar confirmed this.

It is possible that Bhutto did agree in Indira Gandhi's presence but dropped the idea when close associates of his vehemently opposed it. I got a whiff of this when I visited Pakistan later. Some said that Bhutto was obliged to abandon the idea because he couldn't sell it in Pakistan. My feeling is that even if there had been such an agreement it would have been akin to the Treaty of Versailles, a humiliating treaty which Germany signed after the First World War that led to the Second World War. Islamabad would not have implemented it because soon after the secession of East Pakistan, Bhutto, or for that matter anyone else, could not have persuaded the country to give up Kashmir which lent unity of a kind to Pakistan.

At the end of the conference Indira Gandhi wrote a letter to Haksar appreciating 'the manner' in which he had handled 'this whole delicate business of talking with the Pakistani delegation'. Dhar felt cut up because there was no mention of him in the letter.

I thought India gained quite a lot at Shimla. For the first time it was agreed that the two countries would hold bilateral talks to settle their problems. This meant that the UN would no longer be in the picture in any future negotiations. Converting the ceasefire line into the Line of Control (LoC) was indeed an important concession on Bhutto's part.

Long after the conference, Dhar called me and left with me the files on his talks with Aziz Ahmed. I was then writing my book *Distant Neighbours*. When the book was later published, Dhar was upset because I had reproduced the different drafts which the two sides had submitted at the Murree meeting.

Dhar said that he would have to face the ire of parliamentarians but I assured him that nothing of the kind would occur. If my reading of MPs served me right, I told him, not one of them would read the book or at least not to the end where the drafts had been reproduced. Many months later, Dhar told me that my reading had proved to be correct. MEA's Ashok Chib told me that a distinguished scholar from America had inquired about the authenticity of the drafts. I do not know of the government's response, if any.

The files Dhar showed me had details of what happened at Murree where India and Pakistan first met after the 1971 war. The first two-day session was as calm as the climate in hilly Murree. The discussions were in English, although Dhar wanted to switch-over to Urdu to add a more informal touch. Aziz Ahmed frankly admitted that even if Urdu was the official language of Pakistan, he for one found it difficult to use, especially when speaking to Dhar who, like other Kashmiri Pundits, spoke fluent Urdu.

A durable settlement was on the top of the tentative agenda that Dhar had carried from New Delhi, and he had been given a directive to include

Kashmir. Aziz Ahmed had been told to give top priority to the POWs, the vacation of territory, and not Kashmir.

In the opening speech Aziz Ahmed spoke about the need for a step-by-step approach, and also referred to reports in some Delhi newspapers that Dhar would 'demand' recognition of the ceasefire line in Kashmir as the international border. In reply, Dhar said that the past history of Indo–Pakistan relations should itself indicate that the step-by-step approach had not succeeded and that they could turn over a new leaf by discussing how they could achieve a durable peace. He contradicted press reports that he had come to dictate anything 'here and now'. The two never produced a joint draft. Bhutto met them but he understandably took Aziz Ahmed's side. He did however say that he wanted the ceasefire line as 'a line of peace', meaning thereby that there should be no cross-border firing or sniping.

The Shimla Agreement remained on paper as had the earlier pacts between India and Pakistan. The problem for Islamabad was that if it were to sort out its problems with India, then what excuse would Pakistan have to explain to its people its economic backwardness and other domestic problems.

Looking back, the Shimla Agreement caused the two sides to fully realize the futility of hostilities. True, there was a misadventure by Pakistan in Kargil in 1999, but, this was the doing of the then Army Chief General Parvez Musharraf. There was no regular war despite the incident. Prime Minister Yusuf Raza Gilani announced in 2011 that the Kashmir problem could never be resolved through war. Both sides had to sit across the table to solve it. That has become Islamabad's policy on the apparently intractable problem of Kashmir.

11

THE EMERGENCY AND AFTER

I was in the Lok Sabha press gallery when Atal Bihari Vajpayee, leader of the Opposition, hailed Indira Gandhi as Durga, the goddess of destruction. The Jana Sangh had never wished Pakistan well, and indeed the party took a fiendish delight in the division of Pakistan, East Pakistan liberating itself from West Pakistan. Indira Gandhi acknowledged the compliment with a smile, behaving in the manner of a Roman emperor returning after a triumphant war.

The Bangladesh war had undoubtedly heightened Indira Gandhi's stature but also lowered the spirits of other political parties which felt demoralized. For a long time there was no protest even over serious government lapses. Also, the political parties were so distant from one another that they did not pose even a semblance of a threat to the government. So trivialized had politics become that Pilu Modi, a Lok Sabha member, would attract attention with the 'I am a CIA agent' badge he flaunted.

Jayaprakash Narayan's was the only voice that caught attention. He was not a member of parliament and stayed mostly in Patna, but whenever he spoke, people took notice of him. His Gandhian background and his refusal to accept any office in the government, even when offered by Nehru, had given JP, as he was popularly known, the halo of asceticism and acceptability. He criticized the ruling Congress for corruption, on the one hand, and regretted the inertia amongst the public, on the other. He believed that the time was favourable to awaken the people to the values and principles which he said the Congress was destroying and giving India the imprint of Indira Gandhi's authoritarian rule.

In fact, what came to be known as the JP Movement was the people's ventilation of pent-up anger against the dishonesty and insolence of public servants and ministers. The protest, which began as a gentle breeze soon developed into a storm. Indira Gandhi had come to embody corruption, not only in terms of money but in the deployment of power. She had humbled the old guard and had no compunction in employing any method to demolish whatever and whosoever she believed stood in her way.

JP was past seventy when he joined issue with her. A Gandhian in approach, he was resentful of the methods she used to govern. I had met him many times and admired his simplicity and the sense of values he evoked. I had often written against Indira Gandhi's misrule, so he was aware of my dislike for her authoritarian governance when he called me one day in 1973 to inaugurate a meeting in Patna and lend my voice to those who had been silenced by the tyranny of her government.

The meeting was held in the heart of the city, the Senate Hall. Lalu Prasad Yadav, president of Patna University Students' Union, was in the chair. Little did I realize then that I was part of a movement that would eventually unseat Indira Gandhi from power.

JP was overwhelmed by the public response because the hall was full, many even squatting outside on the road. I made a brief introductory speech, regretting the falling standards of integrity in public life. JP spoke at length and reminded people of the value system that India had followed during the freedom struggle and in the days of Nehru and Shastri. His emphasis was on a return to a values-based system, and he promised the audience that he would speak to them on the following day at Gandhi Maidan, a large open space, to spell out his programme.

I did not stay for the subsequent meeting which I learnt later attracted a large gathering of his supporters. However, before my departure JP gave me a recorded interview talking about his future plans. To my horror, however, there was nothing recorded because I had inadvertently switched the recorder to the silent mode. Therefore, whatever I could recall I reproduced in the *Statesman* story, as the first lead. He spelt out before me his programme which epitomized *parivartan* (change) in the country. He told me that he would go to the people and mobilize them to replace the Congress government headed by Indira Gandhi and provide an alternative with new people and a new party which he named Janata. Even so, at Gandhi Maidan he did not raise the demand for fresh elections but gave the public the slogan of *parivartan*.

With that determination, he went to Gujarat to lend support to the Students' Nav Nirman agitation which led to the fall of the state government headed by Chimanbhai Patel of dubious reputation. *Gujarat main shore hai, Chaman Bhai chor hai* [There is a noise in Gujarat, brother Chaman is a thief]. It was a call against corruption in high places.

The success at Ahmedabad gave JP heart and he was surprised to find his support increasing well beyond his expectations. The demand gathered into a protest for the resignation of the prime minister who was assailed for her corrupt and autocratic rule. The basic departure in her approach was that the politics which since Independence had had a consensual element began bearing her personal domineering stamp. She, in fact, began going out of her way to rub her political opponent the wrong way.

JP founded the Yuva Chatra Sangh to bring students to the vanguard of his movement. They began protest marches in Patna against unemployment, corruption, and inflation. The scene appears so familiar in the present time. Old Gandhians and the socialists who were waiting in the wings jumped in to try to convert it into a mass movement.

🪷

I was unhappy in the *Statesman*. Irani had reduced me to the position of consulting editor from resident editor. He then wanted me to vacate my room as well, and asked me to sit somewhere else. Subsequently, he withdrew my peon and telephone too. What hurt me most was that a colleague and a friend, Nihal Singh, tried to effect the changes. It was in fact he who conveyed Irani's decision to me. Nihal's attitude exuded authority which was humiliating. I could understand Irani's action but not those of Nihal who himself subsequently suffered at Irani's hands and had to leave the *Statesman*. The only person who stood by me during those days was my secretary, G. Barret. She refused to work with Nihal and preferred to stay on with me. I was reduced to writing only my weekly column, 'Between the Lines'. Irani tried to stop that too but did not succeed because the editor N.J. Nanporia refused to permit that.

In fact, my support to Nanporia when Irani wanted to get rid of him was the reason for Irani's annoyance with me. There was a time when during a visit to Calcutta, the headquarters of the *Statesman*, he put me up at his house 'to give a message to the staff', as he explained. He hated journalists as a class, probably because he was not accepted by the fraternity even when he appointed himself as the *Statesman*'s editor-in-chief. Once he told Inder Kumar Gujral, then the information minister, that the government should tell him if it wanted the *Statesman* to take a particular line. Surprisingly, Irani was commended by the Bengal intelligentsia when he wrote a daily column 'Caveat'. His vehement criticism of New Delhi was the only thing lapped up by Bengalis, who tend to be anti-Centre.

Ram Nath Goenka (RNG), owner of the *Indian Express*, knew all about the *Statesman* through Irani, who claimed to be his younger son, next to RNG's own son, B.D. Goenka. One day RNG invited me to breakfast, famous for its idli-dosa, and offered me the job of editor of the Express News Service. Before I could react, he said he knew that I had been reduced to a zero in the *Statesman*. I joined the *Indian Express* in March 1975, even though I was aware that RNG was close to the Jana Sangh and had once won a Lok Sabha seat on their ticket. To his credit, he never tried to impose the Jana Sangh views on the paper and left it to us, journalists, to run it.

The protest against Indira Gandhi was gaining momentum. I was glad to be in the *Express* which openly supported JP and his movement. It was heavenly living in that atmosphere of defiance. To me it appeared as if one was back in the days of the national struggle, this time determined to usher in the dawn of economic independence which had eluded us after winning independence for our nation.

I was surprised when, within a couple of weeks of my joining, RNG asked me to write a story that Prime Minister Indira Gandhi proposed to suspend the constitution and lock up the opposition leaders, including JP. I could not get any confirmation and therefore did not do the story. This notwithstanding, I found the same story appearing on the front-page of *Motherland*, the official organ of the Jana Sangh.

I could never imagine that Nehru's daughter would ever do something so autocratic even though she was on a warpath against JP. The demand for *parivartan* got translated into a demand for the resignation of Prime Minister Indira Gandhi, particularly because she had won the elections on a promise to eradicate poverty (*garibi hatao*) but had done little to reduce it.

This was also the time when I was collecting material for my book, *India after Nehru*. When I met M.O. Mathai, Nehru's personal secretary to get his inputs, he was willing to talk about days with Nehru provided I reported him accurately. I was surprised at this condition because I did not have a reputation for putting words into people's mouth. Sensing my embarrassment, he said he would be saying 'certain things' which I might be reluctant to report. He volunteered to sign the transcript of the discussion we were to have.

My first question to him was: 'Why were pandits summoned from Kashi and why was sandalwood used for Nehru's cremation?' 'This was all Indira's doing,' said Mathai, 'You can check with Vijayalakshmi Pandit who rang me to express her horror.' Nehru, he said, was against all such practises and he had denounced them throughout his life. Still, according to Shraddha Mata, a godwoman, Nehru many times showed her his palm to learn what the line of fortune said about his future.

'How would you assess Indira Gandhi?' I asked him. Before saying anything he reminded me of my promise to include everything he said in my book and he was willing to sign my notes after every interview. I emphasized to him that as a journalist I had to check with the persons on whom he might have commented or seek confirmation through some other source. Mathai did not want to continue with the interview until I promised I would use what he said. The second day when I rang him he hung up the telephone and refused to entertain any further calls from me.

A few days after this, when RNG was in Delhi, we discussed the *Express*. RNG also told me that he had employed Feroze Gandhi, a fearless Lok Sabha member and Indira Gandhi's husband, at the instance of Jawaharlal Nehru. However, Indira was not very happy. Eventually, RNG said he had to ask

Feroze Gandhi to leave. What he tried to convey was that there was some friction between Indira Gandhi and her husband. I cannot comment on this but I recall visiting the place overlooking Paris where Feroze proposed to her. It was a green landscape dotted with small tenements. I had never hitherto realized that Paris was so green. On the steps where I was watching the scenic beauty Feroze had offered Indira a ring which she put on her finger as a sign of consent. Although she lived with her father when she was in Delhi, Feroze would often visit Nehru's residence.

I wondered whether I should pick up the thread with Mathai where I had left it off, but before I could decide on an interview with him, my book, *The Judgement: An Inside story of the Emergency* (1975–77), hit the market. The publishers of my book sent me Mathai's manuscript of *Years with Nehru* and wanted me to advise them whether they should publish it or not. He had devoted nearly three pages to me, calling me all kinds of names because I had described him as Nehru's aide in my book *India After Nehru*. He certainly occupied a higher position, whatever his designation. I had seen him talking to Pant, standing with his leg on the chair opposite Pant. I had called him Nehru's aide in a general sense because he was much more than a special assistant.

I advised the publishers to print the book except the chapter 'She', where he had written about his escapades. I found the writing in poor taste. The publishers scrupulously followed my advice. Some days after the book was finally published, I found a cyclostyled copy of the chapter, 'She', on my table in the office. My peon was on leave. The one sitting in the veranda had no idea who had come to leave the papers in my room. I tried to find out from other peons but drew a blank. I rang up the publishers and gave them hell. They denied ever parting with the chapter which they claimed was with them in a locked almirah. I learnt subsequently that the cyclostyled chapter, had been circulated widely to the amusement of many.

After Indira Gandhi returned to power in 1980, two IB officials came one day to my cabin, inquiring who could have circulated the chapter. They wanted to know if I had anyone in mind. I told them the publishers had not done so. Then who did it? I had not the faintest idea. They did eventually locate the person.

I was not surprised when Mathai was denied the Congress seat in the Rajya Sabha from Kerala, his home state where he had settled. His name was on top of the list sent by State Congress Committee. One Congress leader told me that Indira Gandhi had herself crossed it out. When I asked why, he said: 'Indira Gandhi was like the communists who forgave critics but not renegades.'

Coming back to the JP Movement, it was spreading like a wildfire because it was representing the people's grievances against Indira Gandhi's performance and misgovernance. Political parties in the Opposition were vying with one another to associate themselves with him. The communists remained distant. The CPI, together with the CPI(M), was part of Indira Gandhi's entourage because of their ideological differences with JP.

The Rashtriya Swayamsewak Sangh (RSS) and its *parivar*, including the Jana Sangh, were keen to hitch their wagon to JP. They were not growing because they were wearing Hindutva on their sleeves, much to the distaste of the common man. However, as they just wanted a platform which could improve their image, they voluntarily threw their support behind JP. However, JP was cautious. The mass movement he was contemplating had no place for parties with a sectarian or communal outlook.

The RSS leaders assured JP that the Jana Sangh would have no contact with them and would integrate with any organization he founded. It was during this time that the question of dual membership arose. JP was insistent that the Jana Sangh members must break ties with the RSS. Both the RSS and the Jana Sangh leaders gave him an undertaking that once a new party was formed the Jana Sangh would merge with it, giving up its separate identity as well as its name. JP was impressed by their readiness to follow him without asking for anything in return.

This was JP's greatest mistake. An emotional man as he was, he was led by his heart. The Jana Sangh wanted credibility by associating themselves with a secular movement in order to obliterate the stigma of Hindu communalism, and they have done well since. Till then they had never crossed the double-digit figure in the Lok Sabha. However, after associating themselves with the JP Movement they were able to win 80 seats when the elections were held in 1977.

Indira Gandhi was perturbed by the JP Movement and wanted to hold talks with him but he was reluctant to have any dialogue, aware that nothing would come out of it. A cabinet minister, D.P. Dhar, brought in S. Mulgaonkar, chief editor of the *Indian Express*, to persuade JP to meet Indira Gandhi. The meeting was a disaster. Indira Gandhi stuck to the stand that the Congress had no money in its coffers, the same point she had made when JP had met her earlier to complain that the Congress had spent nearly Rs 10 crores to get Nandini Satpati elected in a by-election to the Orissa assembly.

There were too many excesses committed by the security forces throughout the country. Even a small protest was suppressed with an iron hand. JP gave a call to the police and the army not to obey the illegal orders of the government: orders to detain people without any grounds or to harass people who opposed the government.

JP was trying to give a moral edge to the movement but it had little effect on Indira Gandhi. She accused him of instigating the police and the armed forces to rise in revolt. Many intellectuals were taken in by her interpretation. His defence was that he did not want the law and order machinery to obey orders which were illegal and unconstitutional. What he did not, however, realize was that the police and security forces had already crossed the Laksaman Rekha of law and morality. The governments at the Centre and in the states had converted them into a willing tool of tyranny.

The battle between JP and Indira Gandhi was now in the open. JP's demand for *parivartan* became a battle-cry as the days passed. He published a weekly, *Freeman*, which was financed by the *Indian Express* to spread his message. Indira Gandhi became increasingly jittery, not only because of JP but also because she feared worse in the case before Allahabad High Court. Her fears were not unfounded.

❈

Justice Jagmohan Lal Sinha debarred (12 June 1975) Indira Gandhi from occupying any electoral post for six years, holding her guilty of corrupt practices during the elections. He was pronouncing his judgement on the petition that Raj Narain, a socialist leader, had filed against Indira Gandhi's election to the Lok Sabha in 1971.

The petition was allowed on two counts. The first was that she had used Yashpal Kapoor, officer on special duty in the prime minister's secretariat, to 'further her election prospects'. Sinha said that although Kapoor had begun electioneering for Indira Gandhi on 7 January 1971 and tendered his resignation only on 13 January, he had continued in government service until 25 January. Indira Gandhi, according to the judge, had 'held herself out as candidate' on 29 December 1970, the day she addressed a news conference in New Delhi and announced her decision to stand for election.

The second impropriety was that she had obtained the assistance of government officials in UP to build rostrums from which she addressed election rallies. The officials had also arranged for loudspeakers and electricity.

However strict the electoral law, I felt that the judgement was like using a hammer to kill a fly. Sinha gave her a fortnight to file an appeal against his judgement in the Supreme Court. Indira Gandhi had never expected such a verdict and therefore had designated no one to file an appeal against it. A local loyalist, V.N. Kher, a lawyer who was subsequently appointed chief justice of India, submitted an application for appeal in a personal capacity.

The Supreme Court was on vacation and the judge for the period was Justice Krishna Iyer. In the judgement he pronounced, he allowed her to continue as prime minister till the disposal of her appeal but forfeited her right to vote in the House. I met Iyer soon after he had delivered the judgement to find out who had met him before he gave his verdict. He named S.A. Dange, a communist leader from Maharashtra and the then serving Supreme Court judge P.N. Bhagwati. The latter reportedly told Iyer: 'Brother, you must consider all aspects before giving your judgement.'

Justice Krishna Iyer told me as recently as November 2009 that the people considered him responsible for the Emergency that Indira Gandhi imposed a few days after the judgement. What Justice Iyer said had a grain of truth and I told him so. I suspect that being a leftist in his leanings he had a soft corner for Indira Gandhi who was said to be left-of-centre. The Left generally supported her because of her nationalization of banks and insurance companies. Some responsibility for what happened during the Emergency rested on the shoulders of Justice Iyer because he gave her the stay.

When I met Justice Sinha at his residence in Allahabad many months after he had delivered the judgement, he told me how a Congress MP had tried to bribe him and how a colleague on the bench told him that he could be elevated to the Supreme Court if he gave the judgement in Indira Gandhi's favour (the judge who said this to Justice J.L. Sinha had to resign when the Janata Dal government came to power after Indira Gandhi's defeat in 1977). How to keep the judgement secret was Sinha's predicament. He wrote the operative part by hand and sent his stenographer on leave. Even so, every government intelligence agency attempted a variety of stratagems to learn about the judgement. Even sadhus were used because Justice Sinha was said to be prone to their influence.

After the Allahabad High Court judgement, Indira Gandhi had thought of stepping down. My guess is that if she had done so and had gone back to the people for a verdict on her electoral offence, offering her apologies, she would have got re-elected. However, two persons dissuaded her from submitting the resignation. One was her principal advisor Sanjay Gandhi, her son, who completely ruled out resignation. The other was Siddhartha Shankar Ray, then West Bengal chief minister, who advised her to impose Emergency. She reportedly told him that India was already under an Emergency following the Bangladesh war. He said what he meant was an internal Emergency which would enable her to suspend fundamental rights and allow her to rule as she wished.

A dropout from Doon School and an apprentice motor mechanic with Rolls Royce in England, Sanjay had no educational qualification but was keen to enter politics. Indira Gandhi's predicament after she had been unseated by the Allahabad High Court provided him with the opportunity he sought. What fascinated him was money and power, and he could see them within his grasp through his mother. Long before the Emergency she would discuss politics with him rather than her elder son Rajiv Gandhi who later became India's prime minister. She would even remark at the dining table that Rajiv, who was an airline pilot at that time, had no understanding of politics whatsoever.

Sanjay was Indira Gandhi's refuge. She was confident that he would help her in her hour of need. He was credited with having given her the election-winning slogan in 1971: 'They say *Indira Hatao* [oust Indira] but I say *Garibi Hatao* [oust poverty].' Now he had to do more than just coin a slogan. He had to tell her how to extricate herself from the legal tangle in which she was enmeshed. Sanjay knew his mother was not one to throw in towel easily, but at that time she was on the verge of doing just that. She had already informally sounded out Kamlapati Tripathi about his stepping in until her appeal at Supreme Court had been disposed of.

Sanjay knew that he had to convince her that she was needed by the country and had to rise above the obligations under the judgement. His chief aide was thirty-five year old R.K. Dhawan, additional private secretary in the prime minister's secretariat. Sanjay used him to manipulate the entire government machinery. He had yet another friend in the ruthless Bansi Lal, chief minister of Haryana, who too had no scruples. Helping Sanjay from the wings was Congress president Dev Kant Barooah who 'proclaimed that India was Indira and Indira was India' (reminiscent of the oath administered to the Nazi youth by Germany's Adolf Hitler).

JP received an urgent message from the opposition parties to come to Delhi to lead their rally. He however declined, being in favour of awaiting the judgement of the Supreme Court on Indira Gandhi's appeal. Little did he suspect that Indira Gandhi had completely different plans.

Within 24 hours after Justice Krishna Iyer's judgement Indira Gandhi imposed the Emergency on the night of 25 June 1975. She did not consult the cabinet and wrote straight to President Fakhruddin Ali Ahmed, beholden to her for the office, that she would have liked to take up the matter with the cabinet but unfortunately it had not been possible that night. She also wrote that 'there is an imminent danger to the security of India being threatened by internal disturbance'.

If a cabinet meeting could be convened at 90 minutes' notice, as was actually the case on the morning of 26 June, there was no reason why a cabinet meeting could not have been held at any time between her first visit to the president at 5 p.m. on 25 June and the actual signature of the proclamation at about 11.00–11.30 p.m. There is sufficient evidence to prove that Indira Gandhi had planned the imposition of the Emergency at least as early as 22 June. She had also shared the idea with some of her political confidants on the morning of 25 June.

When I went to meet Y.B. Chavan and Jagjivan Ram at their homes on 26 June, I found intelligence officials noting down the car registration numbers and names of people coming to visit them. Chavan was afraid to meet me and Jagjivan Ram, who met me for a minute, looked nervous. All that Jagjivan Ram told me was that he was expecting to be arrested. When he uttered these words he took off the receiver from the telephone in the room, aware that his phone was being tapped. Earlier he had told me that he expected the Supreme Court to give her only a qualified stay because the court had never granted a clear stay in such cases. He thought the Supreme Court judgement would be the time to rise in revolt. 'We can afford to wait till then,' he said. I thought him too cowardly to lead such a revolt.

Indira Gandhi did not explain why action was being taken only after the Allahabad judgement; why the enforcement of the ordinary law could not deal with indiscipline in factories and campuses, and why normal laws could not cope with whatever else was not well with the nation.

That would have been hard to explain, so perhaps she felt there was no purpose in attempting it. She realized her credibility was low; she said at a meeting to condole the death of Lalit Narayan Mishra, 'Even if I were to be killed they would say that I myself had got it done.' Mishra was a dear friend. He rang me up at midnight before going to Samastipur, that he had handed his resignation to her personally. He sadly remarked that he would be killed at Samastipur and put down the phone. It proved to be true. He was murdered at Samastipur the following day. The murder mystery has not been resolved to this day.

Indira Gandhi's one person rule was making her more and more intolerant. She loved the story of Jeanne d'Arc. As a child, Indira would wrap her arm around a pillar, raise the other hand high and proclaim that she would lead her people to freedom some day, just as her role model, her father, had done. Instead, she led the country to disaster. There was no one either in her party or the cabinet to tell her that she was taking a wrong course.

Barooah flirted with right-wing communists because that gave him a veneer of ideology which went down well in an underdeveloped country. That did not please Sanjay Gandhi who called him a commie but the common threat they faced from the Opposition brought Barooah and Sanjay together, at least for the time being.

The first step they took was to get a crowd together to testify to Indira Gandhi's popularity. This was an exercise they had undertaken many times before. Trucks were requisitioned and sent to villages to bring people who were paid and provided with free food for the day. Congress leaders in Punjab, Haryana, UP, and Rajasthan were rung up by R.K. Dhawan to organize rallies.

So crude was the exhibition of support for Indira Gandhi that some Congress MPs took exception to the populist demonstrations. Her reply was simply: 'They are spontaneous.' She even attacked the media for not giving adequate coverage to the support she enjoyed. She would tell audiences that editors would change headlines in tomorrow's paper to run down the massive demonstrations in her support.

There was not a single report of apprehension of any serious breakdown of the law and order situation or deterioration in economic conditions from any public functionary. The official records of that time, be it secret, confidential, or public, and newspaper reports, are unanimous that there was no untoward event or even a hint of that to justify the imposition of Emergency. Why indeed was there such an acute and immediate need for it arose only after the Allahabad High Court judgement.

People at large were quite unaware of what the Emergency signified; they were dazed and confused. It gradually dawned upon them that the democratic system in which they had put their faith for over 25 years had been derailed. Fundamental rights were suspended and judicial powers curtailed. A customer reportedly walked into a book store in Delhi in those days and asked for a copy of the constitution, 'Sorry, we do not stock periodicals,' replied the shopkeeper.

Nearly a lakh of people were detained. JP and other opposition leaders were also put behind bars. A series of totally illegal and unwarranted actions followed involving untold human misery and suffering. In the absence of any explanation, Indira Gandhi took a political decision of dire significance in a desperate endeavour to save herself from consequences of a judicial verdict against her.

Swaran Singh did raise the point at the cabinet that as an Emergency had already been imposed was there need for another? Two ministers, K.C. Pant and Karan Singh, after the cabinet meeting, discussed between themselves the bad name the Emergency would give to the country but they were so cowed down by fear that they obeyed Sanjay Gandhi, now the master of their universe.

The press was gagged, effective dissent was smothered, and democratic values suppressed. High handed and arbitrary actions were undertaken with impunity. Tyrants sprouted at all levels; tyrants whose claim to authority was largely based on their proximity to the seat of power. No one from her own family supported Indira Gandhi in the imposition of the Emergency; Rajiv Gandhi and his wife, Sonia, were unhappy and reportedly did not participate in the political discussions at the dining table, largely confining themselves to their room.

Vijayalakshmi Pandit was openly critical of the Emergency. It is said that there was a very unpleasant meeting when she called on Indira Gandhi to voice her concern over the Emergency. Vijayalakshmi did not, however, campaign when the Janata Dal repeatedly requested her to address meetings during the polls.

Nayantara Sehgal, her daughter, was one of the most outspoken critics of the Emergency, but in any event she and Indira Gandhi never got along well. Nayantara became particularly bitter when she found that she was not a welcome guest at Indira Gandhi's house. One remark she made in my presence was that when 'Mamu (Jawaharlal Nehru) was alive even our dog was welcome at that house but now none of us, not even my mother, is welcome.'

Only a handful of civil servants stood their ground, others were too scared to lose their jobs. Some found in it an opportunity to occupy high positions on the understanding that they would carry out illegal orders. Sanjay Gandhi converted the civil servants into a servile breed; the willing tools of tyranny. They have not to this day recovered from the loss of esteem in the eyes of the public if not their own. They wield authority, not respect. Their political masters know that bureaucrats are beholden to them because they are partners in the loot in which both of them indulge without a twinge of conscience.

There was no doubting the mood of triumph in the prime minister's house. The entire operation on the night of 26 June was painless. George Fernandes, the labour leader; Nanaji Deshmukh and Subramaniam Swami, both Jana Sangh members; and a few others went 'underground' but all the important leaders were arrested.

'I told you nothing would happen,' Sanjay chided his mother. Bansi Lal said he had expected that no one would dare to rise against them. Word was sent to Allahabad to 'fix' Justice Sinha. All the papers relating to his career were screened, his family members harassed, and he was shadowed by the police all the time.

Inder Kumar Gujral, once a member of her kitchen cabinet, took umbrage when Sanjay Gandhi ordered him over the phone to do something about the press. Inder reportedly said that he was a colleague of his mother and not a person at his (Sanjay's) beck and call. Vidya Charan Shukla took over from Gujral who was transferred to the Planning Commission on 28 June. P.N. Haksar, once her principal secretary, was already hibernating there after his removal from the PMO.

Shukla was as enthusiastic as Sanjay Gandhi to get the censorship machinery going at the very earliest. Till then the publication of the local newspapers was stopped by cutting off power supply to their offices and presses. The censorship rules were hurriedly copied from the home ministry manual which had been prepared after the 1962 India–China war. I, as information officer had participated in the meetings where the manual was finalized. Little did I anticipate then that the same manual would be used for purposes of censorship.

Indira Gandhi was initially nervous, and felt it was too early to say that all had gone well. Most chief ministers, however, reported that 'the situation is under control'. On the streets of Delhi, the pall of fear hung heavy. Life was otherwise outwardly normal. The *Statesman* published a photograph by the gifted photographer Raghu Rai that told all: it showed a man peddling a cycle with two children on it, a woman walking behind, and scores of policemen standing all around. The caption said that life was normal in Chandni Chowk (a censor official without realizing the message the photo conveyed 'passed' it and was transferred the very next day).

The cyclostyled forms of MISA (Maintenance of Internal Security Act) orders came in handy to many district magistrates who put their signatures to blank warrants and left the rest to the police. Arrests were made in accordance with lists prepared earlier on the basis of intelligence records. No wonder then that the police raided a house in Agra to arrest a person who had died in 1968.

In Haryana it became normal practice for the government to arrest anyone under MISA and Defence of India Rules (DIR), two measures to detain people without trial. No grounds were required to detain anyone, high or low, friend or foe. During their detention, political prisoners were treated as common criminals.

In other parts of the country, newspapers more or less obeyed the orders of authorities. In Kerala which was under the rule of the CPM, there was no strict observation of censorship rules. Sanjay Gandhi wanted to impose central rule in the state but Indira Gandhi stopped him from doing so.

The Maharashtra High Court Bar Association was the first in the country to condemn Indira Gandhi's authoritarian rule. Ram Jethmalani, president of the All India Bar Association, compared her to Mussolini and Hitler, although he had argued that as the Supreme Court had given her a stay it should be respected. The bar associations in many other states followed suit, but for reasons unknown, the West Bengal Bar Association remained silent.

Gujarat escaped the rigours of the Emergency because of the United Front government in the state. Chief Minister Babubhai Patel wanted to speak over the radio but was not given permission by the Centre. That was his first brush with the Emergency. The Centre sent out instructions to states to round up Jana Sangh and other political leaders. Babubhai did not oblige, and when he finally arrested them, he did so under DIR which enabled an arrested person to be released on bail, a recourse which was denied to a MISA detenu. Defiant, Babubhai said in an interview that he would ensure that civil liberty activists were encouraged to wear black badges, fly black flags from their homes, and hang on their doors the preamble to the Indian constitution which stressed human rights. Public demonstrations included silent marches, student processions, hunger strikes, and sit-ins at public places.

The state gradually became a refuge for hundreds of Indira Gandhi's critics from all over India. Navnirman student leaders would have probably suffered had there been no Babubhai government to shield them, and it was they who had brought down the Chimanbhai Patel ministry in 1974.

Tamil Nadu defied censorship. Still, the DMK government, headed by M. Karunanidhi, did not follow a policy of open defiance and declared that it would carry out Delhi's directives 'acceptable to us'. Unofficially, the DMK was against the Emergency. When I met Karunanidhi to seek his support for anti-Emergency activity he was afraid to do anything in public. He said he could at best help me start an underground newspaper which, he made very clear, should be distributed outside the state.

In West Bengal, from Chief Minister Sidhartha Shankar Ray down to the foot constable, everyone found the Emergency powers useful to settle old scores, personal and political. Two journalists, Gourkishore Ghosh and Barun Sengupta of *Anand Bazar Patrika*, who were critical of the chief minister, were arrested. Ghosh had criticized the latter on political grounds in a booklet, *Kalikata*, but Sengupta's attack was personal. It was easy to arrest Ghosh but Sengupta fled West Bengal and stayed in Delhi for quite a while, enjoying the protection of Sanjay, an indication of the strained relations between Sanjay Gandhi and the West Bengal chief minister. Eventually the police arrested him, and he was badly treated in jail, largely because of the chief minister's annoyance.

I had been warned by London's *New Statesman* correspondent, who had met me two days earlier before the imposition of Emergency that his information was that the constitution would be suspended, the top leadership detained, and the press gagged. I had politely admonished him that India was a democracy and such things did not happen here. The same correspondent wanted to know what lay in the future after the imposition of the Emergency. I told him I did not know because the nation had never faced such a situation before. He sympathized with me. I remarked that the third world countries had enjoyed democracy as long as their rulers had allowed it. India was different, I told myself. It had gone through a long struggle to win freedom for its people and would in the long run retain it.

After the Emergency, when the Justice J.C. Shah Commission examined the excesses, it said:

> Absence of the freedom of the press and the severity of the censorship rules coupled with ad hoc authoritarian oral orders, rendered the channels of communication over the subcontinent choked and polluted.

The commission warned:

> The nation owes it to the present and the succeeding generations to ensure that the administrative set up is not subverted in future in the manner it was done to serve the personal ends of any one individual or a group of individuals in or near the government.

It was shocking to observe the ease with which Indira Gandhi and Sanjay were able to assume control over the entire administrative machinery throughout the country and the willingness with which officials and other government employees accepted this. District magistrates and police commissioners obediently carried out instructions coming from Indira Gandhi and her son. 'Where was the steel frame?' I wondered. Was it a house of cards that collapsed when an autocrat took over? What would have happened to government servants had they not obeyed illegal and whimsical orders? At worst, they could have been transferred. It showed the extent to which Indira Gandhi would go to hold on to power. She was always an empress but had now become grossly imperious.

It was disappointing, to say the least, the way the media and more specifically the journalists reacted to the new situation. Nearly all of them caved in, stricken by an epidemic of fear. However, there were a few exceptions. Two English language journals which had been critical of India's Emergency regulations were forced to stop publication. One was the weekly *Opinion*, punished by the Maharashtra state government because it had 'violated' the censorship rules. The other periodical, the monthly *Seminar*, decided to voluntarily cease publication after they rejected a government order to submit their copy to the censor authorities. The courageous couple, Romesh Thapar and his bold wife Raj, wrote in the final issue that *Seminar* 'cannot surrender the integrity and right of free expression in this way'. No newspaper published the news of the closures of *Seminar* and *Opinion*.

I knew Romesh Thapar when he was a member of Indira Gandhi's 'Kitchen cabinet' but I had kept a distance from him then for that very reason. Raj contacted my wife when I was in jail. We became close friends, and that included their chirpy daughter Mala. What impressed me about Raj and Romesh was not their ideological background but their commitment to freedom which they doggedly defended.

L.K. Advani was quite right in chiding journalists after the Emergency: 'You were asked to bend but you chose to crawl.' My feeling is that virtually the entire tribe of journalists had been spoilt by the attention they received from the establishment and the corporate sector. It was well known that at selected press conferences they were doled out suit-lengths and promoters' shares. Any sense of independence had been corroded. Some of them in fact had no real commitment to the profession. The truth was that the press was already too nice, too refined, and only too willing to 'accommodate'. The ground was therefore fertile for the imposition of censorship. By contrast, the journalists in Pakistan showed courage in the face of imposition of martial law. They did not mince words in criticizing the military regime, some 120 went to jail, and 13 received lashes from the police.

What really worried me was not indiscriminate detentions or the atrocities committed during the Emergency but the destruction of institutions and the ejection of all morality from politics. For most, the dividing line between right and wrong, moral and immoral, ceased to exist.

Indira Gandhi and I used to be good friends. As the chairperson of the Citizens' Committee, which Nehru had constituted during China's attack to mobilize public opinion, she had got to know me well because I was the committee's channel to the press. As the home ministry's information officer, that was my job. We would often discuss the country's political situation. At one time, I expressed my wish to join politics. She conveyed this to my friend Inder Gujral, who said that he was surprised to learn that I had 'political ambitions'.

My quarrel with Mrs Gandhi began when I criticized her for using the government machinery to fight against the old guard in the Congress party. She did not believe in the correctness of methods but only in results.

When the Emergency was imposed I wrote a letter to Indira Gandhi to criticize her dictatorial rule and press censorship. I wrote:

> Madam, it is always difficult for a newspaperman to decide when he should reveal what. In the process of doing so he knows he runs the risk of annoying someone somewhere. In the case of the government, the tendency to hide the

truth and feel horrified once it is revealed is greater than in any individual. Somehow those who occupy high positions in the administration labour under the belief that they – and they alone – know what the nation should be told, how and when, and they are annoyed if any news which they do not wish to be revealed appears in print. In a free society – and you have repeatedly said after the Emergency that you have faith in such a concept – the press has a duty to inform the public. This is sometimes an unpleasant task, but it has to be performed because a free society is founded on free information. If the press were to publish only government handouts or official statements to which it is reduced today, who will pinpoint lapses, deficiencies, or errors?

The reply on her behalf came from Sharda Prasad, her information adviser. He said:

If censorship was introduced in the last few weeks it was not because of any personal or governmental hyper-sensitivitiness but because certain newspapers had become part and parcel of [the] opposition front. When these parties had to be prevented from carrying out their plans to disrupt national life, their principal organs of propaganda had also naturally to be restrained from stirring up trouble. Restrictions on the press have indeed contributed to the situation being under control in the last few days. Freedom of the press is part of the personal freedom which in any country is temporarily abridged in times of national emergency.

What hurt me most was a comment Indira Gandhi made in the presence of a few editors who had gone to 'congratulate' her for imposing the Emergency. She asked them what had happened to the big names in journalism because not a dog had 'barked'. I went round to some offices of newspapers and news-agencies to request journalists to assemble at the Press Club of India the following morning at 10 a.m. (28 June 1975). To my surprise, 103 journalists, including some editors, came. I had drafted the resolution at home and it was passed: 'We the journalists assembled here deplore the imposition of censorship and urge upon the government to remove it immediately. We also demand the release of journalists already detained.' I sent the resolution to the president, the prime minister, and minister for information and broadcasting under my signature.

For the first time I give the list of the 27 journalists who signed the resolution which I had left at the club table after the meeting. I thought it politic to remove the list from the Press Club and kept it with me. The names, in the order of signature, are: N. Mukherjee, R. Bajpai, B.H. Sinha, Raju Nagarajan, A. Mani, Sumi Sridharan, Ashim Chowdhury, V. Raghvan, Anand Vardhan, Virender Kapoor, S.C. Raje, Subhas Kirpekar, A. Rahman, Arvind Ghose, Balbir Punj, V.P. Bhatia, Vijay Kranti, Vedpratap Vedic, Om Prakash,

Prabhash Joshi, U.A. Sumya Prakash, Gopal Sharma, Chand Joshi, Irfan Khan, Jayant Mehta, S. Bhagnagar, and R.D. Gupta.

As the news spread, V.C. Shukla rang up, asking me to meet him. The first question he asked was: 'Where is the love letter?' I replied laughingly, 'It is in a safe deposit'. Shukla's tone changed and he threatened: 'You can be arrested.' 'Many people are telling me to detain you,' he repeated. When I said that I must be on the list of Yunus Khan, Indira Gandhi's ambassador-at-large, Shukla remained silent, but his authoritative, bullying tone surprised me. He said that I had been hobnobbing with foreign journalists and he in particular mentioned the name of Peter Hazelhurst, the principal representative of the *Times*, London. As a correspondent of the *Times*, I knew him well. He was one of India's best friends and had stood by it during the Bangladesh operation in 1971. Soon after his arrival in New Delhi on 26 June he had come to my house and discussed the state of affairs of the free Indian press. Shukla said that it would be unwise for me to be seen in Peter's company. I told him that it was not possible for me to comply with his wishes.

Raising his voice, Shukla said, 'We are going to fix up these foreign journalists; they have been pampered too much.' I could guess that the adverse reaction to the Emergency in the US, the UK, and Europe had rattled the government. The foreign press had rightly sensed that India was slipping into dictatorship and that Indira Gandhi was casting personal liberties into the dustbin of ordinances and constitutional amendments. Before long Peter Hazelhurst was expelled from India.

My weekly article in the *Indian Express* appeared on the day (3 July 1975) I met Shukla. Entitled 'Not Enough Mr Bhutto', it was about Zulfikar Ali Bhutto and Pakistan, comparing his presidency with that of Field Marshal Ayub Khan. My point was: 'The worst part is the suffocation of the people. The press is gagged and statements by the Opposition are suppressed. Even minor criticism is not tolerated.' Shukla said that those in government were not fools. Anyone could deduce that I was referring to Indira Gandhi and the Emergency. That of course had been my intention and I could have thought of no better way of hoodwinking the censors.

I wrote two more articles in the subsequent weeks. On 10 July, I reviewed American history to mark the US bicentennial celebrations and wrote:

> Those who preached democracy were seen to have bloodstained hands. The exit of President Nixon, even though he had won the largest majority that any American President ever had, was because of a gullible press and public opinion.

On 17 July, in a piece entitled 'The Tasks before Students', I again employed the allegorical technique by quoting Voltaire:

Not long ago a distinguished company was discussing the trite and frivolous question, who was the greatest man—Caesar, Alexander, Tamerlane or Cromwell. Someone answered that without doubt it was Isaac Newton, and rightly so, for it is he who masters our minds with the force of truth, to whom we owe reverence and not to those who enslave them by violence ... students should become doctors, engineers, or professors but never journalists.

I had to stop writing the column because the *Indian Express* was informed by censor officials that 'no article written by Shri Kuldip Nayar either in his name or written by him under any pseudonym should be published in your newspaper without being submitted for the scrutiny by the censor'.

Indira Gandhi claimed that she was working within the ambit of the constitution and defended her action in the name of saving democracy. She had to emphasize this because she loathed the word authoritarian used in conjunction with her name. However dictatorial the governance, the democratic façade had to be maintained. As George Orwell said, 'It is almost universally felt that when we call a country democratic, we are praising it: consequently the dictator of every kind of regime claims that it is a democracy.'

Surprisingly, Margaret Thatcher, at a press conference in Delhi defended Indira Gandhi. When I reminded her about her defence of Indira Gandhi in London when I was high commissioner, Margaret Thatcher said: 'I found her isolated.' This defence sounded odd. Traits of her authoritarian personality resembled Indira Gandhi's way of functioning.

Socialist International decided to send a delegation on 15 July, including former West German Chancellor Willy Brandt, and Irish Posts and Telegraphs Minister Connor Cruise O'Brien to visit JP in his place of detention. New Delhi, however, refused permission on the ground that it would be 'gross interference in India's internal affairs'. In response, Socialist International said 'all socialists must now feel a great sense of personal tragedy at what is happening to India'.

Official opinion in the West was that India had lost its democracy for all times to come and, however painful, they might as well accept this rather than annoy Indira Gandhi. US Secretary of State Henry Kissinger discussed the matter in the State Department and came to the conclusion that it would be easier to deal with New Delhi now. Indira Gandhi's policy would be 'pragmatic'; one of his aides said at the meeting: 'You mean, purchasable.'

Press censorship began to be used for party and personal ends. The censor would disallow news items or even statements by Congress or Youth Congress leaders simply because they did not fit in with the 'demands' of the Emergency. V.C. Shukla was forever in touch with R.K. Dhawan, and through him Sanjay Gandhi. Whichever state Shukla visited, he told the censor and media not to report on the dissensions within the Congress. The chief ministers used censorship to black out criticism against them and their group. Punjab

Congress president Mohinder Singh Gill found it difficult to get his statements published because Chief Minister Zail Singh had instructed the censor officials not to allow Gill's observations to appear in the press. Information Minister Subrata Mukherjee in West Bengal told the censor's office not to clear any news against his group.

I was distressed to see on Doordarshan Shabana Azmi and few other artists singing a chorus. It was entertainment of sorts during the Emergency to spread the message of normalcy.

※

I was on the panel for the selection of deputy principal officers at the UPSC office when another expert, Nikhil Chakravarti, a renowned leftist journalist, who strongly upheld the freedom of press, warned me that my house could be searched. I shared this information with my family over dinner. Rajiv, my younger son, collected my papers and deposited the bundle at the house of one of his friends. Two days later, when a police officer knocked at our door on the morning of 24 July, I told him that he could search the house but there was no objectionable material. He said he had come to arrest me and showed me the warrant. The first thing I did was to inform the UPSC secretary that I would be unable to serve on the panel because I was being arrested.

The grounds of my detention had been concocted, as the then additional deputy commissioner told me later when he was a secretary to the government. He said he had received orders from R.K. Dhawan for my arrest. When we didn't find anything against you, he said, we rang him up to say that we had consulted the superintendent of police and found no ground for arrest. Dhawan said that they had to arrest me because Sanjay Gandhi had ordered it. Then they concocted a story that I had gone to Jama Masjid to incite Muslims against the government. In the Intelligence Bureau diary there was a noting that I had once had lunch with the Shahi Imam at Jama Masjid.

In Washington, India's ambassador, Triloki Nath Kaul, said that he did not know the details of the offences committed by Kuldip Nayar. 'I know Nayar,' the ambassador said. 'He is a friend of mine. He is supposed to have sent some dispatches abroad surreptitiously, which is a violation of the law.'

In a cable sent to Indira Gandhi, the editor of the *Times*, London, said, 'Nayar has not sent any dispatches to the *Times* which do not comply with Indian censorship; we have of course not asked him to do so.'

District Magistrate Sushil Kumar stated at the hearings of the Shah Commission that the order to arrest Nayar came to him from the prime minister's house through Navin Chawla, the lieutenant-governor's secretary, who was later appointed chief election commissioner by the Manmohan Singh government. The superintendent of police who arrested me deposed that the grounds for Nayar's arrest were prepared two or three days after his arrest. This was done on the basis of information provided to him by K.S. Bajwa, SP (CID). Bajwa, however, denied having passed on any information about me. P.S. Bhinder testified that he 'came to know' of Nayar's arrest from K.D. Nayyar, S.P., and had no hand in the arrest. The only thing he did was to ask his officials to treat Kuldip Nayar with 'due courtesy' because he was an eminent journalist.

In this case too, Lt Governor Krishan Chand 'merely acted' on orders from the 'super Prime Minister, Sanjay Gandhi'. Krishan Chand said that he was unhappy about my arrest as he knew me but Om Mehta told him that Indira Gandhi was keen that I be arrested.

Dhawan's explanation for the arrest, as he told me later, was my stature as a journalist. Sanjay Gandhi, he said, wanted to silence the top journalists after imposing press censorship. At the discussion, Dhawan said that my name was the first because I was considered the tallest.

Then I rang RNG and Malgoankar to inform them of my arrest. They were not surprised. My wife rang up members of our family. By the time I finished my breakfast my sister's familiar blue Fiat car turned into the crescent where our flat was located. My mother, her limbs shaking because she suffered from Parkinson's disease, remained in the car, but my sister, father, and father-in-law embraced me. My father was weeping but my father-in-law, who had experienced many years of imprisonment under the British, was composed. He jocularly remarked that he would be the next to be arrested. 'I shall follow you, because I have also sent her a letter,' he said, and sure enough he too was subsequently detained.

My mother was dry-eyed. Why should she cry? she asked. She was proud that her son was going to jail for a cause. I was on the point of breaking down, but she calmed me. 'Don't worry about us,' she said, 'we shall be all right and await your return.' My sister Raj said, 'You are a leader now', her eyes wet. Bharti hid her face and Rajiv wept openly as I got into the police jeep. At the end of it all there was something of an anticlimax. The jeep had a weak battery and would not start; I had to push it until the engine showed signs of life.

'Tiger caged,' was how the SHO conveyed the news of my arrest to his superintendent of police over a wireless set. That was funny, but I was looking back, longingly, at my dear ones still waving me farewell. Some stretched their arms, and then I lost them as the jeep took a turn.

'You know, I finished reading your book *Distant Neighbours* (1973) only last week,' said Assistant Police Commissioner Brar at the police station. 'I very much wanted to meet you but had never imagined that the meeting would be in such a manner.' I stopped him from saying anything further, remarking, 'Well, you have to do your duty, however unpleasant.' 'No, this one will be always on my conscience,' he said. 'I have arrested an innocent person,' and was unable to say more because he was in tears. He abruptly left the room.

I felt sorry for him. For a policeman, he was too sensitive, too humane. Otherwise, perhaps my image of the police as merely a force armed with lathis and no feelings was unfounded. For a long time I gazed out through the barred window. There was a woman plaiting a girl's long hair, probably a mother and daughter. How free and happy they looked. I was already beginning to have the oppressive sense of claustrophobia that imprisonment induces. A radio was playing loudly in the background. I thought it would probably be many months or years before I listened to music again. I love Hindustani classical music and attended virtually every concert held in Delhi and had the privilege of listening to Ustad Bade Ghulam Ali Khan, Begum Akhtar, and MS Subbulakshmi.

Life in jail was a curious experience. Straight from an air-conditioned room I was transported to a ward which had a room with 24 beds and one ceiling fan. The most difficult thing was coming to terms with the dry latrine. Subsequently, a long-term convict, my namesake, serving as a sweeper, sympathized with my plight. He would wake me up after cleaning the latrine. This exclusive facility did not last long because other detainees would rush to the latrine as soon as they saw Kuldip approaching my bed.

I often recall my first meal in jail. I was still speaking to other inmates when there was a sound of a spoon being beaten against a plate. This was a call for lunch. I reached for the food while it was sufficiently hot to keep the flies at bay. Someone however stopped me, 'Wait, there will be mantras first'. It was the prayer that the RSS recited at its *shakhas*. Hands were then stretched towards the food. This time I stopped them. I had spotted three Muslims whom I knew, and it was with them that I had spent a week after the Hindu–Muslim riots in Delhi's Kishangunj area a year earlier to find out from them what they had gone through. Theirs had been a harrowing experience, as I had then written in the *Statesman*.

I asked them, 'Don't you say Bismillah?'

'Yes, but only among ourselves,' they said.

'Say it loudly,' I said, and from that day onward, the Hindu prayer was followed by the Muslim one before every meal.

The dal was watery and the chappatis half made. When a second helping of dal was doled out I could see a few flies floating on the surface. I was horrified, but the person sitting next to me said, 'Don't worry, you will get used to them'. He was right. After a few days I became so accustomed to the flies that I would simply fish them out and begin eating without hesitation.

The following day I saw my father-in-law, Bhim Sen Sachar, walking in. I thought he had come to deliver the bedding which I had not brought along, and he permitted my delusion to continue for a while. When I thanked him for his effort, he said with a smile, 'You had left many things behind and I thought I would meet you and give them to you.' Little did I realize then that such a meeting (*mulaquat*) can take place only at the *phatak* (main gate) and that no 'outsider', apart from a member of the staff, was allowed into the jail.

My fellow prisoners were aware of this and they spoke amongst themselves, saying that it was now the turn of Gandhians to be arrested. My father-in-law had been a supporter of Gandhi since 1919 when he abandoned his studies to respond to his call for non-cooperation with the British. One prisoner remarked that if Indira Gandhi could go to the extent of arresting a person who had been chief minister of Punjab, governor of Orissa and Andhra Pradesh, and India's high commissioner to Sri Lanka, she was capable of going to any lengths.

My father-in-law told me how he and seven of his colleagues in Lajpat Bhawan had written to the prime minister to protest against the detentions and the press restrictions. Their letter too quoted Nehru's words, as I had done when alluding to the freedom of press. Indira Gandhi suspected, as I learnt later, that I had provided them with the relevant quotation.

The drudgery of jail was nerve-wracking. The long day was followed by a long night. One night I was awoken by the noise of children not far from where I was sleeping. To my horror I discovered a barred cell with bolted doors in which there were scores of boys crying loudly. I spoke to a few to find out why they were there but couldn't make any head or tail of what they said. In the morning I found the cell empty.

I asked the warden about the boys. He laughed at my inquiry. The boys, he said, had been in prison for years, without trial. They were not registered when they were brought in. They were picked up from the roadside to be used as helpers. Their number rose when there were more prisoners. Very few boys were released because they were needed in one jail or another in the country and were transferred wherever the need arose. The warden told me that some of them had been there for six to seven years. As they came from poor families, they were not easily returned.

After speaking to one of the boys, our helper, I found that he had been brought to the jail only three days ago. His employer who lived in Defence Colony had sent him to bring a pan at around 9:00 p.m. The prowling police picked him up and handed him over to the jail authorities. Justice Krishna Iyer wrote about their plight in a judgement after reading my book entitled *In Jail* (1978). I am sure the practice continues in some form or another to this day despite tall claims about jail reforms.

I experienced a miracle in jail. One night I dreamt of the *pir*. He was sitting on a wooden chair near the grave in the garden of our house in Sialkot. I could recognize both the grave and the chair. This was the *pir* to whom we had bade farewell before leaving our house in Sialkot. Even today I can feel his presence: an aged individual with a *tasbi* in his hand and a green cloth covering his chest and shoulder. His face, with a long white beard, radiated a glow. All he said was that I would be released the following Thursday (*jumeraat*). He disappeared and I abruptly woke up and found some of my ward's inmates saying their prayers. It was dawn.

I thought the dream reflected my desire to be released soon. The profile of the *pir* was something which I had probably imagined after reading books in

Persian and Urdu, but I was keen to find out whether what he had said would prove to be true.

The following day was the day of *mulakat* (meeting), once in fortnight, when my wife and my brother-in-law, Rajinder Sachar, came to meet me. I didn't tell them about my dream but asked them about the fate of the habius corpus petition which my wife had filed at the Delhi High Court. Rajinder, who was then chief justice of Sikkim High Court, told me that the petition would not succeed because the judiciary was itself panic-stricken. The various inquiries, he said, had revealed that I would be released along with other leaders. I asked my wife to send me a quilt, a table lamp, and some books because it appeared that it would be a long sojourn.

At an earlier meeting, my wife and younger son Rajiv had brought with them Chinese food which they knew I enjoyed. The superintendent sat watching us. What could one say when one's heart was full? We tried to make small conversation. I inquired about Sudhir, my eldest son. Bharti said that he was waiting outside, as only two persons were allowed in. I looked through the barred window and saw him standing on the road, and when I shouted his name he waved. He had come by train all the way from Kanpur, where he was working, to meet me, and looked wretched at not having been allowed to accompany my wife and Rajiv.

After Rajinder's visit I was edgy. Three days later, on Thursday, I was agog with expectation. My eyes were fixed on the gate waiting for someone to come with an order for my release. Nothing of the kind happened. After dinner, the jailer came to say that someone wanted to meet me. I followed him. A young man greeted me outside the ward and introduced himself as the deputy commissioner of Delhi. He said that on his way to the jail, Dhawan had telephoned to convey to him that Indira Gandhi had enquired about my health. I told him that there was nothing wrong with my health apart from the fact that the jail was overcrowded and dirty. He explained that the jail was intended to accommodate only a couple of hundred prisoners, but had four or five times that number. I discovered he was the son-in-law of a colleague of mine in the PIB. It was almost 11 p.m. when he left. I wondered about his visit, and particularly the *pir's* assurance that I would be released on Thursday. Nothing of that kind had however transpired.

The jailor woke me up the following morning to convey the government's order for my unconditional release. He wanted me to collect my things and leave in the taxi he had summoned to drop me home. I was keen to learn when the order was received. He said that it had been signed by the deputy commissioner a day before, on Thursday (*jumeraat*), but it was so late that he (the jailer) had decided to release me the following morning. I was humbled. The *pir's* prophecy had proved to be true. I have never experienced the same kind of presence again. There have been so many problems in my life when I have begged him for advice but he has never reappeared.

Bidding goodbye to my jail-mates, even if for only three months, was sad. I felt as if I was leaving a part of my heart behind. They wanted me to meet Sheikh Abdullah and persuade him to raise his voice against the Emergency. They expected me to resume my weekly column. Some of them said they would remain in touch with me after their release. None did, except the convict Kuldip after he had served his term.

My release was not a surprise for my wife and children because Giri Lal Jain, editor of the *Times of India,* had told them about the government's advice not to publish the news of my release. It had been tough on my family because no relative or journalist or personal friends of mine had dared to contact them during the three months I was in jail. Giri was at least frank. He said he was afraid but his wife had been in touch with mine. A couple of her close friends, however, visited every day.

My paper, the *Indian Express*, had challenged my detention and found for my defence Dr V.M. Tarkunde, formerly judge at Bombay High Court and a great defender of civil rights. He volunteered to take up my case and Soli Sorabji came from Bombay where he was practising, neither charging any fees. It was a habeas corpus petition on behalf of my wife.

Hearing of this in jail I became hopeful of an early release. Raj Narain, who used to go to the court for his case against Indira Gandhi's election, told me that there were bright prospects that my case would succeed. Fear, I thought, had infected the judiciary too, but the judges hearing my case were bold and courageous. The division bench comprising Justices S. Rangarajan and R.N. Aggarwal said in their judgement that here was a person who had not been attached to any political party and yet been arrested just for performing his duty as a journalist. The constitution permitted freedom of the press and he was within his right to criticize the government.

Justice Rangarajan said that Kuldip Nayar 'has been a dedicated journalist with no affiliation to any political party. He has been the member of Press Council of India. He only wrote a weekly column, so how could he be considered a subversive element?' The court also complained that it had not been supplied any material on the basis of which the decision to detain Kuldip Nayar had been taken, nor had the court been told about the 'specific' act that had led to his detention. The two-bench judge ordered that the grounds for which I had been detained be 'quashed and the detenue is directed to be set at liberty'.

I was in the court when the government stated that as I had been released there was no necessity for a judgement to be pronounced. Justice Rangarajan however told the authorities that he had asked them on many occasions that if Kuldip Nayar was to be released the bench would not write the judgement, but now that they had written it, they wanted to pronounce it. I got up from my seat to request the bench to pronounce the verdict.

The government was vindictive. It did not touch me again but took action against the two judges Rangarajan and Agarwal. Rangarajan was transferred to

Guwahati where he proved to be the best judge the court ever had. Agarwal, acting high court judge, was reverted to his position as a sessions judge. He indeed paid a very heavy price for his judgement.

༺༻

The case on the validity of the Emergency was still pending in the Supreme Court, it came up for hearing in December 1975. The verdict was considered so important that former Attorney General C.K. Daftary, president of the Bar Association, approached the Chief Justice of India A.N. Ray to set up a bench of the five seniormost judges to hear habeas corpus petitions. Ray did so, although he was surprised at the request. The seniormost judges on the bench were: H.R. Khanna, M.H. Beg, Y.V. Chandrachud, and P.N. Bhagwati, apart from the chief justice.

The government raised a preliminary objection: the president had suspended Article 21 when he imposed the Emergency and therefore no action could be brought relating to it. Daftary argued that the right to freedom did not arise from any particular Article of the constitution but from the inherent compulsion arising from the principle of rule of law. The executive was obliged to honour the principle because the right to freedom, a basic feature of the constitution, was central to the system.

The suspension of the right to enforce Article 21, said Daftary, did not automatically entail the suspension of the rule of law. Even during the Emergency, 'the rule of law was not and cannot be suspended'. Daftary's case was that Article 21 was the sole repository to the right to life, personal liberty, and even the right to move any court. If enforcement of the right was suspended, the detainees had no locus standi.

A brilliant lawyer from Bombay, Nani Palkhivala, said India should bid farewell to democracy if the basic freedoms guaranteed by the constitution were to be snuffed out by the executive. Fundamental rights were not at the mercy of any government's fiat, but a product of people's struggle for Independence, he said.

Justice Khanna was visibly upset over the government's defence that the suspension of fundamental rights was justified during the Emergency, and agreed with Daftary. Bhagwati and Chandrachud too appeared distraught and tended to side with Khanna. However, the scenario rapidly changed. Bhagwati was the first to go over to the government side, Beg was already with Ray. This meant that the case was already going in favour of the government. A few days later, even Chandrachud changed sides, leaving Khanna isolated.

Why did Bhagwati and Chandrachud change their views? Was it the fear that the misuse of powers under the Emergency had generated or was it sheer self-interest? Whatever the compulsions of Bhagwati and Chandrachud, the then law minister H.R. Gokhale was happy. All the habeas corpus petitions were rejected by 4–1 (when Palkhivala and Soli Sorabji received a cryptic message, four to one, they presumed it was a victory: 4 in their favour 1 against, but to their horror the judgement went the other way around).

Many years later, I asked H.R. Bharadwaj, close to Indira Gandhi, why and how Bhagwati and Chandrachud came to the government side and joined hands with Chief Justice Ray and Justice Beg. Bharadwaj said:

> Bhagwati, as you know, was neither here nor there, oscillating between the government and judicial compulsion. Therefore, he was not a problem. Chandrachud was managed through the Brahmin lobby, headed by law minister Gokhale. It took some time but he came along.

Chief Justice Ray said in his judgement that when there was a public threat, the protective law which provided everyone security had to give way to the interests of the state. Beg said that if the locus standi of detainees was suspended, no one was entitled to get the right enforced on their behalf. Chandrachud avoided any comment on the merit of the case. He said that president's proclamation of Emergency was final, conclusive, and non-justiciable. Bhagwati, an exponent of human rights, enunciated the weakest opinion. He said that in the ultimate analysis, protection of personal liberty and the supremacy of law must be governed by the constitution itself and as persons had been detained in accordance with the law, they had no remedy.

Khanna's dissenting judgement was devastating. He said the question was not whether there could be curtailment of personal liberty but whether the law, speaking through the authority of the courts, could be absolutely silenced and rendered mute because of such a threat. He ruled that 'even during an Emergency the state has no power to deprive a person of his life or personal liberty without the authority of law. That is the essential postulate and basic assumption of the rule of law in every civilized society'. Khanna wrote the judgement long before he delivered it, well aware that Bhagwati and Chandrachud had changed their stance and that his verdict would cost him the office of chief justice.

Khanna's judgement raised the hope of those who had seen even the tallest in the country caving in. Palkhivala wrote in an article in the *New York Times* after the judgement that statues of Khanna should be raised throughout the country because he had dared to speak the truth in the face of all manner of danger. We in the *Indian Express* reproduced the article, daring the government, but there was no word from the chief censor.

Sure enough, the government superseded Khanna and appointed his junior, Beg, as the chief justice of India. Khanna did not oblige the government by resigning and stayed on to be a ray of hope in an otherwise dismal showing on the part of the judiciary.

When the Emergency was lifted (on 21 March 1977), Chandrachud was the first to express his regrets. He could not explain why he had sided with the government. But what use was his regret because he had not stood up when he needed to stand up to be counted. Bhagwati was now most critical of the excesses committed during the Emergency but did not say anything about his judgement. He tried to atone for his sins by pronouncing pro-labour and pro-liberty judgements. No one was however willing to forgive him. Both of them remained in the doghouse for as long as they were on the bench. The Supreme Court Bar Association passed a resolution against the two for having delivered the judgement.

Ray did not stop at the judgement, justifying the suspension of fundamental rights. He wanted to rescind the verdict on the inviolate nature of the basic structure of the constitution. At his own initiative, he set up a bench of eleven judges to review the thesis of basic structure. Palkhivala probably touched the heights which no other lawyer had done in defending the concept of basic structure. He said this was the soul of the constitution which no one could violate. He asked Ray on whose authority he had constituted the bench to review the basic structure which was the very essence of the constitutional system. Ray said that some state attorney generals had requested him to do so. The attorney general from Tamil Nadu contradicted Ray, saying that no state attorney general had made such a request. Ray had no choice other than to dissolve the bench.

Chandrachud faced some difficulties in his appointment as chief justice because when his turn came the Janata Party government had been voted in, defeating Indira Gandhi. He was saved by Morarji Desai, the then prime minister, who was a stickler for form. Morarji did not favour Chandrachud's supersession, although he was fully aware of the judgement he had delivered. The then president, N. Sanjiva Reddy, also played a role because he too felt that traditions were far more important than punishment. He did not want to follow Indira Gandhi's example of destroying the institution.

I tried to pick up the thread of protest where I had left it off before I was jailed. However, my efforts bore no fruit. I found journalists were afraid to say anything about the Emergency in public, and editors proved to be the most cowardly. It appeared as if they had been co-opted by the system.

As a member of the press council, I approached the chairman, Justice N. Rajagopala Ayyangar, a retired Supreme Court judge to request him to convene a meeting of the council to discuss the censorship. He said that it would be futile because no newspaper would publish whatever was decided. I argued that some day the Emergency would be lifted and posterity would like to know what the Press Council, the highest body defending the freedom of the press, had done when censorship was imposed. The question, I said, was not whether the decision would appear in the press or not but whether the Press Council would register its protest.

Reluctantly, he convened a meeting of local Press Council members. I found to my horror that although most members were critical of censorship, none of them were willing to go on record or pass any resolution, I was still more disappointed to read in the White Paper, issued by the Ministry of Information and Broadcasting, after the Emergency, that Justice N.R. Ayyangar had played false. He had written a letter to V.C. Shukla informing him that he had been able to stop a resolution against censorship being passed. He lauded his role: 'I was able to convince them [local Press Council members] that this [the resolution] is not necessary or desirable.'

A couple of weeks after my release, Prem Bhatia, then the editor of *Tribune*, organized a dinner for some intimate friends to talk things over. Satish Gujral and his wife, my wife and I, Inder Malhotra, and Rami Chhabra and her husband were there. It was more or less the old *Statesman* crowd. Our conversation centred on the Emergency. No one could guess how long the tunnel would prove to be but all agreed that the administration had been reduced to a brute machine to carry out Sanjay Gandhi's orders. Indira Gandhi, it seemed, was intractable to any suggestion for normalization. One remark that everyone made was that it would be difficult to repair the institutions she had destroyed.

Little did anyone suspect that someone from among us would report our conversation verbatim to Mohammed Yunus Khan, the cruel face of the dynasty? Yunus called Satish Gujral's brother, Inder Gujral, who happened to be in town, having come from Moscow where he was India's envoy. Yunus, a Pathan, threatened to take action against each one present at the dinner and have their property confiscated for conspiring against the state.

Once we learnt that the entire conversation had reached Indira Gandhi, each one of us tried to guess who could have been the stool pigeon. One individual suspected the other; Satish came to my house to check whether I had divulged the conversation to 'make up with the government'. That was his judgement on my integrity! We were all nonplussed but could not pinpoint who was responsible. After the Emergency, Inder Malhotra himself admitted to Chhabra, present at the dinner, that he had done so. True, he was on the establishment's side, but it still escapes me what need there was for him to go to Yunus to report a private conversation?

We, in the *Indian Express*, were happy that our circulation was rising by the day. People had come to associate the newspaper with defiance of the Emergency. Whatever we wrote was given an interpretation which we had by no stretch of the imagination intended. We were however very careful not to give the government any opportunity to prosecute us. We raised the price of the paper but the circulation just kept rising. We were selling around two lakh copies a day in Delhi alone. RNG said that he had no money to buy more newsprint so we were obliged to restrict circulation.

As promised to my jailmates, I went to Srinagar to request Sheikh Abdullah to criticize the Emergency. He told me that she (Indira Gandhi) was in such a foul mood that she would arrest him as well. Shamim Ahmad Shamim, a friend who was a Lok Sabha member, received me at the airport. He told me not be shocked if I found that Sher-e-Kashmir had turned into a *giddad Kashmir*. The Sheikh came to my hotel and embraced me while observing: 'You too have become Haji.' In reply to my request for an interview he said he would call me. After about a week he invited me to lunch at which his family was present. Even after reminding him about the interview he did not fix any date or time.

Shamim appreciated my predicament. He told me that Sheikh Abdullah would not say anything on the Emergency on record. Shamim suggested that we write an interview and attribute it to him. Shamim said that Sheikh Abdullah would not dare to contradict it. The gist of the interview which ran as a lead story was that he had appealed to Indira Gandhi to have a 're-look on the Emergency' because 'it had served its purpose'. Both of us were careful not to use the words 'lift the Emergency' but attributed to Sheikh Abdullah the view that 'a long period of restrictive measures loses its effectiveness'. We were confident that Sheikh Abdullah would not issue any contradiction as I had told him that the eyes of detenue were fixed on him for help. He did not contradict the interview but told me after the Emergency that he would not have given a better interview than the one I had written.

⚜

The Emergency was beginning to yield diminishing returns. Either Indira Gandhi, as dictators are wont, could instill fear of death in people's minds or brainwash them. She was not cut for the first and she had no patience for the second. She proposed some amendments to the constitution to institute harsh laws and extended the tenure of Lok Sabha from five to six years. Two leaders, stormy petrel Madhu Limaye and fiery Sharad Yadav, resigned from the House in protest. Both upheld the traditions of the socialists in India.

People were further alienated by amendments to the constitution to restrict their freedom and the extension of the Lok Sabha's tenure by an additional year. A high-power committee which the Congress had appointed on 27 February 1976 under the chairmanship of Swaran Singh submitted its report which the government adopted more or less in toto. The report read like an essay on a police state. 'It would have been worse if I were not there,' Swaran Singh told me. 'She wanted the presidential system but we have buried it once and for all,' he said.

Nearly 300 educationists, artists, and writers maintained, in a signed petition sent to Indira Gandhi, that 'the present parliament has neither the political nor the moral authority to effect fundamental changes in the constitution'. The non-communist opposition, particularly the CPI(M) refused to have any discussion with Congress party committee on constitutional amendments and boycotted the special parliament session convened on 25 October to pass the necessary Bill. The CPI was, however, on her side.

A joint statement issued by the non-Left opposition parties said that the amendments would 'eliminate the whole system of checks and balances provided in the constitution and leave the arbitrary exercise of authority to the detriment of the citizen'.

All the individuals who had benefited from Indira Gandhi's rule were pressed into service to justify the amendments. This was invariably her tactic whenever she faced a problem. Former chief justice of India and chairman of the Law Commission, P.B. Gajendragadkar argued in her defence:

When Indian democracy embarks upon its missions of justifying the legitimate but expanding hopes and aspirations of citizens and establishing a new social order based on social equality and economic justice, it may have to make suitable laws from time to time to achieve that purpose.

Leftist intellectuals, who had a great fascination for Indira Gandhi's authoritarianism, hailed these 'revolutionary steps'. I also heard that her 'leftist lurch' had forced the rightist JP to launch a movement.

Indira Gandhi lashed out at her opponents in parliament on the grounds that 'those who want to fix the constitution in a rigid and unalterable frame are entirely out of tune with the spirit of new India'. She had transferred as many as sixteen judges who she said had not reconciled themselves to the 'demands of the emergency'.

The self-immolation of Prabhakar Sharma, working in the Acharya Vinobha Bhave camp, sent a shock-wave throughout the country, including Indira Gandhi's establishment. When immolating himself at Surgaon outside Wardha in Maharashtra on 11 October 1976 in protest against Indira Gandhi's dictatorial methods of governance, he said in a letter:

Forgetting God and humanity and arming itself with wide, brutal powers the government last year deprived the newspapers of their freedom of expression and attacked all those qualities of Indian living which can be decent, great and noble. This year it has shamelessly attacked the nation's spiritual and non-violent civilization.

Vinobha vainly sought to meet Prabhakar who had found the former sympathetic to Indira Gandhi. Vinobha had defended the Emergency in the name of *anushasan* (discipline). Nirmala Deshpande acted as the link between Vinobha and Indira Gandhi, and her dislike of JP was in proportion to her admiration for Indira Gandhi. JP, once a close follower of Vinobha, no longer enjoyed popularity in the ashram.

When I visited Vinobha Bhave's ashram during those days to interview him, he criticized JP's arrest but justified 'strong action' to ensure people's obedience to the call of discipline. What about democracy? I asked. He considered 'the discipline' that Indira Gandhi had sought to impose as being a reflection of the steps that needed to be taken to safeguard democracy.

JP's detention was revoked on 4 December 1976. The deputy commissioner of Chandigarh, where JP was detained, wrote to the government that JP's health was failing. This report eventually found its way to Bansi Lal's desk. His response was that he should be left to die [*Susrey ko marne do*]. Although all restrictions on JP were 'removed' he was kept under surveillance. The intelligence department monitored his movements, kept track of his visitors, and examined his letters and speeches very closely, just in case …

In meeting later, JP admitted to me that Indira Gandhi was on the top of the world. She was indeed hailed as Goddess Durga and it sometimes appeared that she believed she embodied that *shakti* (power). She knew exactly how to dress for the best effect: in a village she wore a plain sari, covering her head demurely; in Kashmir she dressed like a Kashmiri; in Punjab she wore a kurta and salwar and even said that she was Punjabi because her younger daughter-in-law, Sanjay's wife, Menaka, was from Punjab. She claimed to be the daughter-in-law of Gujarat because her husband Feroze Gandhi, a fearless member of the Lok Sabha, was a Gujarati. She refrained from mentioning Sonia Gandhi lest the question of her foreign nationality was raised. She was aware all these things went down well with the common people, and indeed they did for some time.

The structure of 'guided democracy' which she had evolved appeared to have acquired a semblance of permanence. Many people across India seemed prepared to accept the political reality that Indira Gandhi had thrust upon them. Many, particularly among the élite, would quite unashamedly maintain: 'We have always needed overlords to govern us. We had the Mughals, we had the British, and now we have Mrs Gandhi. Is that so bad?'

Sanjay had consolidated his political influence. No state chief minister thought his visit to Delhi was complete until he had met Sanjay. They all vied with one another in inviting him to their state and by demonstrating his popularity through government-sponsored rallies.

For Sanjay, political management had come easily; he began building up his own political strength through the Youth Congress which he formally joined and which Barooah asked him to activate. I was at Chandigarh when the inauguration ceremony took place. The editor of *Patriot,* Edatata Narayanan, a left-wing newspaper, met me and rhetorically asked: 'Is this the beginning of the end.' I did not comment because in his editorials he had been supporting Indira Gandhi.

Sanjay manoeuvred to eject Priyaranjan Das Munshi of West Bengal from the presidentship of the Youth Congress and replaced him with a dependable Punjabi girl, Ambika Soni, who had the dubious distinction of having slapped a young socialist, Vijay Pratap, outside the gate of Indira Gandhi's residence.

Shukla reported to Sanjay that nearly all the newspapers and journalists had begun 'behaving'. They no longer represented a threat and were acting as their own censors. Even so, the Prevention of Publication of Objectionable Matter Act of pre-Independence days was revived through an ordinance to prohibit the publication of 'words, signs, or visible representation' that spread disaffection. A group of obliging editors prepared a code of ethics for newspapers. It was a curious 3,000-word exhortation that did not even once refer to the freedom of the press.

The government also withdrew the accreditation of over forty newspaper correspondents. These journalists were permitted to continue to represent their newspapers, but were deprived of such privileges as admission to major news conferences and sessions of parliament (I was one among those who were denied accreditation).

The ten-year-old Press Council of India was dissolved on 31 December 1975. Here the pressure of Kishan Kumar Birla, owner of *Hindustan Times* worked. He was very close to Sanjay because the Birlas provided free advice and other assistance to get the Maruti car on the road. K.K. Birla was the defendant in a complaint filed before the Press Council against the termination of the services of B.G. Verghese, editor of *Hindustan Times*. It was an open secret that the action against Verghese was taken at the instance of 'some members of the ruling party who were inimical to press freedom'.

K.K. Birla had learnt from a discussion of the case in the Council that the judgement would go against him. It did, but it was never pronounced. However, the draft judgement prepared by the Council's chairman on the basis of his informal discussions with the members, among whom I was one, indicated that Birla should be indicted.

The draft judgement stated that the termination of Verghese's service was clearly a violation of the freedom of the press and editorial independence. The Press Council also condemned the attempt by K.K. Birla to prevent the publication of the correspondence between him and Verghese. The verdict could not be delivered because the council was dissolved by then.

The immunity extended to journalists to report parliamentary proceedings was also withdrawn. Sanjay was afraid that the press would splash in its pages all that was said in parliament on the misuse of the Emergency and the Maruti scandal. Ironically, it was Feroze Gandhi, Sanjay's father, who had brought forward a Bill to help the press to freely report the proceedings in the two Houses of parliament. At one time Indira Gandhi wanted the Bill to stay but Sanjay disagreed and had his way. There was no room for 'sentiments in the administration', he told his mother.

Even though the press had become a kind of government gazette, exercising self-censorship to the extent of not even using the JP health bulletins without clearance from the government, Indira Gandhi and her son were not satisfied. There was the *Indian Express* chain of newspapers that had still not fallen into line.

The government first pressed RNG to dismiss Ajit Bhattacharjea and me, the two senior editors. RNG said he could not do so because of the Working Journalists Act, which was applicable in our case. Then the government asked for our transfer to places like Sikkim and Nagaland. He argued that this was tantamount to victimization. Goenka told me in private that he was under pressure to take action against both of us but he would not let either of us go.

RNG was then asked to sell his publications. He took some time to tell the government that he was willing to do so provided he got 'a fair price' and that too 'in white'. While he was in the midst of 'negotiations' with the government, he suffered a heart attack.

B.D. Goenka, his son, preferred to side with the establishment. The government appointed a majority of its own nominees on the *Indian Express* board with K.K. Birla as the chairman. The first decision of the board was to retire Malgaonkar, the editor-in-chief. Birla summoned both Ajit Bhattacharjea and me. He asked me to write in favour of Sanjay Gandhi. I told him I would have done so had I found him doing anything worthwhile. He cut short the conversation. I thought his pep talk was intended to threaten me.

Kamal Nath was one of the *Indian Express* board members. He knew B.D. Goenka and I had met him earlier. The first thing Kamal Nath told me was that they would appoint me as chief editor if I wrote in their favour. As he was a Punjabi, we would exchange a word or two if and when we ran into each other at the *Express* office where the board meetings were held.

Many names were bandied about in relation to the post of chief editorship to fill the vacancy left by Malgaonkar. The position was offered to one of our colleagues, Suman Dubey, but he declined it. Eventually Md. Shamim's name was finalized. How could a film critic from the *Times of India* be our chief editor? we wondered.

B.D. Goenka rang me up and asked me to meet Kamal Nath and ask him to refrain from making the appointment. I told him I hardly knew him. The board was to meet in the morning, according to Goenka. At that time it was 10.30 p.m.

I however rang up Kamal Nath and went to meet him at Oberoi Hotel where he was staying. I suggested to him that he should appoint someone senior to us and certainly not a film critic. He asked me to suggest some names. I told him that for the time being the editor of the *Financial Express*, V. Narasimha Rao could combine the two posts. I was aware of his strong views about the Emergency. Kamal Nath accepted my suggestion for the 'time being'. However, Kamal Nath regretted the decision later because Narasimha ran the *Express* as we all wished him to do. I must say that he saved the newspaper's reputation and at the same time permitted us to write whatever we chose between the lines.

I had not visited the Press Club since my release from jail and just happened to drop in there one day. V. C. Shukla was there and this was our first encounter since my detention. He himself initiated a discussion on my arrest. He was on the defensive and told me that he had done his utmost to prevent it. I did not believe him and told him that to his face. We were once quite close but the detention had snapped the relationship. He said, 'Kuldip, you got one million dollar worth of publicity'.

Somewhere I also ran into Om Mehta, minister of state for home affairs. He was at that time in charge of the ministry because the home minister, Brahmananda Reddy, was not a member of Sanjay Gandhi's inner coterie. Om asked me cynically how I had enjoyed 'our jail'. I countered by asking him why they had allowed it to get so dirty. Laughingly, he said that their intention had not been to send me to Ashoka Hotel.

I once was at a press conference called by Sanjay Gandhi. It was a placid affair. The fear generated by the Emergency had palpably caused pressmen to err on the side of caution. No one asked him any inconvenient questions, and I just sat there impassively facing him, observing him closely. He oozed confidence and did not appear to be someone who would have had a second thought about the excesses for which he was responsible.

Notwithstanding virtual control over the press, Shukla spoke of 'restructuring the entire press industry so as to make it accountable and answerable to the people, society, and the country'. His underlying meaning suggested a permanent arrangement that was not dependent on the special powers available under the Emergency.

For this purpose, the amalgamation of the two major English news agencies, PTI and UNI, and two Hindi news agencies, Hindustan Samachar and Samachar Bharti, into a single entity was deemed essential. That would mean only a single point of control. Shukla used the known arm-twisting methods against newspaper proprietors and owners of news agencies to bring them to agree to a single agency which later came to be known as Samachar. It began functioning on 1 February 1976 and G. Kasturi, editor of the *Hindu*, was appointed its chairman. I failed to understand how a person like him, who always spoke about a free press and courage preferred to carry the stigma of being termed stooge demonstrated no resistance.

While the reorganization of the press was in progress, Sanjay focused his attention on the more important issue of restructuring the government. He had always told his mother that left to him, he would 'change the entire government', and replace one-fourth of its fifty-four member council of ministers with representatives of the Youth Congress. He was already scrutinizing senior appointments at the Centre. Bureaucrats too were summoned to 1 Safdarjang Road, Indira Gandhi's residence, and both politicians and bureaucrats were interviewed by Sanjay and R.K. Dhawan for eligibility.

This was not all. Sanjay wanted his men in the cabinet and in the states to ensure that his instructions were fully complied with. He had Bansi Lal, a hundred per cent loyal and committed leader, inducted into the cabinet. For some reason Bansi Lal wanted the defence ministry and got it.

Bansi Lal did not however wish to be isolated from his principality, Haryana, and therefore his successor as chief minister, Banarasi Das Gupta (Bansi Lal himself had chosen him), was told that Bansi Lal would continue to remain the 'real chief minister' and that he should 'listen' to him.

Indira Gandhi also bowed to Sanjay's wishes to get rid of the eighty-year-old minister, Uma Shankar Dikshit. For her it was a major decision because as the party treasurer since the 1971 elections, he had collected and distributed crores of rupees on her behalf. Of late, she had been somewhat unhappy with him because she found his daughter-in-law, Sheila Dikshit, interfering in the administration. Indira Gandhi had already transferred Dikshit's son, a distinguished civil servant, out of Delhi to keep the meddling daughter-in-law at arm's length but Sheila had stayed back to help her father-in-law. Indira Gandhi had experience in dealing with daughters-in-law. Some time earlier she had curbed the power of another daughter-in-law, the *bahuji* of Kamlapati Tripathi when he was brought to Delhi.

Dikshit's exit from the cabinet (he was soon appointed governor of Karnataka) shocked other ministers. If it could happen to him, it could happen to any of them. This caused them to become even more servile.

Haksar, once her principal secretary, did not however stop corresponding with her. He protested against the raid on the Pandit brothers, close relations of his, at Connaught Place in New Delhi. Sanjay had ordered the raids because he wanted to send a message to show who controlled the government, and the truth was that the transfer of Haksar from the PMO was at Sanjay's behest. Once Yashpal Kapoor asked me rhetorically: 'How can we have a communist in the prime minister's office?' Sanjay loathed both Haksar and Dhar but Indira Gandhi valued their advice.

A few persons, whom Indira Gandhi respected, found no respite from the authoritarian rule nor from the whimsical administration run by Sanjay Gandhi's caucus and voiced their exasperation. The advice of her personal friends in the West to hold elections and a similar suggestion by Haksar, supported by P.N. Dhar, Haksar's successor, made her consider this seriously.

Indira Gandhi was gratified by an official report that her popularity graph was high and decided to relax the Emergency. Sanjay was furious when he learnt that apart from doing that, she was contemplating holding elections. He did not want any polls to be held for many years into the future. There was heated discussion between the two but he had to tone down his objections when he found she was adamant.

Whatever Indira Gandhi's compulsions might have been to go to the polls, her decision to hold elections was an admission that no system could work without the consent and concurrence of the people. In a way, she paid tribute to the patience and sufferings of people during the Emergency, and the truth is that it was they, the illiterate, the backward, and the poor who eventually triumphed.

She proved what was heard all the time that Indira Gandhi was uncomfortable with the Emergency. Someone said she was riding a tiger which she dearly wished to dismount. Holding fresh elections seemed to be the only way for her to retrieve the situation. As a newsman, I suspected that something akin to an election was in the offing but despite my best efforts could obtain no confirmation of this. Being a persona non-grata, no Congress leader or bureaucrat wished to have anything to do with me.

One day a police officer from Punjab, apparently in the IB, whispered to me at a reception that elections were in the offing. His inference was from an order he had received to assess the prospects of the various political parties if polls were to be immediately held. It was a valuable lead but the problem was how to verify it.

I knew Kamal Nath after he was inducted as director of the board of the *Indian Express*. I went to his house early one morning. His wife was having tea, so I introduced myself as Kamal Nath's friend. She had heard my name, offered me a cup of tea, and told me that her husband was sleeping. Within a few minutes, Kamal Nath emerged from the room through a connecting door and joined us in the balcony.

After he had poured a cup of tea for himself, I asked him straightaway which constituency Sanjay Gandhi would be contesting from. He was taken aback but did not try to evade the question. He said it had not yet been decided because they were awaiting the return of an emissary who had gone to Ahmedabad jail to meet Chandra Shekhar, a radical Congressman who had been a consistent critic of Indira Gandhi. Kamal Nath further said that the Congress wanted a rapprochement with him. I imagined that this implied that elections could be held in the coming few weeks. When I asked him how soon the elections would be held he asked where I had received information about the impending elections. That only confirmed the story.

I knew I had not obtained sufficient information to break the news but decided to take the risk. At worst they would rearrest me, and this I argued to myself would not be too difficult. One stint of imprisonment had given me confidence in dealing with such a predicament.

All editions of the *Express* ran the story as a banner in bold type. A little after midnight, RNG, by now in harness after the heart attack, rang me from Bombay to find out more about the story. All that he said was: 'Hope you are right.' I assured him that elections were only a few weeks away. He was overjoyed to hear that because his future or, for that matter, of the newspaper, depended upon a change in government.

Only a few days earlier he had told me that he was at the end of the road. He had exhausted his resources during the 19 months of the Emergency, and keeping the *Indian Express* running was his first priority because it had brought him both fame and wealth.

RNG had then asked me if I could arrange a meeting with Khushwant Singh who was close to Menaka Gandhi, Sanjay Gandhi's wife. Khushwant Singh had taught me company law at Law College in Lahore, and I had always addressed him as Professor Sahib, even when he had become a Gandhi family sycophant, praised them unabashedly, and justified the Emergency. I was indebted to him because he had promised to publish my articles when I told him that I might be obliged to leave the *Indian Express*.

The meeting between RNG and Khushwant Singh was fruitful. RNG offered him the position of editor-in-chief. Once Khushwant Singh accepted the offer, RNG told him that he didn't need to trouble himself about the emoluments. Khushwant Singh said that he would give his management a notice and join the *Express* in a fortnight or so. The news spread like wildfire. Inder Malhotra from the *Times of India* rang me up to confirm the Khushwant story. In the end, however, Khushwant Singh did not join the *Express* because no written offer was sent to him. As soon as RNG saw my story about elections he told me not to pursue the offer to Khushwant Singh.

It was still early in the morning when I received a call from the chief censorship officer, Harry D'Penha who had been a colleague of mine at the PIB. He told me that he had been asked to contradict the election story and issue a warning to me that such news items could result in my arrest once again. That eventuality did not occur because within a few days of my scoop, elections were announced. The Emergency was, however, relaxed to enable public meetings to be held and other forms of canvassing to take place.

JP rushed from Patna and got the editors of the *Express* together at the paper's guest-house. He was in favour of boycotting the polls. His argument was: 'How can fair elections be held when the Emergency has not been withdrawn but only relaxed?' Would people dare to vote? To test the water, JP wanted to hold a public meeting at the Ramlila ground. The crowd overflowed on roads surrounding the ground. JP then requested us to propose the names of candidates. Better people should be harnessed for clean politics, he said, but did not ensure that.

My information was that he had left most of the selection to L.K. Advani, Chandra Shekhar, and Jagjivan Ram. All three got their 'own men' to contest. They had come together when JP had threatened that he would not participate in the poll campaigns if they did not form a single, united party. It was then that the Janata Party was constituted and comprised the various political parties with their leaders pushing their own nominees for election. Very few state leaders had a say. The Akali Dal was however the boss in Punjab.

The Akali Dal leader Prakash Singh Badal came to my office and requested me to contest from Chandigarh. I had no hesitation in declining his offer. I told him that some people should stay out in order to be in a position to criticize the government when necessary. Badal argued that I could do that from within but I stuck to my stand after consulting my wife who said that as both our sons had yet to complete their education we still needed the *Express* salary.

I, however, often look back and wonder whether I should have taken the plunge. The bickering in the Janata Party often made me think that if I had joined politics I could possibly have been of some help in resolving differences. A few friends who had been in jail with me did their utmost to persuade me to join the party and abandon journalism. My father-in-law had also advised me when we were together in Tihar jail that I should carry a *jhola* over my shoulders and travel the country to awaken people to Gandhian values. He said: 'We'll have to persuade your wife [his daughter],' but she firmly rejected the idea. The real reason I did not take the plunge was my sense that I could reach out to and influence more people through my columns. But I have been proved wrong; there is no alternative to parliament, for that is where the real power lies.

I was disappointed over the selection of candidates. After all, the party, the Janata Party, which was formed in the wake of the Emergency, should have encompassed people who believed in *parivartan*, the message to overhaul the system that JP broadcast when initiating the poll campaign.

Most people thought, and newspapermen were no exception, that the polls would be a very close race, with Indira Gandhi's party having a slight edge over the opposition. It was difficult for anyone to have imagined that Nehru's daughter, or for that matter the Congress which had been in power since Independence, could be defeated. This was indeed the impression in the West. Though small Scandinavian countries did not lose hope in the prospect of the Indian people reaffirming their faith in democracy, all the larger nations were on Indira Gandhi's side. At one time, West Germany had warned India that if ever any German correspondent was expelled from New Delhi, it would cut off aid. Now the same country's envoy in New Delhi was convinced that Indira Gandhi was the ideal leader for India. Privately, he rationalized that if all Western countries were to turn against her, she would tilt towards the Soviet Union.

British High Commissioner Michael Walker told London that they had better accept Indira Gandhi and forget about democracy. US Ambassador William B. Saxbe was all in favour of Indira Gandhi from the day she had accepted his invitation to a private dinner party. She was the only one who stood between India and chaos, he told Washington. He was on friendly terms with Sanjay who openly favoured free enterprise. Saxbe had arranged collaboration between Maruti and International Harvester, a US firm.

From among the major countries, the Soviet Union's was the sole voice predicting Indira Gandhi's defeat. Russian officials informed the Indian embassy in Moscow that things did not look favourable for her and that they were concerned.

Elections were held in March 1977 and the people in all the northern states of India rejected the Congress outright. They demanded the restoration of their personal freedom and all that they had lost during the 19 months of the Emergency. Their revolt was not only against forced sterilization but against the system which had left them with no recourse to seek remedy against any form of injustice: the police would not write reports, newspapers would not print their grievances, the courts would not entertain their applications, and neighbours would not, out of fear, come to their help.

The defeat of the Congress was phenomenal. It was able to muster only 153 seats as against 350 in the 1971 elections, the Janata Party won 298. The Congress did not win a single seat out of 84 in UP, 54 in Bihar, 13 in Punjab, 11 in Haryana, and 6 in Delhi. It won 1 seat in Madhya Pradesh, 1 in Rajasthan, 3 in West Bengal, 4 in Orissa, and 10 each in Assam and Gujarat.

While the Janata swept the north, it fared poorly in south India, winning one seat each in Andhra Pradesh, Tamil Nadu, and Karnataka. Obviously, the Janata wave did not sweep through the Vindhyas; it was apparent that the excesses in southern India had been fewer and tales of torture had not reached them.

The thunderous victory of the Janata Party, which fought on the plank of democracy and freedom, came as a great surprise to the intelligentsia in India and the people in the West. Both were cut off from the people. Little did they realize that the poor loved their liberty as much as anyone else. Their approach might not have been sophisticated or ideologically pure but their faith in what they considered democracy was unflinching. A vote gave them the power to elect the leader they wanted and they used it to prove that they were the real masters. Indira Gandhi and her party had usurped that right and this was their judgement.

I honestly believe that Indira Gandhi's defeat saved the country and its democratic structure. Had she returned to power at that time, she would have felt that what Sanjay was doing was right. An open society, strengthened by free and fair elections, is a sine qua non for a country's unity and homogeneity. Pakistan knows this from its experience.

An apology by the Congress might have atoned for some of the sins of its leaders. What about the government machinery? The police were most to blame, but the condemnation was due in equal measure to the services as a whole. Was there any soul-searching on the part of public functionaries? I don't think so. The result was that the honest and upright among them were harassed to such a degree that others thought it wise not to fall foul of their political masters. The younger among them learnt that out-of-turn promotions and cushy jobs were available only if they were 'obedient'.

A few days after the elections I flew to Lucknow to visit Rae Bareilly, Indira Gandhi's constituency. I wanted to meet Vinod Malhotra, the deputy commissioner, who was also the returning officer (RO) and compliment him for the courage he had demonstrated in announcing her defeat. He could not have had any inkling that the Congress had been routed from the entirety of northern India. No radio broadcasts were permitted when counting was in progress nor were results announced till the evening.

The deputy commissioner's residence was located at the back of his office. A peon took in my card and Malhotra came out and guided me to his office. My question was simple: What persuaded him to decide to announce the result? He said that he could judge from the first round of counting that Indira Gandhi was losing. M.L. Fotedar, her agent, had got the ballots counted thrice. Om Mehta rang him twice and R.K. Dhawan thrice asking him not to declare the result.

Then Malhotra took me to his house, where his wife with a small child in her lap was sitting on a charpai. He said that when Indira Gandhi's defeat was confirmed and reconfirmed, he went to consult his wife. He told her that if he were to announce the result, they would have to face Indira Gandhi's wrath because she would return through a by-election. He presumed that her defeat was a freak and that the Congress party would win a majority.

Malhotra's wife told me that when he sought her advice she told him: '*Hum bartan maanj lange magar baimani nahi karenge.* [We shall clean utensils but not indulge in dishonesty].' This gave him courage to announce the result. After Indira Gandhi's return to power in 1980 I reached him with great difficulty to find out if he was alright. He had been transferred to some routine posting outside Lucknow. He requested me not to contact him again as he had had 'enough of it'.

I was in the midst of writing *The Judgement*, an account of some 19 months of the Emergency, when Kamal Nath, by now a senior Congress MP, asked me how I could write about the Emergency without meeting Sanjay.

I said I would like to interview him, and asked whether Sanjay would meet me. Kamal Nath took me to Indira Gandhi's residence at 1 Safdarjang Road. The house wore a forlorn look, rather like a battlefield after a defeat. Bundles of papers and pieces of furniture were strewn all over; no sign of a visitor, no crowd to bid them farewell. Indira Gandhi was standing at the front porch. She saw me and initially moved towards me, but then retraced her steps and went inside.

Sanjay was standing under a tree, and this became the venue of the interview. He was wearing a white kurta-pyjama, the familiar attire in which he appeared in photographs. I had seen him once at a press conference.

Kamal Nath left us when we began talking. Sanjay's first inquiry was whether I knew who would be the leader of the Janata parliamentary party. I said that it appeared that Morarji Desai would be the eventual choice. Sanjay remarked that in that case the government would last. If Jagjivan Ram were to take over, he said, the entire edifice would collapse within a few months. His animus against Jagjivan Ram was understandable because he was a senior minister with a large dalit following, who left the Congress when elections were announced.

Sanjay had heard about the book I was writing. Strangely, he asked me not to include any part of our conversation. I told him that I would honour his request but it made little sense if he wanted his side of the story to be known. He had his way and I did not include anything he said in *The Judgement*. I have however no obligation after his death and am therefore disclosing the gist of our conversation for the first time.

The first question I asked Sanjay was how he thought that they would get away with it: the Emergency, the authoritarian rule, and the rest? He said there was no challenge to them and that they could have carried on with the Emergency for at least 20 to 25 years or more until they felt confident that they had changed people's ways of thinking.

In their scheme of things, he said, there would have been no elections and they would have ruled from Delhi, with the help of provincial satraps like Bansi Lal from Haryana and like-minded bureaucrats in other states. It would have been a different kind of governance, with power centralized in Delhi. I recalled that Kamal Nath had during the Emergency given me the manuscript of a book arguing along the same lines and detailing the machinery such a government would establish to rule with the help of police and some selected bureaucrats.

In the scheme of Sanjay's rule, there was no Congress leader of eminence and experience. Anyone who wanted to be part of the form of governance he was contemplating had to believe in a state completely devoid of fundamental rights, freedom of speech and expression. The judiciary would have to function accordingly.

'Then why did you hold elections?' I asked Sanjay. He didn't, he said. He was opposed to it to the very end. It was his mother's doing. 'You should ask her,' he said. By then Indira Gandhi reappeared at the porch, probably wondering what we were discussing, but then rapidly retraced her steps.

How would such a system have worked when we had a constitution to guarantee us certain rights? Sanjay said that the Emergency would not have been lifted and every right would have remained suspended. I told him that I had heard rumours that before holding elections, his mother and he had contemplated handing over the country to the army. He said that this was not true, and was in all probability right.

It seems that some in the military had toyed with different ideas. Air Marshal Om Mehta had told me that 'some of them had sat once to discuss whether the military should take over. Who would take the lead was not clear. Besides, what daunted action was the unknown after the takeover. No one had the heart to demolish the democratic structure once and for all.'

His predecessor, Air Marshal Idris Latif, was suspicious of the army which never took either the air force or the navy into confidence. After his retirement he wrote to the then Prime Minister Atal Bihari Vajpayee to warn him against parcelling the country into areas and sub-areas, the jargon that the army used in cantonments and elsewhere. He requested him not to ever agree to the creation of the post of chief of the military staff lest he should become a dictator. Idris made the same points to Prime Minister Manmohan Singh. Neither of them replied to his request.

At a meeting which took place at Indira Gandhi's residence, after the defeat of the Congress, she pulled out Bansi Lal's resignation letter from her bag and handed it over to Y.B. Chavan, not to D.K. Barooah, and not before she had got everyone to agree that the entire working committee should collectively resign, sharing the blame for the party's debacle. She added: As one who led the government, I unreservedly own full responsibility for this defeat. I am not interested in finding alibis or excuses for myself, nor am I interested in shielding anyone. I have no caucus to defend or group to fight against. I have never functioned as a group leader.

Enthusiastic Janata Party MPs took an oath of honesty, transparency, and integrity at Rajghat. Some party supporters were also invited; I was not. At the swearing-in ceremony itself, the race for the prime-ministership began and it appeared that Jagjivan Ram had a majority. JP, who was ultimately asked to nominate the individual, selected Morarji Desai. He explained to me that he could not have nominated Jagjivan Ram because he had in parliament sponsored the resolution supporting the imposition of Emergency. JP emphasized unity in the party so that they could collectively implement the promises that had been made. 'I hoped the Janata experiment, bringing regional parties together to fight the elections on one symbol would work.' This notwithstanding, I saw the same party crumbling before my eyes. The ambition and arrogance of the leaders occupying senior positions undid the Janata.

I was particularly unhappy to see the same Jana Sangh men in key positions, bringing with them the same prejudice and parochialism. I would see the RSS men in Advani's room whenever I met him. For the Jana Sangh, the Janata party was a means, not an end in itself. It succeeded in its goal of diluting, though not washing off, its communal credentials by advancing the argument that it was an intrinsic part of the Janata Party which advocated secularism.

The functioning of the Janata Party was not very different from that of the Congress. Instead of Sanjay Gandhi, the government had to reckon with Kanti Desai, Morarji's son, who was equally ruthless and wanting in integrity, but happily not wielding the authority that Sanjay did. However, I felt so concerned that I complained to Morarji that his son was fixing up deals or contracts for huge sums of money. I requested him to at least eject him from the PM's residence which gave him the stamp of authority. Morarji refused to do so, on the plea that he had once lost his daughter who had committed suicide after he had admonished her. In fact, I found Morarji as impossible as I had found him many years earlier when he was in the wilderness: self-righteous, obstinate, and hugely arrogant.

I felt it was my duty to write against the non-performance of the Janata government. When it dismissed the nine Congress-ruled state governments, I wrote that such an action might be constitutionally correct but was morally wrong. I reminded the party of the expectations the people had placed upon them.

Morarji rang me to warn that my writings were actionable and that he could put me behind bars. I told him that Indira Gandhi had done that and he too was at liberty to follow suit. He calmed down and said that if my purpose was not to destroy the government, I should not be writing in the way I had. I said in reply: 'Morarjibhai, the government will fall because of its own misdeeds, not because of my writings.'

On the other hand, I found myself suddenly becoming popular in Indira Gandhi's circles. Sharda Prasad, Indira Gandhi's press adviser, met me once during my regular walk in the Lodi gardens and shook my hand firmly and remarked: 'Greater strength to your pen.'

The down and out Kamal Nath met me and sought my help to enable him and Sanjay Gandhi go abroad. The latter's passport had been impounded. I told him that they would never allow Sanjay Gandhi to travel abroad. As far as he was concerned, I told him that if I knew the system, the Delhi and Bombay airports must have been told not to permit him (Kamal Nath) to go abroad but he could try Madras. Two years later when he met me, he told that my tip had worked and he was able to leave the country via Madras.

The pressure to punish Indira Gandhi for her misdeeds was so relentless and most cabinet members were so insistent for some action that the party demanded her arrest. Morarji was an exception. He wrote on the file that no government action was called for because she had been punished by the people by defeating her at the polls. Charan Singh was, however, adamant as was the socialist block in the party. Members belonging to Jana Sangh were hawkish.

※

RNG felt defeated within the Janata Party because he had wanted Jagjivan Ram to become prime minister. With all his behind-the-scene activities he was keen to retain the number one position for the *Indian Express* as it had been during the Emergency. He asked me to do whatever I could to sustain the increase in circulation. He was willing to hire more hands. I told him that during the Emergency the newspaper had come to represent a sentiment which was selling. That ended with the withdrawal of the Emergency. I was proved to be right. We lost all the additional circulation we had gained.

It was during these days that RNG thought it was the best time to implement his dream of publishing an edition of the *Indian Express* from every state capital. I went to Chandigarh to bring out the Punjab and Haryana edition, but retained my position in Delhi. I would spend three days at Chandigarh and four in Delhi.

I hired many journalists but two of the recruits, Shekhar Gupta and Madhu Kishwar, became celebrities. Shekhar Gupta called me his 'guru' but showed no respect when he stopped my fortnightly column. By then he had become all in all in the *Express*, circumstances having helped him to occupy the position of editor-in-chief. He also became abnormally affluent as well as arrogant. I liked him when he was a simple straightforward journalist at Chandigarh.

What shocked me was that RNG removed V.K. Narasimha, who as editor-in-chief had kept the defiant stance of the *Indian Express* intact, a couple of days after Indira Gandhi lost power. His name was removed from the print line and substituted by Malgaonkar's, without Narasimha's knowledge. He resigned to register his protest. The entire senior editorial staff signed a petition against Goenka's action. I was approached to sign it. I told them that I would do so but after speaking to Goenka who was in the guest-house. I asked if the news about Narasimha's removal was correct. He said he had to restore Malgaonkar to his position to correct the wrong done to him. 'Was it necessary to do so in the manner you have,' I asked. He said that he should have reverted Narasimha to his original position at the *Financial Express* and seemed regretful.

When I told him about the revolt in the office he said they should not forget what he had gone through during the Emergency. I could see repentance on his face. He wanted me to go to Narasimha's house and bring him back. I went there and found him sitting on the floor having a cup of coffee his wife had prepared. I requested him to rejoin as editor of the *Financial Express* and assured him that RNG was apologetic.

For Narasimha the question of joining the Express group again did not arise. He asked me how long had I known RNG. Before I could reply, he said: 'Kuldip, I have known him for 30 years. Goenka has not changed. He is as selfish as ever.' How courageous and noble a man was Narasimha, I thought. He had no job to go to and yet took a stand whenever there was an attack on his dignity. I had close relations with the *Deccan Herald* family and got him posted as editor-in-chief of the newspaper.

While I was in Delhi over the weekend, B.D. Goenka went to Chandigarh on 6 August 1977 and inaugurated the edition published from there without informing me. That was how the Goenkas functioned. They did things at the spur of the moment and showed that like whimsical owners they could do anything at any time. The *Express* at Chandigarh did not give much of competition to the well-established *Tribune* but managed to jolt it.

One day, Prakash Singh Badal, then Punjab chief minister, dropped into my office. As we had known each other for many years, I thought he wanted to surprise me. It was indeed a surprise because he wanted me to propose my name for the state's governor. I told him that I did not have sufficient grey hair to occupy such a position but he paid no heed to my misgivings and sent the proposal to New Delhi.

I used to meet Home Minister Charan Singh at least twice a month. As usual I went to him during my sojourn at Delhi. He informed me about Badal's recommendation. Charan Singh said that he had proposed my name as an experiment in having a joint governor of Punjab and Haryana. I did not join issue with him because I knew that Morarji would reject my name. I was right. He had not forgotten that I had 'helped' Shastri to become prime minister. Vajpayee's proposal to appoint me as Indian envoy to Pakistan met the same fate. 'What has Morarji against you,' inquired Vajpayee when he got back the file rejecting my name.

The Janata Party faced a crisis from its inception on 23 January 1977. Too many groups of different affiliations were not combining well either within the party or government. The chasm between Morarji Desai and Charan Singh began opening up soon after the Janata Party government took its oath of office in march 1977. This told upon the party's unity as well as on the government's coherence. The two differed on the appointment of a commission to examine the excesses committed by Indira Gandhi during the Emergency. Morarji was not opposed to an enquiry against excesses committed but did not want to single out Indira Gandhi because he felt that she had already been punished by the people. Charan Singh differed and had his way because all his cabinet colleagues supported him on the appointment of the commission as well as her prosecution.

When it came to prosecuting Indira Gandhi, the case picked up was when she had 'lied' as a prime minister in her reply to a question on the Maruti car, her son's project. Also, she had been found mixed up in the purchase of jeeps for her party's propaganda during the polls. The Lok Sabha passed a resolution for her arrest.

As the House adjourned, I could see Congress women MPs surrounding Indira Gandhi to defy the execution of her arrest. It was the CBI that arrested her and she refused to seek bail. An FIR was registered on the morning of 3 October 1977. That very day N.K. Singh, an IPS officer of exceptional ability and moral courage, gave her a copy of the FIR. She was accused of misusing her official position and deriving pecuniary benefit in the procurement of jeeps for election purposes.

N.K. Singh was heckled by senior Congress leaders when he went to Indira Gandhi's residence to arrest her at around 8 p.m. Rajiv and Sanjay Gandhi followed her in a car. A place at Bhadkal Lake had been arranged for her detention. The railway crossing between Faridabad and the lake was closed. She got out of the car and said on the culvert that she would abide by her lawyer's advice. A large crowd had gathered and began shouting slogans for her release. Looking at the situation, N.K. Singh took her to the officer's mess of the Delhi police in Old Delhi. She felt comfortable there and spent the night.

The following day, 4 October, Indira Gandhi was produced in a magistrate's court and the police had a hard time controlling her supporters. The magistrate wanted evidence against Indira Gandhi in support of the charges made against her. He was told that the FIR had been registered only the previous day and that the evidence was still being collected. The magistrate sought to know what the prosecution wanted him to do. There was no reply. He summarily discharged her on the ground that there was no evidence given in support of her detention. She was never rearrested. (The magistrate was duly rewarded when Indira Gandhi returned to power in 1980.)

N.K. Singh was held responsible for the fiasco and removed from his position. The poor man was the first victim of Indira Gandhi when she resumed prime-ministership, being asked to proceed on leave. Worse however was the attack on him by Bansi Lal's policemen. He would have been killed had we not got a clue at the *Express*. We rushed a reporter along with a photographer to his house at Gurgaon. The CBI intervened and asked the Haryana police chief to spell out N.K.'s crime. He was dragged to court in connection with a 'criminal case' but was released by the magistrate on a personal bond. There were no voices condemning Bansi Lal's action. I met N.K. Singh a few years later when he was contesting an election from Bihar. He did not make it; honest and straightforward individuals rarely do.

The Justice J.C. Shah Commission, a one man commission, which was appointed to look into the excesses committed during the Emergency, was unaware of Indira Gandhi's arrest. Shah resigned because he did not approve of her arrest when he was in the midst of an inquiry. He had received 48,000 complaints against her but they were yet to be processed. I met him before he flew back to Bombay and wondered how she could have been arrested without consulting him. His reading was that they had given Indira Gandhi credibility by arresting her. Shah was eventually persuaded by Morarji to return to the commission.

As I look back I think that Indira Gandhi's arrest was not viewed with favour by the people and elicited sympathy for her. She exploited the government's ineptitude in filing an ill-prepared case without proper documentation. Doubts arose in people's minds, and many began questioning the entire basis of the inquiry.

The daily broadcast of the commission's proceedings after a while proved to be counter-productive. Indians are a curious people. When they feel that the guilty have been punished they forget the wrongs and forgive them. In Indira Gandhi's case the general belief was that the electorate had punished her sufficiently. When thereafter she was pilloried in parliament and at the Shah Commission, people thought that the Janata government was hitting her when she was already down. Whispering campaigns in her favour, initiated by those who had been tainted by their misdeeds during the Emergency, received encouragement. Many even felt that 'some strong' action had been necessary to establish 'discipline'. The Emergency had been a bitter pill which had to be administered.

The pro-Emergency group even spread the impression that democracy was not suited to India's genius, as many foreigners claimed. Many did not even see anything wrong in the return of Sanjay Gandhi who, the commission said, 'was not answerable to anybody', or Bansi Lal who, the commission said, was an example of 'an authoritarian chief minister'.

In the meanwhile, officers who had cooperated with the commission began dragging their feet. The fear that Indira Gandhi might return one day silenced them. What could they do when they saw some top political leaders changing their tone and colour?

Open differences within the Janata Party, virtually from the outset, only served to alienate the public. When I met Morarji to draw his attention to the growing disillusionment with the government consequent to the bickering at the top, he said there were a few disgruntled elements which he would pulverize. Charan Singh's attitude was equally unaccommodating.

When Indira Gandhi was unceremoniously defeated people felt that they had won freedom all over again, saying openly that the Janata Party's victory had given them a second Independence (*doosri azadi*). They would rebuild the country and bring about the change that JP had promised. Unfortunately, the Janata leaders did not rise to public expectations. Most of them were the same old faces, tarnished with misdeeds; old wine in a new bottle. The defeat of Mrs Gandhi had given people hope of a new lease of life, different from whimsical personal and sterile rule. Now disappointment and disillusionment began being writ large.

I went to Patna to meet JP. He too was feeling let down with the way government was functioning. I asked him to intervene because people had voted in his name and he should not fail them. To my surprise, he told me that 'nobody listens to me'. These words had a familiar ring. Mahatma Gandhi too had expressed helplessness when Nehru and Patel had accepted Partition without consulting him.

My plea to JP was that he should go back to the people to apprise them of his inability to bring about the change he had promised because the government paid no heed to his advice or principles. He said he could not travel because of his ill health. What he said was true. He was on dialysis as a result of a kidney malfunction.

On my return to Delhi, I told Morarji about JP's sense of disillusionment. Rather than speaking of remedial measures to improve the Janata government's performance, Morarji said: 'What does he think of himself. Is he Gandhi? I did not even go to meet Gandhi.' Morarji's obduracy did not surprise me. He was known for his rigidity. He was a rightist at a time when a poor country like India needed someone who was at least left of centre. Only socialists like Madhu Limaye, Janata Party's general secretary, could share JP's grief, not many others.

In fact, the Janata government had made its indifferent attitude to JP amply clear from the outset when he returned from the US after medical treatment. The Air India plane stopped at Delhi on its onward journey to Bombay. The government had deputed Information Minister Purshottam Kaushik to receive JP at the airport on the government's behalf. JP had at least expected, as he told me, Babu Jagjivan Ram, who was known to him because both came from the same state, Bihar, to have come to receive him. Jagjivan Ram was however miffed with him because he had claimed the support of the majority of Janata members and yet JP had preferred Morarji to him.

RNG, who wielded a lot of influence in the Janata government, began settling scores with individuals he did not like. One among them was Dhirubhai Ambani. He provided Arun Shourie, who had, like a paratrooper, landed as executive editor of the *Indian Express,* with material relating to Ambani. Arun Shourie, who had come into the *Indian Express* through Nanaji Deshmukh, an RSS stalwart, used the material to make 'disclosures' against Ambani. So strong was the impact of repeated campaigns by the *Express* that the shares of Ambani's Reliance company came tumbling down. Goenka and Ambani subsequently mended fences.

I met Dhirubhai for the first time when I was waiting for someone at the Taj on Mansingh Road, New Delhi. He came up to me and asked if I was Kuldip Nayar. When I replied in the affirmative, he said that he was Dhirubhai. I was flabbergasted and inquired, 'the Dhirubhai?' He told me that he had been reading my articles from his college days. In reply I said: 'See, where you are and where I am.' The following day he sent me a box of chocolates.

12

THE JANATA PARTY GOVERNMENT
A Case of Musical Chairs and a detour
to Afghanistan and Pakistan

The Janata government's first task was to undo the excesses committed by Indira Gandhi, and particularly so by her son, Sanjay, and to revive the institutions she had destroyed in order to concentrate power in herself.

However, within a few months of forming the government, it dismissed all the Congress-run state governments. Though this was constitutionally correct, it was morally wrong. It set a precedent which Indira Gandhi followed when she returned to power in 1980. I openly criticized the Janata Party's dismissal of these state governments. RNG told me that the party leaders had not liked my criticism of the new government.

The Janata government withdrew the various amendments to Article 42, undertaken in the name of providing 'just and humane conditions' of work. The word 'secular', which had been included in the preamble to the constitution, was retained. Education, which had been placed on the concurrent list, had been a state subject since the introduction of the constitution. The Janata government let it remain in the former category although it encroached on the exclusive domain of the states. This created problems 35 years later when the Centre included in the constitution the Right to Education (RTE) for every child between the ages of 6 and 14 years. The Right to Education was an epoch-making measure but it suffered from infirmities. For example, élite private schools still continue to bar poor students and those of lower-caste and lower-income families though entitled to equal education. Remedial measures to fulfill this fundamental right are still being attempted.

Through the 44th Constitutional Amendment Act, the Janata government made the proclamation of Emergency as difficult as possible. Internal disturbance, not amounting to armed rebellion, would not be a ground for the issue of such a proclamation. The maximum duration of an Emergency was fixed at three years rather than the earlier stipulation of an indefinite continuance at the discretion of the prime minister and the cabinet. Indira Gandhi had extended the tenure of parliament to six years, which was reduced to five years as was originally provided in the constitution.

The amendments could not undo the damage Indira Gandhi had inflicted. One irreparable blow was the free hand given to the police. The force had carried out the most barbaric acts at her behest and on behalf of her coterie. The Janata Party appointed a National Police Commission under the chairmanship of Dharma Vira, a very senior retired bureaucrat, to make recommendations in order to ensure that the force was not used for acts of oppression or to chastise opponents of the government. The principal purpose of this commission was to end political transfers. The force was administered by a law the British had enacted in 1888.

When I spoke to Dharma Vira he admitted that the police was misused by the administration and the only remedy was to stop whimsical transfers of top officials. His formula was to keep the force isolated from political interference. I wondered if this would be acceptable even to Janata's chief ministers like Devi Lal in Haryana and Lalu Prasad Yadav in Bihar.

The report was pigeonholed by Indira Gandhi. She had a grievance against some police officials who had prepared a report about the 'excesses' during her regime. Therefore, at a function over which she was presiding, she stopped the gallantry awards once R.K. Dhawan whispered in her ears that they were being rewarded for post-Emergency inquiries.

The report, finally retrieved after her death, had suggested the formation of a board in every state comprising the home minister, the inspector general of police, the leader of the Opposition, a high court judge, and three apolitical persons. The board was meant to supervise the recruitment and the transfer of policemen. No state government was willing to implement the report. The matter went up to the Supreme Court and it appointed a committee to monitor police reforms. The result of this was no different. Chairperson K.T. Thomas reported to the Supreme Court that he had spoken to the chief ministers of the states individually and had found each of them was against the board. He said: 'They laugh and ask me: "Why did I win the election if I do not have even the power to decide about my own police officers".'

The Janata government motivated by high ideals should have overhauled the system which reeked of misuse of power and corruption going right to the top but the leaders in authority were no different from their predecessors. Where JP went wrong was in leaving the selection of ministers to leaders like Morarji Desai, Charan Singh, and L.K. Advani. They were more interested in their 'own persons' rather than in having clean and capable ministers. Those who came to hold senior positions at the Centre and the Janata-led states were mostly of the old ilk: ambitious, power hungry, and unprincipled. There was no vision, no idealism, not even any inclination to implement JP's core message of *parivartan* to which the electorate had responded with great expectation.

Indeed, Prime Minister Morarji Desai proved to be the greatest disappointment. He was rigid and arrogant. The long spell in the wilderness had left him bitter, and had fired him with a desire to settle old scores with all those who had ever crossed his path in politics.

Had there been a free election in the Janata Party, Jagjivan Ram would have won hands down. He was disappointed when JP was entrusted with the task of selecting the leader of the parliamentary party. Jagjivan Ram knew that JP had not forgiven him for his alliance with Indira Gandhi even after letting it to be known that he would revolt against her if she imposed the Emergency.

'I had no option,' JP said, when I drew his attention to Morarji's uncompromising attitude. 'I could not make Jagjivan Ram the prime minister because he had sponsored the Emergency resolution, and Charan Singh did not have sufficient support in the party. Therefore, Morarji was the obvious choice.'

After a few weeks of enthusiasm over the first non-Congress government at the Centre, people felt disillusioned over the same old system taking over and the same old tainted people getting prominent positions. The intelligence agencies were back to their familiar activity, collecting information on critics and opponents. The same unethical and illegal methods that Sanjay Gandhi had adopted were now being used against Congressmen with impunity, particularly in the states. A new set of bureaucrats who claimed to have suffered during Indira Gandhi's rule came to the fore. A few, very few, unsoiled hands achieved importance in the new government but they were largely ineffective.

What could be considered a change was in foreign policy. Morarji Desai and the Minister of External Affairs Atal Bihari Vajpayee began moving away from the course adopted by the Congress government. Both Pakistan and China had celebrated the ouster of Indira Gandhi, who had adopted a hard-line posture against them. In 1979, Vajpayee was the first foreign minister to visit China after 1962 aggression but he had to cut his visit short when he found that during his visit China had attacked Vietnam, India's friend. Even so, the Vajpayee visit subsequently had a demonstrable effect.

The Morarji government stopped India's support for the guerrillas loyal to Sheikh Mujibur Rahman, still fighting against the military government in Dhaka. New Delhi announced a desire to achieve 'genuine' non-alignment in the Cold War, which had been the long-standing national policy.

Morarji Desai was morally against nuclear weapons for India. He once said, 'We can drive out any aggressor even without the bomb,' adding, 'if China were to throw an atomic bomb on the Indian border, she would create an impenetrable barrier for herself'. At his first press conference as prime minister he expressed doubt as to whether a nuclear programme would be useful for India and suggested returning to 'cottage industry'.

Morarji Desai verbally agreed to 'reject future nuclear explosions' even though New Delhi did not formally accept this provision. In return, President Jimmy Carter promised that he would authorize one more pending shipment of US nuclear fuel supplies to India. In 1978, however, the US Congress intervened and officially blocked the administration from exporting nuclear fuel to India by passing the Nuclear Non-Proliferation Act.

The new government withdrew all charges against the 25 accused in the Baroda dynamite case, which included the new Minister for Industries George Fernandes. As railway minister he had reinstated the railway employees dismissed after the May 1974 strike.

The Morarji Desai government also appointed the one-man Justice J.C. Shah Commission to investigate allegations of corruption and human rights abuses by members of her government, the Congress party, and the police force. Specific inquiries were instituted into Sanjay Gandhi's management of the state-owned Maruti Udyog Ltd., and the activities of former Defence Minister Bansi Lal. Both Indira and her son Sanjay were charged with allegations of corruption.

True, Indira Gandhi's defeat had given the nation, particularly in the north, a sense that the country had won independence once again (*doosri azadi*), without realizing that the instruments for *parivartan* were the same ambitious politicians and the same old breed of bureaucrats out of touch with the requirements of the day and having their own agenda.

It was sad to see a group of people who had wholeheartedly rejected Indira Gandhi bickering amongst themselves, both at the Centre and in the states. The people had never imagined that the principal occupation of ministers would be to pull one another down. Senior leaders would meet at Morarji's house to sort out their differences but disperse without resolving them. This was disappointing because the people wanted the government to deliver.

I met Morarji Desai and Charan Singh in order to appeal to them to work as a team. Morarji said that he was determined to reduce Charan Singh to Churan Singh. The meeting with Charan Singh was equally disappointing. He wondered how he could accept Morarji as his leader when he (Morarji) had won election with only 20,000 votes as against even an unknown Janata Party candidate securing a majority of at least a lakh of votes. When I saw neither an end to infighting nor even the government showing a modicum of performance, I wrote a strong open letter to JP pointing out the aims and values of his agitation against Indira Gandhi's government and its complete lack of realization under the present one. My plea was, 'What Delhi represents today cannot be to your [JP] liking, nor is it to the liking of the people'.

Nothing improved in terms of governance, nor did JP's letter to Janata Party president Chandra Shekhar had an impact. The letter which JP wrote after 15 months of Janata government rule was indicative of JP's anguish and pain. His was a warning that if the party continued its infighting and failed to fulfill the hopes kindled amongst the people with the formation of the Janata government, there was a danger of a re-emergence of dictatorial forces and tendencies.

The Janata government's functioning did not improve. I remember visiting Bombay in those days and meeting Justice J.C. Shah who headed the commission. He was very disappointed by the Centre's performance and said that governance was in fact worse now than under Indira Gandhi.

Pursuing his whimsical policy, Morarji ousted both Charan Singh and his Man Friday Raj Narain from the cabinet. Pressure from Vajpayee and Advani, then information minister, brought Charan Singh back into the cabinet, but they were unable to reinstate Raj Narain as health minister. This indeed proved to be the biggest error committed by the Janata Party leaders. Madhu Limaye, a socialist colleague of Raj Narain, warned me that if he was not reinstated, he would wreck the government. This proved to be the case.

Raj Narain made no secret of his ambition to replace Morarji with Charan Singh as prime minister. Other socialist associates of Raj Narain did not want to disturb Morarji, fearing that were they to rock the boat it might sink. Desperate, Raj Narain contacted Sanjay Gandhi who did not take him seriously at that time believing it was too early for that to happen.

The functioning of the Janata Party as a team was becoming more and more of a formality. The different constituents of the party began operating on their own. The Jana Sangh continued to behave as an unofficial handmaiden of the RSS even after joining the government.

JP also felt cheated. The Jana Sangh leaders had pledged to him that they would delink their association with RSS but did not do so. When I told JP to ask the Jana Sangh to live up to their pledge, he said that he had tried but had not succeeded. 'It's a betrayal,' JP regretted, and it was this issue that eventually split the Janata Party.

The old Congressmen and the socialists who constituted the majority passed a resolution asking the old Jana Sangh members to sever their connections with the RSS (the resolution was passed by a majority of one, Dinesh Singh, who was a Congress plant). Members of the Jana Sangh, in turn, insisted on retaining their dual membership which the other units of the Janata Party could not tolerate, and that was the beginning of the end. Ultimately, the old Jana Sangh members walked out of the party, Advani being the most prominent among them. They founded another party, the Bharatiya Janata Party (BJP) in 1980.

To Raj Narain's delight, Sanjay Gandhi took the initiative and showed interest in the move to dislodge the Janata Party government and install Charan Singh as prime minister with the support of the Congress. Raj Narain felt aggrieved because he had been asked to apologize to party President Chandra Shekhar for a snide remark he had made about him. Raj Narain embarked in all seriousness on his plan to break the Janata Party government. The session of parliament scheduled to be held in a few days' time became critical because the differences between Morarji Desai and Charan Singh appeared to be coming to a head. The demise of the Janata government seemed imminent. However, in 1979, during the last few months of the government it appointed the Mandal Commission to 'identify the socially or educationally backward' sections of the backward castes.

Madhu Limaye, Janata's general secretary, who knew Morarji and Charan Singh well, could have probably sorted out things. He had however taken to his head that splitting the Janata was a historical necessity. It was dialectical materialism of sorts. Even after the return of Indira Gandhi he argued with me that the demise of the Janata Party was in the interest of the country.

❦

Devi Lal, a senior Janata Party leader and a close supporter of Charan Singh, rang me to convey that he was giving me a 'scoop that the Morarji Desai government would fall in the ensuing parliament session'. Every day, he said, four or five MPs from the Lok Sabha would resign from the Janata Party government until it was reduced to a minority. And this is what exactly happened. The Congress sponsored motion of no-confidence came in handy to the Charan Singh group.

When I checked with Congress leader Y.B. Chavan on how he assessed the prospect of the motion he had moved against the government, Chavan said: 'Kuldip, *maarne to chale they billi, lekin mar gaya sher* [We began with the intention of killing a cat, but in the process a lion has got killed].' What could they do? He was still not certain whether the Janata government would finally fall.

When George Fernandes defended the Morarji government on one day and vehemently criticized it the next, I inferred that the game was over. I felt sorry for him because his role as a trade union leader and as a valiant fighter during the Emergency had been exemplary. I did not however know then that a person like him could change colours in 24 hours, first defending the government and then criticizing it with equal vehemence.

When Jagjivan Ram stepped in to marshal support in his favour, he found it easy to muster a majority in the House. Morarji was not however ready to step down from the leadership of the parliamentary party. When I spoke to Morarji he said that as he did not enjoy a majority in the House he would step down from prime-ministership, but not from the party leadership. It was a convoluted way of viewing things but then Morarji was never known for logical thinking.

The no-confidence motion was carried with the support of Charan Singh's men, resulting in the resignation of the Morarji government. There was great pressure on President N. Sanjiva Reddy to invite Jagjivan Ram to form the government but he did not. He explained that as the government led by the Janata Party had been defeated in the House there was no logic in inviting another leader from the same party. Technically he was correct, but Jagjivan Ram might have saved the Janata Party government because Charan Singh had doubts about the support offered by the Congress.

President Reddy asked Charan Singh to form government and prove his strength on the floor of the House. It was a real anticlimax because Charan Singh was seeking the support of Indira Gandhi who was not only his adversary but had imposed the Emergency. Charan Singh was the same person who had told me in jail that if they came to power, he would have the Congress leaders whipped at a public square.

The Congress support to Charan Singh actually proved to be a ruse to break the Janata Party government and hold fresh elections. It was all Sanjay Gandhi's doing. Indira Gandhi did not believe him when he told her about his first meeting with Raj Narain regarding the plan to unseat the Morarji Desai government but the stratagem did please her. Raj Narain, a bold fighter in the struggle against the Emergency and an experienced political hand proved to be naïve and played into Sanjay Gandhi's hands. Strange, a socialist leader like Raj Narain with his ideological commitment, proved just as avaricious for office as anyone else.

Charan Singh's fears proved to be true. He told me that he did not call on Indira Gandhi as Sanjay had insisted. He was trying to convince me that he had 'saved his honour'. He resigned before proving his strength on the floor of Lok Sabha.

For a while the idea took shape to support Charan Singh when the Congress left him high and dry, but the Janata Party members were so bitter against him that the proposal was not implemented. The Janata Party government could have been saved and some adjustments made later, but politics, when dominated by anger and irrationality, is not given to rational tactics. The Janata government had lasted less than three years (Charan Singh was prime minister from 28 July 1979 to 14 January 1980).

This was when President Sanjiva Reddy toyed with the idea of inviting Sheikh Abdullah to become the caretaker prime minister until fresh elections were held. Under the constitution, it was up to the president to nominate anyone he considered fit to lead a caretaker government. Eventually, President Reddy established a precedent by nominating (28 July 1979) the outgoing prime minister, Charan Singh, as the leader of the caretaker government.

In the seventh general elections held in 1980, Indira Gandhi won with a clear majority in a 545-member Lok Sabha: 351 seats against the Janata Party's 32. It was a huge debacle for the latter but this should not have come as surprise because as Vajpayee told me after campaigning, he saw anger on the faces of voters and predicted the party's defeat.

The cine world had floated the National Party to contest the elections in the Seventh Lok Sabha elections and had invited me to Bombay to address them. However, when the time for elections came they did not field any candidate.

Indira Gandhi for her part made anxious inquiries about the National Party when she saw a host of advertisements on its behalf, but that was all.

The Janata Party experiment failed. It was obvious that the persons who held the reins of government at the Centre and the states had neither the commitment to what JP had preached nor faith in the economic emancipation of the bottom tiers of the people. For them, the removal of Indira Gandhi was an opportunity to occupy positions of power and make money. Once that was achieved, they threw to the winds all talk of principled politics or a clean polity. In fact, they did not have it in them to lead a revolution for *parivartan*.

The nation was disillusioned and had never imagined that the change would mean a change only in masters; new persons sitting in the emptied chairs, with no difference either in the polity or policies.

I wish the Emergency had continued for a few more years. The rigours of detention and harsh rule might have tested the commitment of those in jail and thrown up leaders with real idealism and values. Morarji Desai, Jagjivan Ram, and Charan Singh had passed the age of idealism. They were angry but self-righteous and lacked any sense of accommodation.

Some of us from civil society, Romesh Thapar, Nikhil Chakravarty, Mrinal Dutta Chaudhary, Rajni Kothari, George Verghese, Raj Krishna, and I, sat together to prepare 'An Agenda for India', to analyze what was happening to our society and to provide some answers to the questions that were plaguing the nation. Our analysis was that the crisis of the Indian polity was a crisis of change. It reflected the widening gap between the base of the polity and its structure.

We stated:

> During the last decade, both political and economic processes had brought sections of the peripheral and deprived social strata into the active political community. Particularly in the north, the intermediate peasant castes had bettered their economic conditions with the aid of new agricultural technology and were no longer willing to accept a political dispensation weighted in favour of the traditionally privileged. This was a process earlier manifested itself in the south.
>
> The dalits, too, were now aware of their rights, thanks to the slowly-changing opportunity structure and the efforts by political parties to mobilize their support. They had begun demanding a change for the better in their conditions. Also, there was an enormous change in the social and political sensibilities in the rest of the active political community. There was a growing demand for purposeful and principled politics, a deep sense of revulsion against the politics of self-aggrandizement and a mounting anger over the neglect of public interest by the political parties and their leaders.

After drafting the agenda we organized a larger meeting of intellectuals to enlist support. Some 250 attended the meeting and endorsed the agenda. Our initiative, however, came too late. Elections were held without any political parties considering our agenda in their manifestos. Indira Gandhi, after becoming prime minister, asked for a copy of the agenda, but I saw no signs of any of our suggestions being adopted by her after assuming power.

Indira Gandhi dismissed the non-Congress governments in the states, following the precedent set by the Janata government. Even so, both she and Sanjay were cautious in their approach. Propaganda on family planning was completely stopped. Once, I asked my friend, Hemwati Nandan Bahuguna, then a central minister, to adopt steps to check the abnormal population growth. He said that no political party would be willing to take it up because it had been one of the major reasons for Indira Gandhi's defeat. I think he was wrong: it was not family planning but forced sterilization that had angered people.

My own stock slumped. I was now shunned. People linked me so much with the Janata government that its failure was considered my failing. More than criticism was cynicism for my 'intellectual input' against the Emergency. Not that it was not opposed but many thought it was preferable to the chaotic and quarrelsome rule of the Janata Party. Indira Gandhi was not a fallen woman but a person who had indulged in excesses and vindictive action because of the situation that protest and satyagraha had created. A minister from Rajasthan, now in the BJP, said that I had shaken the nation once but the rule that followed made people direly feel the absence of Indira Gandhi.

Indira Gandhi had won convincingly at the polls but had not yet assumed power. Charan Singh was still the prime minister but had no idea how he should react to the attack on Afghanistan by the Soviet Union in December 1979. Foreign Secretary T.N. Kaul formulated a pro-Soviet policy. He sought Indira Gandhi's advice and she wanted India to remain neutral as she saw in Afghanistan a war in the making between the US and the Soviet Union. At her bidding India abstained during the UN vote on Moscow's aggression. This approach made New Delhi unpopular in the West.

I recalled several memories associated with Afghanistan. Some years earlier when I had arrived from Delhi, a person whispered in my ear at Kabul airport that Murtaza Bhutto, son of Zulfikar Ali Bhutto, had invited me to dinner that evening, and that he would pick me up from my hotel. I had gone to Afghanistan to interview President Mohammed Daud Khan.

Murtaza told me at dinner that he had visited India several times and wanted to set up an émigré government in Delhi. He was disappointed that Indira Gandhi was opposed to his proposal, but was certain that she was otherwise willing to help. He said that his organization, Al-Zulfiqar, had conducted raids in Pakistan and wanted to increase their frequency. He gave me the impression that he was receiving assistance from India. I could not figure out why he told me all these things at our very first meeting. Ajmal Khatak, part of the Pakhtoonistan movement, too was there at the dinner. He had taken shelter in Afghanistan from Pakistan's rulers and recalled his association with Khan Abdul Ghaffar Khan.

When Murtaza was assassinated in Karachi I wondered whether he had been eliminated because of a family dispute or because of his past activities to which the Pakistan government was inimical. There were family disputes and it was an open secret that he hated Asif Ali Zardari, husband of his sister Benazir Bhutto.

After interviewing Mohammad Daud Khan I could sense that he was over-complacent in his palatial palace and did not know much about the communist movement which was taking shape in Afghanistan with Moscow's assistance. Kabul in those days was a typical middle-eastern town, bustling throughout the evening and resounding with loud music, garnished with sizzling kebabs with the crowd often breaking out into a traditional dance. There was an overall atmosphere of joy and abandon.

When the local communists killed Daud, I thought that India had lost a friend and the day might come when the government in Kabul would be unfriendly to New Delhi. My misgivings proved unfounded.

In fact, when A.B. Vajpayee, then minister of external affairs, visited Kabul he was taken aback at the suggestion of Prime Minister Hafizullah Amin, leader of the Khalaq Communist Party, that India and Afghanistan should jointly wage a war against Pakistan and divide the country between them.

Indeed, Kabul was very hostile to Islamabad because Pakistan had repeatedly referred to Afghanistan as its strategic depth. Zulfikar Ali Bhutto had visited Afghanistan several times, first as Pakistan's foreign minister and then as prime minister to persuade Kabul to tailor its policies to suit Pakistan's overall strategic policies. Amin told me during an interview that Bhutto had expressed his displeasure over the close relations between Afghanistan and India. That still remains Pakistan's grouse.

When Babrak Kamal, leader of another communist faction, Parcham came to Kabul aboard a Soviet tank on 24 December 1979, and overthrew the Amin government it was clear that Moscow had yielded to the request by local communists to station its forces in Afghanistan. As events unfolded, it became clear that Babrak's impatience to achieve power proved the undoing of both Afghanistan and the Soviet Union.

I was then working as a correspondent for the *Times* (London). They were keen that I interview Babrak. He did not mince words and wanted the Russian forces to be permanently stationed in Afghanistan. His plan was to convert the Islamic Republic of Afghanistan into a communist state within the Eastern bloc. This became evident when the government introduced in schools and colleges many books extolling the virtues of communism. This was against the grain of the Islamic ethos that Afghanistan had nurtured for centuries. People showed their resentment but had little recourse against the might of the State backed by Russia. When, however, the opportunity presented itself they revolted.

Washington was concerned about the Soviet Union's stranglehold over Afghanistan. Pakistan too felt uneasy but was helpless. This was when the Taliban made an appearance and felt confident. The US was able to convince General Zia-ul-Haq, Pakistan's martial law administrator, that he create a force of fundamentalists, who would fight in the defence of Islam. Unconcerned by the motivation of these men, the US purpose was to bleed the Soviet Union. Blinded with its own goals the US thought nothing of creating a Frankenstein which would one day threaten the peaceful existence of the people living in the area its sole concern being to combat the Soviet Union. The US literally opened the vaults of its treasury to fund and arm Pakistan and the fundamentalist. Pakistan's President General Zia-ul-Haq was able to exact the price having earlier rejected the limited US aid as peanuts and even obtain sophisticated arms for a fight against India.

New Delhi's neutrality or, for that matter, its tilt towards Moscow, infuriated the Afghans. Indians were hated at that time for doing nothing to securing Kabul's sovereignty. Indian journalists coming from Kabul told me that the Afghans who went out of the way to shake their hands now kept a distance and even abused them.

This was the time when an organization named Al Qaeda came into existence and formulated a philosophy of fundamentalism to fire up the Taliban. I did not ascribe much significance to either Al Qaeda or the Taliban because I was certain that the Soviet Union would never leave Afghanistan. In my book, *A Report on Afghanistan* (1981) I predicted that the Soviet Union would convert Afghanistan, like Finland, into a satellite state. I was proved wrong because the Taliban, after training in arms, converted their fight into a religious war and in the process won the support of the Afghan people. The supply of weapons by the US was crucial and it spared no resources to give the Taliban and Zia whatever they sought. No think-tank in the US imagined at the time that the day would come when the Taliban would become a menace for the rest of the world.

Grounded in madrassas with no formal education other than religious, the young men coming from there were fanatics who believed that they must bring back the Islamic way of life which, according to them meant no music, no education for women, and no freedom of thought. As a force they came to be known as Taliban.

Zia and Washington financed maulvis, brainwashed young men and fired them with Islamic fervour to die for a place in *bhisat* (heaven) to expel the communists, the infidels who did not even believe in God, from Afghanistan.

The US's interest lay solely in defeating the Soviet Union, its adversary in the Cold War. Zia was well aware that the US was desperate to enlist Pakistan's support given its location and he could dictate the price.

Today Pakistan is fighting against the Taliban not because they are fundamentalists but because they have brought terrorism to the country. The nation was shaken when they captured the Swat Valley. Their closure of girls' schools and ban on music horrified the people. They feared that they might occupy Islamabad. Ayesha Siddiqa, an expert on the Pakistan military, who visited Delhi when Swat was under the Taliban, told me that if they were to capture Islamabad, lakhs of Pakistanis would cross into India. How many would you kill? She was well aware that the Pakistan army was mixed up with the Taliban and the Inter Services Intelligence (ISI) used them to further their foreign policy against India.

There was no doubt in my mind that Zia's creation in Pakistan of 'Mumalquat Deen' (land of religion) inflicted the greatest harm to his country. The seed of bigotism sown by him had sprouted in the form of the Taliban. It was unfortunate that even a progressive leader like Benazir Bhutto blessed the Taliban and proudly said: 'They are my children.'

Curiously, Zia felt so much at home with me that he invited me to Pakistan through his foreign secretary who came to Delhi within a month of my earlier visit. I declined the invitation but met Zia when I went to Pakistan. He once hosted a lunch in my honour at which there were some ministers too. I told him that if he were to hold free elections, I would win. Many present at the lunch nodded their assent.

Because of my equation with Zia, Yahya Bakhtiyar, my senior in Law College, Lahore, asked me to find out from him, with whom the mercy petition was pending, what he was going to do with Bhutto. In fact, this was a suggestion by Bhutto who had read in the press that I was in town to interview Zia. Bhutto had been tried for 'murder' and given the death sentence.

The following day when I interviewed Zia I began my questions on Indo–Pakistan relations but what I really wanted to know was whether or not Bhutto would be executed. I therefore soon switched over to questions on Bhutto's mercy petition pending with Zia. 'I believe you are under a lot of pressure from foreign countries like America and Saudi Arabia to commute Bhutto's death sentence,' I said. Zia vehemently denied any pressure, either from Washington or from Riyadh. He said there was a process for the disposal of a mercy petition which he had already initiated.

The cursory manner in which he spoke about the mercy petition reflected his contempt for Bhutto. I inferred that Zia was determined to hang him. I asked Zia about the procedure. He said it was up to him to decide about the mercy petition. He had only to ring Lahore, where the crime had been committed, to complete the formality. He did not elaborate on the kind of information he was seeking but the confidence he exuded led me to believe that he had already made up his mind to hang Bhutto and now all that was left was the legal formality.

Once again I pressed Zia to tell me when the entire procedure would be completed and when he would take a final decision. He asked me when I was returning to India. I told him the following day. His, 'Oh', in response, revealed his intention. I came to the conclusion that he was going to hang Bhutto, and would do that very soon.

I narrated the entire interview to Bakhtiyar on the same day and expressed my fears. Later when I met Bakhtiyar before leaving for India he told me that Bhutto's reaction to my interview was entirely different. Bhutto was convinced that he would not be hanged. He believed his death sentence would be commuted as a result of pressure from outside. 'Kuldip got it wrong,' Bhutto said.

Within a couple of days of my arrival in Delhi I heard that Bhutto had been hanged (Bhutto was hanged at central jail, Rawalpindi, on 4 April 1979). Zia took only the BBC Correspondent Mark Tully into confidence and told him about the execution. The Indian public reacted strongly against the hanging. There were demonstrations in Delhi and elsewhere to condemn Zia who was called a 'murderer'. Morarji Desai, who was then prime minister, merely said that it an internal matter of Pakistan. Pakistanis were undoubtedly unhappy over Bhutto's execution but were afraid to voice their protest in public. I was disappointed over this response. Here were the people who Bhutto told me would come on to the streets if ever the military took over the country, but they did not dare to utter a word against Zia.

My contact with Zia snapped when I criticized the hanging and described him as a ruthless dictator. His press secretary, Brigadier Siddiq Salik, met me subsequently in Delhi when Zia was on an official visit to India. I asked him why Zia was not giving me an interview. He said that after I had described him as a ruthless dictator he did not wish to meet me. However, Salik told me that Zia was seriously considering restoring civilian rule and holding elections. He said that the point he was pondering over was whether it would do any good if the status quo was disturbed.

I was surprised when Zia was killed by a bomb blast in his plane on 17 August 1988. I have done my utmost to find out who was responsible for his killing. I suspect it was the US, and in support of this surmise I can only say that after Zia's plane was blown up, a Pakistani military officer entered India and flew on to the US. Our government was aware of this, and I wish I knew more about it.

Once the Soviet forces withdrew after suffering heavy losses, the US dropped Afghanistan like a hot potato. A large number of weapons were left behind, but more deadly was a battle-hardened force that was fired by the principle of jehad as they interpreted it. It was this force that unseated the communist government of Mohammad Najibullah Ahmadzai, the then president, and hanged him. His family had earlier fled to Delhi.

The Taliban constituted a government that would strictly adhere to the 'traditional tenets' of Islam, the first Islamic fundamentalist government in the world. People worldwide were horrified when the government banned music, made the burqa compulsory, and stopped girls studying in high school. The Taliban destroyed many historic Buddhist statues, the largest and most magnificent the rock-cut figure of the Buddha at Bamiyan.

Pakistan was the only country to accord recognition to the Taliban government in Kabul. This was ominous. India was seriously concerned about the Taliban government and the nexus between Pakistan and Kabul. Indira Gandhi, who was in power, secretly discussed the matter with the US which was still angry over India's abstention on the Afghanistan vote in the UN.

I rarely had an occasion to meet Indira Gandhi during her post-Emergency prime-ministership. The only opportunity I got was at a function where we folded hands in namaste. This time she was in command and not Sanjay Gandhi. She, however, lost him soon after her return to power.

On 23 June 1980, Raj Thapar, a close friend, rang me to tell about the crash of Sanjay Gandhi's plane. Sanjay was an adventurous pilot. A few days after the crash, his mother-in-law, Menaka's mother, rang me to say that it was sabotage, not a crash. She wanted me to find out how another aircraft could have been flying above Sanjay's plane. I had not heard that before and was unable to verify whether another plane had flown above Sanjay's. What was factually correct was that Indira Gandhi revisited the site of the crash and collected 'something'. What it was still remains a mystery. Could it have been Sanjay's account number in a Swiss bank?

Indira Gandhi's return to power resulted in my leaving the *Indian Express*. Soon after her assumption of power, RNG called me to his room and told me that he wanted to make up with her. 'You know…,' he said but did not complete the sentence. He said he wanted to effect drastic changes in the top editorial staff but did not elaborate. What he was hinting at was evident.

I did not understand whether he was under pressure or whether he was doing so on his own accord to placate the new establishment. The man who doughtily fought against the Emergency was now wanting to ride Indira Gandhi's bandwagon.

A couple of months later, he told me that Malgaonkar, the then editor, would leave the post and function as an advisor. The new editor, he said, would be Nihal Singh, then resident editor with the *Statesman,* who had worked under me as a political correspondent. Then he looked at me and asked what I would do. I told him that I would submit my resignation because that was what he wanted. I recalled the conversation I had with him earlier when he had given me a hint.

Ajit Bhattacharjea, also a marked man during the Emergency, resigned at the same time. A cryptic announcement appeared in the newspaper thanking us for our 'services to the paper'. Strange that the struggle we had waged together during the Emergency ended without even a proper farewell. I told RNG that I would start a syndicate service to disseminate my column and wondered whether his paper would be interested in subscribing to it. He said he would let me know but never did.

Indira Gandhi was not the same person after Sanjay Gandhi's death. Outwardly she stoically bore her grief but those near her told me that she was broken from within. Soon after Sanjay's death, she evicted Menaka, his widow, from her house and that too at the unearthly hour of 11 p.m. Menaka was politically ambitious and wanted to play an active role but Indira Gandhi offered her only the position of social secretary. She did not want even remotely any friction to affect her plan to ensure Rajiv Gandhi's succession.

He was a pilot and initially expressed his unwillingness to join politics. Sonia Gandhi, his wife, was reportedly vehemently against his joining politics. However, the entire country was certain that he would be Indira Gandhi's successor. One day, long before the succession, I checked with R.K. Dhawan who candidly said that whatever the denials, and there would be many, Rajiv Gandhi would be installed as prime minister.

There was some drama in Menaka's departure from the prime minister's house. Indira Gandhi refused to leave Varun, Menaka's only child, and locked herself with him for two hours. A senior police officer told Indira Gandhi that they would be in a fix if Menaka were to go to a police station and file an FIR. To the police's relief, Indira Gandhi relented but wanted Menaka out of her house immediately at the dead of night, which was very chilly at that time. Menaka took a taxi and went to her mother's house. In consequence Indira Gandhi was viewed as a harsh and unsympathetic mother-in-law.

Indira Gandhi's priority during those days was what had come to be known as the Sikh problem. It was she who had carved a Punjabi *suba* from the united Punjab and it was now she who concluded that she had to curb the Akalis.

13

OPERATION BLUESTAR
Punjab in Flames

When I first met Jarnail Singh Bhindranwale, he was already cast in his role of both hero and villain. He was as prominent as Sant Harcharan Singh Longowal, the head of the Akali Dal. Although the demand for a Punjabi *suba* had been conceded (the Punjabi-speaking districts were grouped together to form Punjab state) the Sikhs were generally unhappy with the solution. They aspired to a separate entity, which the formation of the new Punjab state did not fulfill, and therefore the community was seeking ways of achieving that much sought-after separate identity. The two sants, Bhindranwale, haughty and violent; Longowal, meek and dignified, were a study in contrast.

Once I caught up with Bhindranwale in his very untidy room and I asked him why he was surrounded by so many armed men toting rifles and Sten guns. His reply, in rustic Punjabi, was to ask why the police carried arms. I told him that the police represented the authority; to which he retorted, 'Let them ever challenge me, and I shall show them who has the authority'.

This was typical of the man. He believed himself to be above the law of the land; an individual who had been chosen by God for a mission. His ambition was to wield so much power that all the police and all the troops in India would not dare challenge him. That was his tragedy. While I was with Bhindranwale, Central Minister Swaran Singh barged in. As I was sitting on the only chair in the room, he squatted on the floor. Before I could offer him the chair, he remarked that he preferred to sit on the floor in the presence of the Sant.

Bhindranwale did not own responsibility for the assassination of Lala Jagat Narain, owner of *Punjab Kesri* and *Hind Samachar* murdered in broad daylight outside Ludhiana. Not even regret was expressed over the murder when Bhindranwale went on to describe Jagat Narain as 'a person who had abused the Sikh *quaum*'. My friend Romesh Chander, Jagat Narain's son and the editor of the two papers, was also murdered by Bhindranwale's supporters. I felt the tragedy all the more acutely because a day before Romesh returned to Jalandhar on an urgent mission he had promised to go to a cinema show with me.

Bhindranwale's emergence on the political landscape of Punjab can be traced back to 1977 when the Akali–Janata government came to power after the Congress defeat in the assembly polls. Zail Singh, the defeated chief minister who later became president of India, was most unhappy, not only because he had lost power but also because the Gurdial Singh Commission appointed to look into his conduct as chief minister, had found him guilty of misuse of power.

It was Sanjay Gandhi, known for his extra-constitutional methods, who suggested that some 'Sant' should be put up to challenge the Akali government. Both Sanjay and Zail Singh, particularly the latter, knew how the former Punjab chief minister Pratap Singh Kairon had fought the Akalis. He had built up Sant Fateh Singh against Master Tara Singh, the Akali leader, who had become a hard nut to crack. Zail Singh and Darbara Singh, who was a CWC member and later became chief minister, selected two persons for Sanjay's evaluation.

As Sanjay's friend, Kamal Nath, a member of parliament, recalled: 'The first one we interviewed did not look a "courageous type". Bhindranwale, strong in tone and tenor, seemed to fit the bill. We would give him money off and on,' Kamal Nath reminisced, 'but we never thought he would turn into a terrorist.' Little did they realize at that time that they were creating a Frankenstein. Zail Singh too maintained contacts with Bhindranwale, although he denied this after he became president.

Bhindranwale got his first opportunity to get into the limelight on 13 April 1978, Baisakhi day, when a band of Sikhs clashed with Nirankaris who called themselves 'Sikh' but were not considered to be so by the community. They were like the Ahmedis who are not considered to be 'Muslim', although they follow the tenets of Islam.

Sixteen Sikhs died in the clash on that Baisakhi day. Bhindranwale said that the killing of Sikhs when an Akali was the state chief minister was outrageous. There was indeed anger in the community throughout the country. Chief Minister Prakash Singh Badal was in Bombay at the time of the incident. He rushed to Amritsar, suspended some police officers, and arrested the Nirankari chief, Gurbachan Singh. This did not however mollify the Sikh community, nor did his call for a boycott of the Nirankaris assuage its feelings.

To add to the Akalis' woes, on the day of the clash, Zail Singh had blessed the foundation of the Dal Khalsa to needle the Akalis, and his supporters paid the bill. The inaugural function of the organization pledged in a resolution 'to preserve and keep alive the concept of the distinct and independent identity of the 'Sikh Panth'. The political goal spelt out was 'the pre-eminence of the Khalsa'.

The important part of the resolution was that 'in Punjab and other states the Centre's interference would be restricted to defence, foreign relations, currency, and general communications', and for these departments, 'Punjab and other states [should] contribute [central funds] in proportion to [their] representation in Parliament'. This eventually took the form of the Anandpur Resolution, which New Delhi interpreted as a demand for secession.

The Akali leaders were on the defensive about the resolution. Whenever I discussed the Anandpur Resolution with them, they would say there were many versions of it. One of them told me that it was Kapur Singh, a former Indian Civil Servant (ICS), dismissed from service, who had drafted the resolution. It was in English, which Fateh Singh, then the Akali president, did not understand. The resolution was only 'explained' to him by Kapur Singh, and Fateh Singh, reportedly, never realized all that was being incorporated in it.

Perhaps Fateh Singh did not understand the implications but the drafting committee had men like Balwant Singh, former Punjab finance minister, Surjit Singh Barnala, former union minister for agriculture, and Gurcharan Singh Tohra, president of the Shiromani Gurdwara Prabandhak Committee (SGPC), as its members. They could have stalled the resolution or watered it down, but there was nothing surprising about this development because, whenever the Akali Dal was in the wilderness, the party adopted a militant stance. The resolution therefore fitted in with and reflected its politics.

Bhindranwale thought that every young Sikh was a potential follower of his. During his discourses he would hark back to the past; to the days when the Sikhs were rulers and called for a restoration of that superiority. He was not impressed by Longowal or his non-violent methods.

It was apparent that Indira Gandhi and the Akalis were on a collision course. The moderate among the Sikhs were in a minority. People like Prakash Singh Badal, Balwant Singh, and S.S. Barnala were not part of the meeting convened by Bhindranwale to consider the future course of action. Punjab education minister, Sukhjinder Singh, who had stated that the Sikhs should establish Khalistan with the assistance of China and Pakistan, attended the meeting, as did Gurcharan Singh Tohra, who had brought along with him Basant Singh Khalsa, who after losing in the Lok Sabha elections had said that the Sikhs should have a separate electorate.

The prime minister could not accept the Akalis' demand for a separate territorial entity for the Sikhs. Longowal was in two minds. The extremists played on his feeling of betrayal, arguing that Indira Gandhi had gone back on her commitment even on religious demands. To placate the moderates, Longowal nominated Badal to be the first to court arrest in a morcha to win a separate state for the Sikhs. Badal, ever ready to go to jail, was elated when he was assured that he would be the first satyagrahi because this coincided with his desire to be the number one.

What, however, clinched the matter was the fear in the minds of the Akalis that Bhindranwale, who had made the Golden Temple the base for his activities, might eventually take over the gurdwara if the Akalis did not show any resistance. More than that, morchas, as the Akalis knew by experience, always became a matter of prestige for the Sikhs and received traditional support from the countryside, with volunteers numbering in the thousands. The Golden Temple automatically became the fulcrum of any such demonstration.

The morcha began on 4 August 1982. Badal was the first satyagrahi, leading a batch of 300, all of whom were arrested when they emerged from the temple for violating the order banning the assembly of more than five persons. This became a daily affair over the next two and half months, and was all very civilized.

The satyagrahis would move out amidst full-throated cries and the beating of drums. Bhindranwale, who was staying in Gurunanak Niwas, in the premises of the Golden Temple, would be surrounded by armed guards followed by a horde of Sikhs. Longowal usually walked almost alone, unnoticed, towards the *niwas*, where the two lived.

Once when I was invited by Harcharan Singh Longowal to witness the movement I wondered why every Akali agitation eventually assumed a religious flavour. Was it because religion and politics were considered two sides of the same coin, *peri* and *meri*, or was it because no morcha could be sustained without it acquiring a religious fervour?

The moderate among the Sikhs were still in control. Longowal did not fail to chide anyone raising demands other than those that the Akalis had made. The day I attended one of these congregations, when a slogan was raised for Khalistan, Longowal not only condemned it but also said that those who raised the slogan were 'agents of the Congress Party' and that the Akalis were strongly opposed to it. Till then he was in control. Bhindranwale who was sitting beside him did not utter a word.

Longowal sent Balwant Singh Ramowalia, MP, to drop me at the railway station. He was closely following the developments and did not hide the fact that there were differences between Longowal and Bhindranwale, and saw the latter increasingly impressing the Sikhs because of his extreme stand. Ramowalia wondered what was in store for the Sikhs. Bidding him goodbye at the railway station, I told him to convey to Longowal that the movement he had built was so large that it even exceeded his comprehension. 'I hope Longowal will be able to control it because I fear Bhindranwale taking it over and using it to support his extremist line'.

Nearly 30,000 Sikhs were arrested within a span of two months. The jails could not accommodate all; some were detained in camps, or even in houses. Thirty-four people died when a bus carrying them ran into a train. The morcha had caught the imagination of the Sikh peasantry and there was no dearth of satyagrahis.

What frightened me was the religious frenzy that Bhindranwale aroused. I wrote strongly to warn the government that the situation could lead to a renewal of the demand for Khalistan. I also met K.C. Pant, then home minister, to suggest he speak to the Akali leaders. I was pained by his comment: 'I do not doubt your patriotism but I feel that you are encouraging the Sikhs.'

On 15 October 1983, on the eve of Diwali, Indira Gandhi released all Akali prisoners. Within a few days of the Akali prisoners' release, Swaran Singh met Longowal and discussed all their demands, most of which were mundane. He persuaded them to accept the request to have the kirtan at the Golden Temple relayed by the Jalandhar station of AIR rather than their having a separate broadcasting station for it. They dropped the demand to rename the Flying Mail from Amritsar, Harmandir Express, realizing that it would be derogatory to tag Harmandir Sahib's name to a train.

The Akali leaders and Indira Gandhi met almost every afternoon. Balwant Singh would come to my place after the talks and give me the gist of what had transpired. One day he startled me when he said that they had requested Indira Gandhi to appoint me as an arbitrator.

Chandigarh did not pose any problem at that time; it was taken for granted that the city would go to Punjab. As regards Fazilka and Abohar, the Akalis claimed that the Punjabi-speaking population was in a majority there. Swaran Singh, however, agreed that a territorial commission should decide on the respective claims of Punjab and Haryana over all areas on the basis of their linguistic composition.

The sharing of river water was a ticklish issue, but the Akalis expressed their willingness to abide by the decision of a Supreme Court judge and did not object to his being assisted by a team of experts. It was left to Swaran Singh to identify the Act under which the reference could be made to draft the terms.

The Anandpur Sahib resolution was the principal snag. Swaran Singh told the Akalis that he could only discuss with them matters concerning Centre–state relations and nothing beyond. The Akalis held several meetings among themselves and watered down the Anandpur Resolution.

The Akalis told Swaran Singh that the resolution principally concerned Centre–state relations and decentralization of power for all the states. The constitution of a commission (June 1983) to define Centre–state relations under former Supreme Court judge, R.S. Sarkaria, grew out of government's discussions with the Akalis. Sarkaria reported that the 'partisan' role of the governor was the cause of strain in union–state relations after the fourth general elections, that is, after Indira Gandhi became prime minister. His comment was on states, including Punjab, where she used the governor to dismiss three Akali governments.

The Akalis proposed a constitution of an all-party parliamentary committee. Their suggestion of including the opposition parties did not please Indira

Gandhi as in their scheme of things the opposition parties would play an integral part in the discussions. However, Swaran Singh deliberated that as in an all-party parliamentary committee, the representation of each party would be proportionate to its strength in parliament and the Congress would have an automatic majority. It was therefore suggested that the Akalis should agree to leave it to Indira Gandhi to appoint a committee to examine the Anandpur Sahib Resolution and give its verdict.

Swaran Singh, who had been keeping Indira Gandhi in the picture, conveyed to her the details of the agreement on the Anandpur Sahib Resolution and the distribution of water, the two principal demands. She accepted the settlement and praised him for his painstaking efforts.

She, however, told him that she would like the matter to be placed before a cabinet subcommittee, which she constituted immediately, with Pranab Mukherjee, R. Venkataraman, P.V. Narasimha Rao, and P.C. Sethi as its members. Swaran Singh placed the formula in detail before the committee and they accepted it; Swaran Singh proposed that the prime minister be informed for final concurrence. The subcommittee members told him that they had full authority to endorse the formula and convey the government's acceptance.

Accordingly, Swaran Singh told the Akalis that the government had approved the formula, and a draft statement too was shown to them. Their leaders, camping in Delhi, wanted to carry the draft with them to Amritsar. As the statement had to be placed before parliament, it was agreed that it would be relayed to them at Amritsar at about the same time that it was placed before parliament.

However, the statement placed before parliament was substantially different from that which had been shown to the Akalis and did not mention all the points in relation to which Swaran Singh had made concessions. It again spoke about seeking the consent of Rajasthan and Haryana before reaching a settlement on the division of water. The Akalis termed this 'a betrayal' and complained to Swaran Singh. He could say nothing because it was apparent that Indira Gandhi had changed her mind at the last minute and the ministerial committee's approval carried no weight.

Swaran Singh could not subsequently tell me what had happened behind the scenes but his guess was that the cabinet subcommittee did not tell Indira Gandhi that the draft statement, which she subsequently changed, had been shown to the Akalis. His inference might have been correct because Indira Gandhi's ministers had no communication with her. Had they told her that they had authorized the statement on their own, they would have faced her wrath, a prospect which all of them wished to avoid, but this would have paved the way for a settlement.

Who bungled at which stage may never be revealed but it is apparent that Indira Gandhi changed her mind after giving her consent to Swaran Singh. My feeling is that she believed that Longowal and Bhindranwale were on the same page. Any concession would mean that the Akalis could convincingly say that they represented the Sikhs, and where would that leave her own Congress party? What she did not realize was that most of the Sikhs wanted an identity of their own and the Akalis had come to represent them.

After the failure of the talks, Swaran Singh vowed not to get involved again. He kept away from negotiations with the Akalis and even when he was repeatedly requested by the PM to play 'some part' he did not agree. Indira Gandhi left the problem, which she could have settled then, hanging. The Akalis still thought that they could retrieve the situation which was being increasingly controlled by Bhindranwale.

The moderates were against Bhindranwale and his approach but were also angry with the government for not doing anything for the community. They had always given in to the hawks and this time was no exception. The feedback to the Akalis was that the Sikhs in the countryside were agitated over police 'encounters', arrests, searches, and the ill-treatment meted out to the families of suspects. This only increased Bhindranwale's following.

The Sikh youth, mostly from villages, were getting educated but there were not enough jobs for them. They were disinclined to return to the rough and tumble of rural life and even their farms (65 per cent) had become uneconomical with the increase in the number of inheritors, each demanding a share. Even though Punjab had benefitted the most from the 'green revolution' there was growing discontent. All these factors contributed to a demand for confrontation with the government.

Bhindranwale's statement that the Hindu police were killing 'innocent Sikhs' added fuel to fire. The Akalis reacted to the 'excesses' by honouring suspects of murder and violence with *saropas* (a robe of honour), petrifying the Hindus even more. At that time, the People's Union for Civil Liberties sponsored a team, with V.M. Tarkunde as chairman, and I as a member, to assess the police excesses against the Sikhs. Amrik Singh, an educationist and a close friend of mine, was also a member of the team. We stated in our report that the police had 'acted like a force taking revenge' and had even set fire to the houses of a few people who had absconded and destroyed utensils, clothes, and whatever other belongings came to hand.

Relatives of these people were harassed and sometimes even detained. Many days after the excesses were committed by the police, we could see how fear-stricken the people were. Villagers gave us the names of some of the police officials involved. Some of them, they said, had a reputation of taking the law into their hands.

However, we could not but condemn the extremist elements that were bent on disturbing peace and glorifying violence. We were shown in Jalandhar, where we ended our trip, photographs of persons who had been charged with murder and rioting being 'honoured'. We learnt to our dismay that even the moderate Sikh leaders were reluctant or afraid to condemn the unlawful acts of the extremists.

The Akali leaders' failure to speak out against the atrocities to people of other religious beliefs was its major blunder. Many Hindus had tried to discuss the state's problems with the Akalis. Virendra, a leading editor from Jalandhar, went to Longowal to tell him that he supported the Akali demands. Romesh Chander, Jagat Narain's son, Hind Samachar's chief editor, wrote that he accepted the validity of the demands. Nonetheless, both of them, like other Hindu leaders, complained that the Akalis were unwilling to talk to them.

The Hindu leaders made no secret of their suspicion that the Akalis were working towards an autonomous Sikh state and that every act of theirs was intended to further that demand. After losing their all in Pakistan, Hindus feared the prospect of being forced into 'another migration' which an autonomous Sikh state would entail.

At that time there was virtually no law and order in Punjab and the Akalis were openly critical of the government for not taking action against the 'culprits', as were the opposition parties, including the BJP and the CPI(M). According to some sources, Bhindranwale even asked Longowal to give a call to the Sikh masses to buy motorcycles and revolvers to kill Hindus in Punjab. This shocked Longowal and he issued a statement to inform the public about Bhindranwale's intentions to challenge the government. There was, however, such intense pressure from the extremists that even Tohra and Longowal preferred to lie low.

Even though it was announced that Guru Nanak Niwas was part of the Golden Temple, Bhindranwale began feeling insecure there. He feared that the Akali leaders would one day call the police into Guru Nanak Niwas and have him arrested.

Longowal was more than ever convinced that the government would not yield till the Hindus in Punjab lent their voice to the Akali demands. The Punjab group in Delhi, comprising Inder Gujral, Lt Gen. J.S. Aurora, Air Marshal Arjan Singh, Justice Rajinder Sachar, Pran Chopra, and I approached Longowal to have a *hukumnama* (edict) issued against the killings. The Akalis' argument was that this would imply an admission that all the killers were Sikhs. However, Longowal appreciated the need for a unilateral gesture to Hindus but Tohra sabotaged it.

With pressure building on the government to do something (the Lok Dal and the BJP in the opposition demanded army action), Bhindranwale apprehended a Central Reserve Police (CRP) swoop and wanted to move to the Akal Takht. However, its head priest, Kirpal Singh, said that he would not allow arms inside the sanctified area. Bhindranwale then complained to Tohra, who persuaded Kirpal Singh to withdraw his objection. What could the head priest do when Tohra, his employer, thought otherwise? On 15 December 1983, Bhindranwale moved to the Akal Takht.

From that very day fortifications began to be constructed inside the temple. New Delhi was worried because it could see the confrontation building.

Although both the prime minister and the home minister assured President Zail Singh that whatever action they took, they would at most send the police within the precincts of the temple, Zail Singh threatened to resign if the government ever changed its mind.

Longowal didn't approve of Bhindranwale moving into the Akal Takht but could do little about it as he was aware that Tohra, president of the SGPC which has all gurdwaras under it, was sympathetic to Bhindranwale. In fact, Tohra for his part was seeking to maintain good relations with both Longowal and Bhindranwale. Violence erupted in Panipat and Jagadhari in Hindi-speaking Haryana; nine Sikhs were killed and three gurdwaras attacked on 19 February 1984. The connivance of the authorities was palpable.

Relations between Hindus and Sikhs were bad enough because of the killing of some Hindus in Punjab but the equation began to come under strain even outside the state. The central government was also panicky because there was horror and anger against the failure to check the rise of terrorism in Punjab. The state machinery, bolstered by the induction of the CRPF and BSF, made elaborate plans to counter the situation. One step was to clear 'undesirable people' from the houses surrounding the Golden Temple, but New Delhi did not give a green signal for this.

Whatever action was contemplated, the Punjab government was conscious that it was essentially a political question which demanded a political solution. State governor B.D. Pande, stated that it was a political matter and his advisers relayed this message to Indira Gandhi whenever they got an opportunity to meet her.

Sant Longowal was reduced to a puppet. Though he was aware of the fortifications as his aides brought him news of arms being brought in trucks carrying ration for the langar. On the other hand, Maj. Gen. Shabeg Singh, hero of the Bangladesh war, was training the extremists within the Golden Temple complex.

Longowal did not do anything to put a stop to all the buildup inside the Akal Takht. For one, he felt he could not do anything to change the situation, two, he was angry with the government of India for not providing him with an escape route, and three, he did not know how many Sikhs he could take with him if the chips were down. He avoided open confrontation with Bhindranwale, but even so, was willing to call off the agitation if the government were to hand over Chandigarh to Punjab in exchange for an equal area to be given to Haryana and to agree to refer all the other demands to a tribunal. He underlined this in many press interviews.

Longowal made yet another attempt to strengthen his depleting ranks. As the Sikhs had been inspired by Bhindranwale to maintain their distinct identity, Longowal demanded an amendment to Article 25 (2) which stated: 'the reference to Hindus shall be construed as including a reference to persons of Sikh, Jain or Buddhist religions...' This did not figure in the Akalis' long list of grievances, nor was the amendment in their short list of demands. By raising the question, moderate Akalis thought that they would be able to regain their flock. 'We had to do something to retrieve our following which Bhindranwale had taken away from us,' one of them explained.

Badal, who was conscious of Hindu sensitivity, opposed the demand for amendment, Balwant Singh remained silent, and Barnala supported Badal. Longowal brought them round by convincing them that Tohra had already secured Congress general secretary Rajiv Gandhi's approval for such an amendment.

The Akalis also announced the boycott of the biennial Rajya Sabha poll. They could have secured one seat, but this went to the Congress because of their non-participation. They also decided to celebrate Azad Panth week. Increasingly, the emphasis was on the Panth and religious homogeneity to impress upon the Sikhs that they were no different from Bhindranwale when it came to protecting the dignity of the community.

What the Akalis had in mind was either a common civil code for all communities or a separate law for the Sikhs. In a letter to New Delhi, Longowal stated that the Hindus had a separate personal law and so had Muslims, then why not the Sikhs? 'Denial of a separate law is an instance of discrimination against the Sikhs.'

The government was in two minds about whether to take on the Akalis or to compromise with them. Narasimha Rao, then home minister, called us, the Punjab Group, and suggested that we hold discussions with the Akalis and persuade them to divide Chandigarh, one part becoming the capital of Punjab and other of Haryana, as if the Centre had agreed to concede the other Akali demands. We were able to persuade the Akalis to agree to split Chandigarh, but the strange thing was that we were unable either to get an appointment with Narasimha Rao or to convey the Akalis' consent to him over the phone. He was simply unavailable so we feared something fishy was in the air.

Our suspicion was strengthened when H.K.L. Bhagat, the then minister for information and broadcasting, came to meet me. He had been sent by Indira Gandhi, as he told me, and asked whether the government should send troops inside the Golden Temple. I replied in the negative, arguing that the Golden Temple was not just a gurdwara but the Sikhs' Vatican. They would consider it a very grievous affront to the entire community.

I did not hear from Bhagat again, but I heard from the president's press secretary, Trilochan Singh, that troops had entered the Golden Temple. When I had met Giani Zail Singh a few days earlier he had said that he had an assurance from Indira Gandhi that she would never send troops into the Golden Temple.

Trilochan Singh was also the first person to tell the president about the army's entry into the Golden Temple. He felt deeply hurt, and particularly by the fact that even though he was the titular commander-in-chief of the Indian armed forces, he had been kept in the dark when the troops moved into the Golden Temple.

I was shocked but not surprised when the army moved into the Golden Temple on 3 June 1984. As a member of the Punjab Group, I felt defeated because Narasimha Rao entrusted us with the task of talking to the Akalis ten days before the army moved into the Golden Temple. I later checked with Brig. Kuldip Singh Brar, leading Operation Bluestar and found that he had been told about the assignment a fortnight earlier. This meant that the government had made up its mind to storm the Golden Temple when Rao spoke to us. Why did he hide the fact from us?

'Tell him that his guests have arrived,' Longowal said, unable to keep the bitterness out of his voice when referring to Bhindranwale. What he had long feared was happening. Troops had taken up positions around the Golden Temple. Reports that the army action was imminent had been in the air for several days. Longowal had been hoping against hope that the inevitable would not happen. Only the previous night had he heard Indira Gandhi's broadcast to the nation about the Punjab crisis and said that 'if any misgiving or doubt on any issue remain, let us sit round the table and find a solution'. How could she first order a military operation and then suggest negotiations? Longowal complained to me later. Besides, even if the Akalis were ready to talk, how could they contact her? All their telephone lines had been cut.

Although curfew was clamped late in the evening, hundreds of pilgrims were still within the precincts of the temple, 3 June being the martyrdom anniversary of the fifth Sikh Guru, Arjun Dev. Longowal was now certain that the army troops would indeed enter the temple complex unless, of course, Bhindranwale surrendered.

Bhindranwale, feeling secure at the Akal Takht, was telling some journalists: 'If the authorities enter the temple, we will teach them such a lesson that the throne of Indira is sure to crumble. We will slice them into small pieces ... Let them come ...'

His information from government sources was precise to the last detail. He knew exactly when the commandos landed at the airport near Ludhiana, and when they moved into Amritsar. He told the journalists that one lakh troops had moved into Punjab and that there would be simultaneous raids on 35 gurdwaras, including the Golden Temple. His second-in-command, Shabeg Singh had no time for journalists on 3 June. He merely said: 'They [the troops] are all over; I have a lot of work to do.'

While the militants seemed to be well posted with what the authorities were planning, the army's own intelligence was scant. It did not know how many extremists were inside the temple, where they were hiding, and what weapons they had. The government's Intelligence Bureau (IB) was unable to provide even details regarding the fortifications inside the temple though it reported the smuggling of arms. The Punjab Intelligence was worse; it did not even report the regular inflow of arms into the precincts of the shrine. Now that it is an open secret that Amrik Singh, president, Sikh Students' Union, was IB's agent (Falcon was his pseudonym), why did the government not have information from within the Golden Temple. Was he a double agent?

Punjab had already plunged into the next phase of violence which was far more dangerous than the first. Pakistan saw in it fertile ground to conduct its proxy war and stepped in. The .303 rifles with Bhindranwale's men were replaced with lethal AK 47s, rocket launchers, grenades, and improvised explosive devices.

Before the army action, Indira Gandhi had put the Disturbed Areas Act on the statute book. That night (4 June 1984) the army exchanged heavy machine-gun fire with the militants entrenched in the Golden Temple and sent batches of 25 commandos inside the temple. 'We will not surrender. We will fight to the last man,' said Bhindranwale, in what was apparently his last interview with a journalist. 'No might in the world can make us bow our head.'

One of the officers commanding a unit on the night of 5 June described how the commandos were mowed down by Sikh militants firing from inside underground tunnels. The military operation had to be temporarily suspended because of the unexpected disaster.

At about 9 p.m. on 6 June, the entire city of 700,000 was plunged into darkness by a power cut. Half an hour later, Amritsar was shaken by powerful shelling, mortar explosions, and machine-gun fire. The big battle had begun and half the city was up on the rooftops watching it. Tracer bullets and flares lit up the sky. The explosions in the Golden Temple rattled doors and windows miles away. While the battle was raging, All India Radio claimed the city was 'calm'. Between 10.30 p.m. and midnight, slogans were heard from the outskirts of the city, raised by villagers trying to march to the Golden Temple from three different directions. The slogan, 'Long live the Sikh religion' and 'Bhindranwale is our leader', were heard briefly and were followed by rapid army machine-gun fire and screams.

Few residents slept that night (7 June). This was when the battle was at its severest, and it ended over twelve hours later, at around 10.00 a.m. By then the curfew had been extended indefinitely and main streets were being heavily patrolled by troops. There were reports of heavy casualties: according to the official, preliminary count, 800 Sikh militants and 200 army men had been killed in the storming of the temple. Among the dead were Bhindranwale and two former Indian army generals who were leading the Sikh militants.

On 8 June, despite the military capture of the Golden Temple, troops still battled pockets of resistance within the complex, and the intermittent sound of mortar and machine-gun fire continued to be heard all over the town. A tank and an armoured personnel carrier outside the shrine as well as an armoured personnel carrier on the marble pathway inside the temple complex lay smouldering. Lt Gen. Ranjit Singh Dyal recalled that 'resistance was so heavy that they could not have cleared the terrorists from the Akal Takht had they not used tanks'. The stench of death pervaded the neighbourhood of the temple.

Brigadier Kuldip Singh Brar first brought in armoured personnel carriers (APC) at 4.10 a.m. from the Guru Ram Das Sarai side to close in on the Akal Takht. However, anti-tank rockets fired from the Akal Takht substantially damaged one. This came as an acute shock to Brar, as no one had suspected that the militants had rockets.

After the destruction of the APC, seven tanks were brought in from the Guru Ram Das Sarai side. The steps leading to the *parikrama* were broken by a tank to facilitate the entry of the others. Some damage was also inflicted to the *parikrama*, a part of it caving in under the weight of the tanks. Once the tanks had been stationed, appeals were made through megaphones to the terrorists to surrender. Nearly 200 of them did, including 22 who had taken position in Harmandir Sahib.

The tanks opened fire in the afternoon of 6 June. Under the cover provided by them, the jawans who had retained a position near the trees in the compound rushed in and captured a portion of the Akal Takht after room-to-room fighting which resulted in heavy casualties on both sides.

The principal assault on the Akal Takht and the basement, which was the terrorists' arsenal, began that evening. This was when an incendiary bomb fell inside the library and set it on fire. The SGPC alleged that the library was set on fire by the army on the morning of 7 June, but it appears to have been an accident, the responsibility for which is difficult to determine. The library had some rare books and manuscripts, including handwritten copies of the Granth Sahib and *hukumnama*s bearing the signatures of several gurus. All that was left of this treasure was a mound of ashes.

The firing from the Akal Takht continued unabated. Earlier, Brar had used the neon lights of the tanks to blind the terrorists while his men crept up, but the lights would burn out. They were more in the nature of flashlights, intended for a brief duration. The Bhindranwale men were able to resume firing as soon as the lights were out. The tanks were then ordered to use their heavy guns. Some shells from tanks stationed on the other side of the *sarovar* missed the Akal Takht and hit Darshini Deori, the entrance to the causeway leading to the Harmandir Sahib, demolishing a part of it.

At around 11 p.m. someone emerged from the Akal Takht and, rushing to the Nishan Sahib, fired off a shot in the air. Some soldiers thought it might have been Bhindranwale's signal of surrender, but whoever it was, he carried no white flag and there was no let up in the firing. The lone man was hit in the leg and when he fell several militants rushed out and dragged him back inside the Akal Takht. A few of them were killed in the process.

The firing from the Akal Takht now lessened. Though it took the army a few more hours till late at night to clear the ground floor and the basement, the battle was clearly over. There were 31 more bodies strewn all over.

How did Bhindranwale die? I put this question to Dyal a fortnight after his body was found. Dyal said: 'It is very difficult to say; a bullet may have hit him or some masonry might have fallen on him.' Could, as the home secretary, M.M. Wali, had speculated, Babbar Khalsa men have killed him? Dyal said: 'This is not possible, not believable.'

Curiously, while there were troops everywhere in the city, there were none at the crematorium. 'The army probably thinks that the ghosts will take care of intruders,' said the man on duty at the crematorium. He and police officials, who were given charge of removing the dead from the temple complex, said that bodies were being brought in municipal garbage trucks round the clock from early 6 June. 'We have been really busy. To add to our woes, we don't have enough wood to burn the dead, and so we are cremating them in heaps of 20 or more,' said the crematorium official.

On 10 June, a reporter found a body of a petty shopkeeper, who apparently had died of starvation and thirst, being pulled out from a wayside stall by troops about 2 kilometres from the Golden Temple. Later, the district police chief admitted in confidence that 6 people and over 1,000 buffaloes had died of starvation because of the strictly-enforced curfew. In Amritsar's Green Avenue district, babies had no milk to drink and residents were largely reduced to eating lentils and homemade bread. A village milkman who tried to bring milk to the area in violation of the curfew was shot dead by soldiers. Some 100 people were killed between 4 and 10 June when the army fired on crowds of Sikh villagers trying to march to the Golden Temple.

I was keen to find out who had ordered the entry of tanks into the Golden Temple. The military officials who were involved in the operation felt that the continuous firing coming from the direction of Akal Takht made the soldiers sitting targets in their exposed positions. Indira Gandhi was woken up by the Chief of Army Staff Krishnaswamy Sundarji for permission to deploy tanks.

Several of the slain Sikh militants were shot at by troops with their hands tied behind their backs. The doctor, whose team examined 400 corpses, including those of 100 women, and 15 to 20 children, said he had conducted postmortems of several Sikhs whose hands were tied behind their backs with cloth from their turbans.

The firing at Guru Nanak Niwas sparked off indiscriminate shooting from the Akal Takht, the library, and some adjoining buildings. The troops fired back. It was probably then that the damage to Harmandir Sahib was caused (it carried the marks of at least 300 bullets). One *bir* (Guru Granth Sahib) was hit by a bullet; the government tried to take away that volume on 13 June by attempting to make the priest an accomplice.

Dyal told me later, 'We did not resort to firing towards the Harmandir Sahib even when the extremists used the place where the *kirtan* was held, to fire at us.' However, one officer who was part of the operation did admit that 'the jawans fired in reply to the firing from the temple'. I did not get any explanation of the attack on the library in the gurdwara even though the army had an aerial photograph of the buildings and knew where each was situated.

Ramowalia miraculously escaped the killing. Six before him, he said, had been shot dead. When his turn came he shouted and raised his hand with the holding the member of parliament card. He was spared and so were a few others who had been lined up against a wall.

It was all over in less than five days. It was a tragedy that could have been averted. Perhaps the community could have been told that if Bhindranwale did not vacate the Golden Temple even an army operation was possible. Perhaps some Sikh leaders and top retired Sikh commanders could have intervened to put an end to the state within the state which Bhindranwale had built.

The Sikhs were not only hurt but also humiliated. R.K. Dhawan, Indira Gandhi's personal assistant, came to my residence within a few days of the Golden Temple operation. He said that Indira Gandhi had sent him to inquire what the government should now do. I was very upset and told him that she had laid the foundation of Khalistan. 'This was precisely what Prime Minister Indira Gandhi anticipated you would say,' Dhawan said.

My advice was that the troops should be immediately withdrawn from the Golden Temple in order to allow the public free access to it; that would allow them to come and vent their pain and serve to provide catharsis to their pent-up rage. I also proposed that the government should have nothing to do with the election of the SGPC and let the community elect its representatives to manage the gurdwaras.

I warned Dhawan that the government should not rebuild the Akal Takht, which had been destroyed during the operation. If I knew anything about Sikhs, I told him, they would prefer to rebuild the Akal Takht themselves and tear down anything the government raised. None of my suggestions were implemented.

Some days later, the troops were withdrawn after Brar, heading the combat force that went into the Golden Temple, bowed before the Granth Sahib to seek forgiveness. It was not the end of the chapter; just the beginning. Punjab went through 10 years of militancy and people lived a miserable life, many losing their near and dear.

Air-Marshal Arjan Singh, Lt Gen. Jagjit Singh Aurora, and I, as members of the Punjab Group, went to the Golden Temple within a few days of Operation Blue Star. The briefing to us was undertaken by Brar, to Arjan Singh and J.S. Aurora separately because they discussed with Brar the operational details which I, a journalist, was not supposed to know.

This discrimination was understandable, but I could not make out the discrimination shown to Arjan Singh and Aurora on a road to Jalandhar. We three were returning in different cars, the two of them in one and I in another. Their car was searched notwithstanding the top positions they had enjoyed in the air force and army respectively. I, clean-shaven, was allowed to proceed without being searched. I also witnessed the discrimination in Delhi when the Sikh police were not given any weapons. The truth was that Sikhs were removed from all sensitive positions, particularly in the intelligence agencies.

The broadcast President Zail Singh made after Operation Bluestar was probably his finest hour. He literally wept over what had happened at the Golden Temple but at the same time he stood by the government. His resignation would have created a crisis for the nation which it could not afford. It would have meant a confrontation between the Sikhs and New Delhi. He resisted all pressure from within the community and flew to Amritsar to offer his apologies but at the same time carried out his duties as president of India.

He told me that he had conveyed his annoyance to Indira Gandhi. This, I argued with him, was not sufficient; he should convey his annoyance in writing. Posterity would need proof and that could not be oral. He agreed with me and poured his heart out in a note that he, as the president, sent to the prime minister. He resisted the community's pressure to resign because as he told me such an act would have made the entire Sikh community suspect in the eyes of Hindus.

Many years later, the government tried to undo the injustice. General J.J. Singh, a Sikh, became the first Sikh chief of staff. Congress President Sonia Gandhi expressed her regrets in 2004 over Operation Bluestar and the massacre of Sikhs in Delhi and elsewhere in 1984.

The suspicion in the minds of Sikhs that they were not trusted ended when Manmohan Singh was elected India's prime minister. His apology at the Golden Temple in 2004 closed the chapter. I have never been able to understand why he was opposed to the resolution I wanted to move in the Rajya Sabha in 2001 (he was the opposition leader) which sought forgiveness from the Punjabis, particularly Sikhs, for Operation Bluestar. He told me that by doing so I would be raking up old controversies. In any event, the chairman of the Rajya Sabha, Krishan Kant, did not permit me to move the resolution.

🕉

Indira Gandhi's assassination was the revenge of radical Sikhs for Operation Bluestar. The IB wanted to replace her Sikh guards but she insisted on their retention lest their transfer send a wrong signal to the Sikh community.

A night before the assassination she returned from Orissa. It was unusual for her to hold a darbar for visitors the day after her return, but she did not cancel it because a well-known actor, Peter Ustinov, had arranged to film her among the people. She gave instructions to R.K. Dhawan regarding the guest list for the dinner she was hosting to welcome Princess Anne from the UK.

It was around 9 a.m. on 30 October 1984 when she walked through the wicket gate, connecting her residence, 1 Safdarjang Road, with 1 Akbar Road, the venue of darbar, with Dhawan following her. A servant passed that way. She stopped to inspect the cups and saucers he was carrying to serve tea to Peter Ustinov, and asked him to go back and get a better tea-set.

At the wicket gate itself, Beant Singh, one of the guards, shot her with his pistol. As she fell to the ground, another guard, Satwant Singh, fired at her with his Sten gun. Dhawan, as he told me, was at a loss to believe what he was witnessing. Beant Singh said in Punjabi: 'We have done what we had to do. Now you can do what you have to do.' Both assailants dropped their weapons and surrendered to the police.

Dhawan looked for an ambulance. There was none. He put her in an ambassador car and took her to the All India Institute of Medical Sciences (AIIMS). The VIP section was closed so she was wheeled into the casualty ward where a team of doctors was waiting. She was dead by then but they still took her to the operation theatre to try to revive her. The BBC announced her death five hours before the official announcement was made at 4 p.m. in India.

Arun Nehru said, as Indira Gandhi was wheeled in, that people in the country would not remain silent and there was bound to be large-scale violence in response to the attack. He told me later in London that *phupi* (aunt) was against Operation Bluestar.

Arun Nehru was not wrong in anticipating violence because the cavalcade of President Zail Singh, who rushed to the AIIMS straight from the airport (he had just returned from abroad), was stoned. Rajiv Gandhi was in Calcutta when Indira Gandhi was assassinated. Zail Singh decided in the plane itself that he would swear in Rajiv Gandhi as prime minister, without waiting for the ruling Congress to elect a leader of its parliamentary party.

Before the arrival of Zail Singh and Rajiv Gandhi in Delhi, the CWC held a hurried meeting to more or less endorse Rajiv Gandhi's candidature. There were, however, two conscientious dissenters. One, Pranab Mukherjee, said that the seniormost person should be the officiating prime minister till Rajiv Gandhi was formally elected by the Congress parliamentary party. Arjun Singh was on a different wicket. He insisted on having Sonia Gandhi as prime minister. Rajiv Gandhi understandably did not include Mukherjee in the government he constituted. Soon he resigned from the prime-ministership to hold early general elections.

14

RAJIV GANDHI

The Bhopal Gas Tragedy, Influx of Migrants into Assam, Operation Brasstacks, My Interview with A.Q. Khan, the Bofors Scandal

Rajiv Gandhi returned to the Lok Sabha with a massive majority, securing 48 per cent of the votes polled and 77 per cent seats, 419 in the 545-member House. His youth and inexperience evoked sympathy, but Arun Singh, Rajiv Gandhi's friend, and Arun Nehru, whom Indira Gandhi had inducted in her council of ministers, formed part of the prime minister's inner circle of advisers and would decide among themselves on important issues before they were addressed in the cabinet. Both were the principal architects of Operation Bluestar.

The troika arrangement initially worked well but broke down due to personal differences. Arun Nehru explained to me that the understanding on the basis of which the arrangement between them was based was vitiated by the media. Press stories of differences that barely existed surfaced. The worst was that Arun Singh or he (Arun Nehru) was played up at Rajiv Gandhi's expense, Rajiv naturally finding this unpalatable. This was too facile an explanation.

My guess is that the importance attached to Arun Singh and Arun Nehru, only ministers of state, was too much for the other ministers to stomach. The cabinet within a cabinet was a form of humiliation which many senior ministers could not take. It was therefore only a matter of time before such an ascorbic circle would end. This happened within a few months of Rajiv Gandhi assuming power.

Stepping into the big shoes of his mother was not easy. Rajiv Gandhi began with the same handicap as his mother. Indira Gandhi had to devalue the rupee under US pressure; Rajiv Gandhi to let off Warren Anderson, chairman of Union Carbide Corporation, which was running an outdated gas plant in Bhopal which leaked, resulting in the death of some 20,000 people on the night of 2-3 December 1984. Rajiv Gandhi rang Arjun

Singh and instructed him to release Anderson and to arrange to fly him to Delhi.

The outdated plant in question, of a model ordered to be closed in Canada, had been installed in Bhopal during the Emergency (1975–77) at the behest of Sanjay Gandhi in the face of serious official objections. I, as correspondent of the *Times*, London, based in Delhi, failed to realize the enormity of the problem and really slipped up. So disturbed was the *Times* that they sent the newspaper's old hand, Trevor Fishlock, a friend of mine, to Bhopal. The troika of Rajiv Gandhi, Arun Singh, and Arun Nehru were in the main faced with two principal issues that beleaguered the nation. One was the question of terror-stricken Punjab and the other Assam, which was in the throes of agitation against the influx of migrants from Bangladesh. The militancy in the wake of Operation Bluestar and the 1984 pogrom against the Sikhs had given a new lease of life to the movement for Khalistan. The militants found the Sikh community in the rural areas willing to help and shelter them when pursued by the paramilitary forces and the police.

I invited Arun Singh and some friends to my home to learn something about what the government had in mind for Punjab. Arun Nehru was sufficiently frank to admit that the situation was bad but not out of control and assured me that they would negotiate an early settlement with moderate Sikh leaders.

Rajiv Gandhi initiated talks with the Akali leaders who were opposed to the Bhindranwale ideology. He believed that if he was able to win over Sikh liberal opinion he would be able to demonstrate to the community that he was sincere about reaching a settlement, and thereby isolate the militants.

K.P.S. Gill was the director general of police in Punjab. He used questionable strong-arm methods with a total disregard for the tenets of human rights. Many innocent people were killed and many remain missing to this day. He had been given a carte-blanche by Chief Minister Beant Singh to bring the situation under control regardless of the consequences. I was a great critic of his, but even so he invited me to address his men at Chandigarh on the violation of human rights. Gill had that kind of courage.

What greatly helped Punjab to eliminate militancy was Islamabad's gesture. It is significant that the civilian government in Pakistan which had come to power in the wake of military rule provided India with the names of the militants who had once taken shelter in Pakistan, and this helped in uprooting militancy from Punjab.

Longowal, the leader of the movement, had realized that his softness towards the terrorists had emboldened them, but his greatest concern was the cleavage between Hindus and Sikhs. He took me along on his rounds in Delhi to meet several Hindu families who had lost family members at the hands of terrorists. Longowal apologized for the killings and worked single-mindedly to bring back the alienated Sikh community into the mainstream.

However, the negotiations made little headway. On one of those days, the prime minister invited me to breakfast to discuss the future of Punjab. I told him that the Sikh psyche had been deeply hurt, first by the army operation at the Golden Temple and then by the large-scale massacre of Sikhs in Delhi and elsewhere. I said that I found no objection to Longowal's interpretation of the Anandpur Sahib Resolution, the state having more powers. Rajiv wanted to know if I could suggest a way out. My advice to him was to cultivate Longowal who was in a mood to settle the issue.

The Sikh Khalistan movement was an insurgency fighting for a separate country. At its height I visited the Golden Temple. Five young Sikhs surrounded me at the premises. They argued that the Sikhs wanted Khalistan because they too wanted a country of their own where they could enjoy the glow of freedom, the words that Nehru had used in another context, and preserve their identity.

I told them that I would not go into the viability of Khalistan but wanted to know how they would achieve it because the nation would fight with its full might against secession. They said that Pakistan and China had promised to send their forces to 'liberate' them. I told them quite frankly that I could not imagine a situation in which China and Pakistan would wage war against India to 'liberate' Punjab and station their troops there to defend it. 'Do not underestimate New Delhi's power,' I told them.

I could judge from their diction and argument that they were well-read in Maoist writings. In fact, some of the posters at the Golden Temple, written in red ink demanding Khalistan, convinced me that the leaders of the terrorists once formed part of an extreme Left movement. They wanted to give me their names but I declined to have them. A terrorist's average life was two years. I was not surprised when one of them met me in Delhi a few years later and informed me that his colleagues had been killed.

It took the government some time to curb terrorism in Punjab. The assassination of Longowal made the common Sikh feel that the gun would not take the community far. The greatest error of the terrorists was that they alienated the Sikh rural population, their principal base of support.

I recall that once an old man came to me all the way from a village in Punjab to tell me how his wife and daughter-in-law had been raped before his own eyes while he was tied in a corner of the room. Many such instances were reported. A common occurrence was of militants going at night to houses in the village and forcing their inmates to cook food for them, and the following morning the security forces taking the inmates to task for having given succour to the militants. The people just got fed up.

The militants killed Beant Singh, the chief minister of Punjab but failed to sustain their movement. The government ruthlessly pursued them and their accomplices, killing scores of them in the process. To this day the number of missing persons does not tally with that of the total number of casualties.

True, terrorism was successfully crushed. Equally true was the allegation that the state itself indulged in terrorism. If ends justified the means, the state would have been entitled to have murdered even suspects, but in a democratic society, even a known murderer is provided with a fair trial in court which alone is entitled to pronounce a verdict and decree the quantum of punishment.

There was a settlement between Longowal and Rajiv Gandhi. Chandigarh was to stay as the shared capital of Punjab and Haryana, administered as a union territory; a committee was appointed to allocate river waters to Punjab and Haryana and the spirit of the Anandpur Sahib resolution was accepted. Justice R.S. Sarkaria was appointed as a one person commission to deal with the demand for autonomy and Centre–state relations.

After the settlement, Rajiv Gandhi jokingly told Longowal that he would need a bullet-proof jacket, akin to what he wore. Had Longowal listened to this advice he would probably have saved his life from the bullets of the terrorists who killed him, believing, as they did, that the settlement was 'a betrayal'.

Rajiv Gandhi was plagued by another major agitation: that of the All Assam Students' Union (AASU). The genesis of this was a determination of the indigenous people of Assam that people who had infiltrated into the state from Bangladesh be expelled. The movement was directed by two AASU leaders, Prafulla Kumar Mahanta and Bhrigu Phukan. When I went to Guwahati to cover the agitation on behalf of the *Indian Express*, I was struck by their integrity and dedication. Both were students at that time but they guided the state-wide agitation extremely well, and for the Assamese their word was a law. Both of them would order the population to defy the curfew imposed by the government and thousands would come out on the streets, and when they proclaimed a people's curfew not a single candle burned, and a curfew declared by the government was not observed. So non-violent was the agitation that at their call hundreds would line up peacefully outside the deputy commissioner's office to violate Section 144, a ban on the assembly of over five persons.

The government appreciated the point that people from across the border should not be allowed to enter India without valid documents but the border between Bangladesh and India was so porous that it could be crossed at many points. The BSF were also partly to blame, allowing many to infiltrate in return for a paltry bribe.

The first time New Delhi detected the infiltration was in 1955 when I was information officer in the home ministry. The influx of migrants reached such proportions that the local population in Assam began to feel it was being crowded out. The AASU espoused the demand that the infiltrators be expelled, in contrast to the Congress party's encouragement of the inflow. When I once raised this question in Bangladesh, it was strongly disputed. However, one MP, who later became the prime minister of Bangladesh, told me in reply to my question, that India should give 'some land' to Bangladesh.

Rajiv Gandhi signed a pact with the AASU in 1985, committing the government to revising the electoral rolls and deleting from them the names of foreigners. That agreement also stated that those who had infiltrated after 1971 would be sent back, but this entire exercise was only on paper without any implementation whatsoever on the ground. Mahanta and Phukan, the students' leaders, founded their own party, the Asom Gana Parishad (AGP), which swept the polls but was unable to evict the Bangladeshis because New Delhi did not cooperate. Later, because of some differences Mahanta and Phukan, split, and paved the way for the return of the Congress.

The number of infiltrators has vastly increased since. My guess is that the Assamese-speaking population in relation to the total population has fallen to about 40 per cent. The Bangladeshis have for their part learnt Assamese and have affirmed, whenever asked, that Assamese is their mother tongue.

Subsequently, when in the Rajya Sabha, I suggested to the then deputy prime minister, L.K. Advani, that work permits be introduced and made available in Dhaka and Chittagong. At one stage it appeared that the government had decided to introduce a work permit system but the bureaucracy and the extremists in the BJP defeated the entire initiative.

I hold former Assam Chief Minister B.P. Chaliha responsible for the division of Assam which once included all the states in the Northeast. He was chief minister when he refused to have English as the official language alongside Assamese. Representatives of the north-eastern states, then called hill-districts and dominated by Christians, declared that they would remain part of Assam provided English was also given the status of official language.

I recall how first Govind Vallabh Pant and then Lal Bahadur Shastri spent days at Guwahati persuading Chaliha to accord English the status of the official language of the state. The Centre also placated the leaders of the hill districts by granting them autonomy within the state of Assam, akin to the Scottish pattern. Nothing however worked, primarily because of Guwahati's chauvinism, and Assam was eventually split into five states: Arunachal Pradesh, Meghalaya, Tripura, Manipur, and Assam.

Mizoram had raised the standard of revolt under the leadership of Pu Laldenga for an autonomous state within India. New Delhi was able to devise a formula to constitute Mizoram as a separate state within the Indian union.

Today the entire Northeast has become a welter of violence, corruption, and extortion. Small states are welcome but when they become too small they are prey to the greed of politicians, contractors, and bureaucrats. The worst fallout of splitting Assam has been the rise of armed groups that rob, extort, and kill people at random. The ULFA (United Liberation Front of Assam) came into being after the Assam Accord of 1985. It has sustained revolt, although it is today considerably weaker than it was earlier.

A number of militant organizations raised the standard of Independence. They initially projected some idealism but lost general support when they indulged in violence, procuring arms from East Pakistan to keep their rebellion alive. Their secessionist demands were patently unacceptable.

As I wrote sympathetically about the ULFA, I imagined I had the support of its leadership and endeavoured to foster conciliation between the government and the ULFA. On one visit to Guwahati, Justice Krishna Iyer and I issued an appeal to the ULFA to initiate a dialogue with New Delhi under our good offices. I learnt that they were willing to do so provided they received free passage and could retain their arms. This happened many years later. There was a ceasefire, not once but several times. The ULFA utilized every ceasefire as an opportunity to consolidate itself. Finding operation from within India difficult, the ULFA leadership took refuge overseas, sometimes in Myanmar, sometimes in Bhutan, and sometimes in Bangladesh. New Delhi improved its relations with all the three countries and made it difficult for the ULFA to remain a formidable force. It was Prime Minister Sheikh Hasina who handed over the ULFA leaders to India.

As a human rights activist, I brought to the Supreme Court's attention the handcuffing of a pro-ULFA editor in a hospital. Distinguished Justice Kuldip Singh ordered that no one should be handcuffed. The police were not surprisingly upset by the order. Today it is illegal to and inhumane handcuff anyone.

⚜

Rajiv Gandhi's new foreign policy began with the dismissal of Indira Gandhi's closest foreign policy adviser, G. Parthasarthy. He was deemed to have been 'a failure' in relation to Sri Lanka. Rajiv Gandhi replaced him with Ronen Sen whom he knew well. This was largely Rajiv's effort to bring in his own favourites, a tradition to which all prime ministers have adhered.

Unlike the Indira Gandhi of later years, Rajiv believed that friendly ties with the US were a key to India's economic and technological growth. In November 1984, when visiting the US, he signed a memorandum of understanding (MoU) on 'Sensitive Commodities and Technologies'. Rajiv should be lauded for introducing computers in government offices at the Centre. Initially, there was resistance to the scheme and I heard people remark that it was a waste of funds, but in time government functionaries began appreciating the utility of computers.

However, not all the changes brought in by Rajiv Gandhi address the fundamental problems of India's painfully slow economic growth which my friend, Raj Krishna, described as the 'Hindu rate of growth'. Rajiv was more interested in military than economic prowess.

India organized a large-scale military exercise, called Brasstacks on the borders of Pakistan and China during November 1986 and March 1987. The chief of the army staff Gen. K.S. Sunderji almost wandered into Pakistan and China while leading the exercise!

Some senior politicians and bureaucrats in Islamabad doubted New Delhi's intentions. It was perhaps they who decided to sound a warning to India that Pakistan had a nuclear bomb. The calculations might have been that my interview with Dr Abdul Qadeer Khan, Pakistan's father of the nuclear bomb, would convey the necessary message. Had I published the interview straightaway, the hands of Abdul Sattar, the Pakistan foreign secretary, who came to India three days after the interview to discuss the pulling back of Indian troops stationed right on the border, might have been strengthened. My idea was, however, to organize the simultaneous publication of the interview in India and abroad. I began the exercise after my return to India on 6 February 1987 and I was able to arrange for publication on 28 February in the UK, Canada, and Hong Kong, apart from India and Pakistan. That is how the controversial bomb interview took place.

Mushahid Hussain, editor of *Muslim*, a daily from Islamabad, invited me to his wedding. He was a close friend who had once met me in Delhi when he was a lecturer, to seek my advice on whether he should take up journalism. I found his writing promising and predicted that he would one day make a good editor if he took to journalism seriously. Mushahid was at the airport to receive me when I landed in Islamabad. He told me that he would give me a wedding gift, and then whispered in my ear that A.Q. Khan, the nuclear scientist, had agreed to meet me. I was flabbergasted. True, I had asked him many times to arrange a meeting with A.Q. Khan but had never imagined he could pull it off.

My lunch on the following day was with Fakhar Zaman, then a minister in the Zia-ul-Haq government, and his wife, Chandi, who later became Pakistan's ambassador to the US. Mushahid rang me at their residence during the lunch that A.Q. Khan would meet me that very evening, and that he (Mushahid) would pick me up from the hotel for the appointment. He made it plain that I would not be permitted to take down notes or carry a tape-recorder.

Khan lived on the outskirts of Islamabad on the undulating hills of Margalla. The road leading to his house was visible from where he lived. As it was dark, Mushahid had switched on the headlights. I inferred that the Intelligence was aware of our trip because just a day earlier a French journalist and a photographer had been beaten up when they had driven just a few yards along that road.

When we reached A.Q. Khan's house, the security guard spoke to Mushahid but did not even look towards me. That convinced me that the interview was sanctioned by the government. Khan was waiting at the veranda to welcome me. As he was leading me to the drawing room he said he had been following my writings and was a 'great fan' of mine.

'They treated me very badly at Bhopal,' from where he graduated, said Khan. He was referring to his migration from India to Pakistan a few years after Partition. I told him that I came from Sialkot and had faced more or less the same privations. 'The cake is delicious,' I said. 'My wife baked it for you,' he replied.

Now that I felt comfortable, I began probing him about whether Pakistan had produced a nuclear bomb. 'Your job must be very difficult,' I said. Indeed it was when he had to do everything from scratch. He oozed confidence and pride.

Khan had been working on the nuclear bomb ever since Prime Minister Indira Gandhi had authorized a nuclear test in India in 1974. Her counterpart, Zulfikar Ali Bhutto, had said that Pakistan would even eat grass to acquire a nuclear bomb. Khan was the cynosure of all eyes in Pakistan, as an individual who would deliver the country nuclear parity with India.

I had heard he was very full of himself, and he matched the description to perfection. I annoyed him when I mentioned in passing that he had been hauled up before a Dutch court in a case for having 'stolen' information from one of their nuclear laboratories. He raised his voice to deny the charge, adding that the court had cleared him.

The question of whether India had tried to penetrate the secrets of Pakistan's nuclear plant pleased him. Laughingly, he said that New Delhi had sent spies for the purpose, among them an Indian army major, but they had all been arrested.

My entire interview was directed towards learning whether or not Pakistan had made a nuclear bomb. He skirted all such questions, brushing me aside whenever I tried to be specific. It appeared to me that he had been permitted to give me this interview but at the same time had been told not to say anything specific. I praised him for being an outstanding scientist and the only one in the subcontinent who had two PhDs, one in metallurgy and the other in physics. I asked him whether he had any foreigner assisting him. He proudly said that his team comprised only Pakistanis.

I thought I would provoke him. Egoist as he was, he might fall for the bait. And he did. I concocted a story and told him that when I was coming to Pakistan, I ran into Dr Homi Sethna, father of India's nuclear bomb, who asked me why I was wasting my time because Pakistan had neither the men nor the material to make such a weapon. Khan was furious and began pounding his hand on the table: 'Tell them we have it; we have it.' Mushahid was taken aback and looked distraught. I followed up Khan's disclosure with the remark that it was easy to make such a claim but it needed to be corroborated. No test had been so far conducted to confirm that Pakistan possessed a nuclear bomb.

He said that they had already tested the bomb in their laboratory. 'Haven't you heard of a prototype plane flying with the help of a simulator? We do not have to explode a nuclear bomb to ascertain its potency. Sensitive and advanced instruments in a laboratory can show the scale of the explosion. We are satisfied with the results.' He said he had developed 'invaluable technology of isotope separation. We have upgraded uranium to 90 per cent to achieve the desired results.'

'Why haven't you announced that you have a nuclear bomb,' I asked him point blank. 'Is it necessary? America has threatened to cut off all its aid.' Khan said their bomb was larger than the one we had exploded in Rajasthan on 18 May 1974. 'The US is aware that Pakistan has a nuclear bomb,' said Khan, 'and what the CIA has been saying about our possessing a nuclear bomb is correct as are the speculations in the foreign media.'

Khan did not say when exactly Pakistan actually came to possess a nuclear bomb. He said that India took 12 years to make it while he took only seven. He narrated how, when he returned to Pakistan from Holland in December 1975, he had the Kahuta plant built. It took three years to complete. That meant it became operational by December 1978 or the beginning of 1979. Pakistan could be said to have acquired the bomb either towards the end of 1985 or in early 1986 (Khan stated in an another interview later that it was 1984).

Khan made no pretence that Pakistan's nuclear programme was for peaceful purposes. 'The word "peaceful" associated with the nuclear programme is humbug. There is no "peaceful bomb". Once you knew how to make reactors, how to produce the plutonium, all of which Pakistan has mastered, it became easy to produce a nuclear bomb.'

Khan now spoke like a member of the ruling élite. He warned me: 'If you ever drive us to the wall, as you did in East Pakistan, we will use the bomb.' What he was trying to convey was that if Pakistan suffered a reverse in a conventional war against India, it would not hesitate to use a nuclear weapon. President General Parvez Musharraf said the same thing five years later.

The first remark Mushahid made in the car while we were returning was: 'He has split the beans. What story will you do? Tell me.' Mushahid said he had to live in the country. The story should not harm him. I offered not to write the story if it would expose him to any danger. He remained silent and did not utter another word for the rest of the journey, lost in thought. He dropped me at the hotel where I reached for a piece of paper to jot down Khan's words, my memory standing me in good stead.

I had dinner that evening with Mushahid who was all the while saying that I had secured a scoop that would shake the world but it was he who would have to pay the price. We worked on the lead of the story, and he was agreeable to: 'Pakistan has the bomb, Dr A.Q. Khan, father of the "Islamic bomb" claimed during a conversation with me, but he would not explicitly say so.'

I met S.K. Singh, then India's high commissioner to Pakistan, the day after I interviewed Dr A.Q. Khan. I did not tell him anything about the interview because I wanted Khan's sensational disclosure on the nuclear bomb to be my scoop. The only newspaper to which I offered to sell the story was Dawn. At Karachi, when I met Hamid Haroon, a friend of mine and a senior executive at Dawn, I asked him if they would like to run the interview. 'Keep us out,' he said, 'it is too hot.'

I was in Lahore a day before my return to India when Shyam Bhatia of the *Observer,* rang me to ask about my stay in Pakistan. He knew about my visit but not that I had met Khan. I asked him if his weekly would be interested in Khan's interview. He said that it all depended upon what I had got, and promised to check. On my return to Delhi, he conveyed to me his weekly's interest in the story (they paid me only £200 for it).

I found the *Observer* a stickler for detail. Even when I had faxed the story, it wanted me to send them my notes. I had already told them that I had not been permitted to take notes, nor to record Khan on tape. I sent them by post the sheets on which I had scribbled or typed notes after the interview, all from memory. Subsequently, there were many telephone conversations between me and the *Observer* office on the story.

The *Observer* was justifiably cautious because Mushahid Hussain had already said under pressure from his government that no interview had taken place and that I had merely accompanied him to deliver to Khan an invitation to his (Mushahid's) forthcoming wedding. The *Observer* wanted to be doubly certain because of a report that an American newspaper had been offered the same story, but had turned it down because they doubted the veracity of the interview. I did not know who had offered them the story; it certainly hadn't been me.

The reason I was keen to have my article published abroad was because in our part of the world people consider a disclosure appearing overseas, particularly in the UK, more authentic than if published in India. It took me an entire month to persuade the *Observer* to run the interview. The day they published it coincided with the day when our national budget was discussed in the press. My anticipation of poor timing proved to be true. My clients, 70-odd newspapers which bought my service, did not run the bomb story as the first lead, but even so all ran it. The disclosure attracted considerable attention.

Favourable comments on my story overwhelmed me. What touched me most was a personal letter from Nikhil Chakravarty, editor of *Mainstream.* He wrote:

> It would be prosaic to merely say that this is a vindication of your journalistic honour. I see it first as a high tribute to you as a person of integrity and, only then, your journalistic acumen. I must say after reading your piece I feel proud of you and once again I offer my sincerest congratulations to you.

The story's publication in the *Observer*, London, lent it authenticity, and provoked the controversy it deserved. Mushahid's retraction did hurt me a little but I could understand his compulsions in Pakistan. Fortunately, he had published the story in his own newspaper and written an editorial on the interview to argue that Pakistan should tell the entire world that it possessed a nuclear bomb, which, he argued, would send a message to New Delhi.

The Pakistanis were angry and demanded Mushahid's head for helping the 'enemy', and that too a Hindu. Many asked for Mushahid's trial for 'treason'. I could not understand why there was such a furore.

I was confident that Gen. Zia-ul-Haq must have been consulted at some stage. As I learnt subsequently, he had actually okayed the interview but did not want Khan to admit that Pakistan had assembled the bomb. Zia tried to retrieve the situation when he told *Time* magazine that Pakistan was only a screwdriver away from manufacturing a nuclear bomb. This did not attract much attention because by then the cat was out of the bag.

Pakistan's predicament was that the bomb story was published during the week when its aid bill was before the US Congress for approval, and of this I had no knowledge. The timing of my story was a pure coincidence. In the meanwhile, Senator John Glenn, the first American to orbit the earth, rang me from Washington to confirm what Khan had said. Still, amidst doubt, President George W. Bush Sr cleared the way for aid to Pakistan by certifying that Pakistan did not possess a nuclear weapon. I think that politics played a role because the US president told a lie when he had with him the reports of his intelligence agencies which unequivocally said that Pakistan had manufactured a nuclear bomb.

During the controversy, someone asked Prime Minister Rajiv Gandhi whether India had conspired with Kuldip Nayar to do the bomb story on the eve of the US aid bill. Rajiv said in reply: 'We can conspire with anyone but not Kuldip Nayar.'

Dr A.Q. Khan went to the British Press Council to allege that there was no story and that Nayar had used a social call to circulate a canard through the *Observer*. The weekly contested the case and both of us, the *Observer* and I, were exonerated. In its observation, the Council said, rejecting Khan's petition, that it had 'no reason to disbelieve Nayar's story'.

Islamabad did not give up. It had a book published in which it was alleged that Pamela Bordes, an Indian model, was used by Kuldip Nayar to seduce the *Observer* editor in order to ensure the publication of the bomb story. The PTI picked up the Pamela portion from the book and ran it a couple of years later. I threatened to sue the agency. M.K. Razdan, then heading the PTI, withdrew the story but never expressed regret. This was a new kind of journalism: disseminating defamatory material and refusing to express any regrets. I left it at that because the agency had after all withdrawn the story. The Pakistan High Commission in Delhi also sought to punish me by refusing to issue a visa to me for nearly five years.

Almost a decade after the story, I met Mushahid at a conference in Dhaka. I asked him if my meeting with Khan was cleared with General Zia-ul-Haq. He replied in the affirmative, that it had all been arranged. Where things went wrong, he said, was that Khan spoke too much and disclosed more than he was supposed to.

To return to Brasstacks led by Gen. Sunderji, Beijing's reaction became clear to me when I visited China at the invitation of the Institute of Foreign Affairs, a prestigious organization. One day my guests fixed an interview for me with a few top retired military officers. Their expressions and behaviour was stern and hostile. Without my touching on the 1962 hostilities between the two countries, they literally pounced on me for Gen. Sunderji's 'foray in their territory'.

Without letting me speak, they said: 'Have you forgotten the thrashing we gave you in 1962? We will again come and punish you, and return as we did then. You do not seem to have learnt any lessons.' The current National Security Advisor Shiv Shankar Menon was then number two at Beijing, and the ambassador was away. I told Menon about the threat and whatever else I had been told. He said someone from the defence ministry would meet me in Delhi. None did, just as no one from the government of India met me to seek details about my interview with Khan.

৯৯

Giani Zail Singh nurtured a grievance for having been kept in the dark about Operation Bluestar, and resolved that one day he would put the government on the mat to ventilate his feelings of hurt. How he should do so was his predicament. The course of action he decided in consultation with me was to withhold his assent to some important bills. He did not have to wait long. An opportunity arose when the Rajiv Gandhi government sent to him for approval a constitutional amendment bill relating to the Shah Bano case.

The Supreme Court had granted a maintenance allowance to Shah Bano, a Muslim divorcee, whose husband had refused to pay her anything beyond the paltry one-time traditional payment, or *meher,* as alimony. The Muslim community considered the judgement interference in their religious affairs. Agitated, Muslims argued that they would themselves decide the quantum of allowance and would ensure its payment, and did not want the court to 'interfere'.

Following the judgement, there were demonstrations by Muslims throughout the country to force New Delhi to effect a constitutional amendment to overrule the 'damage' the Supreme Court had caused to Muslims. Rajiv Gandhi, with an eye on the elections, thought he would placate Muslims by using a constitutional amendment to nullify the Supreme Court's judgement. It was naïve of him to think in those terms. Subsequently, when he realized that Hindus had been seriously upset by the constitutional amendment brought about by the Shah Bano case, he had the locks of the disputed Babri Masjid–Ram Janmabhoomi Temple at Ayodhya opened. He in this way tried to run with the hare and hunt with the hounds. The nation is still suffering as a consequence of these two actions of his.

When the bill to undo the judgement on Shah Bano's maintenance allowance reached Zail Singh for assent, he saw it as an opportunity to hit back at the government. I used to meet Zail Singh regularly in those days, but he had avoided meeting me when he was home minister. 'Mrs Indira Gandhi did not like our meeting,' he explained to me when I once met him in the Central Hall of parliament. Now, as president, he sent for me when this bill relating to the Shah Bano case reached him.

We discussed the repercussions of a refusal on his part to assent to the bill. Eventually, he realized that a negative response from him would displease Muslims, and he did not want to get embroiled in a situation fraught with religious overtones. At the same time, he did not want to miss the opportunity to embarrass the government. Finally, he decided to assent to the bill to the great relief of Rajiv Gandhi, who had sent Buta Singh to Rashtrapati Bhavan to placate him. Buta Singh told Zail Singh in Punjabi: '*Thwadda hi putter hai* [He is your son]'. Buta Singh takes credit for dissuading Zail Singh from dismissing Rajiv Gandhi as prime minister.

I informed Zail Singh that the Postal Bill, which was being discussed in parliament in those days, was his best bet. He was ready with his knife to hurt the government when the bill reached him for assent. The Postal Bill authorized the government to open anyone's mail. The intelligence agencies were already doing this surreptitiously but the government wanted to make it legal.

When Zail Singh and I discussed the issue we had anticipated that refusal to give assent would evoke a popular response in favour of rejection. The public, jealous of its privacy, would hail the president's step. This was precisely what happened and Zail Singh's refusal was my scoop.

The government's reaction was wild. It stopped sending the president the cabinet papers, telegrams from foreign missions, and the like. This was against the constitution. Zail Singh protested against the government action. He argued that he had a constitutional right to receive copies of government papers just as he was also entitled to ask to see any document. The government however felt that it was within its right to bypass him and Zail Singh's protest, even though publicly voiced, had no effect on Rajiv Gandhi.

Zail Singh did not give up. He thought of some other way of embarrassing the government. This proved to be his Achilles heel. The *Indian Express*, which was largely critical of Rajiv Gandhi, came in handy for the president. He wrote a vituperative letter to the prime minister, drafted by the then editor of the *Express* S. Mulgaonkar and the RSS ideologue S. Gurumurthy at the newspaper's guest-house in Sunder Nagar, New Delhi. As Zail Singh had made some changes in the draft, the letter which appeared in the newspaper was slightly different from the one that had been originally drafted. Both Zail Singh and the *Indian Express* cut a sorry figure when the government raided the guest-house and recovered the draft with Mulgaonkar's corrections.

The letter adversely affected the support Zail Singh had enjoyed. He was viewed as a president settling personal scores with Rajiv Gandhi at the expense of the smooth functioning of the government.

At one time the president was inclined to give approval to a petition by the well-known cartoonist and journalist, Rajinder Puri, seeking permission to prosecute Prime Minister Rajiv Gandhi on allegations of corruption. However, in the wake of the letter incident, any move by Zail Singh would have smacked of personal vendetta so he rejected the petition. He, however, told me that had he not been a Sikh, he would have given permission for prosecution. I think he was right. Some in the Congress had already planned to impeach Zail Singh if he gave permission. The assassination of Indira Gandhi by her Sikh personal guards had made the Sikh community suspect and therefore Zail Singh's fears were not unjustified.

🕉

As the country faced the 9th Lok Sabha elections in 1989, the Rajiv Gandhi government was facing corruption charges in defence contracts. The most damaging was the $285 million contract with Swedish arms company Bofors for supply of 155 mm Howitzer field guns. The army was in favour of another variant which should normally have been purchased because in the course of testing, its performance was superior. Rajiv Gandhi imposed his choice based on kickbacks received rather than merit. Later, the then chief-of-army staff Gen. K.S. Sunderji, admitted that the French howitzer which the army had selected was superior to that from Bofors.

Indeed, the word corruption was substituted by Bofors during the Lok Sabha elections. The disclosure came from Norway where an enterprising radio channel broadcast the full story. Rajiv Gandhi had bent all the rules to order Bofors' howitzers. Even the circumstantial evidence testified to his involvement. A close friend of his told me that Rajiv Gandhi had opened a new account abroad and had deposited the kickbacks there. This benefited his Italian in-laws, parents of Sonia Gandhi. Ottavio Quattrocchi, an Italian middleman in Delhi, close to Sonia Gandhi and Rajiv Gandhi, was responsible for the clandestine payment.

Quattrocchi had once threatened to sue me for defamation because of what I had written about his 'nefarious activities' in my book *The Judegement* (1977). He escaped punishment for all he had done and was eventually allowed to leave India, the CBI ensuring that no harm came to an individual so close to the dynasty. When I checked with some senior officers in the agency, their reply was that there were orders from above. H.R. Bharadwaj told me in Bangalore that he had 'put everything in order' before moving to Karnataka as governor.

According to former CBI director Joginder Singh, Quattrocchi was aware in advance of every move the agency proposed to take against him. For example, he was shown all official papers before he appeared for extradition proceedings at a Malaysian court.

I once asked Foreign Minister Madhavsinh Solanki in the Narasimha Rao government about the documents he had delivered to the Swedish government regarding the kickbacks. New Delhi was keen that the Swedish authorities remained silent. He did not comment on the documents but said that the Bofors gun deal was 'as messy as Narmada's non-use of water'.

It was a coincidence that one day (3 January 2011) before the CBI was to submit a plea in the court to close the case, the income-tax appellate tribunal pronounced its judgement that Ottavio Quattrocchi was the recipient of kickbacks amounting to Rs 41 crore and demanded that income tax be paid on the income earned. Congress General Secretary Digvijay Singh, ever adept at rescuing chestnuts from fire for the party, said it was a deliberate leak by a government official to complicate the Bofors case. Digvijay Singh's loyalty to the Sonia Gandhi family was understandable but not his efforts to distort facts. The appellate court signed the judgement on 31 December 2010 and the press only learnt of it on 3 January 2011 so it was not just a day earlier as Digvijay Singh had alleged.

The official spokesman's rationalization was that it was a civil, not a criminal suit. Whatever the nomenclature given to it, kickbacks remained kickbacks. The question was not a legal but a moral issue. I recall that Mahatma Gandhi had made the same remark when a CWC member, Ishwar Singh Kweshwar defended his non-payment of Rs 500 on the plea that it was time-barred. The creditor had sent a postcard to the Mahatma. Gandhi told Kweshwar that the issue was not a legal but a moral question.

It was the Bofors scandal that led V.P. Singh, finance minister in Rajiv's government, to resign. In him, the non-BJP opposition, then in the wilderness, found a leader who could possibly provide an alternative to the ruling Congress. Indeed, V.P. Singh cobbled together the Janata Dal, consisting of his Jan Morcha (the ex-Congressmen who had been defeated in the late 1980s), socialists seeking a new home after the Janata Party had collapsed, the Lok Dal of Haryana's Chief Minister Devi Lal, and the Telugu Desam party of Andhra Pradesh. The Janata Dal soon emerged as a political party which sought to identify itself with the economic and social aspirations of the cultivating peasantry drawn from the lower castes or Other Backward Classes (OBCs), from the Hindi heartland: UP and Bihar.

The Congress which had won 421 seats in the previous Lok Sabha was reduced to 197 seats in the elections held in 1989. This was indeed a wholesale people's rejection of the party. Rajiv Gandhi rightly decided to sit in the Opposition even though the Congress was the single largest party in the House. He regarded the election results as a verdict against him and his party. This was an honest and courageous appraisal, and I felt he had established a healthy precedent.

⚜

Rajiv Gandhi was assassinated on 21 May 1991. It was his last public meeting in Sriperumbudur, a town approximately 30 miles from Chennai.

Rajiv Gandhi's assassination was the handiwork of the Liberation Tigers of Tamil Eelam (LTTE) suicide bomber Thenmozhi Rajaratnam who came to be known as Gayatri. It was evident that the LTTE avenged their anger over the introduction of the Indian Peace Keeping Force (IPKF) which went to Sri Lanka to help the government curb internal conflicts. This was despite the fact that Rajiv Gandhi was in touch with Prabhakaran, the LTTE chief who had appeared to have given his consent to the IPKF operation to bring law and order to the country.

I did not know Rajiv Gandhi well but felt that India had lost him just at a time when he had matured as a leader. Now he really knew what prime-ministership meant. His greatest contribution was the revival of panchayats. As prime minister he had rightly initiated legislation to transfer power to them. That experiment has won growing appreciation with the passage of time notwithstanding the burgeoning corruption and nepotism that has penetrated the grassroots.

Jawaharlal Nehru, his great-grandfather, dreamt of a scientific temper enveloping India. Rajiv, to a degree, brought that dream to life. He was technology savvy and introduced computers in government offices. Sam Pitroda, his friend, helped him to lay the foundation for the software revolution that has contributed significantly to India's economic growth.

In Priyanka Gandhi's visit to jail to meet Gayatri, Sonia Gandhi's family showed the courage to come to terms with the tragedy. It is a pity that the process which should have ended with the release of Gayatri, after serving the term to which she was sentenced, was not taken to its logical corollary. That indeed is the tragedy of the Congress party which sometimes demonstrates Mahatma Gandhi's trait of forgiveness but surrenders to the exigencies of politics.

15

V.P. SINGH AS PRIME MINISTER
Kashmir, My Appointment as High Commissioner in the UK, and the Implementation of the Mandal Commission Recommendations

Indian politics took a dramatically different configuration in 1989. The Congress party won even less than 40 per cent of the vote in comparison to 48 per cent in 1984. The Muslims, constituting some 15 per cent of the electorate, by and large voted against the Congress. The party won 197 Lok Sabha seats in a House of 545. Rajiv Gandhi himself volunteered to sit in the Opposition although the Congress was the largest party in the House. His plea was that the people had shown no confidence in his governance through a vastly reduced vote. I felt that it was an example which the nation had not known earlier and there was general applause for his courageous step. Vishwanath Pratap Singh, leader of Jan Morcha, was able to harness the support of the BJP and the Left to head the new government.

However, Chandra Shekhar, a leader of significance in the party, was opposed to him and in favour of another stalwart, Devi Lal, who too commanded support in the party but far less than V.P. Singh. A contest seemed inevitable.

There was no doubt that V.P. Singh had a majority among the Lok Sabha members in the Janata Dal. He had the Bofors gun scandal as his election plank, and it was his personal victory. The voters expected him to become prime minister. As a well-wisher of the party I took upon myself the responsibility of averting a contest. I approached Arun Nehru, then a close associate of V.P. Singh. Arun favoured a consensus but not at the latter's expense.

I knew Devi Lal well and met him on the morning of the party's election. Devi Lal had no illusions about himself. He said that V.P. Singh would make a better prime minister but his dilemma was that he had given his word to Chandra Shekhar that he would contest for leadership. I knew it was Chandra Shekhar's move to stall V.P. Singh's election as leader. Chandra Shekhar was the kind of politician who would split a party or bolt from it if he did not have his way. The split I feared might bring the Congress back to power, and I saw no signs that the party had learnt any lessons from the Emergency. Devi Lal requested Chandra Shekhar to meet him at Orissa Bhawan and took me along. Biju Patnaik, the senior leader from Orissa, was already there at Chandra Shekhar's request. It was clear that the party would split if V.P. Singh was not accepted as prime minister. Chandra Shekhar announced that he had requested Madhu Dandavate to propose Devi Lal's name which he would second. Sensing Chandra Shekhar's strong opposition to V.P. Singh, I suggested to Devi Lal that he should accept Chandra Shekhar's formulation. Devi Lal agreed but wanted to know why.

When we drove together to parliament, I told him that once his name was proposed and seconded, he should forego the honour and propose V.P. Singh's name. Devi Lal was agreeable to this because he was unhappy at the thought of betraying Chandra Shekhar. I mollified him by giving him an analogy from the *Mahabharata*. Yudhisthar, I told him, agreed to say that Ashwathama, the elephant, had died in the battle. The Kauravas had a leading warrior, Dronacharya's son, his namesake, and had proved too good for the Pandavas. Yudhisthar did not lie but used this for their own purposes, drowning the word 'elephant' amidst a beat of drums, seeking to shatter the morale of the Kauravas.

I told Devi Lal that he would fulfill the word he had given to Chandra Shekhar by remaining the leader momentarily and it did not matter if he subsequently stepped down. He accepted my reasoning. No one except Devi Lal, Ashwani Kumar, editor of *Punjab Kesari,* and I were aware of the formula. As agreed, Dandavate proposed Devi Lal's name and Chandra Shekhar seconded it. True to his word, Devi Lal rose from his seat and proposed the name of V.P. Singh as his successor. Through oversight no one had been asked to second V.P. Singh's name, and this Ajit Singh did when he realized that there was no one else to do it.

V.P. Singh was unanimously elected but by then the UNI ticker had announced Devi Lal's name. The agency's reporter had run to a nearby telephone booth, as reporters from news agencies are wont to do, to be the first to relay the news. My heart missed a beat when Devi Lal took some time to rise up to announce his withdrawal. He said he wanted to remain the *tau* (elder uncle), as he was popularly known. V.P. Singh appointed Devi Lal deputy prime minister.

When I went to congratulate Devi Lal at his house, he was surrounded by members of his family who badgered him for having accepted the number two position when he could have been prime minister. He assured them that the word deputy would vanish in a few months' time. Om Prakash Chautala, Devi Lal's son who later became Haryana's chief minister, never forgave me for not allowing his father to become prime minister, believing that I had conspired to make V.P. Singh prime minister.

Soon after the V.P. Singh government assumed charge in December 1989, Home Minister Mufti Mohammad Sayeed requested me to go to Srinagar and assess the situation on behalf of the government. I told him that anyone based in Delhi could gauge that the state was slipping into chaos as a consequence of the rising levels of militancy. This notwithstanding, he was insistent.

On my arrival in Srinagar I rang up Abdul Ghani Lone, an eminent Kashmiri leader and a personal friend of mine. He dissuaded me from visiting his house on the ground that in his locality there were a large number of militants who had returned from Pakistan after being trained and armed.

Lone came to Hotel Broadway where I was staying and spent two hours discussing Kashmir. He said that these boys had refused Pakistan's overtures for years but when they found that the state election in 1988 had been rigged they lost faith in the ballot box and chose the gun. I told him that the National Conference had no need to rig the elections because Chief Minister Farooq Abdullah would in any case have won by a small margin. Lone said that Farooq was afraid of losing elections and rigged them in order to leave nothing to chance.

I told Lone that New Delhi might be willing to have a dialogue with 'the boys', and his view was that India should first re-establish its authority in Kashmir because its writ did not run there. What should Delhi do? I asked him. 'You will have to kill at least 20,000 people before you can establish your authority.'

On my return to Delhi, I told Mufti Mohammad Sayeed that 'we are reaping what you had sown'. His laconic reply was that they had made many mistakes in the past but were now prepared to rectify them. By then he had had his daughter, Rubaiya, released from the militants who had kidnapped her. Foreign Minister Inder Kumar Gujral himself went to Srinagar to negotiate the terms of her release. This only proved how effete the Indian polity was.

Lone proved to be correct. His figure was 20,000 but twice that number were killed. The security forces and the militants clashed throughout Kashmir and inflicted heavy casualties on each other.

The militants were optimistic about 'releasing Kashmir from the clutches of New Delhi'. On an earlier visit to the Valley I was told in Anantnag that on my next visit to Kashmir I would require a visa from the 'liberators'. Anantnag would by then be renamed Islamabad.

Kashmiri leaders, including Lone, were detained without trial. That was when the torture chambers, called Papa One and Papa Two, were established. Apparently, they were interrogation centres where indescribable cruelties were committed. As a human rights activist I probed a few cases and found a deliberate, devious official plan.

I also saw numerous barricades in Srinagar and could sense the embers of revolt and alienation suggesting that a massive conflagration was in the offing. I couldn't figure out exactly what the conflagration would result in but it appeared evident that the pro-India elements would face difficult times and in due course be greatly diminished in numbers.

My analysis was that after the rigged state elections of 1987, notwithstanding many assurances from the government to the contrary, the youth in Kashmir, who had till then trusted the ballot, had completely lost faith in the system. Disillusioned, these youths crossed into Pakistan to get arms, believing that the bullet alone could achieve what the ballot had failed to do.

They were wrong because they underestimated India's might and the degree to which it would go to confront them. The militants represented quite a formidable force when they returned from Pakistan after being trained and obtaining weapons. There were open clashes in various parts of the Valley and thousands died over the years in pursuit of their ideals.

The security forces were unable to differentiate between the militants and others, some of whom were sympathizers of the militants' cause. Village after village was surrounded and subjected to brutal and indiscriminate searches. The attitude of the security forces was akin to that of a force entering enemy territory, fired more with the idea of inflicting punishment rather then attempting to genuinely find incriminating evidence. Therefore the security forces became extremely unpopular and India more distant. If ever the history of *zulum* by the security forces is recorded, the interrogation centres in Kashmir will rank quite high up the ladder.

I had often gone to Kashmir in the days when militancy was high and visited the houses of the aggrieved. The recurrent complaint was that young men were picked up by the security forces, some after registering their names with the local police station, but the majority did not return.

The reports which we, activists, wrote each time after returning from Kashmir were unfavourably viewed by New Delhi and we were characterized as 'apologists for the militants'. The reports were quoted at length by the Pakistan authorities at the UN and international conferences. However, the trips helped us develop personal relations with the Hurriyat leaders. A few still visit me at my house in New Delhi.

At one dinner party at my home, which some Hurriyat leaders attended, a television channel announced that India had successfully exploded a nuclear device. Prof. Abdul Ghani, a Hurriyat leader, remarked at the dinner table that he now saw a role for Kashmir as a bridge between India and Pakistan.

Prof. Abdul Ghani was present at a meeting at which I asked Syed Ali Shah Geelani, a hard-liner, about the return of Kashmiri pandits to their homes. Geelani said that this would have to wait until the Kashmir problem was resolved. I argued that it was unfair because most of the pandits had been driven out forcibly, apart from a few who left at the instance of Jagmohan, then the state governor. Geelani stuck to his position then, but many years later told me he had been wrong. The Kashmiri pandits were entitled to return to their homes. Very few did and those who returned left again because they found they were not welcome.

The plight of victims suffering at the hands of the security forces, on the one hand, and the militants on the other, was so much on my mind when

I became a Rajya Sabha MP that I allocated Rs 50 lakh of the MPLADS (Member of Parliament Local Area Development Scheme), for the welfare of victims' families. Initially, the parliament secretariat did not accept inclusion of victims of the state's violence as valid recipients. I eventually won my point that a widow or an orphan was entitled to receive assistance whether the bread-earner had died at the hands of security forces or the militants. A sympathetic female deputy commissioner at Srinagar identified 37 families for rehabilitation. My next allocation went to the victims of violence in Assam.

۞

After Sheikh Abdullah's death in 1953, my contact with Kashmir lessened each year. I knew Farooq Abdullah well but did not share the same proximity to him which I had with his father. In fact, I was in Srinagar on Abdullah's Sheikh invitation to celebrate Farooq's successor as the president of the National Conference. It was a large crowd and Begum Sahiba, the Sheikh's wife, remarked that 'you (Sheikh) never received such a reception; not even when you took over as the prime minister of Jammu & Kashmir'.

This was towards the end of 2010, when I interacted with young Kashmiris in Delhi and Srinagar. I found some of them eager to revive the two-nation theory, little realizing that a secular India would be utterly shocked to hear that. They even threatened to start a movement for an alliance with Pakistan if India did not concede their demand for *azadi*, but what nipped this tendency in the bud was the precarious state in which Pakistan was at that time.

Indeed, of late, politics in Kashmir appears to be taking a new direction. The demand for self-determination remains as strong as earlier but the *azadi* constituency has acquired greater self-confidence in its ability to take on India. The stone-pelters, however, representing the angry youth, were aware that they needed to find a peaceful solution to their demand. Their movement did not last long. This may be because of Kashmir's increasing faith in non-violent agitation. The voice of youth, who speak from the experience of growing up in the years of terror in the 1990s, is becoming increasingly more audible on the streets as well as in media discourses and elsewhere. Yasin Malik takes the credit of diverting the Kashmiris from a pro-Pakistan approach to one for *azadi*.

In all these respects, 2010 was a watershed year. The understanding in the society as a whole was to move away from the gun towards a democratic solution of the issues involved. This does provide New Delhi some space and civil society can also contribute. The trouble is, however, that the government in Delhi has not been able to strike a chord of trust with the Hurriyat or other separatist forces and therefore the latter has concluded that the only way to the Valley is through Islamabad rather than directly. The role of interlocutors, appointed by New Delhi, has been of little help because their brief was limited and the expectations of Kashmiris were high.

The sum total of such developments amount to very little because secession by the Valley will never be acceptable to Indian society, however accommodative it may become in the years ahead. The best that can happen is that India may be brought round to amending the constitution in order to arrive at a genuinely federal arrangement and find a place in that for an autonomous Kashmir. What the Kashmiris have to understand is that India may one day accept their separate identity outside the constitution but it would love to be within India.

🪷

I did not witness much of the working of the V.P. Singh government because I went to London as India's high commissioner in 1990. I was at a party at India International Centre in New Delhi when Foreign Minister Inder Kumar Gujral took me aside and asked me whether I would go as India's envoy to the UK. I was surprised because I had never expected or contemplated such an appointment.

I asked, 'Why not Islamabad?' He said that should I be appointed as such there would be many expectations in Pakistan which I would be in no position to fulfill. He told me that I would be able to do more useful work in London, an influential centre of the media.

It was a difficult decision because, as a human-rights activist and as a journalist, it would be odd to become part of the establishment. What eventually persuaded me was Gujral's argument that I might be able to bring the Sikh community back into the mainstream. London was the hub of the Khalistan movement. I sought and received cabinet status in order to be effective. This helped me to circumvent the babus in government.

The news about my selection was leaked to the press even before the proposal reached London. This was an embarrassment and there was a mixed reaction. One comment was that I had been rewarded for my consistent criticism of Indira Gandhi and her son, Rajiv. For many, I was a welcome choice. Some said that my wings had been clipped. Indeed, I had not spared the Janata government (1977-9) when it had failed to live up to its electoral promises.

The press fraternity was uncertain about how I would fare in the field of diplomacy. I sensed an element of jealousy in some of their remarks. The Indian Foreign Service itself was far from happy because I was an outsider, although the fact was that London had rarely gone to a serving foreign service officer. Some retired hands of the MEA openly said that Gujral would rue the day he chose me. A few of my colleagues at the Citizens for Democracy (CFD), a voluntary organization I headed, were disappointed. They felt I was leaving for a cushy, 'phoren' job.

The briefing at the MEA was perfunctory. No one seemed to take me seriously. Was it a bias against an outsider or an intrinsic part of the nonchalant manner in which I found the foreign office functioning? The atmosphere at

South Block was officious. When I went from room to room to meet the secretary, additional secretary, deputy secretary, and the officers below them I was addressed as 'Sir', probably because of the rank of cabinet minister I enjoyed. I detected a ring of formality but not respect. This became more apparent when they phoned me because most of them would get their stenographers to ring before picking up the phone themselves. The protocol section was worse and I had to speak to Foreign Secretary S.K. Singh even to get my luggage cleared at the airport.

'There are a few key files you must see before you go,' S.K. told me. He and I had been friends for years. I was familiar with his pompous, patronizing style, but he was knowledgeable and intelligent. Whatever his views, he carried out instructions diligently. Gujral never felt comfortable with him; a case of trust deficit. I could sense the tension between the two. Such a relationship between a minister and his secretary could not long subsist and I was not at all surprised when S.K. resigned a few weeks later to make way for Muchkund Dubey.

The external affairs ministry never showed me any files. When I persisted, I was told that copies of all the documents were available in the archives of the high commission in London. This proved to be incorrect because I never found any worthwhile 'files' there. Whatever was shown to me was disjointed and routine. It is possible that the 'key files' were purposely kept away from me, or there were no 'key files', as Salman Haidar, deputy high commissioner, put it. Whatever the truth, a former Indian foreign service hand, Mani Shankar Aiyar, complained to Rajiv Gandhi, his mentor, that I was making 'copious notes' from the files.

The government was keen that I quickly assume charge as President R. Venkataraman was scheduled to pay a state visit to the UK in early April 1990. We were well into March but there was still no word from London on the acceptance of my appointment. The delay was reportedly because of my writings against Margaret Thatcher, the then British prime minister. I had called her authoritarian and going the way of Indira Gandhi, a close friend of hers. The agreement did, however, eventually arrive, albeit somewhat late.

Before my departure, I was able to call on the president and vice-president. I also spent about an hour with Rajiv Gandhi, then the leader of the Opposition. I found him well informed in foreign affairs and candid in his comments. I told him I wished I had met him earlier, and he reciprocated the sentiment.

One person whom I was unable to meet was Prime Minister V.P. Singh, who did not respond to several requests, not even to a formal communication from the Ministry of External Affairs about the date of my departure. I left for London after writing to him: 'Even as a journalist I tried twice to meet you; this time the reason was important because I wanted to talk about my assignment in London.' I subsequently received a note of regret from him.

A British protocol officer welcomed me at Heathrow. A superintendent of police from Scotland Yard, also present, warned me about the security hazards faced by the Indian high commissioner. He wanted me to travel in a police vehicle which my predecessor, P.C. Alexander, had used during his tenure. I refused but was unable to shake off the British security officer, who remained with me until I left London.

Presenting my credentials to the Queen was a laborious exercise. It began with a ride in a buggy drawn by three horses (a special dispensation for envoys from the Commonwealth, for others there were only two!). It was a comic sight, because the Marshal Chief of Protocol, an officer in a tail coat, followed the carriage, keeping pace with the trotting horses from the Royal stables. In my case, the ride was for 4 km, from the high commissioner's residence at Kensington Gardens, known as Millionaires' Row, to the palace.

When I presented my credentials to the Queen I found myself face to face with an individual I had seen in photographs on innumerable occasions. She was somewhat different from her photographs, having grown greyer and heavier. She was friendly and informal, and advised my wife, who joined me at the palace, to always carry a shawl with her as the London weather was very unpredictable. The exercise ended with an informal tea reception. It was a boring affair, too officious and too long. There were no photographers because the Queen does not allow any photographs to be taken within the palace.

During my short stint in London what struck me most was the fiendish pleasure that successful Indians settled in England took in humiliating the British. Many Indian settlers had made a great success of their lives, having generally arrived in London with a few pounds in their pockets and become millionaires, a few even billionaires. This spoke well of their hard work and dedication. For them, it was a form of revenge on the British, once their rulers.

They would hire Britishers as their chauffeurs or house attendants and made it a point to parade them before me whenever I visited their homes. The security man, who accompanied me to the Indian houses, would often remark ruefully after a visit, 'How rich these people are.'

President Venkataraman's formal talks with Margaret Thatcher were held in the cabinet room at 10 Downing Street. She told us that the table around which we sat was the one where the momentous decision on the transfer of power to India was taken. I marvelled how an ordinary, green flannelled, long, rectangular, wooden table could have played such a significant role in a matter affecting the destinies of millions!

During his talks with Margaret Thatcher, the president concentrated on Pakistan's complicity in Punjab and Kashmir. She expressed no surprise. He also introduced South Africa, to her chagrin, to make the point that perceptions of India and the UK were poles apart when it came to racial matters.

Thatcher's lunch, also at 10 Downing Street, was a crowded affair: a five-course meal was served in less than an hour to approximately 200 invitees at large tables in a room where even half the number would have been too many. I thought a buffet would have been a far better idea but the British are fastidious in such matters. They do not have buffets when they entertain guests, particularly from foreign countries. For them it is preposterous to even imagine that the prime minister would host anything but a sit-down meal for a visiting president.

I met some familiar faces at the lunch. Film-maker David Lean was in a wheelchair. A good-looking man, his was a friendly handshake. Though he said he did not want to talk about films, he warmly recalled the shooting of *A Passage to India* (which I thought was more of a passage to England; underlining the stereotyped India with which the British are most comfortable). For a man who had married five times, he looked amazingly relaxed.

Richard Attenborough, director of the film *Gandhi*, and a man who always looks pleased with himself, was there too. We had met in Delhi earlier, but he did not remember. This is the problem with British celebrities or the British generally; you have to be introduced to them anew every time you meet them.

I sat next to Margaret Thatcher and spoke to her for nearly two hours on a variety of subjects. She was communicative and forthright. She said she had refused to visit a gurdwara despite many invitations. 'Those people killed Mrs Gandhi,' she said. 'What kind of people must they be!' She compared the violence in Punjab with the Irish Republican Army's (IRA) terrorism. 'Of course, yours is on a bigger scale,' she said. She was reticent on Kashmir, though she did say that nothing should be done at the expense of India's unity and integrity.

As our conversation progressed, Margaret Thatcher spoke about her personal problems, pouring her heart out to a person who had met her only two days earlier. Her son, she said, had to move to the US because of the 'wild charges' (of using his position to get favours from the government) made against him. She missed her grandchildren but she considered it a price she had to pay to be in politics.

I remarked that ethical standards were disappearing from politics and that our own experience in India was that politicians enjoyed hitting each other below the belt. She said that in Britain it was worse. They would 'kick you' and even when you had fallen, they would not stop hitting you.

She recalled her intimate relationship with Indira Gandhi. 'Even when we differed, our personal equation, did not suffer,' she said. 'We often spoke to each other over the phone,' at times only to 'talk'. Her impression of Rajiv Gandhi was that he was 'sweet boy' but she made no claim of having any rapport with him.

For mid-March, the weather in London was surprisingly pleasant. The snow-melt of winter had washed the exteriors of the buildings clean. The stores were bright with goods and the pavements were dotted with the people in a variety of sartorial attire. Above all, there were no tongas, and no scooters.

I had first visited London in 1948 on my way to the US. Then I was a student seeking a degree in journalism. I remembered how excited I had been walking through the city's streets for hours. Indian history was scattered throughout London. I also recalled the time when, as a schoolboy, I had received a lash from a cane inflicted by a white policeman for being part of a procession in my home town, Sialkot, clamouring for India's Independence. Again, in August 1942, I was detained at a police station for a few hours in Sialkot for responding to Mahatma Gandhi's 'Quit India' call against the British and organizing a strike at the British-run Murray College where I had studied before going to Lahore.

India House, which was the chancery, is a heritage property. When Sir Herbert Baker designed the building in 1920, he provided high ceiling and a huge central dome. Murals have been painted on many of its walls. The most striking feature of the paintings adorning India House is the organic link with contemporary movements in Indian art, especially the Bengal School.

I found portraits most of the of national leaders hanging in the reception hall on the first floor, Maulana Azad's portrait conspicuous by its absence. I requested M.F. Hussain to paint one. He promised to make one but did not, busy as he was with other more profitable ventures.

My first shock at India House was that the Indian high commission's main gate was not open to Sikhs. Through an aperture in the door the security man would scrutinize the visitors and tell a Sikh to enter through the back door. I was aghast by this discrimination. I asked Salman Haider why Sikhs were barred entrance from the front gate. He said that P.C. Alexander, who believed that most Sikhs in London were sympathetic to terrorists, had ordered this.

Alexander had been Prime Minister Indira Gandhi's principal secretary and had been affected by her assassination by her Sikh security guards. I had in fact, before coming to London, gone to Chennai to meet him and get a briefing on the workings of the high commission. He asked me about my priorities. I told him that I wanted to bridge the gap between the Sikh community and India. He had a fit and warned me against fraternizing with the Sikhs who he said were responsible for the assassination of Indira Gandhi. I told him that some Sikhs were responsible, but not the entire community. I saw no change in his attitude after my remark.

In any event, I ordered that the gate be opened to all without any discrimination. The following day I received a telegram from a committee of secretaries to the Government of India warning me that I would be held responsible should any harm befall high commission personnel who I was exposing to security hazards. I rang up Gujral to identify the species to which this committee belonged. He said I should deal with the matter in the manner I saw fit.

Apparently, some officials at the high commission were unhappy with my decision because a top Scotland Yard officer met me to protest against the decision to throw open the gate. He told me that the British government would not be responsible for the security of high commission personnel. He toned down when I told him that we would in turn withdraw the 24-hour security provided to the British high commissioner in Delhi. The opening of the gate was welcomed by the Sikh community.

As the attempt to bring back the Sikhs into the Indian mainstream had been my principal motivation for accepting the assignment, I planned to approach the community which had not forgotten either Operation Bluestar in 1984 or the massacre of Sikhs in the wake of Indira Gandhi's assassination.

I was probably hasty in my first step. I decided to visit, along with my wife, the largest gurdwara in London, at Havelock in Southall. This was a locality which could be mistaken for Amritsar, Jalandhar, or Ludhiana, just as Wembley could have formed any part of Gujarat. The gurdwara was then under the control of militants. Some young Sikhs had got wind of my visit and decided to stage a demonstration.

No sooner had my wife and I entered the gurdwara than slogans of 'Indian dogs go back' and 'Khalistan Zindabad' resounded and I was pushed around by the saffron-turbaned youths. This did not daunt me or my wife. The British security man accompanying us asked us to turn back but we made our way to the inner sanctum where the Granth Sahib was placed. We bowed before it and withdrew.

As it was a Sunday, there was a congregation of nearly 2,000 Sikhs. They sat quietly, oblivious of what had happened at the entrance. On our way out, I was jostled so vigorously that I nearly fell. The security man rushed me to the car and my chauffeur, Avtar Singh, a Sikh, drove me off at break-neck speed. In the melee, I was unable to retrieve my shoes but my wife did. She and Salman joined me later at a Hindu temple where we were welcomed.

I wanted to visit a mosque as well but was advised to do so on a Friday. The visit did not eventually materialize because even after planning a reception in my honour, the Indian Muslims in London cancelled it. They did not want to stick their necks out as the community was strongly influenced by Pakistan. The former Indian deputy high commissioner to the UK, Azim Hussain, living in London, had warned me about the Muslims' attitude.

The Pakistan high commissioner, Shahriyar Khan, was clearly solicitous towards the Muslims in London. His wife told us that they were reluctant to entertain Hindus in their home because the Muslims did not like it. However, the Muslims in Leicester, mostly Bohras, were quite liberal in their attitude. They invited me to inaugurate a mosque, a rare honour for a non-Muslim.

The gurdwara incident ruffled public opinion in India. Gujral rang me up and advised me to be cautious. The jostling I had received had a favourable fallout in the UK. The majority of Sikhs were generally critical of the demonstration staged against me because I was considered 'sympathetic' to them. I had in my writings condemned Operation Bluestar and the massacre of Sikhs in 1984.

Soon after the incident, some leaders of the Sikh community met me at the high commission to apologize for the behaviour of the 'boys'. The community wanted to make amends and therefore I was subsequently inundated with invitations from gurdwaras from all over the UK.

I found the Sikhs a community with moderate views. They had strong ties with Hindus, particularly those from Punjab. Operation Bluestar had, however, alienated the community which enabled those of an extreme persuasion to exploit the injured feelings evoked by the fact that those guilty of the 1984 massacre of Sikhs in Delhi and elsewhere had not been brought to justice.

I was startled by the initiative of the Sikh Human Rights group within a fortnight of my arrival. One of its representatives met me at my house after consulting some militant organizations and argued for 'a negotiated settlement of the Punjab problem'. I told him that the talks could take place on condition that the solution arrived at would be within the parameters of the Indian constitution.

Two days later he sent me a long letter which stated: 'Your government's recent statements indicating its willingness to talk to any Sikh organization regardless of its political policy opens up the avenue of talks as a serious and useful possibility.' Despite my telling him that no settlement was possible at the expense of India's unity, he said in his letter that 'the government has to show a genuine attitude towards talks by avoiding putting constraints regarding allegiance to the political structure or constitution of India'.

When he met me he told me that the proposition of a 'status within India' was acceptable to them provided there was a guarantee of the Sikh identity, its culture, and its traditions. I told him that the two Houses of parliament might be willing to pass a resolution providing assurances regarding Sikh culture and identity. He would not say whether the resolution alone would suffice. I asked him to clearly spell out his demands to enable me to forward them to New Delhi. He did not return, nor did I report the letter or the meeting to New Delhi.

The turning point came at a huge Sikh congregation in London. I appealed them to differentiate between the government and the country. I told them that if the government failed to fulfill its promises, such as bringing the perpetrators of the 1984 massacre to justice, it could be defeated in the next elections. After all, Indira Gandhi had been swept out of power at the polls. If, however, I argued, India as a country was harmed it would be as much their loss as of other Indians because the country belonged to all, be they Hindu, Sikh, or Muslim. Sacrifices made for the country by Sikhs were no less than those made by others. This went down well with most of the people.

When this was followed up by multi-entry visa for people of Indian origin in the UK for five years for five pounds there was great jubilation. The Sikhs came in hordes to India and returned happy. This atmosphere was a setback for the Khalistanis who, I thought, could have been defeated had there been speedy justice in the 1984 pogrom. Foreign Secretary Douglas Hurd congratulated me for my initiative to reach out to the Sikhs. He said he had vainly suggested the same thing to my predecessor. I could see the initial reservations of the Sikhs gradually melting away. The open-door policy had worked.

I also took up the revision of the 'black list' bearing the names of Sikhs debarred entry into India to whom the high commission had no authority to grant a visa without individual reference to the home ministry. At my request, two officers came from New Delhi who, together with the commission's officers, reduced the list of 500-odd to 20. Even the extremists admitted that Hindus and Sikhs had once again begun mixing freely, which had more or less ceased post-1984.

Indeed, the atmosphere had been transformed. This was apparent at a meeting where, from an audience which was 90 per cent Sikh, I collected $ 15,000 (Rs 7 lakh) for the flood victims of Andhra Pradesh.

Another change I made, and instructed my staff accordingly, was not to interfere in the local affairs of the Sikhs. On one occasion a few Sikh leaders approached me for financial assistance to pursue their legal case to wrest the gurdwaras from the hands of militants. I refused to interfere and did not allow officials in the commission to do so. The community was, in any case, making its own efforts to clean up its affairs.

News stories on my contacts with the Sikhs and my visits to gurdwaras did not elicit a favourable reaction from Congress MPs, and the party's supporters in the UK. A couple of them even went so far as to issue a statement criticizing me for 'placating the Khalistanis'. The former minister of state for foreign affairs, K. Natwar Singh, said in a statement that I was behaving as if I was accredited to Southall, where most of the Sikhs lived, rather than to Whitehall. It was the kind of comment I expected from someone like him.

What upset me most was Inder Gujral's telephone call on this issue. He said there was an increasing impression in parliamentary circles that I was hobnobbing with the Khalistanis. He should have known me better because both of us had been close associates in the Punjab Group which had helped the Akalis and the government to hold talks. It was evident he was under pressure, and wanted me to issue a contradiction because some Congress members sought to raise the issue in parliament in the form of a short-notice question.

I issued the contradiction, ruling out talks with 'supporters of Khalistan until they abandoned their demand for secession'. The storm in Delhi blew over but some bureaucrats, who had disapproved of my opening the front gate of the high commission to Sikhs and their accessibility to me, continued to be hostile.

The Gujaratis in the UK outnumber the Punjabis and are a disciplined community; richer but quieter. I attended my functions organized by them and I found women serving food which they had cooked themselves. At one of the functions I met

Chimanbhai Patel, the then Gujarat chief minister, who had come to London to sell bonds for the construction of the Narmada dam. The name of Mahatma Gandhi went down particularly well in Gujarati circles. I often shared with them my experience of attending Gandhi's prayer meetings in Delhi.

My first political report from London was on the defeat of the Conservatives in a by-election in mid-Staffordshire within days of my arrival. I had a feeling this might prove similar to the Allahabad by-election after which V.P. Singh's caravan began rolling till Rajiv Gandhi's Congress government fell in 1989.

At a dinner hosted by a leading Gujarati solicitor, S.H. Ruparell, in honour of Britain's Deputy Prime Minister Geoffrey Howe, I raised many eyebrows when I said that I did not wish to see the end of Conservative rule during my tenure. As it happened, Margaret Thatcher lost her prime-ministership just before I left London.

Tony Benn, a Labour radical, told me that those wearing 'grey suits' had advised her to quit. I recalled one of our conversations when she said that political opponents 'within your own party stab you in the back'. Something like that happened even though she was otherwise on the top of the world because the UK and US had won the Cold War and the Soviet Union had collapsed. When I congratulated her for defeating communism, she said: 'Mr High Commissioner there is yet another enemy before the West named Islam. I am therefore not surprised when Washington and London are going out of the way to pick on the Islamic world.'

Since the middle of 1989 the party had slumped in the opinion polls and its image had been mauled. Margaret Thatcher's own personal popularity was at an all time low. She had administered harsh medicine after becoming prime minister, ruthlessly cutting subsidies and remorselessly privatizing state-owned industry inviting a head-on collision with the trade unions. In so doing, she had succeeded in eradicating many of the ills afflicting the British economy. The price for this had however been high in terms of unemployment and a divided nation.

What seemed to have worked in the 1980s and saw the UK grow more rapidly than all its European competitors barring Germany did not seem to be succeeding any longer. Margaret Thatcher and the Conservatives thought they had found a formula for inflation-free growth were shocked when 1989 proved to be a year of considerable economic hardship.

How far I had left journalism behind dawned upon me when I heard about the hanging, by the Iraqi authorities, of the London *Observer* correspondent, Farzad Bazoft. I wanted to issue a statement to protest the murder of a journalist who was only doing his duty but Salman Haider advised me to desist from any public comment. He appreciated my feelings but reminded me that I was no longer a journalist and that anything I said could be misconstrued. All I had intended was not a policy statement, but just an expression of grief over the execution of a journalist.

After Salman's advice, I checked with Gujral, who sternly told me not to issue any statement that might annoy Iraq. He said over the phone that he was trying to improve relations with Iraq following Iran's uncompromising attitude on Kashmir. I thereupon tore up the statement I had prepared. I, who had once defied Indira Gandhi on press censorship just fretted and fumed, and eventually remained silent.

It was very apparent that whenever the British government spoke about the state of Jammu & Kashmir, it only mentioned Muslim-majority Kashmir, none of the other parts of the state figuring anywhere, neither the Hindu-majority Jammu nor Buddhist-majority Ladakh.

The British press did not discuss the integration of Kashmir with India but only UN resolutions concerning the Kashmir Valley. Forever critical, the press took us to task for disturbances in the Valley. I joined issue with the *Independent,* a leading British daily, sending it a letter for publication which, inter alia, said:

> What India is defending in the State is not its territory alone. It is fighting to preserve the principle of secularism which sustains the Indian democratic structure. India did not accept the partition of the subcontinent on religious grounds. Nor will it now accept the demand that a Muslim area can secede from the Union on the basis of religion … your editorial has missed the real point: how does India reconcile a religious demand of the five million Muslims in the Kashmir valley with its secular dispensation where the Muslims number 110 million, in excess of Pakistan's population? This is not the "politics of weakness but the politics of commitment to secularism".

Pakistan issued a contradiction challenging my thesis of secularism. Aware that Margaret Thatcher had recently visited Moscow, I asked her about her meeting with President Mikhail Gorbachov. She said he had asked her how he could stop the two republics of the Soviet Union slipping away from his hands. She said she had told him to visit India and see how people of different religions, castes, and regions had been able to coexist for centuries. Then she turned towards me and asked: 'Mr High Commissioner, what do you attribute it to?' It was a question for which I was entirely unprepared.

I told her that we in India did not see things as either black or white. We believe that there is a grey area which we continue expanding, and that is the essence of our pluralism; the glue that sustains it is a spirit of accommodation and sense of tolerance. She nodded in agreement, but in my heart I felt that the glue that united such sentiments was drying up and that in India the spirit of tolerance was gradually dissipating. A delegation from the local Soviet embassy met me a few days later and expressed its desire to visit India. A large team from Moscow visited New Delhi to study our experiment with pluralism.

Soon after the end of the Emergency, I was invited to one of the RSS *shakhas* (cadres). The entire programme was Hindu in content and anti-Muslim in spirit. The *sanchalaks* (members) did not like my speech because I emphasized on our secular ethos and the pluralistic core of our national struggle.

The British foreign office had a largely Col. Blimp attitude, nose up and treated India patronizingly or cursorily, seldom normally. Once when the Gujarati community sought special facilities of travel for their head, the British foreign office made me attend a junior level meeting to underline the point that even for a minor concession the high commissioner must come in person to plead the case.

The worst example was that of Foreign Secretary Douglas Hurd summoning me to his office and alleging that India was smuggling arms into Iraq in ships in which we were transporting food supplies on humanitarian grounds. I denied the allegation, saying that the US and UK forces had already searched our ships twice and had found nothing. Still not convinced, Hurd said that they would maintain a close watch, not a pleasant remark to make to a friendly country.

There were some other instances that made me feel that India was being intentionally slighted. When I took up the case of the return of the Koh-i-noor diamond to India, the response was an imperious regal negative, with the British government disinclined to enter into a debate on the subject. However, I argued with its foreign office about how Lord Dalhousie had forcibly seized the Koh-i-noor from Dalip Singh, the son of Maharaja Ranjit Singh, who originally owned it and wore it on his turban. Dalhousie was so secretive about the spiriting away of the Koh-i-noor from India that he took the diamond through the South Africa route rather than the regular one through the Suez.

I cited to the British government the UNESCO resolution that colonizers must return the relics seized by them to their countries of origin. I failed to make any headway because the British government just stonewalled the issue. However, one individual who sustained my effort was our servant Murli, who had accompanied us to see the Indian jewels in the Tower of London. He told me after seeing the Koh-i-noor: '*Babuji ise zaroor le jana. Yeh heera hamara hai.* [Sir, we must take this diamond back because it is ours'].

In fact, the British have in their custody thousands of relics that should rightly be the property of the subcontinent. When the Nehru Gallery was opened at the Victoria and Albert Museum in 1990, during the last days of my tenure, only a part of the treasure in the museum's basement was displayed. I asked the then curator how much had been displayed. She said: 'Only 5 per cent.' I offered to take some of the relics to India at our expense, promising to return them safely after they had been displayed in various parts of India. I was brusquely brushed aside as if the objects were their property. I did not find our government particularly concerned about the issue, as if they had reconciled themselves to the loss of objets d'art like the Koh-i-noor. When I subsequently took up the case as MP with Foreign Minister Jaswant Singh he appealed to me not to press my point in the interest of good relations between New Delhi and London.

An even more reprehensible act on the part of British government was the distribution of books, documents, maps, and other historical material in the India Office Library among various libraries in the UK. The India Office Library held all the original documents concerning the 150-year-long British imperial rule and the national struggles waged against it. A treasure-trove of documents about India and its history, extending even to the Mughal period and earlier, they provided essential source material for historians and researchers in single venue. Now they are all scattered.

It is true that India and Pakistan could not agree on the division of the India Office Library and its documents but that did not mean its appropriation by the UK. There was a time in the early 1980s when India, Pakistan, and Bangladesh jointly demanded all the material stored in the India Office Library, but the British government dragged its feet and linked the division of the library with other problems.

I once suggested to the British foreign office that they hand over all the material to Pakistan with which we and Bangladesh would negotiate a share. There was no response. The British foreign office has no intention of returning the most valuable material which attracts research scholars from all over the world to the UK. Even the photostat copies we obtained of some documents for the Indira Gandhi Centre in Delhi were acquired at a huge price.

I found too many Research and Analysis Wing (RAW) men at the high commission working under sundry designations. Although they were headed by a soft-spoken poet, Keki N. Daruwala, who later became director of RAW, their methods were dubious. I asked Salman what their role was. His cryptic reply was: 'They keep an eye on us.' I suggested to New Delhi that their number be cut, but was told that the agency was directly under the control of prime minister who did not favour any reduction.

I was receiving top secret reports on the Sikhs from the RAW, but after reading two or three reports I discontinued them because I had read more or less the same thing a few days earlier in the Punjabi newspapers.

I detected an element of racism in the UK towards the non-white population. This was the time when one conservative MP made the most provocative statement that people from India and Pakistan settled in the UK were not Britishers because they cheered cricket teams from their respective countries playing against the English national team. Innumerable instances of discrimination against people of Indian origin were brought to the high commission's notice, but the Commission preferred to distance itself from such complaints because the people settled there were British citizens and it was for London to attend to their grievances.

I must admit that my contact with British foreign office was very limited. Salman maintained the link on regular basis but we both went one day to a briefing on how Iraq was attempting to arm itself with weapons of mass destruction and defying world opinion. I could see that the UK was building up a case against Saddam Hussain.

Gujral stopped off in London on his way to the US. He had met Saddam Hussain and his impression was that Iraq had 'something' up its sleeve and would not be an easy target for the West. Saddam Hussain had told him that the war was over oil and had pointed out how the West had manipulated everything: oil was cheap but the technology expensive because it came from the West.

I had invited the top journalists and experts on Iraq to meet Gujral over lunch. He made out that Iraq would not be easy to occupy. This surprised them because their information was that Saddam Hussain's surrender would be just a matter of days. The experts got the impression that India was standing behind Saddam Hussain. Notwithstanding our efforts to dispel such an impression, British journalists did not hide their contempt for Gujral's assessment. I was so confused that I checked with the high commission's bright air attaché Vinod Patni whether Saddam Hussain was as powerful as Gujral had made him out to be. Patni said that Saddam Hussain's surrender would occur under a week after the attack. He too had been surprised at how differently the Indian foreign minister viewed the situation.

One person with whom I did not discuss politics but everything else under the sun, was the writer, Nirad C. Chaudhuri. He was past ninety and lived in a modest house in Oxford. Chaudhuri was as much part of the UK as were memories of the Raj. I delayed calling on him till I found a rare vintage wine selected by Salman, a connoisseur. I could see Chaudhuri's eyes light up when I presented it to him. Clad in dhoti and kurta, he was at the gate to receive me. (I had become punctual to a fault in the UK.)

Chaudhuri was justifiably indignant about the letter he had received intimating him about my proposed visit. A junior bureaucrat from the high commission had written that 'he had the privilege of informing Chaudhuri that the high commissioner had kindly agreed' to meet him. In fact, it was the other way round. The truth was that I had wanted to meet him and he had kindly agreed to do so.

Chaudhuri was, however, even more indignant about the substandard quality of the stationery used by the high commission. The officer concerned was not to blame for this because that was all the high commission had to offer given the niggardly budget. I had brought my own hand-made paper stationery from India at my expense. We had just begun talking when his wife walked in. She wanted to be there because, as she told me, she had read my writings for years in the *Statesman*. Unlike Nirad Chaudhuri, she seemed ill at ease in the UK.

'I am writing in Bengali these days,' Chaudhuri said. 'Whatever I write is being lapped up by the people of West Bengal.' By no stretch of the imagination could he be described as a modest individual but he was highly respected in the UK. His impeccable use of the English language and his knowledge of British history were the envy of educated and the knowledgeable Englishmen. A few days before I met him, he had admonished the British in a letter to the editor of a London daily for succumbing to Europe's dictats on unity and integration.

He told me he felt as much at home in the UK as in India. The 'hypocrisy of Indians' still bothered him but he was no longer an angry man; only a saddened one. Laughingly, he wondered why India was always referring to a conspiracy to dismantle it. Time had mellowed him. Like most men of his age, he was fond of his grandchildren and spoke at length about them. What struck me about him was his child-like dependence on his wife. After every sentence he looked towards her as if seeking her approval for everything he said.

Another person I recall meeting while I was in the UK was Salman Rushdie. I found him much more interesting than his books. He was so natural, not having to tailor his expression and views to suit anyone. He is better reflected in conversations than in his writings because, face to face, he does not say anything just for effect. My judgement may, however, be faulty because we spent only three hours together.

The threat to his life and two years' hiding following the publication of his book, *The Satanic Verses*, had affected him but not broken him. When I met him, he was planning moves to make peace with the liberals in Islamic society, particularly in Egypt.

'I thought I would buy a house in Bombay and spend more time there than in London,' he said, 'but what do I do now with Hindu chauvinism taking over India?' He added, 'I can predict India's disintegration if it jettisons secularism.'

He blamed Indira Gandhi for having compromised over secularism. 'Looking back, it is she who pampered Hindu chauvinism for votes.' I told him that there might be a spurt of religious frenzy among the Hindus but it would not last long. 'All this is just for the elections,' I assured him. 'As soon as they are over, the tide of fundamentalism will subside.' Rushdie was not convinced that my reading was correct. 'Indian society is becoming increasingly intolerant and communal,' he stressed.

He concurred with my view that fundamentalism was the greatest threat to democracy. I told him about the discussion that I had had with Margaret Thatcher when she had said that 'Islamic fundamentalism was the greatest threat to the world after the defeat of communism.' Rushdie took pride in having taken on some fundamentalist Muslim beliefs and chided Hindu liberals for not having done the same in relation to Hinduism.

Khushwant Singh, was quite high on the list of people who Rushdie felt had let him down. He was referring to Khushwant's advice to Penguin not to publish *The Satanic Verses*. Subsequently when I asked Khushwant about it, he said: 'As a consulting editor to the publishing house, I told them that the book would offend Muslims and create problems.' He said he was not discussing the merits of the book when he spoke about religious susceptibilities. Khushwant felt hurt that Rushdie had misunderstood him.

Rushdie was uncompromising about Kashmir. He wanted India to concede the right of self-determination to Kashmiri Muslims. When I tried to advance the argument that if Kashmiri Muslims opted out of the Indian union this might adversely affect the Muslims in the rest of India, he said that Indian Muslims were not hostages; they were Indian citizens who were entitled to equal rights. He did not believe that Kashmiri Muslims wanted to join Pakistan; they sought independence.

❁

Farooq Abdullah met me in London when I was high commissioner. I advised him, in the presence of his entire family which I had invited for lunch, not to return to the Valley for at least ten years because it was possible that he could become relevant after the passage of that time. George Fernandes, railway minister in the V.P. Singh government, took him back almost directly from my house, where they held protracted discussions, to Delhi. I was proved correct. He had returned too early to the same type of politics.

I was recuperating from a minor operation in 1990 when India's Chief Justice Sabyasachi Mukherejee arrived in London on his way back from the US. On his arrival he suffered a heart attack at a friend's house where he was staying. The high commission took him to the Royal Free Hospital, one of the best in London. Justice Mukherjee suffered another severe heart attack and died in hospital on 25 September 1990. The high commission sent Salman Haider to accompany the body to Delhi and my wife accompanied Mukherjee's wife to provide her with solace during the long journey.

There was a concerted attack on me in the Lok Sabha for Mukherjee's death. Subsequently, Rabi Ray, the Lok Sabha speaker, told me that he had no idea that the permission granted to the BJP MP, Ghuman Lal Lodha, to make a reference to Mukherjee's death would turn into a full-scale attack on me. Chandra Shekhar, who called me 'a social climber', took over from Lodha and then it was a free-for-all.

It was a god-sent opportunity for the Congress, which was licking its wounds inflicted by my vehement indictment of the Emergency. Vasant Sathe, Dinesh Singh, and Jaffer Sharief were all staunch defenders of Indira Gandhi's authoritarian rule which I had defied.

Arrogant P. Chidambaram, whom I had described as 'a whiz kid' during Rajiv Gandhi's stewardship, was the angriest of all. K.K. Venugopal, president of the Supreme Court Bar Association, was instrumental in having a resolution passed by the general body of the association, condemning the Indian high commission's 'indifference and negligent' treatment of Mukherjee during his illness.

I asked Atal Bihari Vajpayee, when he was staying with me in London, why the criticism from the BJP had been feeble. He said that he had told his party men that the Congress was playing politics and they should not become party to it.

Chandra Shekhar's grievance, as he explained later to his friends, was that on two occasions I had stood in the way of his becoming prime minister, once in 1977, when the Janata Party assumed office, and then when the Janata Dal, a new party that he and some Janata party members cobbled together in order to form a government. Though his assessment was correct, he overestimated the extent of the influence I wielded.

He could not have become prime minister in 1977 because at that time the choice was between Morarji Desai and Jagjivan Ram. Chandra Shekhar was not even in the picture. True, I knew many Janata leaders, particularly Jayaprakash Narayan, who played a decisive role in choosing the prime minister, but it had been a problem just to get Chandra Shekhar elected as the president of the Janata Party. He could not conceivably have become prime minister in 1990 because the loyalty of members was split between V.P. Singh and Devi Lal.

Dhirendra Singh, an IAS officer, attached to Mukherjee, wanted to cover up any blame accruing to him. He told the one-judge inquiry commission that the high commission was differentiating between private and official visits. Such matters do not come up before the high commissioner and are dealt with by the high commission in accordance with instructions received from Delhi. In Mukherjee's case, the Supreme Court said that he was on a private visit to London. The high commission did not, however, draw any distinction between official and private, providing all the facilities he and his wife would have enjoyed had they been on an official visit.

This is my diary noting of the time:

> Apart from my sense of personal hurt – and that was very strong – what was painful was to see how politics in India was being trivialized for party purposes. At a time when the Congress government was collapsing, the economy going to pieces, Kashmir and Punjab burning and of course, the Ayodhya dispute heading for a showdown, it was unbelievable that parliament should spend three days on a non-issue. However, one lesson came through clearly to me: it is all too easy to criticize the bureaucracy from outside but the reality within can be very different.

I insisted on an inquiry although the then Prime Minister Chandra Shekhar was not overly keen on one and reportedly remarked: 'the purpose has been served.' Judge Chinappa Reddy was appointed and I appeared before him in Delhi. He exonerated me and the high commission from providing 'inadequate medical facilities' to Mukherjee. In fact, the judge commended the high commission for all it had done and dispelled the impression that the Royal Free Hospital was a second-rate medical institution. The only stricture, if it can be so called, of the judge was that the deputy high commissioner and high commission should have helped Mrs Mukherjee to properly express herself because she had only a limited knowledge of English. The case eventually came to the Supreme Court where Chief Justice J.S. Verma held that there was nothing against Kuldip Nayar.

卐

I was still in London when V.P. Singh announced (1990) the implementation of the recommendations of the Mandal Commission Report on Other Backward Classes (OBC). V.P. Singh was one of the most controversial politicians, and though his impact on politics might have stirred division, his tenure led to the implementation of the Mandal Commission recommendations which Indira Gandhi had kept under wraps. For the first time, the educationally and socially backward classes, also referred to as OBCs, got reservation in government jobs and admission to institutions of higher education. V.P. Singh had, however, to pay a price as the upper castes and the intelligentsia, who felt threatened by the Mandalization of politics, came out on to the streets in protest against his policies. His critics averred that his sudden love for the OBCs was a panic reaction to the threat posed by Devi Lal, who was uncomfortable under his leadership.

V.P. Singh never wavered in his commitment to the Mandal cause. He told me that he might have 'lost a leg but had scored a goal'. His credibility among the minorities, particularly Muslims, was very high.

The truth is that political considerations compelled V.P. Singh to implement the Mandal Commission recommendations. Both he and Deputy Prime Minister Devi Lal had been at loggerheads from the very outset. Devi Lal wanted to have an equal say in key appointments and share the discretionary powers which the prime minister enjoyed. Devi Lal announced a political rally at India Gate and threatened to bring lakhs of people to demonstrate his strength.

To counter the demonstration, V.P. Singh, on the eve of Devi Lal's rally, played the Mandal card, i.e. announced reservations for the OBCs. The upper classes, however, felt that a gauntlet had been thrown at them and they picked it up and replied with ferocity. Delhi was engulfed by disturbances. During that time it was difficult even to drive a car without a sticker declaring: 'I am not an OBC'.

When I returned from London, I was approached by some young men with an anti-Mandal agenda who asked me to lead them against reservations for the OBCs. I was aware that V.P. Singh had brought in the reforms for purely political reasons but declined to join the anti-Mandal agitation. I thought the reforms represented a churning in society and might help it vomit out the poison in the body politic. I kept aloof from the issue, neither supporting nor opposing the pro- or anti-Mandal elements. I was however disappointed by the way in which the OBC leaders, once in the forefront of the JP Movement, fattened themselves in the name of their community; the 'creamy layer' which the Supreme Court has debarred from the benefits of reservation who have by their actions trivialized the issue.

When the OBC question was raised on the pretext of enumerating castes in the 2011 census I was furious. I failed to understand the argument that by counting the number of OBCs, the nation would learn the number of 'poor' in their caste. Poor is poor, regardless of caste. For me, the eradication of caste from our lexicon is essential for India in its attempts to establish a democratic, pluralistic nation. Gandhi, Nehru, and JP have all fought for a caste-less society.

The implementation of the Mandal Commission recommendations projected V.P. Singh as a veritable messiah of social justice in the eyes of the marginalized castes. At the same time, it generated unrest with upper-caste youth taking to the streets of north India, a few even attempting to immolate themselves in protest against what they considered the 'darkening of their future'.

This aspect came to light during the proceedings of the Liberahan Commission which was examining the demolition of the Babri Masjid. In fact, V.P. Singh, the author of the Mandal reforms, said in his deposition that L.K. Advani undertook the *rath* yatra in 1990 to counter the Mandal Commission's report because the BJP was apprehensive that it might lose the support of the middle classes if the party did not oppose the report. It preferred to play the religious card which V.P. Singh believed the BJP regarded as a proper riposte to the repercussions of the Mandal issue.

V.P. Singh was not at all equipped to run a minority government, particularly because he had powerful detractors like Chandra Shekhar within his own party. I have reason to believe that he asked Lalu Prasad Yadav, chief minister of Bihar, to stop the yatra and arrest L.K. Advani. Hearing this, Atal Bihari Vajpayee went to the president to withdraw the BJP's support to the V.P. Singh government. V.P Singh did not resign even then because he expected the Congress to support him when he was fighting a battle to sustain secularism, but the Congress did not oblige. V.P. Singh lost the vote of confidence in the Lok Sabha in November 1990.

Atal Bihari Vajpayee gave me a different reason for his withdrawal of support to the V.P. Singh government, as not being precipitated by the arrest of Advani. He said that had V.P. Singh not implemented the Mandal Commission recommendation the BJP would have continued its support. 'If there had been no Mandal we would not have used *kamandal* [a vessel used for prayer],' said Vajpayee.

卐

I resigned from my post as high commissioner as soon as I heard that the V.P. Singh's government had fallen (10 November 1990). I was a political appointee and had no business to continue after the government which had appointed me was no longer in power. News of the fall of V.P. Singh's government and my resignation were broadcast by All India Radio in a single bulletin.

On my departure, the House of Commons, in an unprecedented gesture, passed a resolution to commend my services.

> That this House notes the contribution of the retiring High Commissioner of India, Shri Kuldip Nayar, to the enhancement of good relations between the people of India and Britain; warmly congratulates him on his initiatives in reducing the visa fees for persons who wish to visit India; commends the energetic and enthusiastic way in which he forged bonds of friendship with the communities of India origin living in Britain; hopes that these positive measures will be continued by his successor.

I was overwhelmed by the response of the British as well as the Indian community which gave me a warm farewell. V.P. Singh and I.K. Gujral sent me congratulatory messages. However, Rajiv Gandhi's comment, when Gujral told him about the House of Commons resolution, was: 'Kuldip must have done something for the British.' To this Gujral's cryptic retort was: 'Yes, we must ask the CBI to inquire.'

V.P. Singh's rule will be remembered because it was he who stopped the *rath* yatra led by L.K. Advani from Somnath temple to Ayodhya (25 September 1990). The BJP's intention was clearly to polarize a pluralist society, and indeed the *rath* yatra did result in a deep gulf developing between Hindus and Muslims.

Even after the yatra began, V.P. Singh, then prime minister, took no action because his government was sustained by the BJP. This was his most grievous error. He should have resigned on 25 September rather than a few months later when the BJP withdrew its support. Had V.P. Singh resigned then it would have strengthened the secular forces. It was clear that the yatra would pollute the atmosphere and provoke communal riots. Inevitably there were clashes between Hindus and Muslims leading to riots in several places. V.P. Singh still did not act because he wanted to cling on to his prime-ministership.

I went to Ayodhya a month before the demolition. To my surprise I found that the people at Faizabad did not welcome outsiders. There was no tension between Hindus and Muslims and it did not look like a city which a few weeks later witnessed the destruction of the masjid. I went to Hanuman Mandir near the disputed mosque and had to approach a Muslim family which for generations had custody of the key to the temple lock.

V.P. Singh was relegated into historical oblivion but kept his promise of creating a more equitable relationship between the lower castes and the agrarian peasantry. At the cabinet level, half the ministerial berths were filled by members of the backward communities. The National Commission for Scheduled Castes and Scheduled Tribes was vested with statutory powers to enforce implementation of governmental programmes, and was headed by a prominent leader from those castes. Most striking was the action taken to redress the neglect since Independence of Babasaheb B.R. Ambedkar, the iconic dalit leader. Soon after V.P. Singh took office, a portrait of Ambedkar was installed in the Central Hall of parliament. His date of birth, 14 April, was declared a national holiday, and the posthumous award of the Bharat Ratna, India's highest civilian honour, was conferred on him. After V.P. Singh's government fell he never returned to active politics, allowing himself the luxury to pursue his passion for painting till renal failure and blood cancer incapacitated him.

My regret is that I never interviewed Dr B.R. Ambedkar. I listened to him from the press gallery piloting the constitution and admired the passion and the conviction with which he put across his point of view on sundry issues. He was personally opposed to reservations for the scheduled castes and scheduled tribes but the general sense of the constituent assembly was in favour of reservations. He pleaded that he did not want 'crutches' for his community but eventually agreed to reservations for ten years on condition that the period would not be extended.

Little did he imagine that leaders from his community would continue to insist on an indefinite extension of the period. This, however, suited the Congress which used the scheduled castes and scheduled tribes as a vote bank for the party. Only in the 1970s did it lose their unquestioned allegiance.

The credit for the latter goes to a devoted worker from Punjab, Kanshi Ram, who founded the Bahujan Samaj Party (BSP) and built it up. He did not reap the fruits of his efforts but his close associate Mayawati's emergence as a significant political leader in UP has proved that Kanshi Ram had assured the dalits a place in the sun.

The blame lies not with the upper castes alone; the politics of votes has got ingrained amongst the dalits too. Their leaders, largely stemming from the 'creamy layer' of society have come to enjoy the spoils of office without adequately articulating the genuine interests of their community.

While piloting the constitution, Dr Ambedkar, the most distinguished leader among the dalits, was able to incorporate in it the numerous safeguards for the Harijans and banning the concept of untouchability. This has not however resolved the problem of untouchability which lies deeply imbedded within the psyche of Hindu society.

What really disturbs me is the stoicism of the dalits who have remained part of a Hindu society in spite of the repression and exploitation they have undergone for centuries. Dr Ambedkar aptly described the situation by borrowing a phrase from Shakespeare: 'It may be your interest to be our masters but how can it be ours to be your slaves?' The oppressive caste system remains more or less intact among Hindus and there has been no movement for decades to reform the society. Liberals lap up the segregation of dalits as much as leaders of the conservatives.

It is true that we have adopted certain rules and conventions to help the scheduled castes and tribes to develop. They deserve such help but, even so I am against any form of reservation, more particularly in relation to jobs. I react strongly against anything that leads to inefficiency and second-rate standards. I want my country to be a first class in everything. When we encourage the second-rate, it handicaps us. Affirmative action, like that adopted in favour of the blacks in America, may be a possible solution. Reservations are making upper-caste youth bitter. Whether now or fifty years hence, India will have to reinterpret reservation and make economic status the criterion for eligibility.

I resumed my syndicated weekly column, 'Between the Lines' after my return from the UK. Even within the brief period of a year when I was in London, Indian journalism had changed dramatically and become owner-driven. For instance, *Anand Bazar Patrika* reflected Aveek Sarkar's views. His father, Asok Sarkar, was a friend of mine so I treated Aveek like a member of the family. He once told me that he was the second most important person in West Bengal after Jyoti Basu, who was then alive. Another editor, a proprietor in the *Indian Express,* was Shekhar Gupta, who was infatuated with himself. His personal views and other considerations shaped the *Indian Express* which was once India's most anti-establishment newspaper.

Much earlier the *Rajasthan Patrika* had stopped publishing my column. The owner, R. C. Kulish, was a personal friend but could not tolerate my criticism of the BJP position. 'I am not against Muslims and I have one servant from the community but they have to be kept in their place,' he told me once. Never did I suspect that he would go so far as to stop the publication of the column. I vainly tried to meet him in Jaipur. Once when in the city, I learnt he was critically ill, so I went to his house and waited to see him but he refused to meet me.

In the case of *Daily Bhaskar*, I stopped my column because it refused to publish my piece on 'paid news'. Although I did not name anyone the newspaper still refused to publish the column. I wrote a letter of protest to the owner and received no response.

My experience with N. Ram, the editor of the *Hindu* was disappointing. I used to write an opinion piece for the newspaper twice a week and a human rights column once a month. He stopped them because I was a friend of Malini

Parthasarthy who, along with N. Ravi, was pushed out of editorial control when they were reduced to a minority in the public limited company that the *Hindu* is. Ram joined G. Kasturi and few others to constitute a majority. Ravi, modest and unassuming, and Malini, a talented journalist, suffered the most but stoically bore the humiliation. When newspapers turn themselves into companies and the majority begins to prevail, the newspaper becomes a purely commercial proposition like any corporate house.

⚜

When the V.P. Singh government fell, the Janata Dal still existed as a party although individual state leaders controlled its constituent parties. Chandra Shekhar, whose principal ambition in life was to become prime minister, was the first claimant. He could not have won a majority in the party without the support of Mulayam Singh Yadav, who eventually rallied to his aid.

Mulayam Singh was on the defensive when he shared with me what induced him to support Chandra Shekhar. Initially he (Mulayam) did not take Chandra Shekhar's call, but when he repeatedly called him, Mulayam Singh picked up the phone. Chandra Shekhar implored him for support in his quest to become prime minister. 'I felt I must help a friend who was after all a socialist,' said Mulayam Singh.

Rajiv Gandhi had already offered outside support to Chandra Shekhar. The latter asked I.K. Gujral to join his cabinet as foreign minister but he declined, the portfolio eventually going to V.C. Shukla, the Goebbels of Emergency disfame. Chandra Shekhar, who had fought against the Emergency, had no compunction in including him in the cabinet for the couple of votes he had at his command. Greed makes curious bedfellows.

I was especially invited to a dinner in honour of Chandra Shekhar and was informed that I was to share a table with Rajiv Gandhi. Suman Dubey, who was close to Rajiv Gandhi, was very insistent that I attend the dinner, but I do not know why Rajiv Gandhi, after shaking hands with me, did not after all share my table.

Chandra Shekhar's brief period of 40 days in power was the most corrupt in the history of India. I was sorry to see the sharp decline of an individual who had once been a 'young Turk' in the Congress and the president of the Janata Party. For Rajiv Gandhi he served the purpose of filling in a blank. Once the Congress felt that its election prospects had improved, it withdrew support from him on the trumped-up charge that Rajiv Gandhi was being shadowed by the CID.

16

NARASIMHA RAO'S GOVERNMENT
Economic Reforms, Yasin Malik and the Kashmir Question, the Babri Masjid-Ramjanmabhoomi Imbroglio, Of Communal Riots and Inquiry Commission Reports, and the Rise of Sonia Gandhi

The election commission announced fresh elections in 1991 because no party was in a position to form a government. The Congress had the largest number of seats in the Lok Sabha, as many as 232 in a House of 545, but was short of a clear majority. Despite the fact that the Congress had gained from the sympathy wave, there was a very low voter turnout. The nation was halfway through the elections when Rajiv Gandhi was assassinated on 21 May 1991. Emotional Chief Election Commissioner T.N. Sheshan halted further polling for a few days. This helped the Congress party, which won more seats in the second phase than in the first. In a way, Rajiv's assassination was responsible for the return of the Congress at the Centre.

Political turmoil apart, Prime Minister Narasimha Rao's government faced a financial crisis. Foreign reserves had dwindled to a level required to pay for the import of petroleum products for a fortnight. Thanks to the fiscal profligacy of the Chandra Shekhar government, the Rao government was even obliged to send 47 tons of gold to the Bank of England as collateral for a loan. It was also forced to take a loan of $1.4 billion from the International Monetary Fund (IMF) to restructure the Indian economy. It was humiliating for the nation but then the British wanted their pound of flesh.

Rao inducted Dr Manmohan Singh, former governor of the Reserve Bank, into his cabinet as finance minister to deal with the acute financial crisis. It was comrade Harkishan Singh Surjeet who had suggested the name of Manmohan Singh. The latter succeeded in the extremely difficult task of moving the Indian economy towards an integrated programme for economic reforms. Rather than being defensive, he went on the offensive. He opened his budget speech more than twenty years ago (24 July 1991) by quoting Victor Hugo: 'No power on Earth can stop an idea whose turn has come.'

He dispensed with the license-quota raj and gave a free hand to the corporate sector. The rupee was devalued by 20 per cent. He opened the door wide to foreign investors, permitting investment in fields that India had jealously guarded and reserved for domestic entrepreneurs. Export subsidies were abolished, tariffs lowered, and the expansion of the public sector was put on hold.

The effect of these measures was that the growth-rate grew substantially, a phenomenon not witnessed earlier. The prime minister, together with Manmohan Singh, thoroughly reviewed the economic liberalization programme, its overall results, and the benefits that could accrue to the people from it. They concluded that globalization was inevitable and Nehru's vision for a socialistic pattern of society was pushed aside in favour of unadulterated capitalism.

We (some anti-globalization elements) founded a group with Ramesh Chauhan, a big name in the mineral water business, to oppose the economic reforms. We would meet every week at Chauhan's house where his charming wife, Zainab, fed us. The entire effort came to nought when Ramesh saw that he was safer with the corporate sector than us, Left-inclined individuals. He wound up the group overnight without consulting any of us.

The Narasimha Rao government was, however, completely discredited by scandals implicating the prime minister in acceptance of bribes, and the unprecedented 'hawala case'. There is sufficient evidence now to prove that Rao personally accepted a suitcase-full of currency notes. Records relating to his appointments and to the visitors' reception at the enquiry office at his house were fudged to show that Lakhubhai Pathak, who had claimed to have given him a suitcase-full of currency notes, never met him or visited the PM's official residence. Karnataka governor H.R. Bharadwaj admitted before me that altering register, etc was not a difficult task. 'Nobody seeks my advice these days, otherwise the 2G or CWG scam could have been managed,' Bharadwaj said.

My contact with Narasimha Rao during his tenure as the prime minister was very limited. He however kept tabs on me. Once I complained to him that intelligence men were tailing me. After attending a dinner at the British counsellor's house two persons in khaki came to my house to inquire about the purpose of my visit. The reply came from the cabinet secretary who said that they had made inquiries and had found no substance to my complaint.

I used to frequently meet Narasimha Rao when he was chief minister of Andhra Pradesh (1971–73). At the time of his leaving the state for Delhi, I told him that he should bear in mind what had happened to Sanjiva Reddy who had faced a hard time at the hands of Indira Gandhi.

Rao, however, ensured that during his tenure Sonia Gandhi made no approaches to the Congress which he indirectly controlled. She was undoubtedly hyphenating at the time but was also waiting for an opportunity to be offered the post of party president without even having to ask for it.

To the disappointment of his pro-socialist followers, Rao pushed for the economic reforms that Rajiv Gandhi had initiated on a small scale. Rao wanted to go full speed ahead and Manmohan Singh, well-versed in this economic paradigm, had ceased to be idealistic and needed no convincing.

Rao was not punctilious in his behaviour and was, as we have seen, even guilty of accepting money for making business transactions 'easy' for individuals and the corporate sector. He would often remark that he did not do anything against his conscience but convinced it to act as the situation demanded.

Rao bribed four MPs from the Jharkhand Mukti Morcha (JMM) to save his government and was the first Indian prime minister to be convicted in a criminal case. CBI Special Judge Ajit Bharihoke found him and former Home Minister Buta Singh guilty in 2001. However, in March 2002, the Delhi High Court acquitted both Rao and Buta Singh, much to the shock of the public.

When Rao was in office, he approached me to persuade Yasin Malik, originally a militant in Kashmir, to break his fast unto death. The IB officials called me to the AIIMS where he was fasting. His demand was that the government should withdraw security forces from Hazratbal shrine in Srinagar.

I felt that Malik's demand for an inquiry was just and that it showed his lack of confidence in the government machinery. I asked him why he had no confidence in Indians. He said he had faith in me [aap ki zaat mein mujhe yakin hai]. I assured him that I would try to get the security forces to vacate the shrine. Rao told state minister for home affairs Rajesh Pilot to follow my advice. A few militants had holed up in Hazratbal shrine. The security forces had surrounded the site and the people of the entire Valley wanted the militants to be allowed safe passage out of the shrine. I was able to persuade the government to withdraw the security forces to some distance and an entire day was spent on the wording of the settlement. I frequently shuttled between Pilot's house and the AIIMS to arrive at a concurrence between the government and Malik.

For the first time I felt that the government's right hand did not know what the left was doing. By the time I reached the AIIMS after obtaining the government's approval on the draft settlement, the doctors were all set to force-feed Malik. He had been tied and one doctor was able to force a tablespoon down his throat. I told the doctors about the settlement. An IB man checked with his officers and only then did the ordeal end. The militants were allowed to escape during the night.

My contact with Malik became intimate and I told him about the futility of using arms which killed but did not convince anyone about his stand on Kashmir. Somewhere I think I was able to touch a chord by what I told him. He gave up violence, became vegetarian, and also had Mahatma Gandhi's photograph hung on the wall of his room. He even convinced the Hurriyat, a body of several organizations fighting for Kashmir's azadi to stop confronting the security forces with violence. The violence currently being undertaken in the Valley is not by the Hurriyat but largely by militants from across the border. Rao once said that the 'sky was the limit' in Kashmir if it remained within India. This was a welcome statement but he did nothing to implement it, becoming too engrossed in the events in Ayodhya where Babri Masjid stood.

🕉

Rao's government will always be held responsible for the demolition of Babri Masjid. The curious thing was that he was conscious of such an eventuality but did virtually nothing to avert it. Once he invited senior journalists to acquaint them with the efforts his government was making to reach a settlement. I asked him which stage they had reached. 'Somewhere,' he said in reply, but there was no serious edge to his voice.

Soon after I witnessed the gathering of the storm, with thousands of *kar sevaks* descending upon Ayodhya and the RSS and the BJP leaders converging on the city. Kalyan Singh was the state chief minister heading a BJP government. The statements he made indicated that he had no intention of protecting Babri Masjid, although the Supreme Court had ordered him to maintain the status quo and his government had given it an undertaking that it would do so.

I wish I had asked G.B. Pant, when I was his information officer, about Babri Masjid. It is now well known that he was sympathetic to the people who placed the idols in the mosque on 23 December 1949. Nehru had warned Pant that 'the whole atmosphere of UP has been changing for the worse from the communal point of view. Indeed, UP is becoming almost a foreign land for me. I do not fit in with them.' Nehru's was a voice of pathos, of a person who had been born and brought up in hate-free UP. He vainly referred to such Congress members who were behind the Hindu fanatics and responsible for the installation of the idols at Babri Masjid.

Pant never replied to Nehru's indignant letter to him in which the latter had argued that there was no historical proof to support the temple theory. Pant, however, wrote a letter to Sardar Patel to argue that the masjid was originally built after demolishing a temple and the entire matter was sub judice.

It was known even then that a local administrator, K.K. Nayar, had placed the idols in the masjid on the night of 22–3 December 1949. The RSS's official organ, the *Organiser*, reported the event as follows: 'On the historic morning of 23 December 1949, the idols of Sri Ramachandra and Sita Devi miraculously appeared at the Janmasthan.' Nayar was rewarded by the RSS in the form of a Lok Sabha ticket given to his wife Shakuntala in 1951, on which she was elected.

After the installation of the idols, an FIR was filed to the effect that two policemen were responsible for the act, and although nothing came of it, it showed that some outsiders were responsible for the mischief and that nothing like a miracle or *pargat* (appearing from nowhere), had occurred as many believers made out.

The Pant government in UP had to put a lock on the gate of the disputed Babri Masjid–Ramjanambhoomi site because of the heated controversy between Hindus and Muslims regarding the origins of the edifice. Muslims claimed that the masjid had stood at Ayodhya since the days of Babur, while Hindus maintained that masjid had been built after demolishing a Rama temple.

The climax came when Babri Masjid was demolished to the last stone on 6 December 1992 by thousands of *kar sevaks* egged on by the BJP and RSS leadership. It was daylight murder of secularism. So delighted were the BJP leaders who witnessed the demolition that they leapt into one another's arms. They said it was a mere structure, yet this structure represented India's secular ethos, the Ganga–Yamuna culture. One newspaper aptly wrote: 'Mahatma Gandhi was shot at on January 30, 1948 but he died on December 6, 1992.'

So widespread was the protest that Advani resigned from the Lok Sabha to wipe off the stains of the demolition. The gesture proved to be a farce because he was not slow in taking back his resignation.

My information was that Rao had connived at the demolition. He sat at puja when the *kar sevaks* began pulling down the mosque and rose only when the last stone had been removed. Madhu Limaye told me that during the puja Rao's aide whispered in his ears that the masjid had been demolished. Within seconds, the puja was over.

When there were riots in the wake of the masjid's demolition, Rao invited some senior journalists to his house. He was at pains to explain to us how his government had made every arrangement to stop the demolition. Rao said that he was betrayed by UP Chief Minister Kalyan Singh. I asked him how a small temple could have been erected overnight at the site when the Centre was at the helm of affairs having dismissed the Kalyan Singh government. Rao said he had attempted to send a contingent of CRPF by plane to Lucknow but they were unable to land because of bad weather. He did not explain the inaction of Central forces at Ayodhya, but assured me that the temple would not be there 'for long'.

Rao tried to wash off the stigma of the demolition of the mosque when he appeared before the Justice Liberhan Commission, appointed to apportion blame for the masjid's destruction.

Admitting that the structure which had been demolished was a mosque, Rao said:

> What else could it be? Was it a dwelling house? When the Government of Uttar Pradesh says that namaz was going on there until 1949, irrespective of the date, what else could it be but a mosque?'

Rao said before the commission:

Personally I was not aware of the *shilanyas* but I can refer the Commission
to Mr Buta Singh, who was then Home Minister, and who according to my
information, was dealing with the subject from day to day. I believe that
he will be able to shed some light on this. [Buta Singh told me when he
was Home Minister that "he would not be a Sikh if he had not got the Ram
temple built at the disputed site".]

Affirming that the demolition structure was a mosque, Rao said:

"What else could it be? Was it a dwelling house? When the Government of
Uttar Pradesh says that namaz was going on there until 1949, irrespective of
the date, what else could it be but a mosque?"

Council for the Commission (Q): "Whether he had come across any anti-
Muslim rhetoric during the Ayodhya movement".

Mr. Rao (Answer): "As you find it today, as it has evolved today over a
period of time, yes it was there".

Q. BJP accused Congress government to get electoral benefits out of
Ramjanmbhoomi movement and the Congress allowed to have shilanyas near
the site of the masjid on Nov. 10, 1989.

Mr. Rao: "Personally I was not aware of the shilanayas but I can refer the
Hon'ble Commission to Mr. Buta Singh, who was then Home Minister, and
who, according to my information, was dealing with the subject from day to
day. I believe that he will be able to shed some light on this."

Q. How do you see the role of VHP and Dharma Sansad?

Mr. Rao: I refused to acknowledge them as organizations.

Q. What about cultural nationalism.

Mr. Rao: "Indian culture went far out of India, it also spread to Indonesia,
Thailand and so many other areas. So the geographical entity which is
called 'India' today is much smaller than what is comprehended in the
phrase "Indian culture'."

The Liberhan Commission gave Rao a clean chit, but a comment of Rahul
Gandhi, Sonia Gandhi's son, was significant. During an election campaign
he said that if someone from the Gandhi family had been there, the masjid
wouldn't have fallen.

That temple is still there under government protection. I learnt later that
State Minister for Home Affairs Rajesh Pilot told Rao that he could remove
the temple overnight but Rao did not allow him to do so. I do not think any
government at the Centre will dare to demolish the temple that has arisen
overnight. Any such step would arouse a groundswell of anger from the majority
community, however reprehensible the demolition of the Babri Masjid.

Rajiv Gandhi too is not immune from the blame because he began his
election campaign from the place adjacent to Babri Masjid and laid the
Shilanayas (on 10 November 1989) despite the Allahabad High Court ruling
that the status quo be maintained at the disputed site.

Advani's *rath* yatra brought the communal politics of the Sangh Parivar, Vishwa Hindu Parishad, Bajrang Dal, and BJP into full focus, and it was self-evident that Advani had an eye on the UP elections. He reaped the harvest when the BJP won 57 seats in UP.

The RSS which assured control of these factions I installed Kalyan Singh as chief minister (24 June 1991) and prepared to demolish the masjid in a planned operation. Kalyan Singh and L.K. Advani's hands were stained with blood of Muslims who were killed in the wake of masjid's demolition.

Liberhan took seventeen years to prepare the report but gave an accurate account of what had happened. The RSS and BJP leaders had toured the entire country collecting money for the construction of the temple and spread communal venom.

Liberhan held 68 persons culpable, including L.K. Advani, Murli Manohar Joshi, Kalyan Singh and, surprisingly, Atal Bihari Vajpayee who appeared to have distanced himself from the Ramjanmabhoomi campaign. (When Vajpayee came to London I was high commissioner. He stayed with me. I asked him why he had come here and not gone to Ayodhya as other BJP leaders were doing. Vajpayee said: '*Jo mandir ke bhagat hain wo Ayodhya gaye aur jo desh ke bhagat hain wo yahan aa gaye.*' [Those who are devotees of the temple have gone there and those who are lovers of the country have come here.']

The Babri Masjid demolition shocked me beyond measure. I knew that the BJP would try to create some mischief there but did not expect the party to go to the extent of destroying the mosque. A few Gandhians rang me from Ayodhya two days before the demolition saying they had been beaten up by RSS workers because of their silent march for the protection of the mosque.

The masjid for me was more than a structure. It represented our pluralistic ethos and the composite culture which we had built brick by brick over the centuries. I was not present at the site but saw everything on television. Subsequently, I watched a documentary which showed all that happened in graphic detail.

That the RSS and its *parivar* were triumphant was not surprising but some of the images, for instance Uma Bharti jumping on Murli Manohar Joshi's shoulders were quite shameful. I was certain about Kalyan Singh's active participation and thought the Supreme Court let him off excessively lightly when it imprisoned him for only one day as punishment for contempt of court. He had brazenly flouted the Supreme Court order to the Uttar Pradesh government to maintain the status quo.

I wondered whether Vajpayee's remark to me at London was serious because the day after the demolition I met him to request that the BJP should make amends. I was horrified when he said: 'Let the temple come up.' My experience tells me that the liberal Vajpayee took a back seat whenever the RSS asserted itself. Liberhan was correct in characterizing Vajpayee as a 'pseudo-moderate'. The observation in the report was: 'There can be no greater betrayal or crime in a democracy and this Commission has no hesitation in condemning these pseudo-moderates for their sins of omission.'

I also met Jaswant Singh, a BJP leader who was then a close friend. I told him that he should resign from the party. He said he had not slept all night and was deeply disturbed by the destruction of the Babri Masjid. 'Suppose I were to resign, tell me which party should I join?', he asked. I told him that was his business but he could not remain in a party that had severely damaged India's pluralism. I could appreciate his feelings but I began distancing myself from him.

Riots in Mumbai broke out when followers of the Shiv Sena and BJP came out on the streets to celebrate the demolition of the masjid raising anti-Muslim slogans, and as had been the case in earlier riots, the police sided with the majority community. The riots shook Narasimha Rao and he sent Defence Minister Sharad Pawar to Mumbai to supervise the arrangements to curb them but did not requisition the army. This reminded me of the 1984 riots in Delhi. A contingent of the army undertook a flag march in Mumbai, as was the case in 1984 in Delhi but only after the full fury of the riots had subsided.

The Government of India appointed Justice B.N. Srikrishna to inquire into the riots of Mumbai during December 1992–January 1993. After the announcement was made there were bomb blasts in Mumbai (25 May 1993). Muslims were so incensed by the masjid's demolition and the murder of so many members of their community that they retaliated. The Srikrishna Commission's terms of reference were expanded to include the bomb blasts.

The Commission's verdict was damning. Shiv Sena leader Bal Thackeray, MP Madhukar Sarpotdar, and other leaders like Gajanan Kirtikar, and Milind Vaidya were directly indicted. The report was also critical of 'Muslim aggression'. Srikrishna also made adverse remarks against the Mumbai police.

I was so impressed by the Srikrishna Report that I rang Justice Srikrishna to congratulate him when I was in Mumbai within a week of the report's publication. I went to personally tell him what a wonderful job he had done to strengthen the cause of justice and fair play. I was surprised to find in his room life-size idols of gods and goddesses and a *kamandal* (a vessel which Hindus carry in water to a temple). Finding me somewhat surprised, Srikrishna said that he was 'a practising Hindu' and went to the temple every day.

Aware of Pawar's proximity to Shiv Sena I did not expect any action against Bal Thackeray but thought the government would take some action, particularly against the police officers mentioned in the Srikrishna Report. Nothing happened and the report was filed like so many others on the riots. One day I rang Srikrishna in Delhi and he remarked that had he known about the fate of the report he would have not accepted chairmanship of the commission. 'I could have disposed of many cases during the time I wasted at the commission.'

I wish the lack of action on the Srikrishna Report had evoked a countrywide debate on Hindu–Muslim relations and the role of the security agencies when dealing with the minority community. Nothing of the kind took place.

The prejudice between the two communities continues to be demonstrated in one form or another. Partition, it seems, has only aggravated the issue and not solved it in any way. The two-nation theory has disturbed the sense of accommodation between the two communities that was shown when they lived together for centuries. The countryside in India remains more or less unaffected and follows ancient traditions and norms. Despite the deliberate policy of the RSS *parivar* to establish a Hindu *rashtra* (nation) the country is by and large pluralistic. In recent times the evidence of Muslim extremism has also surfaced but appears to take inspiration more from across the border than from what happens within India. For the past two years the evidence of Hindu terrorism has also come to the fore. This is ominous for the future.

Studies by the home ministry have revealed that communal riots have their source more or less in equal proportion, 50 per cent instigated by Hindus and 50 per cent by Muslims. The studies have, however, shown that the loss of Muslim lives is far in excess of Hindu lives. Another disturbing aspect which the studies have revealed is that over the years the rioters have developed a passion to kill rather than injure.

Of some twenty-five inquiry reports on riots in India which I have analyzed I have found that the same old issues such as playing music in front of a mosque, the route of a procession, and raising provocative slogans lead to the initial trouble which essentially testifies to the failure of intelligence to anticipate a riot or identify extremists seeking to foment trouble. The authorities choose to take only perfunctory action, if any at all, before a riot occurs, which is generally one sided because the police tend to side with the majority community.

Inquiry commissions appointed in the 1970s and later make one point in common: the anti-Muslim policy of the RSS has fouled the atmosphere. Even at places where Hindus and Muslims have lived peacefully for centuries, the RSS has been able to foul the environment. There are innumerable examples of this.

⁂

The Congress cauldron was boiling, not because of the Babri Masjid's demolition but because of internal conflicts. Sonia Gandhi never liked Narasimha Rao, particularly when he assumed both leadership of the Congress party and its government. She did not want to join issue with him, preferring to remain aloof from party matters. Even so, the infighting within the Congress and its shrinking space in the country bothered her. Many Congress leaders from the Centre and the states met her individually to appeal to her to lead the party. To them she seemed the only person who represented the consensus in the party.

Her inclination was to stay away from politics, as she had advised her husband to do. Even so, she was convinced that the future of the country was interlinked with the future of the Congress. Her gravest concern was that communal forces, representing the BJP were claiming the political space. The only occasion I spoke to her she came across as a committed secularist who firmly believed that pluralism was the bedrock of Indian society. She devoted 50 minutes out of one hour to underline how democracy and whatever economic plan the nation had in mind would go awry if communalism was not suppressed. I could gauge that she was coming around to the view that she would have to join politics if she wanted to fight against communalism and that the only instrument she had for this was the Congress.

Had she wanted the party's presidentship she could have merely sent a message to Sitaram Kesri, who was holding the charge, to resign and he would have obeyed her even if Rao had opposed the move. Kesri told me that she wanted to publicly demonstrate the strength she wielded in the Congress. She therefore held a parallel meeting of key Congress leaders at the very time when Kesri called them to his house. Virtually no one came for Kesri's meeting and he resigned. He went out, unwept and unsung although he had been the party's treasurer for many decades. He was hardly a person to evoke attention because he was involved in too many scandals and undesirable people in the country. My regret was over the manner in which he was pushed out. Did this reflect Congress culture? During Sonia Gandhi's tenure as party chief, the Congress blossomed and went from strength to strength.

※

In the elections in 1996, the BJP was the largest party with 161 seats. The Congress under Sonia Gandhi won 140, trailing the BJP by 21. I was therefore surprised to hear the BJP claim that it would be able to muster sufficient votes to prove its majority. President K.R. Narayanan's decision to give it an opportunity to prove its majority on the floor of the House was that it was the largest party in the Lok Sabha. I did not see any other political party supporting the BJP and wondered how it would reach the magic figure of 277 in the 545-member House. On the thirteenth day, before seeking the vote of confidence, Prime Minister Atal Bihari Vajpayee said that he was going to submit the resignation of his government because no party had agreed to support them. I saw from the press gallery the first BJP government since Independence resigning. It had been a foolhardy exercise destined to end unceremoniously.

The Congress party had no choice other than to support a hastily cobbled together 15-party minority government. This was the United Front coalition which came to power with the sole purpose of 'containing communal forces and consolidating the secular forces'. That was how first Deve Gowda and then Inder Gujral became prime ministers.

Once the Congress party decided to support Third Front candidates comprising non-Congress and non-BJP members it became clear that one among them could become prime minister. Their first choice was V.P. Singh but he vanished from his house and could not be traced. All eyes turned towards Jyoti Basu, the then communist chief minister of West Bengal. He was inclined to accept the offer provided his party's politburo permitted him to do so, but permission was denied. Anil Biswas, the then CPM general secretary in West Bengal was quite adamant. He explained to me that they did not wish to form a government until their party achieved a majority in the Lok Sabha. I told him that such an expectation was a pipe dream.

The hardliners, who held the majority in the politburo, were ideologically correct but they lost an opportunity which Jyoti Basu later described as a 'historic blunder'. The problem with most politburo members was that they had little contact with the outside world, and this was illustrated by the photographs they displayed at their office. They were of Stalin, Lenin, Engels, and Karl Marx; they continued to live in a world that had collapsed after the end of the Cold War in 1990. The hardliners could not visualize the boost the party would have got and its expanded base with Jyoti Basu at the helm of affairs. I knew Jyoti Basu well and felt that India had lost an opportunity to be ruled by an individual with a strong commitment to the amelioration of the conditions of the poor.

When Jyoti Basu declined, the Third Front settled on Deve Gowda from Karnataka whose name was proposed by Lalu Prasad Yadav. Perhaps the name of Ram Krishna Hegde, also from Karnataka, would have won the day if he had been present at the meeting. However, as he told me later, he was intentionally misled about the venue of the meeting.

Deve Gowda was a disaster as prime minister (from June 1996 to April 1997). He claimed he would perform miracles for Indian farmers but got mixed with dubious deals through his Man Friday C.M. Ibrahim who was the information minister in his government.

Deve Gowda's known contribution was the Ganga water sharing accord signed on 12 December 1996 between him and the Bangladesh Prime Minister Sheikh Hasina. The Farakka Barrage Agreement, as it is called, owed a lot to then West Bengal Chief Minister Jyoti Basu. He agreed to release more water than he had been willing to do earlier. This was a great sacrifice on his part as he had built the second Hooghly bridge sufficiently high to allow the passage of large ships to the Calcutta port. Besides that, Haldia port was also endangered because the silt in the Hooghly might not one day allow tankers to reach the oil refineries.

Basu's gesture was hailed by Bangladesh. Many years later, Mamata Banerjee, the West Bengal chief minister, let down Dhaka, particularly Prime Minister Manmohan Singh, when she did not honour her word to release more water from the River Teesta. She changed her mind because of the Communist threat. This lost India Bangladesh's goodwill.

The Congress was soon 'disillusioned' with Deve Gowda and wanted the Third Front to elect a new leader. Harkishan Singh Surjeet, the CPM general secretary, who was Deve Gowda's mentor, tried his utmost to sustain his prime-ministership but the ambitious Sitaram Kesri, then heading the Congress, had his eye on the office. He found no support either within his own party or from the Third Front. The Congress was still unable to muster the necessary support it sought. The party which had provided the Third Front with the numbers necessary for its survival as a government insisted on a new leader. Deve Gowda had no choice but to submit his resignation. The fact was that Sonia Gandhi wanted more time for the Congress to rehabilitate itself.

The names of Inder Gujral and Chandrababu Naidu came up. The CPM general secretary, Harkishan Singh Surjeet, again opposed both but did not pursue the matter. He zeroed in on Mulayam Singh Yadav and brought Jyoti Basu around to accept his candidature. Basu counted a great deal because the communist members represented a sizeable chunk of the Third Front.

Surjeet was strongly opposed to Gujral, having scores to settle with him from the days when they were both members of the communist party in Lahore. It was a miracle therefore that Gujral did eventually become prime minister.

As luck would have it Surjeet had to go to Moscow on the day the Third Front was to elect a leader. Gujral was a friend of mine and I was keen that he become prime minister. He rang me up and asked me to meet Jyoti Basu at Bangla Bhawan in Delhi on the morning of the election. When I met him, Sitaram Yechuri was sitting with him. I cautioned Jyoti Basu that Mulayam Singh had a reputation of sorts, and Yechuri confirmed this. It appeared that Jyoti Basu was not particularly against Gujral but had gone along with Surjeet because he depended upon 'his judgement' in such matters. Jyoti Basu agreed that Gujral would make a better prime minister than Mulayam Singh, and the latter was considered for deputy prime-ministership. Gujral did not however favour the proposal and I think that Naidu could have got the post but he said that he had to strengthen his party in Andhra Pradesh, the Telugu Desam. At that time N.T. Rama Rao's wife, Lakshmi Parvathi, posed a challenge by presenting herself as her husband's successor. Gujral was rung up. By the time I contacted his home, he had already been conveyed the news and was closeted with Basu.

The Gujral government (April 1997–March 1998) was known for its accommodation with neighbouring countries. He respected their sensitivities and went to great lengths to fulfill these. This policy of placating neighbours even at the cost of compromising some of our own interests became known as the 'Gujral Doctrine'. This without doubt brought about a marked improvement in our relations with Pakistan.

At the summit at Male, Gujral was able to persuade the then Pakistan Prime Minister Nawaz Sharif to resume trade between the two countries and at the same time to appoint a committee to discuss Kashmir. The important point here was that trade would not be dependent on the progress of talks on Kashmir.

The two prime ministers also agreed to institute a barter system to enable both India and Pakistan to exchange goods, without, for the time being, having to bother about the adverse balance of trade. Sadly, the mind-set of the bureaucrats from Pakistan ruined the deal. One of them said during the meeting: '*Mian sahib,* what about Kashmir?' Nawaz Sharif remained silent and then went on to discuss trade with Gujral. Trade was, however, never resumed and it became apparent that the bureaucrat's remark proved to be the last word.

On Kashmir, Gujral and I had frequent long discussions and we agreed that an autonomous status within India was the way out. As prime minister, he declared during his visit to Srinagar that the solution had to be within the parameters of the Indian union, but not necessarily within the ambit of the Indian constitution. There was a strong adverse reaction to this statement and Gujral had to change his position and announce that what he had meant was within the limits of the constitution. Both RAW and IB blamed me for Gujral's original statement.

When Gujral was prime minister, Yasin Malik was again imprisoned in Delhi for having threatened to go on a fast outside parliament to protest against oppression in the Valley. CPI leader Indrajit Gupta was the home minister then.

I met him in connection with Yasin Malik's release. Indrajit Gupta was himself unhappy about the detention. His secretary rang up the jail authorities, and I got him released. Parliament was still in session then. The following day some members attacked Indrajit Gupta for 'hobnobbing with the separatists'. His response was that he wished he could contact more and more of them and persuade them to join the mainstream.

While Gujral was at the helm, he undertook a tour of South Africa and Egypt in October 1997. I accompanied him as a journalist. My purpose was to see the country where Gandhi had experimented with his satyagraha, an antidote to the class struggle, because a satyagrahi was required to purify himself in order to serve the society without any ulterior motive. I visited the railway station where a pamphlet is available relating how Gandhiji was thrown out of a first-class railway compartment exclusively reserved for whites.

When visiting various parts in South Africa, particularly Cape Town, I felt that by and large the blacks still lived at the margins. True, apartheid had been dismantled and political power transferred to the blacks but the reality was that both the blacks and whites still lived in two different worlds, the former still generally poor and the latter abnormally well off. I found the blacks frustrated that they still had not received their due in their own country. The whites owned vast tracts of land, lived in luxurious villas, and held top jobs in the bureaucracy. I wondered whether the country was sitting on a volcano which would burst one day. The presence of Nelson Mandela had a soothing impact, but for how long it was difficult to gauge.

It was my long cherished desire to meet Nelson Mandela. He had retired from the position of president he had occupied after the apartheid had ended. I asked him how long the blacks would wait. He said that Mahatma Gandhi had taught them that violence or force did not solve any problem; generosity and forgiveness were the ultimate values.

I changed the subject and asked him how he had spent some twenty-three years in the jail on an island which was visible from Cape Town. He said that the jail staff had been kind to him and allowed him and his comrades in jail to be together all the time. 'Every piece of news reached us,' he said, 'and we knew that we would one day win the right to rule ourselves.'

What surprised me was his preference for Nehru over Gandhi. South Africa wanted to pursue Nehru's path of rebuilding the country and imbibed his approach of harnessing the support of their erstwhile British rulers to develop the country. Nehru had built institutions like parliament and the judiciary. These had ensured that India would remain democratic and pluralistic, Mandela said. He had created an atmosphere that radiated self-confidence and self-reliance and permitted the development of a normal and friendly relationship with the British.

My meeting with Mandela was a memorable moment in my life. Later, at night, there was a banquet in honour of Gujral where Mandela broke into dance and dragged Gujral on to the floor.

While we were on a state visit to South Africa, at home, a constitutional crisis awaited Gujral. Joginder Singh, director CBI, was determined to arrest Bihar Chief Minister Lalu Prasad Yadav with the help of a local army contingent because the deputy commissioner had refused to do so. Gujral got Lalu to step down and his wife, straight from the kitchen, sworn in.

Gujral's bonanza to government servants on the recommendations of the pay commission was too heavy a burden on the exchequer at a time when India was not in sound economic health. Had he implemented the other recommendations, such as the 30 per cent cut in the bureaucracy and extended working hours, some balance might have been struck. Gujral was under pressure from the trade unions and the Left. The hike unbalanced the Central budget and was beyond the capacity of the states when they too were obliged to follow suit.

Kesari's personal ambition did not permit another non-Congress government to continue and therefore fresh elections were inevitable. By then I was in the Rajya Sabha to which Gujral government had nominated me.

17

MY TRYST WITH PARLIAMENT

The Right to Information Act, Kashmir and Pakistan, the Terrorist Attack on Parliament, Elections to the Rajya Sabha, Vajpayee's Bus Ride to Lahore

With mixed feelings I entered the Rajya Sabha: mixed because I held the House in high esteem and had witnessed some of the most eloquent addresses by distinguished orators and dedicated public servants as Bhupesh Gupta, Hiren Mukherjee, and Hridaynath Kunzru. In the face of this I found myself vastly inadequate in terms of eloquence or erudition. I also had reservations about how the political parties would react to my presence because I had relentlessly criticized them in my columns. Would I be able to make any substantial contribution to the deliberations and the legislation in the House was the question uppermost in my mind.

I was delighted to find my entire family in the visitors' gallery when I took oath in the Rajya Sabha. My wife Bharti was there as well as my sister, Raj, brother-in-law, Rajinder Sachar, their daughter Madhu, my daughters-in-law, the two Kavitas (both of them have the same name), my sons, Sudhir and Rajiv, and my grandchildren, Mandira, Kartik, and Kanika. They were thrilled to see me taking a seat in the house.

The first thing I did after taking the oath was to send a statement of assets, my own and those of my wife, to Chairman Krishan Kant. The Rajya Sabha secretary told me that there was no such practice and the secretariat did not know what they should do with a declaration of assets. I told him that he should file it wherever he thought fit and should compare it with that I submitted the following year.

Subsequently, when the business of the House was marred by frequent walk outs and forced adjournments, I wrote to the chairman that I did not wish to draw any allowances on days when the House failed to transact any business. The chairman was nonplussed and referred the matter to the law ministry. I was happy to learn that the ministry was agreeable to my proposal.

I continued this practice to forego the daily allowance whenever the House did not transact any business.

The coldest reception as a Rajya Sabha member I received was from Congress MPs. They nurtured a grievance over my vehement criticism of Indira Gandhi's rule during the Emergency. I found even Manmohan Singh, then the leader of the Opposition, who knew me personally, deliberately distancing himself as if afraid to be on familiar terms with me.

My nomination was for eminence in journalism (literature). Six more joined me to fill the vacancies. Under the constitution, the President of India could nominate twelve members, one-third retiring every year, for having 'special knowledge or practical experience in respect of ... literature, science, art and social service'.

The BJP was understandably angry with me because of my criticism of their policy for Hindutva, but even so several of its members were warmer than the Congressmen. The greater part of my six-year tenure (1997–2003) was during the National Democratic Alliance (NDA) coalition government, headed by Atal Bihari Vajpayee. He was at least civil and polite to me. We had once been very close. I, together with the late J.D. Sethi, an economist, used to have tea with him virtually every evening. Vajpayee was fond of *jalebis* and *kachoris* and so were we. These two delicacies were specially brought from Chandni Chowk.

My maiden speech, which lasted 30 minutes, focused on the nation's failure to establish a secular polity. I wondered where we had gone wrong and why our efforts had not shown results. True, I ascribed most of the blame on communal forces without naming any specific party and lamented that the secular forces had not been sufficiently strong or cohesive to prevail. I reminded the House of the nation's struggle for Independence under Mahatma Gandhi who preached secularism to his last breath.

When I came to the contribution made by Jayaprakash Narayan to the country I saw Pranab Mukherjee leaving. He was in fact formal and distant throughout my tenure in the Rajya Sabha. Even when he was the chairman of the Parliamentary Standing Committee on Home Affairs, of which I was a member, he was correct but not warm.

I recalled his phone call to the *Statesman* when I was resident editor, requesting me to have tea at his house. He held no government office then. We three, including his wife, sat on the floor and sipped tea which she had prepared. They had very little furniture and no servant. This reflected the austere living style of an average Bengali who had moved from a state to the nation's capital. His wife was a struggling dancer seeking to gain recognition. When he requested me to give her publicity, I realized why he had invited me to his house.

I met the same Mukherjee some years later during the Emergency. His house exuded opulence and the sitting room was cluttered with stylish furniture, plush carpets, and sparkling silver. He was then commerce minister, a trusted hand of Sanjay Gandhi.

In Rajya Sabha, the nominated members sat together in the centre of the hall. Dr Raja Ramanna, a distinguished scientist, sat to my left and the famous film director Mrinal Sen to my right. Shabana Azmi was at the beginning of the row. As Mrinal showed up very rarely, Shabana and I sat together most of the time. I had great respect for her as an actor, yet finding her next to me made me happy in a different way. Though I did not attempt to flirt with her, the temptation was there. Her attitude was so matter-of-fact that she deterred me. Once I told her that despite my best efforts she did not care a fig. Her reply was: *aisi bhi baat nahin*.

We would discuss a variety of subjects, largely concerning poverty in India. She was doing commendable work for the people living in the slums of Mumbai. We were like-minded in the sense both of us were secular in our outlook and left-of-centre in ideology. One thing about which we strongly concurred was that marriage should be a contract for a fixed period and automatically end after the expiry of this. She would often urge me to reply to Arun Shourie, a BJP member, who frequently expressed his jingoistic views laced with the BJP ideology.

Dr Ramanna once related to me how Saddam Hussain had, when he visited Baghdad, offered him a blank cheque for know-how for the construction of a nuclear device. Saddam was surprised when Ramanna refused to divulge any details. Ramanna never visited Iraq again for fear of Saddam's ire. Before meeting as members of the Rajya Sabha Ramanna and I had met at Tirupati, the temple town, where we both received awards for contributions in our respective fields. He confided to me then that both Pakistan and India had nuclear bombs. The information about Pakistan came as a surprise because its possession of a nuclear device became public much later.

Within a few days of my nomination to the Rajya Sabha, a member of the House met me to inquire what I proposed to do with my Member of Parliament Local Area Development (MPLAD) allocation of a crore of rupees. Before I could reply, he said that I need only sign the papers for withdrawal of the fund allotted to me and he would give me Rs 50 lakhs. I was shocked by the offer, but asked how this was managed. He said that on paper a bridge or a road would be constructed and then washed away by rains. This would also enable the sanctioning authorities to receive their share from the money drawn.

I was disappointed with the nonchalant atmosphere in the Rajya Sabha. Both the content and quality of speeches had fallen very substantially since I had covered the Rajya Sabha some 45 years earlier. Most members would look at the press gallery whenever their turn came and often spoke only for effect. A few even distributed a prepared copy of their speech among journalists.

I was also disappointed that even the best presentations went unreported or were cursorily dismissed by the media. Once the chairman of the Rajya Sabha consulted me on how they could get the proceedings reported in the media. I told him that it was largely dependent on the reporters covering parliament or the space a newspaper devoted to parliament on a particular day.

I suggested that meetings of the parliamentary standing committees be thrown open to the press to motivate greater coverage. Both the Speaker of the Lok Sabha and the chairman of the Rajya Sabha opposed the idea. I could see little logic in their rejection because the proceedings of standing committees were recorded verbatim, including the testimonies of bureaucrats, experts, and other outsiders, and placed on the table of the House, along with the report. Therefore, the argument of secrecy did not hold.

Somnath Chatterjee, the Speaker during those years, did some PR exercise and invited editors and senior journalists in batches to his house to persuade them to carry the proceedings in parliament. Nothing came of the exercise. A noisy, boisterous House still made a far better story than a serious, well-researched presentation by an MP.

During his tenure, Chatterjee did pioneering work in inviting intellectuals, legal luminaries, and other eminent persons to the three round-table conferences he convened to discuss the situation in the country. The public never learnt about such an exercise which was a serious attempt on the speaker's part to diagnose the nation's ills. How the conditions prevailing in India could be improved was the subject of the conference I attended. In my presentation I dwelt upon how the total negation of morality from politics had adversely affected all aspects of life in India.

Somnath Chatterjee and I became quite friendly. He confided in me how hurt he was when the Communist Party of India (Marxist) unilaterally expelled him and cancelled his membership of the party. The fault ascribed to him had been that he had presided over the debate on the nuclear energy agreement with the US. The CPM was totally opposed to any such understanding with the US. He wondered how he could have avoided presiding over the debate when he considered the issue crucial for the nation. He could not have run away from the responsibility of maintaining decorum when he saw how hopelessly divided the House was. He said he would have carried out the party's fiat to resign after the fate of the bill had been decided. I believe the decision to expel him was that of the hard-line Prakash Karat, and in consequence the CPM lost an honest and dedicated leader of the masses.

I invited Chatterjee to speak at the function I held to release my book *Without Fear* on Shaheed Bhagat Singh's life. He was very complimentary about the book and said it was the work of someone who had lived through the ups and downs both of the freedom movement and of the march of free India. 'In more ways than one, Shri Nayar has been one of the activists in that march and one who has walked by the values that our Founding Fathers cherished.'

I was a member of the Standing Committee on Home Affairs when it was entrusted with the Right to Information Bill (RTI). We discussed it threadbare and I was constantly in touch with Aruna Roy, a pioneer of the Right to Information movement to learn what she thought of its provisions. I defended her points of view at the committee.

Many of Aruna's suggestions were incorporated in the bill. Sometimes I consulted her over my mobile while at the meeting of the standing committee. The bill did not fulfill all her expectations. She advised me to accept whatever was offered so that the country would at least have some legislation to establish a citizen's right to information.

When some of my suggestions were accepted I left it at that. I had not, however, anticipated the revolutionary effect the act would have in bringing about some transparency in the government. I knew there were some loopholes but I had never imagined that officials would exploit those to keep most secrets under wraps, on the plea that the discloser of this or that piece of information was not in the 'public interest'.

A few years earlier Aruna Roy had invited me to Bhilwara in Rajasthan where she and some villagers were sitting in a dharna to demand the right to information. I sat in the burning sun to demonstrate my solidarity with what she was doing.

Subsequently, I participated in many other agitations for the same purpose. Twice or thrice, I headed the delegation to meet the then state Chief Minister Bhairon Singh Shekhawat, to demand access to details of expenditure incurred on projects in the rural areas of Rajasthan. I told him how his own engineers had appeared before the public in certain villages and made a clean breast of their dishonesty and admitted to having pilfered funds allocated for a particular project. Bhairon Singh did nothing about it.

Many months later Shekhawat met me to inform that the demand we had made had already been granted in the Gazette notification he had brought with him. I have never been able to resolve the mystery of the notification because if there had been one he would have shown it to us much earlier.

I used the RTI facilities in 2008 when I wanted access to the Henderson Brookes inquiry report on the 1962 border debacle with China. This was written by two senior army officers, Lt Gen. Henderson Brooks and Lt Gen. Prem Bhagat. Their report is nearly fifty years old and yet the government has kept it under wraps.

The government got away under cover of 'public interest'. Nowhere in the world has the army been able to deprive the public on facts on such an important chapter in India's history for such a long period under the cover of secrecy. It is a pity that the Central Information Commission comprising two retired civil servants, Wajahat Habibullah and M.L. Sharma, were unable to rise above the hangover of their loyalty to the establishment. They rejected my plea to make the report public. Even so, I would say that Wajahat Habibullah has expanded the contours of the act. I have disagreed with him sometimes but there was no doubt about his commitment to transparency.

The non-disclosure of the report confirms my view that the army in India is a sacred cow. The public, particularly the media, is so circumspect when it comes to discussing the armed forces that even mild criticism is avoided, lest it should adversely affect the 'morale' of the armed forces. This craven attitude has allowed the armed forces to get away even with murder.

The commission's verdict was so palpably wrong that it went against the grain of intelligence. It considered the issue of the India–China border to be 'alive' because of the 'ongoing negotiations' between the two countries. It did not want to lift the lid from a scandal of cowardice and arrogance. The commission should be aware that the negotiations began long before the hostilities, and were in progress when I was information officer with the then home minister, G.B. Pant, in 1957.

The former chief of the army staff, General V.P. Malik reacted appropriately to the withholding of the report. He publicly criticized the judgement, arguing that it was not in the public interest to keep the 1962 report secret. He said that both weaponry and tactics had undergone an enormous transformation since those days so there was no question of secrecy in the national interest.

My feeling is that as the responsibility for the India–China war had been laid at Nehru's door the government was unwilling to make the report public. It is amusing that Justice Hamoodur Rahman should lay the blame on the army, not politicians for Pakistan's defeat in Bangladesh while the Henderson Brooks Commission headed by a former army officer absolved the men from the services and held politicians responsible. A war lost because of the failure of the army and the then rulers' ineptness can neither endanger external nor internal security. My appeal against the order at the Delhi High Court is still pending.

When the bill to spell out the control over CBI came before the home affairs parliamentary committee, I was still a member of it. The Chief Justice of India J.S. Verma had proposed in a hawala case an independent Directorate of Prosecution (DOP) control the CBI. No political party – all of them were represented in the committee – wanted the CBI to become autonomous. I was disappointed when Justice Verma's proposal was rejected and administrative control of the government was endorsed. So much so, that the committee restored the Single Directive which the Supreme Court had thrown out. The Single Directive meant that the government's permission was required before initiating an enquiry or action against joint secretaries and officers above them. There is hardly any minister who does not use the CBI for his or her party's interests. Details of the 2G Spectrum scandal, now revealed by the CBI, shows how ministers flouted all rules in the allotment of licences and were in league with corporate houses.

At the standing committee on home affairs we also discussed Kashmir and visited the state once when Pranab Mukherjee was still the chairman. However, it was disappointing that no one from the Hurriyat, the Bar, or the students met us. Even so, we wrote a long report, underlining the state's 'permanent' integration with India. The committee was reluctant to venture beyond the beaten track.

Farooq Abdullah, who was the state chief minister, had done better. Leading the National Conference, he got the state assembly to pass a resolution that Kashmir should return to the status it enjoyed immediately after its accession to India in 1951. The resolution reiterated that New Delhi would only exercise control over foreign affairs, defence, and communications, the three subjects which the Maharaja of Jammu & Kashmir had ceded to the Centre when signing the instrument of accession. The standing committee was unhappy about the resolution but even more so about the violence that had begun overtaking the valley. The alienation was so palpable that I could taste it.

While in Srinagar, I received a call from Prime Minister Vajpayee to request Farooq not to press the state assembly resolution. I met him over breakfast and conveyed the request which he accepted. I wondered why New Delhi was not willing to honour even the terms of the instrument of accession. How then could there be any meeting point with the Hurriyat which had demanded *azadi*.

However, Vajpayee never consulted me on Pakistan. In fact, one day, when intervening in the debate on the general budget he made an observation relating me and Pakistan. I had gone to the Notice Room of the Rajya Sabha to make an urgent call. In my absence Vajpayee looked toward my vacant seat and said: 'Where has he gone? To Pakistan?' Some leftist members protested his comment, and told me about it when I returned to my seat. Vajpayee responded that it had been a jocular remark. Even so, the anti-Pakistan feeling was strong in the BJP. Vajpayee was an exception because he realized that without an equation with Islamabad he would not receive the attention he sought from world leaders.

The party's bias was clear from the uproar an observation of mine evoked during a speech by Deputy Prime Minister L.K. Advani. He was blaming the ISI for the minutest disturbance in any part of India. Standing up in the House, I said the reaction in Pakistan was no different. Whenever there was even a tyre burst on any road they blamed RAW. The anger voiced by the BJP members to my observation was so noisy and prolonged that I was at a loss to understand why this was so. They demanded the deletion of my remark from the parliamentary proceedings, and the chairman ordered this to be done.

I was shocked when the BJP's unofficial organ, the *Pioneer*, demanded my impeachment the following day. I knew that it was a command performance because the editor was nominated to the Rajya Sabha by the BJP government. Even so, I wrote to the newspaper to register my protest against the charge of

India's betrayal in an editorial. The newspaper published my letter along with two others, one in my support and another against.

I also sent a complaint to the Privileges Committee of the House, arguing that the newspaper had violated a member's right by demanding his impeachment for views he was at full liberty to express. Najma Heptullah, deputy chairperson, was the head of the committee. For months I did not hear anything about my privilege motion. When I asked her about it, she cursorily remarked that it had been dropped because the editor had expressed regret. I said it was surprising that I had not been summoned by the committee and that its decision had not been communicated to me as was the practice. She did not heed my protest. For the first time I felt that even the privileges committee had given a judgement to suit the ruling party's position. I was therefore not surprised at all when the BJP gave her a Rajya Sabha ticket.

I got many threatening calls from Hindu chauvinists. I reproduce part of one letter which I received: 'I have been going through your articles for the last several years and have concluded that opposing Hinduism is your only and only "motto", which certainly is not expected from journalist of your calibre.'

Almost a decade later I was attacked for having attended a seminar convened by Ghulam Nabi Fai in Washington. He had been arrested as Pakistan's spy working for ISI on its Kashmir agenda. Those were the days when Washington and Islamabad were distancing from each other and asking their respective intelligence agents working in their countries to leave. This was a fallout of Osama Bin Laden's killing in Abbottabad at the hands of US navy SEALS.

I had been called a pro-Pakistani earlier but this time at least one television channel working for *aman* (peace) between the two countries characterized me as an 'anti-India intellectual'. I took the criticism as an instance of their ventilation of prejudice. I was unaware of who was financing Fai when I attended the one-day conference held at Capitol Hill. Some hot-headed Kashmiris, who have settled in Middle East, brought before the meeting a resolution to support Kashmir's *azadi*. I vehemently opposed it, as did the other three Indian participants. All that happened was the issue of a statement urging upon India and Pakistan a peaceful and amicable resolution of the Kashmir issue.

I do feel, however, that the Indian mission in Washington should have warned us against attending the seminar which they knew about. I had in fact contacted the embassy much in advance and shared details about the seminar.

What however surprises me is that all journalists go on free and lavish junkets organized by the US, UK, Germany and other countries without compunction but when it comes to Pakistan there is a deep prejudice. If it is a question of ethics, then all hospitality from other countries, including our own, should be refused but double standards prevail.

I found in the Rajya Sabha that the BJP was out to polarize the country and convert it from a secular to a Hindu state. The BJP was forever seeking any issue to communalize the atmosphere because that is their fundamental agenda. To them Pakistan is an enemy country. I do not agree with this formulation. True, Pakistan is intransigent but it is a neighbour with whom we have to live in peace, recognizing its sovereignty and independence of action. India and Pakistan have already fought three wars but neither has totally supervened. Now that both the nations have nuclear weapons the question of an all-out war doesn't arise. Even so, some fanatics and the Hindutva brigade want to wage a war but they too will one day have to realize that there is no alternative to peace.

***

A proposal before the committee on information was whether foreign equity should be available to the media. This question was confined to the press because television channels had already entered into contracts with foreign networks. I argued that foreign equity was of no benefit to India because the Indian press was inferior to none. Foreign journalists were no better than ours. At that time I carried the day. I found almost all the members, particularly Chairman Somnath Chatterjee, on my side.

On the virtually negligible opposition side was my friend, the late Narinder Mohan, editor of *Jagran*. He, however, had the last laugh because the craze for globalization made the Congress government to agree some years later to 26 per cent equity for foreigners.

In fact, all this began when Manmohan Singh was finance minister in the Narasimha Rao government and N.K.P. Salve was minister for information and broadcasting. I was able to persuade Salve to postpone the proposal for foreign equity in the mass media till after the polls which were due. He agreed and the press got a breather because the Congress lost the elections. It was, however, a different story altogether when the Congress returned to power. Foreign equity was one of the economic reforms which the party was proud to undertake.

One regrettable aspect of the standing committees' tours was its extraordinarily lavish life-style. Members were accommodated in 5-star hotels, provided with personal cars, and presented with gifts, all at the expense of one or other of the public-sector undertakings. I pointed out to Chairman Somnath Chatterjee that this was a waste of public funds and members should stay at the MLA hostels in various states. The chairman was not happy with the way things were conducted but rationalized the practice by saying that if members enjoyed luxury once in a while I should not object. Several years later, he wrote against the waste of public funds by the standing committees.

I had completed almost two-third of my tenure when terrorists attacked Parliament House on 13 December 2001. There was no business in the Rajya Sabha on that day and, as had been the case the day before, the chairman adjourned the house till Friday morning. I was making my way towards the exit near the Rajya Sabha when I remembered I had to take a form for a short-notice question. The Notice Office is just a few yards away from the entrance to the Rajya Sabha.

I initially ignored the few shots I heard, but then the shots continued uninterrupted and seemed to be coming from more than one direction. I was more curious than afraid. I rushed to the veranda that runs between the offices and the outer stone wall of Parliament House. There were security men running up and down. One of them said openly, 'We have been asking for arms but the home ministry has been rejecting our demand.'

Now, the shots were becoming louder than earlier. The assailants had also moved to other positions it appeared from the way the firing had spread. I walked leisurely to the main entrance of parliament, the door of which was closed. Within a few seconds I heard a loud explosion, followed by another.

It never occurred to me that the main wooden gate of Parliament House could be smashed and the assailants could march in. The massive walls of Parliament House gave me a curious sense of security. After 10–15 minutes of firing, I heard a bell ringing and sirens blaring a warning. Probably an afterthought; someone had suddenly remembered the safety rules.

The rumour among members was that one assailant had escaped and was hiding somewhere in inside the building. Security personnel scurried hither and thither. I was locked up in a lobby for 45 minutes after which I was let out, I went to the courtyard within Parliament House where life-size statues of Jawaharlal Nehru and Abul Kalam Azad stood. I wondered whether it had ever crossed their minds that one day the institution of democracy which they had nourished with their blood would be sullied by the blood of those who believed in violence and murder. The terrorists had shot at the guard when they were stopped at the gate. The police intervened and four militants were killed. Five policemen and security guards also lost their lives.

Tempers were frayed in the Central Hall. Two hours after the first shot was heard, the minister for parliamentary affairs, Pramod Mahajan, stood up on a table in the hall to announce that MPs could now leave, women first. The members of parliament were not panicky even in the first instance but appeared more than relieved when they heard that all was over. Information and Broadcasting Minister Sushma Swaraj refused to go with the caravan of women. I heard her saying something like, 'Let me find out what really happened'. By then, the army had arrived. The defence minister had personally rung up to summon the force. I saw some members thanking him, including those who had sought his resignation. It was a curious kind of camaraderie, reflecting a unity which the country assumes when confronting an external threat.

Was this an act of war? Parliament represents India's sovereignty. Alternatively, was it only the work of some bigoted extremists who had been brainwashed to understand the normal functioning of a society such as India's? I saw the body of one of the terrorists lying outside Parliament House's main gate and some pieces of luggage littered around. Democracy is an idea; a nation's determination that extremists can never understand. They only strengthen the belief that no price is too high to sustain freedom and democracy. I returned to parliament the following day as usual, as others did, to reaffirm our faith in the institution and to warn the assailants and their masters to keep their hands off.

Pramod Mahajan, who was the minister in charge of BJP's parliamentary affairs, was totally against my becoming a member of any of the committees. As we, the nominated and independent members had formed a group we were entitled to a seat in any of the House committees. He would say he was willing to nominate anyone as member but not Kuldip Nayar. I even wrote a letter to A.B. Vajpayee to draw attention to Mahajan's remark but did not receive even an acknowledgement. Mahajan was angry because I had criticized him in my columns. The first time he read one of the columns he rang me up to inquire how he could improve his image, to which I suggested that he could do so 'by talking less'.

Before Mahajan's order could prevail I had been elected to the Joint Committee on the Central Vigilance Commission Bill, 1999. In their judgement (December 1987) the Supreme Court had struck down, what had come to be known as the 'single directive'. This meant that the CBI could not investigate high-ranking bureaucrats (joint secretaries and above) without the prior sanction of the government.

After the first meeting of the committee I wrote a letter to Sharad Pawar, who was the chairman, to let every member of the committee declare his or her assets. I received no reply. When I raised this point during the committee's meeting, members laughed at my proposal and resumed their discussion.

The joint committee rejected the Supreme Court decision and restored the status quo ante. The result was that the government once again acquired powers to shield pliant and like-minded 'delinquent officers'. Such public servants who carry out the nefarious diktats of their political masters go scot free because permission for their prosecution is not forthcoming.

The report was unanimous barring my dissenting note in which I, inter alia, said:

> Some sort of quid pro quo has come to be established. The officer concerned may be making money on the side and his political bosses may be shutting their eyes to this because of 'services' rendered to them. Corrupt officers

have come to rule the roost due to their proximity to the seats of power. Increasingly, public servants are ceasing to be aware of what is right and may not have even desire to act according to what is right.

In my note I referred to the N.N. Vohra Committee Report which had pointed out the existence of a nexus between politicians, civil servants, and criminals; a mafia parallel to the government. 'If there is a prima facie case against anyone the CBI should straightaway move against him or her whether or not their rank is joint secretary or above'.

MPs from the Left sided with the government at the committee meetings. When I criticized them they promised to support me when the necessary legislation came before the House, but to my dismay they too went along with the government. I realized that the communists, who had governments in West Bengal, Kerala, and Tripura, were under the 'same compulsions' as the central government. It was strange to see the establishment and the Opposition uniting when it came to their personal interests.

⚙

The worst act of the Rajya Sabha was to amend a bill relating to election to the House. The operative clause substituted India in place of state. The amendment did away with the requirement of domicile for a Rajya Sabha member. According to the parliamentary rules and the spirit of the constitution, a candidate to the Rajya Sabha had to be 'ordinarily a resident of that state'. The substitution of word India and the deletion of state made a mockery of the constitution makers because they had provided for two Houses in parliament, one, the House of the people (Lok Sabha) for the country as a whole, and the second, the House of states (Rajya Sabha) to represent the states.

The bill also sought to do away with the secrecy of voting, fundamental in a democratic polity. A state legislature is not an auction house where a show of hands decides who among the members had garnered this or that number of votes. Money had begun playing a decisive role because a buyer could see for himself the number of votes he would get. In the past, some members would exercise their vote against the party's directive but now, according to the new bill, they had to show the ballot paper to the party's agent, and violation would cost them their membership. Curiously, election to the upper house in the states continued to be as of old, through a secret ballot, but the procedure for the Rajya Sabha was to be changed.

When the bill was passed despite my one member opposition, I wrote an article pointing out how the complexion of the Rajya Sabha had been changed. After reading the article, former President R. Venkataraman, a member of the constituent assembly, wrote to me that the amendment would defeat the real purpose of the Rajya Sabha, which was to give representation to the states. He referred to his discussion with the then law minister B.R. Ambedkar who had piloted the bill in the constituent assembly. Ambedkar had assured him that the purpose was to institute one house of the people and another representing the states.

On the basis of Venkataraman's letter and my article which appeared in the *Indian Express,* I wrote to the then Chief Justice of India V.N. Kher to argue that the new method of election to the Rajya Sabha defeated the letter and spirit of the constitution. Treating my letter as a public interest litigation (PIL), he immediately arranged for a hearing, about which the Registrar informed me just a night before.

I went, accompanied by my brother-in-law, former Chief Justice Rajinder Sachar. When I appeared before a division bench, presided over by the chief justice, the latter insisted on my arguing the case. 'We have read you and we want to hear you,' he said. I was somewhat nervous, but nonetheless stood before the bench and said that when I was studying at Law College, Lahore, my greatest ambition was to appear before the highest court of the land. I was unable to pursue the legal profession because of Partition and entered journalism. 'My dream has been realized today,' I said.

My plea was that the amendment had defeated the real purpose of the Rajya Sabha; the representation of states in parliament. Under the new dispensation, any person from any part of the country could get elected to the Rajya Sabha, without his or her being a resident of the state, and unfamiliar with its language and culture.

The division bench accepted my petition and stayed the elections to the Rajya Sabha and asked the constitution bench to decide upon the validity of the amendment. When I asked one judge on the division bench at a reception that very day why they had taken so little time in accepting my plea, he said: 'You were precise and to the point'. I wondered then whether I had missed my true vocation.

A lawyer representing the EC too was present at the hearing. I had sent the commission a copy of my letter to the chief justice. Even so, the commission went ahead with a notification of elections to the Rajya Sabha. I again knocked at the door of the Supreme Court. The vacation judge, Justice Ruma Paul, granted me a stay and ordered the EC to stop the process of Rajya Sabha elections until the disposal of my case. It created a furore in civil society.

The government woke up and appealed against Justice Paul's order to the division bench. As expected, the division bench, headed by Justice K.G. Balakrishnan, lifted the stay and ordered an early hearing of my case by the constitution bench. To the delight of the Congress and the BJP, the election to the Rajya Sabha was held.

Justice Santosh Hegde was heading the constitution bench at that time. He was willing to take up the case, but the opposition lawyers said that they would need some time to place their point of view before the court. The real reason was that they did not want to face a tough judge like Hegde, known for his integrity and independence, who they knew would soon be retiring.

The case did not come up for hearing for several months. Chief Justice Y.K. Sabarwal, after assuming office, constituted a five-judge bench to hear the case. It was heard daily for nearly two weeks. Justice Sachar and Fali Nariman argued on my behalf while Solicitor General Ghulam Vahanvati, now attorney general, opposed the petition. Arun Jaitley also chipped in on behalf of the Opposition. The judgement was reserved for a few days, but when it was pronounced it was a unanimous 5 to 0 verdict in favour of the government's point of view. It was a perverse judgement, and I said so in an interview to the media.

The court upheld the amendment which had done away with the residential qualification for a member of the Rajya Sabha and introduced an open rather than a secret ballot. The court failed to appreciate the role of the Rajya Sabha which was now in effect no longer a council of states but a council of freelancers.

The Supreme Court saw no merit in the elected member being from the state concerned, arguing that 'the electorate that is electing him is required by law to do so'. It was strange logic to justify the election of an outsider. The point at issue was not who could be elected but who could represent the state. Obviously, a person who normally lived in the state should be preferred to someone who had not, the former being familiar with the region's culture, problems, and aspirations.

My feeling is that the judges had political considerations at the back of their minds in arriving at the verdict. They were aware that Dr Manmohan Singh was a Rajya Sabha member from Assam and did not reside in the state. The domicile qualification, if retained, would have morally embarrassed him, although his membership had been legally upheld by the Supreme Court.

The Supreme Court gave a new title to the Rajya Sabha as a revising house. It was an independent house with its own duties and obligations whose role was not secondary to that of the Lok Sabha. All bills, except those relating to money matters, could be introduced in the Rajya Sabha. In matters concerning the states, the Rajya Sabha came first. All questions relating to the central services and the like were to be initiated in the Rajya Sabha. If the Supreme Court logic were to be accepted, the Lok Sabha would become a revising house for whatever emerged from Rajya Sabha. The bench had failed to understand that.

It is sad that the Supreme Court judgement has opened doors of the Rajya Sabha to money bags, the mafia, or the undesirable. It is becoming a hunting ground for those who have clout or deep pockets. Political bosses are now free to bring their favourites into the House from any nook and corner of India. The constitution lays down that only twelve members will be nominated to the Rajya Sabha. Now the entire strength of the House will be nominated by our political masters.

During my tenure as a member of the Rajya Sabha three general elections took place (1996, 1998, and 1999). In the 1998 election A.B. Vajpayee lost by a single vote. However, during his 13-month tenure he had the nuclear device exploded to go down in history. Vajpayee had asked the atomic scientists even in 1996, when he came to power, to explode the bomb. They were not, however, able to do so because his government lasted only thirteen days. Now they had all the necessary time.

India conducted five nuclear tests in Pokhran in May 1998, three on the 11th and two on the 13th. The US intelligence agencies failed to detect from air the movement of vehicles and men to Pokhran, the site of the explosion. Former Prime Minister Narasimha Rao had tried to explode a nuclear device but the US had detected the movement of vehicles from the air and stalled his initiative. The BJP government ensured that all movements took place stealthily in the dead of night.

President Bill Clinton was furious about the nuclear tests and announced all manner of sanctions to punish India, snapping all ties to ban the import of even low-level technology from the US. The enthusiasm in the country was at such a high pitch at that time that nobody bothered about what the US said or did.

Vajpayee, however, also realized that if he had to face Washington's wrath he must try to normalize relations with Islamabad. At Srinagar he declared that he would be travelling by a bus from Amritsar to Lahore meet Pakistan's Prime Minister Nawaz Sharif. This announcement transformed the atmosphere not only in the two parts of Kashmir but also in India and Pakistan. Vajpayee's words evoked a sense of expectation.

Two days before the bus journey the Pakistan high commissioner met me at a reception. He complained that the list of passengers notified to them comprised only secretaries to the Government of India and some other top-level officials. He said this was a good opportunity for the leaders of different political parties to travel by bus and meet leaders of the political parties in Pakistan. I told him that transporting politicians and secretaries in the bus was undertaking a useless exercise. I suggested that writers and artists be included. I took up the matter with prime minister's principal secretary, Brajesh Mishra (who I knew of through his father D.P. Mishra, a friend), at the reception itself. He said he favoured my proposal and promised to place it before the prime minister. Vajpayee welcomed the idea. (While Morarji Desai was prime minister he had at the instance of his friend D.P. Mishra's suggestion, superseded many foreign service officers to appoint Brajesh, his son, as India's representative to the UN.)

I was informed by the prime minister's press secretary Ashok Tandon that I was to travel in the prime minister's bus. I had been critical of the BJP but the criticism did not come in the way of selection. We flew to Amritsar where the chief minister of Punjab Prakash Singh Badal joined us.

With drum-beaters and a colourful bhangra party in front, the bus moved slowly towards the border. It was a ceremonial departure over in a few minutes. The bus was full of people who had distinguished themselves in the fields of film, dance, literature, and journalism. I remember among the passengers Dev Anand, Javed Akhtar, and Mallika Sarabhai. Scores of journalists and photographers had gone ahead, to the other side of the border to report the arrival of bus carrying the Indian prime minister, men of letters, and artistes.

It was a short trip of about 25 kilometre from Amritsar to the border. When travelling towards Pakistan, Vajpayee called me and showed me a message he had received: Twelve Hindus had been killed in the upper reaches of Jammu. 'What should I do?', he asked me. He had to bear in mind Indian public opinion. I said that terrorists had always tried to sabotage talks between India and Pakistan. This was yet another example of that.

Soon after I came back to my seat, I could hear the beat of drums from the Pakistan side; we were in fact on Pakistan soil. The ceremony was short and simple. The then Prime Minister Nawaz Sharif hugged Vajpayee and welcomed him. The three service chiefs of Pakistan registered their presence but did not salute the Indian prime minister. It was a defiance of sorts but they probably nurtured a guilt conscience because they had already planned the Kargil war.

During Vajpayee's stay at Lahore, a roadmap was prepared for the solution of the problems between India and Pakistan, including Kashmir. According to Mushahid Hussain, who was the minister in waiting, both sides came to an understanding that they would establish a back channel to discuss possible solutions within a fixed time-frame.

৯৯

During the last months of his 1998 government, the Vajpayee government lost its majority in the Lok Sabha because the AIADMK withdrew its support. Fresh polls seemed inevitable, but President K.R. Narayanan, wishing to avoid the huge expenditure on elections, invited the next largest party, the Congress, to form the government.

Sonia Gandhi was keen to become prime minister. She was able to cobble together the required numbers apart from the thirteen votes of Mulayam Singh Yadav, which would give her a majority. As she had assured the president that she would be able to form the government she used the CPM to win Mulayam Singh over to her side. Mulayam Singh, however, stipulated that his Samajwadi Party should be represented in her cabinet. She, on her part had publicly made it clear that hers would be a purely Congress government.

She had to eat humble pie and tell the president that she had not been able to muster sufficient support. Her image took a bit of a beating but she put up a brave face. Her inability to form the government resulted in fresh elections in 1999 with Vajpayee in charge of the interim government. This was the practice followed earlier.

18

THE BJP AT THE HELM
The Kandahar Hijack, the Kargil War,
and the Gujarat Riots

The elections of 1999 did not give any party an absolute majority. This had now began to be a pattern and it inevitably started an era of coalition politics. I welcomed it from one point of view: the states would have a say in the formulation of countrywide policies and not be treated as a supplicants by the Centre. However, I was concerned that an all-India perspective would weaken and with time the states might become so powerful that the centrifugal elements might assert themselves. India's unity was not a major worry but emotional integration was.

The BJP emerged once again as the single largest party. It realized more than ever that it could not form the government on its own. This time it was able to persuade the RSS that if the BJP was to come to power it would have to hold in abeyance two of its major planks, the mandir issue and abrogation of Article 370 giving Kashmir a special status. Reassurance on these two issues persuaded some regional parties to join the BJP-sponsored coalition, the National Democratic Alliance (NDA). A surprising catch was Ram Vilas Paswan who had denounced the BJP communalism at every given opportunity.

I was not therefore surprised when a woman BJP member roundly abused him when he became a minister in the NDA government. Sitting in a row next to me in the House, she asked me how he had the gumption to become an ally of a party which he had abused all the time.

The bonhomie which Vajpayee had developed after the accord with Pakistan's Nawaz Sharif during his last government plummeted because of the release of terrorists by the BJP government at Kandahar on 31 December 1999. Some seven days earlier an Indian Airlines airbus had been hijacked by Harkat-ul-Mujahideen, a Pakistan-based terrorist group. There were some 170 passengers on board. The plane landed at Amritsar for refuelling because

Captain Anil Sharma had told the hijackers, whose guns were pointed at him, that he had insufficient fuel to fly to Kandahar.

The authorities at Amritsar, where the plane landed for refuelling, bungled badly as did Delhi. They were unable to place an impediment on the runway at Amritsar to prevent the plane from taking off fearing that the hijackers would shoot them from the plane itself. Pakistan, on close terms then with the Taliban government ruling Afghanistan, fuelled the plane at Lahore and allowed it to fly to Kandahar despite repeated requests by India that they detain the plane.

The hijackers initially demanded the release of 35 Islamic militants in Indian jails and $200 million in cash but the Indian negotiators succeeded in persuading the hijackers to reduce their demands to the release of three prisoners. These were Maulana Masood Azhar (who founded Jaish-e-Mohammed in 2000 which gained notoriety for its alleged role in the 2001 attack on the Indian parliament), Ahmed Omar Saeed Sheikh (arrested in 2002 by the Pakistani authorities for the abduction and murder of Daniel Pearl), and Mushtaq Ahmed Zargar (who trained Islamic militants in Pakistan-administered Kashmir). The government agreed to release the three terrorists who were in a jail in Jammu. No rules were followed and despite protest by jail authorities, the hostages were whisked away and in Delhi put on the plane bound for Kandahar.

It was a hard decision for the Vajpayee government to take, having earlier declared that it would not release the terrorists at any cost. The government relented when relations of the passengers sat in dharna outside the residence of the prime minister.

The cabinet met and decided that it had no option but to meet the demands of the terrorists. Foreign Minister Jaswant Singh travelled in the plane carrying the three terrorists claiming it was his personal decision: Indeed, it was. '*Hum se to kisi ne poochha nahi* [nobody asked me],' Vajpayee told me at an iftar party at Hyderabad House on the day Jaswant Singh flew to Kandahar. It was understandable that BJP had no choice when the hijackers threatened to kill all the passengers on board and had stabbed one dissenting passenger. What was not however comprehensible was Jaswant Singh travelling in the plane as if he was escorting the terrorists to Kandahar. The nation felt horrified even though relieved that the hostages had been released.

Already stung by the Kargil war, India linked the Kandahar incident to Pakistan's hard and unfriendly policy towards New Delhi. It was a total betrayal of trust when General Musharraf initiated the Kargil war. He gave me no explanation when I met him later except that the 1971 debacle at Bangladesh was still fresh in the mind of the Pakistani armed forces.

During the brief conversation, he said that he had kept the then Prime Minister Nawaz Sharif informed about Kargil all along. The later stoutly denied this when I met him at Jeddah, banished from Pakistan. Nawaz Sharif said that what Musharraf had told him was that a few teams of soldiers had been sent to Kargil to exert pressure on India to solve the Kashmir issue. This reminded me of Ayub's complaint that Bhutto never told him about infiltrators sent to Kashmir in 1964.

There was a great deal of anger in India over Kargil. People were particularly incensed that the Indian government had failed to detect the positioning of militants and the Pakistan army at key points along the border. It appeared that Musharraf had begun the operation as soon as Vajpayee returned to India from Lahore.

There were demands from senior quarters that India should make a surgical air strike to destroy the militant training camps in Pakistan and 'Azad' Kashmir. Vinod Putney was in charge of the proposed operation. I met him somewhere to inquire how the operation was going because the rumour was that Pakistan had cut off our supply line to Kashmir. He contradicted that but regretted that his request for a surgical strike into Pakistan had been rejected. Vajpayee had himself turned it down fearing that the strike might escalate into a full-scale war. The air force pounded Pakistan's entrenched positions in Kargil but did not go beyond that. (After the Kargil war ended, the air chief complained that the army had informed the air force only when the former was in the midst of hostilities. The complaint was not new because no army chief had ever taken either the air or naval chiefs into confidence before initiating any operation.)

In parliament there was uproar over Kargil and many demanded an attack on Pakistan. Vajpayee rejected the demand but promised to take some firm action later. After few reverses India was able to recapture Kargil and many Pakistani soldiers were isolated and under attack on the Kargil heights.

Nawaz Sharif told me how Musharraf came running to him and begged him to seek US intervention to enable peaceful withdrawal of the Pakistan army. Nawaz Sharif said that even though it was 4 July, US Independence day, he called President Bill Clinton and sought an appointment that very day. Clinton immediately contacted Vajpayee and persuaded him to let the Pakistani army retreat.

The Pakistan government lost face but it was more Musharraf's bravado that was defeated. He explained to Nawaz Sharif that there had been a miscalculation, and that the strategy had been sound. People in Pakistan felt let down because they had been fed on a false story that Kargil had been forcibly seized from India by the Pakistan army.

Nawaz Sharif punished Musharraf by removing him from the position of chief of army staff when he was still on a trip to Sri Lanka. Musharraf's loyal commanders, however, staged a coup and Pakistan was back under military rule. Nawaz Sharif and his brother Shabaz Sharif were arrested. Nawaz Sharif described his six months' detention as the worst torture anyone could have inflicted upon him. 'It was like a black hole,' he said, describing the prison to me.

Nawaz Sahrif's imprisonment, and even more so the imposition of military rule in Pakistan, dismayed New Delhi. Vajpayee was at his seat in the Rajya Sabha when I went to him to ask what had happened. Nawaz Sharif, he said, paid the price for his 'friendship with us'. Vajpayee was concerned for Nawaz Sharif's safety but volunteered information regarding the behind the scene talks on Kashmir: 'Kuldip we were almost there; almost 80 per cent.' When I asked him to elaborate on the 80 per cent, Vajpayee remained silent.

Niaz Naik was Pakistan's representative and R.K. Mishra represented India at the back-channel discussions. Niaz told me that they were discussing the Chenab line which meant the entire Valley was to be jointly administered by India and Pakistan. I asked him to tell me more. He promised to do so at our next meeting but that never took place because he passed away. R.K. Mishra was very reticent and died without revealing anything.

Many years later, the back channel between India and Pakistan was restored. By this time the Congress-led government was in power and India's former high commissioner to Pakistan, Satish Lamba, served as the back channel. He too said that substantial progress had been made but assured me that it had been agreed that no division of Jammu & Kashmir would take place on the basis of religion and that the present borders would not be changed, although they could become 'irrelevant'.

Another confirmation of a settlement of sorts came from Pakistan's foreign minister Khurshid Kasuri who said at a reception at the Pakistan high commissioner's residence at Delhi that the Kashmir issue had been settled and that an agreement would be signed 'soon' by Prime Minister Manmohan Singh at Islamabad. When I met Kasuri, then out of power, in Lahore, he said that the agreement could not be signed because of the lawyers' agitation in Pakistan. The scenario changed after the lawyers' agitation was over: the Pakistan People's Party had assumed power in Islamabad.

In 2010, I asked Pakistan Foreign Secretary Salman Bashir, when he came to Delhi to meet his counterpart Nirupama Rao, whether Kashmir had figured in their discussions. He replied in the affirmative, but the most significant remark he made was in reply to my inquiry whether the ground covered behind the scenes would have to be once more retraced. He said they would pick up the thread from where it had been left off. 'We will resume from the stage already reached,' said Bashir. I thought I would make my suggestions in the light of the experience I had gained after following the Indo–Pakistan relationship for sixty years.

My formula on Kashmir is that both India and Pakistan should integrate the areas they occupy in their country and soften the border between the two Kashmirs. New Delhi should transfer all powers, except defence and foreign affairs, to the state of Jammu & Kashmir with Islamabad following suit in Azad Kashmir. The elected members of Jammu & Kashmir should sit in the Pakistan National Assembly and the elected members of Azad Kashmir in the

Lok Sabha. This should be the full and final settlement, with a withdrawal of the complaint pending before the UN.

꧁

The Vajpayee government had been four years in power when the Gujarat riots broke out (28 February 2002). The former cabinet secretary, Zafar Saifullah, rang me up suggesting that we should immediately go to Baroda and Ahmedabad where Muslims had been killed by the hundreds. Md. Arif Khan, former central minister, accompanied us. We flew to Baroda where a few NGOs, human rights activists, and Gandhians had gathered to discuss how the riots had suddenly engulfed parts of Gujarat. They warned us that the police could come at any time and imprison all. Fear was writ large on their faces.

One NGO who had come from Ahmedabad told me how the entire city had been mapped out locality by locality within a few hours of the Godhra incident where some forty-nine *kar sevaks* had been burnt alive in a train bound for Ahmedabad. Areas, houses, shops, and factories owned by Muslims in Ahmedabad were marked out and the specific task of killing, looting, and burning was assigned to different groups. They were in touch with 'their bosses' who directed them over mobile phones. A pamphlet was distributed to urge Hindus to boycott the Muslims economically and refuse to buy anything from their shops and to conduct no transactions with them.

The police behaved as if the force had been given instructions 'not to interfere'. The then President Narayanan wrote a letter to prime minister Vajpayee and chief minister Modi to call the army immediately and order it to shoot at sight. He did not get even acknowledgments for his letters to the two leaders. Subsequently, a top police officer said in an affidavit that he was present when Chief Minister Narendra Modi had ordered the killing of Muslims. During the riots, the *New York Times* had got hold of transcripts of conversations between the police control room and officers on the streets. The advice was to allow Muslim houses to burn and to prevent aid from reaching the victims. Elsewhere in Gujarat it was worse. The police instigated and protected the rioters. Seeing the plight of the victims and the refugee camps I wept profusely.

The day of Partition was recreated before my eyes. At that time too the police were hand in glove with the rioters, or for that matter, the killers. What was perceived as 'the call of religion' had transformed thousands of ordinary people into a horde of criminals engaging in atrocities that even hardcore criminals would scarcely dare to engage in.

Even then, as in Gujarat, there was little remorse on the part of society at large. I for my part felt a spontaneous kinship with the refugees. They too had left behind their hearths and homes, friends and dreams as I had done when I left my home town, Sialkot. Their plight was however more harrowing because they were refugees in their own country like the Kashmiri Pandits. I was also reminded of the 1984 riots in Delhi where 3,000 Sikhs were butchered in broad daylight.

We also visited the site where the Godhra incident had taken place. Reconstructing the tragedy, we found that the train had left Godhra station at 7.50 a.m. on 27 February 2002. Some *kar sevaks* were still on the platform washing their faces or teasing some vendors. One *kar sevak* pulled the chain to stop the train. When the train started moving after five minutes, the chain was pulled again at 7.58 a.m., this time in three different compartments. The authorities had yet to identify who was responsible for this. When the train halted at a distance of 800 metres from the station, the train was stoned and the bogie S-6 was set on fire.

An inquiry committee instituted by the railways headed by Justice U.C. Banerjee placed the responsibility on the kar sevaks. However, the Justice Nanavati Report said that it was a pre-planned conspiracy by local Muslims in collaboration with the ISI. Haji Umarji, a local cleric, presided over the meeting of Muslims where this conspiracy was hatched. They bought 140 litres of petrol, cut open the vestibule between S-6 and S-7, spread the petrol and burnt the coach. Nanavati arrived at this conclusion without even a single eyewitness to the burning of the train.

I have no doubt that the attack was well planned, otherwise it would not have been possible for a mob of 500 carrying petrol and kerosene to assemble in three minutes in an area that can only be reached by running through thorn-bushes. I have walked in the area adjacent to the rail track.

Godhra however pales into insignificance when compared with the 'retaliation' in Ahmedabad, Baroda, and some other cities, and even in the countryside. Ten districts out of 23 in Gujarat were affected. The official figures of those killed is put at 800. Nearly one lakh men, women, and children were forced to live in inhuman conditions in what are called refugee camps.

Why the Centre merely hummed and hawed and did nothing was understandable bearing in mind the infighting within the BJP. It was a confrontation between the hawks and the doves. That also explained why the prime minister did not immediately go to Gujarat.

Many in the BJP believed that occurrences such as in Gujarat, would consolidate Hindus on its side. A few like the prime minister and Foreign Minister Jaswant Singh believed otherwise but they remained silent. They were afraid of the RSS hardliners who had initiated the thesis of Hindu consolidation and found no fault with Modi, an RSS *pracharak*.

I wrote a letter to the prime minister in which I said:

> the riots in the state were not Hindu–Muslim clashes in the sense of two communities fighting each other. It was really a pogrom; a well-planned and executed scheme … I found that the bureaucracy and the police had been communalized. There are instances to show that the government machinery

was biased as if there were unwritten instructions not to act against the rioters. Chief Minister Narendra Modi should have been asked to resign long ago.

I suggested that the one-man commission be expanded to a three-member panel to be presided over by a Supreme Court judge. The CBI, not the state security establishment should be given the charge of the investigation. Of course, I received no reply.

Vajpayee however rang me up on the eve of his visit to Gujarat. He asked me what he should do when he had already delayed a visit to the state. I told him that he must admonish Modi in public and deliberately lose his temper in order to let the people know how angry he was about his lapses. I told him I could understand his dilemma: he could not, on the one hand, dismiss the Modi government and, on the other, could not condone what he had done.

Vajpayee did more or less that. He lost his temper when he visited refugee camps and gave the chief minister a piece of his mind in public hearing. His visit went down well, but later when he flew to Goa, he was brainwashed by Arun Shourie and Arun Jaitley who were sitting on either side of him. The speech he made at Goa referred less to the riots and more to Islam. He said that 'Hindus were living peacefully everywhere but wherever Muslims are they do not want to live peacefully'.

The Gujarat riots would have gone unnoticed as just another riot in the country had the English language dailies and 24×7 TV networks not followed up the carnage to demonstrate that it was a case of genocide. They were able to confirm the impression that the killings and looting were pre-planned and Modi and his ministers were behind the atrocities.

It was tragic that the Gujarat riots came at a time when Muslims had begun joining the mainstream. Their faith in the constitutional guarantee of equality had been deepening and their confidence in the country's secular ethos steadily rising.

Even after Partition, their romance with Pakistan had not ended, although they had felt let down. The liberation of Bangladesh, however, with one Muslim region cutting itself off from another, disillusioned the Indian Muslim community. For better or for worse, it accepted the fait accompli and began developing an identity that was neither theocratic nor pan-Islamic but wedded to the soil.

How can one otherwise explain their deliberately distancing themselves from the issues that captured the imagination of the Muslim world at large? India, after Indonesia, has the largest Muslim population in the world but Indian Muslims did not participate in a jehad elsewhere. Take, for example, Afghanistan. Pakistani Muslims fought alongside the Taliban against the US-backed Northern Alliance. So much so, that Islamabad took Washington's permission to evacuate them. Some Bangladeshi Muslims were also found in Afghanistan, but no Indian Muslim.

Nearer home, take Kashmir. You find Muslims of different countries participating in spreading violence in the Valley, but no Muslim from elsewhere in India. Even their support for autonomy is lacking. The silence of Indian Muslims on such issues is often misunderstood, yet they have seldom said or done anything which they feel does not represent their sense of country.

What happened in Gujarat has indeed jolted the community. On the one hand, they were surprised at the reaction of those who were driven to such desperation that they went to the extent of burning the coaches of the Sabarmati Express at Godhra. On the other, the community suffered disproportionately when it came to 'retaliation'.

The worst thing was that no Muslim victim was rehabilitated by the state and even when New Delhi sent funds for this Modi returned them. He converted the killings into Gujarat's prestige as if his critics were challenging the state, not him for the crimes he had committed. He succeeded in winning the subsequent assembly elections but this happens in autocratic states where the top man changes the very nature of the people. The Gujaratis were taken in by the argument that it was their prestige which was at stake rather than meting out justice to thousands of Muslims who had suffered in what is known as Modi's pogrom.

True, the Gujarat fire did not spread to the rest of India, barring stray incidents in three or four cities. That is of little satisfaction to the community given the periodic communal conflagrations. Their fears have heightened because they find the authorities deliberately inactive, the police partial, and the government more interested in covering up its tracks than in punishing the guilty. In fact, the community increasingly feels that a Hindu–Muslim riot generally evolves into a Muslim–police clash. The proposal to have a mixed force in every state has remained just that: a proposal.

The greatest challenge facing the community and the country is how to change the biased mind-set of the police. Almost equally challenging is how to stop the injection of communal poison by the RSS *parivar* in the states under BJP rule and elsewhere. Still more daunting is the reformation of the police force which tends to suspect Muslims and pick up their youth from the scene of a bomb blast or other such incidents.

The Gujarat riots proved to be a millstone around the BJP's neck. Its slogan of 'India Shining' did not sell and the secular countryside rose against it. In the general election of 2004, the tally of BJP's seats in the Lok Sabha fell to 138 in the 545-member House. BJP leaders attributed their defeat to over-confidence. The truth however was that the Gujarat riots and Modi's role in the mass murder of Muslims turned civil society against the party. A few movies and books on Gujarat indicate that the conscience of civil society was deeply hurt but its voice is so muffled that it is primarily confined to the media.

19

THE MANMOHAN SINGH GOVERNMENT
The Second Phase of Economic Reforms, the Indo-US Nuclear Deal, and the Mumbai Terrorist Attack

The 2004 election results came as a surprise. The BJP was over-confident of forming the government as the head of the National Democratic Alliance (NDA) and convinced that its slogan, 'India Shining' would work in its favour. This notwithstanding, it won only 138 seats and its allies too lost much ground.

I was not enamoured of the BJP government, concerned about their communal predilections, and it was an open secret that the party was only the political arm of the RSS. Although most were certain that the BJP would return to power at the Centre, I had my doubts. I believed that most Hindus were pluralistic in their outlook. If that were not the case, the 80 per cent would have converted India into a Hindu Rashtra. I preferred Congress government because I felt it was the lesser evil.

The Congress unexpectedly won 145 seats, albeit only 7 more than the BJP, but parties ideologically akin to the former made a good showing. The Left won 60 seats, corrupt Lalu Prasad Yadav's Rashtriya Janata Dal (RJD) 24, and casteist Mulayam's Samajwadi Party (SP) 36 seats in the elections. The Congress constituted a United Progressive Alliance (UPA) and appointed Sonia Gandhi as its chairperson.

Within the Congress party there was a strong demand that Sonia Gandhi should head the government. I was surprised that Mulayam Singh, who had earlier refused her 13 votes which would have enabled congress to from the government, now did an about turn and supported the UPA.

I wanted the Congress to win the elections with Manmohan Singh as the prime minister and Sonia Gandhi as the party president, and that was precisely what happened. I had, however, never imagined that Manmohan Singh would only be an instrument in her hands and that she would be so dominant in the government that not even a minor appointment could be made or a meaningful decision taken without her concurrence. As the days of the government in office passed, Manmohan Singh began to be considered a stalking horse.

However, there was a lot of drama in the Congress parliamentary party before Manmohan Singh was finally nominated by Sonia Gandhi. The venue, the Central Hall of parliament, had the government-owned Doordarshan to disseminate the entire day-long proceedings of the members' demand for Sonia to become prime minister. Some wept, some staged a dharna and some threatened not to leave the hall until Sonia agreed to become PM. Rahul Gandhi too jumped into the fray to say that her mother had won the election and should become PM. I watched the drama which became boring after a while.

That she allowed the pantomime to be staged was understandable in order to let everyone know where the real power lay. Manmohan Singh for his part was not overly happy. My sympathy lay with him and I was happy to find that there would be a break from dynasty.

Sonia Gandhi had to her credit a record of secularism but there were many shortcomings. Major among them was a trait of authoritarianism which she had copied from her mother-in-law, Indira Gandhi. I did not want her to be the country's prime minister. When it appeared that the Congress would be forming the government, Ramoji Rao, editor of *Eenadu*, a self-made man and a friend for the last five decades, rang me up and asked me to do something to prevent the humiliation of India being ruled by an Italian. He represented the general opinion. I assured him, on the basis of a hunch, that she would not become prime minister.

I suspected that her plan was to bring in her son, Rahul Gandhi, at an appropriate opportunity. Her own election would have made it difficult for her to have her son succeed because the party and the country would not have reacted favourably to such a dynastic monopoly. Rahul Gandhi, who had returned from abroad, could easily succeed Manmohan Singh after spending some time in the organization learning the ropes. This was precisely the route she adopted.

Sonia Gandhi overlooked her daughter, Priyanka, who had been an extraordinarily successful election campaigner and had been more popular among the masses than Rahul. Manmohan Singh had worked under Sonia as the Opposition leader in the Rajya Sabha and proved through his loyalty that he would be her Man Friday. I still remember that when I proposed in the House that another commission be appointed to examine the 1984 Sikh killings, the then Home Minister L.K. Advani accepted the suggestion but wanted the leader of Opposition, Manmohan Singh, to concur. I went to his seat and beseeched him to support the proposal but he remained silent. He announced the party's acceptance of the proposal the following day because he needed to get Sonia Gandhi's concurrence. A bureaucrat by training, he could be depended upon to do her bidding. It was Sonia Gandhi who drew up a list of cabinet ministers and showed it to him later.

It was an open secret that the key files went to 10 Janpath, her residence, for her approval. Envoys abroad were also chosen by her and posted to places she indicated. The credit for successfully running this dual-headed system goes to Manmohan Singh, not to her. I cannot think of anyone else among the ministers or Congress leaders who could have handled matters so efficiently and so obediently. For forms sake, Sonia referred to him as prime minister whenever she spoke to others, including foreigners. She was punctilious in her behaviour even at party meetings yet everyone was aware of who was the boss.

What disillusioned Manmohan Singh a few years later was that all roads led to 10 Janpath. He was distressed but compromised with or overlooked such instances because this was the price he had to pay to remain prime minister. After some years he told a few friends that he was fed up. Was he? Very few sacrifice their positions when forced to choose between office and the wilderness. Manmohan Singh is not one of them. Had he resigned when his reputation was lessening because of his concurrence with the decisions Sonia Gandhi took, he would have saved his reputation which continued to plummet.

As Sonia wielded so much authority she thought it politic to seek the advice of social activists and intellectuals she preferred. She appointed a National Advisory Committee (NAC) drawing members from among NGOs and retired bureaucrats to scrutinize the government proposals to ensure that they would conform to the people's needs. Members of the NAC were people who had an unblemished record of integrity and had earned kudos in their respective fields. The fact, however, remained that they were not elected and yet were taking important decisions, also sometimes being privy to documents which ministers or top bureaucrats did only after taking an oath of secrecy.

The rationale of appointment to the NAC was probably the suggestion by Plato in his book, *The Republic*, that a person from among the intellectuals should be nominated so as to allow him to rule without the pressure of plebeians.

This NAC was akin to the Central Citizens' Committee which Nehru had appointed under the chairmanship of Indira Gandhi to mobilize public opinion during India's war with China in 1962. Indira Gandhi then had no locus standi. The committee gave her an official status and facilities. Sonia visibly had all the power and still sought to run a form of parallel government which would be effective and bear no responsibility.

Manmohan Singh's principal contribution to the nation was the economic reforms initiated from 1991 (he was finance minister in the Narasimha Rao government from 1991 to 1996). He ended the licence-raj system and took major steps to integrate the Indian economy with the world economy. This was, however, not an unmixed blessing because the process of concentration of wealth in fewer hands had led to the growing strength and clout of the private sector and foreign investors in the decision-making process. It was globalization and a free market economy with a vengeance.

The Congress dismantled the structure that Nehru had built to put the public sector at the commanding heights of the economy. He spoke of 'a third way which takes the best from all existing systems – the Russian, the American, and others – and seeks to create something suited to India's own history and philosophy'. Yet the fact remains that the growth rate during his tenure averaged 3.5 per cent.

The Gandhians were most upset by the direction the economy took under Manmohan Singh and held many meetings, which I also attended, to initiate a Satyagraha to revive self-sufficiency through development of the rural economy based on the cottage industries that had been decimated by unbridled capitalism.

After the First Five Year Plan, Nehru had realized that the fruits of industrialization were not reaching the common man as he had visualized. He had then set up a committee. Manmohan Singh did not appoint such a committee although the GDP was averaging a growth of 8 to 9 per cent per annum. However, a government-blessed committee headed by Arjun Sengupta (2010), a distinguished economist and once part of Indira Gandhi's entourage, said that 70 per cent of the people in India earned less than $2 (approximately Rs 100) and 41 per cent of them not even $1.

Manmohan Singh's response was the legislation of the Mahatma Gandhi National Rural Employment Guarantee Act (MGNREGA), a job guarantee scheme for rural India. The worst thing to happen during Manmohan Singh's tenure was the setting of Special Economic Zones (SEZs) which were greatly resented by NGOs. What the zones meant was the acquisition by the government of large tracts of land (with negligible compensation) 'in the public interest' and handed over to Indian and foreign industrialists at much less than the market price. The government in this way brought back the era of feudal lords who converted the best agricultural land into industrial units, hotels, and places of entertainment. The setting up of SEZs was eventually abandoned after protests by NGOs but the government continued to acquire land in (public interest) and hand it over to industrialists and businessmen.

The CPM government in West Bengal burnt its fingers by giving land to the Tatas for their small car project (Nano) at Singur. There were large-scale protests in the region, but the worst repercussions were in Nandigram where farmers did not surrender any land and barricaded their villages to keep the government and CPM cadres at bay.

This was CPM's first clash with the farmers who were unwilling to fall in line. This was also the most striking example of a people-oriented party using every method at its command, including its cadres assisted by the state police, to help rich industrialists. Many farmers died during the confrontation, but what was worse was that of hitherto disciplined party cadres behaving like rabble and indulging in rape, loot, and murder.

When I met CPM General Secretary Prakash Karat at his office in Delhi he admitted that the state government had handled the situation badly but regretted that the intellectuals who had supported the CPM had turned against the party and even dubbed them fascist. He was referring to Medha Patkar who openly attacked the CPM. The West Bengal government not only lost the project but also prestige and people support. This became evident when Mamata Banerjee's party, the Trinamool Congress (TMC), routed the CPM government in the state elections of 2011 after having ruled the state for almost thirty-four years. In a landslide victory, the TMC and its allies won 226 seats in a House of 294. However, at the Centre, the Left, with its 60 odd seats, was a strong supporter of Manmohan Singh. The situation changed when he made the India–US nuclear treaty a prestige issue. The treaty, opposed by an influential section in the US itself, was the result of Manmohan Singh's personal rapport with US President George W. Bush Jr. It took three years for the deal to fructify because India had to overcome the hurdles of a hostile International Atomic Energy Agency (IAEA) and a suspicious US Congress. The deal separated the civil and military nuclear facilities in India and opened up all the civilian nuclear plants, thirty-five in all, to IAEA inspection.

Politically the deal hurt the Congress and Manmohan Singh personally. It was generally viewed as a step opening up India to US pressure and influence. The Congress lost the support of the Left which had also given the party a liberal image. The Congress continued to remain in office but it was a weak government and forever on the defensive.

It is an open secret that before the vote in parliament on the nuclear deal the Manmohan Singh government made 'certain deals' with some small political parties and independent members to win them over. The motion was carried by 19 votes. Some members disobeyed the whip by abstaining or crossing the floor. The BJP dramatized the cash-for-votes accusation by displaying wads of currency notes in the House. The whole thing misfired in the sense that the then Speaker, Somnath Chatterjee greatly disapproved of the tamasha and ordered a probe which the Delhi Police did not take seriously for three years until the Supreme Court stepped in. The astonishing part is that nobody from the Congress, which had benefited from the situation and had survived the no-confidence motion, was held responsible. It was obvious who was responsible for Delhi Police delay as the force fell directly under the home ministry. A really positive achievement of the Manmohan Singh government was the enactment of the Right to Information Act (RTI).

✸

India also witnessed, during Manmohan Singh's tenure, a well-planned attack on Mumbai on 26 November 2008. The Pakistan government had prior knowledge of it. Hafiz Sayed's Lashkar-e-Taiba and Pakistan's ISI (Inter-Services Intelligence) had planned the attack from their soil and had sent some ten Pakistani terrorists by boat from Karachi to attack the Taj Mahal and Oberoi hotels, the Jewish Synagogue, Cama Hospital, Leopold Café, and the CST killing in all some 175 people. The attack continued for three days. One Pakistani terrorist, Ajmal Kasab, was arrested and confessed to his involvement in the attack and that of his Pakistani collaborators.

The entire country reacted with anger and universal condemnation of Pakistan because, for the first time, the entire attack was graphically captured live on Indian television screens. Anti-Pakistan feeling ran high but was somewhat assuaged when Prime Minister Manmohan Singh met Pakistan's Prime Minister Syed Yusuf Raza Gilani at Sharm-el-Sheikh, Egypt, on 16 July 2009. The latter admitted that his government had no control over the army which used ISI to mastermind the entire operation. Apparently, it was a hush-hush affair, as Riaz Khokhar, the Pakistan high commissioner in Delhi at that time told me that he was not aware of the attack. He was sufficiently frank to admit that if Pakistan was behind it and, as India suspected, it was an act of war.

Former Prime Minister Nawaz Sharif said openly that the terrorists had used Pakistani soil to plan the operation, and criticism hurt Islamabad the most. Manmohan Singh and Gilani did reaffirm their resolve to fight terrorism and cooperate with each other, and yet it was the first time an Indian prime minister had declared that talks with Pakistan would continue uninterrupted, and be kept separate from India's concerns on terrorism emanating from Pakistani soil. Another statement which an Indian prime minister made for the first time was an acknowledgement that he did 'have some information' on the unrest in Baluchistan. The allegation that New Delhi was giving money to the Baluchistan nationalist leaders was confirmation of sorts and Pakistan went to town about this.

So strong and widespread was the criticism of Manmohan Singh for separating Indo–Pakistan talks from terrorism emanating from Pakistan that there was no follow up to the Sharm-el-Sheikh meeting. New Delhi was particularly incensed by Hafiz Sayed's free movement in Pakistan notwithstanding clear evidence of his involvement in the Mumbai attack and continuing anti-India tirades and activities. Action against him was seen as a litmus test of Pakistan's sincerity.

No doubt, Pakistan has itself paid a heavy price for terrorism which it blessed to engage India while standing behind the scenes. But the terrorists have become a Frankenstein to devour the creator. They pose a problem to the region. During my visits to Pakistan after the Mumbai attack I did not find any evidence to show that Islamabad was keen on punishing the terrorists. The intelligentsia felt sorry that such an attack had taken place but seemed helpless. No one was willing to show the candle to the ISI.

For having mentioned Baluchistan, Manmohan Singh faced strident criticism because this was the first time that the Indian government had said anything on the subject despite Pakistan's relentless propaganda about it. The Manmohan Singh–Gilani meeting did not really break the ice and the two countries stood apart as usual.

Eventually, New Delhi made a move to invite the Pakistan foreign secretary for talks, which too failed. At a reception at Pakistan House in Delhi I asked Foreign Secretary Salman Bashir why the talks failed. 'We are the prisoners of the past,' he said. That in a nutshell describes the failure of interactions between India and Pakistan to normalize relations. Subsequently, the two countries shed some of the hostility for economic reasons. Pakistan extended Most Favoured Nation (MFN) status to India, which had already done so a decade earlier. The breakthrough in the trade relationship came in 2012 when Pakistan agreed to a negative list, that is, the items which India could not export numbering roughly 1500. I felt that the trade between the two countries would eventually be free and lead to the solution of other problems. I did expect hiccups but was optimistic that the goods would flow from one side to the other. However, the transit facilities to Afghanistan and the countries beyond did not seem to be coming through. New Delhi should have made more efforts to use the road through Pakistan to Afghanistan because it would have opened the markets of Central Asia.

There is no set formula I can apply to assess the performance of Dr Manmohan Singh or his government. Instances of good or bad governance are available, more bad than good. Even so, two of India's founding fathers identified a criterion to measure the success of a government. Mahatma Gandhi's yardstick was to identify the poorest individual in the country and determine how far his life had improved. Jawaharlal Nehru said that the touchstone should be how far any government 'enables the individual to rise above his petty self and think in terms of the good of all'.

On either count, neither Manmohan Singh nor his government has fared well. True, there has been economic growth, but this has manifested itself more in high-rise buildings, dazzling TV networks, opulent plazas, big dams and large industrial estates than in the infrastructure or in the improvement of the lot of the common man. Nehru once observed that high economic progress was not his dream of tomorrow's India if it lost its spiritual heritage in the process. I too believe in this dictum.

Economic inequalities and inequities have galloped without restraint. Far from seeing any improvement in their standard of living, the poor have not been able to maintain their abysmal standard of living, nor do the prospects ahead auger hope. Those below the poverty line may have fallen to 40 per cent of the population according to the official records but no reduction in poverty is visible. The Planning Commission goes on changing the definition of poverty to keep the figure low. The middle class has felt the squeeze all the time.

That the Manmohan Singh cabinet is not a cohesive unit came to the fore in 2011 when differences simmered all the time among senior ministers, particularly Pranab Mukherjee and P. Chidambaram. Neither could reconcile to Sonia Gandhi's choice of Manmohan Singh. They considered him a loyal bureaucrat planted in the political field which was beyond his depth and qualification. Pranab knew that Sonia Gandhi did not trust him for the top job because her husband too had nurtured doubts about him.

Chidambaram thought that his ability for exceeded that of Manmohan Singh. On several occasions, Sonia Gandhi intervened to ensure that the other Congress ministers in the cabinet supported him. My information was that Manmohan Singh gave it back to them, when a 2G spectrum (relating to mobiles) note by the finance ministry was made public. The note said that Chidambaram, then the finance minister, could have stalled the allotment of licences had he insisted on their being auctioned. Chidambaram suspected that Pranab Mukherjee was responsible. Pranab, as finance minister, got a private detective agency to have his office checked because he thought that the home minister had bugged his room. The private agency found the spots which were used for bugging although this had ceased when the search was conducted a search.

The 2G spectrum note was given out by the prime minister's office, not by the finance ministry. This was done in response to a query under the RTI by a BJP activist. I vainly tried to find out whether Sonia Gandhi suspected Manmohan Singh but it was clear that she did not hold either Pranab or Chidambaram responsible for any harm they caused to each other. She was keen on the two staying together and got them to realize that both were making a mountain out of a molehill.

I do not want to assess Manmohan Singh's term as prime minister because he is still in harness. I can, however, say that the hopes I had pinned on him have been dashed. His government could have performed far better and at least given a semblance of governance to the country. His failure, particularly after the CPM withdrew their support, is palpable. His explanation is that the coalition dharma, meaning thereby the compromises he has to make to get the support of his allies, left him with very little leeway. He may be right but his helplessness has cost the nation dearly.

The Manmohan Singh government will go down in history as the most corrupt period faced by the nation. When members of the ruling party and their allies are caught siphoning off money, no rules are considered sacrosanct and no values are sacred. The government could have at least introduced a better Lokpal Bill but Manmohan Singh did not appear his own master when it was being prepared or introduced. His helplessness in face of the forces against which he has to contend is pathetic. He could have resigned from prime-ministership and in that way, at least in part, redeemed his reputation.

I confess that I have dealt with the last decade cursorily because I have very little information which has not appeared in print. My two friends, Kailash Prakash and Krishna, both former Secretaries to the Government of India, told me that readers expected from me some word of guidance. I am hardly the person to undertake this because even I have been searching for 'an avtar' for my country.

I do however feel that if the idea of India is to mean anything we must try to bring back morality to politics. India has been known for its value system not the riches. We should refurbish the Laxman Rekha to differentiate moral from immoral, right from wrong, a line which has got effaced over the years.

Nehruvian thinking led me to believe that a democratic society with individual freedom and a dominant public sector could coexist. My experience nullifies such a possibility. One thing which is clearer to me than before is that our future depends on the quality of our people and their capacity to work.

True, the polity has been trivialized by political, religious and economic forces. In the midst of rivalries among them the country's development has lagged behind. Disillusionment and frustration, and the inevitable fallout, violence, have engulfed certain areas in the absence of integrity and development.

India is always a story of shadows and sunshine. Which of the two prevails at a particular time gives it bad or good name. The last decade or so is no exception apart from the fact that the shadows have lengthened. Corruption has darkened the skies and exposed a system reeking with graft. An utter want of governance has added to the woes of the nation.

Regional politics has replaced national thinking. I see this growing at the expense of the Centre or the national point of view. Federalism is the answer but how do we ensure that the states do not become prey to local chauvinism, caste temptations, and religious pulls and pressures. An all-India perspective is necessary, but this is not possible when the states provide a majority to a political party to remain in power.

The time has come to think seriously about a presidential form of government providing the individual elected a fixed tenure, of say five years, to function without requiring maneuvering a majority in Lok Sabha. She/he will be responsible for an all-round development ensuing that the states do not encroach upon the subjects the constitution has given to the Centre. Safeguards can be built in to ensure that the president does not turn into a dictator.

I feel that the next few years will be really challenging. Probably what India's first Prime Minister Jawaharlal Nehru said, that the following generations were sentenced to hard work, is true. The confidence which the people have developed in themselves and in their country, sustains hope that India will see the sunlight increasing and the shadows receding.

Epilogue

Injustice still hurts me just the same way as it did over sixty years ago, and among my very few friends are those who similarly care about the violation of basic values. Indeed, my instincts from a very early age have been to recognize such people who suffered victimization and marginalization. I have worked with them in Kashmir as they searched for an identity, in Bihar where land-grabbers have fraudulently seized people's land, and elsewhere where large dams have been constructed, evicting thousands of farmers and tribesmen.

Indeed, seeking a responsive chord wherever and whenever it was possible to find it has been a guiding principle for me which made religious and political boundaries becoming largely irrelevant. The young Muslim who protected my parents at Sialkot railway station during Partition was a human being first and a Pakistani second. He earned my gratitude and loyalty forever. Hindus who likewise risked their own lives by sheltering Muslims in 1947 or Sikhs in 1984 belong to the élite group of eternal heroes.

While harking back to the past, I may have romanticized some of the experiences of both Hindus and Muslims but in doing so I was only projecting the harrowing times that the three countries, India, Pakistan, and Bangladesh, endured. All of them were born out of blood and they separated from their kith and kin to find their individual ethos and identity.

All I know is that in my case the plight of others has touched me so deeply that I have sometimes made their sufferings mine. When I crossed the border on 13 September 1947 I had seen so much blood and destruction in the name of religion that I vowed to myself that the new India which we were going to build would know no deaths due to differences in religion or caste. I therefore wept when I witnessed the mass-murder of Sikhs in 1984 and saw a repetition of such inhumanity in Gujarat in 2002, viewing it as a microcosm of the communal violence I had witnessed in 1947: the same refugee camps, similar stories of rapes, and the expulsion of innocent Muslim families from their hearths and homes. Gujarat caused me to ponder on how distant we still were from the vow I had undertaken over six decades ago to help transform India into a genuinely secular polity.

I cannot count how many threats and the hate mail I have received in my journalistic career. They have largely emanated from Hindus who believe that I take a pro-Muslim and pro-Pakistan stand. I cannot pretend that I am the only person, journalist or writer, who has received threats or hate mail. Nor can I say that I am the only witness to horrific days in 1947 and subsequently. Perhaps others have written more eloquently about those times. All I know is that I too have cried to myself at night and sensed a personal sense of helplessness that comes from the absence of a foundation on which to build.

I recall that when I brought home to my mother my first salary, a paltry sum even by the standards of the time, she told me how she had dreamt that I would one day be rolling in wealth. Then she said: 'You will be a great man one day, but I shall not be there to see you.'

She breathed her last before my eyes. In the same way, I felt helpless when my sister, Raj, died a few months ago. She was the closest friend I had. I remember requesting the police who knocked on my door during the Emergency to delay my detention till I had met her. Raj's last note with a *rakhi* said: 'My dearest brother who has been everything to me in my life, my guide, my friend and my saviour. If only all brothers could be like you this world would be an excellent place to live. How proud I am of you.' Perhaps it was my parents who drilled it into me that you can only find respect for yourself if you respect others.

It may not have been obvious to me as a young man, but good journalism is all about exposing injustice and highlighting heroes, regardless of the consequences. Therefore, although my teenage brain may have impelled me to become a lawyer, my human instincts were actually marching in a different direction. Looking back, it now seems obvious that I was destined to embrace the world of journalism. It was only a matter of how and when. In the event, it has been a long stint notwithstanding the realization that I could have prospered more elsewhere. In my profession what haunts me is that I do not write better. I should after having spent over fifty years in journalism.

India is engulfed in a series of crises, a new one taking hold before the last one has ended. I blame the political parties most for failing to reach a consensus on the basic issues concerning the country. That is probably why there is less of India and more in terms of regional, religious, and ethnic identities. I have found the youth disappointed and disillusioned, taking to careerism and consumerism rather than working for an egalitarian society and towards deepening India's ethos of secularism and democratic socialism. True, the young have of late awoken to the cancer of corruption that seethes within the system yet they remain devoid of ideals, without ideological moorings like lamps without oil. My fear is that they may some day seek desperate remedies. Will they succeed? I do not know, but what I do know is that if the means to achieve an end are vitiated the ends are bound to be debased. That is what Mahatma Gandhi taught us. I wish the country would follow him more than the economic and social pundits who have before them grand and extravagant visions unsuited to India's genius.

The Delhi durbar, as the political cauldron is known in Delhi, has been full of intrigues. I saw them from close quarters for the first two decades after Independence and watched it keenly later from outside. It was like the times immemorial: the fight for the top job. First it was who would be the raja, has now changed into who would be the prime minister. No method was mean enough to grab the top position and no method was spared to suppress the opponents within and without the party, although the emphasis was on the value system. The battle for succession was as full of intrigue after Nehru as was after Shastri. Things became more sordid after the death of these two leaders.

I have seen very few living within their means. Someone has helped them by somebody from somewhere. The entry of corporate sector in is a recent phenomenon. In fact, those who have preferred to adopt a simple austere life are very few, resisting all temptations. Probably what holds good for political leaders also holds good for journalists and others.

My contact with the youth has been limited. They are resentful of what goes on in the name of politics but very few among them are willing to soil their hands with dirt and come to the field to challenge the entrenched elements. I am not taking a despondent view of the present but I do feel consumerism is embracing the youth rapidly.

It is healthy that my generation is fading away. As Romain Rolland says in his book, *Jean Christopher*, man must die for a child to be born like the day which must consume itself in the darkness of night for a new dawn. An individual must be born again and again as must a human soul or self. This is a journey from the horrible to the sublime. It does not end the quest.

ANNEXURES

1

ANNEXURE
The Indian Media

Journalism as a profession has changed a great deal from what it was in our times. I feel an acute sense of disappointment, not only because it has deteriorated in quality and direction but also because I do not see journalists attempting to revive the values once practised. The proliferation of newspapers and television channels has no doubt affected the quality of content, particularly reporting. Too many individuals are competing for the same space. What appalls me most is that editorial primacy has been sacrificed at the altar of commercialism and vested interests. It hurts to see many journalists bending backwards to remain handmaidens of the proprietors, on the one hand, and of the establishment, on the other. This is so different from what we were used to.

At that time, proprietors left us alone to get on with the job of reporting, commenting on current political developments, and the like. I concede that there was a Lakshman Rekha which stopped us from transgressing beyond certain norms of free expression. It was, however, understood that journalists would not slant their story in a particular direction, nor make personal attacks on any leader in the government or political party. Also, the question of 'paid news' just didn't arise.

Today the bulk of our newspapers and television channels are owned and run as family enterprises. The proprietors are usually the real editors, even when they have a front man called 'editor'. A few newspapers have members of their family formally trained. The *Hindu* took pride in this but N. Ram, the editor-in-chief, has stopped that practise which the newspaper adhered to for 140 years. He has appointed a professional editor and also a CEO, probably to underline that the journalism is an industry, not a profession.

Shamlal once told me that he as the editor of the *Times of India,* was never rung up by Shanti Prasad Jain, the then owner of the newspaper, and that the latter did not even remotely suggest to him which line he should adopt on any particular subject. Throughout Shamlal's long tenure, Shanti Prasad never expressed his disapproval of anything the editor wrote. By contrast, the attitude of his son, Ashok Jain, who inherited Bennett Coleman & Co., publisher of the *Times of India,* was quite different. He was committed to commercial success and would ensure that the newspaper did not come into conflict with his business interests or those he promoted. Giri Lal Jain, the then editor of the *Times of India*, rang me up one day to ask whether I could speak to Ashok Jain, whom I knew well, to get Samir Jain, his son, off his back. Giri said that Ashok Jain, whatever his preferences, treated him well but Samir's attitude was humiliating. Inder Malhotra once recounted to me how senior journalists were made by Samir to sit on the floor in his room to write out the names of invitees on cards sent by the organization.

I flew to Bombay and spoke to Ashok who frankly said he would have no hesitation in supporting his son because the latter had increased the revenue tenfold, from Rs 8 lakhs to Rs 80 lakhs. 'I can hire many Giri Lal Jains if I pay more but not a Samir,' said Ashok. I conveyed this to Giri who did not last long with the newspaper.

The reason why the *Statesman* adopted an independent line even after the induction of C.R. Irani of the Swatantra Party as managing director was the influence of J.R.D. Tata. It is another matter that he caved in when the CPM took over in West Bengal. N.J. Nanporia, the editor, would tell me that Irani was afraid to suggest anything to him because he knew that 'I [Nanporia] can speak to JRD directly'. During the Emergency, Irani bought majority shares in the *Statesman* at book value because the owners were petrified and did not want to have anything to do with the *Statesman* or any other newspaper.

In the *Indian Express*, RNG did not interfere until Indira Gandhi returned to power in 1980. He would see the morning newspaper, which in those days was printed at midnight. Even if he noticed that a story was incorrect – he had wide contacts and knew what was happening in political circles – he would not stop its publication. He would tell me (I was the editor of the Express News Service) that such and such correspondent had got it all wrong; nothing beyond that.

Another instance of proprietor's whimsical attitude was the dismissal of Vinod Mehta from *India Post* owned by Vijaypat Singhania. Vinod was a very close friend. I was so worked up by his dismissal that I convened a public meeting at Constitution House and asked Vinod to come from Mumbai and address it. The hall was full. I was disappointed when he did not say a word against his proprietor, much less against the cult of proprietorship. He read my thoughts and said, 'You are mistaken if you thought I would say anything about proprietors. I have to look for another job.'

It is difficult to think of an ideal structure for the ownership of newspapers or television channels. I suggest that the leading ones should have an Ombudsman to ensure that they adhere to the policy enunciated by them. The Ombudsman should ensure that the employees are not shunted out by the proprietor, as Ram did in the *Hindu* to force N. Ravi and Malini Parthsarthy to resign.

Another suggestion is to separate the financial side from the editorial one. I mean that editor should have an annual allocation which he manages and the proprietor should not interfere so long as editor remains within the budget. Any additional financial demands should be worked out between the two.

In our days, the business or the advertisement department would maintain a distance from the editorial section because they were aware that we did not welcome even their managers. Whenever a press note or some other material came from them, we just threw it into the wastepaper basket. Even when they wrote B.M. (Business Must), it made no difference. Today a new innovation called CEO has been introduced in newspapers as if the press was an industry or business house. The CEOs matter more than editors. Some newspapers, like the *Times of India,* have no editor. They proudly pronounce that the market is more important than the editorial content and are proud to sell news columns. That is how the term 'paid news' has come into currency, although the practice has been misused by regional papers beyond all limits.

The Emergency in 1975–77 was the watershed. The way journalists capitulated and got co-opted by the establishment led proprietors to wonder whether they were at all indispensable. If they were willing to obediently follow the government's diktats why not those of their paymasters? Many leading newspapers have to obtain the approval of their proprietor for the editorial they write and for the articles they use. Nearly all proprietors have their political prejudices and preferences.

The contract system under which a newspaper hires a journalist for a particular period of time was introduced after the Emergency. This goes against the letter and spirit of the Working Journalists Act which Jawaharlal Nehru had passed in parliament to guarantee a journalist his/her job. He said that as they would be working independently and objectively they ran the risk of annoying either the proprietor or the government. Nehru argued that while the former had the power to exert pressure on and even sack a journalist if s/he did not heed instructions, the other had the authority to influence the proprietor to sack 'uncomfortable' journalists. I have consulted some legal authorities who say that the contract system violates the Working Journalists Act and is therefore ultra vires. Despite my pleas, the various journalist unions have not gone to court to challenge the contract system.

The reason Nehru took steps to ensure the permanency of journalists' jobs was because he felt that there was no opposition to the Congress worth the name. He wanted the press to be a critic of the government and point out where it had erred. He also ensured that the Indians would own the newspapers run by the British. The *Statesman* in Calcutta and the *Times of India* in Bombay, the *Mail* in Madras, and the *Pioneer* in Lucknow changed hands from foreigners to Indians.

I have known journalists leaving one newspaper for another to improve their prospects but can count on the fingers of one hand those who resigned on a point of principle. There was a time when journalists preferred resignation to regimentation. This profession is notorious for unemployment. Once Frank Moraes, a leading editor then working for the *Indian Express,* asked Challapati Rao, another doyen of journalism, what he (Rao) thought was the reality about an editor's relationship to the owner. Rao said that Frank Moraes was the myth while Goenka was the reality. Frank used to write a weekly column titled 'Myth and Reality'.

Journalists have for their part reconciled themselves to the situation of being at the mercy of proprietors. Journalists had won the battle when Prime Minister Rajiv Gandhi had sought to introduce an anti-defamation bill which, if enacted, would have restricted the freedom of the press. There was a strong old Indian-style protest at India Gate. Even Goenka joined the demonstration, holding aloft a placard that screamed: 'I am against the anti-defamation bill.' What animated the atmosphere was the unity of journalists who had risen in force against the government's effort to silence them.

The protest reignited, at least momentarily, the old spirit of speaking out. I wrote the oath: 'If ever the freedom of the press is threatened we cannot and will not remain silent.' During the agitation, Amitabh Bachchan, who was then a member of the Lok

Sabha, called on me. He had moved into my neighbourhood, Vasant Vihar. I told him how Rajiv Gandhi, a friend of his, had completely alienated the press because of the anti-defamation bill. He must have spoken to Rajiv because the bill was withdrawn within 24 hours of Amitabh's visit.

The government has learnt its lesson and I doubt whether it will venture to restrict the freedom of the press in the foreseeable future even though it may have constituted a Group of Ministers to find ways to 'supervise' the press. Electronic media is facing the challenge but I do not find anyone picking up the gauntlet. My real concern stems from the corporate sector which is dictating who will write a column where and say what. It may be the remark of a cynic but it is true that the news is written on the back of advertisements. This has become starkly apparent with the involvement of journalists in the lobbying by Nira Radia along with ministers and top bureaucrats for leading industrialists like Ratan Tata and Mukesh Ambani. Radia quit the business when the recordings of her conversations and that of those she pressurized was leaked to the media.

The corporate sector dictates not only to small but also to large newspapers on the line they should or should not adopt on important economic matters. The rivalry within the corporate sector is also affecting the press because the comparatively more powerful industrialist can arm twist a newspaper proprietor and advise him or her not to run the advertisement of a rival. There is something in what Lord Northcliffe, the newspaper magnate in the UK, said: 'News is what somebody, somewhere wants to suppress. Everything else is advertising.'

As there are many foreign players both in the corporate sector and the share markets, they too have begun to have a 'say'. The foreign equity of 26 per cent in the media, permitted by the government is a Trojan horse, dangerous in the long run. We have our traditions and cultural values which are not appreciated by foreign equity-holders; they are not sensitive to our ways. As I have said elsewhere, I am firmly opposed to foreign equity in the news media.

Freedom of the press is as much a moral concept as is the right to freedom of speech. A shallow, unthinking attitude on the part of newspapers gets reflected in the news stories and articles they publish. Reporters do not always cross-check the information they receive and often write one-sided versions of events and about people of no consequence. Often good stories are not followed up properly and planted stories make it to the front page. Even factual information provided by a newspaper is often incorrect, and for a price.

The term 'paid news' became official after the 2008 Lok Sabha election when packages were openly offered: covering favourable news, photographs, and archives in support. I took this up with the EC and implored it to appoint a committee to investigate the allegations. Some party leaders had assured me that they would inform the committee about the amount they had paid to particular newspapers and journalists. The EC took up one case. However, the Press Council of India appointed a committee which investigated the charges. The report was first suppressed and then altered because the council members, under pressure from their owners, could not reach a consensus. Some portion of the report is as follows:

> In recent years, corruption in the Indian media has gone way beyond the corruption of individual journalists and specific media organizations—from "planting" information and views in lieu of favors received in cash

or kind, to more institutionalized and organized forms of corruption wherein newspapers and television channels receive funds for publishing or broadcasting information in favor of particular individuals, corporate entities, representatives of political parties and candidates contesting elections, that is sought to be disguised as "news".

News is meant to be objective, fair, and neutral, and that is what sets apart such information and opinion from advertisements that are paid for by corporate houses, government organizations, or individuals. What happens when the distinction between news and advertisements begins to blur, when advertisements double up as news, or when 'news' is published in favour of a particular politician through sale of editorial space? In such situations, the reader or the viewer is in no position to distinguish between news reports and advertisements /advertorials.

Corruption is not confined to politicians, public servants, or the corporate world. The media too has blackened its face. Not only have reporters or correspondents changed their copy or withheld information for a consideration, but they are also involved in scams, vis-a-vis the appellate income tax tribunal. Stories about them are related in whispers but, for obvious reasons, rarely in print. I do believe there should be greater transparency in relation to editors.

My suggestion to the Editor's Guild of India was that editors should annually file with the Press Council of India a list of their assets and that of their spouse. If they did not wish the press council to come into the picture, they could post their assets on the Internet. Like Caesar's wife, editors should not only be honest but seen to be so. My suggestion was not to the liking of many editors.

Honesty in money matters is important for editors but it is crucial in the running of newspapers. The printed word is still gospel truth for our readers. I know of editors who mould their writings to please the powers that be at the time and that do a U-turn when there is a change of government. Different political parties when they come to power use advertisements to influence the media. Ninety-five per cent of the newspapers in India cannot resist this temptation because government advertisements constitute a substantial part of their revenue. The television networks are no different.

The Centre and the states should set up autonomous boards, headed by an eminent person or former high court judge, to determine the distribution of advertisements. This is public money and its misuse is a dishonest practice for which ministers should be held responsible.

Speaking the truth is dependent on your basic attitude towards people. If it is people-friendly, if you genuinely like being with people, if you are sufficiently interested in listening to what they say they will freely confide in you. Will Rogers, the legendary American folk philosopher, used to say: 'there are no strangers; only friends I have not met'. That should be a good reporter's attitude to people.

Cynicism or pessimism in the conditions that exist is not the correct approach. A beginning has already been made in the form of the Right to Information Act. It is limited, but it is for us all to expand its boundaries.

What has disappointed me most is the compromises that journalists make to advance their careers. Indeed, success has become synonymous with passiveness. If you know how to get along, you advance in life and begin to believe that talent does not matter, but conformism does.

If the lives of successful men and women were to be traced, most of them belonged to the tribe which knew how to get along. They never came in anyone else's way, they never walked out of step, they never made anything an issue. Their preference was to remain silent and when, at all if they chose to speak, they were seldom out of tune. Some would criticize them for playing it safe but by any yardstick they were successful and climbed higher and higher up the ladder.

Intellectuals are no better. Conformism has become the badge of their community. They rationalize every occurrence in their lives. Independent thinking is only a facade behind which they live in security and prosperity. The rule, 'I sing the song of him whose bread I eat', sums up their philosophy. They would do anything to retain what they have. It is not that they do not appreciate the value of sacrifice or the suffering of others, but it is a precept they want others to follow but not themselves.

Whether journalists believe in anything at all is difficult to say but my general impression is they are primarily interested in themselves. They may speak about values, and they ceaselessly speak about principles but it is material rewards that they hanker after. I realize that change is the law of life, and that there cannot be any progress without change. However, are journalists bringing about change? In the words of a philosopher, 'No doubt, when modesty was made a virtue, it was a very advantageous thing for the fools, for everyone is expected to speak of himself as if he were one'.

Ascribing information to 'reliable sources', or 'government sources' is a convenient path to shirk responsibility. Similar phrases are also often used in political reportage to enable the creation of stories from mere hearsay, conjecture, and speculation. Identification of the sources from which the information publicized has been obtained is an accepted professional practice, except in stated and specified circumstances. Widespread use of such phrases as 'it is believed', 'it is understood', 'according to sources' or no mention of a source at all opens the road wide to speculation, exaggeration, planted and even invented stories being passed off as authentic news.

To ensure credibility, sources of news items should be identifiable by name and/or designation or at least credible proximity to the informant. In the event of confidentiality being sought, the reporter must assume responsibility for the credibility of the source and it is the responsibility of the copy editor to ensure that the claim is genuine. These rules must be made known to the editorial staff and the readers. If broken, offenders must be punished and the case publicized to maintain the credibility of the media and to check inclusion of planted stories.

While I agree that self-regulation is no regulation there should be a code of ethics which journalists should follow to the last word. Any control, big or small, will end in some form of censorship. What Jawaharlal Nehru said at the All India Editor Conference holds good: 'By imposing restrictions you do not change anything. You merely suppress the manifestation of certain things, thereby causing the idea and the thought underlying them to spread further. Therefore, I would have a completely free press with all the dangers involved in the wrong use of that freedom than a suppressed or regulated press.'

2

ANNEXURE
Human Rights and the Environment

I owe my initiation into the field of human rights to Justice V.M. Tarkunde, a simple and modest individual who pioneered the movement in India to provide safeguards to the people against government excesses. After resigning from the Maharashtra High Court he came to Delhi to practise in the Supreme Court. Without charging a fee, he would appear on behalf of those who fought for social causes. He contested my case too without a fee.

My detention during the Emergency made me more sensitive to human suffering, and I was profoundly affected when I encountered young boys languishing in jail as under trials. I was jolted when I heard their tales of privation. Their faces haunted me. I had seen abject poverty when as a journalist I travelled through parts of UP, Bihar, and Orissa. That memory had faded with time, but violations of human rights were like arrows piercing my consciousness.

Jayaprakash Narayan had founded People's Union of Civil Liberties (PUCL) and the Citizens for Democracy (CFD) organizations. The first was concerned with cases of human rights violations, while the second focused on the Indian democratic system and espoused causes relating to secularism, the grant of autonomy to Kashmir, and the rights of the north-eastern states, particularly Nagaland, within the Indian union.

Tarkunde persuaded me to join the CFD which I went on to head. Many years later, some undesirable elements were able to capture the organization and caused its demise. It is a terrible shame and a slur on those who worked in the organization that they purloined the Rs 1 lakh deposited in the name of the organization. I was able to revive the CFD only in the second half of 2011.

Tarkunde was a radical humanist, but his association with JP motivated him to take up the thread of *parivartan* from where JP had left it. Both were convinced that what was necessary for India was *sampurna kranti* (total revolution).

Tarkunde and I found that the youth associated with JP, particularly those from Sangharsh Vahini, remained committed to working towards a value-based system but lacked leadership. We convened a meeting of Sangharsh Vahini and other social service organizations working at grassroots, to chalk out a programme that would enable them all to work from a single platform and pursue JP's unfinished agenda.

The meeting lasted for three days at Bodh Gaya in Bihar. It was a futile exercise and both of us felt dejected because all the time 'points of order' were being raised to stall the meeting. The entire atmosphere was completely vitiated and our effort ended in a whimper. To our dismay, what we found was that most of the participating NGOs were regular recipients of funds from abroad. We could see the schism between those who received money from abroad and those who did not.

Nothing came out of our deliberations, although we divided the work among five zones and selected five paid workers from among them to mobilize opinion in favour of total revolution. We hoped against hope that they would eventually work at the grassroots to organize people for *sampurna kranti* but were proved wrong because within a year the organizers had taken to some other vocation.

I realized at the meeting how the youth just wanted to encash the sacrifices they had made during the JP Movement. The essential truth was that the fire in their bellies had been extinguished and they were like any other individuals seeking to feather their own nest. Still many died unsung working to bring JP's message for change true.

True, movements owe their origin to persons thrown up in particular historical circumstances, and both Gandhi during the Independence movement, and JP when he was pitted against authoritarianism, were able to take advantage of these to generate revolution. These movements nonetheless fired the middle class which took upon itself a leadership role. Sadly, consumerism has overpowered the youth today and they have given up fighting against the ills of our society.

Recently, I found the Gandhian Anna Hazare trying to revive the same spirit of defiance. His target was corruption that had corroded the vitals of the system. It was a great tribute to his simplicity and integrity that the middle class civil society for the first time after the JP Movement came on to the streets in large numbers in his support. The protest had the making of a movement for *parivartan*. Hazare's concentration was on the appointment of the Lokpal (ombudsman) to combat corruption. The nation, shaken by the corruption leading up to the Commonwealth Games (CWG) and 2G spectrum allocation responded with a positive energy. The loss to the exchequer from these two instances alone was estimated at Rs 30,00,000 crore.

What was lacking in the movement was that it did not include the common man's priority of *roti, kapda aur makan*. Even violations of human rights were kept out of the purview of protest. The government presented to the nation a watered down version of the Lokpal Bill which once again demonstrated that the government was not serious about tackling corruption. The administrative control of the government over the CBI (Central Bureau of Investigation) could not be acceptable to Anna because the agency was used by the party in power to put pressure to initiate one case or to suppress another. Several CBI directors have told me how they felt handicapped because of government instructions to favour the guilty.

I myself tried to find grounds for conciliation between Prime Minister Manmohan Singh and Anna Hazare on the Jan Lokpal Bill. When I heard Manmohan Singh saying on television that the government was open to a 'discussion or dialogue' on the Lokpal Bill placed before parliament, I saw a chink of opportunity. That very afternoon, I went to meet Hazare whom I knew a little and found him prepared for a compromise provided the three basic issues were substantially met.

The first condition was the independence of the judiciary. I suggested that a Lokpal be set up exclusively for the judiciary. Hazare readily agreed to this. The second was the inclusion of the prime minister. Hazare was willing to divide the office in two parts, one relating to governance and the other to acts of corruption. He only wanted to pursue the instance of corruption if prima facie a case was established. The third condition was the independence of the CBI. Hazare agreed to place the organization under the jurisdiction of the Supreme Court until an acceptable Lokpal Bill was passed in parliament.

I did not speak to the prime minister directly, but someone who knew him personally conveyed what Hazare had conceded. The prime minister's reply was not helpful. He said that Hazare should put his views before the Parliamentary Standing Committee which was discussing the matter. The plea that he should invite Hazare to a special meeting of all political parties was also rejected. The entire exercise came to naught.

In the field of human rights I found the National Human Rights Commission (NHRC) wanting in many respects. The exclusion of Jammu & Kashmir and the armed forces from its ambit is an obvious lacuna. Its greatest limitation is that it has no investigative mechanism of its own to investigate allegations as I discovered from experience.

There was a fake encounter at Ansal Plaza, a posh shopping centre, where two Kashmiris were killed in the basement car parking. A doctor who was a witness challenged the encounter in his statement to the press. The government did not move. I petitioned the Human Rights Commission when retired Chief Justice J.S. Verma was its chairman. He readily ordered an inquiry, but this was conducted by the very same police force that had killed the two Kashmiris in the encounter. The inquiry, the text of which the commission forwarded to me was a sham. The police reiterated its earlier stand that no fake encounter had occurred.

Another complaint I filed with the NHRC was on the return of Khalid Masood's body to Pakistan. There were conjectures about how he died. One was that he died of torture while in detention in a prison in Gurgaon. The commission rejected the petition without any inquiry.

Yet another futile protest was on the appointment of a former CBI director to the Human Rights Commission. He had shown favour to the then Home Minister Lal Krishna Advani by dropping the case against him relating to the demolition of the Babri Masjid. I lost the case in the Supreme Court which held that a person from the police had every right to become a member of the commission. The court missed the central issue or chose to do so.

My contact with Medha Patkar, leading an agitation against the Narmada Dam, was at her invitation to the site. When I went there I saw a temple with its long obelisk that had not yet been submerged in water. I agreed with her in principle that small dams were preferable to large ones because the extent of displacement of the population in the former was relatively lower. A network of small dams could also irrigate the same proportion of land and the devastation caused in the event of a natural disaster would also be substantially lower.

Gujaratis misunderstood the purpose of the agitation. They told me that it was 'their Kashmir' and that they would take to the gun if the dam was not constructed. They were hardly concerned about the rehabilitation of those who had been forcibly evicted from their homes to make way for the area of submergence.

In the Narmada case, there was an award that the people who were sought to be shifted as a consequence of the construction of the dam should be compensated with land plus a rehabilitation grant. This was not entirely implemented either in Gujarat, Madhya Pradesh, or Maharashtra. Medha had reluctantly come around to accepting the height of the dam to a particular point on condition that all those who were uprooted would be fully rehabilitated and compensated. As time passed, however, we found that all the three states, in particular Madhya Pradesh, fudged the records to show that they had rehabilitated the uprooted.

Tarkunde and I were invited by Gandhians in Ahmedabad to discuss the dam. We found them all in favour of the dam to its maximum height but at the same time they assured us that the rehabilitation of the uprooted was their first concern. One of them even threatened if the dam was not constructed, Gujarat would erupt into violence. Tarkunde and I issued a statement, emphasizing that the promised rehabilitation package was an essential aspect of the construction of the dam. We also appealed to Medha Patkar and others to divert their attention from the dam to the rehabilitation of the displaced people. She surprised us by observing that she herself was concentrating on the rehabilitation aspect.

However, there was insufficient land to redistribute. Medha was so upset by this that she undertook a fast unto death. Rajinder Sachar and I were among those who sat in dharna with her at Jantar Mantar. Prime Minister Manmohan Singh called Rajinder on his mobile and sought his assistance. We both went to his house where the minister for water resources, Saifuddin Ahmed Soz, and Ahmed Patel, Sonia Gandhi's adviser, were closeted with the prime minister. Ahmed Patel from Gujarat was supporting the line, his state had taken. Rehabilitation might have shortcomings but this should not stop the construction of the dam, he argued.

Both of us requested the prime minister to send a team headed by Soz to assess the rehabilitation in MP. He agreed and promised to stop work on the dam if the report found fault with the rehabilitation process. Medha did not give up her fast but waited for the report. Soz and Meera Kumar, who subsequently became the Lok Sabha speaker, visited MP and described the rehabilitation process as a 'farce'. The prime minister did not stop the construction of the dam but the Supreme Court took stern notice of this and suspended construction until the rehabilitation norms had been complied with. Nevertheless, the legal wrangling did not stop the Gujarat government from building the dam to the desired height.

One night, after Rajinder and I had returned from the dharna, the police picked up Medha at night and took her forcibly to the AIIMS. With great difficulty we persuaded Medha to end her fast but the pain etched on the faces of those who had been evicted from the dam site, some of whom were present at the dharna, has remained etched in my memory, as does the remark of one of them: '*Babuji, ham nay kabhi nehi dekha ke garib kisan ko zamin ke badle zamin mila* [I have never seen a poor farmer getting land in exchange for land'].

I had a curious sense of satisfaction when I was invited in 2010 to a seminar on Narmada at Ahmedabad convened to express the view that the dam had failed to fulfill even the modest benefits expected from it. Those who were present at the seminar included Sanad Mehta and Madhav Rao Solanki. Both were once fanatically in favour of the dam.

I was also one of the demonstrators in Vienna against the Indian delegation, headed by Dr Manmohan Singh, at a conference on human rights and the environment, but I hid myself behind a tree lest Manmohan Singh should see me. I think that my class instincts

got the better of me. I took many years to transform myself when I participated in virtually every dharna organized by farmers and the poor at Jantar Mantar.

Whether the Maoists violate human rights may be questioned by some but I think that their methods vitiate the end they have in view. In response to their violence, India's democracy is being undermined. The government is enacting draconian laws and restricting legitimate democratic space. Such steps remind one of repressive periods, such as the Emergency period in India, the McCarthy era in the US, Apartheid in South Africa, the pre-unification stir in East Germany, and the Soviet Union's repression in Hungry. The Indian government's increasingly authoritarian measures are creating an environment where legitimate non-violent means of discussion, debate, or dissent are being relentlessly stifled.

A circular issued by the Ministry of Home Affairs on 6 May 2010 is a chilling example of moves to suppress the freedom of speech. Citing Section 39 of the Unlawful Activities (Prevention) Act (UAPA), the MHA threatened imprisonment for those who 'supported' Maoists, implying that 'NGOs/intellectuals' or other members of the public who propagate their ideology' will be subject to punishment under this anti-terrorism law. I do not concur with the ideology of the Maoists but how can a democratic government take action against those who adhere to it.

That the circular was issued shortly after the publication of reports on the Maoists by prominent writers and activists Arundhati Roy and Gautam Navlakha, Delhi editor of the highly respected academic periodical *Economic and Political Weekly,* indicate that the government's threat was targeted directly at them and others seeking to critically examine the issue of Maoist violence and the state's response to it. I also criticized the Public Safety Act.

I received a letter from Home Minister P. Chidambaram questioning my arguments on the contraction of democratic space. He said: 'Nevertheless, it may be remembered that the power is vested in the Court and not in the Executive Government. It is the Court hearing the bail application that will decide whether bail should be granted or not, and if the bail is not granted, what should be the period of custody of the accused.'

In my reply I said: 'This legislation is so draconian and anti-democratic that any one committed to the rights of individuals and human rights will face serious embarrassment amongst groups discussing India's commitment to human rights. It is this personal pain that I was pointing out in my article and I hope you will consider it in that light as home minister of our country. The detention of Binayak Sen under the UAPA points to its indiscriminate and partisan use.'

I thought that the violence attributed to Dr Binayak Sen, a medical practitioner in Chhattisgarh, was an alibi to cover up his detention under the Public Safety Act. I wrote to Chhattisgarh Chief Minister Raman Singh seeking Binayak's transfer to Vellore hospital for better medical attention. I was aware that the chief minister's pet child was the Salwa Judum, a force he constituted to let people 'defend' themselves against 'violence' by the Naxalites. This force, declared illegal by the Supreme Court, has been above the law and indulges in all manner of activities, including violence, against the Maoists or those the government regards as Maoists. What the chief minister has really done is to pit adivasis against adivasis, changing a peaceful environment into a land of violence and murder with the authorities playing a dubious and negative role.

We are witnessing a virtual war in the hitherto peaceful and tranquil forests. The area of conflict is steadily growing. It is no secret that the state has arrayed a formidable paramilitary force against the Maoists who are portrayed as the most dangerous internal security threat to India. The worst affected area is the Dandakaranya region, which was promised a 'special deal' by Prime Minister Jawaharlal Nehru in 1958 while inaugurating the Dandakaranya Development Authority, beginning with the settlement of displaced persons from Bangladesh. That promise was, however, soon forgotten.

I do not approve of the cult of violence that the Maoists have adopted. A murder is a murder whatever the name you give it. Mahatma Gandhi said that if your means are vitiated so are your ends bound to be. Any goal achieved by wading through a pool of blood is not worth achieving. Disregarding the means is the essence of dictatorship; democracy represents the will of the people, not through the bullet but through the ballot. The killings in which the Maoists have indulged cannot in any way be justified, and indeed through such acts they have distorted the very economic philosophy which they represent: From each according to his capacity and to each according to his need.

The sense of growing authoritarianism is also indicated in the recent killing of CPI (Maoist) spokesman Azad (Cherukuri Rajkumar), along with a journalist Hemchandra Pandey, in what was labelled an 'encounter'. Before Azad was killed he was reportedly in correspondence with Home Minister P. Chidambaram through an intermediary, Swami Agnivesh, in an attempt to broker a temporary ceasefire and initiate talks between the government and the Maoists. He told me he had a terrible experience and described the government as 'dishonest in its efforts'. The killing of Azad cast serious doubts on the state's professed intention to debate the issue. He had provided insights into the Maoist ideology, motivations, and strategy. Azad was attempting to garner support amongst Maoists to initiate talks with the government.

The Maoist violence is more than a law and order problem and requires solutions that address social and economic inequalities. The state, however, continues to push ahead with its increasingly authoritarian approach to tackle the problem. It is no secret that arrayed against the Maoists, who are portrayed as the worst internal security threat in the country, the maximum possible police and paramilitary force the state can muster is used and justified.

In the face of the government's preference for violence against the Maoists over action against vested interests, the problem has become extremely intractable. A more reasoned strategy would be to ensure that the issues are debated as thoroughly and widely as possible and that the social and cultural life in the tribal areas is not disrupted and uprooted. Above all, the crazy rush to set-up industrial plants there in the name of development has to stop. Tribes-people are entitled to seek clarity on concerns, interests, and grievances, the root causes, and areas of possible future political solutions. They are also entitled to learn about and comment on the laws and policies that are ostensibly intended to safeguard their security and the national interest. Limiting the free circulation of ideals not only diminishes plurality and diversity, but entirely undermines democracy itself.

I have written and spoken about the environment at several seminars but never realized the reality of the imminent threat to it until one day I woke up to its destruction in the area where I live. My house is in Vasant Vihar which I built in the 1960s after getting land from a government servant housing society when I was information officer in the home ministry.

The government's proposal was to connect the road on which schools were situated with the airport. How could the authorities have taken such a step without thinking about the schoolchildren affected? I complained to the police but they did not react, and were in fact in favour of the suggestion. I was horrified when I learnt that the road was part of a plan to construct seven five-star hotels on the forest land in the locality which later came to be known as Vasant Kunj. I wrote a letter to the CJI under a PIL plea pointing out how the road and hotels would destroy the ecology encompassed by the centuries' old ridge in the area. I also pointed out the low groundwater level in the area.

Taking notice of my complaint, officiating Chief Justice Kuldip Singh, a judge literally worshipped by environmentalists, issued a stay order in my favour. The authority was also required to provide an assurance in writing that they would never construct the proposed road. Lawyers were irritated and one of them said that I would be responsible for the 'biggest slum in Asia'. Nearly twenty years later that small patch of forest land is an oasis amidst a concrete jungle.

The builder mafia did not however relent in their efforts. They were able to get the Supreme Court to release a portion of the forest for which I had obtained a stay order. Why Justices B.N. Kripal and J.C. Verma permitted the destruction of forest land is beyond me. However, some of us constituted a group of environmentalists and held demonstrations and sat in dharna to stop high-rise buildings mushrooming in that area. The government appointed a committee which endorsed our argument that there was insufficient water in the area to support such construction.

This notwithstanding, malls and a range of other buildings have mushroomed despite the stay order and the case we fought in the Supreme Court. Justice Ajit Pasayat did not initially agree to stop the building until our objection was disposed of. Later, when the malls were two-third complete he pronounced that it was too late to do anything. He, however, said that a heavy fine should be imposed on the builders for having violated environmental guidelines.

When the construction of the malls were at full swing I discovered through RTI that the fine imposed was only a lakh of rupees. The building mafias have won. What amazes me is how, through liberal deployment of financial resources, they were able to surmount every impediment, whether judicial or other. Jairam Ramesh did not control the ministry at that time and therefore it is hypothetical to guess whether he would have done anything. The way in which he ordered the demolition of other buildings in Mumbai for not having obtained environmental clearance sustains the hope that an appreciation of green areas has begun to take root.

Even so, the defence ministry, in my limited experience, is immune to such considerations. It built flats for accommodation of service officers on the ridge without any clearance. I have written to the last two defence ministers, first George Fernandes and then A.K. Anthony, raising objections but both have turned down my request to leave the ridge free of construction because of the forest cover it provides, and serves as one of the few green lungs of Delhi. At a public hearing, which the government had ordered, at one time the plea adopted by representatives of the defence ministry was amusing. They said they had to be in proximity to the airport to enable them to reach their planes expeditiously in the event of an external attack. Apparently, they got away with this argument because the ridge is dotted with apartments for defence personnel which is altogether illegal.

Our group of environmentalists, headed by Vikram Soni, a scientist, fighting for clean environment, tried to have the venue of the Commonwealth Games changed because the proposed village for athletes was to be built on the bank of the Yamuna. The Akshardham temple was raised on the bed of Yamuna during the Vajpayee government. Prior to the construction of the temple I had written to Vajpayee about it but his reply was that there was no such proposal and yet the temple came up. The BJP government violated all environmental norms in permitting its construction.

When the Commonwealth Games flats were to be built, I approached the central minister, the late Arjun Singh, who convened a meeting of a group of ministers to hear us. We demonstrated before them how the concrete poured on the banks of the Yamuna would end the prospect of drawing water from the sand, which has a quality of absorbing water as does a sponge. This water could be easily sucked out and could supply drinking water to the entire population of Delhi.

Apparently, the government was not willing to change the site because the argument was that they had gone too far in their preparations to build the village. Jaipal Reddy, then minister for urban development, did ask me if there was any alternative. I told him that they could erect collapsible structures which could be dismantled once the games were over. This was mere talk because the venue was not changed. Too many hands had their fingers in pie which subsequently became one of India's biggest scams.

3

ANNEXURE
Indo-Pak Relations

For me, the partition of India is not an academic subject, which can be analysed and discussed dispassionately, but a series of incidents etched in my memory that haunt me to this day. Our house in Sialkot, the town in Pakistan where I was born and where my father was a well-known and well-loved medical physician; my father's Muslim friends whom we referred to individually as *chacha* (uncle); the shops from which we bought chocolates, lozenges, and chewing gum; the school where I studied, my teachers; close friends, many of them Muslim; our affectionate Muslim neighbours; the wonderful food we ate. The searing days of Partition; the savage riots, of burning, looting, killing, when men became beasts; how we left Sialkot without knowing that we would never return to our home and how I got a few inches of space in an old army jeep driving to India. How, when we were passing Wazirabad, about 30 miles from Sialkot, we saw long lines of haggard refugees attempting to trek to India; an old Sikh, with a flowing beard flecked with grey, who tried to hand over his young and only grandson to me pleading pitifully, 'He is all we have. Please, take him to India. At least, *he* should live'; the young woman who tried to thrust her child into the jeep imploring, 'I shall locate you when we cross over to India and collect my son. Please take him with you'; how it broke my heart when we could not accommodate either of the two children because there was not an inch of free space in the jeep; the never-ending waves of refugees with terror-sculpted faces going to India or coming to Pakistan along the same road ...

> *Life for me has been no crystal stair.*
> *It's had tacks in it,*
> *And splinters,*
> *And boards torn up*
> *And places with no carpet on the floor*

These lines from 'Mother to Son' by Langston Hughes (from Hewz), the American poet, aptly sums up the history of Indo–Pak relations.

The course of Indo–Pak relations, like the course of Shakespeare's 'true love', never ran smooth. Right from the day after the constitution of Pakistan was adopted there were problems: exchange of documents, compensation, Junagarh, infiltration into Kashmir, the 1965 war, the Bangladesh war, Kargil ... and so the list meanders on endlessly. Not all the perfumes of the Tashkent and Shimla agreements, nor of the bus yatra to Lahore could sweeten relations between the two countries. As for the present, distrust and suspicion has overtaken the two countries. There is no conflict but there is no settlement either. No hostility but no harmony either. Both continue to remain, though geographically side by side, distant neighbours.

Immediately after the constitution of Pakistan, Mohammed Ali Jinnah assured its citizens: 'You may belong to any religion or caste or creed; that has nothing to do with fundamental principle that we are citizens and equal citizens of one State.' This was, however, an empty assurance which was never translated into action, perhaps because Jinnah died soon thereafter. Religious elements interpreted the new Muslim state in their own way.

India, though a secular state, could not give the same status to the minorities as the majority enjoyed. The coexistence by the two principal communities, Hindus and Muslim, has developed into a way of living. The unfortunate part is that Muslims have been driven to live in separate localities, mostly slums. As the Muslim middle class had by and large migrated to Pakistan, the Hindu middle class came to develop exclusively Hindu environs uninfluenced by Muslim culture or people.

I recall that when I met Rafaqat Ali and his professor wife Mausuma in Delhi, her first remark was: 'We can always take shelter at your house when Hindus want to turn us out from our place.' I realized then how insecure Muslims felt after six decades of Independence. They still suffer from the same fear.

The sharpest thorn in Indo–Pak relations has been Kashmir. Nothing has bedeviled them more than this beautiful mountainous state. Kashmiris say that their state is 'a heaven on earth', but this 'heaven' has played hell with Indo–Pak relations from the very outset. Maharaja Hari Singh, its ruler, was more to blame than anyone else for this dispute. Had he decided on Kashmir's accession before 15 August 1947, when Lord Louis Mountbatten, the Crown representative, had the authority to see it through, there would have been no trouble and no Kashmir problem. After Independence, both India and Pakistan claimed the state.

Blinkered political leaders and bureaucrats on both sides, rather than bridging the gulf between the two countries, have only widened it. This is because they find that the more rigid the approach they espouse against the country across the border, the higher they rise in public esteem.

Foreign powers have also contributed a great deal in keeping the two countries apart. Through arms and economic assistance, they have stoked the fires of enmity. They have been following a 'keep-them-divided' policy, either to preserve their 'spheres of influence' and 'area of interest' or to maintain the so-called 'balance of power' in the region.

Another reason which may have contributed to the worsening relations between the two countries is a lack of leaders of stature. Jinnah died shortly after the constitution of Pakistan, Mahatma Gandhi was assassinated within a year of India's Independence. Pakistan had, after Jinnah, leaders like Liaquat Ali Khan, Ayub Khan, Yahya Khan, Zia-ul-Haq, and Zulfikar Ali Bhutto who sorely lacked Jinnah's stature. After the death of

Pandit Jawaharlal Nehru, in India too there were no great leaders to speak of. Had Gandhi been alive – he announced that after Partition he would live in Karachi – and had Pakistan a leader of Jinnah's stature, Indo–Pak relations might have taken a very different turn for the better.

I say, 'might have', because I am not certain that this would have been the outcome. Sometimes I think there is much truth in what Nehru said: 'Even if Kashmir were to be handed over to Pakistan on a platter, Pakistan would think of some other way to keep its quarrel with India alive because Kashmir was only a symptom of a disease and that disease was hatred of India.' I have a feeling that Pakistan seeks to keep that hatred alive because it is that which provides it with its ethos, its raison d'etre. This is evident to me in the textbooks the students are taught.

Sheikh Mujib-ur-Rehman, the Bangladesh leader, once told me in an interview: All along Pakistan has preached four things: one, Islam is in danger; two, the Hindu is a kafir; three, India is the enemy; and four, Kashmir must be conquered. The Pakistanis have been fed on this propaganda for many years. The hate campaign unleashed in that country is even against the tenets of Islam. Unless there is a change in the mentality of the people of Pakistan, they cannot get out of their make-believe world.

The political parties in India with a communal outlook have been muddying the water. There is a limited liberal opinion which understands the plight in which Pakistan is enmeshed. A very few in the government are willing to provide some flexibility to improve relations with Pakistan. There is no point in arguing about who is responsible for the situation. The moot point is that the situation must change, and the easing of visa restrictions, preferably its abolition, would help people-to-people contact which is currently very limited.

Yet, relations between the two countries might have been normal had Pakistan not been taken over by the military within a few years of Independence. The country has gone through three coups and even when the army has returned to the barracks its writ has run without any opposition. India has failed to appreciate the problems that the people in Pakistan face because of army control, on the one hand, and the pressure of fundamentalism, on the other. A more liberal attitude would have helped. Both New Delhi and Islamabad have to realize that there is no alternative to peace.

What then can bring about this change? Many things. The subcontinent can carve out its own destiny in accordance with its own genius if foreign powers allow it to do so and if the two nations are allowed to look within, not without. With time, they may be able to forget their animosity and mistrust. Jinnah himself once underscored this point: 'Some nations have killed millions of each other's and yet, an enemy of today is a friend of tomorrow. That is history.' He thought India and Pakistan would be like the US and Canada.

Normalization is the first necessary precondition to kick-start a new era in Indo–Pak relations. Economic and cultural relations will develop from there. All this means that there should be soft borders to enable the people of the two countries to intermingle freely. Such continuing contact will clear up the doubts and banish the fears that have taken root in the minds of the people of the two nations. This continuing dialogue will not only ease tension and mute jingoism but its fallout may even help restore democracy in Pakistan.

The importance of such an interchange also lies in its strengthening our of secular ethos, because otherwise many people in India, harping on the sentiments of Partition, can transform anti-Pakistan feelings into anti-Muslim feelings. Once I told Benazir Bhutto at London a few days before her assassination at Karachi that India could give democracy to Pakistan and Pakistan to India its determination to fight against all odds to remain secular. She said: 'I shall make the subcontinent borderless.' She gave me a copy of document, a charter for democracy, signed by her and former prime minister Nawaz Sharif.

The charter opened with words: 'We the elected leaders of Pakistan have deliberated on the political crisis in our beloved homeland, the threats to its survival, the erosion of the federation's unity, the military's subordination of all state institutions, the marginalization of civil society, the mockery of the Constitution and representative institutions, growing poverty, unemployment and inequality, brutalization of society, breakdown of rule of law and, the unprecedented hardships facing our people under a military dictatorship, which has pushed our beloved country to the brink of a total disaster.'

As for Kashmir, it is not an insoluble problem and can be resolved through mutual cooperation and understanding. Some proposals for an agreement that does not alter the existing borders have won the support of governments on both sides. What Pakistan must bear in mind is that India will never agree to another partition on the basis of religion. I think that the state of Jammu & Kashmir can get all the autonomy, even outside the constitution but not outside the Indian union.

Trade and commerce between the two countries must be accelerated. Communication and transport facilities should be restored and people-to-people contacts must be encouraged. If these things happen, a favourable atmosphere would be generated to sort out other problems and cut Kashmir's Gordian knot.

An economic common market, involving India, Pakistan, and Bangladesh, is another way of easing the tension. Though the idea is good, it may not mature for quite a while in the future because India is a developed country in comparison with the other two, but the idea is worth pursuing. When I spoke to Zulfikar Ali Bhutto in 1972, he said, that a European model of economic union would take some years to mature; not until Pakistan had developed economically.

I feel that the charter of democracy which Benazir Bhutto and Nawaz Sharif signed in London when both were in the wilderness can be applicable to the subcontinent as a whole. It spoke of democracy without dictators or military leaders destroying or diluting it and at the same time promised a welfare state. I also hope that an economic union like that in Europe will develop one day and a single visa that will enable people to travel and trade in the entire South Asian region.

I am confident that the high walls of fear and distrust will crumble one day and that the two nations, without sacrificing their separate identities, will work together for the common good. This is the faith that has sustained me ever since I left Sialkot, over sixty years ago and it is the straw I have clutched in the sea of hatred and hostility that has engulfed the subcontinent.

When I crossed over to India, I never felt that I had left an enemy country, but a country full of friends who I would meet again soon. I have visited Pakistan many times since and interviewed its leaders. Even now I go to the India–Pakistan border at Wagah in Punjab every year on the night of 14–15 August and light candles of peace and friendship in the company of many from India as well as Pakistan. I started with 10–12 people in 1992. In 2011 there was a crowd of more than a lakh. The idea has caught up and it is now a peoples' movement for friendship with Pakistan.

I have found that any word of kinship finds a response. Once in Karachi, when I was heading a parliamentary delegation, I found that people had tears in their eyes when I said that we were of the same blood and would never abandon them. This view is, however, far removed from the official one.

I still remember meeting Benazir Bhutto in Lahore in 1993 when she praised my efforts and told me not to falter in my endeavour to improve relations between India and Pakistan. She said: 'You people may be successful one day. We, the governments, will not get anywhere.'

That afternoon I had an appointment with Nawaz Sharif, then prime minister. He endorsed the idea and offered all the help he personally and his government could provide. During the discussion he made the famous observations: 'We can neither take Kashmir from you forcibly nor can you give it on a platter peacefully.'

The response from the Pakistan side has been limited. The army and religious organizations have been against the initiative. In the past two years, the Pakistan People's Party has sent some representatives to the border. For the first time, our side opened the iron gates in 2009, although the Pakistan authorities kept theirs shut.

From the Pakistan side the people-to-people contact was initiated by Dr Mubashir Hussain. He was joined by Asma Jehangir, Jugnu Mohsin, and I.A. Rehman. Subsequently, Aitzaz Hussain, his wife Bushra, Iqbal Haider, and Chaudhary Manzoor have joined the movement. On our side Manak, Romesh, Gogi, Rajinder Sachar, and Mahesh Bhatt are some of the persons who push the caravan of peace despite all odds. Girl students from both sides have joined in and Nandita Das's efforts to get children from both sides to play cricket have also contributed to improve relations. However, the governments, particularly Pakistan's, are not enthusiastic about encouraging people-to-people contacts although they pay lip service to the initiative.

Nevertheless, I have found Islamabad more forthcoming than New Delhi in certain matters. In 2010, when we took up the question of the release of fishermen languishing in jails even after having served their sentences, Pakistan released virtually all the Indian prisoners. In India we had to meet Sonia Gandhi to get some Pakistani fishermen released.

This is, however, a perennial problem. Both governments wreak vengeance on fishermen who stray into each other's water because there is yet no agreement on territorial waters. Indeed, much worse is the plight of prisoners from either country. They suffer from the fallout of the enmity between the two countries. Persons like Assad Mufti, a Pakistani settled in Holland are rare. He is secular and boldly takes India's side. In his view, the Pakistan establishment is in the way of normalization between the two countries.

The other day I was reading a book in which I found this verse (*rubai*) of Omar Khayyam, the great Sufi poet of Persia. I will quote it as the highest ideal I can think of, which I wish always remained in my heart and in the hearts of all Indians and Pakistanis:

> *So it be written in the Book of Love,*
> *I do not care about that Book above;*
> *Erase my name or write it as you will,*
> *So I be written in the Book of love.*

Index